OCT 02 2012

CHICAGO

★ ★ ★ *City of* ★ ★ ★
Neighborhoods

CHICAGO

★ ★ *City of* ★ ★
Neighborhoods

HISTORIES & TOURS

DOMINIC A. PACYGA   ELLEN SKERRETT

WITH A FOREWORD BY M.W. NEWMAN

 LOYOLA UNIVERSITY PRESS/CHICAGO

Book design by C.L. Tornatore

Cover design by Aristarch Kirsch, C.L. Tornatore

Cover typography design by Robert Horn, Aristarch Kirsch

Library of Congress Cataloging in Publication Data

Pacyga, Dominic A.
  Chicago, city of neighborhoods.

  Bibliography p. 559
  Includes index.
    1. Chicago (Ill.)—Description—1981   —Tours.
2. Historic buildings—Illinois—Chicago—Guide-books.
3. Chicago (Ill.)—History. I. Skerrett, Ellen. II. Title.
F548. 18.P33 1986   917.73'110443   85-19833
ISBN 0-8294-0497-X (Paper)   ISBN 0-8294-0518-6 (Cloth)

to Johanna and Mary

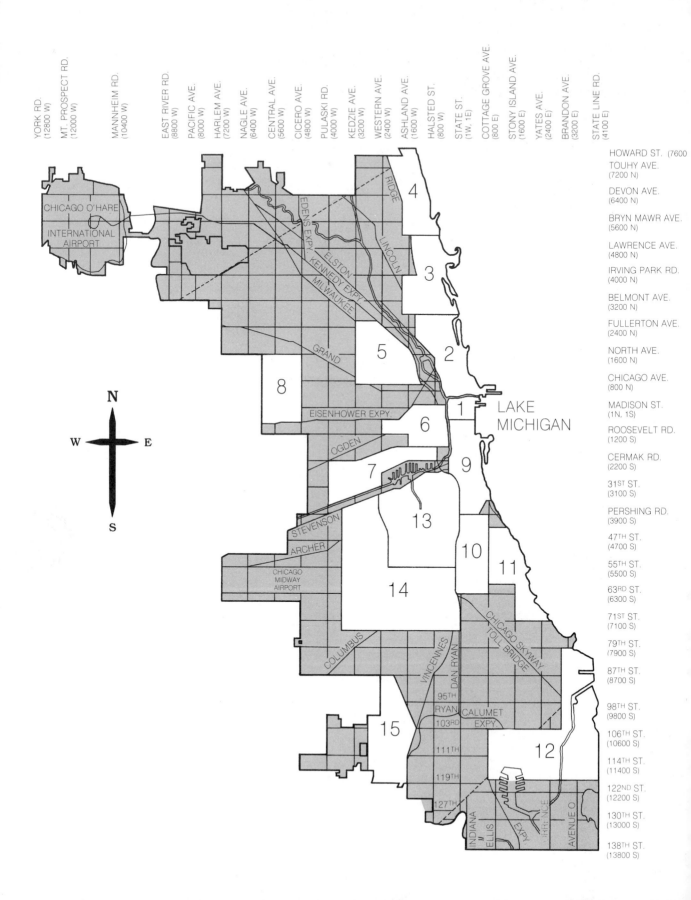

YORK RD. (12800 W)
MT. PROSPECT RD. (12000 W)
MANNHEIM RD. (10400 W)
EAST RIVER RD. (8800 W)
PACIFIC AVE. (8000 W)
HARLEM AVE. (7200 W)
NAGLE AVE. (6400 W)
CENTRAL AVE. (5600 W)
CICERO AVE. (4800 W)
PULASKI RD. (4000 W)
KEDZIE AVE. (3200 W)
WESTERN AVE. (2400 W)
ASHLAND AVE. (1600 W)
HALSTED ST. (800 W)
STATE ST. (1W, 1E)
COTTAGE GROVE AVE. (800 E)
STONY ISLAND AVE. (1600 E)
YATES AVE. (2400 E)
BRANDON AVE. (3200 E)
STATE LINE RD. (4100 E)

HOWARD ST. (7600
TOUHY AVE. (7200 N)
DEVON AVE. (6400 N)
BRYN MAWR AVE. (5600 N)
LAWRENCE AVE. (4800 N)
IRVING PARK RD. (4000 N)
BELMONT AVE. (3200 N)
FULLERTON AVE. (2400 N)
NORTH AVE. (1600 N)
CHICAGO AVE. (800 N)
MADISON ST. (1N, 1S)
ROOSEVELT RD. (1200 S)
CERMAK RD. (2200 S)
31ST ST. (3100 S)
PERSHING RD. (3900 S)
47TH ST. (4700 S)
55TH ST. (5500 S)
63RD ST. (6300 S)
71ST ST. (7100 S)
79TH ST. (7900 S)
87TH ST. (8700 S)
98TH ST. (9800 S)
106TH ST. (10600 S)
114TH ST. (11400 S)
122ND ST. (12200 S)
130TH ST. (13000 S)
138TH ST. (13800 S)

CHICAGO O'HARE INTERNATIONAL AIRPORT

LAKE MICHIGAN

CHICAGO MIDWAY AIRPORT

N
W   E
S

Contents

Foreword

The town runs blotchy gray if you look at it fast. Along the expressways it blurs into neon and weary factories, a heavy-boned, hard-breathing place, all sinew, with muscles even in its head. No one ever will mistake it for San Francisco or Savannah. A spacious town, to be sure; but gracious, rarely. There has been no time for that.

One day, perhaps, the whole sweating place heaved out of the earth and socked in for good. Over the years it swelled like mad, but something happened and hunks of it now barely hang on. Weedy lots, wrinkled buildings, acres of billboards, miles of train tracks—the town is no Miss America, although maybe it's Mister America, still pumping iron even after losing the title. A town as tough as they come and as tough as they go, too.

There's a river but it's no Seine: a working-stiff stream, green where it should be blue, flowing backwards and emptying on St. Louis. On the land, a million-legged iron treadmill screeches over the streets and circles back on itself, groaning by night. It's the Elevated, nearly a century old in some of its pinned and bolted bones and a reminder that the town has years on it now but that it keeps going and that it still connects.

The town, of course, is Chicago. Along the money-green lakefront it's one city and back of the skyline it's another. It has had a long run as a city of neighborhoods, although some of them are lost now, vanished in the memory gap that divides the haves and have-nots. Anyone willing to explore, though, will find surprises: surviving neighborhoods, reviving neighborhoods, and even abiding ones. The town is no lost city although it surely has strayed and has sacrificed living pieces of itself.

Getting such a place together in one big civic formula is a job for a sociologist or maybe a contortionist. You begin with the ingredients, and they're mixed. No city is all one thing, anyway, and this one is part yesterday, part tomorrow, part problem, part solution: an iron city going somewhere but not quite sure where as it puts aside a century of assembly lines and heads for a century of light lines to the moon.

You won't see it that way, though, if you stay on the expressways that split the town's crust. Oh, you'll see looming shapes of church spires and they make you wonder how they happened to get here in such breathtaking numbers. You'll see the business towers that grab lakeside sky and excite the air.

And there are hints of neighborhoods that hold the town in place: working-class wooden houses from another time, with working folk still living in them, sometimes six to a room in old Pilsen; surprisingly delicate graystones housing third-generation families in Wrigleyville, say; bungalows and two-flats and apartments on street after street; stylish high-rises with lake views in a city with an architectural lineage tracing to Louis Sullivan, Frank Lloyd Wright, and Mies van der Rohe.

To see it all clearly, you get off the expressway and wheel onto the streets. They're packed, they're swollen, and the shopping strips are cluttered with storefront sign glare and the dust of the generations piled at the curbs. And along with all this, thousands of taverns, hog-wild gas stations, shaggy parking lots, and tons of housing projects. And for that matter, whatever became of Hyde Park's 55th Street?

And yet—you look again at these streets where Chicago lives and the town turns out to be full of householders with careful lawns. And maples and honey locusts on secluded streets. All the streets run straight to infinite horizons and too many of them are gap-toothed, but the good ones use every inch. And there are places that look like townhouse London or moneyed Manhattan or Kansas City or Milwaukee, and some perhaps look better, and there are great streaks of beauty, and isn't that amazing?

The town is rich in rugged brick buildings, made to last. And, everywhere, hardy people, weathered, solid—citizens in forests of stone and steel. A place at once vast, familiar, strange, ferocious, sprawling flat but enduring, and always itself, with sweat and history in every sidewalk.

And then you begin to sense that the blur is untangling. The town sorts itself into neighborhood spaces, into social classes, into languages and nationalities and colors, into parishes and school districts and shopping streets and block clubs and bus routes. And into hope and dreams, for that matter. It's a dreamer's town, for all of its harshness. Some of it is writhing, some waiting, some being reborn. It's passe, it's fresh, it's gone and it's coming, and as it sheds one skin it grows another. It's a town that never stops, a neighborhood for the world.

The best place to put your finger on its pulse is on the streets where we live. Many of them are described and defined with loving insight in this historical guide to a city of rooted landmarks and changing faces: a city of challenging purposes and abundant life, mingling its yesterdays and tomorrows in a throbbing here and now.

M. W. Newman

Introduction

Chicago has had a rich and flamboyant history. From Rogers Park to Austin to the steel mill neighborhoods tucked away near the Indiana border, generations of Chicagoans have created a vital city with a long and colorful tradition. Chicago has been called the Garden City, the Windy City, Hog Butcher to the World, and the City That Works. But its most enduring title is the City of Neighborhoods.

Everyone seems to know what a neighborhood is, but few can define it. "My neighborhood" may mean a street corner, a block or two, or a large geographical area like Lincoln Park. Early social scientists claimed that neighborhoods belonged to the world of small towns and rural areas. Urban dwellers knew differently. From the mid-nineteenth century on, Chicagoans have created a wide variety of neighborhoods, from the Gold Coast to "Little Hell."

Chicago neighborhoods usually developed around some economic base. This might have been a stock yard, a steel mill, a university, park, or real estate subdivision. The economic base often became a symbol of the area, such as Back of the Yards or Wicker Park. Whatever the economic or symbolic base may have been, it determined much of the character and future of the neighborhood which grew up around it.

Neighborhoods were created to protect and nurture families, and families in turn gave stability to urban areas. Many of Chicago's original settlers were single men, immigrant laborers who sought their fortunes in the steel mills and packinghouses. Industrial sections of the city did not become neighborhoods until families predominated. Likewise, early real estate developers sought to attract families to the new homes that dotted the prairies of Lake View, South Lawndale, and Morgan Park.

Although *neighborhood* is a geographical term, it implies much more than geography. Because neighborhoods are social entities too, many people refer to them as "communities." While neighborhoods may indeed be communities, they are generally more diverse in terms of structure and organization. Whereas communities imply common interests or common institutions, neighborhoods have always included people of various ethnic, racial, and economic backgrounds.

From the 1830s on, Chicago neighborhoods have experienced ethnic and racial changes. When the French moved in, the Indians moved out, and the city has been changing ever since. In some neighborhoods ethnic succession occurred peacefully, while in others the battle for neighborhood turf was hotly contested. As the following histories reveal, Chicago neighborhoods are remarkably resilient, and they continue their day-to-day life rather successfully, even in the face of dramatic economic changes.

For generations of Chicagoans, neighborhoods reduced the awesome experience of urban life to a human scale. Institutions, especially churches and synagogues, were often catalysts for neighborhood development. More than just houses of worship, church buildings were also social and communal centers. In addition to religious services and organizations, the churches often founded and supported credit unions, fraternal societies, youth organizations, poetry and theatrical circles. Parochial schools maintained religious and cultural traditions among Chicago's diverse ethnic groups, and they played a vital role in both community and neighborhood development.

Other institutions which contributed to neighborhood life included public schools, parks, fraternal organizations, funeral homes, small shops, restaurants, and the ever-present tavern. Some of the warmest memories which neighborhood residents have revolve around these "third places" away from work and family where social interaction took place. Chicago's neighborhoods were once filled with meeting places like these where neighbors discussed local events, politics, and family matters. In the face of changing entertainment and shopping habits, Chicago's small commercial strips carry on this traditional function.

For generations of urban dwellers, the most familiar place in the neighborhood has been the block. Chicago's grid system of streets divides the city into thousands of these small units. It is on the block that the term *neighbor* is most meaningful. Sidewalks, backyards, gangways, and alleys still provide the first playgrounds for most Chicago children. Front porches, fences, and corners are the meeting places of adults, and these form the gossip network for both men and women. The corner tavern as well as the now almost extinct "Ma and Pa" grocery store were important local institutions which served the block as well as the larger neighborhood.

This book about Chicago neighborhoods continues a long tradition. As early as the 1860s, guidebooks have documented the city's rapid rise from a frontier town to an urban metropolis. Because of their tremendous role in creating and sustaining the city, we believe Chicago neighborhoods deserve special attention. Our focus in this book is historical. In addition to describing the origins and development of the neighborhoods, we have selected historic and contemporary photographs to illustrate the changes which have taken place in the neighborhoods over the years.

The fifteen suggested tours are based on the neighborhood histories. Be sure to read the histories first, then set out on the tours. The tours point out institutions and buildings which have played an important role in neighborhood growth. Many of the tours trace the historic development of individual neighborhoods, from the oldest settlements to the newest sections. The tours are designed to provide a specific route through each neighborhood, but as Chicagoans well know, many a two-way street has been changed to one-way, apparently overnight. We must leave the adjustments to your own ingenuity.

We hope this book will promote a greater interest in and appreciation for Chicago's neighborhoods. Far from being relics of the past, the neighborhoods are alive and dynamic, and the city very much needs them if it is to survive.

Dominic A. Pacyga
Ellen Skerrett

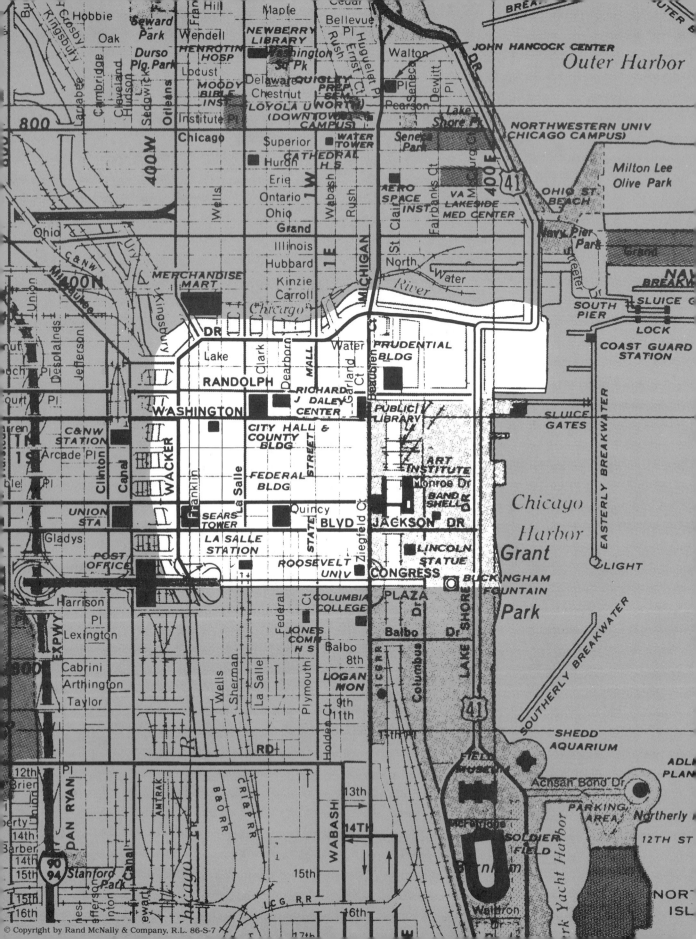

The Loop

The history of early Chicago begins near the mouth of the Chicago River. As early as 1673 the river attracted the French explorers Father Jacques Marquette and Louis Jolliet. After they discovered the waterway, it became a major route for French *voyageurs, engagés,* and explorers, who raised the flag of the Bourbons over the western frontier. In 1763, after the French and Indian War, the territory passed to British control. The mouth of the river was a natural place for a settlement. But no permanent settlement was made in the area until about 1781 when Jean Baptiste Point du Sable, a French-speaking black man, arrived and built a cabin on the north bank of the main stream, where the Chicago River flows into the lake. Du Sable's home became a center of economic activity in the Northern Illinois country. Trappers and traders stopped at Jean Baptiste's to sell their furs or simply to visit as they plied their trade along the rivers and lakes of the Old Northwest.

The American victory over the British in 1783 in the War of Independence saw the future Chicago area come under the new government, nominally at least. But the war did not bring about any significant changes in the area. Logistically it was difficult for the fledgling republic to assert its control over the territory. British troops and a sizeable number of French-Indian and British traders still held control. The campaign of General "Mad" Anthony Wayne against pro-British Indians in the 1790s ended with the Treaty of Greenville in 1795. This treaty recognized the mouth of the Chicago River as a strategic place, which was ceded to the United States government by the Indian nations. Wayne advised the Secretary of War to establish a fort there, but the government was unable to do this until the summer of 1803, when troops arrived to erect the first Fort Dearborn under the command of Captain John Whistler. By the spring of 1804 a wooden fort stood just about where the south end of the Michigan Avenue Bridge stands today.

The establishment of a military installation here immediately attracted more traders and Indians. Du Sable had already left the area by the time the army arrived. In 1800 he had sold his cabin to Jean La Lime and disapeared from history. Four years later John Kinzie arrived, and he soon became the principal fur trader in the area. Fort Dearborn became the center of economic activity as trappers and traders gathered around it. The small settlement was

Michigan Avenue Bridge Bas Relief. The reliefs on the bridge pylons commemorate events in the history of Chicago. The bridge itself is located a few feet from the original site of Fort Dearborn. Pictured here is The Defense *executed by Henry Hering.*
(G. Lane)

already ethnically diverse. Most of the soldiers were American, whereas the traders were American, British, and Scotch, and they traded with French-Indian *engagés*.

Frontier life was often dull, and Fort Dearborn stood well beyond the area of white settlement. Whiskey flowed freely between the traders and the Indians, and this became a bone of contention between the fort and the settlement. In 1812 Captain Whistler and his officers were removed from the post because of a feud between the Kinzie and Whistler families over whiskey and the Indian trade. Political influence was a factor even at this early date in Chicago's history. Captain Nathan Heald was sent to replace Whistler as commander of Fort Dearborn.

War clouds were gathering in the east as the British navy continued to disregard American maritime rights. Meanwhile, Tecumseh, the great Shawnee Indian chief, was gaining influence all over the old Northwest Territory. Tecumseh watched and waited as war broke out between the United States and Great Britain in June of 1812. When the American invasion of Canada failed and Fort Michilimackinac fell to the British army, thus threatening Detroit, Tecumseh sent out word that the Americans could be driven back to the Atlantic Ocean.

While the American forces in the West were retreating towards Detroit, Captain Heald was ordered to abandon Fort Dearborn and march with the settlers to aid in the defense of Detroit. On August 15, 1812 Heald led a small column of regular troops, militia, women, and children out of the fort and south along the lakefront. Indian braves attacked the column near what is today the intersection of 18th Street and Calumet Avenue. Thirty-nine men, among them Captain William Wells, two women, and twelve children were killed, a score were wounded, and others were captured. American control of Chicago had ended after nine short years. The U.S. Army did not return until July 4, 1816 to rebuild Fort Dearborn at its old location near the mouth of the Chicago River.

The new fort created certain geographical and economic patterns that would eventually influence Chicago's "Loop." Traders again flocked to Chicago because of the protection afforded by the military, and a marketplace developed along the south bank of the river west of the fort. As the population grew over the next twenty years, this area became the commercial center of the town. The South Water Street market and Lake Street were the first economic centers of the settlement. Wolf Point to the west, where the river splits, was also a site of development. Here, by 1831, stood the legendary Wolf Tavern and Sam Miller's Public House. The Sauganash Hotel, owned by Mark Beaubien,

Equestrian Statues of Indians. Ivan Mestrovic's twin statues of Indians flank Congress Street where it enters Grant Park.
(G. Lane)

stood on the south bank of the river, closer to the fort. Today the Apparel Mart across from Wolf Point, and Wacker Drive marks the site of the old south bank trading center.

In 1833 Chicago was incorporated as a town, and in 1837 it became a city with 4,170 inhabitants. The small settlement of log cabins had swiftly become a major Western town, and it would soon be a city of national and even world importance. Already in the summer of 1837 seventeen lawyers were making a living in Chicago. Lawyers and litigation were another sign of developing urbanization. Land speculation was a major business in the city then, just as it is now. The two lots which Mark Beaubien purchased for his Sauganash Hotel for $120 in 1830 rose in value to $108,000 by 1853. The population continued to grow from year to year, decade to decade. And so did the land values.

Since the economic life of the early city centered around the river, it is not suprising that Lake Street became Chicago's first principal thoroughfare. The city's most important businesses were located on both sides of Lake Street from Wabash to Wells. By the late 1850s many brightly-colored three- to five-story Italianate style buildings lined the street. John Mills Van Osdel, Chicago's first architect, designed the first cast-iron building in the city in 1856. His designs set the style for the buildings on Lake Street before the fire.

Chicago continued to grow at a phenomenal rate. The city's population grew from just under 30,000 in 1840 to 109,260 ten years later. By the outbreak of the Civil War in 1861, over 300,000 people lived in Chicago. The area that would later become the Loop reached residential and economic maturity by this time. It was a very different central city than the one we know today. The area was not yet segregated by function. It was both residential and commercial. Wealthy people lived in the central business district, especially south of Van Buren Street. Wabash Avenue was known as the street of churches because prominent Protestant congregations built large houses of worship in what is today the South Loop. Wealthy people lived close to the center of the expanding city in order to be close to where they worked. Limited transportation facilities made it desirable to live close in.

Working-class people also lived in the central area. Immigrants from Ireland, Germany, and Scandinavia lived on the outskirts of today's business district. Old St. Mary's Church, St. Peter's, and St. Patrick's remain in the Loop today, or just outside it, as reminders of this period of development. The poor lived close to the rich before the Chicago Fire, once again because of limited transportation.

Lake Street, between Clark and LaSalle, 1860. This lithograph shows the work of raising an entire block of buildings four feet to the new street grade. Lake Street was Chicago's principal retail district in the years before Potter Palmer developed State Street south of Lake.

(Courtesy Chicago Historical Society)

Workers walked to work. Immigrant shanty towns and densely packed tenements stood near the river. Some immigrant workers also lived in alley slum dwellings behind the impressive looking business blocks. Residential integration and social segregation remained the order of the day until new means of transportation and the Chicago Fire drastically changed the city after the Civil War.

In 1860 Chicago's commerce and industry still centered around the Chicago River close to the lake. But entrepreneurs were beginning to look for new locations away from the central business district. River traffic had become much too heavy, and pollution problems were already developing. Besides this, the new technology of the railroad was making manufacturers less dependent on the river. Two of Chicago's major industries moved away from the central city at this time. In the early 1860s a few meatpacking plants moved to the South Branch of the Chicago River in Bridgeport. Then in 1865, when the Union Stock Yard opened on 39th Street to the southwest of the city, the remaining plants moved to the Town of Lake. Steel makers also looked for new locations away from the crowded banks of the Chicago River. In 1875 the first steel mill opened on the Calumet River and began a trend which would make the far southeast side of Chicago a steel-producing center that would eventually surpass Pittsburgh in tonnage. As the mills, packinghouses, and factories left the downtown area, so did the workers.

The Chicago Fire also contributed to the outward movement of the working-class neighborhoods. A little after nine o'clock on Sunday evening, October 8, 1871 a fire broke out in the O'Leary barn on DeKoven Street near Jefferson in the Irish "Patch," just southwest of downtown, where the Fire Academy stands today. No one knows how the fire began, but once it started, the O'Leary name was linked with the tragedy, and by Tuesday morning most of Chicago was a smoldering ruins. Nothing could stop the inferno as it first consumed the wooden houses of the Patch then attacked the "fire-proof" buildings downtown. Mrs. O'Leary's house stood untouched as the fire burned an average of sixty-five acres per hour and destroyed the proud, young city. Over 1,600 acres lay in ashes from the Near West Side to the lake and up to Fullerton Avenue north of the river. To many people the fire seemed to mark the end of Chicago.

To many others, however, it presented an opportunity. The fire did not touch the industry that had moved to the outskirts of the city. While the fire consumed the lakefront, the Union Stock Yard continued its processing of hogs, cattle, and sheep. The newer grain elevators away from downtown were ready to take on additional produce. Railroad tracks, twisted and destroyed near the heart of the city, still came in from the East. Money, too, soon arrived. The Chicago Fire drastically affected the insurance business, but investors soon saw that the city had great potential for new growth. The important Eastern connections that had helped to create Chicago now helped to resurrect it. The city rose like a phoenix from the fire.

Fire of 1871, looking north on Clark Street from Cook County Court House and City Hall.
(Courtesy Chicago Historical Society)

Pillar of Fire, *Jefferson and DeKoven Streets. 1985. This bronze sculpture by Egon Weiner at the Chicago Fire Academy marks the site of the O'Leary barn where the Chicago Fire began on October 8. 1871.* (G. Lane)

Working-class people suffered greatly from the fire. The well-to-do, who lived in the south part of the "Loop" along Wabash and Michigan Avenues, were less affected. Those who had already made the move to the Prairie Avenue district were untouched. The city council quickly took control of the rebuilding process. It forbade the construction of wooden buildings in the burned-out district; this had been the basic type of housing for the poor and the working class. The new law permitted only brick or stone buildings in and adjacent to the downtown area. Therefore, workers and their families had to move to outlying industrial districts, like Bridgeport and West Town, in order to find cheaper rents in frame buildings. The O'Leary family, for instance, moved to Canaryville, just east of the Union Stock Yard.

A new central business district grew out of the ashes of October 1871. Within a very short time the downtown area was even more impressive than it had been before the tragedy. In one sense, the Chicago Fire can be thought of as a massive unintended urban renewal project. The old city was gone, and in its place stood a new one. Van Osdel and other architects quickly got involved in the reconstruction of buildings which they had originally designed. Over twenty cast-iron fronts reappeared on Lake Street, still a busy retail district. The Page Brothers' building, which stands today at the southeast corner of State and Lake Streets, is typical of the construction of this period. Standing five stories high, the structure included a steam elevator. Van Osdel's original design for this building had the cast-iron front on Lake Street, though it also had a small storefront on State. The construction of principal facades along Lake Street changed, however, as State Street grew in importance and surpassed Lake in the 1870s as Chicago's princpal thoroughfare.

State Street's preeminence as a retail business district did not occur overnight. The Chicago entrepreneur and real estate developer Potter Palmer played a crucial role in the development of State Street. Palmer had made a fortune in cotton speculation during the Civil War, and when the fighting ended, he turned his attention to real estate. In 1867 he purchased three-quarters of a mile of property on State Street south of Lake. Most of the buildings on this property had been wooden. The developer knocked down the shacks at State and Monroe and built the fabulous Palmer House. He also convinced Field, Leiter and Company to move its wholesale dry goods and retail store from Lake Street to State Street. This major company, now on the northeast corner of State and Washington, provided the commercial anchor Palmer needed for continued development. Other retail stores soon replaced the small buildings that had

contained livery stables, saloons, laundries, and
working-class housing on the new State Street. The first
Palmer House, designed by John Van Osdel, opened on
September 26, 1870. Within ten years State Street had
become the center of Chicago's retail business.

Indeed, the fire hastened a process that had been going
on for some time; that is, the sorting out by function of the
various parts of the central business district. Different
sections would play different roles in the economic, social,
political, and cultural life of the city. While the retail district
prospered along State Street, government was centered at
City Hall on Clark Street. Entertainment could be found
along Randolph west of State Street. And cultural life
flourished along Michigan Avenue from the Chicago Public
Library to the Auditorium Building. This cultural center was
not allowed to expand into Grant Park, but it overflowed onto
the lakefront south of Roosevelt Road. After 1911 the Field
Museum of Natural History, the Shedd Aquarium, the Adler
Planetarium, and Soldier Field were located there. LaSalle
Street became the center of Chicago's financial district. The
area south of Van Buren Street on State and Plymouth Court
was the vice district.

*Caryatid near the south entrance
of the Field Museum, 1985.*
(G. Lane)

One example of this sorting-out trend can be seen in
what happened along South Wabash Avenue after the fire.
Before the Chicago Fire, Wabash Avenue was a quiet street
of fine homes and churches. The beautiful First Presbyterian
Church and St. Paul's Universalist Church stood below
Adams on Wabash. A popular skating rink occupied the
northeast corner of Wabash and Jackson. This was a
well-to-do area which, even before the fire, had begun to
change. In the 1860s Chicago's music businesses were
located on Clark Steeet near the entertainment district on
Randolph. The Crosby Opera House opened in 1865 on
Washington Boulevard between State and Dearborn. The
downtown area had begun to differentiate by function.

The fire accelerated this trend. The wealthy moved their
homes away from the center of the city to Prairie Avenue
and even to the distant suburbs of Hyde Park and
Washington Park. The economic success of State Street
transformed the southern part of the central business
district. The fire actually moved many of the retail
businesses temporarily into the former homes of the wealthy
on South Wabash and Michigan Avenues. Once the business
community returned to the heart of the city, these older
homes were given over to other enterprises or turned into
cheap housing. The wealthy had moved on.

Meanwhile, other businesses looked for downtown
locations at reasonable rents. The music industry began to

*Field Museum of Natural History,
Twelfth Street at Lake Shore Drive,
1937. This photo shows the
construction of the foot bridge over
Lake Shore Drive. The Field
Museum moved to this site from
Jackson Park in 1919.*
(Chicago Park District, courtesy R. Wroble)

*A. Kroch and Company Bookstore,
26 West Monroe Street, c.1907.
Chicago quickly became the
publishing center of the Midwest.
By the time of the Fire in 1871,
there were sixty-eight bookstores
in the city.*
(Courtesy Kroch's & Brentano's)

Visiting Santa, the Boston Store, northwest corner of State and Madison, 1910. This family photograph is typical of what might be found in many Chicago family albums. Visiting the Loop for Christmas has been a longstanding Chicago tradition.

locate in new commercial buildings going up along Wabash Avenue. By 1891 the W.W. Kimball Company, maker of organs and pianos, opened its showroom on the southwest corner of Wabash and Jackson. In 1916 the company built the sixteen-story Kimball Building on this site; the building today houses De Paul University's Lewis Center. Across the street at the northeast corner, where a skating rink had stood, the Lyon & Healy Company built their new headquarters, also in 1916. These two companies provided the anchors for Chicago's Music Row, but other firms located along Wabash Avenue as well. At the very south end of Music Row stood the landmark Auditorium Building, linking the cultural institutions of Michigan Avenue with the music firms on Wabash.

The extension of the elevated trains into the downtown area in the 1890s reinforced the popular nickname of "the Loop," which had originated from the lines of Chicago's once-extensive cable car system. The trains also lowered land values and rents on Wabash Avenue. Until the elevated structure was built, Wabash Avenue merchants claimed that their street would become the retail center of the city. But once the tracks were constructed and the noise of the elevated trains began, the dream of challenging State Street disappeared.

The sixty-year period from about 1880 to 1945 was the Loop's heyday. All roads led to the downtown area. Chicago's central business district developed into the transportation center of Northern Illinois. The various transit lines that linked the city with outlying areas all converged on the Loop.

First the horse drawn streetcars, then the cable cars which appeared in 1881, and finally the trolley cars and elevated lines connected outlying neighborhoods to the city's center. Commuter railroads, like the Illinois Central and the Chicago and North Western, also converged on the Loop. Finally, by the end of the first decade of the twentieth century, the electric interurban trains tied Chicago to its satellite cities, Milwaukee, Joliet, Aurora, Elgin, South Bend, and many others.

This transportation network made the Loop a regional shopping and business center. No other place could compete with it. The large central business districts of the time were made possible by mass transportation systems. The "streetcar city" presented definite opportunities to the urban dweller. Retail and other businesses had to locate close to mass transportation if they were to succeed. Before the streetcar, Chicago was compact and crowded. With the coming of the streetcar, the middle class could join the wealthy on the fringes of the city and the outlying residential neighborhoods began to grow. The Loop lost its role as a residential area. The poor and the well-to-do abandoned the central city as commerce and government expanded. Warehouses also replaced the old "Patch" on the south edge of the Loop. Immigrants flooded the North, South, and West Sides of the city. By the last decade of the nineteenth century, the new transportation technology had created a new Chicago and transformed the Loop.

The Chicago created by the streetcars, railroads, and elevated trains became a showplace of American architecture. The fire of 1871 afforded tremendous opportunities to the young architects who flocked to the city. The Chicago School of Architecture emerged and actually transformed the way the nation and the world thought about buildings. The leader of the young architects who came to Chicago after the Civil War was William Le Baron Jenney. Trained in Paris, he served in the Union Army as an engineer and came to Chicago in 1868. Jenney pioneered new structural methods, especially the skeleton frame, which made it possible to build the first real skyscraper, the Home Insurance Building, in 1884-85. Because of increasing land values and the popularity of downtown locations, Chicago's buildings became taller and taller, creating the modern cityscape so familiar to us. Chicago architects Holabird & Roche, Adler & Sullivan, and Burnham & Root created the designs that set the style for the American city.

The Chicago Loop also became a major entertainment center. This was partly a response to the needs of the city, but also those of the business community and the convention trade. Hotels were centered in the Loop. Many of

Mich. Ave. Chicago.   10/13-13.

Michigan Avenue, 1913. This view
across a yet unlandscaped Grant
Park shows Chicago's emerging
skyline. A. Montgomery Ward,
whose spired building is seen in
the distance, led the civic crusade
to keep downtown Chicago's view
of the lake free from obstacles.
(C.R. Childs, courtesy G. Schmalgemeier)

Blackstone Hotel, Michigan
Avenue at Balbo, c.1909. Marshall
and Fox designed this hotel which
opened in 1909. Two- and
three-story residences filled the
block just south of the Blackstone
until the mid-1920s when the
construction of the Stevens Hotel
began, now the Chicago Hilton
and Towers.
(C.R. Childs, courtesy G. Schmalgemeier)

The Walnut Room in the Bismark Hotel, 1945. The Loop reached its zenith as an entertainment center during the era of the big bands. The couples pictured here are dining at the Bismark Hotel, Randolph at Wells Streets.

them stood along South Michigan Avenue below Van Buren Street. This hotel district stood close to the railroad stations of the South Loop; and the railroads, of course, provided the major form of interurban transportation from the mid-nineteenth until the mid-twentieth century. Large railroad stations, like the Illinois Central Station, the Polk Street Station, the LaSalle Street Station, and the Grand Central Station, were all in the South Loop. Other hotels served the financial and business districts within the area.

This large and vital Loop was largely the result of the technology of its day, that is, of rail transportation designed for long-distance hauling and for moving people within the city. The Loop began to decline in certain respects when the technology changed. This occured after World War II as the automobile came into more general use. The car made it possible to shop in neighborhood shopping centers and to do business away from the center of the city. A growing trend toward decentralization began in the 1920s and continued through the 1970s.

The period after 1945 saw the rapid development of suburban shopping centers that catered to the automobile. Slowly at first, then much more rapidly, these outlying retail districts drained dollars away from the Loop. Industries also began to move corporate headquarters out of the city close to expressways and especially closer to O'Hare Airport, to the northwest of the city.

But the Loop continued to show a good deal of vitality in the 1950s and afterwards. The construction of the Prudential Building in 1955 broke the ice jam in downtown construction that had lasted since the Great Depression. A renaissance in office building construction has taken place over the last twenty-eight years. This economic boom, however, did not directly effect the retail district on State Street. Here decline began to set in, especially as North Michigan Avenue captured a significant part of the city's retail trade. In 1978 the city turned State Street between Wacker Drive and Congress Parkway into a mall. At first this seemed to be an unpopular move, but Chicagoans have gotten used to the new traffic patterns. But the mall did not stem the decline of State Street as a retail center. Especially at the south end of the street, many retailers closed their stores and moved on. Goldblatt's, Sears, and Montgomery Ward left the strip. Lytton's, a long time State Street store, first announced it was leaving then decided to keep a smaller store in the Loop at its old location. The old Sears store at State and Congress is being turned into a combined retail and office building. The Goldblatt building at State and Jackson is scheduled to become the new home of the Chicago Public Library. There are new directions and new developments in the city and in the Loop once again.

The growth of North Michigan Avenue as a retail center was influenced by two factors connected with State Street. The first was a racial factor. Many retailers abandoned South and West Side shopping centers as racial change took place in those neighborhoods. This left large parts of black Chicago with few or no retail shopping centers. But the transit lines still led to the Loop, and the downtown shopping district became the only alternative for many of these people. This trend created a sort of retail white flight from the Loop. The higher-priced stores which wanted to stay in the city opened new locations on the more fashionable North Michigan Avenue. These retailers began calling the shopping strip north of the river the "New Downtown." The second factor was a change in function that saw the Loop return to an earlier pattern of settlement.

After nearly a century, the Loop suddenly began to acquire a residential population once again. The first step in this direction was the construction of Marina Towers (1960-64) on the North Bank of the Chicago River. These twin sixty-story towers designed by Bertrand Goldberg ushered in a new era in the history of downtown Chicago. Standing at the north end of the Loop on Dearborn Street, they rise above the river on a street that is known for its architectural excellence.

Between 1963 and 1981 the downtown residential district expanded eastward with such highrises as Outer Drive East at 400 E. Randolph, the Columbus Plaza Apartments at 233 E. Wacker Drive, and Doral Plaza at 155 N. Michigan.

While Marina Towers began this residential return to the heart of Chicago, the North Loop redevelopment bogged down for a time in politics and competing plans. The South Loop, however, began to prosper as a residential area with private development. Old office and loft buildings underwent a renewal that began in the 1970s and has continued into the 1980s. The South Loop has become a popular place to live and has recently been christened Burnham Park. Its major development has been the conversion of old loft buildings on Printer's Row, along Dearborn and Plymouth Court, into condominiums or rental apartments. These conversions were supplemented by the new townhouses and apartments of Dearborn Park, which was heralded by Mayor Michael Bilandic in the late 1970s as Chicago's newest neighborhood. Since that time the trend has continued with the construction of River City just south of the Loop and the new Presidential Towers just west of the Loop. All of these developments have brought residents back into the central city. Most of these people, however, tend to be single or couples without children. Generally speaking, it is still difficult to attract families into the central city.

All of this new development has occurred with the hope that it will help retail sales on State Street and keep Chicago's downtown a vital shopping center. While State Street has not fared badly at all when compared to central business districts in other American cities, it has continued to change. Developers are looking at State Street as a site for more office towers. Although Michigan Avenue has taken some of the trade from State Street, the retail center of the city still remains close to its historical and geographical center. The Loop is now redeveloping as a residential and commercial district. That does not mean that its retail functions will disappear, it simply means that they will be altered in proportion to new functions. The presence of apartments in old office and loft buildings may also mean that more entertainment will return to the Loop. All these developments will create a new and very interesting Loop.

(Top right) Dearborn Park housing development, State, Polk, Clark, and Roosevelt Road, 1985. This modern development in the South Loop contains townhouses, low- and highrise condominiums, as well as recreational facilities. (G. Lane)

(Bottom right) River City, east bank of the Chicago River south of Harrison Street, 1985. The South Loop developed into a major residential area in the 1980s. Pictured here are the squat towers of Bertrand Goldberg's River City, a new residential complex along the river's South Branch. By 1985, over 9,000 people lived in the South Loop area. (G. Lane)

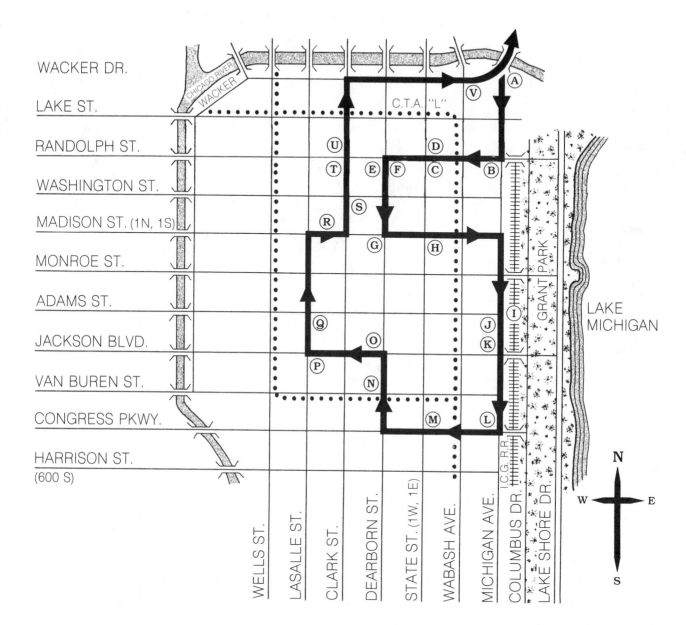

WACKER DR.

LAKE ST.

RANDOLPH ST.

WASHINGTON ST.

MADISON ST. (1N, 1S)

MONROE ST.

ADAMS ST.

JACKSON BLVD.

VAN BUREN ST.

CONGRESS PKWY.

HARRISON ST.
(600 S)

C.T.A. "L"

CHICAGO RIVER
WACKER

LAKE
MICHIGAN

GRANT PARK

WELLS ST.

LASALLE ST.

CLARK ST.

DEARBORN ST.

STATE ST. (1W, 1E)

WABASH AVE.

MICHIGAN AVE.

COLUMBUS DR.

I.C.G. R.R.

LAKE SHORE DR.

N
W   E
S

Loop Tour

The Loop tour, which begins at the south end of the Michigan Avenue Bridge, is the only walking tour in our book. The reason for this is simple, it is difficult to drive the Loop and look at its sights. Use this guide to look around and get acquainted with a part of Chicago which continues to be vital and whose history is the history of the city itself. While architects and building styles will be pointed out, this walk around Chicago's central business district deals, for the most part, with function: the role that various parts of the Loop played in the life of the city.

Walking time: about 2 hours.

Ⓐ Walk south on Michigan to Randolph Street. The site of the **Michigan Avenue Bridge** marks the point of origin of the settlement of Chicago. The cabin of Jean Baptiste Point du Sable, Chicago's first permanent resident, was located near the north pylon of the bridge in what is now Pioneer Court. Fort Dearborn stood on the south bank of the river. Sidewalk markers commemorate the military base established here in 1803. The bridge, part of the 1909 Burnham Plan for Chicago, opened in 1920 and paved the way for the development of the Near North Side. Within ten years the old warehouses that once lined the river disappeared and were replaced by the office buildings which still accent this entranceway to the city.

Elevator doors, 333 N. Michigan Avenue Building, 1985. The elevator doors of this Art Moderne building carry figures sculptured by Edgar Miller. (G. Lane)

Alfred S. Alschuler designed the **Stone Container Building** (1923) at the southwest corner of Wacker Drive and Michigan Avenue. This structure, originally known as the London Guarantee Building, is distinctive for the Greco-Roman lantern on its roof.

Across Michigan Avenue at the southeast corner is the **333 North Michigan Avenue Building** (1928) designed by Holabird and Root. This Art Moderne structure includes exquisite elevator doors done in relief by Chicago artist Edgar Miller.

One block south at 230 North Michigan stands the **Carbide and Carbon Building** by the Burnham Brothers, sons of the great planner and architect. This forty-story structure was designed just before the Great Depression. It is distinguished by a dark green and gold terra-cotta tower.

(B) Proceed south on Michigan Avenue, turn right at Randolph, and walk three blocks west to Dearborn Street. The **Cultural Center of the Chicago Public Library** stands on the southwest corner of Michigan and Randolph. Originally built as the city's central library in 1897 and designed by Shepley, Rutan, and Coolidge, this building was thoroughly renovated in 1977 under the guidance of the firm of Holabird and Root. Included in the Cultural Center is the large G.A.R. Museum dedicated to the Northern soldiers of the Civil War. This building marks the north end of the Michigan Avenue cultural district. Once the street was built up with cultural institutions and businesses, the area immediately to the south of Grant Park became a cultural "annex" of Michigan Avenue. The Field Museum of Natural History, the Shedd Aquarium, and the Adler Planetarium are located along the lakefront south of Roosevelt Road.

(C) At the southeast corner of State and Randolph stands the **Marshall Field & Company** department store, designed in several phases (1892, 1902, 1906, 1907, and 1914) by D.H. Burnham & Company. The portion at State and Washington marks the site of three previous buildings used by the partnership of Field and Leiter. The company moved to State Street in the late 1860s after Marshall Field was persuaded by Potter Palmer that this underused street would become the retail heart of the city. The Field and Leiter store gave the Chicago real estate entrepreneur a much-needed anchor for the development of State Street into "that great street."

(D) The grand old **Chicago Theatre** stands on the east side of State Street north of Randolph. This movie palace, opened in 1921 and designed by C.W. and G.L. Rapp, has a special place in the hearts of Chicagoans who remember the stage shows that featured many of the greatest names of show business in the 1920s, 1930s, and 1940s. One of Chicago's largest movie houses, the theater seats 3,980 people. The building was designated a Chicago landmark in 1983 despite protests by its owners. Plans have been drawn up to turn the old movie house into a center for the performing arts.

(Left) Stone Container Building, Michigan Avenue at Wacker Drive, 1985. This building faces the Chicago River and forms with the Wrigley Building an impressive architectural gateway to the city.
(G. Lane)

Chicago Theatre, east side of State Street near Randolph, 1985. Plans for the redevelopment of this Beaux Arts style structure as a performing arts center are crucial for North Loop redevelopment. Rapp and Rapp designed this landmark building for the Balaban and Katz theater chain in 1921. (G. Lane)

(E) Randolph Street west of State Street was an early entertainment district for Chicagoans. The State Street location of the Chicago Theatre and the State-Lake Theater, which was across the street from it, marked the eastern end of this area. Chicago's major vaudeville and movie theaters were on or near Randolph Street. Old Heidelberg, once located just west of State Street, was a favorite place for Chicagoans to dine out, as was Henrici's farther west on Randolph in a building which stood on the site of the Daley Civic Center.

Several important historical and architectural landmarks stand at the corner of Randolph and

Dearborn. On the northeast corner is the eight-story **Delaware Building** built in 1872. This Italianate structure, designed by Wheelock and Thomas, was one of the first structures built after the Chicago Fire and is a fine example of an early commercial building in Chicago.

The building which dominates this intersection, however, is the thirty-one-story **Daley Civic Center** built in 1965. It is made of Cor-Ten steel that has oxidized to its present rust brown color. The Daley Center acts as a link between the old entertainment zone, which has faded drastically over the last twenty years, and the political heart of the city on Clark Street. Holabird and Roche's combined **County Building and City Hall** (1907,

*(Right) Delaware Building,
northeast corner of Dearborn and
Randolph, 1980. This landmark
building, completed in 1874, is
typical of office and retail
structures built in Chicago before
and just after the Chicago Fire.*
(Bob Thall, courtesy Commission on Chicago
Landmarks)

*The Picasso sculpture, Daley
Center Plaza, 1985. One of four
plazas on or near Dearborn Street
between Jackson and Randolph,
this one is heavily used and
contains Chicago's famous Picasso
sculpture.*   (G. Lane)

1911) stands directly across Clark Street from the Daley Center. Noontime concerts are held through most of the year in the Daley Center Plaza or in the center itself, depending on the weather.

Two movie houses also occupy corners at Dearborn and Randolph. The **Woods Theatre** and its two twin neighbors to the north, the **Selwyn** and **Harris Theatres**, are under consideration for preservation and rehabilitation as a theatre row that would link up to the Chicago Theatre on State Street. All of these plans, however, are dependent on attracting funds for North Loop redevelopment.

(F) Walk south along Dearborn Street to Washington. The **McCarthy Building** stands on the northeast corner of the intersection. It was designed by Chicago's first professional architect, John M. Van Osdel in 1872, and like the Delaware Building, it recalls the pre-Civil War style of architecture. Van Osdel designed many Loop area buildings both before and just after the Chicago Fire of October 1871. During the eighteen months following the fire, Van Osdel designed about one and one-half miles of building frontage in Chicago. The McCarthy Building is one of only two known Van Osdel structures still standing in the Loop. The other is the Page Brothers Building at 177-91 North State Street, also built in 1872.

The **Daley Center Plaza** is on the northwest corner of Dearborn and Washington. This very public space contains the famous Chicago **Picasso**. Erected in 1967, this work is still a controversial piece of public art. In the more than eighteen years that it has graced the Daley Center Plaza, the 136-ton work has become a universal symbol of Chicago.

Across Washington Street, in a narrow court, stands the work of another eminent Spanish artist. Joan Miro's *Chicago* joined Picasso's untitled work in the late 1970s.

(G) Continue south on Dearborn Street to Madison. The **First National Bank Building and Plaza** stands on the block bounded by Dearborn, Madison, Clark, and Monroe. The building was constructed in 1969, and the plaza followed four years later. The 850-foot building is sheathed in gray-speckled granite and bronze-tinted glass. The sweep of the A-shaped structure immediately

captures the eye and draws it skyward. This plaza, like its neighbor at the Daley Center, is the home of another famous work of modern art. Marc Chagall's *Four Seasons* mosaic covers the sides and top of a rectangular block fourteen feet high and seventy feet long. It highlights this plaza, which is one of the most popular open spaces in the city. Through the collection of major sculptures by Miro, Picasso, Chagall, and Alexander Calder, Dearborn Street has become an important repository for modern public sculpture.

(H) Go east on Madison to State Street. This corner marks the center of the city's street grid. Chicago's streets are numbered to the east, west, north, and south from this intersection. Once one of the busiest corners in the world, this intersection marks the center of the State Street retail district.

On the southeast corner stands the **Carson Pirie Scott** store designed by Louis Sullivan in 1899 and 1903. It was enlarged in 1905 by D.H. Burnham and Company, and again in 1960 by Holabird and Root. These architects, however, remained loyal to Sullivan's original plan. The intricate floral design of the ornamentation on the the two first floors is clearly Sullivan's. Notice also the use of the Chicago window throughout the building, allowing light and air into the interior of the department store. The Schlesinger and Mayer Company originally owned the edifice. Carson's purchased it in 1904.

The firm of Holabird and Roche designed the **Wieboldt's** store, formerly the Mandel Brothers store building, on the northeast corner. This firm also planned the State-Madison Building which formerly was occupied by the Boston Store on the northwest corner.

Carson Pirie Scott Building, southeast corner State and Madison, 1985. Louis Sullivan's monumental department store was built in stages betweeen 1899 and 1904. Elegant iron work accents the first two floors of the building.
(G. Lane)

(I) Walk east on Madison to Michigan Avenue and then south to Adams Street. The **Art Institute of Chicago** stands at the head of Adams Street. The original building opened in 1892 and is French Renaissance in style. This institution has played an important role in the cultural life of Chicago for over one hundred years. It marks the center of the Michigan Avenue Cultural District. The museum's holdings are among the finest in the world. The School of the Art Institute is a world-renowned institution.

The Art Institute of Chicago, Michigan at Adams, 1985. This building, designed by the architects Shepley, Rutan and Coolidge, was built in 1892. Before this the Art Institute occupied a building at the southwest corner of Van Buren and Michigan. (G. Lane)

(J) Proceed south on Michigan Avenue. At 220 South Michigan stands the **Theodore Thomas Orchestra Hall.** The building is owned by the Orchestral Association and houses the Chicago Symphony Orchestra founded by Theodore Thomas in 1898. D.H. Burnham and Company designed the hall which was dedicated late in 1904. Harry Weese planned the 1969 restoration. The symphony orchestra moved here in 1905 from its former headquarters in the Auditorium Building at the south end of the Michigan Avenue district.

(K) South of Orchestra Hall, at the northwest corner of Jackson and Michigan, stands another Burnham-designed structure, the seventeen-story terra-cotta clad **Railway Exchange Building** (1904). The Santa Fe Company has recently renovated the structure, and it promises to be an anchor for the revitalization of South Michigan Avenue as an important office center. The building features an impressive atrium and skylight.

(L) Proceed south to Congress Parkway. The **Fine Arts Building** stands at 410 S. Michigan Avenue. Originally designed as a wagon showroom for the Studebaker Company by Solon S. Beman, who planned George Pullman's model city on the Southeast Side, this structure has served Chicago and the Midwest as an important cultural center since 1898. It, along with the Auditorium immediately to the south, has been the home of many an aspiring artist in Chicago. The building originally housed two theaters. But these have been remodeled into four, now showing art films.

At the corner of Congress and Michigan stands Adler & Sullivan's **Auditorium Building** (1889). Now occupied by **Roosevelt University,** it is one of Chicago's most famous cultural and architectural landmarks. The structure originally included a hotel and office building as well as the renowned Auditorium Theatre. The original Auditorium Hotel lobby can still be appreciated as you enter the building from the Michigan Avenue side. This building provided the southern anchor for the Michigan Avenue cultural district as well as for "Music Row," which was located on Wabash Avenue south of Adams Street.

Auditorium Building, at Michigan, Congress, and Wabash, 1985. Adler and Sullivan's architectural masterpiece (1889) anchors the south end of the Michigan Avenue cultural district. Today Roosevelt University occupies the structure. The Auditorium Theatre is an exquisite Sullivan design with some of the finest acoustics in the world. (G. Lane)

Today Roosevelt University provides an important anchor for the redevelopment of the South Loop. Several institutions of higher learning have settled in the South Loop, including Roosevelt and De Paul Universities, as well as Columbia College. Together they have provided a sound institutional foundation as the Loop has gone through a transition period. Once again Michigan Avenue and Wabash Avenue are serving the city as important cultural centers, even if in a different context.

(M) Walk west along Congress to State Street. At the northeast corner stands the former **Sears Roebuck** store. The father of the skyscraper, William Le Baron Jenney, designed this department store in 1891. Levi Z. Leiter, the former partner of Marshall Field, erected this building as an income property. Upon completion it was leased by the Siegel, Cooper & Co. department store. It was later occupied by a cooperative department store under the Leiter name. Sears purchased the store in the 1920s and billed it as the "World's Largest Store." The Sears-owned radio station received its call letters, WLS, from this sobriquet. The building is a fine example of the commercial style for which the Chicago School was famous. Sears left the Loop in 1983, and today the store is being renovated for both commercial and office space.

The former Sears store marks the southern boundary of the State Street Mall. The mall cost $17 million when it was constructed in 1978 and is said to

Manhattan Building, 431 S. Dearborn, 1985. William Le Baron Jenney, father of the Chicago School of Architecture, designed this edifice in 1889, and it opened two years later. It was one of the first tall office buildings to use skeleton construction throughout.
(G. Lane)

accommodate more buses than any other thoroughfare in the nation. While originally a controversial project, the mall has come to be accepted by most Chicagoans. It has not, however, brought about the hoped-for revitalization of the city's old retail center. Since the mall opened, Goldblatt's, Montgomery Ward, and Sears have closed their State Street stores. South State Street is now seen as a choice area for office tower development. The function of State Street seems to be changing as the economy of the city has shifted over the last thirty years.

(N) Continue walking west on Congress to Dearborn. Go north on Dearborn to Van Buren Street. This part of the walk is marked by four important office buildings. One, William Le Baron Jenney's **Manhattan Building** at 431

S. Dearborn (1890), was one of the first tall office buildings to use skeleton construction throughout. It has been remodeled as a downtown residential structure and represents the northernmost thrust of the apartment conversion trend that has hit the South Loop since the late 1970s. While this part of Chicago has recently been renamed Burnham Park, in honor of the great architect and planner, many people continue to call it the South Loop.

The **Old Colony Building** at 407 S. Dearborn was completed in 1893 after plans by Holabird and Roche. Directly across the street stands the **Fisher Building,** on the northeast corner of Van Buren and Dearborn. This is another Burnham building, whose steel frame skeleton is apparent despite the use of terra-cotta detailed in rather elaborate Gothic ornamentation. The Fisher Building's bay windows helped the architect to achieve a notable openness and lightness in this building.

On the west side of Dearborn between Van Buren and Jackson stands the venerable **Monadnock Building.** Holabird and Roche designed the southern half of the building in 1893 to compliment the northern half done by Burnham and Root two years earlier. Its stark silhouette suggests the New England mountain it was named for. While Root's building is the tallest wall-bearing masonry structure in Chicago—its walls are six feet wide at the base—the Holabird and Roche section is of more conventional steel-framed construction. The Monadnock is perhaps the fullest expression of John Root's power as an architect. The **Chicago Architecture Foundation's ArchiCenter** is located in the Monadnock Building. This center includes a fine bookstore dealing with Chicago's architectural heritage. Public lectures and tours are also offered through the ArchiCenter.

(O) Continue north to Jackson. On the northwest corner stands the **Kluczynski Building and Plaza.** Across the street stands the **Dirksen Building.** Ludwig Mies van der Rohe designed these structures (including the low-rise post office on the plaza) as the **Federal Center and Plaza,** which was constructed between 1964 and 1975. The plaza, like the two others on Dearborn, is adorned by a sculpture. A fifty-three foot red stabile by Alexander Calder called *Flamingo* ornaments this public space.

Monadnock Building, southwest corner Jackson and Dearborn, 1985. This trim, sixteen-story building (1891) was the tallest ever built with masonry, wall-bearing construction. (G. Lane)

(P) Proceed west on Jackson Boulevard to LaSalle Street. LaSalle street is the financial heart of Chicago's Central Business District. The magnificent **Board of Trade Building,** designed by Holabird and Root in 1929, just before the financial panic that brought on the Great Depression, dominates this canyon-like street. This is the second Board of Trade Building to be located on this site. The first commodity exchange designed in 1885 by W.W. Boyington, who also designed the Water Tower on North Michigan Avenue, had a 300-foot tower that had to be removed in 1895 because of structural problems. At the top of the present building stands a statue of Ceres, the Greek goddess of grain, 609 feet above LaSalle Street. The actual trading of commodities can be seen from the visitors's gallery every business day from 10:30 a.m. to 1:00 p.m.

(Q) Go north on LaSalle to Adams. The **Rookery** dominates this intersection with its powerful columns and stonework. Burnham and Root designed the building, which was built between 1885 and 1888. It is one of the oldest forerunners of the modern skyscraper. Shops and offices surround the first-floor light court. The building is naturally lighted from four sides and from the central light well. The glass-covered lobby court provided one of the more bold and exciting innovations in modern civic architecture. In 1905 the Rookery was further enhanced by the work of Frank Lloyd Wright, who remodeled the lobby with gold and white marble detailing.

(R) Continue north on LaSalle to Madison and walk east to Clark Street. **St. Peter's Church** is located at 110 West Madison Street. German Catholics founded this parish in 1846. The original church stood on Washington Street between Wells and Franklin. A second church at the corner of Clark and Polk Streets housed the parish from 1875 until the present church opened in 1953. The church serves aproximately 500,000 Roman Catholics who work in the Loop. The structure has only one window, a Gothic stained glass window which faces Madison and is dedicated to Mary, Queen of Peace. The church offers fifteen Masses each weekday. It is estimated that 20,000 persons attend services each week.

(Left) The Rookery Lobby, 209 S. LaSalle, 1972. This interior view of Burnham and Root's Rookery Building shows the lobby as remodeled by Frank Lloyd Wright in 1905. Wright replaced Root's elaborate ornament with ironwork in a simple geometric design and added huge rectangular planters.
(Courtesy Commission on Chicago Landmarks))

The **Chicago Loop Synagogue** is located just south of the intersection of Clark and Madison at 16 South Clark Street. Designed by Loebl, Schlossman and Bennett in 1957, it includes a wonderful stained glass composition by Abraham Rattner on the theme "Let there be light!" The Loop Synagogue acts as the city's central synagogue. It was founded in 1929.

(S) Walk north on Clark to Washington Street. The **Chicago Temple Building** soars above the intersection of Clark and Washington. The Temple has twenty-one stories plus an eight-story spire. The French Gothic design stands out among the Loop skyscrapers. Architects Holabird and Roche designed this unique combination office building and church for the First United Methodist Church in the early 1920s. Westminster chimes sound from the tower and are heard throughout the Loop. The building claims the world's tallest spire topped with a cross 568 feet above the street. The First United Methodist church is the mother church of all Methodist churches in Chicago.

(T) On the northwest corner of Clark and Washington stands the combination **County Building and City Hall.** The County Building is the older of the twin buildings designed by Holabird and Roche. Its Beaux-Arts classicism was typical of civic architecture in the first decades of this century. The heavy Corinthian columns quickly establish the importance of the buildings. Clark Street has developed as the government center of Chicago and even of Cook County. For those interested in doing research on Chicago's history, City Hall contains the excellent Municipal Reference Library.

County Building and City Hall, Clark, Washington, LaSalle, and Randolph Streets, 1985. This block-square neoclassical structure was designed by Chicago architects Holabird and Roche and was completed in 1911. (G. Lane)

(U) Continue north on Clark Street. At the northwest corner of Randolph and Clark stands the 1.2 million square foot **State of Illinois Building.** This Helmut Jahn design opened to much fanfare on May 6, 1985. The huge rotunda and the large open spaces that include office and retail space make this a unique structure. The building is the home of over fifty state agencies. It includes three floors of restaurants and shops, an art gallery, and a six hundred seat auditorium. Tours begin at the information booth. Jean Dubuffet's ten-ton white fiberglass sculpture, *Monument With Standing Beast* stands at the main entrance.

State of Illinois Building, Clark, Randolph, LaSalle, and Lake Streets, 1985. This monumental office building with retail space was designed by Helmut Jahn and completed in 1985. (G. Lane)

South Water Street Market, c.1917. This busy produce market was removed to a site two miles southwest of the Loop in the 1920s and replaced with the two-level Wacker Drive specified in Burnham and Bennett's Chicago Plan of 1909.

(Courtesy Commission on Chicago Landmarks)

(V) Walk north to Wacker Drive and then turn right and proceed to Michigan Avenue. The **Seventeenth Church of Christ Scientist** is located on the corner of Wacker, South Water Street, and Wabash. Harry Weese designed this place of worship in 1968. This entire area was renovated after the Burnham Plan (1909) called for the removal of the South Water Street Market from the Loop and the creation of the Michigan Avenue Bridge. Wacker Drive replaced the old market place in 1926. Three years later modern buildings joined this formal riverfront as part of Chicago's gateway to the lake.

Heald Square, directly across Wacker Drive from the church, commemorates the ill-fated commander of Fort Dearborn at the time of the massacre in 1812. Sculptured figures by Lorado Taft of Revolutionary notables Robert Morris, George Washington, and Haym Salomon adorn the square.

17-8635

Near North Side

2

In many respects, the Near North Side is one of the best known places in Chicago. The historic Water Tower, which survived the Chicago Fire of 1871, is one of the city's most enduring symbols. A stark reminder of Chicago's past, it now stands in the midst of the city's most fashionable district. When the Water Tower was completed in 1869, it was one of the tallest structures in the city. Today it is dwarfed by newer Chicago landmarks such as the John Hancock Building, Water Tower Place, One Magnificent Mile, and the Olympia Centre.

The Near North Side, which extends roughly from the Chicago River to Diversey Parkway, was not always the city's Gold Coast. Shoppers at glittering Water Tower Place might find it hard to believe, but in the 1850s and 1860s the surrounding area was a hodgepodge of breweries, shipyards, factories, and immigrant slums, with only a few fashionable homes. Although the Rush Street Bridge connected this section of Chicago to the business district in 1856, crossing the river posed a formidable problem until 1920 when the Michigan Avenue Bridge opened.

In the 1920s North Michigan Avenue was just one of several important commercial strips outside the Loop. Now it is Chicago's premier shopping district, inviting comparisons with New York's Fifth Avenue. Although few single-family homes remain in the immediate vicinity, high-rise construction has boosted the residential population of the area around Chicago Avenue. According to the 1980 census, about 30,000 people lived east of State Street between the river and North Avenue. Nearly half of this population was concentrated between Chicago Avenue and Division Street. Like much of the Near North Side, the Gold Coast is populated mostly by single men and women and married couples without children.

One of the most dramatic changes to occur on the Near North Side in recent years has been the expansion of the Gold Coast to embrace the neighborhoods of Old Town and Lincoln Park. Twenty years ago, most Chicagoans would not have believed that the area between Division Street and Diversey Parkway would become the most popular residential district in Chicago. While some urban renewal has taken place here, for the most part the old houses and apartments have been restored and upgraded. Besides restoring greystones and row houses to their former glory, young professionals have transformed nineteenth-century laborers'

The Water Tower, Michigan at Chicago Avenue, 1985. Designed by W.W. Boyington and completed in 1869, the Water Tower is one of Chicago's most famous landmarks.
(G. Lane)

homes into upper-middle-class residences. Even more significant, within the past decade real estate developers have renovated factories and built new townhouses and highrises in areas previously considered too dangerous to live in. Not only have these entrepreneurs increased the city's supply of middle- and upper-middle-class housing, but they have realigned the boundaries of the Gold Coast.

For more than a century the Near North Side has been an area of great contrasts. Our Near North Side history focuses on the Gold Coast as well as its backyard, an area once known as Little Hell, and it includes the outlying neighborhoods of Old Town and Lincoln Park.

Gold Coast

The Germans were the first ethnic group to settle in large numbers on the Near North Side. Because so many German immigrants were craftsmen and skilled workers, their communities tended to be prosperous, and they supported a rich cultural life as well. In addition to their many beer gardens, restaurants, saloons, and small businesses, the Germans established singing societies and charitable institutions. Three pioneer German congregations which continue in existence today trace their origins to the Near North Side; they are First St. Paul's Evangelical Lutheran Church (1846), now at 1301 N. LaSalle Street; St. Joseph Catholic Church (1846), at Hill and Orleans Streets; and St. Pauls (1848), which moved to Kemper Place and Orchard Street in 1898.

By the 1850s large numbers of Irish and Swedes had also settled on the Near North Side where they found jobs in the shipyards along the north bank of the river and in large manufacturing plants like McCormick's Reaper Works. The early Irish settlement on the North Side was known as Kilgubbin because it was composed of peasants who had been evicted in the 1840s from three large estates in Kilgubbin, County Cork, Ireland. Kilgubbin was centered along Market (Orleans) Street between Kinzie and Erie, and it expanded north of Chicago Avenue during the next two decades. By the 1860s Irish squatters had built shanties on the land between the forks of the North Branch of the river, around Division Street. In due time this remote section of the city came to be known as Goose Island, a reference to the wildfowl that were kept by the immigrant Irish.

For hundreds of North Side Irish, the focal point of their community was Holy Name parish. Being unwilling to worship in the German church of St. Joseph, the Irish

Catholics attended Mass in the chapel of St. Mary of the Lake University, Chicago's first institution of higher learning. From 1846 until its abrupt closing by Bishop James Duggan in 1866, St. Mary of the Lake University occupied the property bounded by Chicago Avenue, State Street, Superior Street, and Cass (Wabash) Avenue. In 1849 Holy Name Chapel was reorganized as a parish, and the congregation built a frame church at the northeast corner of State and Superior Streets, on the present site of Holy Name Cathedral.

Chicago's first Swedish colony was located west of Wells Street, between the North Branch of the river and Erie Street. The Swedish population here expanded rapidly despite the ravages of a cholera epidemic in the late 1840s and early 1850s. By the 1860s the Swedes were displacing the German residents in the area. When the Deutsche Haus opened in 1856 at Grand and Wells, it was the cultural center of Chicago's North Side German community. In less than ten years, however, this area was a densely populated Swedish district. The Germans moved northward, relocating their churches and other institutions.

In 1864 the members of First St. Paul's Lutheran congregation built a new church at the northwest corner of Superior and Franklin Streets. In 1865 German Catholics dedicated their new St. Joseph Church at the northeast corner of Chicago and Cass (Wabash). Two years later German Jews began worshiping nearby in the North Side Hebrew Temple.

Throughout the nineteenth century North Michigan Avenue, then known as Pine Street, remained relatively undeveloped. Dearborn Street, on the other hand, contained a mix of residences, businesses, churches, and other institutions. North Market Hall, for example, built in the 1840s at Dearborn and Hubbard Streets, was one of three public market houses in Chicago. Over the years this

building was the scene of lively political gatherings. Stephen A. Douglas attempted to defend the Kansas-Nebraska Bill here in 1854, but was shouted down by an angry mob. After the Chicago Fire of 1871 destroyed the North Market Hall, a Criminal Court building and jail was built on the site. This structure was replaced in 1892 by a new building, which still occupies the site and is now being renovated for use as offices.

In 1868 the Chicago Historical Society built its first permanent home at the northwest corner of Dearborn and Ontario, catty-corner from the Westminster Presbyterian Church. Organized in 1856, the Historical Society has been a North Side institution for more than 125 years.

Just as Chicago's Germans were moving north of Grand Avenue, so too were the city's elite. In the 1860s the area around Washington Square Park at Dearborn and Delaware Place developed into a fashionable neighborhood populated mostly by American-born Protestants of English descent. These families built stately homes along LaSalle, Dearborn, and Cass (Wabash), and they worshiped at some of the city's most prominent churches, among them St. James Episcopal (1857), at Wabash and Huron; New England Congregational (1867), at Dearborn and Delaware; and Unity Church (1869), at Dearborn and Walton. This last church, destroyed by the Fire of 1871, was rebuilt in 1873, was acquired by the Medinah Temple Association in 1903, and became the Scottish Rite Cathedral when Medinah's new mosque opened at 600 N. Wabash in 1912.

On October 8, 1871, just hours before the Chicago Fire began, the new congregation known as Fourth Presbyterian worshiped for the first time in its new church at Grand and Wabash. Fourth Presbyterian was formed by a merger of two early North Side churches, North Presbyterian and Westminster. Of the 321 founding members of Fourth Presbyterian, all but five lost their homes in the conflagration.

The Chicago Fire of October 8th and 9th, 1871 burned down most of the Near North Side, homes and businesses and churches, from the river all the way up to Fullerton Avenue. After the fire many wealthy Chicagoans moved south of the river to the Prairie Avenue district. Others stayed on the North Side and built brownstones and mansions east of Dearborn Street. Congregations such as Unity and New England faced the task of rebuilding churches that had only recently been opened for worship. Older congregations such as Holy Name and St. James Episcopal also rebuilt their houses of worship. Several North Side churches sought out new locations after the fire. Fourth

(Top left) The Church of St. James, built in 1857 at the southeast corner of Wabash and Huron, was reconstructed after the Fire of 1871. The oldest Episcopal church in the city, St. James is now the cathedral for the Episcopal diocese of Chicago. (G. Lane, 1980)

(Top right) Unity Church, which opened in 1869 at the southeast corner of Dearborn and Walton, was one of the Near North Side's most prestigious congregations. Designed by Robert Collyer, the church was completely destroyed in the Chicago Fire, but was rebuilt and rededicated in 1874. As a result of changing residential patterns, Unity Church was sold in 1903 to the Medinah Temple Association. Since 1912, it has been known as the Scottish Rite Cathedral. (J.Ficner)

(Bottom left) The Chicago Historical Society occupied this building at 632 N. Dearborn from 1896 to 1932 when it moved into its present quarters in Lincoln Park. The granite-walled structure designed by Henry Ives Cobb has recently taken on new life as the Limelight nightclub. (G. Lane)

State Parkway looking north from Division Street. c.1911. The trolley car lines linked this part of the Gold Coast with downtown Chicago.
(C.R. Childs, courtesy G. Schmalgemeier)

Presbyterian constructed a new building at Rush and Superior in 1874, and German Catholics of St. Joseph parish built a new Gothic church at Hill and Orleans in 1878.

The fire wiped out the frame houses of Chicago's Germans and Swedes as well as the original Kilgubbin, but it spared the squatters' shanties on Goose Island. The aftermath of the city's first complete urban renewal program was almost as disastrous as the fire itself. Hundreds of "temporary" shanties were constructed north of Chicago Avenue and west of Wells Street. Crowded together on narrow lots, these clapboard houses provided shelter for the refugees of the fire. But far from being temporary, many of these shanties continued to be used late into the 1930s.

To a remarkable extent, rebuilding after the Chicago Fire reinforced earlier patterns of settlement. The well-to-do residential district around Washington Square Park expanded steadily over the next twenty years. Already by 1873 ten new houses had been built along Rush Street between Grand and Ohio on land which had formerly been vacant. In 1875 R. Hall McCormick built a mansion at 660 N. Rush Street. Four years later Cyrus Hall McCormick moved into his mansion across the street at 675 N. Rush. So many McCormick relatives built homes nearby that this section of the Near North Side came to be known as "McCormickville." The two McCormick mansions which still survive now function as restaurants. The L. Hamilton

McCormick home at 631 N. Rush Street was known for many years as the Kungsholm Scandinavian Restaurant. Today it is Lawry's. Chicago's oldest French restaurant, Chez Paul, operates in the former R. Hall McCormick residence at 660 N. Rush.

Much of Chicago's present-day Gold Coast owes its existence to Potter Palmer, the wealthy State Street merchant who built a $1 million castle in 1882 at what is now 1350 N. Lake Shore Drive. This swampy area near Lake Michigan was soon gentrified as socialites built splendid homes between Bellevue and Burton Place. William Borden's turreted mansion at 1020 N. Lake Shore Drive was one of the area's showplaces in 1883. In 1892 Byron Lathrop's three-story Georgian mansion was completed at 120 E. Bellevue Place. Since 1922 it has been the home of the Fortnightly Club, Chicago's oldest women's club.

When Archbishop Patrick A. Feehan moved into his many-chimneyed residence at 1555 N. State Parkway in 1885, most of the surrounding neighborhood was uninhabited. But not for long. After the turn of the century the Archdiocese sold its property south of the episcopal residence and it was subdivided for homes. Wealthy Chicagoans hired architects to design spacious brownstones along Dearborn, State Parkway, and Astor Street. While many of the city's elite had forsaken the North Side for Prairie Avenue and Jackson Boulevard, the trend northward was now unmistakable. More and more, the Gold Coast's housing expanded to include high-class apartment buildings, many of them designed by Benjamin Marshall. The building boom, which continued throughout the 1920s, transformed this section of the Near North Side into the city's most prominent residential district.

Improvements in nearby Lincoln Park further enhanced the reputation of the Gold Coast. Lincoln Park traces its origins to the city's cemetery, located just beyond North Avenue, in the 1840s. (A Catholic cemetery occupied property between Schiller and North Avenues.) As the city expanded northward, concerns over sanitation prompted the closing of both burial grounds. Mass exhumations took place, and bodies were reinterred in two new cemeteries which were established in 1859 along the Chicago and North Western Railroad line: Rosehill, near Thorndale Avenue, and Calvary, near Evanston.

Lincoln Park opened to the public in 1868, and during the next forty years it became one of the city's most beautiful parks. In addition to its system of lagoons, flower conservatory, and zoo, Lincoln Park is the site of the Chicago Academy of Sciences (1893), and since 1932, the Chicago Historical Society. At the turn of the century Lincoln Park was also one of Chicago's most popular public places with an average attendance of 100,000 people on warm summer Sundays. In 1908 one Chicago writer commented that, "Nothing could be more gratifying to the settlement worker, the philanthropist and the social economist than the sight of groups of families—almost innumerable—with their luncheons and other comforts, that dot the lawn stretches of Lincoln Park."

A photograph taken from the top of the Water Tower in 1888 vividly illustrates the humble beginnings of the Gold Coast. A few mansions can be seen along Lake Shore Drive near Bellevue Place, but just north of Chicago Avenue the neighborhood consisted of many frame houses built close together, some below grade. In the midst of these were blacksmith shops and saloons such as Michael Donoghue's "sample room" on Chestnut, just east of Pine. When the Pine Street Land Association was formed in 1892 to promote a residential district east of Pine Street (Michigan Avenue) between Lake Shore Drive and Pearson, nearly half the site was under water.

The desolation of this area did not deter George Wellington Streeter from staking his claim. In 1886 Streeter took up residence on a small boat which had run aground just south of Chicago Avenue. He subsequently laid claim to more than 150 acres of landfill, arguing that this territory was not included in the original federal land grant which established the State of Illinois. Until his death in 1921, the "Squatter King" waged a spirited battle to defend his holdings. Although he was unsuccessful, the area bounded by East Lake Shore Drive, Michigan Avenue, the river, and the lake still bears his name—Streeterville.

The upgrading of the Near North Side around the Water Tower only happened gradually. Some institutions, like the North Chicago Hebrew Congregation, regarded LaSalle Street as a more promising location. Now known as Temple Sholom, this congregation began to build a synagogue at Rush and Walton in 1884. Due to harassment by Irish and German gangs, however, they decided not to complete their building. Instead, they moved again, to LaSalle and Goethe Streets, where they dedicated a new temple in 1895. Near this site, Chicago's first Jewish hospital operated from 1868 until it was destroyed in the Chicago Fire.

Wealthy German and Swedish families put their mark on the neighborhood in the vicinity of LaSalle Street. In 1889 the Germania Club moved into new quarters at 1536 N. Clark; the building, which stands today, was designed by the architectural firm of Addison & Fiedler. The club began in 1865 when three hundred Civil War veterans sang at President Abraham Lincoln's funeral. Another German

Chicago's emerging Gold Coast, 1888. In the distance, turreted mansions and greystones flank the new Lake Shore Drive at Bellevue Place. In the foreground along Chestnut Street are frame buildings and fire "shanties" constructed after the Great Fire of 1871. (Courtesy Chicago Historical Society)

The synagogue constructed by Temple Sholom in 1895 at LaSalle and Goethe was purchased by First St. Paul's Evangelical Lutheran Church in 1910. Chicago's oldest Lutheran congregation, First St. Paul's has been a North Side institution since 1846. In 1970 the congregation constructed a modern church building on this site.
(Courtesy G. Schmalgemier)

institution nearby was the Red Star Inn at 1528 N. Clark Street. Although this popular restaurant was demolished to make way for Sandburg Village, the Germania Club survived and in recent years its Victorian complex has included such tenants as the Merchandise National Bank and Women's Workout World.

In 1896 Swedish Chicagoans established a club at 1258 N. LaSalle Street. Over the years the distinctive blue-and-white buildings of the Swedish Club were a North Side landmark. Although the club closed in 1984, its buildings are being renovated as part of a new apartment complex.

Flanked by the Gold Coast on the east and working-class districts to the west, LaSalle Street symbolized the division between rich and poor on Chicago's Near North Side. While much of the street's fine housing has survived, even more remarkable is the number of institutions which continue to anchor this busy North Side thoroughfare.

In 1875 Dwight L. Moody's new church opened at the northwest corner of Chicago Avenue and LaSalle Street, now the site of the Moody Bible Institute. Moody's Sunday School, founded in 1858, developed into one of the largest denominations in Chicago, and its missionaries are known throughout the world. The Moody Church, which occupies a large site just north of North Avenue, between Clark and LaSalle streets, was dedicated in 1925.

Another institution whose influence extended beyond the immediate neighborhood was St. Vincent's Hospital and Orphan Asylum. It was founded in 1881 by the Sisters of Charity at 721 N. LaSalle Street. The present building, now known as the Catholic Charities Near North Center, dates from 1931.

LaSalle Street's churches have served many, many people since the late nineteenth century. The oldest structure, the LaSalle Street Church at 1136 N. LaSalle, was dedicated in 1886. It originally housed Chicago's first English-speaking Lutheran congregation, known as Holy Trinity Church, which is now located at 1218 W. Addison Street. Across the street at 1133 N. LaSalle is the historic Church of the Ascension. This Episcopal congregation was organized in 1857, and its present house of worship dates from 1887. The Annunciation Cathedral, housing the oldest Greek Orthodox congregation in Chicago, was built in 1911 at 1017 N. LaSalle. LaSalle Street's newest church building houses the city's oldest German congregation, First St. Paul's Evangelical Lutheran Church (1970) at 1301 N. LaSalle. The Missouri Synod was founded at First St. Paul's, and the present church also marks the site of the North Side's first synagogue, Temple Sholom.

Little Hell

While LaSalle Street north of Chicago Avenue developed as a middle-class residential enclave in the 1870s and 1880s, the neighborhood to the west remained a working-class district and a port of entry for Swedish immigrants. In the years following the Fire, the area bounded by Chicago Avenue, Wells Street, Division Street, and the river became the largest Swedish "town" outside of Sweden and Finland. As late as the 1890s, nearly ten thousand foreign-born Swedes lived in this area.

When the red brick church at Cleveland and Elm Streets was built in 1889 by the First Swedish Baptist Church, it was located in the heart of Chicago's "Swede Town." After moving to Lake View, the Swedes sold their church to Wayman A.M.E. Church in 1919. The oldest black congregation in the area, Wayman A.M.E. now stands in the midst of the Cabrini-Green public housing project. (G. Lane)

According to Ulf Beijbom, Chicago Avenue was the main business district as well as the south boundary of "Swede Town," and for years it was known as "Swedish Clodhoppers' Lane." Immigrant Swedes organized fraternal groups, dramatic clubs, and singing societies as a way of preserving their culture, and they established churches, hospitals, orphanages, and old people's homes which met their special needs in the city. Among the many institutions formed by Chicago's Swedes were Augustana Hospital, Augustana College and Theological Seminary, and North Park College.

The churches were by far the most important institutions in Swede Town, and they were quickly rebuilt after the Fire. Members of St. Ansgarius Episcopal, the oldest Swedish congregation in Chicago, built a red brick Gothic church at 845 N. Sedgwick, which was opened on Christmas Eve 1872. The original St. Ansgarius Church was known throughout Swede Town as the "Jenny Lind Church," because the famous Swedish singer contributed more than $1,000 towards its construction in 1851.

Families who belonged to the Swedish Evangelical Lutheran Immanuel congregation cleaned and stacked bricks from the ruins of their old church. These were used in the construction of a new church at Sedgwick and Hobbie Streets in 1875. Between 1880 and 1890 four more Swedish churches were constructed, all within the small territory bounded by Chicago, Orleans, Elm, and Milton (Cleveland).

The Swedish colony on the Near North Side was highly organized, and it provided a welcome structure for newly arrived immigrants. Many Swedish newcomers were skilled craftsmen—carpenters, cabinetmakers, iron molders—and community leaders were proud that their countrymen were conspicuously absent from the criminal court docket. The Swedes in Chicago gained a reputation for being law-abiding citizens; large numbers of them also became homeowners and landlords.

Following a long-standing Chicago custom, Swedish families on the Near North Side lived in frame houses until they could afford to build brick residences. To make way for the new house, the frame building was often moved to the back of the lot. One Swedish writer applauded this pattern of homebuilding, arguing that: "Long ago the Swedes of Chicago solved the question of workingmen's homes which is agitating industrial communities everywhere, thus setting an example worthy of emulation in other parts of the world." Although new brick homes indicated growing prosperity among the Swedes, the same could not be said for the Irish and Italian families who often rented the rear tenements. Not only did these 1870s wooden buildings pose a fire hazard, but they generally lacked adequate ventilation and sanitary facilities.

So intense were the flames and smoke from the gas plant at Crosby and Hobbie Streets that the surrounding neighborhood as well as nearby Goose Island earned the sobriquet "Little Hell." John J. Flinn called attention to this section of the Near North Side in 1890 when he included it in a Chicago guidebook. In addition to commenting on the number of fire shanties which remained in the area, Flinn discussed the neighborhood's reputation as a "terror district." He noted that gang problems had declined because "most of the desperate characters who infested the district have been killed or sent to the penitentiary or driven out of the city."

According to the Chicago *Tribune*, the notorious Hatch House gang on Market Street (Orleans) terrorized families in this neighborhood for years. Among the district's criminals were "Clabby" Burns, Eddie Hall, "Kid" Murphy, and "Cooney the Fox." Swedish homeowners and landlords appealed to the police for protection, and before long holdups ceased and there were "no more revolver fights in the darkness with heads stuck out of lighted windows to see whether a friend or a foe had been shot." At the request of long-time residents, the City Council changed the name of Market Street to Orleans. While the name change gave a new air of respectability to the area, it could not solve the neighborhood's continuing problem, ethnic rivalry.

In the early years it was Irish-Swedish conflict which put Little Hell on the map. By the turn of the century the notoriety passed to the Italians. On May 6, 1900 Swedish homeowners held a meeting with the intention of driving the Italians out of the neighborhood. According to the Chicago *Tribune*, Swedish residents denounced Italians because they "steal street paving blocks for firewood. . .dwell crowded together in a filthy manner, breeding disease, noise, and constant feuds." When the Italians learned that Swedes planned to raise their rents, they held a counter demonstration—in a Swedish hall!

After 1900 more and more Swedish families left the neighborhood for newer residential districts. Some moved to the Belmont-Sheffield area in Lake View, others settled around Foster Avenue and Clark Street in Andersonville. Although some of the pioneer Swedish churches remained in Swede Town for another decade, one by one they closed or moved further north in the city.

Just as the Swedes had displaced earlier German residents, so also the Italians eventually dominated the area between Grand Avenue and Division Street. The early Italian settlement on the Near North Side was composed largely of immigrants from Genoa and Naples. The Assumption of the Blessed Virgin Mary Church, the first Italian Catholic church in Chicago, was dedicated in 1886 on Illinois Street, just west of Franklin. The Italians who settled in the area around Chicago Avenue during the 1880s and 1890s were overwhelmingly Sicilian. Many came from the same villages, and they reestablished Old World customs in Chicago, such as the *Festa* in honor of the Blessed Virgin Mary. For more than fifty years St. Philip Benizi Church at Oak Street and Gault Court (Cambridge Avenue) was the center of the Near North Side Sicilian community. The streets around the church were the scene of lively festivals and processions. Indeed, the "flight of the angels" across Oak Street was the highlight of the annual August 15th *Festa*. Young girls dressed in white were suspended from strong ropes through pulleys. Their journeys began from buildings on opposite sides of Oak Street; and when the "angels" met above the Blessed Mother's shrine, they recited a long prayer.

Like the Market Street gang of the 1880s, Black Hand extortioners terrorized neighborhood residents around the turn of the century. So many unsolved murders occurred in the area around Oak and Milton (Cleveland) that by 1911 the intersection was known as "Death Corner." In 1908 a number of Italians formed the White Hand Society in hopes of bettering their social standing in Chicago. From their office in the Masonic building downtown, members of the White Hand Society promised protection to "all of our countrymen who receive threatening letters from the Black Hand."

Protestant churches which had established missions for German immigrants in the 1880s turned their attention to the Italians of the Near North Side. The Eli Bates House at Larrabee and Elm Streets and the Olivet Institute at 1441 N. Cleveland were church-sponsored settlements which carried on "splendid and inspiring activities for the betterment of the poor of this district." Missionaries from Moody Bible Institute began their work among the Italians of the Near

Rev. Luigi Giambastiani, OSM, pastor of St. Philip Benizi Church, welcomes new tenants to the Cabrini Homes, 1942. These low-rise brick buildings replaced slum housing just north of Chicago Avenue and west of Sedgwick Street in "Little Hell."
(Courtesy The Chicago Catholic)

North Side in 1911. Although gospel workers were at a disadvantage in this heavily Catholic district, they did make some headway. In 1923 the Moody Italian Mission reported that, "Gradually the open street became our arena where the good fight of faith was waged."

One building which bears witness to the conflict between Protestants and Catholics in the Italian community stands near the intersection of Clybourn, Larrabee, and Evergreen. Now known as Strangers Home Missionary Baptist Church, this building was constructed in 1901 by Ascension Episcopal Church on LaSalle Street. Despite the efforts of an Italian-speaking clergyman, the church did not take root. In 1927 it was rechristened San Marcello Mission, and for nearly fifty years it functioned as a Catholic church.

As Italians in the area prospered, many moved further north and west in the city, following the path blazed by Germans, Irish, and Swedes. For those who remained on the Near North Side, housing conditions were grim. Homes and apartments constructed in the 1880s and 1890s had deteriorated, and frame houses from the 1870s were virtually uninhabitable.

In 1941 Works Progress Administration workers began demolishing dilapidated two- and three-story buildings in the 800 block of Cambridge Avenue to make way for a Chicago Housing Authority project. These new low-rise buildings occupied a site just north of Chicago Avenue between Larrabee and Hudson. At the suggestion of Rev. Louis

Giambastiani, OSM, pastor of St. Philip Benizi Church, the homes were named in honor of Mother Frances Cabrini. As head of the Missionary Sisters of the Sacred Heart, Mother Cabrini had opened the Assumption, BVM, school on Erie Street in 1899, and in 1905 she founded Columbus Hospital. (In 1946 Frances Cabrini became the first United States citizen canonized by the Catholic Church.)

Although a large number of tenants in the new Cabrini Homes were Italian, the project included black families as well as white. When the Cabrini Homes opened in 1942, preference was given to war workers or servicemen who earned less than $2,100 a year. As late as 1947 forty percent of the tenants in Cabrini Homes were veterans.

Blacks had lived in the area around Chicago Avenue since the early 1920s, but their numbers grew dramatically during World War II as a result of migration from the South. Although most newcomers settled on the South Side of Chicago where they found ready employment in the stockyards and steel mills, hundreds moved into homes in Little Hell. According to an Urban League survey, black families in Near North Side rear tenements often paid more for rent than the Italian families who lived in the houses at the front of the lots.

Spurred by the success of the Cabrini Homes, the Chicago Housing Authority in 1950 announced plans for more than two thousand new dwelling units in the area around Division and Orleans Streets. In a 1951 field report for the CHA, J.S. Fuerst noted that the Cabrini Homes had somewhat slowed the process of resegregation in the area. Because tenants had been selected according to the racial composition of the area in 1941, the Cabrini Homes remained seventy-five percent white, even though during the intervening years the surrounding neighborhood had become eighty percent black.

Fuerst's report sounded an ominous note for the new housing planned by the CHA. Because first priority would be granted to eligible families already living in the area, he predicted that the new project would contain "a far larger number of broken families receiving public assistance than exists in the total population."

Although CHA planners believed that two-story rowhouse units were the best type of housing for families with children, cost limitations prevented rowhouse construction. Instead, fifteen highrises ranging in size from seven to nineteen stories were built between 1956 and 1959. The new red brick structures were called the Cabrini Extension, but they had little in common with the low-rise apartments of 1942. In its annual report for 1957, the CHA noted that while skyscraper living "may not be ideal for the family with children, it has advantages that should not be overlooked." Because tall buildings occupied only a small portion of the land, they freed the rest of the site for playgrounds and courtyards. The report noted that the new projects contrasted sharply with "the cluttered grid pattern of streets and alleys" below. Furthermore, the high-rise galleries eliminated inside corridors, providing open porches where children could play and adults could visit. This feature of the project "adds zest to living in the new home for some families who formerly had to come out of basements to see daylight."

When the Cabrini Extension highrises were completed in 1959, the project's racial composition was approximately seventy-five percent black. The highrise at 500 W. Oak was known as the "International Building" because its 262 families represented many different ethnic backgrounds, among them German, Chinese, Puerto Rican, Negro, Swedish, Irish, and Italian. But the highrises did not remain integrated for long. By the time the nearby William Green housing project at Division and Larrabee Streets was dedicated in 1962, the surrounding neighborhood had become almost totally black. Despite the fact that Cabrini-Green was by then an entirely black housing project, CHA officials were optimistic that the new highrises would revitalize this section of the Near North Side and forever banish memories of Little Hell.

Critics of the highrises pointed out that unlike Sandburg Village to the east, which was developed during the 1960s, Cabrini-Green was intended for families with children. The difficulties of supervising thousands of children from fifteen stories up soon became apparent. So many children live in the project—nearly 10,000 in 1981—that this section of the Near North Side can hardly be called a neighborhood in the traditional sense. Although residents of Chicago's public housing have always been poor, the most important change to occur in Cabrini-Green during the past twenty years has been the decline of two-parent households. Today, single mothers, many of them barely out of their teens, head seventy-six percent of the households in the project. Gang-related violence is a constant worry for residents. Indeed, fear about safety and gang warfare have prompted many families to move out of Cabrini-Green when financially they could least afford to leave.

While the Cabrini-Green highrises were a vast improvement over the substandard housing that had previously existed in the area, they virtually destroyed the institutional structure of the neighborhood. Along with deteriorated housing went the shops and small businesses that had provided jobs and stability. Although black churches in the neighborhood such as St. Matthew Methodist, 1000 N. Orleans; St. Joseph, 1101 N. Orleans; Holy Family Lutheran, 542 W. Hobbie; and Wayman A.M.E., 509 W. Elm, remained in the neighborhood and expanded their programs, they could hardly meet the needs of more than 15,000 residents. Far from being a solution to the complex urban problems of poverty and racial segregation, the Cabrini-Green highrises are the modern version of the "relief shanties" which plagued Little Hell in the half century after the Chicago Fire.

Old Town

Although Germans began to settle in "Old Town" as early as the 1850s, the district bounded by Division, LaSalle, Armitage, and Halsted Streets experienced its greatest growth after the Chicago Fire. Pushed by the Swedes from the south, the German population continued to move north of Division Street in the 1880s and 1890s. Because of the location of early streetcar lines, the west end of this neighborhood developed more rapidly than the eastern part. In 1879, for example, Germans celebrated the Cannstadter Volkfest by decorating Sedgwick Street between Division and Goethe with colorful flags, garlands, and evergreens. As the line of march passed Sigel (Evergreen) Street on its way to Ogden Grove, a man dressed as "Duke Ulrich" reviewed the parade. According to the Chicago *Tribune,* the bogus duke was suspended from a clothes basket and "kept alive by large potations of lager-beer which he drew up in a dinner pail with a string."

Improvements in transportation did much to open up the Old Town area and connect it with the downtown business district as well as with Lincoln Park to the north. Streetcar lines along Lincoln Avenue, Clybourn Avenue, Larrabee, and Sedgwick Streets provided German workers with access to factories along the Chicago River such as the North Western Terra Cotta works at Clybourn and Wrightwood.

In the 1890s construction began on the Northwestern Elevated line, the predecessor of the CTA rapid transit line. North of Chicago Avenue, the tracks were constructed between Franklin and Orleans Streets, for what is today's Ravenswood line. The elevated road curved west along North Avenue and then northwest across Bissell to Sheffield Avenue. Although the elevated tracks forced the relocation of

The brick and frame buildings of SS. Benedict and Scholastica Academy in the German parish of St. Joseph at Hill and Orleans Streets were typical of post-fire construction in the 1870s. Despite its location in one of the most congested parts of the city, the academy included landscaped gardens in keeping with its status as a "select school."
(Courtesy St. Scholastica Priory Archives)

Alexian Brothers Hospital, the parish complex of St. Joseph remained intact, albeit flanked by girders of steel.

Unlike certain parts of Lake View which remained sparsely settled, Old Town and the Lincoln Park area were well developed by the turn of the century. Although the elevated railroad did not spark a building boom in this section of the North Side, it played a significant role in urbanizing the area north of Division Street. In addition to providing inexpensive transportation to the downtown business district, the "L" with its stations at two-block intervals promoted commercial development along Division Street, North Avenue, Halsted Street, and Armitage Avenue.

One of the central institutions in Old Town was St. Michael parish, organized by German Catholics in 1852 when the surrounding area consisted mainly of prairies and farmland. The wealthy German brewer Michael Diversey donated land for the new parish, and in 1866 construction began on the massive brick building which stands today at the southeast corner of Eugenie and Cleveland Streets. Although the walls of St. Michael church remained standing after the fire of 1871, the rest of the parish buildings and the parishioners' homes were destroyed. German Catholics rebuilt the church in 1873, and in 1888 the steeple was added.

By 1892 St. Michael's was the largest German parish in Chicago. Indeed, it completely overshadowed the predominantly Irish parish of Immaculate Conception, which had been founded in 1859 just a few blocks south in the 1400 block of North Park Avenue.

At the turn of the century North Avenue was known as German Broadway, and its shops, small businesses, restaurants, and saloons extended west to the intersection of Clybourn and Halsted. There were large businesses nearby such as the Western Wheel Works at Schiller and Wells, Siebens Brewery at 1470 N. Larrabee, the Oscar Mayer Sausage Company at 1241 N. Sedgwick, and the Seeburg Piano Manufacturing Company at 1500 N. Dayton. These companies were an important source of employment for residents of Old Town, and they contributed much to the economic stability of the neighborhood.

In the late 1890s the pioneer German parish of St. Joseph at Hill and Orleans Streets began to decline in numbers as families sought newer housing further north in the city. This same trend was reflected in church development among German Lutherans. In 1895 *Die Abendpost* noted that the German Evangelical Johannes congregation had left its old chapel at North Park Avenue and Eugenie Street and relocated at Dickens and Mohawk. Their new church quarters had been vacated by an English-speaking congregation who no longer felt at home in the rapidly developing German neighborhood.

Perhaps the most significant move made by a German congregation occurred in 1898 when St. Pauls parishioners left their old church at Ohio and LaSalle Streets and began worshiping in a new building at Orchard Street and Kemper Place, just a few blocks from Lincoln Park.

The opening of the Robert A. Waller High School at Orchard and Center (Armitage) in 1901 provided further evidence of the German movement north from Old Town to Lincoln Park. This modern building replaced the old North Division High School located at Wendell and Wells Streets since 1883. Before long the area surrounding Waller High School was built up with duplexes and apartment buildings, many of them owned by German-Americans.

Although Old Town continued to be a predominantly German neighborhood well into the 1930s, change was taking place rapidly. According to Vivien Palmer, between

The tower of St. Michael Church at Cleveland and Eugenie Streets is one of Old Town's landmarks. Built by German Catholics in 1869, St. Michael's was gutted by the fire of 1871. The present structure dates from 1873 and the steeple from 1888.

(G. Lane)

1910 and 1920 the old German Broadway had become "decidedly a Hungarian shopping street, its stores owned by Russian Jews . . . but replete with advertisements to attract the Hungarian trade." During this period Old Town's German Jewish population also relocated. Anshe Emet Synagogue had been a neighborhood institution at 1263 N. Sedgwick Street since 1893. In 1922 the congregation moved to 627 W. Patterson Street, just north of Addison near Broadway.

The construction of the Ogden Avenue extension in 1920 also left its mark on the neighborhood. More than two hundred homes in the area were demolished to make way for the overpass which connected this part of the North Side with Union Park on the West Side. Much of Old Town's housing dated from the early 1870s, and it was fast becoming dilapidated. In 1928 construction began on the Marshall Field Garden Apartments bounded by Evergreen, Blackhawk, Sedgwick, and Hudson streets. Although this five-story walkup complex replaced run-down housing, few poor people in the neighborhood could afford the rent, which ranged from $35 to $63 a month. Moreover, as Thomas Philpott has reported, the managers of the Garden Apartments incurred high vacancy rates "rather than fill empty apartments with black families."

By the 1930s several thousand black people lived in the Little Hell neighborhood just south of Division Street. While there was little conflict between black and Italian families in this district, both groups suffered from a lack of adequate housing. In November 1934 CHA officials announced a slum clearance program for sixty-seven acres between Division and Blackhawk streets, from Ogden Avenue east to Sedgwick. The project would provide homes for 2,500 families at a cost of $12.5 million. However, area residents protested so strongly that the CHA dismissed condemnation proceedings on October 30, 1936. Research compiled by the Federal Writers Project in 1935 revealed that this part of the Near North Side contained a large number of German institutions, among them the German-American Civic Association, numerous singing clubs, and meeting places such as Mozart Hall at 1534 N. Clybourn, and Yondorf Hall at the northeast corner of North Avenue and Halsted. Today the Golden Ox restaurant at 1578 N. Clybourn is a reminder of the once-flourishing German institutional life of Old Town.

The ethnic composition of this neighborhood expanded after World War II to include Italians, blacks, and Orientals. In the 1960s Spanish-speaking families, mostly Puerto Rican, moved into Old Town. Because of relatively inexpensive rents, the area also attracted a number of musicians and artists, and since 1950 the Old Town Art Fair has been one of the community's main events.

By 1962 the area around Division Street west of Sedgwick was a black community, dominated by the massive highrises known as the William Green project. A very different kind of urban renewal was then occurring at the east end of Old Town, along LaSalle and Clark Streets. The first part of the huge Sandburg Village complex, completed in 1966, included nearly two thousand apartments in 28-story highrises. As its promoters hoped it would, Sandburg Village attracted thousands of young, predominantly white young men and women to this part of the Near North Side. Before long new bars opened on Division Street between Clark and State, and they became popular meeting places for the area's newest residents.

During the 1960s Wells Street in Old Town also took on new life as a commercial district and a tourist attraction. Although most of the shops which catered to the "flower children" are long gone, a number of institutions survived and prospered, among them Second City Theater and Piper's Alley, a small shopping center at 1608 N. Wells Street. Nearby on Clark Street at North Avenue, a new Latin School was completed in 1969 and the Chicago Historical Society opened a modern addition in 1972.

Old Town residents anticipated the national trend toward renovating Victorian frame cottages, brownstones, and Italianate and Queen Anne style homes. Over the years much of the neighborhood's housing had been carefully preserved, especially in the Old Town Triangle area formed by North Avenue, Clark Street, and the Ogden Avenue Mall. Moreover, the Lincoln Park Conservation Association founded in 1954 and the Old Town Triangle Association have taken an active role in directing urban renewal. Improvements to the area included the widening of North Avenue and the construction of Ogden Corners. This 45-unit townhouse development, located along North Avenue at Ogden, was the area's first housing built on urban renewal land.

Just as St. Michael church rose from the ashes of the Chicago Fire of 1871, new church buildings were constructed in conjunction with the Lincoln Park urban renewal program. In 1971 Japanese-Americans dedicated the distinctive Midwest Buddhist Temple at 435 W. Menomonee. Two years later work began at the southwest corner of Wisconsin and Orleans on the Church of the Three Crosses. This congregation was formed by the merger of two pioneer Old Town churches, St. James United Church of Christ and Second Evangelical United Brethren.

In 1976 the Chicago City Council designated the Old Town Triangle area as a landmark district. In testimony supporting the designation, Rev. Donald F. Miller, C.Ss.R., pastor of St. Michael's parish, argued that, "The real strength of Chicago lies not in the Sears Towers, or the Hancock Centers, but in the neighborhoods such as this one. Chicago, to be humanly alive, must sustain little homes inhabited by the common man."

Ironically, by the mid-1970s Old Town was fast becoming a high-priced residential district. So great was the demand for housing among young urban professionals that rents in the neighborhood began to skyrocket. Old-time German and Italian families soon learned that their workingmen's cottages and brick buildings were valued at more than $100,000. New construction in the neighborhood included $200,000 townhouses along Larrabee Street and highrises on Wells Street north of North Avenue. By 1980 the median value of owner-occupied dwellings in Old Town ranged from $118,000 between Halsted and Larrabee to $186,000 in the area bounded by North Avenue, Clark Street, Armitage, and Sedgwick.

The project known as St. Michael's Mews symbolizes the speed with which gentrification occurred in Old Town. When the Redemptorist priests of St. Michael's parish built a new grammar school in 1961 at 1620 N. Hudson, area residents regarded the building as a good omen, a sign of the neighborhood's stability. But few people could have predicted that within twenty years Old Town would no longer be a family-oriented community. Parochial school enrollment figures told the tale. St. Michael's was once a parish with thousands of children, but by 1979 only 160 children attended its grade school. In order to ensure the continued existence of St. Michael's Church, the Redemptorists sold the former grammar school and high school buildings, the high school gymnasium, a power plant, and the former monastery of the Brothers of Mary to Lincoln Plaza Company, a private redevelopment team. Today the condominiums and townhouses of St. Michael's Mews offer eloquent testimony to the demographic changes which have occurred in Old Town, once the home of Chicago's largest German Catholic community.

Although many minority families can no longer afford to live in Old Town, a number of apartments have been constructed for moderate income families and the elderly. One of the most successful of these projects, Evergreen Terrace, occupies the site bounded by Goethe, Evergreen, Cleveland, and Sedgwick. According to William Moorehead, who conceived the plan for the new housing in 1968, there have been few turnovers in the all-black complex since its first building opened in 1977. In contrast to nearby Cabrini-Green, applicants at Evergreen Terrace undergo a strict screening process that includes a credit check, housekeeping inspection, and interviews with heads of households and their children.

In recent years young professionals as well as real estate developers have renovated buildings at the edges of Old Town. The $10.5 million Willow-Dayton project in 1979, for example, was built around the former Schulien's restaurant at 1800 N. Halsted Street. Willow-Dayton's success as an apartment-townhouse complex spurred more renovation along Halsted—all the way to North Avenue. Not only have existing houses been rehabilitated, but new condominiums have been constructed too. And in 1984 work began at 1707 N. Halsted on a new building for one of Chicago's oldest institutions, the Juvenile Protective Association. From a near slum, Halsted Street has emerged as one of the North Side's most important thoroughfares. Indeed, the area around Halsted and Armitage is anchored by a fashionable shopping district whose antique stores, restaurants, and bars draw patrons from all over the city.

New ventures such as Atrium Village and Cobbler Square have expanded the boundaries of the Gold Coast to a degree that urban planners would have found unimaginable in the 1960s. Atrium Village, which opened in 1978 at the southwest corner of Division and Wells Streets, was unusual in several respects. Funded by a coalition of churches—Fourth Presbyterian, LaSalle Street, St. Matthew Methodist, and Holy Family Lutheran—it was situated in the shadow of Cabrini-Green. Unlike much of the Near North Side's housing stock, this mid-rise and townhouse complex was designed for families with children. Atrium Village includes a private day care program known as Lake Shore Teaching and Learning Center, which draws students from throughout the area.

One of the newest rehabilitation programs on the Near North Side is known as Cobbler Square, located two blocks north of Atrium Village at Schiller and Wells. Developers of this project consider it to be the "residential anchor for south Old Town." Architect Kenneth Schroeder transformed factory buildings into a self-contained complex of 295 apartments, many of them with lofts. The oldest building in the complex dates from 1889 when it housed the Western Wheel Works, the largest bicycle manufacturer in the world. From 1911 to 1981 the red brick buildings were the headquarters of the Dr. Scholl footwear company. An important link with Old Town's past, Cobbler Square seeks to tap the Near North Side rental market.

Of all the rehabilitation and new construction that has occurred in Old Town since 1970, the New City YMCA (1981) at Halsted and Clybourn combines a consciousness of the

Cobbler Square, Old Town's newest rental apartment complex, originally housed the Western Wheel Works, the largest bicycle manufacturer in the world in the 1890s. After 1911, the red brick buildings were the headquarters of the Dr. Scholl footwear company.
(G. Lane, 1985)

neighborhood's past with a concern for its future. According to William G. Kuntz, the Y's senior executive for human and community development, the association has tried to "create the neighborhood of tomorrow" where racial and economic integration will become a reality. YMCA officials took great care in planning this facility, which is poised between the Cabrini-Green housing complex on the south and the affluent Lincoln Park community on the north. Architect Ralph Youngren designed the new building in such a way that it unites the industrial district to the west with the residential areas to the north and south.

Lincoln Park

The Lincoln Park neighborhood extends westward from the lake between Armitage Avenue on the south to Diversey Parkway on the north. Over the years its boundaries have been the subject of much dispute. Some area residents claim their neighborhood extends to North Avenue, others say it goes west to Clybourn. In recent years homeowners living around Belden and Sheffield have begun to call their neighborhood De Paul, after the Catholic college that was established here in 1898. Complicating matters even further is the fact that nearly ten civic groups claim specific boundaries within Lincoln Park, from Wrightwood to Sheffield and Park West.

The original settlement in Lincoln Park centered around McCormick Theological Seminary. As a result of a $100,000 gift from Cyrus Hall McCormick, the Presbyterian Theology Seminary moved to Chicago from New Albany, Indiana in 1859. After occupying temporary locations downtown and on the Near North Side, the seminary established its campus in 1863 on twenty acres of land donated by Joseph Sheffield and William Ogden. This property, located just south of Fullerton and west of Halsted, was then at the very edge of Chicago. The seminary's holdings also extended north into Lake View where William Lill and Michael Diversey had donated five acres of land.

When construction began on Ewing Hall in 1863, there were no homes in the vicinity. The seminary was one of the few North Side institutions to escape destruction in the Chicago Fire of 1871, and its location proved to be a promising one in the years to come. As the student body increased, new buildings were constructed, among them a chapel (1876), McCormick Hall (1884), and Fowler Hall (1887). In 1886 the seminary was officially renamed McCormick in memory of the wealthy industrialist who had died two years earlier.

(Top left) The six-story Bedford stone structure at the northeast corner of Webster and Kenmore was built in 1907 for St. Vincent's College, founded on this site in 1898. Chartered as De Paul University in 1907, the school's Lincoln Park campus remained relatively small until the 1960s and 1970s.
(C.R. Childs, courtesy G. Schmalgemeier)

(Bottom left) Founded in 1863, McCormick Theological Seminary on Halsted between Fullerton and Belden was Lincoln Park's foremost institution. It set the architectural standard for the neighborhood and attracted middle-class Presbyterian families to this part of the North Side. These buildings were demolished in the early 1960s as part of the Lincoln Park Conservation Program.
(Courtesy Commission on Chicago Landmarks)

The McCormick Seminary was instrumental in the formation of several North Side churches, among them the Fullerton Avenue Presbyterian Church (1864), the First German Presbyterian Church (1873), and the Lake View Presbyterian Church (1888). After a "thorough exploration of the neighborhood" in 1884, Presbyterian officials decided to build two new churches, one at 600 W. Fullerton and the other at Belden and Halsted. The old wooden Presbyterian church at 530 W. Fullerton was sold to the Episcopal Church of Our Saviour, which subsequently built a Romanesque structure on the site. The Episcopalians moved eastward toward the lake to escape the "encroachment of business at Belden and Lincoln." Early restrictions against streetcar lines on Fullerton between Halsted and the lake ensured the desirability of this thoroughfare for generations to come.

Beginning in 1882 the seminary devised a novel plan to augment tuition—building and renting six houses on its property. This proved to be so successful that by 1887 the seminary owned fifty-five houses, thirty-six on Belden and Fullerton and nineteen on Montana and Dunning (Altgeld) Streets in Lake View. In 1889 the seminary decided to sell its houses in Lake View and invest the proceeds so that it could build "homes of a better class" on the seminary grounds. The resulting project, now known as the McCormick row houses, included eighteen homes on Chalmers Place, a private street just south of Fullerton. A distinctive feature of this arrangement was the location of a professor's home at the end of each row of houses.

By 1892 McCormick Theological Seminary was one of the largest landowners in the Lincoln Park area with holdings valued at $1.3 million. In his 1893 history of the institution, Le Roy Halsey noted that, "The improvement of the (seminary) grounds with handsome residences, with their intelligent occupants, has added not a little to the . . . beauty and growth of the neighborhood."

While McCormick Theological Seminary exerted tremendous influence in the early days of Lincoln Park, the neighborhood did not develop as a Presbyterian stronghold. In the 1880s, for example, a thriving German community existed north of Fullerton between Orchard and Southport. Once a part of Lake View, this area was annexed to Chicago in 1889. German Lutherans built the Deutsche Evangelical Bethlehem Church at Diversey and Lewis (Magnolia) in 1885. Here on June 25, 1885, graduates of Lake View High School received their diplomas and listened to the welcoming address—in German. Other community institutions included Lake View's Public School No. 2 at Diversey and Seminary, later renamed Louis Agassiz, and the Lincoln Turners hall at Diversey and Sheffield. A German Evangelical Lutheran church opened in 1886 at Sheffield and Mariana (Schubert); it continues in existence today as St. George Greek Orthodox Church.

Another German settlement was located near Wrightwood and Clark on the site of the former Wright's Grove, a favorite picnic ground for German *Saengerfests*. In 1894 the estate of Dr. Henry M. Hobart at Wrightwood and Hampden Court was sold and built up with homes. At 503 W. Wrightwood Francis J. Dewes built a spacious European-style mansion. Nearby at Diversey and Lake View was E.J. Lehmann's home, now the site of the Elks National Memorial. By 1898 German Lutherans had established another institution in the area, St. Pauls Church at Orchard and Kemper Place. The German Catholic population of this district also increased, and in 1905 a group of prominent German Americans established St. Clement Church at Deming Place and Orchard.

In the shadow of McCormick Theological Seminary another Catholic community took shape. When St. Vincent de Paul parish was established in 1875, it was located in the "bleak regions of Nickersonville." Much of the surrounding area was farmland, but it was quickly built up with homes in the aftermath of the Chicago Fire. The first church of St. Vincent de Paul at Webster and Kenmore could not have constrasted more sharply with the buildings of McCormick Seminary. In 1876 the Chicago *Times* noted that, "The edifice might pass for a factory, a brewery, or a hospital, anything else but a church."

So rapidly did the Catholic population of this district increase that before long two new parishes were formed, St. Josaphat (Kashubian) in 1883 at Belden and Southport, and St. Teresa (German) in 1889 at Armitage and Kenmore. The German-speaking Poles of St. Josaphat's formed a cohesive community around their church, and they earned a reputation over the years as spirited defenders of their neighborhood. In the late 1880s, for example, members of the parish removed tracks of the Milwaukee Road Railroad to protest the spur line which cut through the heart of their Kashubian settlement. In the 1890s the construction of the Northwestern "L" line prompted the relocation of another Catholic institution in Lincoln Park. The Alexian Brothers Hospital, founded in the 1860s in the Old Town area, was directly in the path of the new elevated railroad line. From 1896 until it moved again in the 1960s to suburban Elk Grove Village, Alexian Brothers Hospital was located at Belden and Racine. The site is now occupied by the Little Sisters of the Poor Center for the Aging (1980).

The Irish and German Catholics of St. Vincent's parish soon had a church of which they could be proud. James J.

The Lutheran congregation of St. Pauls, following the northward movement of Germans into Lincoln Park, built this Gothic structure at Orchard and Kemper Place in 1898. After this church was destroyed by fire in 1955, a modern building was erected on the site.

(C.R. Childs, courtesy G. Schmalgemeier)

Egan designed the French Romanesque structure which stands today at the northwest corner of Webster and Sheffield. In 1898, one year after the new church opened, the Vincentians established St. Vincent's College. Chartered as De Paul University in 1907, this institution claims more than 70,000 graduates.

The last Catholic institution established at the west end of Lincoln Park was St. Augustine Home for the Aged at 2358 N. Sheffield. Although the Little Sisters of the Poor began their work here in 1884, they could not afford to complete the building's superstructure until 1898. The massive, four-story red brick building was completed according to plans drawn by Egan & Prindiville, and it soon became a familiar sight to riders on the nearby "L."

Aside from its appeal as a fine residential district, Lincoln Park also attracted many hospitals. Over the years these institutions played an important role in the development of the neighborhood, and today they are the largest employers in the Lincoln Park area. In the early years each hospital served a distinct group. The nationally known Children's Memorial Hospital which occupies the triangle created by Fullerton, Lincoln, and Orchard was founded in 1882 as the Maurice Porter Memorial Hospital. Augustana Hospital, established in 1884 at the southeast corner of Lincoln and Cleveland, was a Swedish Lutheran institution. Grant Hospital, which opened in 1884 at 2225 N. Lincoln, served a German clientele. St. Joseph Catholic Hospital, now at 2900 N. Lake Shore Drive, was located at Dickens and Burling from 1871 to 1964. Another Catholic hospital, known as Columbus, opened in 1905 in the old Lincoln Park Sanitarium at Lake View Avenue and Deming Place.

Throughout the 1920s and 1930s, Lincoln Park continued as a high-class residential district. While the area east of Clark Street contained the newest housing, many homes in the west end of the neighborhood dated from the 1880s. Compounding the problem of deteriorated housing was the fact that many units were converted during World War II into rooming houses. The population of this area declined throughout the 1950s as families left Lincoln Park for the suburbs or for neighborhoods further north and west in the city.

As early as the 1940s, the City of Chicago's Department of Research recognized the area around McCormick Theological Seminary and De Paul University as a possible site for redevelopment. In *44 Cities,* Helen Monchow noted that, "The large amount of institutionally held real estate in this vicinity would seem to furnish a starting point for some comprehensive scheme of redevelopment which would focus on the educational centers as the nuclei."

St. Augustine Home for the Aged opened in 1898 at 2358 N. Sheffield. Once home to the elderly poor, this red brick building is now a luxury apartment complex known as The Sanctuary. (G. Lane, 1985)

The neighborhood's turnaround began in 1956 when the Community Conservation Board of Chicago designated Lincoln Park as an urban renewal area. Unlike parts of the South Side where blocks of homes were demolished to make way for new housing, rewewal occurred here at a slower pace. In 1961 the Conservation Board published a study of local institutions, with proposed redevelopment plans. As a result of such planning, institutions such as Grant Hospital, St. Joseph Hospital, De Paul University, and McCormick Seminary demolished obsolete buildings and expanded their facilities.

In 1962 McCormick Seminary built a new library as well as a new chapel just west of Halsted Street. In 1969 a three-story administration building was opened near Fullerton Avenue. De Paul University also embarked on a program of expansion. In 1963 the university spent $750,000 for the city block bounded by Fullerton, Seminary, Belden, and Kenmore. Here the new Schmitt Academic and Activities Center were constructed.

Within a few years, however, McCormick Theological Seminary announced its decision to affiliate with the University of Chicago Divinity School and move to Hyde Park. Ironically, Hyde Park had been the first choice of Presbyterian officials when they discussed the relocation of the seminary to Chicago in 1857! McCormick Seminary's move south proved to be a windfall for De Paul University. In 1976 the university purchased McCormick's west campus, and in the following year the east campus with its three new facilities. As a result of these purchases, De Paul's Lincoln Park campus now includes twenty-six buildings on twenty-five acres.

Fullerton Parkway looking west from Cleveland Avenue, 1937. High class residential construction in the 1880s and 1890s made Fullerton one of Lincoln Park's most fashionable streets. Large-scale rehabilitation since the 1960s has upgraded the neighborhood's housing stock and restored Lincoln Park's reputation as an upper middle-class enclave. (Chicago Park District, courtesy R. Wroble)

According to the 1980 census, 37,000 persons lived in that part of Lincoln Park bounded by Armitage, Southport, Diversey, and Lake Michigan, a decrease of 5,000 residents since 1970. While the population east of Sheffield appears to have stabilized, figures for the west end of the neighborhood indicate that tremendous changes have occurred there in the past ten years. Not only did the median price of owner-occupied units soar during the 1970s, but this part of the neighborhood lost 4,000 residents. As a result of condominium conversions and escalating rents, many Hispanic families were forced to move from the area, a trend which continues through the 1980s. Just as significant was the decline in the number of young children. In 1970 children accounted for nearly twenty-five percent of the population west of Sheffield Avenue. By 1980 they represented only ten percent.

More and more, middle-class families are unable to afford the high cost of Lincoln Park housing. Indeed, between 1970 and 1980 the median value of owner-occupied buildings in the area west of Sheffield between Fullerton and Diversey has jumped dramatically. Caught in the crunch, a number of middle-class families have left Lincoln Park for North Side neighborhoods such as Lake View, Edgewater, and Rogers Park where housing prices have not yet skyrocketed.

Two recent rehabilitation programs west of Sheffield Avenue underscore the changes which have taken place in Lincoln Park. The former St. Augustine Home for the Aged at 2358 N. Sheffield has been converted into luxury apartments and renamed The Sanctuary. A few blocks west on Fullerton at Southport, the former Milwaukee Road building has taken on new life as the Lincoln Park Retirement and Geriatric Center.

Since the 1960s Lincoln Avenue has become the neighborhood's nightlife district, and its numerous bars, restaurants, and theaters attract patrons from all over the city and suburbs. Although the lack of adequate parking remains one of the area's most persistent problems, in recent years the amount of open green space within the community has increased. For residents who live a distance from the lakefront, Oz Park at the intersection of Lincoln, Webster, and Larrabee and the new Jonquil Park at Wrightwood and Sheffield provide much-needed "breathing spots."

After more than a century, Lincoln Park once again has become an exclusive residential district, forming the north boundary of Chicago's Gold Coast.

(Left) When Waller High School opened at Armitage and Orchard in 1901, it served the neighborhood's growing German-American community. By the 1960s, Waller was known as a tough "inner-city" school. Renamed Lincoln Park High School in 1979, the school now serves neighborhood youth as well as students from the Gold Coast.
(J. Ficner)

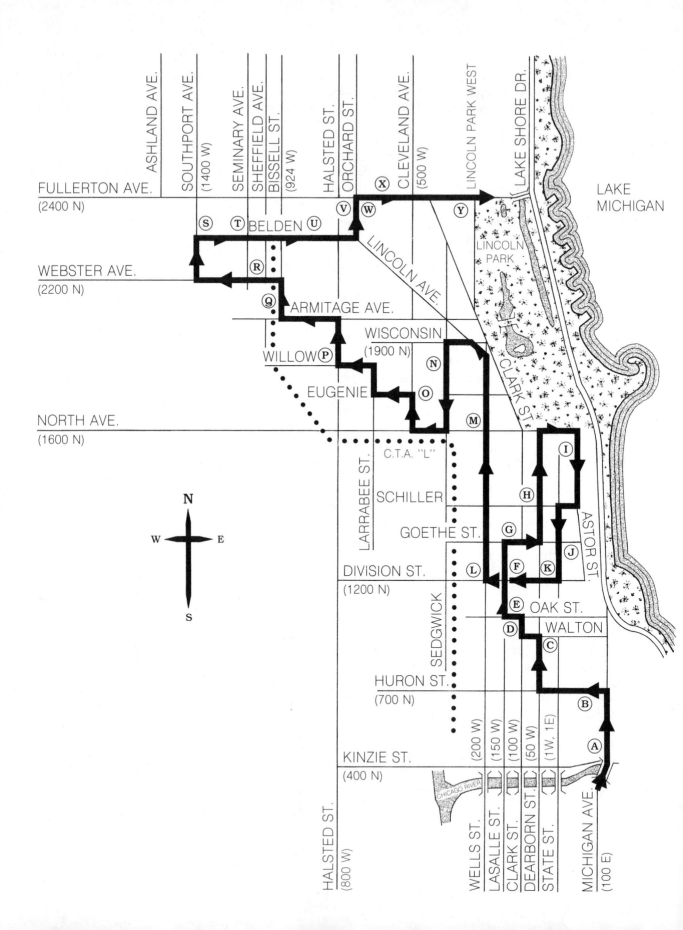

Near North Side Tour

This tour begins at Wacker Drive and North Michigan Avenue and wends its way north to Fullerton Avenue. It focuses on the Gold Coast and it includes the outlying neighborhoods of Old Town and Lincoln Park.

Driving time: about 2 hours.

(A) The opening of the double-decked **Michigan Avenue Bridge** in 1920 finally made the Near North Side accessible to downtown Chicago. As the bas-relief on the southwest bridge tower testifies, this spot marks the site of Fort Dearborn (1803), Chicago's first permanent settlement. Although North Michigan Avenue is now Chicago's most fashionable thoroughfare, in the early 1900s it was a narrow street containing a mix of factories, shops, and residences. In the 1909 Plan of Chicago, however, architects Daniel H. Burnham and Edward Bennett predicted that Michigan Avenue would probably carry "the heaviest movement of any street in the world." Beginning in 1916, Michigan Avenue was widened from Randolph to Erie Streets. By 1921, the **Drake Hotel** at 140 E. Walton anchored the north end of Michigan Avenue and the **Wrigley Building** had opened as North Michigan Avenue's first skyscraper.

In keeping with Burnham and Bennett's plans, the Michigan Avenue Bridge accommodated automobile traffic on its upper deck and trucks below. The completion of Wacker Drive in 1926 further assured North Michigan Avenue's future as an important commercial district. Throughout the 1920s, modern offices, hotels, and shops were constructed along the avenue, notably the **Tribune Tower** (1925), 435 N. Michigan; **Saks Fifth Avenue** (1929), 669 N. Michigan; the **Allerton Hotel** (1924), 701 N. Michigan; and the **Palmolive** (now Playboy) **Building** (1929), 919 N. Michigan. Although the scale of North Michigan Avenue has been altered in recent years by the construction of high-rise hotels, offices, condominiums, and shopping malls, it continues to be Chicago's "Magnificent Mile."

(B) Turn left at Huron Street (700 North) and go four blocks west to Dearborn Street. The **Episcopal Cathedral of St. James** at the southeast corner of Huron and Wabash dates from 1857, when this part of the Near North Side was sparsely settled. The oldest Episcopal church in Chicago, this structure was rebuilt following the Chicago Fire of 1871. St. James now serves as the cathedral for the Episcopal diocese of Chicago, which includes 140 congregations from Lake Michigan west to the Mississippi River.

(C) Turn right on Dearborn Street (50 West) and go north to Walton (930 North); then west on Walton to Clark Street. Dearborn was one of the North Side's early fashionable residential streets. By the 1940s, however, the street's once elegant brownstones had been converted into rooming houses. In recent years the entire area south of Chicago Avenue has been upgraded. Indeed, the thirty-three-story apartment complex known as **Asbury Plaza** (1981) at 750 N. Dearborn was the first new building constructed on this section of Dearborn Street since the 1920s.

Just north of Chicago Avenue is the **Washington Square** district, which takes its name from the small park bounded by Delaware, Dearborn, Walton, and Clark. Washington Square Park was one of Chicago's first parks, and it has a colorful history. On April 21, 1855 during the Lager Beer Riot, angry Germans gathered here to protest the Common Council's ordinance which raised liquor license fees to $300 per year. The Chicago *Tribune* denounced "Lager Beer swilling and Sabbath breaking Germans" who wished to preserve their custom of Continental Sundays. The Germans finally triumphed, and their beer gardens remained an important part of Chicago neighborhood life until Prohibition in 1920.

By the 1920s, Washington Square was known as Bughouse Square because so many soap-box orators gathered here on Sunday evenings. The nearby "Dill Pickle" Club at the rear of the Tooker mansion, 863 N. Dearborn, was the center of the Near North Side's flourishing literary community. In the past decade Washington Square has regained its status as a wealthy residential district. In addition to renovating 1880s townhouses, urban pioneers have attempted to reclaim the park from local prostitutes.

Washington Square Park, c.1909. In the background is Newberry Library, designed by Henry Ives Cobb and opened in 1893. (C.R. Childs, courtesy G. Schmalgemeier)

Among the historic buildings that surround Washington Square are the **Scottish Rite Cathedral** at 915 N. Dearborn, which was rebuilt after the Fire as Unity Church in 1874, and **Newberry Library,** 60 W. Walton. (The New England Congregational Church at the southeast corner of Dearborn and Delaware was destroyed by fire in 1936 and never rebuilt.)

The Newberry Library, one of the nation's foremost research libraries, was designed by Henry Ives Cobb and constructed in 1892 on the site of Mahlon D. Ogden's estate. A new addition, completed in 1982, provides the Newberry with state-of-the-art storage facilities.

(D) Turn right onto Clark Street from Walton and continue one block north to Oak Street. Go west on Oak to LaSalle Street, then turn north. **Henrotin Hospital** at 111 W. Oak, was founded in 1886 as the Chicago Policlinic Hospital "to furnish practical instruction" for Chicago physicians. In 1889 a modern clinic building was constructed at 221 W. Chicago. As the institution grew, larger quarters were needed. In 1907 a new hospital opened at the southeast corner of Oak and LaSalle. It was named for Fernand Henrotin, president of the Policlinic's board of trustees, who had died in 1906. This building was demolished when LaSalle Street was widened in 1930. The present hospital complex includes a Y-shaped building opened in 1935 and a five-story addition completed in 1968.

When Annunciation Church was
built in 1911, LaSalle Street
contained many single-family
homes. The Greek Orthodox
Cathedral was designed by
architects Worthmann &
Steinbach. (G. Lane, 1980)

(Top right) The Chicago Policlinic,
nucleus of Henrotin Hospital,
occupied this building at 222 W.
Chicago Avenue from 1889 to
1924. In 1907, a new Henrotin
Hospital was built at the
southeast corner of LaSalle and
Oak Streets.
(Courtesy G. Schmalgemeier)

(Right) LaSalle Towers, northeast
corner of LaSalle and Division,
1985. This was one of many
apartment hotels constructed on
Chicago's Gold Coast in the 1920s.
As part of a renovation program in
1980, artist Richard Haas
transformed the building's exterior
with trompe l'oeil murals. (G. Lane)

(E) After decades as a rooming house district, North LaSalle Street is undergoing a renaissance. Once again considered part of Chicago's Gold Coast, it includes a mix of nineteenth-century townhouses, student housing for **Moody Bible Institute,** nursing homes, and modern apartment buildings. The decline of once-fashionable LaSalle Street began in 1930 after the street was widened to accommodate automobile traffic heading for Chicago's financial district. While older townhouses lost only their front yards, newer buildings sacrificed portions of their exteriors. LaSalle Street's churches remain as vivid reminders of this street's heyday as a residential district: **Annunciation Greek Orthodox Cathedral,** 1017 N. LaSalle; **Ascension Episcopal,** 1133 N. LaSalle; and **LaSalle Street Church,** 1136 N. LaSalle.

(F) One of the most unusual buildings in Chicago is **LaSalle Towers** at the northeast corner of Division and LaSalle. In 1980, artist Richard Haas transformed the exterior of this l920s apartment hotel with "trompe l'oeil" (trick of the eye) murals. The south facade honors the memory of Chicago architects Louis Sullivan, Daniel Burnham, John Wellborn Root, and Frank Lioyd Wright. Also on the south exterior of the building, Haas painted an arch reminiscent of that on Sullivan's Transportation Building at the Columbian Exposition of 1893. The "windows" of this building "reflect" the Chicago Board of Trade in the distance at LaSalle and Jackson. The east wall of the building continues Haas's tribute to Chicago's architectural heritage with replicas of Chicago bay windows, which create the illusion of depth. On the north wall of LaSalle Towers Haas painted architect Adolph Loos's design for the Chicago Tribune Tower competition in 1922. More than 200 architects from the United States and around the world entered the competition, which was won by the New York firm of Hood & Howells.

On the west side of LaSalle at 1258 is the former **Swedish Club,** now part of a new apartment complex.

(G) At Goethe Street (1300 North) turn east and continue to Dearborn Street. The modern brick church, **First St. Paul's Evangelical Lutheran** at 1301 N. LaSalle, stands

Dearborn Parkway, looking north from Burton Place, 1937. Although highrises have altered the scale and density of the Gold Coast, many of these homes remain today in this elite residential district.
(Chicago Park District, courtesy R. Wroble)

in the midst of the Carl Sandburg condominium complex. "An old church in a new day," First St. Paul's is Chicago's oldest Lutheran congregation, founded in 1846 at Ohio and LaSalle. When the parishioners split in 1848 over the question of church creed, the congregation known as First St. Paul's built a new church on Grand Avenue in what was then the center of the North Side German community. A larger church, constructed in 1864 at Superior and Franklin, was destroyed in the Chicago Fire of 1871. Evangelical Lutherans rebuilt this church in 1872 and continued to worship there until 1910, when they purchased the former North Chicago Hebrew Synagogue (Temple Sholom) at LaSalle and Goethe. In 1970 First St. Paul's built this modern church designed by architect Edward Dart.

(H) At Dearborn Street turn left and continue all the way to North Boulevard. The Three Arts Club at the northeast corner of Goethe and Dearborn is a Chicago Landmark, designed by Holabird & Roche. Founded in 1912 to provide young women artists, musicians, and actresses with a safe place to live in the city, the Three Arts Club is the last of six such residences located throughout the world.

St. Chrysostom's Episcopal Church at 1424 N. Dearborn recalls the era when Dearborn was home to Chicago's elite. The parish dates from 1894, and the present Gothic church was dedicated in 1926. St. Chrysostom's is well known for its 43-bell carillon, which was made in Croydon, England and donated by Charles R. Crane, a Chicago steel manufacturer.

As you turn right onto North Boulevard from Dearborn Street, the **Chicago Historical Society** is visible to your left. This museum and library of Chicago and American history has been a North Side institution for more than 125 years. The complex in Lincoln Park was built in two stages, the colonial red-brick structure in 1932 and the modern white limestone addition in 1972.

(I) Go two blocks east on North Boulevard, then turn right on Astor Street. At 1555 N. State Parkway is the red brick Queen Anne style mansion built in 1885 for Catholic archbishop Patrick A. Feehan. The oldest house on Chicago's Gold Coast, the archbishop's residence was constructed on the site of the city's first Catholic cemetery. Architect Alfred F. Pashley designed the many-chimneyed mansion, which has been a landmark for generations of Chicagoans.

Go south on Astor Street to Schiller. Astor Street contains fine examples of high-class residential construction, ranging in style from Queen Anne to Richardsonian Romanesque to Georgian Revival.

The **May house** at 1443 N. Astor (1891) bears a resemblance to H.H. Richardson's Glessner House at 1800 S. Prairie Avenue. The 1929 **Russell house** at 1444 N. Astor was designed in the Art Deco style by Holabird and Root. Although three highrises were constructed in the 1300 block of Astor Street in the 1920s, far more typical of the area's housing was the single-family residence known as the **Joseph T. Ryerson house** at 1406 N. Astor. According to the Commission on Chicago Historical and Architectural Landmarks, David Adler designed this home after Parisian *hotels* of the Second Empire.

At the southeast corner of Astor and Schiller is the **James Charnley house,** designated a Chicago landmark in 1972. It was designed by the firm of Adler & Sullivan in 1892 and shows the genius of those men and that of the young Frank Lloyd Wright who was then in the firm.

*East Lake Shore Drive, 1985.
When the Drake Hotel at Michigan
and Walton opened in 1920, the
Chicago* Tribune *predicted that:
"Its location fixes a new social
focus, around which will grow a
small new city of theaters, clubs
and fashionable shops." In April
1985, this section of East Lake
Shore Drive was officially
designated a Chicago Landmark
District.*
(Bob Thall, courtesy Commission on Chicago
Landmarks)

(J) Turn right on Schiller and go west to State Parkway;
turn left and go south on State to Division Street. At
1340 N. State Parkway is the **George S. Isham house,**
designed in 1889 by James Gamble Rogers. One of the
Gold Coast's earliest residences, it attained notoriety in
the 1960s as the Chicago residence of magazine
publisher Hugh Hefner. It is now used as a dormitory by
the School of the Art Institute.

   This stretch of North State Parkway includes the
Ambassador East Hotel, 1301 N. State, home of the
famous "Pump Room" and the Ambassador West at 1300
N. State with its famous "Guildhall." Although the
Churchill Hotel at 1255 N. State Parkway was converted
into condominiums in the late 1970s, Eugene Sage's
restaurant continues in its twelfth year at this location.

Division St. E. from State, Chicago, Ill.

15731.

Division Street, looking east from State, c.1911. Over the years, this section of Division has remained a mix of townhouses, greystones, and flat buildings with a few commercial structures.

(C.R. Childs, courtesy G. Schmalgemeier)

(K) At Division Street, turn right and go four blocks west to Wells Street. This section of Division Street is the Gold Coast's best known nightlife area. When Butch McGuire opened his saloon at 20 W. Division in 1961, the surrounding neighborhood contained vestiges of Chicago's Bohemian community. The construction of nearby Sandburg Village in 1962 did much to attract single young white Loop workers and airline flight attendants to this part of the Near North Side. In recent years, luxury townhouses have been constructed along Clark Street and modern convenience stores have opened nearby on Division. Although the condominium boom of the 1970s diminished the number of renters in the area, Division Street continues to attract patrons from all over the city and suburbs.

(L) At Wells Street, turn right and go north three-fourths of a mile to Lincoln Avenue. Once the dividing line between the "Gold Coast and the Slum," Wells Street has been upgraded with new housing and shops. At the southwest corner of Division and Wells is **Atrium Village,** a successful apartment complex built in 1978 on "no man's land" between the Cabrini-Green public housing project and the highrises of the Gold Coast. Architect George Schipporeit, who designed Lake Point Tower, designed this unique complex, which includes a double atrium building with interior landscaping.

At 1206 N. Wells is the **House of Glunz,** a wine merchant and family business that dates back to 1888, when this part of the neighborhood was predominantly German.

One of the most interesting renovation projects in recent years is **Cobbler Square** (1985) at 1350 N. Wells Street. Once a factory complex housing the Western Wheel Works and later Dr. Scholl's Footwear, the buildings were readapted for residential use by architect Kenneth A. Schroeder.

(M) **Piper's Alley** at 1608 N. Wells is the home of Second City, the improvisational theater company established in 1960. Piper's Alley is named after Henry Piper's bakery which occupied this site in the 1880s. Throughout the 1960s, Piper's Alley was a popular tourist attraction noted for its boutiques, theater, and shops which catered to Old Town's artists and "flower children." Stanley Tigerman redesigned the complex in 1975.

(N) At the juncture of Wells and Lincoln, continue north on Lincoln to Wisconsin Street (1900 North). Turn left on Wisconsin, go west to Sedgwick (400 West), then south (left) on Sedgwick to North Avenue. Although the Old Town Triangle District is well known for its interesting mix of frame cottages and brick homes, it also includes such modern structures as the **Church of the Three Crosses** (1973) at the southwest corner of Wisconsin and Orleans. Along Sedgwick Street between Wisconsin and Menomonee are ten luxury townhouses designed by Chicago's leading architects. Just one block south, however, Sedgwick is lined with workingmen's cottages and brick flat buildings which date from the 1870s to the 1890s, when Old Town was a thriving German community.

In the l960s, Piper's Alley with its theater, psychedelic shops, and boutiques was one of Old Town's best known tourist attractions. Today the small shopping mall at 1608 N. Wells reflects the neighborhood's transformation into an upper middle-class area.
(G. Lane, 1985)

These two-story frame and brick houses in the 1600 block of N. Cleveland were typical of the Old Town homes constructed after the Chicago Fire of 1871. (D. Pacyga)

(O) Turn right at North Avenue and go west to Cleveland (500 West). Go north on Cleveland to Eugenie Street. **St. Michael's** parish was Chicago's largest German Catholic community in the 1890s. The massive Bavarian Baroque church at the corner of Cleveland and Eugenie was begun in 1866. Only the walls of St. Michael's remained standing after the Chicago Fire of 1871. The structure was rebuilt and rededicated in 1873. Over the years St. Michael's parish provided a complete system of education, from grammar school through high school. In recent years, however, parts of the parish plant have been transformed into **St. Michael's Mews,** an expensive townhouse and condominium complex. After decades as a German institution, St. Michael's became an ethnically diverse parish serving Italian, Spanish-speaking, and black families in Old Town. Today the congregation includes young white professionals as well as older neighborhood residents.

(P) Follow Eugenie Street west to Larrabee, then north (right) on Larrabee one block to Willow Street (1746 North). New townhouses along Larrabee Street replaced ramshackle buildings in the western section of Old Town. Go four blocks west on Willow to Halsted Street. One sign of ethnic change in the area is the **Pilgrim Missionary Baptist Church** at 725 W. Willow. Originally a German church, the building now houses a black congregation.

At Halsted Street, turn right and go north to Armitage Avenue (2000 North). Generations of Chicagoans knew the imposing brick building at the northwest corner of Willow and Halsted as **Matt Schulien's restaurant.** The German restaurateur entertained his patrons with "goldfish" swallowing tricks and gard cames. The tradition continues at 2100 W. Irving Park, where Schulien's restaurant has been located since 1955. Today the building on Halsted Street forms the anchor of the Willow-Dayton complex, the first major renovation project in the area, begun in 1979. Since that time, renovation and new building along Halsted Street has continued at a record pace, all the way from North Avenue to Fullerton.

(Q) Turn left at Armitage and go three blocks west to Bissell Street (924 West), then two blocks north on Bissell to Webster Avenue (2200 North). The brick row houses on the west side of Bissell Street are typical of the housing stock in the Sheffield Historic District. At the time the "L" tracks were laid between Sheffield and Bissell in 1897, this neighborhood was completely built up.

(R) Turn left at Webster and go nine blocks west to Southport Avenue (1400 West). **St. Vincent de Paul Church,** at the northwest corner of Webster and Sheffield, was built between 1895 and 1897. Designed by architect James J. Egan, this edifice compared favorably with the buildings of nearby **McCormick Theological Seminary.** A national depression notwithstanding, parishioners devised many ways to finance their new church. The most unusual was a "popular voting contest" in October 1896 between Illinois Governor John Peter Altgeld and his Republican

This Victorian house at 1838 N. Lincoln Park West, built in 1874, was the boyhood home of Charles Wacker, after whom Wacker Drive is named. He aggressively promoted the plan which replaced the old South Water Street Market in the 1920s with a modern double-decked street at the river's edge. (D. Pacyga)

opponent, John R. Tanner. Although Altgeld won St. Vincent's contest, Tanner won the gubernatorial election in November.

Webster Avenue between Racine and Southport was the center of Chicago's Roumanian community in the late 1920s. Workers employed in the nearby North Western Terra Cotta factory and the Deering Harvester Plant contributed generously to the construction of the **Assumption of the Holy Virgin Roumanian Greek Orthodox Church** (1915) at 1339 W. Webster. Now a private home, the building recalls the days when it was a popular meeting place for the North Side Roumanian community.

Arthur J. Schmitt Academic Center, 2323 N. Seminary, 1985. When this center opened in 1967, it was the first new classroom building constructed on De Paul University's Lincoln Park campus since 1938. In the mid-1970s, De Paul acquired the buildings and grounds of nearby McCormick Theological Seminary, making it the largest institution in the neighborhood west of Halsted Street. (G. Lane)

(S) Turn right at Southport Avenue and go one block north
to Belden Avenue. **St. Josaphat** parish was the city's
first Kashubian Catholic congregation. German-speaking
Poles established their parish in 1884 and built the
present St. Josaphat Church in 1902. Architect William
J. Brinkman designed this Romanesque gem with its
distinctive maroon and gold coffered ceiling. Turn right
on Belden and go fourteen short blocks east on Belden
to Orchard Street (700 West).

Historically, this part of the Near North Side has
been isolated from the larger Lincoln Park community.
In recent years, factories along the Milwaukee Road's
spur line have closed, and the area is now ripe for
redevelopment. Local real estate dealers have financed
the construction of new townhouses such as Lakewood
Commons on Lakewood between Fullerton and Belden,
and plans are under way for a Treasure Island grocery
store at Lakewood and Clybourn.

(T) **De Paul University** was founded in 1898 in the original
St. Vincent church building at the northeast corner of
Webster and Kenmore. In addition to its Lincoln Park
campus, De Paul also maintains a downtown campus
centered at Wabash and Jackson. The university has
contributed much to the stability of the Lincoln Park
neighborhood, and in recent years the area west of
Sheffield Avenue has come to be known as De Paul.
Predominantly a commuter college, De Paul University
broke ground on June 20, 1985 for a new dormitory at
Clifton and Fullerton. When completed, the building will
increase the university's resident housing to 950
students.

(U) The former campus of **McCormick Theological
Seminary** was bounded by Fullerton, Bissell, Belden,
and Halsted. The school's original buildings, constructed
between 1864 and 1896, were demolished in the 1960s
as part of the Lincoln Park urban renewal program.
Although the seminary subsequently constructed a new
library, chapel, and administration building, declining
enrollment and economic considerations prompted the

institution's move to Hyde Park in 1973. Nearby De Paul University now owns the buildings and campus of the former Presbyterian seminary. However, the fifty-eight McCormick row houses located along Fullerton, Belden, and Chalmers Place are privately owned.

(V) Turn left at Orchard Street and go north to Fullerton Parkway. The nationally known **Children's Memorial Hospital,** a Lincoln Park institution since 1882, occupies the land bounded by Lincoln, Fullerton, and Orchard. In addition to a modern steel and glass building at Lincoln and Fullerton (1963, 1982), Children's Memorial includes the brown brick structures on the west side of Orchard known as the Agnes Wilson Building and the Nellie A. Black Building.

(W) At 2335 N. Orchard is **St. Pauls United Church of Christ,** a neo-Gothic structure dedicated in 1959. When the 1898 church building on Orchard Street was destroyed by fire in 1955, the congregation financed a new structure designed by Benjamin Franklin Olson.

(X) Turn right onto Fullerton Parkway and go east to the Fullerton Avenue entrance to Lake Shore Drive. In the 1880s and 1890s, Fullerton Parkway was a fashionable residential street with elegant brownstones and spacious mansions. An early ordinance prohibited streetcars along the parkway, and the ban remains in effect today. (However, while buses are not permitted between Clark and Halsted Streets, automobile traffic is particularly heavy.) Not only was Fullerton one of the North Side's most exclusive streets, but it contained two of Lincoln Park's most prominent institutions, **Fullerton Presbyterian Church** (now known as Lincoln Park Presbyterian), and the **Episcopal Church of Our Saviour.** In the 1880s both congregations constructed beautiful churches which blended in well with the area's fine homes. The **Lincoln Park Presbyterian Church** at 600 W. Fullerton Parkway was completed in 1888, and the nearby **Church of Our Saviour** at 530 W. Fullerton dates from 1889.

Clark Street is one of Lincoln Park's most important commercial strips, and its mix of small shops, restaurants, and bars provides a steady stream of pedestrian traffic at all hours of the day and night. Just east of Clark Street at 320 W. Fullerton is the **Aztec Apartment Building,** constructed in 1916 on the site of the former Aztec Tennis Club. High-class apartments such as the Aztec contributed to Lincoln Park's reputation as a fashionable residential district in the 1920s.

Intersection of Clark and Fullerton, c.1910. As Lincoln Park was built up with apartment buildings, small shops emerged along Clark Street.
(Courtesy G. Schmalgemeier)

Damen
Winchester
Honore
Ravenswood
Summerdale
Paulina
Ashland
Cla
Balmoral
Wayne
Lakewood
Magnolia
BRO
14
Winthrop
Kenmore
SHERIDAN

Berwyn
Farragut
FOSTER
41
FOSTER AVE. BEACH
Lincoln

AMUNDSEN H S
Winon
Carmen
Winona
Carmen
Argyle
Margate Ter
Castlewood Ter

mac
rk
Winona
Winnemac
Argyle
Winnemac
Argyle
Broadway
Ainslie
Gunnison
Gunnison

BETHANY METHODIST HOSP
Hermitage
Paulina
Ainslie
St. Boniface Cemetery
Lawrence
CHICAGO LAKESHORE HOSP

Seeley
4800
Chase Park
Lakeside Pl
Leland
Eastwood
Wilson
Windsor
Clarendon Community Center Park

CITY COL OF CHGO-TRUMAN COLLEGE
Racine
Broadway
Dover
Beacon
Malden
Magnolia
Clifton
Agatite
Clarendon
WEISS MEM HOSP
FRANK CUENO MEM HOSP

Simonds
LAKE SHORE DR
Marine Dr
Lawrence
PARKING AREA
Wilson Dr
Montrose Dr
PARKING AREA

MONTROSE-WILSON BEACH

RAVENSWOOD HOSP MEDICAL CENTER
Sunnyside

Winchester
Wolcott
Honore
Pensacola
Cullom
Hutchinson
Berteau
Warner
Belle Plaine
Cuyler
Montrose
Graceland Cemetery
Clark
First German Lutheran Cemetery
Kenmore
SHERIDAN
Pensacola
Cullom
Hazel
Hutchinson
Gordon
Belle Plaine
Cuyler
Junior Ter
Dayton
Buena Ter
U.S. PUBLIC HEALTH SERVICE OUT PATIENT CLINIC
Bittersweet Pl

2000
1600
LAKE VIEW H S
Irving Park
19
Montrose
800

Waveland Ave. Golf Course

Larchmont
Berenice
Pl
Patterson

Ravenswood
Hermitage
Paulina
Marshfield
Ashland
Bosworth
Greenview
Janssen
Grace
Byron
Hebrew Cem
Wunder Cem
HEART OF MARY
AMERICAN HOSP OF CHICAGO
Dakin
Wilton
Sheridan
Grace
Bradley Pl
Gill Park
Sheridan Rd
Broadway
Pine Grove
41
Addison Dr
BIRD SANCTUARY

Lincoln
1200
Sheil Park
Southport
Wayne
Lakewood
Magnolia
Racine
Clifton
Alta Vista
WRIGLEY FIELD (CUBS)
Waveland
ADDISON
3600
Patterson
Belmont Harbor Dr
Belmont Harbor

Eddy
Cornelia
Newport
Roscoe
Melrose
Eddy
Newport
Greenview
Henderson School
Gross Park
Clifton
Seminary
Kenmore
Sheffield
Fremont
Reta
Roscoe
Dayton
Brompton
Cornelia
Elaine Pl
Buckingham Pl
Melrose
Stratford Pl
Hawthorne Pl
Roscoe
Aldine

Belmont
3200

Seeley
Damen
Wolcott
Honore
Fletcher
Nelson
Wellington
George
Hamlin Park
Barry
Nelson
Oakdale
ILL MASONIC MEDICAL CENTER
Wellington
ST. SEBASTIAN H S
George
Wolfram
DIVERSEY
Fletcher
Briar Pl
California Ter
Barry
Waterloo Ct
Broadway
Cambridge
Hudson
Pine Grove
Surf
SHERIDAN RD
Lake Shore Dr West
Commonwealth
Hampden Ct
Diversey Dr
Commonwealth
ST JOSEPH HOSPITAL
2800 PKWY

Hoyne
C&NW
Paulina
Marshfield
Bosworth
Greenview
Janssen
Magnolia
Schubert
Drummond Pl
Wilton
Mildred
Dayton
Schubert
Drummond
Wrightwood
Draper
Lill
Wrightwood
Burling
Orchard
Cambridge
Pine Grove
Lehmann Ct
Wrightwood
Deming
St James
ELKS MEM
GOVERNOR OGLESBY MON.
COLUMBUS HOSP
North Lagoon
Park
Linco

© Copyright by Rand McNally & Company R.L. 86-S-7 pk.

3

Mid-North Side

Ever since the Chicago Cubs' 1984 divisional championship when they played to capacity crowds, controversy has swirled around "Beautiful Wrigley Field" at the intersection of Clark and Addison in the Lake View neighborhood. When this park opened in 1914, baseball was a daytime sport, and the Wrigley family continued the tradition long after night games became popular in the late 1930s. Over the years North Siders have strongly supported the state statute and city ordinance prohibiting electric lights in Wrigley Field. When the Chicago Tribune Company, owners of the Cubs since 1981, sought to have the ordinance struck down, local residents and the Lake View Citizens Council fought back. The community scored a major victory on March 25, 1985 when Cook County Circuit Court Judge Richard L. Curry issued an opinion upholding existing ordinances banning lights in Wrigley Field. In their fight to preserve the residential character of their neighborhood, "Wrigleyville" homeowners focused new attention on Lake View, one of Chicago's oldest neighborhoods. Our focus in this section will be first on Old Lake View, then East Lake View/New Town, Wrigleyville, Buena Park, and Uptown.

Lake View

When the city of Lake View was annexed in 1889, Chicago acquired a well-organized community. Indeed, Lake View had been incorporated as a township in 1857, and it claimed the territory bounded by Fullerton, Western, Devon, and Lake Michigan. Within this extensive area were the villages of Ravenswood, Bowmanville, Summerdale, Andersonville, Rose Hill, Gross Park, and Belle Plaine.

From the 1830s through the 1850s the area between Diversey and Irving Park was sparsely settled. Immigrants from Germany and Luxembourg established farms here, and before long Lake View was the principal source of Chicago's flourishing celery trade.

On July 4, 1854 James B. Rees and E.E. Hundley opened a hotel at Grace Street and the lakeshore. According to local historian Helen Zatterberg, the inn was known as the Lake View House because of its unbroken view of Lake Michigan. When Lake View township was organized, it took its name from the hotel.

In the early years, transportation to downtown Chicago was a difficult business. Homeowners in the vicinity of the Lake View House funded the construction of a plank road between Montrose and Diversey. The Lake View Plank Road (now known as Broadway) continued south along the Green Bay Road (Clark Street) to the township limits at Fullerton Avenue. In 1856 a stagecoach route was established from the Lake View House to Chicago, and in the following year omnibuses made the trip twice a day, except Sunday.

Although a number of wealthy Chicagoans built country houses along the lakeshore, this part of Lake View remained largely undeveloped. In 1869 a reporter for the Chicago *Times* noted that, "The great need of the Lake View suburbs is a steam railway running along the lake shore . . ."

After the Chicago Fire of 1871, a number of Swedish families moved to the area around Belmont and Sheffield from the Near North Side. Here they established a community which continued to grow in numbers throughout the nineteenth century. According to one historian, by 1900 newly-arrived Swedish immigrants went directly to Lake View, bypassing the city's original Swede Town on the Near North Side.

The first public building to be erected in Lake View was the Town Hall (1872) at the northwest corner of Addison and Halsted. Once the center of local government for the township, the site continues the tradition up to the present time. For decades now the building on this corner has housed the Town Hall station of the Chicago Police Department.

Another important institution in Old Lake View was the high school, which opened in 1874 at Irving Park and Ashland on land which had been donated by the Graceland Cemetery Association. One of the earliest township high schools, Lake View has been part of the Chicago public school system since 1889.

Residents of Old Lake View found ready employment in factories such as the Deering Iron Works along the North Branch of the Chicago River. In the 1870s and 1880s the area bounded by Diversey, Ashland, Wellington, and Ravenswood was the center of Chicago's brickmaking industry. In 1905 the area's industrial base expanded to include the Stewart Warner Company at 1826 W. Diversey, one of the largest employers in Lake View.

Lake View's public schools give an idea of how the community took shape. Although School No.1 was established in the 1860s at the northwest corner of Broadway and Aldine, the area of greatest growth occurred near School No. 2 at Diversey and Seminary. The two-story brick school on Diversey was a four-room structure when it opened in 1878. In less than ten years it had fourteen classrooms, and it ranked as one of the town's most substantial buildings,

Lake View Town Hall, built in 1872 at Halsted and Addison, was the center of government for Lake View township and included the area's first police station. The brick building now located on this site is known as the Town Hall station of the Chicago Police Department.

(Courtesy Chicago Public Library, Sulzer Regional Library)

valued at $45,000. According to A.T. Andreas, children accounted for one-third of Lake View's population of 12,824 in 1884. To meet the needs of these youngsters, new schools were built at Wrightwood and Ashland (1882), and Orchard and Wrightwood (1883).

In the early 1880s S.E. Gross promoted the development of the area bounded by Wellington, Southport, George, and Herndon (Lakewood). Because this section of Lake View was located outside the fire limits, property owners were allowed to build frame houses. Although the supply of brick nearby was plentiful, workingmen preferred the less expensive wooden balloon-frame houses which ranged in price from $700 to $1,200. Indeed, Lake View's many building and loan associations did much to promote home ownership among the area's families.

Like the Swedes, German people also moved northward into Lake View from early settlements near Chicago Avenue. Two of the area's pioneer German churches, St. Alphonsus (1882) and St. Luke's (1884) are still important institutions in this community after more than one hundred years.

In 1882 Redemptorist priests established St. Alphonsus parish as a mission of St. Michael parish in Old Town. Rev. Joseph Essing, C.Ss.R., settled the controversy over where the Catholic church should be located when he purchased five acres of land bounded by Wellington, Southport, Oakdale, and Greenview, just west of Gross's subdivision. The German parish of St. Alphonsus played a significant role in attracting Catholic families to the area.

St. Luke Evangelical Lutheran Church at Belmont and Greenview was founded as a branch of St. James Church at Hoyne and Wellington Avenues. Like St. Alphonsus, St. Luke's also operated a parochial school where children learned their lessons in German and English. The parishes of St. Alphonsus and St. Luke's built massive complexes which became the focal points for the area's large German Catholic and Lutheran populations.

The history of the Birren Funeral Home illustrates the successive moves made by Germans on the North Side. Shortly after Heinrich Birren arrived in Chicago from Luxembourg in 1848, he settled near Chicago Avenue and Pine Street (Michigan Avenue) in the vicinity of the German parish of St. Joseph. In 1859 he established an undertaking business and subsequently moved to Eugenie and Wells, a short distance from St. Michael Church. Birren's son, Peter, moved north in 1885 to 2927 N. Lincoln Avenue, thus becoming Lake View's first undertaker. Since 1926 the Birren Funeral Parlor has been located catty-corner from St. Alphonsus Church.

Unlike other suburban towns such as Austin, Morgan Park, and Hyde Park, which enforced strict ordinances against saloons, Lake View had its own saloonkeepers' society. On the second and fourth Fridays of every month the town's saloonkeepers met in the Masonic hall at the southwest corner of Diversey and Racine to "protect and defend their common interests by all lawful means and measures."

German beer gardens and saloons were important gathering places for early Lake View residents. Among the notable spots where Germans continued their tradition of the "Continental Sunday" were the Bismarck Gardens at Halsted and Grace, and Christian Fisher's "Summer Family Resort and Restaurant" at Lake View Avenue and Surf Street. As in other German neighborhoods, residents established musical societies such as the Lake View *Liedertafel,* the Lake View Maennerchor, and the St. Cecilia *Liederkrantz.* Lake View's flourishing community life was reflected in its many lodges and societies and in its large number of meeting halls, among them the Music Hall on Lincoln Avenue at Sheffield; Hillinger's hall at 1001 W. Belmont; and Jung's hall at 3004 N. Lincoln, headquarters of the German Citizens' Club.

Although Germans formed the largest ethnic group in Lake View, a sizeable Swedish settlement also

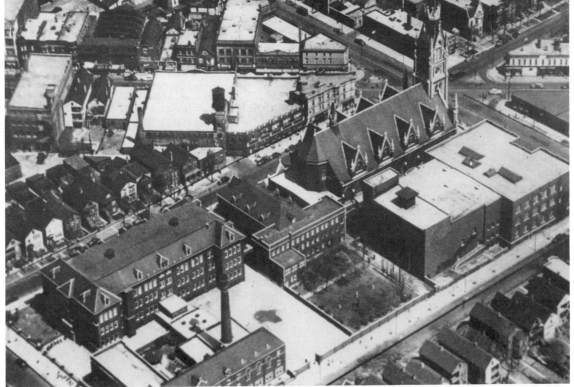

St. Alphonsus parish buildings fill the block bounded by Wellington, Southport, Oakdale, and Greenview. Located in the heart of Lake View, St. Alphonsus was a classic example of a nineteenth-century urban German Catholic community.
(Courtesy The Chicago Catholic)

developed—on the site of an old Jewish cemetery known as Anshe Maariv, located at Belmont and Clark. In the space of just a few years, Lake View's Swedes had established three churches along Barry Avenue: Elim Swedish Methodist Episcopal (1883), Trinity Lutheran (1883), and Lake View Mission Covenant (1886).

The Lake View Directory for 1886 reveals a well-organized community with a network of small businesses—meat markets, pharmacies, florists, grocers, and saloons. According to one local booster, the area's population continued to increase as "people left the city to make their home in this suburb, and the houses they have erected show that . . . they have come to stay."

By the late 1880s Lake View residents had established a wide range of churches which became important community institutions; among them were the Lake View Presbyterian Church, 3600 N. Broadway; the Lake View Congregational Church, Lill and Seminary; Centennial Deutsche Methodist Church, at George and Seminary; the Third Deutsche Evangelical Reformed Friends Church, Wellington and Sheffield; Our Lady of Mount Carmel Church, Wellington and Wilton; and the Sheffield Avenue Methodist Episcopal Church, George and Sheffield. In 1894 English-speaking Irish and German Catholics established St. Andrew parish at Addison and Paulina.

Over the years a number of churches relocated in Lake View from the Near North Side. The First Swedish Baptist Church, for example, moved in 1911 from Elm and Milton (Cleveland) Streets. Once a densely populated Swedish area, that neighborhood experienced considerable ethnic change as "Swedish street meetings had given way to Roman Catholic (Italian) processions." Since its own founding in 1866, First Swedish Baptist had established fifteen other churches in Chicago, making it the "mother church" of the Midwest Baptist Conference. Following its move to 1242 W. Addison Street, First Swedish Baptist changed its name to the Addison Street Baptist Church in 1935. After nearly 120 years the congregation continues in existence, a link with Chicago's original Swedish settlement.

Another pioneer North Side congregation that moved to Lake View was Holy Trinity, Chicago's oldest English-speaking Lutheran church. In 1914 members of this congregation left their former church building at 1136 N. LaSalle Street and built a new house of worship at 1218 W. Addison Street.

Improved transportation contributed to the development of Lake View after it was annexed to Chicago in 1889. The Chicago and North Western Railroad and the Milwaukee Road Railroad both provided commuter service to downtown Chicago, and streetcar lines along Lincoln and Clark connected Lake View with communities to the north and south. In 1900 service began on the Northwestern Elevated line between Wilson Avenue and Lake Street. The tracks of the "L" line were constructed just east of Sheffield Avenue, with stations at Diversey, Wellington, Belmont, Roscoe, Addison, Grace, and Sheridan (Irving Park). By 1908 residents of West Lake View had their own branch line, known as the Ravenswood "L," which joined the main line at Belmont Avenue.

The "L" line along Sheffield together with the extension of streetcar lines north of Fullerton sparked commercial development along Belmont Avenue. Among the shops in the area were Max A.R. Matthews' hardware store at 1224 W. Belmont and George Rasmussen's grocery store at 1328 W. Belmont, the birthplace of the National Tea Company. In 1902 local businessmen began to promote development of the "triple transfer corner" of Lincoln-Belmont-Ashland.

One of the pioneer merchants in the area was H.C. Struve who opened a dry goods store in 1904 at 3167 N. Lincoln Avenue. In 1911 William A. Wieboldt financed the construction of the Lincoln Building at the southeast corner of Lincoln and Belmont on the site of the former Math Jung tavern. From his office in the new commercial building, Wieboldt drew up plans for an eight-story department store, which was completed in 1917 at 3267 N. Lincoln Avenue. Then as now, Wieboldt's anchored the shopping district which developed around the intersection of Lincoln, Belmont, and Ashland Avenues.

More than just a neighborhood shopping area, this commercial district attracted patrons who lived as far north as Bowmanville and Niles Center (Skokie). By the 1920s Lincoln-Belmont was the largest retail furniture district outside the Loop. In 1922 a Chicago *Daily News* reporter commented that the Lake View shopping center with its "cash and carry" customers was one of the most stable in the city. Because its residents were employed in a variety of occupations, from factories to Loop offices, Lake View was not as hard hit during the Depression as other "one-economy" neighborhoods.

When the Lake View Trust and Savings Bank, founded in 1905, began construction of its present building at 3201 N. Ashland in 1913, much of the surrounding neighborhood consisted of modest frame houses. Indeed, as late as 1922 reporter Harry Beardsley noted the existence of scores of "old, almost ramshackle buildings" and he predicted that, "When the building boom hits here the old timers will be pulled down by the dozen." While some homes were razed to make way for brick apartment buildings, most of the area's

The construction of Wieboldt's department store in 1916-17 near the intersection of Lincoln, Belmont, and Ashland put Lake View's shopping district on the map.
(Courtesy Chicago Public Library, Sulzer Regional Library)

These frame buildings, constructed in the 1880s, were razed in 1913 to make way for the modern Lake View Trust & Savings Bank, 3201 N. Ashland.
(Courtesy Chicago Public Library, Sulzer Regional Library)

housing stock remained intact. At the time Illinois Masonic Hospital purchased the former Chicago Union Hospital in 1921, for example, Wellington Avenue still contained many frame houses, relics of Lake View's suburban era. Established to care for "indigent Master Masons and their families," Illinois Masonic at 836 W. Wellington has expanded both its physical plant and its mission. Since its first addition in 1926, the hospital has increased its capacity from 53 to 566 beds. Now the largest fraternal hospital in the world, Illinois Masonic cares for patients without regard to race, creed, or color.

Population throughout Lake View continued to increase in the 1930s and 1940s. Among the newcomers to the neighborhood were Korean families who established a Methodist church at 826 W. Oakdale in 1932. The Korean community in Chicago remained relatively small until the 1960s. Because so many immigrants were professionals with medical training, they tended to settle near the hospitals where they were employed. In their rapid move up the economic ladder, however, Korean families have moved farther north and west, beyond Lake View, establishing businesses and churches in such neighborhoods as Ravenswood, Rogers Park, Albany Park, and Irving Park.

The Japanese community in Lake View dates from the 1940s. After meeting for six years in the Torrey chapel of Moody Church on the Near North Side, a group of Issei and Nisei arranged to buy the old German church at 954 W. Wellington. Dedicated in 1950 as the Lakeside Japanese Christian Church, this was the first church building to be purchased by a Japanese group in Chicago. Because so many Japanese families have moved to the suburbs, their old community in Lake View has declined in numbers. Although Lakeside Christian continues as a predominantly Japanese church, it now serves worshipers of many nationalities.

Despite the fact that Lake View's Swedish population had been declining steadily since the 1930s, the community continued to support a number of its pioneer institutions. From 1883 until it merged in 1970, Trinity Lutheran Church at Barry and Seminary was a Lake View landmark. After a series of discussions in 1969, members of Trinity joined nearby Messiah Evangelical Lutheran Church to form a new congregation known as Resurrection. Messiah Lutheran, founded in 1896, was the first English-speaking congregation in the Augustana Lutheran Synod, and its church building at Seminary and School Streets dates from 1925.

By the mid-1970s the old Swedish area around Belmont and Sheffield had become a Latino district. According to one estimate, in 1974 there were 2,000 Spanish-speaking people living in the area around Wrigley Field between Halsted and Racine. By 1980 this area had expanded considerably, west to Southport, north to Grace, and south to Diversey. Indeed, the latest census figures indicate that people of Spanish origin live in all parts of Old Lake View, and they constitute approximately one-quarter of the area's population.

The conversion of apartments into condominiums has not occurred as swiftly in Old Lake View as in the area east of Halsted Street. According to the 1980 census, home ownership figures remained very high among the 40,000 persons who lived in the area bounded by Diversey, Clark, Irving Park, and Ravenswood. Whether Hispanic families will be priced out of the neighborhood, as happened in Old Town and Lincoln Park, remains to be seen. Nevertheless, despite a decline in population since 1970, this part of the neighborhood includes a high percentage of children, a tradition preserved since Lake View's early days.

Trinity Swedish Evangelical Lutheran Church. 1100 W. Barry, c.1907. When Trinity Church was dedicated in 1897, Barry Avenue was the center of Lake View's Swedish district. Today the former Swedish church is known as Iglesia del Valle.
(Courtesy G. Schmalgemeier)

In the 1970s Japanese and Korean people opened many shops and restaurants along Clark Street from Belmont to Addison. And in recent years Spanish-owned businesses have opened along Belmont in close proximity to older ethnic institutions such as Ann Sather's Restaurant, 927 W. Belmont, and the Toguri Mercantile Company, at 851 W. Belmont.

Signs of change within Old Lake View include the rededication of the old Norwegian Lutheran Church at 1017 W. Roscoe as the North Side Islamic Mosque and the renovation of the Elim Swedish Methodist Episcopal Church at 1017 W. Barry into condominiums. The old Trinity Lutheran Church down the street from Elim is now known as Iglesia del Valle, and its former parochial school at 1034 W. Barry has taken on new life as the Mo-Ming Dance and Arts Center.

In 1983-84 two theaters reopened in the Lake View neighborhood, reversing a city-wide trend. Under new ownership, the Music Box Theater at 3733 N. Southport has been restored to its 1929 grandeur, a perfect setting for vintage movies. The Victorian Theater at 3145 N. Sheffield, built in 1912 as a vaudeville house, featured German operettas during the 1920s. Today the "Old Vic" is a showcase for live music. These two theaters extend the boundaries of Old Lake View's performing arts district, which includes the Steppenwolf Theater, 2851 N. Halsted, and the Organic Theater, 3319 N. Clark.

At the west end of Lake View, the Lincoln-Belmont shopping district has undergone a facelift, and it continues to be one of Chicago's major retail districts. In the heart of Old Lake View, the neighborhood's German traditions continue through such institutions as Zum Deutschen Eck restaurant, 2924 N. Southport; Kuhn's Delicatessen, 3053 N. Lincoln; Meyer Import Delicatessen, 3306 N. Lincoln; Dinkel's Bakery, 3329 N. Lincoln; the Schwaben Stube restaurant, 3500 N. Lincoln; and the Paulina Market, 3501 N. Lincoln. Indeed, after more than a century, some German is still spoken in the churches of St. Luke and St. Alphonsus.

East Lake View/New Town

Whereas Old Lake View developed as a community of workingmen's families in frame homes, brick buildings predominanted in the area east of Halsted Street. Time, of course, was a factor. When S.E. Gross laid out his subdivision along Wellington Avenue in the 1880s, there was not yet much residential construction near the lake. Even more important for the future of this area, however, was the ordinance establishing fire limits in the district bounded by Fullerton, Halsted, Belmont, and Lake Michigan. Shortly before its annexation to Chicago in 1889, the city council of Lake View passed an ordinance requiring the use of fireproof materials in all public buildings and businesses. No structure over two stories could be built unless fireproof materials were used in the exterior walls. Moreover, the council ruled that it was unlawful to build or repair any frame building within the new limits if damage to the structure exceeded fifty percent of its value. This attempt to ensure high-class construction paid off. As a result of the building boom of the 1890s, the area east of Halsted took shape as a modern urban neighborhood of flat buildings and greystones. The extension of the Broadway and Clark streetcar lines accelerated the area's development as a residential district, and it also led to the formation of a new commercial center known as Clark-Diversey.

Unlike Old Lake View, the area close to Lake Michigan supported few ethnic institutions. The families who moved into the apartments and homes that were built on the site of old German beer gardens were mostly native-born Americans of English, German, or Irish descent. Like other emerging communities along the lakeshore, East Lake View was a middle-class residential district.

Our Lady of Mount Carmel parish illustrates how Catholic parishes adapted to the changing needs of their congregations as they became Americanized. When this

The Brewster Apartments (left), at Pine Grove and Diversey Parkway, c.1907. One of Chicago's first highrise apartments (1893), the Brewster was designed by E. Hill Turnock. His generous use of skylights assured apartment dwellers of bright, airy rooms.
(C.R. Childs, courtesy G. Schmalgemeier)

These greystones along Pine Grove north of Grace Street were typical of the high-class residential construction in East Lake View. Uniform setbacks as well as similar building designs and materials contributed to the street's harmonious scale.
(C.R. Childs, courtesy G. Schmalgemeier)

parish was founded in 1886, Lake View was just beginning to develop as a suburban community. Rather than attend the German parish of St. Alphonsus, English-speaking Irish and German Catholics built a small frame church at the corner of Wellington and Wilton. Beginning in 1904, the parish school was located at 728 W. Belmont in the old Academy of Our Lady of Mount Carmel. When the Sisters of Mercy opened their private academy in 1888, the surrounding area was sparsely settled. After the turn of the century, however, Catholics were among the new homeowners and renters in the area. Catholic officials responded to the shift in population by relocating Our Lady of Mount Carmel Church.

In 1912 Archbishop James E. Quigley established St. Sebastian parish for Catholics living west of Clark Street in Old Lake View. The people of Our Lady of Mount Carmel parish, living east of Clark Street, subsequently built a beautiful English Gothic church at 690 W. Belmont in 1914. Not only was the new church a symbol of middle-class Catholic respectability, but it compared favorably with the older St. Peter's Church, located across the street and a little to the east on Belmont Avenue.

St. Peter Episcopal parish began in 1888 in a private home on Fletcher Street, and within six years the cornerstone of the present Gothic church was laid. Following its dedication in 1895, St. Peter's became one of the North Side's most prestigious congregations.

Another sign of the neighborhood's development was the new Nettlehorst public school at 3532 N. Broadway, which dates from 1893. This brick building replaced an earlier schoolhouse in the 3300 block of Broadway that had served as Lake View School No. 1.

Among the new residents in East Lake View were German Jews who had moved into this district from other neighborhoods on the North Side. In 1908 members of Emanuel Congregation built a new synagogue at 701 W. Buckingham Place. Since the late 1890s this congregation had been located in the Lincoln Park neighborhood at the southeast corner of Burling and Belden.

In moving to East Lake View, two North Side institutions selected sites on Pine Grove Avenue, one of the area's most fashionable addresses. In 1907 the Madames of the Sacred Heart moved their academy for girls from State Street and Chicago Avenue into twin greystones at 3540 N. Pine Grove. The school remained at this location until 1929, when the present Academy of the Sacred Heart was built at 6250 N. Sheridan Road.

In 1910 Temple Sholom built a new synagogue at 3760 N. Pine Grove. For fifteen years members of this congregation had worshiped in a synagogue at LaSalle and Goethe Streets. In 1922 Anshe Emet, another North Side Jewish congregation, moved into the area and built a synagogue at 627 W. Patterson, near Broadway. For many members of this congregation the move to East Lake View from Chicago's "Old Town" (1263 N. Sedgwick) was a sure sign of economic and social mobility.

In the 1920s single-family residences and flat buildings east of Clark Street were demolished to make way for high-rise buildings and apartment hotels. While a few mansions remained on Commonwealth Avenue, Sheridan Road was built up with luxury highrises. Like other sections of the North Side, East Lake View prospered as a high-class residential area. Its proximity to downtown as well as its location near Lake Michigan made it especially attractive to white collar workers.

The 1920s proved to be a high water mark in terms of construction for the city as a whole. One of the most important structures built in East Lake View during this period was Temple Sholom at 3480 N. Lake Shore Drive. Completed just before the Depression, the new Temple Sholom was an architectural masterpiece, and it compared favorably with new synagogues constructed in Rogers Park and Hyde Park. Even more important, Temple Sholom became a community center for families who lived in the area's highrises, a function it continues today. (The older synagogue building at 3760 N. Pine Grove took on new life as Anshe Emet.)

The ethnic composition of East Lake View remained fairly stable until the 1950s. Among the new groups who settled in the area at that time were Japanese-Americans who had come to Chicago after living in West Coast "relocation camps" during World War II. Displaced once again by urban renewal in the area around Clark and Division Streets, many families moved farther north. In 1947 Japanese families organized Christ Church, and eight years later they acquired Temple Emanuel at 701 W. Buckingham. The Jewish congregation moved to Edgewater where it built a modern synagogue at 5959 N. Sheridan Road.

New steel-and-glass highrises built in East Lake View during the 1950s and 1960s did much to increase the neighborhood's density. These high-priced buildings were generally confined to Lake Shore Drive and such main arterial streets as Diversey and Belmont. But a different kind of apartment building known as the "four-plus-one" began to show up in large numbers on the side streets of the neighborhood. In order to save money and make the maximum use of a site, builders sunk the ground floor of these buildings below grade for parking and constructed four residential floors above. The four-plus-ones were often located as close to the sidewalk as possible, with no provision for yards. The Lake View Citizens Council launched a successful drive to prevent further construction of these apartments which had replaced so many of the neighborhood's greystone buildings.

According to a 1973 study, 73,000 persons per square mile then lived in the Lake View area, constituting a higher density than Manhattan. When this part of East Lake View was built up, few families owned automobiles. By the mid-1970s, however, community leaders claimed there were 2,000 more resident-owned autos than parking spaces. Soaring real estate prices forced many minority families to leave the neighborhood, a fact reflected in the declining population of Nettlehorst School. Between 1969 and 1974 enrollment dropped from 1,500 to 700 students.

Throughout the 1970s new restaurants, bars, and boutiques which catered primarily to young adults opened along Broadway. As a result of increasing rents in the area, many older merchants sold their stores. New shopkeepers promoted the name "New Town," but a number of longtime residents disliked the term because it conjured up images of the 1960s tourist strip in Old Town. Indeed, arrests for prostitution increased dramatically as Broadway became a nightlife spot. The Clark-Diversey shopping district, on the other hand, attracted new restaurants and shops, but not at the expense of well-established businesses. The $10 million renovation of the Century Theater, 2828 N. Clark, into a mall further enhanced the vitality of the Clark Street shopping strip.

Between 1970 and 1980 the area bounded by Diversey, Halsted, Irving Park, and Lake Michigan declined in

Wellington Avenue looking east across Sheridan, 1936. Although Sheridan Road was built up with highrise apartments in the l920s, this stretch of Wellington continued as an enclave of single-family homes.
(Chicago Park District, courtesy R. Wroble)

population from 47,586 to 43,251. During this period, however, condominium conversions, especially east of Broadway, contributed greatly to the stability of the neighborhood. Condominiums now account for more than forty percent of the housing units in the area east of Halsted between Addison and Irving Park.

One of the newest buildings in the area, Rienzi Plaza, symbolizes the vast changes which have occurred in this part of East Lake View. At the turn of the century a four-story hotel stood at the intersection of Broadway and Diversey. At its rear were the Rienzi Gardens (named after the Wagner opera), where local families gathered on Sundays to hear band concerts. In the 1920s a new eight-story hotel was built on the site, and it kept the Rienzi name. According to Ben Laverty, the last resident manager of the Rienzi Hotel, the building belonged to the era when men and women traveled by railroad and ship. At the end of each floor was a special room for storing steamer and wardrobe trunks. The present Rienzi Plaza is a twenty-story high-rise complex which opened in October 1981. But far from displacing longtime residents, the building includes a special section for senior citizens. Nearly fifty residents of the old hotel now live in the new highrise, thus preserving the Rienzi tradition.

Wrigleyville

Since the 1970s two new neighborhoods have emerged in the shadow of Uptown on Chicago's North Side. These neighborhoods, known as Wrigleyville and Buena Park, occupy the area east of Graceland Cemetery between Addison and Montrose. In the l920s the bright-light district around Wilson and Broadway obscured the smaller

The Bismarck Gardens at Halsted and Grace Streets was one of Lake View's many German beer gardens. Until Prohibition in 1920, the Continental Sunday was a Chicago tradition, especially among the city's North Side Germans. Today Faith Tabernacle Church marks the site of the old Bismarck Gardens.

(H.B. Brooks, courtesy G. Schmalgemeier)

residential areas to the south. But Wrigleyville and Buena Park have recently been "discovered" by young professionals and real estate dealers interested in rehabbing Chicago's dwindling housing stock. Within a few years home values have soared, and these areas are fast becoming the Lincoln Park of the Mid-North Side.

Wrigleyville, a long-established part of the Lake View neighborhood, claims the area bounded roughly by Clark, Irving Park Road, Halsted, and the Ravenswood "L" tracks at Newport Avenue. As renovation continues in the area, it is likely that one or more of these boundaries will be extended.

Graceland Cemetery, established in 1860, borders Wrigleyville and Buena Park on the west. The cemetery's carefully cultivated grounds made it a favorite place for family outings in the nineteenth century, and its "architectural monuments" continue to attract Chicago sightseers.

Long before Wrigley Field was built, this part of the North Side boasted a popular entertainment spot at Halsted and Grace Streets. Known by various names over the years—De Berg's Gardens, Bismarck Gardens, and Marigold

Gardens—it operated as a German beer garden in the 1890s
and later as a vaudeville house and ballroom. In its heyday
as a sports center, Marigold Gardens drew upwards of 7,000
people to its outdoor boxing matches. In 1963 Faith
Tabernacle Church purchased the arena and remodeled it
into a house of worship.

In the years following the turn of the century, the streets
north of Addison were built up with apartment buildings
and greystones. The completion of the Northwestern
Elevated line to Howard Street in 1908 provided residents
with inexpensive transportation downtown and later to the
"Uptown" commercial and theater district which emerged
around Wilson Avenue. Moreover, the Halsted and Broadway
streetcar lines made this part of the North Side one of the
most accessible in the city.

One of the area's earliest institutions was the House of
the Good Shepherd at 1126 W. Grace Street. In 1904 the
nuns who operated the Magdalen Asylum in the German
parish of St. Joseph purchased land just east of Clark Street
on Grace. Here they constructed a new building to continue
their work with young women who had been "exploited or
whose conduct brought them to the attention of the police or
other city officials." Over the years the Sisters of the Good
Shepherd have cared for wards of the juvenile court and
delinquent girls assigned by the Department of Corrections
and more recently for battered women and their children
and unwed mothers.

This community's best known institution is Wrigley
Field, home of the Chicago Cubs, which opened at the corner
of Clark and Addison on April 23, 1914. In its early years
the park was known as Weeghman Park, after Charles
Henry Weeghman, owner of the Chicago Federal League
baseball team. (In 1916 Weeghman purchased the Chicago
Cubs and consolidated the team with the Chi-Feds, known
for a brief time as the "Whales.")

According to Richard Lindberg, the new baseball field on
Addison Street was modeled after the New York Polo
Grounds, where the New York Giants played ball in 1911.
Weeghman hired Zachary Taylor Davis to design the facility,
which originally had a seating capacity of 14,000. An upper
deck was added in 1927 after William Wrigley, Jr.,
purchased the team.

Like Comiskey Park on the South Side, also designed by
Zachary Davis, Weeghman Field was located close to an "L"
stop; and since the first Cubs game on April 20, 1916,
thousands of loyal fans have commuted to watch the Cubs
play ball. The North Side park replaced an earlier baseball

Lorado Taft's sculpture Eternal
Silence, *is one of many
architecturally important
monuments in Graceland
Cemetery.* (G. Lane)

field on the West Side, located at Polk and Wood Streets, now in the heart of the West Side Medical Center.

Photographs published on opening day show how much this neighborhood has retained its original character. Solid greystone buildings flank the ballpark, and automobiles line the surrounding streets, evidence that congestion was as much a problem then as it is now.

Although the area around Wrigley Field has been familiar to generations of Chicago baseball fans, only in recent years has attention been focused on the neighborhood's architecture. On September 15, 1971, the City Council officially recognized the Alta Vista Terrace District as a Chicago landmark. This small section of the neighborhood, bounded by Grace, Kenmore, Byron, and Seminary, was cited for its townhouses, whose "distinctly human scale creates a unity and harmony rarely found elsewhere in the city."

More and more young couples have been investing "sweat equity" in Wrigleyville's homes, renovating and restoring buildings with great care. By the late 1970s property values had soared and rents soon followed. And yet, in comparison with housing costs on the Gold Coast and in Lincoln Park, newcomers regard this neighborhood as affordable.

The area around Wrigley Field continued to be a stable residential neighborhood throughout the 1960s. However, like other parts of the city, Wrigleyville declined in population during the past twenty years. Between 1970 and 1980, for example, the number of area residents decreased from 11,537 to 8,512. According to the 1980 census, persons of Spanish origin constituted nearly thirty percent of the neighborhood, and the black population about ten percent.

If present trends persist, it is likely that Wrigleyville will continue to be a predominantly white community with a sizeable Hispanic component. As of 1980, the percentage of children in the neighborhood remained relatively high, an indication that young families have settled in the area along with single men and women.

The controversy over lights in Wrigley Field has engendered a new sense of community among the diverse people who make up this neighborhood. In the years to come the big question will continue to be: Will the Chicago Cubs leave Wrigleyville for a stadium where they can play night games? While some residents would be happy to bid the team and park adieu, others subscribe to Bill Veeck's view that the Cubs have "squatters rights." Despite the obvious problems of congestion associated with the ballpark, many Wrigleyville residents would mourn the relocation of the Cubs because this would put an end to many jobs, much business, and a longstanding tradition of daytime baseball.

Buena Park

One of the most amazing developments to occur on the
North Side in the 1980s has been the secession of Edgewater
and Buena Park from the community area known as
Uptown. Although both neighborhoods are every bit as
urban as Uptown, their middle-class origins are far more
apparent. Not only has the housing stock in Edgewater and
Buena Park remained intact, but residents in both
neighborhoods have succeeded in upgrading property which
was once threatened by the wrecker's ball.

The community of Buena Park derives its name from the
sixty-acre estate of James B. Waller. About 1860 Waller built
a brick Italianate mansion in Lake View township which he
named "Buena." This area soon attracted the attention of
government officials who decided that it was a perfect
setting for the U.S. Marine Hospital, "the harbor of refuge for
those following a sea-faring life." This institution, dedicated
to the care of retired and ill sailors, recalled Chicago's early
prominence as a port city. For years after the Marine
Hospital opened in 1873, its landscaped gardens were a
popular tourist attraction. (The Disney Magnet School, 4140
N. Marine Drive, occupies the site of the hospital today.)

Another showplace in the Buena Park area was S.H.
Kerfoot's summer home and gardens at Irving Park and the
lakefront. In 1869 a Chicago *Times* reporter noted that
Kerfoot had improved his eleven-acre tract by planting "rich
groves of ash, cherry, basswood, white birch, golden-lark . . .
and lawns of the brightest and most cheerful green."
Although only a few homes had been built here at that time,
the area's superb grounds set this district apart from other
sections of the city and suburbs.

In 1889 Buena Park became part of the city of Chicago
as a result of the annexation of Lake View. However, its
development was definitely suburban-oriented. As Daniel M.
Bluestone wrote in his report for the National Register of
Historic Places, architects designed the neighborhood's
single-family homes and apartments in keeping with "the
prevailing suburban ideal of light, air, and open space."

One of Buena Park's first subdivisions was known as
Gordon Terrace. In contrast to many parts of the city where
homes were constructed from readymade plans, this
subdivision was carefully planned. In 1889 real estate
developers Charles U. Gordon and Francis T. Simmons hired
the architectural firm of Jenny & Mundie to design their
family homes as well as other homes on the block.

In 1893 John C. Scales commissioned architect George
W. Maher to design a house in his new subdivision along

In 1894, George W. Maher designed this elaborate Queen Anne home at 840 W. Hutchinson Street for John Scales. The home is now part of the Buena Park Historic District.

(B. Crane, courtesy Commission on Chicago Landmarks)

Kenesaw Terrace (now Hutchinson). Not only is the Scales house at 840 W. Hutchinson one of the oldest homes in the area, but it has been described by Bluestone as Buena Park's "most flamboyant and exotic Queen Anne."

By the turn of the century Buena Park was well on its way to becoming the North Side's most fashionable residential district. The tradition of lavish house-building continued as families hired architects to design spacious brick homes along Hutchinson, Junior Terrace, Cuyler, Cullom, and Hazel. As in other lakefront neighborhoods, Buena Park soon included a number of apartment buildings. Although these buildings increased the area's density, they did not detract from its suburban character. According to Bluestone, courtyard buildings such as the Pattington (1902) at 660 W. Irving Park Road "eliminated the noisy, unattractive light and air shafts of earlier apartment buildings and provided the amenity of a suburban residential lawn visible from each of the seventy-five apartments."

St. Mary of the Lake Church, 4210 N. Sheridan Road, c.1925. When Henry Schlacks designed this church, dedicated in 1917, the Buena Park neighborhood was a fashionable residential district of single-family homes and new apartment buildings.

(H.B. Brooks, courtesy The Chicago Catholic)

Whereas the Pattington contained apartments as large as nine rooms, suitable for small families, new apartment construction after 1910 featured one- and two-room kitchenettes. These apartments, with their "beds-in-a-door," were models of efficiency, and they attracted young men and women as well as childless married couples. As a result of the apartment building boom, Buena Park reached residential maturity by the 1920s. Although the area was no longer an enclave of single-family homes, it retained its reputation as a high-class district. Apartment hotels such as the Monterey at 4300 N. Clarendon provided residents with spectacular views of Lake Michigan as well as easy access to Clarendon Beach. When it opened in 1914, Clarendon Beach was the city's largest public bathing spot, attracting thousands of Chicagoans every week.

Just as Buena Park's apartment buildings blended in well with its single-family dwellings, so too did its main institutions. James B. Waller, father of Buena Park, was instrumental in forming the Buena Memorial Presbyterian

Church, and his wife, Lucy, provided land for a new house of worship in her will. The distinctive design of Buena Park Memorial Church (1922) is enhanced by its location on a triangular site formed by the intersection of Sheridan Road and Broadway.

St. Mary of the Lake parish, established in 1901 by English-speaking Catholics, soon outgrew its frame church on Sheridan Road between Cuyler and Belle Plaine. The pastor hired Henry Schlacks, Chicago's best known ecclesiastical architect, to design a new church which was built on the site of the Robert A. Waller home, 4210 N. Sheridan Road. (The Waller home was moved around the corner, to 1026 W. Buena.) St. Mary of the Lake Church, dedicated in 1917, is a striking example of Roman basilica-style architecture, and Schlacks modeled its free-standing tower after the ancient campanile of St. Pudentiana in Rome.

The third major institution in Buena Park, The Immaculata High School, continued the neighborhood's tradition of architectural excellence. In 1921 the Sisters of Charity of the Blessed Virgin Mary hired Barry Byrne to design the school's new building, which opened for classes in September 1922. After serving more than three generations of Catholic women, The Immaculata High School at 640 W. Irving Park Road closed in 1981. Since 1983 the stately brown brick building with its red tile roof has housed the American Islamic College.

Over the years Buena Park's single-family homes have contributed much to the stability of the area. Recent construction, such as the Waterford Condominiums (1973) at 4170 N. Marine Drive, has increased the number of housing units in the neighborhood. According to the 1980 census, nearly forty-two percent of the housing units located east of Clarendon between Irving Park and Lawrence were owner-occupied, and condominiums accounted for sixty-five percent of the housing stock.

Buena Park's rebirth dates from 1983 when the City of Chicago officially recognized the area bounded by Irving Park, Sheridan, Montrose, and Marine Drive as a separate community area. The Buena Park Association spearheaded the drive for neighborhood recognition. But before residents could redeem their community's reputation as a middle-class residential district, they had to clean up the neighborhood. This meant battling slum landlords, gangs, prostitution, and drug traffic. By the mid-1980s the renovation boom was well underway, involving an estimated sixty percent of the homes. Encouraged by large-scale rehabilitation throughout the North Side, Buena Park residents hope to preserve the area's ethnic and racial mix as they upgrade the neighborhood.

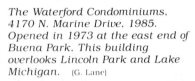

The Waterford Condominiums, 4170 N. Marine Drive, 1985. Opened in 1973 at the east end of Buena Park. This building overlooks Lincoln Park and Lake Michigan. (G. Lane)

Uptown

The Uptown neighborhood, bounded roughly by Montrose, Clark, Foster, and Lake Michigan, experienced one of the most rapid developments of any Chicago community. By the 1890s relatively few homes had been built in the Argyle Park subdivision around Ainslie and Kenmore and the Sheridan Park area between Graceland and St. Boniface cemeteries. The real growth of the neighborhood occurred after 1900 when the Northwestern Elevated line began service from its terminal at Wilson and Broadway. This new elevated railroad was located just east of the old Milwaukee Road Railroad line, and it soon surpassed it in terms of ridership to the downtown business district. The "L" sparked a residential and commercial building boom that quickly transformed the prairies around Wilson Avenue into a densely populated district.

In his study of the North Side elevated system, James Leslie Davis claimed that the area around Wilson Avenue was first known as South Edgewater. According to Edward Marciniak, director of Loyola University's Institute of Urban Life, the community was christened "Uptown" in the 1920s by Broadway and Wilson Avenue merchants who "borrowed the name from a fashionable department store." In any case, the neighborhood quickly gained a reputation as a high-class residential district containing a wide variety of housing, from single-family homes to apartment hotels.

At the turn of the century Uptown was a real estate developer's dream. Not only were there acres of vacant land available for building, but the area's location near the rapid transit line and the lakefront made it especially attractive as a residential district. Like Edgewater to the north and Buena Park to the south, Uptown contained a small area of single-family dwellings, which were concentrated in the Sheridan Park subdivision east of Clark between Montrose and Lawrence. According to Martin Tangora, Sheridan Park included two governors of Illinois among its well-to-do residents: John P. Altgeld, who moved to Dover Street just north of Wilson from the Lake View neighborhood; and Edward F. Dunne, who lived at Beacon and Sunnyside.

Uptown was built up during the great age of public transportation when few Chicagoans owned automobiles. Because of its central location on the North Side rapid transit line, the Wilson Avenue shopping district emerged as one of the most important commercial centers outside the Loop. Wilson Avenue was also an important transfer point for commuters on the Milwaukee Road's express trains.

By 1910 Chicago was the center of America's new moving picture industry, and Uptown boasted the pioneer film studio known as Essanay at 1333 W. Argyle Street.

Dover Street looking south from Wilson Avenue, c.1910. Fine homes provided gracious living for middle-class residents of the Sheridan Park subdivision in Uptown.

(C.R. Childs, courtesy G. Schmalgemeier)

Before the movie industry moved to Hollywood, California, a number of motion pictures were filmed at Essanay Studios, including the Wallace Beery "Sweedie" comedies and Charlie Chaplin's only Chicago film, "His New Job."

Although Essanay Studios closed in 1918, Uptown's reputation as a film center continued. Among the splendid theaters which operated in the area were the Uptown, 4816 N. Broadway; the Riviera, 4746 N. Racine; and the Lakeside, at 4730 N. Sheridan. The neighborhood's most famous showplace, however, was the lavish Aragon Ballroom which opened in 1926 at 1106 W. Lawrence Avenue. For nearly thirty years the Aragon featured Big Band music. Even after the popularity of ballroom dancing waned, the Aragon survived—first as a roller rink, then as a boxing and wrestling arena, a discotheque, and more recently as a gathering place for fans of rock and Latin American music.

High-rise apartments and apartment hotels constructed east of Broadway did much to increase Uptown's density. By their very nature, however, apartment hotels discouraged community building. While some young married couples moved from apartment hotels into family homes west of Racine Avenue, most did not remain in the area for extended periods. Thus even before the Depression struck, Uptown was well on its way to becoming a transient district.

During World War II many single-family homes in the area were converted into rooming houses, and apartments were subdivided into smaller units. Largely because of its cheap rents, Uptown became a port of entry for thousands of

Appalachian whites and American Indians who moved to Chicago during the 1950s and 1960s. No longer the city's bright-light district, Uptown fell on hard times, and its once fashionable housing stock continued to deteriorate. Indeed, Jack Meltzer in his 1962 study estimated that nearly fifty percent of all the neighborhood's housing units were the result of massive conversions.

Unlike Edgewater to the north, which had remained a stable community, Uptown's population was highly mobile. Compounding the problem of neighborhood stability was the fact that many Southern whites and American Indians did not regard their residence in the city as permanent. Not only did they move several times within the Uptown neighborhood, but they tended to return to their family homes for long periods. Throughout the 1960s and 1970s, Uptown's population expanded to include Cubans, Koreans, Hispanics, Arabs, and blacks. The newest immigrants to settle in the area are Indo-Chinese refugees from Vietnam, Thailand, Laos, and Cambodia.

Over the years Uptown's churches have played a major role in fostering community life. Among the neighborhood's pioneer institutions which have survived the turbulent changes in the area are St. Thomas of Canterbury parish, 4815 N. Kenmore; North Shore Congregation Agudas Achim, 5029 N. Kenmore; and the People's Church, 941 W. Lawrence, where Dr. Preston Bradley once preached to overflowing crowds.

When St. Thomas of Canterbury was founded in 1916, it

Wilson Avenue district, looking east from Broadway, c.1924. In the 1920s, Uptown was one of the largest retail centers outside Chicago's Loop. In the distance are the Sheridan Plaza Hotel, 936 W. Wilson; the Chelsea Hotel, 920 W. Wilson; and the Uptown Baptist Church, 1011 W. Wilson. (Kaufmann & Fabry, courtesy The Chicago Catholic)

was considered to be one of the most "American" parishes in the Chicago archdiocese, and its colonial style church was the first of its kind in Catholic Chicago. In addition to serving the poor and the elderly who live in Uptown's Kenmore Avenue district, St. Thomas of Canterbury is also the center of Chicago's growing Vietnamese Catholic community.

One of the neighborhood's newest institutions is Uptown Baptist Church at 1011 W. Wilson Avenue. Established in 1981, the congregation worships in the Gothic church built in 1906 by members of the North Shore Congregational Church. Uptown Baptist serves a cross section of neighborhood residents, from Spanish-speaking to Vietnamese, Cambodian, Laotian, and Hmong families.

During the past twenty years city planners, welfare workers, community activists, and sociologists have regarded Uptown as a case study in urban blight and poverty. Controversy has flared over such critical issues as shelter care facilities, subsidized housing, and education. For example, a number of community activists protested the construction of Harry S. Truman College at Wilson and Racine Avenues because it displaced more than 1,000 families who lived on the site. Even after the institution opened in 1976, the debate continued: Would area residents benefit more by academic training or by job training?

Not far from Truman College is another school, St. Augustine College, which occupies the former Essanay Studios offices at 1333 W. Argyle. The only bilingual college in the Midwest, St. Augustine was established by Dr. Carlos Plazas with backing from the Spanish Episcopal Services, a branch of the Episcopal Diocese of Chicago. When the school opened in 1980, Dr. Plazas expressed his hope that, "Just as the beginning of movies here marked the start of an era in American culture, . . . the beginning of a bilingual college will mark the start of an era in Hispanic culture."

In the 1960s and 1970s, critics charged that Uptown was a dumping ground for the poor and for mental patients who had been released from state facilities. As a result of government programs, most new housing was intended for minority families or the elderly. Indeed, according to a Chicago Housing Authority advisory committee report in 1984, Uptown included 5,300 federally subsidized housing units, more than in the Robert Taylor or Cabrini-Green housing projects. In recent years, however, a significant amount of rehabilitation and new construction has taken place in Uptown, and this bodes well for the future of the neighborhood.

At the southwest corner of Uptown, middle-class professionals and "urban pioneers" have begun to restore single-family homes and flat buildings in the Sheridan Park subdivision. A number of buildings in the Wilson-Broadway commercial district have been renovated, especially the Uptown National Bank at 4753 N. Broadway. The former Kemper Life Insurance building at 4750 N. Sheridan now houses the Ecumenical Institute of Chicago.

Pensacola Place, at Montrose and Sheridan, provides city residents with a neighborhood shopping strip complete with parking lot, a rare commodity in the Uptown neighborhood. Between Sheridan Park and Pensacola Place lies the Winthrop-Kenmore corridor. Although some of the deteriorated housing in this strip has been destroyed by fire or the wrecker's ball, many buildings have been rehabbed. While it is difficult to predict just how extensive Uptown's renaissance will be, it is likely that the area will remain one of Chicago's most diverse neighborhoods. Beyond the renovation of existing housing units, the neighborhood's future rests with decisions made by the area's three main organizations, the Uptown Center Hull House Association, 4520 N. Beacon; the Voice of the People, 4927 N. Kenmore; and the Uptown Chicago Commission, 4753 N. Broadway.

Whereas many Chicago neighborhoods have lost their ethnic flavor as a result of gentrification, Uptown may reverse this trend. Originally settled by second- and third-generation Americans, Uptown's future may well be that of an ethnic neighborhood. Indeed, in recent years Argyle Street between Sheridan and Broadway has emerged as a new Chicago Chinatown. Indo-Chinese refugees have established restaurants and businesses, and they have begun to buy apartment buildings in the area. If Lam Ton, owner of the Mekong restaurant, 4953 N. Broadway, and his fellow merchants have their way, Chinese-style gates will soon stand at either end of the Argyle Street business strip. More than just a symbol of Chicago's new Chinatown, the gates would bear witness to the city's newest immigrants who are forming a cohesive community in Uptown.

Argmore building, northwest corner Argyle and Kenmore, 1985. Built around 1915, this building replaced a spacious single-family home. Today, Argyle Street between Sheridan and Broadway is Chicago's new Chinatown, with shops and restaurants owned by Indo-Chinese refugees from Vietnam, Laos, and Cambodia. (J. Ficner)

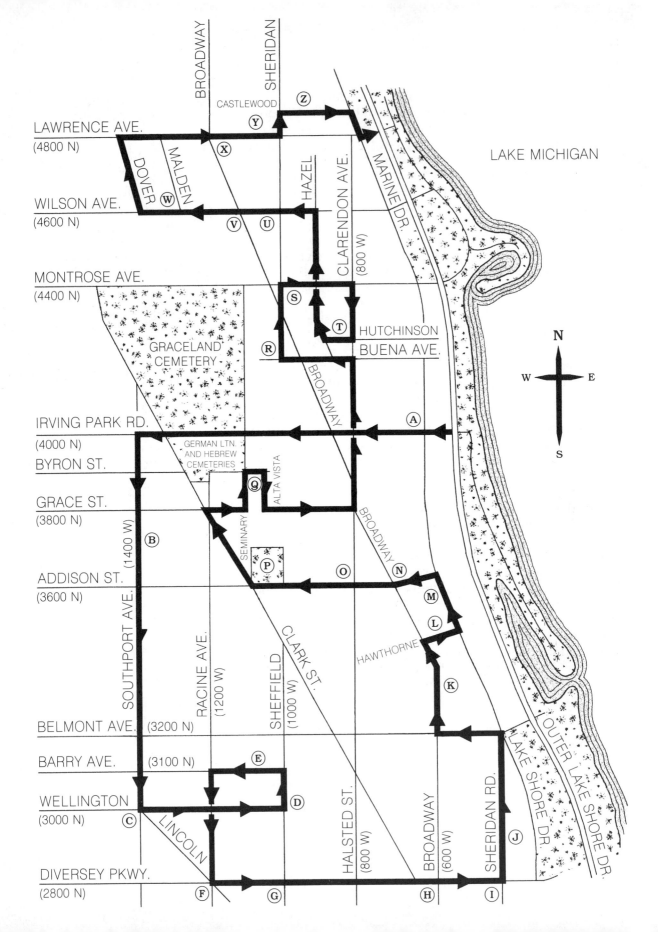

Mid-North Side Tour

This tour begins at Lake Shore Drive and Irving Park Road, goes west through the heart of Old Lake View, then east again to "New Town," then north through Wrigleyville, Buena Park, and Uptown.

Driving time: about 1½ hours.

(A) Go west on Irving Park Road to Southport Avenue (1400 West). The brown brick structure at 640 W. Irving Park Road was built in 1922 as **The Immaculata High School for Girls.** Barry Byrne's design made this one of the most beautiful school buildings in Chicago. In 1977 the structure was added to the National Register of Historic Places. Although declining enrollment and rising costs prompted the Sisters of Charity of the Blessed Virgin Mary to close The Immaculata in 1981, the building continues in use as a school. Since 1983 it has housed the American Islamic College.

The stretch of Irving Park Road between Kenmore Avenue and Clark Street could be called "cemetery row." To the north is the **First German Lutheran Cemetery** and **Graceland Cemetery,** Chicago's most architecturally significant burial ground. To the south is **Wunder's Cemetery,** named after the pastor of First St. Paul's Evangelical Lutheran Church, and also a small **Hebrew cemetery.**

(B) Turn left at Southport and go sixteen blocks south to Wellington Avenue (3000 North).

The **Music Box Theater,** built in 1929 at 3733 N. Southport, has been carefully renovated by owners Chris Carlo and Robert Chaney. In addition to its beautifully restored lobby and theater, the Music Box boasts the last working neon and incandescent marquee in the city.

In recent years the balloon-frame houses of Old Lake View have taken on new life. Built as workers' housing, they are still priced within the range of young families and single people. In block after block, along Southport and elsewhere in the neighborhood, homeowners have enhanced the exteriors of their buildings—some with aluminum siding, others with authentic Victorian color schemes.

The Music Box Theater at 3733 N. Southport Avenue, built in 1929 and recently renovated, boasts the last working neon and incandescent marquee in the city of Chicago. (G. Lane, 1985)

One of Lake View's oldest buildings is the Masonic Hall, built in 1885 at the intersection of Diversey and Racine. Here German saloonkeepers met on a regular basis to discuss trends in their trade. (G. Lane. 1985)

(C) The massive Gothic church of **St. Alphonsus** at 2950 N. Southport was built by a German Catholic congregation in 1897. Although Chicago's North Side German community has diminished since the l930s, St. Alphonsus remains one of the few distinctly German parishes in the city.

This church at the northeast corner of Wellington and Sheffield gives a classic example of ethnic change in Lake View. Built by a German congregation in the l880s, it became the Lakeside Japanese Christian Church in 1950.
(G. Lane, 1985)

(D) Turn left at Wellington and go six blocks east to Sheffield (1000 West). The church at the northeast corner of Wellington and Sheffield was built by a German congregation in the 1880s. In 1950 it was rechristened the **Lakeside Japanese Christian Church,** the first house of worship purchased by a Japanese group in Chicago.

(E) Turn left and go one block north on Sheffield to Barry Avenue (3100 North). Go left on Barry four short blocks to Racine Avenue (1200 West). Barry Avenue formed the heart of Lake View's old Swedish community. The changing ethnic and economic composition of the neighborhood is reflected in the new uses of Swede Town's historic church buildings. The former **Elim Swedish Methodist Episcopal Church** (1898) at 1017 W. Barry has been converted into condominiums; the former Trinity Lutheran school (1924) at 1034 W. Barry is now the **Mo-Ming Dance and Arts Center;** and the old Trinity Lutheran Church at 1100 W. Barry houses a Spanish-speaking congregation known as **Iglesia del Valle.**

(F) Turn left on Racine and go six short blocks south to Diversey Avenue (2800 North). The red brick building at 2756 N. Racine has a colorful history. Built in 1885 as the **Lake View Masonic Hall,** it was one of the community's most popular gathering places. In addition to the Masons, Lake View saloonkeepers met here on a regular basis to discuss trends in the liquor business. The Racine-Diversey corporation has restored this Lake View landmark, which now houses Marks Ltd. Clothing Store.

(G) Turn left on Diversey and go about ten blocks east to Sheridan Road (400 West). The **Lincoln Turners Hall** at 1019 W. Diversey was one of Lake View's many German institutions. Founded in 1885 as the Lincoln Turnverein, the athletic club built the present structure in 1922.

(H) At Clark Street, in East Lake View, the area's housing stock changes dramatically. In contrast to the balloon-frame houses of Old Lake View, this part of the North Side includes high-rise apartments, greystones, four-plus-ones, and brick flat buildings. **Rienzi Plaza** at 600 W. Diversey is a modern high-rise apartment complex built on the site of an old hotel. Just down the street, at 2800 N. Pine Grove, is the historic **Brewster Apartments,** constructed in 1893. One of the first high-rise elevator apartment buildings in Chicago, the Brewster Apartments were light and airy, thanks to architect E. Hill Turnock's generous use of skylights.

The Goethe statue in Lincoln Park at Diversey was dedicated on June 13, 1914, just a few weeks before the outbreak of World War I. Once regarded as the city's premier ethnic group, Chicago's Germans soon found themselves the target of an Americanization program. Indeed, after the United States entered the war, the Goethe statue was placed in storage to preserve it from destruction.
(G. Lane, 1985)

(I) Turn left on Sheridan Road and go six blocks north to Belmont Avenue (3200 North). The southwest and northwest corners of Diversey and Sheridan originally contained single-family homes, built when this part of the North Side was a new residential district. In the 1880s E.J. Lehmann built a mansion on the south side of Diversey at Sheridan Road. It was torn down to make way for the $3.5 million **Elks National Memorial Building,** dedicated in 1926 in memory of the Elks who fought in World War I.

Peter Schloesser's red-brick mansion stood at the northwest corner of Sheridan and Diversey for more than five decades after it was constructed in 1885. On August 30, 1950 the Amalgamated Meatcutters dedicated their new headquarters on the site of the old Schloesser mansion. According to Chicago author John Drury, the modern structure with its series of wide stone steps and cylindrical decoration "gives the effect of a butcher's chopping block." Since 1985 the building has housed the **Ida and Norman H. Stone Medical Center,** affiliated with nearby St. Joseph Hospital.

On the southeast corner of Diversey and Sheridan stands the **Goethe Memorial statue** by sculptor Hermann Hahn, which was erected by the German-American community of Chicago and unveiled in 1914.

(J) **St. Joseph's** modern hospital, one block east of Sheridan Road at 2900 N. Lake Shore Drive, is one of East Lake View's institutional anchors. The Daughters of Charity established this hospital in 1868 at Clark and Diversey. In 1871 they cared for victims of the Chicago Fire in their "new" building at Dickens and Burling. After nearly a century of service in the heart of Lincoln Park, the Sisters of Charity built a skyscraper hospital on Lake Shore Drive in 1964.

(K) At Belmont Avenue, turn left and go west to Broadway. Turn right and follow Broadway as it wends north to Hawthorne Place (3418 North). Broadway was originally known as the Lake View Plank Road and later as Evanston Avenue. The fire-ravaged hulk of the **Evanston Avenue Methodist Episcopal Church** (1901) at Buckingham Place is the sole reminder of Broadway's former name.

In the 1970s Broadway earned the sobriquet "New Town" because it eclipsed the tourist strip on Wells Street in Old Town. However, area homeowners prefer to call their neighborhood East Lake View, a name which has historic as well as geographic significance. Broadway's many bars and nightlife spots contribute to the area's congestion, and longtime residents have supported police efforts to crack down on prostitution.

(L) Turn right onto Hawthorne Place (3418 North) and continue to Lake Shore Drive. Hawthorne Place with its fine homes is a world away from the hustle and bustle of Broadway. Unlike neighboring streets in the area, Hawthorne Place has survived intact as an enclave of single-family homes. When John and Benjamin McConnell established this subdivision in 1883, the area was part of Lake View. Even after annexation to Chicago in 1889, however, Hawthorne Place retained its suburban character. The oldest house on the block, 568 W. Hawthorne, was built in 1884 by Benjamin McConnell. About 1885, his brother John moved into a red brick structure at 546 W. Hawthorne. In December 1984 the **Chicago City Day School,** 541 W. Hawthorne Place, purchased at auction the **Herman Hettler house,** constructed in 1892 at 567 W. Hawthorne. The American Society of Interior Designers subsequently designated the mansion as Chicago's first "Showcase" home. The three-story Victorian home is now being restored to its former glory—including a tea pavilion that was added at the time of the Columbian Exposition of 1893.

The stone columns of Temple Sholom, 3480 N. Lake Shore Drive, are richly ornamented with Byzantine motifs. Dedicated in 1930, this synagogue has served generations of Jewish families in East Lake View. (G. Lane, 1985)

(M) Turn left and go north on Lake Shore Drive to Addison Street (3600 North). **Temple Sholom** (1930) at 3480 N. Lake Shore Drive is one of East Lake View's best known houses of worship. The Lannon stone structure with its Byzantine motifs was designed in 1921 by three young student architects, Gerald Loebl, Norman J. Schlossman, and John Demuth. Established in 1867, Temple Sholom is the North Side's oldest Reform congregation. At a time when Chicago's Jewish community is predominantly suburban, Temple Sholom continues as a flourishing center of Jewish life in the city.

(N) Turn west on Addison Street and continue three-quarters of a mile to Clark Street. When **Lake View Presbyterian Church** at 3600 N. Broadway was constructed in 1888, this area was sparsely settled. In keeping with their conviction that the district would prosper, Presbyterian families commissioned the well-known architectural firm of Burnham & Root to design a church. Just as the congregation predicted, there was an influx of Presbyterian families in Lake View, and in the 1890s the shingle-style church on Broadway was enlarged.

The brick building at the northwest corner of Addison and Halsted is known as the **Town Hall station** of the Chicago Police Department. The station marks the site of Lake View's Town Hall (1872), hence its name.

Turn right at Clark Street and go north to Grace Street (3800 North), then go east on Grace. **Wrigley Field** is one of Chicago's famous landmarks, the second baseball park in the city designed by Zachary Taylor Davis. Originally known as Weeghman Park (1914), it was renamed Wrigley Field after William Wrigley, Jr. purchased the Chicago Cubs in 1926.

At 1126 W. Grace is the **House of the Good Shepherd,** a residential center for women and girls in need, operated by the Sisters of the Good Shepherd at various locations in Chicago since 1859.

Aerial view of Wrigley Field looking south toward the Loop. Built in 1914 on the site of the original Chicago Lutheran Theological Seminary, the baseball park was designed by Zachary Taylor Davis. In recent years, the surrounding neighborhood has taken on a new identity as "Wrigleyville" and residents have waged a vigorous campaign to prevent night baseball in the park.
(Courtesy The Chicago Cubs)

Doorway in Alta Vista Terrace. Known as the Street of Forty Doors, Alta Vista Terrace was developed between 1900 and 1904 by S.E. Gross. Gross made a fortune building balloon-frame houses in Chicago neighborhoods such as Back of the Yards and Lake View. In contrast, his Alta Vista homes were constructed of brick to resemble London townhouses. (G. Lane. 1985)

(Q) While the **Alta Vista Historic District** is not inaccessible by car, it is reached by a circuitous route. Continue east on Grace to Seminary (1100 West with a little park adjoining it), then one block north on Seminary to Byron. Go east on Byron to Alta Vista. S.E. Gross's subdivision provides a sharp contrast to the frame workers' houses he built in Old Lake View and Back of the Yards. Most of the brick townhouses along Alta Vista were constructed between 1900 and 1904. The narrowness of Alta Vista contributes to the European flavor of the street. Known as the "street of forty doors," Alta Vista was designated a Chicago landmark in 1971.

(R) Turn left on Grace Street from Alta Vista and go six blocks east to Broadway-Halsted (800 West). Turn left on Broadway and go one and one-half blocks north, staying to the right as Halsted becomes Clarendon. Go north on Clarendon to Buena Avenue (4200 North), turn west and go three blocks to Sheridan Road, then go north on Sheridan to Montrose (4400 North). The Buena Park neighborhood, once considered part of Uptown, has recently established a separate identity as an historic district. As Daniel M. Bluestone argues in his report for the National Register of Historic Places, Buena Park's suburban-style single-family residences "influenced the architectural style and plan of succeeding apartment designs."

St. Mary of the Lake Church (1917), 4210 N. Sheridan Road, is one of Henry J. Schlacks's finest church buildings. In creating this model of a Roman basilica, Schlacks patterned the church's campanile after the tower of St. Pudentiana's in Rome.

Just north of St. Mary's at 4242 N. Sheridan is the six-story **Buena Terrace Apartments** (1920), designed and owned by the same architect. One of the few residential buildings designed by Schlacks, the Terrace Apartments incorporate elements of his ecclesiastical structures.

(S) The **Buena Park Memorial Presbyterian Church** occupies an unusual triangular-shaped site formed by the intersection of Sheridan and Broadway. James B.

Waller, Buena Park's founder, played a leading role in the establishment of this parish. A bequest in his wife's will provided money for the construction of the present Gothic building in 1922 according to the plans of architect Ivar Viehe-Naess.

(T) Turn right onto Montrose and go three blocks east to Clarendon (800 West). On the south side of Montrose between Sheridan and Hazel is a modern shopping center and apartment complex designed by Stanley Tigerman. Known as **Pensacola Place,** it is named after one of Buena Park's small curving streets. M.W. Newman has described Pensacola Place and the nearby **Boardwalk Apartments** at 4343 N. Clarendon, also designed by Tigerman, as "the crossroads leading to a new Uptown."

On the north side of Montrose at Clarendon is the **Frank J. Cuneo Hospital,** designed by Belli and Belli architects and opened in 1942 by the Missionary Sisters of the Sacred Heart, who also conduct Columbus and Cabrini Hospitals in Chicago.

Turn right on Clarendon and go three blocks south to Hutchinson Street (4232 North), then west on Hutchinson to Hazel. The **Hutchinson Street Historic District** is one of Buena Park's most famous subdivisions. These single-family homes, built between 1894 and 1921, represent a wide range of architectural styles, from Queen Anne to Richardsonian Romanesque and Prairie School. Chicago architect George W. Maher designed five homes along Hutchinson Street: 750, 817, 826, 839, and 840—the exuberant Queen Anne style house built for John Scales. At the turn of the century, Maher also designed many of the mansions along Sheridan Road in Edgewater and Rogers Park which were later torn down to make way for highrises. Maher's Hutchinson Street homes survived intact, and they continue to provide gracious living near Chicago's north lakefront. Turn right on Hazel and go north to Wilson Avenue (4600 North, four blocks north of Montrose).

A typical Hutchinson Street home designed by George W. Maher. Over the years, this part of the Buena Park neighborhood has retained its status as a high-class residential district. (G. Lane, 1985)

(U) Turn left on Wilson and go west about nine blocks, under the "L" tracks to Dover Street (1400 West). Wilson Avenue has long been synonymous with the Uptown

The Uptown National Bank, southeast corner of Broadway and Lawrence, was built in 1924 during the neighborhood's heyday as a commercial center and nightlife district. The architectural firm of Marshall & Fox designed this terra-cotta structure which has recently been restored to its former glory. (G. Lane. 1985)

neighborhood. In the 1920s apartment hotels and palatial movie theaters made Uptown the North Side's bright-light district. After more than three decades as an economically depressed area, there are signs that Uptown is rebuilding. **Chelsea House,** a retirement hotel at 920 W. Wilson; the **Uptown Baptist Church** at 1011 W. Wilson; and the **McJunkin block** at 4550 N. Broadway are examples of Uptown's high-class construction.

(V) Just west of the rapid transit line is **Harry S. Truman Junior College.** When this institution opened in 1976, it was widely heralded as the beginning of Uptown's rebirth. The community college serves the North Side of Chicago as well as Uptown's Appalachian whites, American Indians, blacks, and Indo-Chinese refugees.

(W) Turn right at Dover Street and go two blocks north to Lawrence Avenue (4800 North). Dover is located in the Sheridan Park subdivision which was built up between 1890 and 1920. Although the district contains mostly brick homes and apartment buildings ranging in size from two to twenty units, a few Victorian frame houses remain.

(X) Turn right on Lawrence Avenue and go about eight blocks east to Sheridan Road. The **Uptown National Bank** at 4753 N. Broadway was built in 1924 on the grand scale according to plans drawn by Marshall & Fox, the architectural firm that designed the Edgewater Beach Hotel and Apartments. This impressive terra-cotta structure, one of the largest office buildings outside the Loop, has been restored to its former grandeur. In addition to housing the Uptown National Bank, the building's tenants include the Uptown Chamber of Commerce, and the Uptown Chicago Commission.

(Y) For generations of Chicagoans, the **Aragon Ballroom** (1926) at 1106 W. Lawrence Avenue was the North Side's most lavish dancing spot. The Moorish-style ballroom with its famous domed ceiling was built at a cost of nearly $2 million dollars. Like the Trianon Ballroom on the South Side, also owned by the Karzas brothers, the Aragon featured Big Band musicians, among them Wayne King, Dick Jurgens, Griff Williams, and Anson Weeks.

(Z) At Sheridan Road, turn left and go north two short blocks to Castlewood Terrace. Then turn right on Castlewood Terrace to Marine Drive. The mansions of Castlewood Terrace recall the era when the Essanay Movie Studios at 1333 W. Argyle put Uptown on the map. Turn right on Marine Drive and go south to the Lawrence Avenue entrance to Lake Shore Drive.

To generations of Chicagoans, the Aragon Ballroom at 1006 W. Lawrence was Uptown's most famous landmark. In addition to its city-wide reputation as the home of Big Band music, the Aragon reached a national audience through live radio broadcasts. (G. Lane. 1985)

Austin
Hull Ter
Hull Ter
ST FRANCIS HOSP
Mulford
Florence
Wesley
Asbury
Harvard Ter
Case
Sherman
Calvary Cemetery
Rogers Ave. Park & Beach
Juneway Ter. Park & Beach
Park
1300
Ashland
Barton
Brummel
Dobson
Elmwood
800
Custer
Callan
Clyde
Juneway
Ter
Haskins
Paulina
Marshfield
Ashland
Jonquil
Ter
Kiwanis Plg Pk
Eastlake Ter
100
BETHESDA HOSPITAL
CHICAGO CITY LIMITS
Howard
Hoyne
Seeley
Birchwood
Wolcott
Fargo
Hermitage
Rogers
1600
Greenview
Howard St. Park & Beach
Rockwell
Maplewood
Campbell
Artesian
ST SCHOLASTICA H S
Pottawattomie Park
Jarvis
Sherwin
Fargo Ave Park & Beach
Jarvis Ave. Park & Beach
Sherwin Ave Park & Beach
Rogers Park
Claremont
Chase
Oakley
Bell
Hamilton
Winchester
2000
Touhy Park
Chase
Chase Ave Park & Beach
WESTERN
7200
Blvd
Touhy
Leone Park & Beach
2400
RIDGE
Damen
Estes
SHERIDAN
Indian Boundary Park
Wolcott
Clark
Paulina
Ashland
Greenleaf
Glenwood
Lunt
LOYOLA BEACH
Paschen Plg. Park
Morse
Loyola Park
Ravenswood
Farwell
Glenwood
Wayne
RD
JEWISH OF CHGO
Oakley
Bell
Hamilton
6800
PRATT
BLVD
Pratt Blvd. Park & Beach
Laurence C. Warren St Pk
Robert A Black Golf Course
BLVD
Honore
Columbia
North Shore
Lakewood
Columbia Ave. Park & Beach
North Shore Ave. Park & Beach
Damen
Wallen
SULLIVAN H S
Albion
Ashland
Bosworth
Winthrop
Albion
Hartigan Park & Beach
Loyola
LOYOLA AVE. BEACH
Loyola
Arthur
Newgard
Arthur
Arthur
Leavitt
Hamilton
Hoyne
Seeley
Schreiber
Schreiber Plg. Park
LOYOLA UNIVERSITY
St Henry Cemetery
Wayne Park
Devon
MUNDELEIN COLLEGE
6400
Highland
Highland
Highland
SHERIDAN RD
Devon Ave Park & Beach
Rosemont
ROSEMONT AVE. BEACH
ACADEMY OF THE SACRED HEART H S
Thome
Thome
Glenwood
Wayne
Magnolia
BROADWAY
Winthrop
Kenmore
Bell
Granville
Berger Park & Beach
Emerson Park
Hermitage
Paulina
Greenview
Hood
Hood
NORTHEAST COMM HOSP
Claremont
Oakley
Damen
Winchester
Wolcott
Glenlake
Glenlake
Glenlake Ave Park & Beach
Green Briar Park
Norwood
Norwood
6000
14
Elmdale
PETERSON
Senn Park
Thorndale
Lane Park & Beach
ARMORY
SENN H S
Rosedale
Thorndale
Ardmore
RD
Maplewood
Ardmore
Rosehill Cemetery
Rosehill Dr
Victoria
RIDGE
Victoria
Ardmore
ARDMORE HOLLYWOOD BEACH
Edgewater
Early
Hollywood
EDGEWATER HOSP
HOLLYWOOD
Campbell
Artesian
WESTERN
5600
Olive
Bryn Mawr
BRYN MAWR
PARKING AREA
Mellin Park
ST GREGORY H S
Gregory
Ravenswood
Ashland
Glenwood
Catalpa
Bowmanville
Rascher
Wolcott
Ravenswood
Clark
Rascher
Balmoral
Lakewood
Magnolia
BROADWAY
Winthrop
Kenmore
SHERIDAN
Summerdale
Rockwell
41
Bell
Hoyne
Damen
Winchester
Honore
Berwyn
Wayne
14
FOSTER AVE. BEACH
Paulina
Farragut
5200
FOSTER
41
AMUNDSEN H S
Winona
Winona
Winona
Carmen
Carmen
Carmen
Lincoln Park
Winnemac Park
Winona
Winnemac
Janssen
Winnemac
Broadway
Argyle
Argyle
Argyle
Argyle
Lincoln
LAKE SHORE
Margate Ter
Simonds
BETHANY METHODIST HOSP
Ainslie
Ainslie
Castlewood Ter

4

Far North Side

While Rogers Park has been known as Community Area 1 since University of Chicago sociologists drew up neighborhood maps in the 1920s, the Edgewater area only recently attained independent status. For nearly fifty years city planners regarded Edgewater as part of the Uptown community. Nevertheless, Edgewater residents preserved their neighborhood's identity, and in the 1970s community leaders waged a successful battle to have the area bounded by Foster, Ravenswood, Devon, and Lake Michigan designated Community Area 77—Edgewater.

As the history of Rogers Park and Edgewater makes clear, these North Side communities share more than just a common boundary. Both areas were originally communities of single-family homes, and their populations grew dramatically after the Northwestern Elevated line was completed to Howard Street in 1908. With stations at three-block intervals, the "L" provided quick, inexpensive transportation to the downtown district. In both Rogers Park and Edgewater, Sheridan Road was a high-class boulevard lined with mansions. Not only did Sheridan Road link Rogers Park and Edgewater with Uptown and other North Side communities, but after the completion of the Lake Shore Drive extension to Foster Avenue in 1933, it provided direct access to downtown Chicago.

Several factors combined to give Rogers Park and Edgewater reputations as cosmopolitan, urban communities. The physical setting along the lakefront and superb transportation facilities appealed to white collar workers and wealthy businessmen alike. As a result of the apartment building boom of the 1920s, Rogers Park and Edgewater were transformed into high-density areas with a combined population of 110,000. While both communities included thousands of renters, both had strong religious and cultural institutions as well, which provided stability and cohesion. Equally important was the fact that no single ethnic group dominated these twin lakefront communities.

Although both Edgewater and Rogers Park remained nearly all white until the 1970s, they enjoyed a long history of ethnic diversity. The Swedish settlement known as Andersonville developed in the southwest corner of Edgewater, and a German community flourished just south of Rosehill Cemetery. Devon Avenue and Ridge marked the center of a Luxembourger community which dated from the 1850s. Irish Catholics were early settlers in Rogers Park and

Edgewater, and after World War II the Jewish population of both communities grew steadily. But the presence of different ethnic groups was far from divisive. Indeed, the second-generation Germans, Swedes, Irish, and Jews shared much in common with native-born Americans of English descent, and the communities they formed within Rogers Park and Edgewater reflected their hopes and desires as Americans.

In their formative years Rogers Park and Edgewater resembled other North Shore suburban communities. But by the 1920s they were very much urban neighborhoods, part of the larger city. The movement of white families to the suburbs accelerated after World War II, and both lakefront communities felt the impact of this national trend. While the construction of new highrises along Sheridan Road did much to offset population losses between 1960 and 1970, both communities suffered from pockets of urban decay.

Largely through the cooperation of area churches and synagogues, two community groups were formed: the Rogers Park Community Council (1954) and the Edgewater Community Council (1960). Both organizations have become powerful forces within their communities, and in recent years the groups have joined together to combat such problems as deteriorated housing, aging commercial strips, absentee landlords, and an overabundance of nursing homes and shelter care facilities. Few Chicago neighborhoods have as clear a sense of direction as Rogers Park and Edgewater. Indeed, their success as urban neighborhoods seems to be directly related to their carefully cultivated identities.

Rogers Park

When Rogers Park was incorporated as a village in 1878, it claimed the territory west of Lake Michigan to Ridge Avenue between Devon and the Indian Boundary Line (now Rogers Avenue). The new village was named for Phillip Rogers, an early landowner whose estate passed to his daughter after his death in 1856. Catherine Rogers's husband, Patrick L. Touhy, was one of the original incorporators of Rogers Park, and he promoted the development of the area between Ridge Avenue and Clark Street.

Ridge Avenue formed a natural boundary for this settlement. Once part of the lakeshore, the Ridge's elevated land was a desirable location for farmers. Because the area near Lake Michigan was marshy, most early residential construction occurred along the Ridge, between Rosehill Cemetery and Evanston. Clark Street, originally known as Green Bay Road, was an important Indian trail, and it later

Lunt Ave.

serin served as the main link between Fort Dearborn in Chicago and Fort Howard in Green Bay, Wisconsin.

The Touhy mansion at the northeast corner of Touhy Avenue and Clark Street was one of the first houses in the district in 1871, and it remained a showplace for years to come. According to local lore, the oak trees surrounding the house once shaded the wigwam of Pottawatomie Chief Black Partridge. But the Touhy backyard held an even greater attraction for area residents: a stone cornerpiece from the old Chicago courthouse which was destroyed in the Great Fire of 1871.

As in other Chicago suburbs, Rogers Park developers sought to attract families to the area by donating land and money for churches. A Methodist church was constructed in 1874 on the south side of Greenleaf Avenue, just east of Wolcott. Over the years several Protestant denominations worshiped in this building until they could afford to build churches of their own. Patrick Touhy contributed generously to the construction of St. Catherine Church at Touhy and Wolcott Avenues in 1875. This frame structure, named for the patron saint of his wife, was destroyed in a fire in 1877. Thereafter, in order to attend Mass, the few Catholic families of Rogers Park had to travel to St. Mary Church in Evanston or to St. Henry Church at Devon and Ridge.

Despite these efforts at community building, Rogers Park remained sparsely settled throughout the l880s. The area's first settlement was concentrated around the Chicago and North Western Railroad depot at Ravenswood and Greenleaf Avenues. Although Rogers Park was linked to downtown Chicago by the North Western Railroad, the community

Elegant Victorian homes along Lunt Avenue recall Rogers Park's origins as a suburban residential district. When this photo was taken, c.1907, the area around Lunt and Ashland was still a forest of birch trees.
(Courtesy G. Schmalgemeier)

actually had more in common with Evanston than it did
with the city to the south. Not only had Rogers Park been
part of Evanston township, but its founding fathers included
such Evanston residents as Luther Greenleaf, Stephen Lunt,
and Charles Morse. Moreover, because Rogers Park lay
within the "four-mile limit" of Northwestern University in
Evanston, no liquor sales were allowed in the area north of
Devon Avenue. Legal challenges to the university's charter
brought no relief, and the "four-mile limit" remained in effect
until after Prohibition. As a result, Rogers Park continued to
be a temperance town even after its annexation to Chicago
in 1893.

Unlike Edgewater to the south, Rogers Park did not
originate as a planned community. Due to the swampy
nature of the land along the lakefront, most residential
construction took place near the "Ridge." However, the
community gradually expanded east of Clark Street,
especially after the Milwaukee Road began commuter service
to downtown Chicago in 1887. This railway cut a swath
through the east end of Rogers Park, a route later followed
by the Northwestern Elevated trains.

Church-building in Rogers Park also followed the
west-to-east development of the neighborhood. In 1886
Episcopalians built St. Paul Church at 1715 W. Lunt. Four
years later the First Congregational Church of Rogers Park
was established at 1701 W. Morse. In 1894 Catholics built
St. Jerome Church directly across the street, at the
northwest corner of Morse and Paulina. As in other
suburban areas, the village's churches were built in close
proximity to one another, and this reinforced the small-town
character of the district.

By the turn of the century, the population was still
centered at the west end of Rogers Park where most of the
businesses, churches, and homes were located. Annexation
to Chicago had been welcomed by property owners in 1893
because it resulted in lower taxes. But the proposal to
establish a North Shore Park District was another matter.
Critics charged that the community "will not need a public
park for twenty years to come." According to the Chicago
Tribune, supporters of the park district included real estate
developers who were anxious to "secure local control of the
lake shore," prevent "objectionable bathing resorts," and have
Sheridan Road declared a boulevard.

One of the most vigorous opponents of the act was S.
Rogers Touhy, grandson of Phillip Rogers. In 1897 he built a
new home at 7339 N. Clark Street, a short distance from the
old Touhy mansion. Like many of his neighbors, Touhy
feared the consequences of designating Sheridan Road a
boulevard. Whereas funeral processions to nearby Calvary

*First Congregational Church of
Rogers Park, 1545 W. Morse, 1918.
After this building was destroyed
by fire in 1925, a new church was
built at a cost of $250,000.*
(C.R. Childs, courtesy G. Schmalgemeier)

Rogers Park Life Saving Station, c.1913. Rogers Park's "street-end" beaches, just east of Sheridan Road, enhanced the quality of neighborhood life.
(C.R. Childs, courtesy G. Schmalgemeier)

Cemetery had formerly used Sheridan Road, they would now be diverted to Clark Street, increasing congestion on an already busy thoroughfare. The referendum was hotly contested, but on May 10, 1900 Rogers Park residents voted 249 to 203 in favor of creating the North Shore Park District in the territory bounded by the city limits on the north, Devon Avenue on the south, the Chicago and North Western tracks on the west, and Lake Michigan on the east.

For more than twenty-five years after its incorporation, Rogers Park remained an isolated district. But the city was growing northward, especially along the route of the Northwestern "L" line which inaugurated service from downtown Chicago to Wilson Avenue in 1900. The fact that so much land remained vacant in Rogers Park was a drawing card for developers and institutions alike. In 1906, for example, the Jesuits from Holy Family parish on the Near West Side purchased a twenty-acre tract of land along Lake Michigan from the Milwaukee Road Railroad. They planned to establish a parish here and build a college, which would eventually become Loyola University. One of the members of the building committee recalled that the area around Devon and Sheridan consisted mainly of dunes and scrub oaks, and he described the territory as windswept, with "plenty of sand." Indeed, when the frame church of St. Ignatius opened in 1907 at Devon and Broadway (the present site of the Granada Theater), its congregation numbered only seven families.

The Jesuits' optimism about the future development of Rogers Park was shared by Benedictine Sisters from the German parish of St. Joseph on the Near North Side. In 1907 the Sisters established their motherhouse at 7340 N. Ridge Avenue, and in the following year they opened a girls' academy there known as St. Scholastica. In 1909 the

Jesuits founded Loyola Academy for boys in a brick building, Dumbach Hall, located just north of Devon Avenue on the lakeshore. The presence of such institutions as St. Scholastica, Loyola Academy, and St. Ignatius parish did much to attract Catholic families to Rogers Park, and this trend continued as second-generation Irish and German families moved out of older neighborhoods on the Near West and Near North Sides of Chicago.

More than any other factor, however, the "L" was responsible for large-scale development in Rogers Park. James Leslie Davis has estimated that when the elevated railroad was completed between Wilson Avenue and Howard Street in 1908, only 2,000 people lived in the area north of Devon and east of Ashland. By 1914 the population of this part of the neighborhood numbered 10,000, and it continued to grow throughout the 1920s.

The building boom which followed the completion of the Northwestern "L" took two forms, residential and commercial. In the area around the Loyola "L" station, two-story brick flat buildings predominated. This type of dwelling appealed to families because they could live in one apartment and rent the other. While commercial districts of various sizes developed around each "L" station, Clark Street continued to be the main shopping district of Rogers Park. Moreover, it contained such important institutions as the police station, post office, and library. The building boom sparked a revitalization of Clark Street. In 1911, for example, a new theater and office building was built on the northeast corner of Clark and Greenleaf, just across the street from Phoenix Hall. Phoenix Hall was an important link to Rogers Park's past. Over the years it had been one of the neighborhood's most important meeting places, serving such diverse groups as the Cumberland Post of the Grand Army of the Republic and the Rogers Park Evangelical Lutheran Church.

Before long the Rogers Park neighborhood bore little resemblance to the village which had become part of Chicago in 1893. Although substantial tracts of land remained undeveloped, the neighborhood acquired even more vacant land in 1915 when the area known as "Germania" was annexed. This section of South Evanston was bounded by Howard Street, the Milwaukee Road railroad tracks, Calvary Cemetery, and Lake Michigan. Because Evanston could not afford to install lights or streets or provide police protection, the area south of the cemetery had been a "no-man's land." Annexation provided Rogers Park with a new northern boundary, and by the 1920s a new commercial district along Howard Street.

When the first parish church of St. Ignatius opened in 1907 on Sheridan Road just north of Devon, this part of Rogers Park was sparsely settled. Following the construction of the present church at Loyola and Glenwood in 1917, the Jesuits sold their Sheridan Road property. In 1923, the Granada Theater rose on the site of the old frame church.
(William T. Kane, S.J. Photo Collection, Loyola University of Chicago Archives)

Clark Street looking north from Devon, c.1909. By the time Rogers Park was annexed to Chicago in 1893, Clark Street had emerged as the area's commercial district. Its streetcar line linked it with Edgewater and other North Side neighborhoods.
(Courtesy G. Schmalgemeier)

The period between 1915 and 1930 marked the golden age of building in Rogers Park. New high-rise apartments, apartment hotels, and courtyard buildings expanded the area's housing stock and contributed to the rapid growth in population. According to the Chicago *Daily News*, in 1922 alone, buildings containing more than 1,500 apartments were under construction in the territory north of Estes and east of Clark Street.

The fastest growing part of the neighborhood was the recently annexed section north of Howard Street. Besides such commercial ventures as the Broadmoor Hotel at the northwest corner of Howard and Bosworth, developers constructed many three- and four-story apartment buildings.

Brick apartment buildings, northeast corner of Sheridan and Howard. c.1912. These flats are typical of many buildings constructed in Rogers Park between 1910 and 1930. Proximity to the lakefront as well as the nearby elevated line made Rogers Park one of Chicago's fastest-growing neighborhoods after World War I.
(Courtesy G. Schmalgemeier)

In 1922, for example, architect Harry L. Dalsey designed a building at 7639 N. Greenview which contained thirty-three apartments. In an attempt to attract families to this section of Rogers Park, Dalsey provided "perambulator stalls in the basement of each apartment" and a playroom for every six units in the building. Moreover, he guaranteed a $25 savings account to every baby born in the building.

Institutional development followed closely on the heels of new residential construction. As the population of Rogers Park increased, so did the membership of its churches. New congregations were formed by Baptists, Christian Scientists, Jews, Lutherans, and Presbyterians, and older denominations expanded their facilities. St. Jerome's led the ecclesiastical building boom in 1916 with its new church at the southwest corner of Lunt and Paulina. In the following year the Renaissance-style church of St. Ignatius opened at the northeast corner of Loyola and Glenwood. In 1919 Baptists moved into their new church which had been completed at 1900 W. Greenleaf. The 1920s continued as an era of great church-building. Among the massive churches constructed in the neighborhood were St. Paul's By the Lake (1926), 7100 N. Ashland; Temple Mizpah (1924), 1615 W. Morse; Rogers Park Congregational Church (1927), 1545 W. Morse; B'nai Zion (1928), 1439 W. Pratt; and the Sixteenth Church of Christ Scientist (1929), at 7201 N. Ashland.

Not only did Rogers Park reach residential maturity in the 1920s, but its institutional base also expanded to include Loyola University and Mundelein College. The transfer of St. Ignatius College from 12th Street to 6525 N. Sheridan Road in 1922 fulfilled the Jesuits' promise to establish a Catholic university on the north shore of Lake Michigan. However,

The Loyola Avenue station of the North-South "L" line, 1937. More than any other factor, the construction of the rapid transit line sparked Rogers Park's building boom and assured the neighborhood's future as a desirable residential district.
(Chicago Park District, courtesy R. Wroble)

because Loyola University maintained a downtown campus as well as professional schools at other sites, its lakeshore campus remained relatively small until the early 1960s. Indeed, the few buildings on Loyola's lakeshore campus were overshadowed when Mundelein College opened its doors at 6363 N. Sheridan Road in 1930. Owned and operated by the Sisters of Charity of the Blessed Virgin Mary, Mundelein was the second Catholic college for women established in Chicago. The building itself is a striking example of Art Deco architecture, and it has been described as "the first self-contained skyscraper college for women in the world."

Throughout the 1930s and 1940s, Rogers Park remained an affluent urban neighborhood. The most important change to occur in the area was the expansion of the Jewish community. By 1950 more than 20,000 Jews lived in Rogers Park, comprising nearly one-third of the neighborhood's population. Many Jewish families moved to the North Side from the Lawndale neighborhood, which had been the city's largest Jewish community since the 1920s. As a result of racial change on the West Side, the Jewish population in the Rogers Park area grew dramatically during the 1950s.

Groups such as the Young Men's Jewish Council realized that the original Jewish community in Rogers Park was expanding and that the district west of Ridge Avenue was fast becoming a new Jewish neighborhood. In his 1950 report on recreational facilities for the Young Men's Jewish Council, Eric Rosenthal noted that most agencies begin work in a neighborhood after it had seen its "heyday." He suggested that Jewish agencies establish themselves in areas where they could "share the years of growth as well as of the inevitable decline." Because of the greater availability of vacant land in West Rogers Park, that community attracted more new synagogues than Rogers Park, and it claimed such important institutions as the High Ridge YMCA (1954), 2424 W. Touhy Avenue, and the Bernard Horwich Jewish Community Center (1959), 3003 W. Touhy Avenue.

Despite the construction of the Chicago Park District fieldhouse in Loyola Park in 1951, modern recreational facilities remained a pressing need in Rogers Park. The area's largest park, Pottawatomie, was located west of Clark Street and north of Rogers Avenue. In the early 1950s the Park District established Touhy Park near the intersection of Sherwin and Paulina. While the Park District maintained Loyola Beach and Park, the City of Chicago owned all the street-end beaches of Rogers Park and Edgewater. In 1962 area residents waged a spirited battle over control of these neighborhood bathing spots. Just as the proposal to create a North Shore Park District had embroiled the community in 1900, so did the fight for local beaches. The Chicago Park District eventually gained control of the former city beaches, and it renamed the Touhy Avenue Beach and Fieldhouse after Sam Leone, a longtime area resident who founded the lifeguard program for the City of Chicago.

Beginning in the late 1960s, the ethnic composition of Rogers Park expanded again as black families moved into the area. While religious and community leaders did much to assure peaceful integration, by 1971 area residents feared that a ghetto was forming in the area north of Howard Street between the Chicago Transit Authority tracks and Greenview Avenue. This section of Rogers Park had fallen on hard times after World War II. Howard Street had prospered as an outlying business district in the 1920s largely because it was an important transfer point for commuters. Not only was Howard Street the terminus of the Clark Street streetcar line, but it was also a "triple terminal" for the "L," the North Western Railroad, and the North Shore electric line which operated between Chicago and Milwaukee from 1919 to 1955.

For years the area north of Devon Avenue had been "dry," a legacy of Northwestern University's charter. Although saloons were permitted on Howard Street after Prohibition ended in 1933, Evanston and its adjoining suburbs retained their ban on liquor. As a result, Howard Street was the "last stop" where North Shore residents could purchase liquor. The area was also a popular spot for college students. During World War II soldiers from Fort Sheridan and sailors from the Great Lakes Naval Training Base frequented the Howard Street saloons, thus contributing to the district's reputation as a transient area. Apartment hotels constructed in the 1920s further exacerbated the problem. These high-rise buildings with their kitchenette and studio apartments were not conducive to a stable residential population. Moreover, in response to the housing shortage after World War II, spacious courtyard apartments were subdivided into smaller units.

Increasingly in the 1960s, Rogers Park residents referred to the area north of Howard Street as the "Juneway Jungle." To aid poor families in this part of the neighborhood, community groups organized legal aid programs, food pantries, and English-language classes for Hispanic and Asian newcomers. Deteriorated housing continued to be a problem, and in the late 1970s the Department of Housing and Urban Development demolished nearly four hundred apartments in the Haskins Triangle area, just east of the CTA tracks.

A very different kind of urban renewal occurred in 1982 as a result of a joint venture by the Chicago Area Renewal Effort Service Corporation (RESCORP) and the Amoco Neighborhood Development Company, a subsidiary of the Standard Oil Company of Indiana. These two organizations took the lead in planning the renovation of twelve courtyard buildings located on Juneway Terrace, Jonquil Terrace, Paulina, Marshfield, Ashland, and Bosworth. The $19.5 million rehabilitation program was funded by private enterprise, the Illinois Housing Development Authority, the City of Chicago, and the U.S. Department of Housing and Urban Development. The renovation and landscaping of these courtyard buildings dramatically changed the appearance of this part of Rogers Park. Even more important, property owners in the vicinity began to upgrade their buildings, further enhancing the success of project "Northpoint."

During the past decade, new Caribbean, Mexican, Korean, Polish, and Chinese restaurants and delicatessens have opened on Howard Street between Greenview and Paulina. These ethnic shops draw patrons from beyond Rogers Park, and they contribute much to the stability of the area. Another sure sign that this part of Rogers Park is on the way up occurred recently when area residents successfully invoked local option laws to close down taverns along Paulina Street, north of Howard.

Rogers Park continues its tradition as a cosmopolitan urban neighborhood. Among newcomers to settle in the area are Soviet Jews, Vietnamese, Hispanics, East Indians, and Koreans. The changing ethnic character of Rogers Park is clearly reflected in the neighborhood's commercial strips. The Morse Avenue business district, for example, once supported many Jewish-owned shops. The best known of these was the Ashkenaz Delicatessen which moved to 1432 W. Morse in 1937 from the West Side of Chicago. It quickly became a North Side institution, patronized by nearly three generations of Rogers Parkers. In part because of the area's declining Jewish population, the Ashkenaz family moved its operations to suburban Wilmette and to Chicago's Gold Coast in the 1970s. The Morse Avenue delicatessen continued to operate under Greek ownership as "Ashkey's" until it was destroyed by fire. Today Korean-owned businesses predominate on Morse Avenue, and these shops serve neighborhood residents as well as an ethnic clientele.

Rogers Park churches offer equally dramatic examples of changing ethnic patterns in the neighborhood. In 1965 a Japanese congregation built a new church at 1630 W. Devon. In recent years Temple Mizpah has become the Korean United Presbyterian Church. The Christian Scientist Church on Ashland is now known as the Apostolic Catholic Assyrian Church of the East (St. George parish). The Rogers Park Women's Club, built in 1916 at the southeast corner of Ashland and Estes, is owned by the Unification Church of America, and the former Masonic Temple at 1716 W. Lunt is now the International Society for Krishna Consciousness.

Although plans for an entertainment district along Howard Street did not materialize in the 1970s, Rogers Park now boasts several resident theater companies. The "Little Theater" movement in this neighborhood dates back to 1926 when the Loyola Community Theater of St. Ignatius parish was established. As its name suggests, the Loyola group produced many plays of interest to the large Catholic community in Rogers Park. Wisdom Bridge Theater Company at 1559 W. Howard Street celebrated its tenth year in Rogers Park in 1985. Since 1982 the Phoenix Theater group has renovated a former Commonwealth Edison substation at 6912 N. Glenwood for its productions. Among the new resident companies in the area are the Immediate Theater, 1146 W. Pratt; the Stormfield Theater, 6443 N. Sheridan; and the Alliance Theater Company, which rents the St. Ignatius parish theater at 1300 W. Loyola Avenue.

Since the 1920s Rogers Park has been predominantly a community of renters. However, during the 1970s many apartments were converted into condominiums, especially in the area east of Sheridan Road. In addition, young couples began to renovate the large single-family homes located west of Broadway. Unlike other lakefront neighborhoods, Rogers Park has not been overbuilt with highrises. But its concentration of nursing homes along Sheridan Road has

Aerial view of Loyola University's lakeshore campus, 1974. Dumbach Hall (center left) was the first building erected, 1909, followed by Cudahy Science Hall (center), 1912. The hip-roofed skyscraper at the upper right is Mundelein College, 1930. The Granada Theater and the "L" tracks are visible in the foreground.
(Loyola University of Chicago Archives)

provoked controversy within the community. Critics charge that the existence of so many of these facilities has changed the character of Sheridan Road from residential to institutional. As a result of community opposition, no new nursing homes have been built in Rogers Park since the mid-1970s.

Two recent public improvement projects illustrate how the neighborhood's past continues to shape Rogers Park. For nearly one hundred years, Clark Street has been the community's major commercial district as well as its civic center. Just as the present public library was built in 1958 at 6907 N. Clark Street near its original location, so too the 24th district police headquarters (1979) at 6464 N. Clark continues the tradition of public buildings on this historic thoroughfare.

Another link with the past is provided by the modern "L" station at Loyola Avenue, which was completed in 1981. The boarding platform offers an unparalleled view of the neighborhood, and the station's name is a constant reminder of Loyola University which played such a prominent role in the development of the area.

Although Rogers Park includes a large proportion of elderly residents, it also has a sizeable student population, which contributes to the vitality of the community. Loyola University and Mundelein College are the largest institutions in the neighborhood, and their influence extends well beyond Devon Avenue and Sheridan Road. Loyola University, for example, is the largest employer in Rogers Park, and in 1977 it inaugurated a $1 million "Walk to Work" program. As a means of encouraging faculty and staff members to live in the area, the university provided five-year loans up to $8,000 at six percent interest. With this seed money, university employees were able to make downpayments on homes or upgrade their property. By 1984 Loyola's "Walk to Work" program accounted for nearly $4 million worth of owner-occupied property in Rogers Park. The benefits of this program now extend to the faculty and staff of Mundelein College also.

For years Loyola students lived in fraternity houses and rented apartments in nearby Edgewater, but the area south of Sheridan Road was never considered part of the campus. All that changed in the early 1980s when the university acquired and remodeled apartment buildings in the 6300 blocks of Winthrop and Kenmore Avenues for use as dormitories. Some of these buildings had been eyesores, and their renovation symbolized a new relationship between Loyola University and the Edgewater community. New campus maps proclaim the fact: for the first time in its history, Loyola's lakeshore campus extends beyond Rogers Park into Edgewater.

Edgewater

At the time that Loyola University was expanding its boundaries, the Edgewater neighborhood regained its status as an independent community. For more than half a century, city and federal officials regarded Edgewater as part of the Uptown neighborhood. The situation was curious for several reasons. Since its founding in the 1880s, Edgewater claimed the territory between Foster and Devon Avenues. Moreover, clubs, churches, and businesses used Edgewater in their titles, and from an early date the name evoked powerful images of an exclusive residential district. So well established was this community's reputation at the turn of the century that the Wilson Avenue district of "Uptown" was originally called South Edgewater.

In 1886 John Lewis Cochran purchased land bounded by Foster, Broadway, Bryn Mawr, and Lake Michigan and subdivided it for homes. Unlike Rogers Park to the north, Edgewater experienced somewhat uniform development. Before construction proceeded on homes, Cochran's subdivision was improved with sewers, macadamized streets, Edison lights, stone curbs, and sidewalks. By the winter of 1887, thirty homes stood along the lakeshore and sixteen more were under construction. According to the Chicago *Inter Ocean*, in one season Edgewater had become "a duplication of Chicago's most famous residence centers and stylish mansions." Although the new suburb was located within the boundaries of Lake View township, the newspaper argued that it should be compared with such

Beginning in 1887, real estate developer J.L. Cochran promoted the growth of Edgewater through advertisements in Chicago newspapers. The ads stressed Edgewater's proximity to Lake Michigan and its location along the Chicago, Milwaukee & St. Paul Railroad line, a route later followed by the "L".
(Courtesy L. Blommaert)

EDGEWATER ELECTRIC CAR LINE

Will Be in Operation by June 1st, 1893.

EDGEWATER Homes } $5,100 —TO— $12,000

Modern, Artistic, With All Conveniences.

FOR SALE | *On Terms That Will Suit You* . . .

1,000 MEN will be put to work at once on construction of New Electric Railway. FIFTY CAR LOADS of material on the ground.

QUICK TRANSPORTATION.

FIFTEEN NEW HOUSES, NO TWO ALIKE—SEE THEM, EDGEWATER— *A Strictly Residence Suburb.*

Take C., M. & St. Paul Railroad to Edgewater. Agent there or salesman at city office will take you to see property free of expense. For terms, etc., apply to

J. L. COCHRAN, 722 Chicago Opera-House.

SUBURBAN REAL ESTATE.

elegant city streets as "Prairie and Calumet avenues . . . Ashland and Washington boulevards, Dearborn and LaSalle avenues."

Edgewater's location along the route of the Milwaukee Road railroad and its proximity to the lakeshore appealed to wealthy families because it provided the amenities of suburban life within commuting distance of the central business district. Even after its annexation to Chicago in 1889, the area retained its suburban flavor. Two institutions which reinforced the exclusive reputation of this community were the Saddle and Cycle Club and the Edgewater Golf Club.

In May 1895 the Saddle and Cycle Club built a clubhouse at Kenmore and Bryn Mawr Avenues. The club's members were prominent Chicagoans whose interests included horseback riding and the popular new sport of cycling. When the City of Chicago formed plans for the renovation of the lakefront in 1898, the Saddle and Cycle Club moved to Foster Avenue, where it has remained ever since.

The Edgewater Golf Club, incorporated in 1898, was something of a neighborhood institution. Although its membership included golfers from various North Side communities, a number of its officers and founding members lived along Kenmore Avenue between Catalpa and Thorndale, in close proximity to the clubhouse at 5658 N. Winthrop. As this area was built up with houses, however, the club opened a larger golf course at Pratt Boulevard and Ridge Avenue in 1912. Despite its location outside the community's boundaries, the golf club continued to be known as Edgewater.

One of the most important buildings in the growing community of Edgewater was the Guild Hall at the southwest corner of Bryn Mawr and Winthrop Avenues. More than just a meeting place, the Guild Hall was used for church services by Episcopalians, Methodists, Presbyterians, and Catholics. Church-formation contributed greatly to the stability of Edgewater. Indeed, all four of the congregations which were established in the area between 1886 and 1900 continue in existence today.

Episcopalians began the church-building process in 1886 when they founded the Church of the Atonement at the southeast corner of Kenmore and Ardmore. In 1889 the Epworth Methodist Church was organized in the home of Mr. and Mrs. L.T.M. Slocum at 5047 N. Kenmore. Massive boulders from the Slocum home in Lake Geneva, Wisconsin were floated down Lake Michigan on barges to Edgewater where they were used in the construction of the present church (1891) at 5253 N. Kenmore. Following a series of public meetings in 1896, area residents voted 23 to 13 to establish a Presbyterian rather than a Congregational

(Top right) One of Edgewater's most important buildings was the Guild Hall, designed by Joseph L. Silsbee and constructed in 1886 at the southwest corner of Bryn Mawr and Winthrop. The Guild Hall housed the real estate offices of Cochran & McCluer and served as the meeting place for the neighborhood's early congregations.
(Courtesy Rev. L. Issleib, Edgewater Presbyterian Church)

(Bottom right) The Edgewater station of the Chicago, Milwaukee & St. Paul Railroad provided residents with quick transportation to downtown Chicago. Located at street level, the railroad tracks were later elevated to accommodate the rapid transit line now known as the Howard "L".
(Courtesy Rev. L. Issleib, Edgewater Presbyterian Church)

(Top left) This frame building on Winthrop near Bryn Mawr housed the Edgewater Presbyterian Church from 1897 to 1903. As membership increased, the congregation built a fieldstone structure designed by George W. Maher at the southwest corner of Bryn Mawr and Kenmore. The present community house at the northeast corner of Bryn Mawr and Kenmore dates from 1927.
(Courtesy L. Blommaert)

(Top right) When Epworth Methodist Church at 5253 N. Kenmore was dedicated in 1891, Kenmore Avenue was a quiet residential street of single-family homes. In 1929 the church auditorium was remodeled and an adjoining community hall constructed.   (Courtesy L. Blommaert)

(Right) The Catholic parish of St. Ita grew from a few families in 1900 to one of the largest congregations on the North Shore by the 1920s. This frame church on Magnolia near Catalpa was replaced in 1927 by a magnificent French Gothic church designed by Henry J. Schlacks.
(Courtesy L. Blommaert)

church. Members of the Edgewater Presbyterian Church first worshiped in a white frame building near the Guild Hall. By 1900 the church was self-supporting, and as membership grew the Presbyterians hired noted architect George W. Maher to design a new fieldstone church which was located at the southwest corner of Kenmore and Bryn Mawr. This church and property were later sold, a hotel was erected on the site, and a beautiful new limestone church was constructed in 1926 across the street on the northeast corner.

The Catholic parish of St. Ita was founded in 1900 to serve fifty-three families in Edgewater. Unlike Protestant denominations which had established their churches on fashionable Kenmore Avenue, the Catholics built a frame church on Catalpa near Magnolia. This part of the neighborhood developed rapidly, and by the time the present St. Ita Church at 5500 N. Broadway was dedicated in 1927, it towered over one of the most important thoroughfares on the North Side.

In the late 1890s the Broadway and Clark streetcar lines were extended to Devon Avenue, connecting Edgewater with the larger city. Residential construction soon followed, especially in the area bounded by Foster, Glenwood, Bryn Mawr, and Broadway. In keeping with Cochran's original plans for Edgewater, single-family homes predominated in this section, and apartment buildings were excluded from nearby Sheridan Road.

Cochran was a moving force behind the construction of the Northwestern Elevated Railroad which extended its service from Wilson Avenue to Howard Street in 1908. The new line included stops at Berwyn and Bryn Mawr, former stations along the Milwaukee Road railroad, as well as two new stations at Thorndale and Granville Avenues. Since the 1880s the Bryn Mawr station of the Milwaukee Road was known as Edgewater, and this name continued to identify the new "L" stop for many years. Likewise, the Granville station of the elevated line was known for a long time as North Edgewater.

The location of the "L" line so close to Sheridan Road did not diminish the desirability of this street. In the early 1900s the Corbett and Connery Lake Shore Addition to Edgewater was platted in the area just north of Foster Avenue and east of Sheridan Road. To ensure the exclusive character of this district, real estate developers divided lots into depths ranging from 250 to 550 feet, and they banned the construction of homes less than thirty feet from Sheridan Road. By 1910 the Edgewater and Rogers Park sections of Sheridan Road were built up with substantial brick mansions with coach houses.

Ebenezer Lutheran Church, 1650 W. Foster Avenue, 1980. Dedicated in 1912, this church was known as Andersonville's Swedish cathedral. It has served generations of Swedish-American families. Andersonville was the third and last major area of settlement for Chicago's North Side Swedes. (G. Lane)

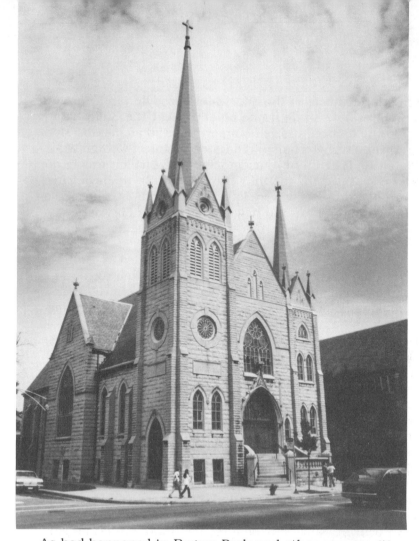

As had happened in Rogers Park and other communities along the route of the elevated line, residential construction boomed during the 1910s and 1920s. A variety of buildings were constructed in Edgewater. West of Clark Street, brick two- and three-flats were built next to frame homes which dated from the 1880s and 1890s. This part of the Edgewater neighborhood included large numbers of Swedes and Germans who had moved into the area from other parts of the North Side. Many of these newcomers found employment in the manufacturing plants located along the Chicago and North Western railroad tracks near Ravenswood Avenue.

For the Swedes especially, Edgewater was an area of third settlement. The city's pioneer Swedish churches, businesses, clubs, and ethnic institutions were all located on the Near North Side in the area bounded by Grand Avenue, Wells Street, Division Street, and the river. By the turn of the century, however, this once flourishing "Swede Town" was fast disintegrating. As early as the 1870s, some Swedish families had established homes in Lake View, around Belmont and Sheffield. In succeeding decades the area around Foster and Clark emerged as an important

Swedish-American colony. In their move northward, Swedes established new churches and transplanted others.

Ebenezer Lutheran Church at 1650 W. Foster Avenue dates from 1892, when Swedish families rented church quarters on Summerdale Avenue near Ashland. Construction of the present "Swedish Cathedral" began in 1904, and Ebenezer Church was finally dedicated in 1912.

Just south of Foster Avenue Swedish families organized Bethany Methodist Episcopal Church, and over the years this congregation built a large church at 5030 N. Ashland as well as a hospital and old people's home at 4950 N. Ashland. Among Chicago's pioneer Swedish congregations to relocate in Edgewater from the Near North Side were the First Swedish Methodist Episcopal Church (1919) at Highland Avenue and Paulina Street, and the Immanuel Lutheran Church (1922) at 1500 W. Elmdale Avenue. Because so many Swedes opened shops on Clark Street, the commercial strip north of Foster Avenue took on a Scandinavian character which persists today in spite of recent ethnic changes in the Andersonville neighborhood.

For German-Americans Edgewater also represented a third area of settlement. Since the 1860s the German population of Chicago had moved steadily northward in the city from Chicago Avenue to such areas as Old Town, Lincoln Park, and Lake View. Although the German population of Edgewater never grew as large as the Swedish, the Germans still made their mark on the neighborhood. The experience of German Catholics is a case in point.

In 1904 a group of German-American men organized St. Gregory parish during a special meeting held in Matthias Evert's saloon, across the street from the Rosehill Cemetery station of the Chicago and North Western railroad. Over the next five decades this congregation built a massive parish plant which includes a Norman Gothic church at 5533 N. Paulina, a grammar school, a coeducational high school, and a gymnasium. So pervasive was the influence of this parish that by 1917, the City Council renamed Edgewater Terrace Gregory Street.

Another prominent institution in the Edgewater community is the Edgewater Hospital at 5700 N. Ashland, which opened its doors as a ninety-bed hospital in January 1929, just before the Great Depression. Additions to the hospital were completed in 1954, 1960, 1968, and 1973, so that today Edgewater Hospital/Mazel Medical Center is a 431-bed hospital with a full range of health services.

Many second- and third-generation Germans, Swedes, and Irish lived in Edgewater, and there was very little inter-ethnic tension. Although a large portion of the neighborhood's housing stock consisted of brick two-flats

East Lounge·Edgewater
Beach Hotel - Chicago, Ill.

East lounge of the Edgewater Beach Hotel. c.1920. To generations of Chicagoans, the Edgewater Beach Hotel at 5349 N. Sheridan was the neighborhood's most famous landmark. Designed by Benjamin Marshall, the hotel operated from 1916 until 1967. It was razed in 1970. Plans have recently been announced for the Sheridan Road Lifecare Community to be built near the site of the old hotel.
(Courtesy G. Schmalgemeier)

and single-family homes, Edgewater was regarded as a high-class residential district. No building symbolized this more than the Edgewater Beach Hotel at 5349 N. Sheridan Road. Soon after this luxury hotel opened in 1916 at the lake's edge, it became a favorite dining and dancing spot for Chicagoans. In the 1920s one of the most prestigious addresses in the area was 5555 N. Sheridan Road—the Edgewater Beach Apartments. Benjamin H. Marshall designed these two Spanish Renaissance style buildings, the hotel and the apartments, and they continued to be neighborhood landmarks for half a century.

One of the most important changes to occur in Edgewater during the 1920s was the construction of apartment hotels and high-rise apartments just west of Sheridan Road. The proximity of the lakefront and excellent transportation to downtown Chicago made the eastern section of Edgewater particularly attractive to white collar workers. Whereas single-family homes once predominated along Kenmore and Winthrop Avenues, by the 1920s high-rise apartments and hotels overshadowed the family residences. Buildings such as the Bryn Mawr Apartment Hotel, 5550 N. Kenmore, and the Winthrop Towers at 6151 N. Winthrop with its built-in "Murphy beds," did much to accelerate the urbanization of Edgewater.

As the apartment houses of the neighborhood multiplied, so too did its population. By the time the Depression halted any further construction, more than sixty thousand people lived within the 1 1/2 square mile area known as Edgewater. In spite of its high density and its many apartments, Edgewater remained a stable middle-class

Looking south on Winthrop Avenue from Thorndale, Chicago, Ill. 14400.

neighborhood. Part of the reason for this had to do with the location of the high-rise apartments. Most high-rise construction during the 1920s occurred east of Broadway. In nearly every other section of Edgewater, single-family homes or low-rise apartment buildings predominated.

One such residential district emerged after 1910 in the territory bounded by Norwood, Clark, Granville, and Broadway. Built up entirely with single-family homes, this area has survived intact, a reminder of an earlier era when cathedral elms shaded many of Edgewater's streets.

The combination of low-rise and high-rise housing contributed greatly to the stability of the neighborhood. Then too, Edgewater did not experience major shifts in its population. Native-born Americans, Swedes, Germans, and Irish continued to stay in the area for more than one generation. One measure of the vitality of this neighborhood was that virtually every denomination in Edgewater increased in membership during the 1920s. While the expansion of existing churches was necessary to accommodate growing congregations, the new buildings were constructed on the grand scale. These houses of worship symbolized the investment the people were willing to make in the future of the Edgewater neighborhood. Indeed, the process of church-building continued well into the 1950s.

The Edgewater Presbyterian Church, for example, seriously considered building a new church in 1926. The congregation had just about decided upon a site when a prominent member suggested that building a Presbyterian church across the street from the Episcopalian Church of the Atonement was inviting trouble. The members agreed,

Looking south on Winthrop Avenue from Thorndale, c.1914. By the 1920s, brick flat buildings, courtyard apartments, and apartment hotels had replaced most of Winthrop's single-family homes.
(C.R. Childs, courtesy G. Schmalgemeier)

Northwest corner of Broadway and Ridge, c.1920s. Modern brick flat buildings, streetlights, and stoplights contrast sharply with older frame structures, relics of Edgewater's days as a suburban residential district.
(Courtesy L. Blommaert)

and in 1927 they gathered for the dedication of the present Presbyterian community house at 1020 W. Bryn Mawr Avenue. Only the onset of the Depression halted plans for a new sanctuary at the corner of Bryn Mawr and Sheridan Road.

Another congregation that looked to Edgewater for its future growth was the North Shore Baptist. Organized in 1905 at Leland and Racine Avenues in the Uptown area, this church followed its members as they moved further north in the city. In 1921 the 450-member congregation built a $250,000 building at Berwyn and Lakewood Avenues; the present sanctuary dates from 1952. For years the red neon sign "North Shore Baptist" proclaimed the existence of this church to riders on the nearby "L." The Baptists' commitment to Edgewater went beyond new church facilities. In 1926 the congregation established a Chinese Mission School, which later became the North Shore Chinese Baptist Church, and in 1957 the Baptists organized a Spanish Sunday School, which later moved to its own church building on Addison near Clark.

The building boom which transformed Edgewater into an urban neighborhood also made possible the erection of massive church complexes such as North Shore Baptist, Edgewater Presbyterian, and St. Gertrude's. When second-generation Irish and German Catholics founded St. Gertrude parish in 1912, the area west of Broadway and north of Thorndale was just beginning to be built up with homes and apartment buildings. The Catholic population of North Edgewater increased rapidly, and in less than twenty years St. Gertrude's boasted a modern parish plant. Indeed, the present St. Gertrude Church, which stands at the northwest corner of Granville and Glenwood, was one of the few houses of worship constructed in Chicago during the Depression.

As a result of the City of Chicago's lakefront expansion program in the 1930s and 1940s, nearly half of Edgewater's original lake frontage was filled in. The landfill program was a mixed blessing for the neighborhood. Although it extended Lincoln Park from Foster Avenue to Ardmore, it also provided for an extension of Lake Shore Drive. Since the 1920s, Sheridan Road had been an important route for automobile traffic. After the opening of the Lake Shore Drive extension to Hollywood Avenue, however, Sheridan Road became one of the city's most heavily traveled thoroughfares. The expansion of the Outer Drive also increased congestion along Foster, Bryn Mawr, Peterson, and Devon Avenues.

Between 1950 and 1960 Edgewater declined in population; this was partially due to the movement of families to North Shore suburbs. But during the 1960s the population increased from 51,000 to 61,000 people. As had happened in the past, this change reflected new developments in the area's housing stock. Modern high-rise apartments which replaced mansions along Sheridan Road accounted for much of the increase in population. These new buildings, triple the size of 1920s highrises, created a canyon effect, walling off the lake from Hollywood to Rosemont Avenues.

Amid the highrises, however, two new houses of worship appeared, St. Andrew Greek Orthodox Church (1956), at 5649 N. Sheridan, and Emanuel Congregation (1959), at 5959 N. Sheridan. Although the Greeks and Jews were among the last denominations to build large complexes in Edgewater, they were no strangers to the area.

The Greek parish of St. Andrew dated from 1926, and for nearly thirty years Greek families worshiped in quarters at the southwest corner of Hollywood and Winthrop.

Long a North Side institution, Emanuel Congregation was organized in 1880 in a hall at Blackhawk and Sedgwick Streets. For many years the synagogue was housed in a former Swedish church on Franklin Street, a Baptist church on Belden Avenue, and in temples at Belden and Burling and at 701 W. Buckingham Place.

For the most part Edgewater residents looked favorably upon the modern high-rise apartments which changed the face of Sheridan Road. However there was no such acceptance of the apartments known as "four-plus-ones" which were built in the 1960s along Kenmore and Winthrop

St. Gertrude Church, northeast corner Glenwood and Granville, c.1935. This beautiful church, dedicated in 1931, was one of the few churches in Chicago completed during the Depression. Founded in 1912, the parish built this massive complex in less than twenty years.
(Courtesy St. Gertrude Church)

*Colvin house, northwest corner
Thorndale and Sheridan, 1985.
Between 1950 and 1974,
single-family homes along
Sheridan Road were razed to
make way for 35 highrise
apartment buildings between
Bryn Mawr and Granville. This is
one of the few remaining houses
on the street* (G. Lane)

Avenues. These buildings were relatively inexpensive to build, and in many cases they replaced housing that was far superior in terms of construction. By placing the garage and lobby entrances of the new buildings below grade, developers gained an extra story, hence the term "four- plus-one." Like apartment hotels of an earlier era, these new buildings attracted single people rather than families.

During the late 1960s and early 1970s, many of Edgewater's apartment hotels became little more than halfway houses for people who had been released from state mental hospitals. Although hundreds of these former patients had been receiving only custodial care, many were unable to make the adjustment to independent living. Not only did Edgewater have one of the largest elderly populations in the city by the early 1970s, but it supported a disproportionate share of shelter care facilities for patients who were dependent upon public aid.

In cooperation with the Rogers Park Community Council, Uptown Chicago, and Organization of the Northeast (ONE), the Edgewater Community Council successfully prevented the proliferation of new shelter care facilities. In recent years the Edgewater Council has devoted much of its energy to improving the Kenmore-Winthrop corridor. In addition to working with managers of individual buildings, the community group has monitored cases in Housing Court, and in 1982 it funded a survey of the area. At least nine buildings once slated for demolition in the strip have been restored, and area residents point with pride to such newly renovated buildings as the Pines of Edgewater, 5518 N. Winthrop, and Winthrop Towers, 6151 N. Winthrop.

A continuing concern of the Edgewater Community Council is recreation facilities for the neighborhood. Beginning in the 1960s, the Council pressured the city and state to purchase the former Edgewater Golf Club at Ridge and Pratt Avenues, thereby preventing the property from being redeveloped with highrises and a shopping center.

In 1984 the Council launched a drive to raise $600,000 to renovate a mansion at 6219 N. Sheridan Road for use as the North Side Cultural Center. The Chicago Park District purchased this building as well as another mansion and coach house at 6205 in 1979. While the Park District is renovating the southern mansion for recreational facilities and park offices, the future of the other building rests with the community. These two single-family dwellings constitute "the last open space on the lakefront," and they are a reminder of the time when Sheridan Road was a boulevard of homes. Indeed, when the Academy of the Sacred Heart opened at 6250 N. Sheridan Road in 1929, its buff-colored building was located in the midst of a residential district. Today the Academy and Hardey Prep, with their modern gym-auditorium facility, are among the few remaining low-rise structures along this stretch of Sheridan Road.

In recent years two fine studies of Edgewater have provided residents with an in-depth look at their community. Jane E. Ratcliffe's 1978 monograph, *A Community in Transition: The Edgewater Community,* analyzes the neighborhood's housing stock and land use patterns as well as the area's changing ethnic composition. In addition to longtime Swedish, Irish, German, Greek, and Jewish families, Edgewater now includes residents of many different ethnic backgrounds, such as Koreans, Cubans, Japanese, Chinese, and Cambodians. Senn High School at 5900 N. Glenwood reflects the area's diversity. Here students from nearly fifty countries learn English as a second language.

In his 1981 study, *Reversing Urban Decline,* Edward Marciniak describes Edgewater as a new kind of urban neighborhood, very different from the traditional Chicago community based on ethnicity, class, or race. Common concerns about housing, schools, safety, and recreation have united residents of many different backgrounds. Not only does Edgewater boast a strong community group, but its network of more than twenty block clubs provides unusual opportunities for citizen participation. A century after its founding, Edgewater remains a vital community, and its residents face the future with a renewed sense of identity.

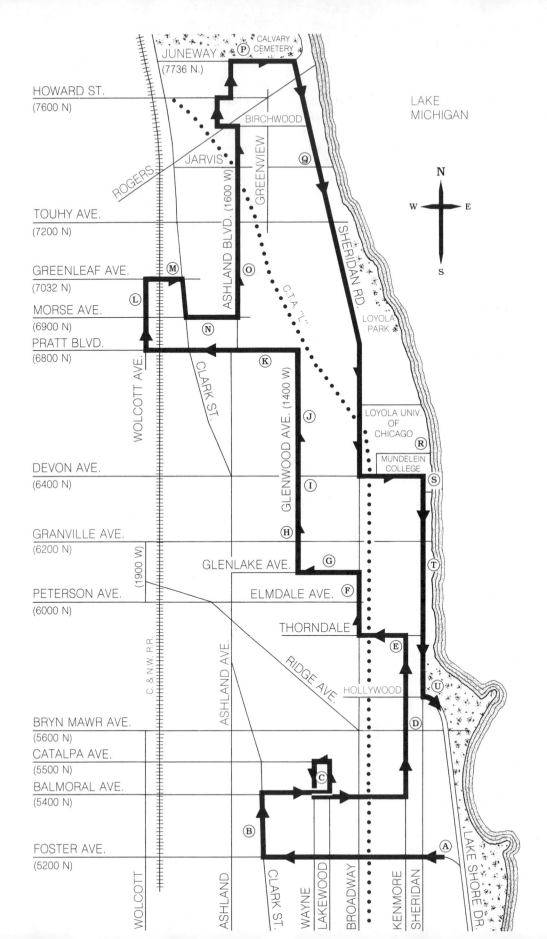

CALVARY
CEMETERY

JUNEWAY
(7736 N.)

Ⓟ

LAKE
MICHIGAN

HOWARD ST.
(7600 N)

BIRCHWOOD

GREENVIEW

ROGERS

JARVIS

Ⓠ

N

W   E

S

TOUHY AVE.
(7200 N)

ASHLAND BLVD. (1600 W)

SHERIDAN RD.

GREENLEAF AVE.
(7032 N)

Ⓜ

Ⓛ

Ⓞ

C.T.A. "L"

MORSE AVE.
(6900 N)

Ⓝ

LOYOLA
PARK

PRATT BLVD.
(6800 N)

WOLCOTT AVE.

CLARK ST.

Ⓚ

GLENWOOD AVE. (1400 W)

Ⓙ

LOYOLA UNIV.
OF
CHICAGO

Ⓡ

DEVON AVE.
(6400 N)

Ⓘ

MUNDELEIN
COLLEGE

Ⓢ

GRANVILLE AVE.
(6200 N)

Ⓗ

(1900 W)

GLENLAKE AVE.

Ⓖ

Ⓣ

PETERSON AVE.
(6000 N)

ELMDALE AVE.

Ⓕ

THORNDALE

C. & N.W. R.R.

ASHLAND AVE.

RIDGE AVE.

Ⓔ

HOLLYWOOD

Ⓤ

BRYN MAWR AVE.
(5600 N)

Ⓓ

CATALPA AVE.
(5500 N)

Ⓒ

BALMORAL AVE.
(5400 N)

Ⓑ

LAKE SHORE DR.

FOSTER AVE.
(5200 N)

Ⓐ

WOLCOTT

ASHLAND

CLARK ST.

WAYNE

LAKEWOOD

BROADWAY

KENMORE

SHERIDAN

Far North Side Tour

This tour begins at Lake Shore Drive and Foster Avenue in the Edgewater neighborhood and continues north into the adjoining community of Rogers Park.

Driving time: about 2 hours.

(A) Exit Lake Shore Drive at Foster Avenue (5200 North) and proceed west on Foster to Clark Street. The **Saddle and Cycle Club,** located behind the green fence at 900 W. Foster Avenue, is one of many institutions that contributed to Edgewater's reputation as a high-class community. Established in 1895 by socially prominent Chicagoans who were interested in cycling and horseback riding, the Saddle and Cycle Club is the only private country club still in existence along Chicago's lakefront.

(B) Turn right at Clark Street and go four blocks north to Balmoral Avenue (5400 North). The Swedish community of **Andersonville** centers along Clark Street, where shops cater to fourth- and fifth-generation Chicago Swedes. Andersonville is the last of Chicago's three North Side Swedish communities. Over the years area merchants remained faithful to such Swedish traditions as Midsummerfest and the daily ritual of street sweeping. Every morning at 10 a.m., a bell ringer clanged his bell, a signal for local merchants to sweep the sidewalks in front of their shops.

This community's pride in its Swedish heritage is reflected in the exhibits of the **Swedish American Museum Association of Chicago,** 5248 N. Clark. This storefront has been embellished with a log cabin facade, a tribute to Swedish pioneers who introduced the idea of log cabins to America. In the midst of ethnic changes, the Andersonville shopping district retains its Swedish flavor. The distinctive **Swedish Tobacco Shop** at 5400 N. Clark, for example, is owned by an Assyrian, Isaac Toma.

(C) Turn right on Balmoral and go three blocks east to Lakewood (1300 West). Turn left at Lakewood and go one block north to Catalpa (5500 North), then west on Catalpa to Wayne. Follow Wayne Avenue south to Balmoral, then five blocks east on Balmoral to Kenmore (1040 West). This small enclave of single-family homes is known as Lakewood—Balmoral, a reminder of the days when Edgewater was a suburban community. Residents of this area have played prominent roles in the campaign to have Edgewater recognized as an independent community with its own boundaries. Since 1921 the **North Shore Baptist Church** at 5244 N. Lakewood has been the largest institution in the Lakewood—Balmoral area.

(D) As you approach the "L" tracks, the starkly modern glass highrise known as the **Park Tower Condominium** is visible ahead of you at 5415 N. Sheridan Road. Turn left on Kenmore and go five blocks north to Thorndale Avenue (5934 North). At the time J.L. Cochran laid out his Edgewater subdivision in the 1880s, Kenmore Avenue was one of the area's select streets, and it subsequently became the favored location for three of the community's earliest churches: **Epworth Methodist**, 5253 N. Kenmore; **Edgewater Presbyterian** at Kenmore and Bryn Mawr; and the **Church of the Atonement** (Episcopal), at 5749 N. Kenmore. Over the years spacious mansions and Victorian homes have been torn down to make way for modern buildings—1920s highrises, 1950s California-style apartments, and Chicago's own "four-plus-one" apartments, whose lobbies and garages are located beneath grade level. In recent years Edgewater residents have spearheaded efforts to upgrade buildings along Kenmore and Winthrop Avenues. The revitalization of the Kenmore—Winthrop corridor has put Edgewater on the map as an urban community with a clear sense of its future.

(E) Turn left at Thorndale and go two blocks west to Broadway (1200 West). The small shopping district near the "L" tracks at Thorndale is typical of the commercial strips which developed along the Edgewater and Rogers Park stations of the North-South rapid transit line. The "L" line, which opened in 1908, followed the route of the old Chicago, Milwaukee, St. Paul & Pacific Railroad from Howard Street to Wilson Avenue.

(Top left) The Saddle & Cycle Club, 900 W. Foster Avenue, is one of Edgewater's oldest institutions; it was founded in 1895. Jarvis Hunt designed this distinctive clubhouse in 1906. (Courtesy T. Samuelson)

(Bottom left) Andersonville merchants hoist their brooms during a Midsummerfest parade down Clark Street, 1960s. For years, businessmen in this Swedish neighborhood swept the sidewalks in front of their shops at 10 o'clock every morning. (Courtesy Swedish American Museum Association)

(F) Turn right at Broadway and go three blocks north to Glenlake Avenue (6100 North). After years of "bookmobile" service, Edgewater residents finally have a permanent library at the northwest corner of Broadway and Elmdale. The Edgewater Community Council vigorously supported construction of the new library (1972). More than just a branch of the Chicago Public Library system, the **Edgewater Library** is a symbol of the community's fight for recognition as a separate neighborhood.

(G) Turn left at Glenlake and go west one long block to Glenwood Avenue (1400 West). This small subdivision of single-family homes has been one of Edgewater's most stable residential districts. It is a classic example of suburban-style living with all the amenities of an urban neighborhood—rapid transit to downtown Chicago, a nearby commercial district, and proximity to the lakefront.

(H) Turn right at Glenwood and go north seven-eighths of a mile to Pratt Boulevard (6800 North). The imposing complex of **St. Gertrude Catholic parish** stands on the southwest and northwest corners of Granville and Glenwood. Many of the area's apartment buildings date from around 1912, the year construction began on the parish's first building at 6220 N. Glenwood. The beautiful English Gothic church, dedicated in 1931, was one of the few houses of worship in Chicago constructed during the Depression.

(I) For generations of Edgewater and Rogers Park Catholics, **John E. Maloney's Funeral Home** at 1359 W. Devon has been a neighborhood landmark. Just down the street at 1300 W. Devon is **Weinstein Brothers Funeral Home,** which has served the area's large Jewish community. Not only was Devon Avenue the dividing line between Edgewater and Rogers Park, but it once marked the beginning of Northwestern University's "four-mile limit." While saloons along Clark Street were an accepted part of neighborhood life in Edgewater in the 1890s, they were strictly prohibited in Rogers Park.

Congregation B'nai Zion, Chicago's first Conservative congregation, built this massive synagogue at 1439 W. Pratt Boulevard in 1928. Founded in 1918, the congregation first worshiped in the former Episcopal church of St. Paul at 1715 W. Lunt. (G. Lane, 1985)

(J) **St. Ignatius Church** at 6555 N. Glenwood was dedicated in 1917, just ten years after the Jesuits built their first church in Rogers Park, a frame building at the northeast corner of Devon and Sheridan Road. Henry J. Schlacks designed the present magnificent structure with its free-standing campanile after the Gesu, the mother church of the Jesuit order in Rome.

(K) Turn left at Pratt Boulevard and go eight blocks west to Wolcott Avenue (1900 West). **Congregation B'nai Zion,** Chicago's first Conservative congregation founded in 1919, built the massive complex at 1439 W. Pratt in 1928. After more than sixty-five years, Congregation B'nai Zion continues as a center of Jewish life in Rogers Park.

(L) Turn right at Wolcott and go four blocks north to Greenleaf Avenue (7032 North), then turn right and go two blocks east on Greenleaf to Clark Street. The Chicago and North Western Railroad tracks pass through the heart of Old Rogers Park. Along Wolcott Avenue are Victorian homes which were among the first buildings constructed in the area. Because of the nearby Ridge and its elevated land, this part of Rogers Park was developed in the 1870s. Nearly thirty years elapsed before residential construction along the lakefront was feasible.

(M) Turn right at Clark and go two blocks south to Morse Avenue (6900 North). Clark Street was Rogers Park's original commercial district as well as its civic center. Clark Street's buildings are a mix of old and new, ranging from **Phoenix Hall** at 7044 N. Clark, an early meeting place, to the **Rogers Park Public Library,** 6907 N. Clark.

(N) Turn left on Morse Avenue and go two blocks east to Ashland Boulevard (1600 West). This stretch of Morse Avenue contains a surprising number of ecclesiastical institutions, among them **St. Jerome Catholic School,** 1706 W. Morse; **Rogers Park Lutheran Church,** 1701 W. Morse; the **Korean United Presbyterian Church,** 1615 W. Morse; and the **United Church of Rogers Park,** 1545 W. Morse. Ethnic change in Rogers Park has occurred peacefully. St. Jerome School, once an Irish Catholic stronghold, now includes students from more than thirty-five ethnic and racial groups. Likewise, the old Temple Mizpah has taken on new life as a Korean Presbyterian church.

(O) Turn left on Ashland and go all the way north to Juneway Terrace (7736 North). One of Chicago's longest streets, Ashland runs from the city limits on the north to 123rd Street on the south. Predominantly a commercial thoroughfare, in Rogers Park Ashland attains the status of a boulevard. As such it has been the favored location for several prominent Rogers Park institutions, notably the **Eugene Field Public School,** 7019 N. Ashland; the former **Rogers Park Women's Club** (now the Unification Church of America), 7077 N. Ashland; **St. Paul's By the Lake** (Episcopal) Church, 7100 N. Ashland; and the **Sixteenth Church of Christ Scientist** (now the Apostolic Catholic Assyrian Church of the East), 7201 N. Ashland. Note: jog left at Birchwood and right at Howard to continue north on Ashland.

Wisdom Bridge Theater at 1559 W. Howard, a Rogers Park institution since 1975, is one of several resident theater companies in the community, making Rogers Park an important center for the performing arts.

The area just north of Howard Street was known as "Germania" when it was part of Evanston, Illinois. After annexation to Chicago in 1915, it was rapidly built up with modern apartment buildings. Following years of decline, there are signs that the "Juneway Jungle" is being transformed into a liveable neighborhood. Since 1982 many of the district's courtyard buildings have been renovated as part of project "Northpoint."

Mundelein College, 6363 Sheridan Road. 1985. Joe W. McCarthy and Nairne W. Fisher designed this Art Deco skyscraper which opened for classes in 1930. In 1980, Mundelein College was listed on the National Register of Historic Buildings. (G. Lane)

(P) Turn right onto Juneway Terrace and go one block east to Sheridan Road. Charles Ferguson, the man who promoted the annexation of "Germania" to Rogers Park in 1915, lived in the white stucco house at 1542 W. Juneway Terrace. Ferguson is also known as the "father of Howard Street" because he financed the construction of the Howard Theater at 1631 W. Howard in 1918.

(Q) Turn right on Sheridan Road and follow it all the way south to the Hollywood Drive exit of Lake Shore Drive.

In the late 1890s the Rogers Park real estate firm of Doland and Jennings began to market single-family homes in the area known as Birchwood, roughly between Touhy and Pratt. Although a number of mansions were constructed along Sheridan Road in the next ten years, the area around Lunt and Ashland was still a forest of birch trees in 1909. One of the few mansions remaining in the area, at 7450 N. Sheridan, is now owned by the Unification Church.

Frank Lloyd Wright designed the **Emil Bach house** at 7415 N. Sheridan in 1915. It was declared a Chicago landmark in 1977.

(R) **Loyola University** at 6525 N. Sheridan Road is Rogers Park's largest institution. In 1907 Jesuits from the West Side parish of Holy Family established St. Ignatius Church at Sheridan and Devon, on the present site of the Granada Theater. The oldest building on Loyola's Lake Shore campus is **Dumbach Hall,** opened in 1909 as Loyola Academy. Other early structures include **Cudahy Science Hall** (1912); **Cudahy Library** (1930); and **Madonna della Strada Chapel** (1939). Beginning in 1966, Loyola University embarked on an ambitious building program which has resulted in a high-rise dormitory, classroom buildings, and a science building. Through its "Walk to Work" program, Loyola University has encouraged staff and faculty to purchase and renovate homes in Rogers Park and Edgewater, thus contributing to the stability of both neighborhoods.

(S) Sheridan Road curves east at Devon Avenue, past **Mundelein College,** Chicago's second Catholic women's college. Joseph McCarthy of Chicago and Nairne Fisher of Dubuque, Iowa designed this Art Deco skyscraper, which opened in September 1930. Financed by the nickels and dimes of students in the BVM Sisters' schools throughout the country, Mundelein is "the first self-contained skyscraper college for women in the world." The building was added to the National Register of Historic Places in 1980.

(T) In 1910, this stretch of Sheridan Road was built up with stately brick homes. The **Albert G. Wheeler mansion** at 6355 N. Sheridan with its magnificent Tiffany-style window, was typical of the high-class construction along Sheridan Road. Like the few homes which remain on Sheridan, the Wheeler "marble mansion" has been converted into institutional use. It is now part of the Mundelein College campus.

The **Academy of the Sacred Heart** and **Hardey Prep** are to your right at 6250 N. Sheridan Road.

In recent years Edgewater residents have tried to raise funds to renovate the former **S.H. Gunder mansion** at 6219 N. Sheridan into a North Side Cultural Center. This building and the mansion at 6205 N. Sheridan, which has been renovated by the Chicago Park District, represent the last open spaces in the canyon of highrises which flank the east side of Sheridan Road.

(U) In the original J.L. Cochran subdivision of Edgewater, local churches selected sites along Kenmore Avenue. By the 1950s, Sheridan Road had become the preferred location for **Emanuel Congregation**, 5959 N. Sheridan, and **St. Andrew Greek Orthodox Church**, 5649 N. Sheridan. Both buildings signaled the end of the church-building boom, which reached its height in Edgewater and Rogers Park in the 1920s.

Milwaukee Avenue Corridor

Milwaukee Avenue is one of Chicago's few diagonal streets. It goes out from the downtown area in a northwesterly direction, eventually reaching the suburbs. The street was originally an Indian trail which followed a buffalo path to the Chicago River. White people later developed it as a plank road to bring farm products into the city. While little development occurred along the street before the Chicago Fire in 1871, after that event Milwaukee Avenue became a major urban thoroughfare. Various ethnic groups, making their way to the neighborhoods of the Northwest Side, used Milwaukee Avenue to move out to what were perceived to be greener pastures. The street has always been an important byway for Chicago and its environs.

Milwaukee Avenue has indeed been a transportation and residential corridor for generations of Chicagoans. Like other neighborhoods that bordered the elevated lines or those that adjoined commuter railroads or streetcar lines, the communities along Milwaukee Avenue acted as corridor communities. People came and went. Ethnicity shifted, but the role of Milwaukee Avenue itself did not. Although the names of the people changed from German and Scandinavian to Polish and Jewish, and then to Hispanic, Milwaukee Avenue continued to play its role as a pathway in and out of the inner city. Its role in the economic and demographic life of Chicago remains much the same today as it always was.

The neighborhood at the lower end of Milwaukee Avenue near the Kennedy Expressway has been known by various names in its long history. The area east of Wood Street was within the original boundaries of Chicago in 1833. Census takers called it West Town. The Polish people who came there in large numbers after 1875 often called it *Stanislowowo-Trojcowo*, after the two major parishes, St. Stanislaus and Holy Trinity, in the area around Division and Noble Streets. Outsiders sometimes called it Polish Downtown or simply Milwaukee and Division. Some residents now refer to the area as East Humboldt Park. Others prefer Wicker Park, a rather gentrified name that is derived from a small neighborhood of mansions and greystones near the intersection of Milwaukee and Damen Avenues. Developers, with an eye to the young urban professionals, would call a much larger territory "Wicker Park" than was ever historically accurate. Another section near the lower part of the Milwaukee Avenue corridor is now known as the Ukrainian Village, because of the attachment which Ukrainian Americans have to their neighborhood around Chicago Avenue and Oakley Boulevard. The various names tell us much about the history of the neighborhoods in the Milwaukee Avenue corridor. They also say something about the future that residents hope to see.

West Town

Mark Noble bought and cleared land for a farm on the Northwest Side in the 1830s, but little settlement took place there until the 1850s. In 1851 Chicago extended its city limits to Western and North Avenues, thus taking in much of the lower Milwaukee Avenue corridor. The earliest settlement centered around the North Western Railroad car shops, just to the northwest of the downtown area. Wooden shacks stood on the prairie near the river. By 1860 the Milwaukee Avenue horsecar line ran northwest from Halsted Street. This transportation link facilitated residential development, and developers soon flocked to the Northwest Side.

Chicago's German population expanded rapidly in the period after the 1848 revolutions in Central Europe and before America's Civil War. Many of these immigrants settled on the North Side. By the 1860s they had begun to cross the North Branch of the Chicago River to the Northwest Side. In 1864 German Catholics in this area petitioned the diocese for a German national parish of their own. For almost two years the German parish of St. Joseph at Superior and Wabash had operated a mission in the new settlement at Chicago Avenue and Carpenter Street. The new congregation of St. Boniface moved the mission church to a lot on Cornell (Chestnut) and Noble, and the German Catholic community had its own parish here with the blessings of Bishop James Duggan.

Even as the German community was setting down roots on the Northwest Side around Division and Noble, another ethnic group was making its way into the neighborhood. Poles settled in the district in large numbers as early as the mid-1860s. Some came to Chicago even earlier, but the large migration did not begin until after 1865. While several Polish emigrés visited and lived in Chicago before him, Anthony Smarzewski-Schermann, who arrived in the 1850s, is considered the founder of Chicago's Polish community. Smarzewski-Schermann soon quit his trade as a carpenter and opened a store to serve the small, almost rural community west of the river. Since he was not only catering to the newly-arrived Poles, he changed his name to the more Germanic Schermann.

The bell tower, St. Boniface Church, northeast corner Noble and Chestnut, 1980. This handsome church, designed by Henry Schlacks, was built in 1902-04 by a German Catholic community in West Town. (A. Kezys)

The Poles and Germans had been rivals for centuries in Eastern Europe. At the time Chicago's Northwest Side was developing, Germany occupied large parts of Polish territory in the form of Prussia and the Austro-Hungarian Empire. In 1871 the newly-created German Empire included parts of northern and western Poland. Old world animosities could not be easily set aside, even in Chicago. While many Germans welcomed their East European neighbors on the near Northwest Side, many others did not. The arrival of Catholic Poles in the parish of St. Boniface caused violence to break out in the small community. Rev. James Marshall, the pastor in the late 1860s, welcomed the Poles. He spoke Polish as well as German and English. And he occasionnaly conducted services in Polish. A group of parishioners who wanted St. Boniface to remain a strictly German parish forced Father Marshall to resign. The arrival of a new pastor, who quickly moved against the radical nationalists, stopped the violence, but change continued. By 1895 the majority of the parishioners of St. Boniface were Kashubes, a Slavic group from German-occupied Poland who spoke a German-Polish dialect. Most of the original Bavarians had left this immediate area and moved to the northwest.

The Poles, meanwhile, flooded into the area. In 1867 they organized the parish of St. Stanislaus Kostka, the first Polish congregation in the diocese of Chicago, on Noble Street several blocks north of St. Boniface. The Resurrectionist priests, a Polish religious order, took charge of the parish in 1869. This was an auspicious event, because this order organized the parish and helped the Polish community spread from this little settlement near the river throughout the Northwest Side. By the turn of the century, St. Stanislaus Kostka had developed into one of the largest Catholic parishes in the world, with reportedly over 5,000 families. In 1908, 4,500 children attended the parochial school. The present church, modeled after one in Krakow, Poland, was dedicated in 1881. Rev. Vincent Barzynski, the legendary leader of the community and founder of many Polish churches in Chicago, built the church and is generally recognized as the primary force behind the expansion of Polish Catholic institutions in Chicago after 1875. He was appointed pastor of the parish in 1874 and remained at St. Stanislaus Kostka until his death in 1899.

Holy Trinity parish, also a Polish Catholic congregation, was organized in 1873 just south of Division Street on Noble, the year before Barzynski's arrival. It posed a real challenge to his authority. The Poles at Holy Trinity decided to take a more nationalistic attitude. Although the founding date for Holy Trinity is celebrated as 1873, it was not recognized as a

St. Stanislaus Kostka Church, southeast corner Noble and Evergreen, 1980. This parish is the mother church of all Polish Roman Catholic congregations in Chicago. At the turn of the century, approximately 40,000 Polish Americans worshiped here.
(A. Kezys)

Holy Trinity Church, 1120 N. Noble, 1980. This splendid example of Renaissance architecture faces the Kennedy Expressway just south of Division Street. The parish maintains its connection with the Polish community despite ethnic changes in the neighborhood. (G. Lane)

separate parish until 1893. There was a controversy here which tore the Polish community apart for twenty years. Historian Joseph Parot traces this battle in Polonia in his excellent book, *Polish Catholics in Chicago.* Barzynski and the parishioners of Holy Trinity were at odds with each other over the question of who owned the Holy Trinity parish property. The diocese eventually had to step in. But before the controversy was settled, there were actual street fights between parishioners of the two Polish parishes—not an isolated event in the history of the Catholic Church in the United States at this time. Polish Catholics, especially, were involved in such controversies, and some of them led to the creation of the Polish National Catholic Church.

The Milwaukee Avenue corridor began to develop rapidly after 1869. In that year the West Park Commissioners established the 207-acre Humboldt Park at California Avenue and Division Street. The Milwaukee Road railroad also constructed a Humboldt station at Bloomingdale and

California Avenues at about this time. In 1895 an elevated
railroad line reached out to Logan Square and Humboldt
Park, providing quick and relatively inexpensive
transportation to the Loop. Local real estate ads appeared in
German at this time, as Western Europeans began to flee
the growing East European population further to the
southeast along Milwaukee Avenue.

This in-migration of Poles and other East Europeans
proved unstoppable. The Milwaukee Avenue corridor became
the largest of the five principal Polish neighborhoods in
Chicago. The other four were the Lower West Side (Pilsen),
Bridgeport, Back of the Yards, and South Chicago. Indeed,
the Milwaukee Avenue-Ashland-Division intersection soon
became known as Polish Downtown. Throughout the first
half of the twentieth century this area was the capital of the
American Polonia. At or near this intersection stood the
headquarters of just about every major Polish organization in
America. The Polish Roman Catholic Union and its rival the
larger Polish National Alliance both had their national
offices here, just a few blocks from each other. The Polish
Women's Alliance occupied a building on Ashland just north
of Milwaukee Avenue. The Polish Welfare League also
occupied a building in the 1300 block of Ashland. These
secular organizations, along with the many Polish churches
that dotted nearby neighborhoods, provided a strong
institutional base for Polonia in the West Town community area.

Polish-owned businesses occupied storefronts along
Milwaukee and Ashland Avenues as well as east and west on
Division Street. Polish and other East European Jews also
settled here and opened stores and other businesses in the
growing immigrant community. The Goldblatt Brothers' first
store opened on Chicago Avenue at Ashland in 1914. The
Jewish merchants replaced German and Scandinavian ones
who had moved further west and northwest. A strong
commercial base thus joined the Polish institutional base in
the neighborhood.

Immigrants, however, came to this area for its
employment opportunities as well as for its Old World
atmosphere. The banks of the North Branch of the Chicago
River filled with manufacturing plants, as did nearby Goose
Island. Tanneries and other industries employed thousands
of the immigrants who came to West Town. The major
industrial section of the community is bounded by Chicago
Avenue on the north, Kinzie Street to the south, the Chicago
River to the east, and California Avenue to the west. In 1910
the population peaked. Ten years later 218,000 people lived
in the lower part of the Milwaukee Avenue corridor.
Forty-four percent of these were foreign born. Poles and

Interior of St. Hyacinth during the dedication of an image of Our Lady of Czestochowa.
(Courtesy The Chicago Catholic)

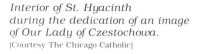

St. Hyacinth Church, 3635 W. George, 1980. This parish in Avondale on the Northwest Side has the largest Polish Catholic congregation in Chicago today.
(G. Lane)

Russian Jews made up the largest part of the group. But even at this time the East Europeans were moving northwest along the Milwaukee Avenue corridor.

St. Hedwig's parish was founded in 1888 at Webster and Hoyne Avenues for Polish Catholics moving northwest. Father Barzynski founded St. Hyacinth's parish in Avondale in 1894, also to serve Poles moving along Milwaukee Avenue. Between 1917 and 1921 parishioners built the present magnificent Renaissance style church with a seating capacity of two thousand. Today in the 1980s St. Hyacinth is the center of the Northwest Side Polonia. Almost half of its parishioners are Poles who came to America within the last twenty years. This speaks to the continuing development of Chicago's Polish community and to the economic and geographic mobility of the group over the years.

Indeed, ethnic change has been a constant factor along the Milwaukee Avenue corridor. Polish people did not make up the entire population of West Town or even of the area around Milwaukee Avenue and Division Street. Ukrainians, Italians, and Jews each had their enclaves, as did the Germans and Scandinavians who first lived in the areas just northwest of the Loop.

As late as the 1880s, German workers still lived in the Milwaukee-Ashland-Division neighborhood. Three of the four Haymarket martyrs lived in the West Town community. As William Adelman has pointed out, Milwaukee Avenue, at the time of the Haymarket Riot, was often called "Dinner Pail Avenue" because of the working-class people who made up the great majority of the local population. The funeral procession for the Haymarket martyrs took place, apropriately enough, down Milwaukee Avenue. Polish, Italian, Jewish, and German workers came out in force for

the funeral procession on Sunday, November 13, 1887.
Nearly a half million people lined the procession route. Local
authorities had hung Albert Parsons, George Engel, August
Spies, and Adolph Fischer on "Black Friday," November 11,
1887. At the time of the funeral, Lucy Parsons and her
family had also moved to West Town and lived at 1129 North
Milwaukee Avenue, today the site of a low-income housing
project. The funeral began at the home of August Spies who
lived near Wicker Park at 2132 Potomac. The park itself, at
Damen and Schiller, was said to be the center of the
anarchist plot to take over Chicago. After the riot, police dug
up Wicker Park in an attempt to find bombs supposedly
planted by Louis Lingg. None were ever found. Lingg
committed suicide the day before his scheduled excecution.
Two of the Haymarket defendants, Samuel Fielden and
Michael Schwab, had their sentences commuted to life
imprisonment by Governor Oglesby the day before the
execution. The jury gave Oscar Neebe a fifteen year
sentence. Governor John Peter Altgeld later pardoned these
survivors on June 26, 1893, the day after a monument was
erected to the four martyrs at Waldheim Cemetery. This
action by the governor partially accounted for his not being
reelected in 1896.

*Hermann Weinhardt House, 2137
W. Pierce, 1893. This house still
stands on Pierce Street looking
much as it did when constructed
in the nineteenth century.*
(Courtesy Chicago Historical Society)

Wicker Park

German middle-class people quickly settled the Wicker Park
area near Damen and North Avenue. Many of these families
owned stores on Milwaukee Avenue. Although the first lot
near Damen and Chicago Avenue was not sold until 1877,
Hoyne Avenue in this district was one of the first paved
streets in the city. The name of the community comes from
Joel and Charles Wicker who donated the park to the city in
1870 in order to enhance their real estate investments in
the area. Many socially prominent Chicagoans lived in this
district, including O.W. Potter, the president of Illinois Steel;
W.A. Wieboldt, the retail merchant; and John Buehler, the
German-American banker. A variety of architectural styles
appeared in the homes around Wicker Park, including
Italianate, Queen Anne, Second Empire, and even Swiss
Chalet. West Park Commissioner Herman Weinhardt built a
"gingerbread" house at 2137 W. Pierce in 1888. The Uihlein
family of the Schlitz brewery in Milwaukee owned one of the
finest homes in the neighborhood. Large and stately houses
on Hoyne, Damen, Pierce, Oakley, and neighboring streets
reflected the new found success of their owners.

For the Germans, the arrival of Poles and other Eastern Europeans in Wicker Park meant change. In 1902 Jan Smulski, a Polish leader and banker, purchased the home of Hans D. Runge, the German-American treasurer of Wolf Brothers Wood Milling Company, at 2138 W. Pierce. By this time the original mansions immediately surrounding Wicker Park had been turned into boarding houses and multiple-family dwellings for the Polish working class.

Polish Americans soon dominated the Wicker Park neighborhood. The Runge-Smulski home became known as the Paderewski house, because the famed Polish pianist played the piano to a crowd from the front porch of the house in the early 1930s. The house later served as the Polish consulate. Paderewski is said to have played the piano in several homes in the Wicker Park area, including the one at 1036 N. Hoyne. Black people lived in Wicker Park along Bell Avenue, a servants' community for the Wicker Park mansions.

Ukranian Village

Eastern Europeans also came to the neighborhood south of Wicker Park, along Chicago Avenue. Ukrainians, Poles, and Slovaks mingled here just as they had on the European steppe. Many of the Ukrainians had been neighbors of the Slovaks in the Hungarian-dominated Carpatho-Ukraine. Others came from Galicia, the westernmost of the Ukrainian provinces. These parts of the Ukraine had been under Polish, Austrian, and Hungarian rule throughout most of their modern history. Ukrainians often referred to themselves as Rusins or Ruthenians, terms derived from the word *Rus*, the ancient name of the Ukraine. Many of these immigrants were Uniate Catholics, sometimes known as Greek Catholics. According to Myron Bohdan Kuropas, Chicago's Ukrainian community can trace its origins to the arrival of Dr. Volodymyr Simenovych around 1890. The founding of St. Nicholas Ruthenian Catholic Church at the corner of Superior and Bishop Streets in 1905 created the institutional base for the Rusin community in Chicago. Ukrainians purchased their first church from a Danish congregation as the neighborhood underwent ethnic change. In 1913 Ukrainian Catholics began construction of the beautiful neo-Byzantine church we see today at the corner of Rice Street and Oakley Boulevard. Rev. Nicholas Strutinsky, who guided the parish from 1907 to 1921, was also an important leader and founding father of the community.

(Top right) Paderewski House, 2138 W. Pierce, 1985. This is one of many stately homes built by well-to-do German Americans which lined the streets of Wicker Park. It was later known as the Paderewski House because the famed Polish pianist and diplomat played the piano from the front porch. (G. Lane)

(Bottom right) St. Nicholas Ukrainian Catholic Cathedral, northeast corner of Rice and Oakley, 1980. This Byzantine style cathedral, modeled after the cathedral of Kiev, was constructed in 1913-15 and was beautifully renovated in 1974-77. (A. Kezys)

The Ukrainians tended to settle near Chicago Avenue, mostly around Oakley Boulevard. Here they built many large churches, turning the boulevard into a street of Orthodox, Uniate, and Roman Catholic churches. In 1916 Ukrainian Baptists built the Ukrainian First Baptist Church on Damen Avenue and George Street. Bielarusians (White Russians) also lived in the neighborhood. If they were Orthodox Christians, they were often assimilated into the Russian or Ukrainian communities. If they were Catholics, they often settled near Poles, and many attended services at Holy Trinity Church on Noble Street.

Poles and Slovaks also built churches on Oakley, further attesting to the ethnic diversity of that part of the Milwaukee Avenue corridor which is known as the Ukrainian Village. The Slovak parish of the Sacred Heart on Huron and Oakley was the sixth Slovak parish to be organized in Chicago. In 1911 Slovaks purchased the building of the Bethlehem Norwegian United Church at Huron and Racine. Parishioners began construction of the church on Oakley in 1916.

Humboldt Park / Logan Square

Jews also settled on the main streets of West Town, but they too began to move northwest and onto the boulevards of the Northwest Side. Large numbers of Polish and Russian Jews moved to Humboldt Park, Logan Square, and the Palmer Square neighborhoods of the Milwaukee Avenue corridor. Jews settled in Logan Square after 1912, but their principal movement to this middle-class area began after the First World War. By 1930 Logan Square's Jewish residents made up one of the neighborhood's largest ethnic communities. The Esther Falkenstein Home at 1917-19 N. Humboldt Boulevard was a principal charitable organization of the North Side Jewish community.

Congregation Beth El, the first synogogue in the West Town area, was founded in 1871 at Huron and May Streets. As Irving Cutler has pointed out, some twenty places of worship eventually served the Jewish people of the Milwaukee Avenue corridor. The West Town Jewish community was also known for its political radicalism. It also had its share of celebrities, including Saul Bellow, Sydney J. Harris, and Michael Todd. Many of the Jewish families of the Milwaukee Avenue corridor eventually moved to Albany Park and the north and northwest suburbs.

Italians also moved across the lower part of the Milwaukee Avenue corridor. In 1874 they organized the first

Italian Catholic parish in Chicago, the Assumption of the Blessed Virgin Mary Church on Illinois Street near Orleans. In 1903 Santa Maria Addolorata Church was founded at Ohio and Sangamon Streets. In July 1904 the Archdiocese of Chicago agreed to establish another Italian parish, Holy Rosary, at 614 N. Western Avenue. This parish almost immediately came under the care of the Scalabrini Fathers. In 1929 as the parish celebrated its silver jubilee, 430 children attended the parochial school and over 10,000 Catholics belonged to the congregation.

In the early years Scandinavians made up a large part of the population in the Milwaukee Avenue corridor. The original Northwest Side Scandinavian community grew up in the area bounded by Chicago Avenue and Division Street between Franklin and Larrabee. In 1870 Swedes organized the Gethsemane Lutheran Church at Huron and May streets. Five years later they organized the Bethlehem Lutheran Church at Sangamon and Milwaukee Avenue. Norwegians also lived in this area. In 1870 the Norwegian Lutheran Bethlehem Church opened on Sangamon and Grand, just south of the Swedes. Fourteen years later the Norwegians had begun to move northwest as the Bethania Lutheran Church opened at Grand and Carpenter. In 1896 St. Johannes Lutheran Church began serving Norwegians at 940 N. Washtenaw near Humboldt Park. Two years earlier, Chicago's Norwegians opened the Norwegian-American Hospital at Thomas and Francisco. This ethnic community was economically and geographically very mobile. They moved north and west as Chicago's housing stock expanded and as Eastern Europeans and Italians moved into their old neighborhoods.

In 1900 the Humboldt Park Swedish Baptist Church opened at Rockwell and Wabansia. The Logan Square Norwegian Baptist Church followed in 1906. Danish Chicagoans came to Logan Square at about this time too, organizing the Trinity Danish Lutheran Church. Chicago's most famous writer of Scandinavian descent, Nelson Algren, lived in the Wicker Park neighborhood.

By 1900 the Milwaukee Avenue corridor had become a microcosm of Chicago's ethnic history. While Scandinavians and Germans made their way northwest, Poles, Ukrainians, Slovaks, other Slavs, Jews, and Italians followed them through the neighborhoods. Milwaukee Avenue provided an upward and outward path from the old neighborhoods of the Near Northwest Side. The various white ethnic groups used it well. As Scandinavians and Germans continued to move out along the avenues, the Northwest Side began to resemble more and more the Eastern European melting pot itself.

Humboldt Park Swedish Baptist Church, c.1913. Several Protestant congregations in the Humboldt Park area can trace their origins to the large Swedish immigration of the last third of the nineteenth century.
(C.R. Childs. courtesy G. Schmalgemeier)

1600 block of N. Troy Street, c.1911. This row of brick and stone two-flats reflects the upward mobility of the various ethnic groups which moved into the Humboldt Park area from neighborhoods closer to the Loop.
(Masure & Leonhard. courtesy G. Schmalgemeier)

Southwest corner of Cleaver and Potomac, 1985. The streets near St. Stanislaus Kostka Church were once filled with Polish-American children. Today Hispanic families dominate the working-class apartments and street corners. (D. Pacyga)

Polish and Yiddish, Ukrainian and Bielarusian, Slovak and Lithuanian, all could be heard along the side streets and avenues of West Town, Logan Square, and Humboldt Park. The ethnic change that had been violently resisted at St. Boniface, as Poles moved into the then German parish, proved overwhelming. By 1950 it seemed that the Milwaukee Avenue corridor would never change. But nothing is forever, especially in Chicago, and especially along Milwaukee Avenue. Change again came to the corridor.

In the 1950s Spanish began to be heard along the streets of West Town, especially in the older sections that had long been identified with Italians, Poles, and Ukrainians. Meanwhile, the construction of the Kennedy Expressway in the late 1950s forced a mass exodus from West Town by many older ethnics. By 1960 some 10,000 Spanish-speaking people, mostly Puerto Rican and Mexican, lived in the area. Six years later that number had jumped to about 40,000. The heart of the Hispanic community was in the area bounded by Ashland, Haddon, Potomac, and California. In 1966 the *Sun-Times* estimated that eighty-five percent of the residents in that area spoke Spanish. Saul Bellow, a former resident of this neighborhood, described the change in *Humboldt's Gift,* calling Division Street a ". . . West Indies slum, resembling parts of San Juan . . ." In 1970 residents of Latin origin made up over thirty-nine percent of West Town's population of about 124,000. Ten years later 56.7 percent of the population, which had decreased to 96,428, was of Latin origin. This lower part of the Milwaukee Avenue corridor today includes the largest Puerto Rican community in Chicago. The number of

Northwest corner of Cleaver and Blackhawk, 1985. Wave after wave of East European and now Hispanic immigrants have lived in the West Town neighborhood. This large brick tenement is typical of those constructed in the late nineteenth century. (D. Pacyga)

(Top right) Humboldt Park, looking east toward California Avenue, 1937. Many fine homes and apartments lined the parks and boulevards of the Northwest Side. (Chicago Park District, courtesy R. Wroble)

(Bottom right) West Town Center, Milwaukee Avenue just west of Ashland, 1985. This new shopping center confirms the continuing vitality of Milwaukee Avenue as a commercial district. (G. Lane)

Mexicans almost equaled the Puerto Rican population in 1980, and Cubans and other Hispanics also live in the neighborhood.

Like the older groups, Puerto Ricans and other Hispanics also moved up the Milwaukee Avenue corridor to Humboldt Park and Logan Square. West Town, however, still serves as a point of entry for new arrivals from Puerto Rico. The gang problem in this area continues to plague the residents. But the Milwaukee Avenue corridor has always had its share of gangs and violence. Nelson Algren described much of the "under life" of this neighborhood in *Man With A Golden Arm*, long before the arrival of Hispanic ethnic groups. Hispanics entering West Town faced a neighborhood with many old and often neglected buildings. In 1980 as in 1880, Milwaukee Avenue provided a home for Chicago's most recent arrivals and the newest members of the working class.

The ethnic changes and the continuing decline of the housing stock around Milwaukee Avenue attracted the attention of the city and federal governments. In the 1950s urban renewal often meant neighborhood removal. The first physical threat to the community came in the late 1950s when city planners proposed the expressway that would eventually be named for John F. Kennedy. Word leaked out that St. Stanislaus Kostka church and school stood in the path of the expressway and would be demolished. The highly-organized Polish-American community rose up in protest, City Hall gave in, and the expressway passed behind

the Polish Catholic landmark. Although the protest saved the church, the highway construction forced over four hundred families out of the parish. Change indeed was coming to West Town.

Another urban renewal crisis developed when urban planners began to think of ways to "rehabilitate" the Milwaukee-Ashland-Division area. In 1958 the Department of Urban Renewal (DUR) declared all of West Town part of a conservation area. At the time no one in the community knew what that meant. There was much anxiety in the lower part of the Milwaukee Avenue corridor. In 1961 the pastors of twenty-two Catholic parishes approached Cardinal Meyer for aid in stemming the flight of parishioners and halting the deterioration of their neighborhoods. The Cardinal asked Monsignor John Egan to help. He in turn enlisted Saul Alinsky to organize the neighborhoods of the Northwest Side. This resulted in the formation of the Northwest Community Organization (NCO). By the time NCO held its first congress, 177 local institutions, including Protestant churches, ethnic fraternal groups, and settlement houses, belonged to the new umbrella organization. The NCO soon found itself at loggerheads with local politicians. Aldermen Matthew Bieszczat and Tom Keane, especially, came into conflict with the new group.

At the heart of the controversy was local control of the urban renewal program. After much debate, both the neighborhood and DUR approved the Noble Square Plan. The twelve-acre project adjoined the Polish church of the Holy Trinity on Noble street. This area was cleared in 1965. Alderman Bieszczat had supported the construction of a Cabrini-Green type project, but NCO fought that proposal, and with the support of Mayor Richard J. Daley the project was scaled down to townhouses and one large apartment tower. After a long delay, construction finally began in December 1968.

Noble Square was not a success by the standards of the community. The project displaced the primarily Polish residents of the twelve-acre site. Most of these families could not move into the new housing because their incomes were too high. The project, which was originally intended to be integrated, soon became a black community in the heart of Polish Downtown. Many of the families in Noble Square formerly lived in nearby Cabrini-Green. Many people on the Northwest Side blamed NCO for the failure of public housing in West Town. But Noble Square has actually proved to be more successful than other poor and moderate income housing in Chicago.

Other urban renewal plans have come and gone. The most controversial was the *Chicago 21* plan put forward by the city in 1973. This plan designated the old Polish

Downtown area as East Humboldt Park and included it in a plan for central city redevelopment. Once again the Northwest Side was up in arms. The community wanted a say in its own urban renewal planning.

In 1977 another controversy broke out in the lower part of the Milwaukee Avenue corridor when the City announced it would designate the Oakley Boulevard-Chicago Avenue area as blighted. The neighborhood was soon at war with City Hall. And the fight began to look like an old-fashioned Chicago ethnic free-for-all as Poles, Latinos, Lithuanians, and others protested a Ukrainian plan for the community which would displace members of these other groups. By the end of the year the City backed down. Chicago-Oakley was saved. The Ukrainians were able to maintain their cultural centers, and the community, now known as the Ukrainian Village, stabilized without displacing its residents. The neighborhood spruced itself up. The homes are clean and well maintained and the neighborhood now attracts further outside investment. Unlike surrounding neighborhoods, the Ukrainian Village is for the most part free of gang graffitti. The neighborhood is well organized and militant about its survival. One neighbor reflected in the *Chicago Daily News* in 1975, "Oh those Ukies—the gang kids are afraid to go near them, afraid they'll get their heads cracked open."

The success of the Ukrainian Village points to yet another change for the lower part of the Milwaukee Avenue corridor and in turn for the whole area. Young urban professionals have been moving into the Wicker Park neighborhood for some time. During the Byrne administration Milwaukee Avenue saw some new investment as an old Wieboldt's store was turned into a shopping mall. Polish and Hispanic stores still line Milwaukee Avenue, but change is in the air—or at least that is what real estate developers would have us believe. When new subsidized housing came to the neighborhood, the new middle-class residents opposed it. Meanwhile, their poorer neighbors fear they will be pushed out of Wicker Park as it undergoes gentrification. Residents of Avondale, Jefferson Park, and other communities farther up Milwaukee Avenue are waiting to see if the poor will be pushed up the street to their neighborhoods.

The Milwaukee Avenue corridor began as ethnic groups marched northwest to new neighborhoods further away from the central business district. It has always acted as a human expressway from the Loop outward. In its 150-year history it has seen much change. Since the 1950s the change has not only been ethnic, but it has shown the influence of big government too. The community has tried, with some success, to control its own destiny. Whether it can continue to do so in the future remains to be seen.

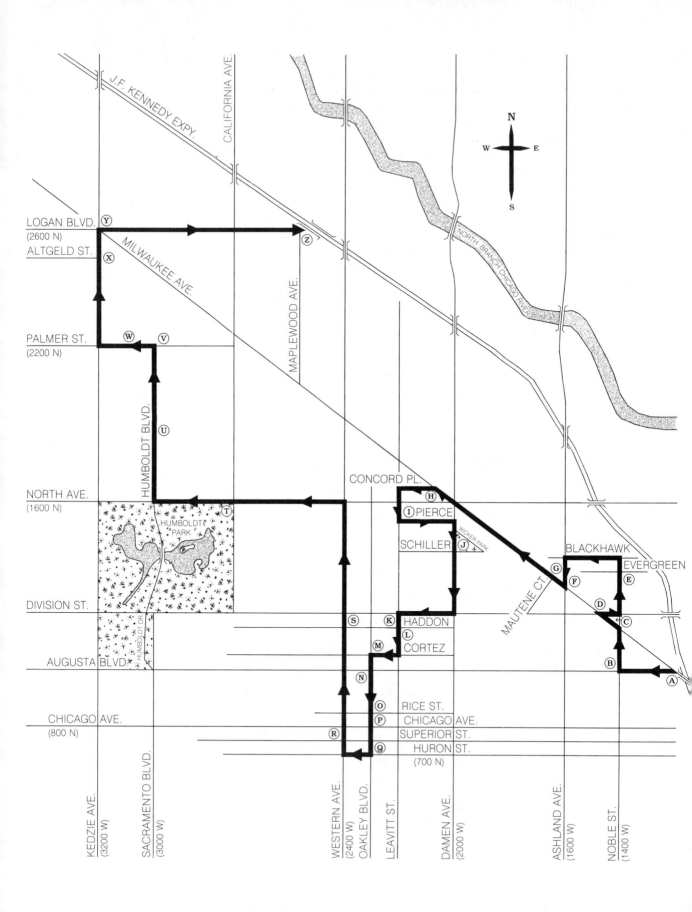

Milwaukee Avenue Corridor Tour

This tour begins just off the Kennedy Expressway at Milwaukee Avenue and Augusta Boulevard (1000 North). It goes through the West Town neighborhood, then through Wicker Park, the Ukrainian Village, then northwest, along Humboldt Park, up Humboldt Boulevard, through Palmer Square and Logan Square, and ends at the Logan Boulevard entrance to the Kennedy Expressway.

Driving time: about 2 hours.

(A) The national headquarters of the **Polish Roman Catholic Union of America** (PRCUA) stands on the southwest corner of Milwaukee and Augusta (1000 North). This fraternal organization was formed in 1873. One of the original founders of the PRCUA was Rev. Vincent Barzynski, who played such an important role in the development of Chicago's Polonia. Also in this building are the Polish Museum and its library and archives. While the museum opened in 1935 as the Museum and Archives of the Polish Roman Catholic Union in America, it took on the name of the **Polish Museum of America** in 1961. This ethnic educational institution is the largest of its kind in the United States. It contains exhibits which deal both with Poland and with Polish America.

Just south and west of the PRCUA you will see the towers of **St. Boniface Church** (1902), which was organized as a German parish in the 1860s, became Polish in the 1920s, and is largely Spanish-speaking today.

(B) Go one block west on Augusta Boulevard and turn right onto Noble Street (1400 West). On the northwest corner stands the **Northwestern University Settlement House.** The sociologist Charles Zeublin founded this organization in 1891. Irving K. Pond, the well known architect of settlement houses and community centers, designed the building, which still operates as a social settlement. Founded two years after Hull House, this institution played an important role in the social service movement.

(C) Go one block north on Noble and make a left onto Milwaukee Avenue. On your right is the **Noble Square Cooperative Housing Project** and **Holy Trinity Church.** This parish was the second Polish congregation founded in Chicago, and the present church dates from 1906. Today it stands overlooking the Kennedy Expressway and the nine-acre townhouse and high-rise housing project which replaced the surrounding neighborhood in the 1960s.

(D) Proceed northwest on Milwaukee Avenue to Division Street (1200 North). Turn right and go east on Division back to Noble. The corner of Division and Milwaukee marks part of the **Polonia Triangle** or the old Polish Downtown. Located near this corner were, at one time, all of the major national organizations in Polish America. The large white terra-cotta building on the northeast corner of the intersection once housed Jan Smulski's Bank Polski. It later became the home of the Polish newspaper *Dziennik Zwiazkowy,* published by the Polish National Alliance. Today it houses a True Value hardware store.

Just east of this is a grey building at 1520 W. Division Street. This was once the home of the **Polish National Alliance** (PNA). The PNA followed the Polish-American population northwest and left this building in the 1970s to relocate at 6100 N. Pulaski Road. Polish Americans founded the PNA in Philadelphia, but it held its first convention in Chicago's Palmer House on September 20, 1880. It is the largest Polish fraternal organization in the United States. One hundred years after its first Chicago meeting the organization had some 302,000 members. The first building owned by the PNA stood at 1406 W. Division Street. Like its rival, the Polish Roman Catholic Union, the PNA is very involved in cultural and youth programs. Also like its rival, it is a major fraternal insurance corporation.

Flanking Division Street at 1443 and 1444 are **Holy Trinity High School** and **Holy Family Academy,** Catholic secondary schools, which have been educating young people in Chicago since the last century.

(Top left) Polish Roman Catholic Union and Polish Museum of America Building, 1985. The P.R.C.U.A. building stands next to the Kennedy Expressway at Augusta Boulevard. The home of Polonia's oldest fraternal organization also houses the largest ethnic museum in America. (J. Ficner)

(Bottom left) Polish Daily Zgoda Building, 1985. Jan Smulski operated his Bank Polski from this white terra-cotta building on the corner of Division and Milwaukee until the 1930s. Later the Polish Daily Zgoda published from this site until it moved to the far Northwest Side in the 1970s. Today a True Value Hardware Store occupies the building. (J. Ficner)

1450 W. Blackhawk Street, 1985. This brick house, constructed in 1896, is typical of the better-quality homes built when West Town was a thriving East European community area.
(G. Lane)

(E) Turn left on Noble and go four blocks north to Blackhawk Street (1500 North). Facing Pulaski Park on the corner of Evergreen and Noble stands the huge Renaissance-style church of **St. Stanislaus Kostka.** This parish, organized in 1867, was the first Polish Catholic congregation in Chicago. It is the mother church of all Polish churches in the city. The building, begun in 1876 and completed five years later, seats 1,500 people. While once among the largest congregations in the world, today about 850 Polish-, Spanish-, and English-speaking families belong to the parish. In 1890 nearly 8,000 families or about 40,000 people called St. Stanislaus Kostka their parish. The area surrounding the church and Pulaski Park was the center of the Northwest Side Polish community.

(F) Turn left on Blackhawk and go four blocks west to Ashland Avenue (1600 West), where you will make another left and go south to Milwaukee Avenue. The housing in this part of West Town is very old and has witnessed the arrival of several waves of newcomers to Chicago. Today the neighborhood is heavily Hispanic, particularly Puerto Rican and Mexican. Older Polish Americans and some recent Polish immigrants still live in the neighborhood. Some professionals have been moving into the area as part of the gentrification of Wicker Park, but this has not yet become a major trend. You will also notice that some of the homes are actually built below grade, that is, their first floors are below street level. This is a result of the city's decision in the 1850s to raise the streets in order to provide better drainage.

As you go south on Ashland Avenue you will pass the former headquarters of the Polish Women's Alliance at 1309 N. Ashland. Like the PNA, this organization has left the West Town area and is now located in suburban Park Ridge. The **Polish Welfare Association** still maintains headquarters at 1303 N. Ashland.

(G) Turn right onto Milwaukee Avenue and proceed northwest. Milwaukee Avenue developed as a major shopping strip in West Town. In 1898 architect Robert C. Berlin planned a new Wieboldt's department store for the popular street. In 1979, after Wieboldt's left the street, the building became the **West Town Center.** Developers hoped that it would provide the nucleus for a

First Communion procession to St. Stanilaus Kostka Church, Noble Street, 1985. This scene reflects the white, black, and Hispanic composition of the parish and the West Town neighborhood today. (A. Chruscinski)

Northwest Tower, corner of Milwaukee, North, and Damen Avenues, 1985. (G. Lane)

revived Milwaukee Avenue shopping center. Included just off Milwaukee and Mautene Court are a Zayre department store and a Jewel/Osco store which represent new investment in the area.

(H) Continue north on Milwaukee Avenue beyond North Avenue to Concord Place (1632 North) and make a left. At the northwest corner of Milwaukee, Damen, and North Avenues stands the twelve-story Art Deco **Northwest Tower.** The architectural firm of Holabird and Root designed this structure, which was built in 1929 just before the Great Depression. The building, which once provided the centerpiece for the area's business community, fell into disrepair and was almost empty by the mid-1970s. A plan for its restoration was announced in 1984.

The elevated station at North Avenue connects Wicker Park with the Loop. The trip takes about eight minutes. As you make the turn on Concord Place, you will pass under the elevated tracks and find yourself on a comfortable and attractive street of elegant greystones. This is a good introduction to the Wicker Park area, a neighborhood of large homes and apartment buildings, which has been undergoing some gentrification since the late 1970s.

(I) Turn left on Leavitt (2200 West) and proceed two blocks south to Pierce (1532 North) and make another left. Continue two blocks east to Damen Avenue (2000 West). Pierce is a street of fine homes. The house at 2141, with a Romanesque front, has an Orthodox cross on its peak. Built in the 1890s, it served as the home of the Ukrainian archbishop of the Russian Orthodox Holy Virgin Protection Church from 1954 to 1971. Herman Weinhardt built the gingerbread house at 2137 W. Pierce in 1888. Hans Runge constructed the building known as the **Paderewski House** across the street at 2138 two years earlier. The famous Polish pianist once played here.

(J) Turn right on Damen and go six blocks south to Division Street (1200 North). Wicker Park, on your left at Schiller and Damen, gives this community its name. In the 1880s mansions surrounded the small park and provided a center for the wealthy German Protestant families who lived in the area. This part of the Milwaukee Avenue corridor went into decline early in the twentieth century.

As you continue south on Damen, you will be passing through a predominantly Hispanic community. While some gentrification has taken place here, this area is still in need of widespread revitalization. Nelson Algren used this neighborhood as the location for many of his novels.

(K) Turn right on Division Street and go two blocks west to Leavitt (2200 West), then turn left (south). **St. Mary of Nazareth Medical Center** and its new emergency helicopter pad stand on the southwest corner of Leavitt and Division. In 1976 this futuristic building replaced a seventy-five year old structure that stood on the corner of Haddon and Leavitt. The Polish community founded St. Mary's as a twenty-four bed hospital in 1894. By the 1930s over two hundred patients could be treated in the facility. The present facility includes nearly five hundred beds. It is operated by the Sisters of the Holy Family of Nazareth.

*Front door and canopy, Holy
Trinity Cathedral, 1121 N. Leavitt,
1980. The simple, flowing patterns
seen here reveal the genius of
Louis Sullivan, who designed this
landmark Chicago church for
Russian immigrants in 1903.*
(G. Lane)

(L) Louis Sullivan's picturesque **Holy Trinity Orthodox
Cathedral** stands on the southeast corner of Haddon
and Leavitt. This is the first of the Orthodox and Greek
Rite churches which adorn this community. Immigrants
from the Carpatho-Ukraine founded the parish in 1892
as St. Vladimir's Russian Orthodox Church. The
congregation engaged Louis Sullivan to build a parish
church that would reflect the provincial churches of
their homeland. Czar Nicholas II donated $4,000 for the
construction of the building. Patriarch Tikhon of Moscow
consecrated the house of worship in 1903. The Russian
Orthodox Church designated this church a cathedral in
1923. It was placed on the National Register of Historic
Places in 1976 and designated a Chicago landmark in 1979.

(M) Continue two blocks south on Leavitt to Cortez (1032
North) and turn right (west). Make a left at Oakley
Boulevard (2300 West). On the northeast corner stands
St. Vladimir's Ukrainian Orthodox Cathedral. This
church, built in 1911, marks the entrance of our tour
into the Ukrainian Village. The parish, which serves
Orthodox Ukrainians, was the first institution
constructed by Ukrainians in the neighborhood.

(N) Go south on Oakley. **St. Helen's Catholic Church** stands on the southwest corner of Augusta and Oakley. Organized in 1913 to serve the growing number of Polish families in the predominantly Irish parish of **St. Mark's** just to the west, this parish reflects the ethnic diversity of the neighborhood which is often called the Ukrainian Village. Parishioners began construction of the present church in 1964. It seats 1,100 people and is built in the form of a fish, the symbol of Christ. At one time more than 2,500 families attended St. Helen's. Today over 1,000 families belong to the parish. While Polish Americans predominate, a growing number of parishioners from the Philipines and India attend services at St. Helen's. Spanish-speaking families tend to belong to St. Mark's.

(O) Continue south on Oakley. A huge neo-Byzantine structure dominates the northeast corner of Rice and Oakley and the surrounding neighborhood. This is **St. Nicholas Ukrainian Catholic Cathedral,** built between 1913 and 1914 by Ukrainian Catholics who follow the Eastern Rite of the Roman Catholic Church. They are sometimes called Uniate Catholics. The founders of this parish came from the western part of the Ukraine (Galicia) and the Carpatho-Ukraine. The parish originally called itself Ruthenian rather than Ukrainian, but this designation was changed on January 28, 1923 as a expression of the people's growing national consciousness.

The parish was founded by fifty-one Rusins (Ukrainians) on December 31, 1905. This group purchased a former Danish Lutheran church at Superior and Bickerdike for $8,000 for their first house of worship. By 1911 it was clear that the growing congregation needed a larger space for worship. After a two-year delay, Bishop Ortynsky blessed the cornerstone of St. Nicholas on November 27, 1913. The congregation celebrated the first divine liturgy in the new edifice on Christmas Day (Julian calendar), January 7, 1915. From that time on St. Nicholas has provided a communal center for Chicago's growing Ukrainian population. In 1968 a division took place which saw 1,100 families leave St. Nicholas and form a new congregation, the parish of SS. Volodymyr and Olha. The break occurred over the decision by the people of St. Nicholas to follow the Gregorian calendar instead of the traditional Julian calendar.

(Left) Ceiling of St. Nicholas Ukrainian Catholic Cathedral, 1980. This elaborate interior recalls the Byzantine heritage of Chicago's Ukrainian community. (A. Kezys)

(P) Continue south on Oakley past Chicago Avenue. Chicago Avenue features many Ukrainian stores and organizations. The **Ukrainian Institute of Modern Art** is at 2318 W. Chicago Avenue. The Ukrainian Congress Committee of America has an office just south of Chicago Avenue on Oakley. The School of Ukrainian Studies is located nearby at 2228 W. Rice Street.

On the northeast corner of Superior and Oakley stands the modern Byzantine-style **SS. Volodymyr and Olha Church.** This very active parish closely observes Ukrainian ethnic traditions. It follows the Eastern Rite of the Catholic Church and uses the traditional Julian calendar. The building itself was built from 1973 to 1975. The huge mosaic over the main entrance commemorates the conversion of the Ukrainians to Christianity in 988 A.D. by St. Volodymyr. It was executed by Hordynsky, Makarenko, and Baransky.

SS. Volodymr and Olha Church, northeast corner Superior and Oakley, 1985. The Ukrainian Catholic community split in two in the l960s over the use of the Gregorian Calendar. This parish staunchly observes the traditional Julian calendar and Ukrainian liturgy. (G. Lane)

(Top left) Southwest corner Oakley and Walton, 1985. The Ukrainian Village neighborhood is attracting a number of young professionals to its well-kept apartments and neatly manicured lawns. The area is easily accessible from the Loop and the Near North Side. (J. Ficner)

(Left) Ukrainian-American Bookstore, 2315 W. Chicago Ave. 1985. The Chicago Avenue and Oakley Boulevard area is home for many Ukrainian businesses. (D. Pacyga)

Roberto Clemente High School, corner of Division and Western, 1985. This modern high school, named for the late Puerto Rican baseball star, reflects the changing ethnic character of the neighborhood. St. Mary of Nazareth Hospital appears to the right of the school. (G. Lane)

(Q) Continue one block south to Huron Street (700 North) and turn right (west). On the northeast corner is the parish church of the **Sacred Heart.** Slovaks also settled in this neighborhood. In 1911 they purchased the Bethlehem Norwegian United Church on Huron and Center (Racine) Avenue and dedicated it on October 22 of that year. Five years later ground was broken for a new parish church at Huron and Oakley. Archbishop George W. Mundelein dedicated the present church on January 17, 1917. Slovaks and Carpatho-Ukrainians were nearby neighbors in Europe. They settled close to each other here as well as in other parts of Chicago.

(R) Go one block west on Huron to Western Avenue. Turn right and go two blocks north to Chicago Avenue. Just west of the intersection of Chicago and Western stands the **Ukrainian National Museum** at 2453 W. Chicago. This institution is a major cultural and historical anchor for the Ukrainian community on the Northwest Side.

Humboldt Boulevard north from Palmer Place, c. 1909. By 1900 Palmer Square had developed into an upper middle-class residential area. It is part of the boulevard system connecting Humboldt Park with Logan Square. Many of these fine homes are now being restored.
(C.R. Childs, courtesy G. Schmalgemeier)

(S) Continue north on Western Avenue. On the southeast corner of Division and Western stands **Roberto Clemente High School.** This modern building serves the Northwest Side and was named for the famous baseball player from Puerto Rico. It provides an important symbol for Chicago's growing Puerto Rican community. Clemente High School replaced the older Tuley High School in the mid-1970s.

Between Hirsch and LeMoyne streets on your right you will see **St. Elizabeth Hospital,** opened in 1887 by the Poor Handmaids of Jesus Christ, which today is a 343-bed facility serving the health-care needs of this multi-ethnic community.

(T) Turn left on North Avenue (1600 N.) and drive twelve blocks west to Humboldt Boulevard (3000 West). This shopping strip along North Avenue developed in the late nineteenth century after the construction of the Northwest Side Elevated line. Originally German and Scandinavian stores predominated in the area. Later Jewish and Polish enterprises dotted the strip. Today Hispanic businesses line the street.

Humboldt Park, first organized in 1869 and designed by architect William Le Baron Jenney, lies to the south of North Avenue between California and Kedzie Avenues. This park includes the only non-lakefront beach in Chicago. The famous landscape architect, Jens Jensen, did much to enhance the design of this park in the early twentieth century.

Old Holy Resurrection Serbian Orthodox Church, 3062 W. Palmer, 1985. This Palmer Square church, built in 1910 by a Protestant congregation, today serves a Serbian Orthodox community.
(G. Lane)

(U) Turn right at Humboldt Boulevard and go six blocks north to Palmer Street (2200 North). This boulevard was part of the greenbelt designed to circle Chicago in the 1870s. German and Scandinavian families built fine homes along this greenway in the 1890s, and they established several Protestant churches which are still located on the boulevard and are serving Hispanic and black congregations. By the time of World War I, Jewish families had settled in the area. Today the neighborhood is predominantly Puerto Rican.

(V) Turn left at Palmer Square and go west to Kedzie Avenue (3200 West). On the east side of Humboldt Boulevard at Palmer is **St. Sylvester Church.** This parish was founded in 1884 to serve English-speaking, that is Irish, families in what was then the Town of Jefferson, Illinois. The cornerstone of the present church was laid on August 19, 1906. Celtic crosses adorn the church, recalling the ethnicity of its founders. Today about two thousand families belong to St. Sylvester parish. These families are of predominantly Hispanic, Polish, German, and Irish backgrounds. St. Sylvester's is a very active Catholic parish.

W Both sides of Palmer Square are occupied by impressive residential structures. Some of these are mansions; others are greystone and other types of apartment buildings. The **Old Holy Resurrection Serbian Orthodox Church** is located at 3062 West Palmer Boulevard. The building was constructed in 1910 by the architectural firm of Worthmann and Steinbach. Palmer Square, along with the larger Logan Square neighborhood, witnessed a rise in land values in the 1970s and 1980s. Young urban professionals have moved into the neighborhood over the last ten years. Residents began an annual Palmer Square Arts Fair in 1978. The square itself is named after Potter Palmer, the famous Chicago real estate developer.

X Turn right on Kedzie and go north toward Logan Square. This boulevard, which connects Logan and Palmer Squares, is also lined with fine homes and apartment buildings. Scandinavians, primarily Norwegians, and Germans owned many of these homes. Later Jewish and Polish families predominated on the boulevard. Today the area is experiencing some regentrification.

Illinois Centennial Monument, Kedzie at Logan Boulevard, 1985. This stately column was erected in 1918 to commemorate the first one hundred years of Illinois. (G. Lane)

Y Continue north on Kedzie to Logan Square (2800 North). As you approach Logan Square, named after Civil War general John A. Logan, you will see Henry Bacon's **Illinois Centennial Monument** dedicated in October 1918. Over ten thousand spectators turned out for the dedication. Evelyn Longman's reliefs depicting the state's history circle the base of the fifty-foot column. This monument gives the entire area a noble quality.

Z Proceed east on Logan Boulevard and follow the signs to the Kennedy Expressway. **St. John Berchmans Church** (1907) stands on the southeast corner of Logan Boulevard and Maplewood Avenue. The archdiocese organized this congregation as a national parish for Belgian Catholics in Chicago in 1903. The parish buildings occupy a full city block. Today Spanish and Polish families make-up the majority of parishioners of this active parish.

The tour ends at the Kennedy Expressway.

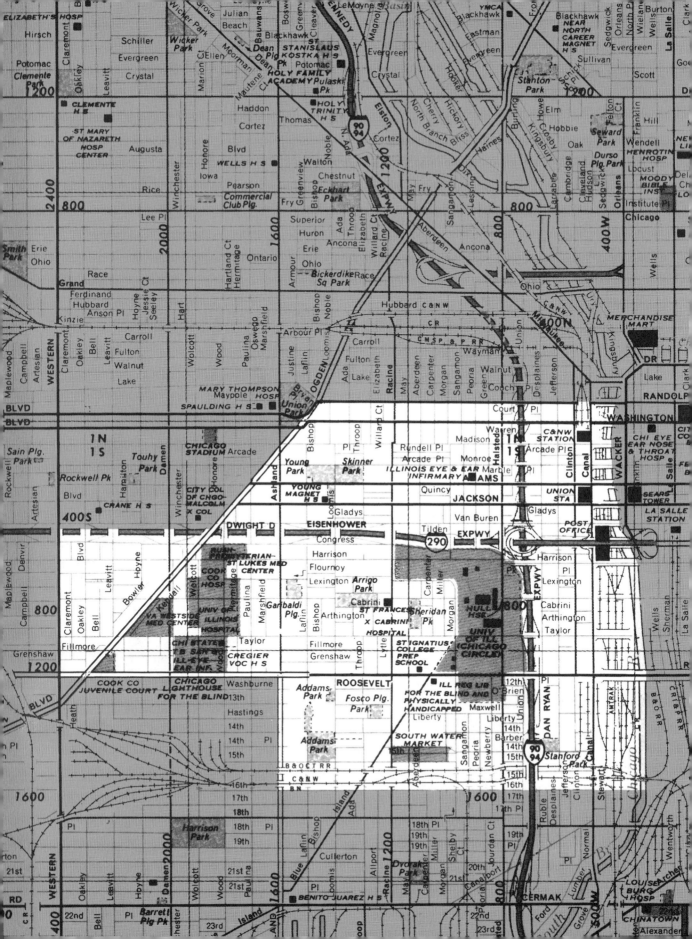

Near West Side

6

Long before the Chicago Fire of 1871 began at DeKoven and Jefferson Streets, the Near West Side was an area of stark contrasts. Wealthy Chicagoans built spacious homes just west of Haymarket Square, the city's open-air market at Randolph and Desplaines Streets. Before long this, section was known as an exclusive residential district, and its boundaries extended westward to Union Park at the intersection of Randolph and Ogden.

As in other nineteenth-century American cities, the rich and poor on Chicago's Near West Side lived close together. At Harrison and Halsted Streets, for example, the notorious "squatter" district known as "Kansas" was composed of several hundred two-room shanties. According to a reporter in 1865, residents used the front room of the house for living quarters, and it contained all the essentials of domestic life: bed, cupboard, and shelves filled with crockery. Cows and pigs lived in the rear room, and creeping vines covered the "solitary window."

From the 1850s on, the Near West Side was a port of entry for immigrants: first German, Bohemian, French, and Irish, and later Eastern European Jews, Greeks, Italians, Mexicans, and Southern blacks. But far from being a "melting pot," the neighborhood was always divided along ethnic, economic, and racial lines. Although large sections of the Near West Side have undergone urban renewal, a number of institutions remain, symbols of the powerful drive to preserve ethnic and religious identities in the New World.

The Near West Side of Chicago encompasses a fairly large area, bounded by Kinzie Street on the north, the Chicago River on the east, the Burlington railroad tracks at l6th Street on the south, and Ogden Avenue on the west.

During its heyday as an exclusive residential district between the Civil War and the turn of the century, the Near West Side included some of Chicago's most fashionable homes and prominent institutions. Although only a few nineteenth-century buildings remain standing today, they evoke a sense of what the area must have been like a century ago. Carter H. Harrison II, five-term mayor of Chicago, recalled that when he was growing up on the Near West Side in the late l860s, only six houses stood on Ashland Avenue between Madison and Congress. Harrison's boyhood home, located at the southwest corner of Ashland

The Episcopal Cathedral of SS.
Peter and Paul, northwest corner of
Washington Boulevard and Peoria
Streets. Erected in 1852 as the
Church of the Atonement, this
limestone structure was enlarged
in 1861-62 after being designated
a cathedral. Once the pride of the
West Side Gold Coast, SS. Peter
and Paul's was destroyed by fire
in 1921.
(Courtesy Episcopal diocese of Chicago)

(Top right) Washington Boulevard
looking west from Bishop Street,
1937. The lofty spire and
limestone facade of the First
Congregational Church (1870) can
be seen just across Union Park in
the distance.
(Chicago Park District, courtesy R. Wroble)

(Bottom right) Hull House complex,
Halsted at Polk Street, c. 1920.
Within six years of its founding,
Hull House was flanked by the
Butler Art Gallery and the
Children's Building. The Hull
House complex, though not the
original house, was demolished in
1963 to make way for the
University of Illinois Chicago
Circle Campus.
(Courtesy Jane Addams Collection, University
of Illinois at Chicago Library)

and Jackson, had been built in 1858 by H.H. Honore, one of
the West Side's early pioneers. Because of its proximity to
the center of the city, however, the area was soon built up.
Washington Boulevard emerged as one of the neighborhood's
most elegant streets, and it contained such prominent
churches as the Episcopal Cathedral of SS. Peter and Paul
(1861) at Peoria Street, First Congregational (1870) at Racine
Avenue, and the Union Park Congregational (1871) at
Ashland Avenue. Union Park Congregational was the
birthplace of the Chicago Theological Seminary, established
in 1858; and First Congregational at Washington Boulevard
and Racine Avenue claimed the distinction of housing the
city government for six weeks after the Chicago Fire.

In the years immediately following the fire, a number of
wealthy Chicagoans looked to the Near West Side as their
future neighborhood. The old residential district along
Washington Boulevard expanded west and south. According
to the *Inter Ocean*, in 1886 the area west of Racine Avenue
between Van Buren and Taylor was the fastest growing
neighborhood on the West Side. The newspaper predicted
that improved transportation over the river, together with
the extension of streetcar lines would make this part of
Chicago "even more attractive . . . as a private residence
district." As the real estate columns of the *Inter Ocean*
attest, during the 1880s and 1890s expensive greystones
and flat buildings were constructed along Macalister Place
(Lexington Avenue), Loomis, Winthrop Court (Bishop), and
Laflin.

Despite new construction along Jackson and Ashland,
however, the Near West Side residential district was

NEW COOK COUNTY
HOSPITAL,
HARRISON & SO,
LINCOLN STS,
CHICAGO

Cook County Hospital, 1835 W. Harrison Street, c.1916. When this photo was taken, Cook County Hospital was a new building in the West Side Medical Center.
(P.L. Huckins, courtesy G. Schmalgemeier)

essentially an island in the midst of a rapidly expanding city. Already in the 1880s, Chicago's business district was moving west of the river, and this trend continued after the turn of the century. Single-family dwellings were demolished to make way for warehouses and light manufacturing plants which clustered around the Randolph Street Market.

Aside from the encroachment of business on the east, the Ashland Boulevard residential district was further limited by the hospital district to the west and the burgeoning ghetto to the south. By 1884 the outlines of the West Side Medical Center were clearly established. Cook County Hospital, the area's main institution, dominated the site bounded by Harrison, Wood, Polk, and Wolcott Streets. Nearby were such flourishing institutions as Rush Medical College, at Harrison and Wood; Rush Medical Hospital, on Wood Street between Congress and Harrison; the College of Physicians and Surgeons, Harrison and Honore; Chicago Homeopathic College, at Flournoy and Wood; and the Women's Medical College on Wolcott.

Although Ashland Boulevard retained its reputation as one of Chicago's most prestigious addresses throughout the 1880s, change was coming swiftly. The construction of Zion Temple in 1885 at the corner of Washington Boulevard and Ogden Avenue offered unmistakable proof that the area's ethnic composition was expanding. Affluent German Jews

*Zion Temple, Washington
Boulevard and Ogden Avenue,
c.1906. Adler & Sullivan designed
this magnificent synagogue in
1885. In less than ten years,
however, most of the congregation
had moved to the Grand
Boulevard neighborhood on
Chicago's South Side.*
(Courtesy Chicago Historical Society)

hired the architectural firm of Adler & Sullivan to design
their magnificent temple, and it compared favorably with the
Third Presbyterian Church (1878) at Ashland and Ogden,
and the new Church of the Epiphany (1885) at Ashland and
Adams.

While improved transportation linked this part of the
Near West Side with downtown Chicago, it also played a role
in breaking up the West Side Gold Coast. By the early 1890s
the intersection of Ogden and Madison was one of the city's
busiest. Hundreds of passengers made connections here
betweeen the Ogden Avenue streetcars and the Madison
Street cable lines. New businesses soon opened along
Madison Street, and office buildings and hotels were erected.

The construction of two elevated railroads, along Lake
Street and along Congress Street, led to more commercial
development in the area. Although these elevated trains
provided inexpensive transportation to the central business
district, many longtime residents felt that the railroads
altered the residential character of their neighborhood.
Middle-class families began to leave the Near West Side for
places like Garfield Park, Austin, and Oak Park, which had
not yet been completely built up. Indeed, nearly the entire
congregation of Zion Temple moved en masse to the South
Side where they dedicated Temple Isaiah at 45th and
Vincennes Avenue in 1899.

Signs that the old residential district on the Near West Side was fast disintegrating occurred as early as 1889, when Second Baptist Church celebrated its 25th anniversary at Morgan and Monroe Streets. According to the parish history, nearly the entire membership had moved a mile or more to the west. One writer called the abandonment of the church "wicked," and he urged present members of Second Baptist to disregard "speculative and social ambitions" in their choice of homes. Despite an expensive renovation program in 1890, members of Second Baptist did not move back into the neighborhood. Membership continued to decline, and in 1912 Second Baptist Church became the headquarters of the Aiken Institute.

Events at nearby Haymarket Square in 1886 also accelerated the breakup of the old West Side Gold Coast. As William J. Adelman has written in his books on Chicago labor history, the West Side was the scene of many bitter strikes and conflicts. In the 1880s workingmen fought for the right to strike and to form unions, and they pressed for better wages and an eight-hour day.

On May 4, 1886, workers gathered in Haymarket Square at Randolph and Desplaines Streets to protest the killing of a worker by police at McCormick's Reaper Plant on Blue Island Avenue the day before. Mayor Carter Harrison visited the rally but saw no reason to disperse the throng. Shortly after the mayor went home, however, a reserve force of 176 policemen from the nearby Desplaines Street station arrived on the scene. Before the crowd could obey Captain William Ward's order to leave, a bomb exploded, killing Chicago policeman Matthias J. Degan. The ensuing violence left six police officers and four civilians dead, with scores of injuries on both sides. Hundreds of suspects were arrested and thirty-one people were formally indicted. However, of the eight men who were ultimately charged with conspiracy in the murder of policeman Degan, only two had been present at Haymarket Square when the bomb exploded. The Haymarket trial was one of the most sensational in American jurisprudence. Four of the Haymarket defendants were hanged; one committed suicide; and three were pardoned by Governor John Peter Altgeld in 1893.

The Haymarket affair sent shock waves through Chicago's working-class communities as well as the city's exclusive residential districts where leading businessmen had built their homes. After 1886 many wealthy Chicagoans no longer felt safe living so close to the site of labor upheavals.

The West End Woman's Club, organized in 1892, worked hard to reestablish the prestige of the neighborhood. In 1904 they built a new clubhouse on Ashland Boulevard at

Monroe, which became the headquarters of the West End Neighborhood Improvement Association, chartered in 1905. As its name suggests, the group sought to "improve alleys, streets, and vacant lots," but its larger purpose involved the establishment of Charles Gunther's American War Museum in Garfield Park. Although the museum was never established, efforts to reclaim the West Side's flagging reputation continued. While some institutions such as Epiphany Church remained in the area and expanded their ministries, others closed as their members moved further west.

After more than forty years as separate institutions, First Congregational and Union Park Congregational merged in 1910, following a fire at the old First Church at Washington Boulevard and Racine Avenue. In that same year Dean Walter T. Sumner of the Episcopal Cathedral of SS. Peter and Paul at Washington Boulevard and Peoria Street summed up the vast changes which had occurred on the Near West Side when he declared:

> The Cathedral, formerly the center of the city's most prosperous residential district, now is the hub of the most wretched colony in the world. Degenerates and criminals, fallen women and vicious men make the West Side territory a region of vice and disease.

While the old Washington Boulevard residential district had all but disappeared in the 1890s, so too had the early immigrant communities of the Near West Side. Lured by the prospects of better living and better working conditions in new subdivisions, second- and third-generation Irish, Germans, and Bohemians left the neighborhood by the thousands. In their wake Jewish, Italian, and Greek immigrants began the process of community-building all over again. Like the earlier immigrant settlements, the new communities were shaped by ethnic and religious rivalries.

In the 1850s and 1860s German, Irish, Bohemian, and French immigrants built frame shanties on the prairies within walking distance of the railroad yards and lumber district along the South Branch of the Chicago River. Strictly a working-class district, this part of the Near West Side soon supported a variety of institutions from churches and schools to saloons and small businesses. By the mid-1860s, ethnic and religious rivalries had left their mark on the neighborhood. In 1854 German Lutherans established Immanuel Church on 12th Street just west of Blue Island Avenue. Nearby, the Jesuits of Holy Family parish built a massive Gothic church in 1860. So intense was Irish-German conflict that in 1864 the Lutherans moved away to Taylor and Sangamon Streets. In 1888 members of

First Immanuel Lutheran moved again and built a new Gothic church which stands today at 1124 S. Ashland Avenue.

By the 1860s the Near West Side was honeycombed with Catholic parishes: St. Patrick (Irish) at Adams and Desplaines Streets, St. Wenceslaus (Bohemian) at DeKoven and Desplaines Streets, St. Francis of Assisi (German) at 12th Street and Newberry Avenue, and Notre Dame (French) at Congress and Halsted Streets. As the largest English-speaking Catholic parish in Chicago, Holy Family included a massive parish complex. Five years after the new church opened on 12th Street, the Jesuits established a large boys' school in the 1200 block of S. Morgan, and in 1870 they opened St. Ignatius College next to Holy Family Church. Now known as St. Ignatius College Prep, this building stands on the site of the original Immanuel Lutheran Church.

In 1860 the Religious of the Sacred Heart moved their girls' academy into the neighborhood—by floating it on a scow down the river from the North Side. The intersection of Taylor and Lytle Streets soon became known throughout Chicago for its boarding school, the Academy of the Sacred Heart. From the 1860s through the 1890s, Sacred Heart alumnae included daughters of Chicago's leading businessmen, Protestant and Catholic. Tuition from boarders was used to defray expenses for the "free school" which served girls from Holy Family parish.

The Chicago Fire of 1871 began at the rear of Patrick and Catherine O'Leary's barn at DeKoven and Jefferson Streets, and it spread northward and eastward, destroying nearly the whole central business district and an area as far north as Fullerton Avenue. Most of the West Side remained intact, and following the fire a "gentrification" of sorts occurred. Three years after the fire a reporter noted that, "The region around Mrs. O'Leary's stable has been rebuilt with comfortable dwellings so that one would hardly know there had ever been any fire there." Indeed, a prosperous Bohemian, Anton Kolar, built a two-story and basement brick residence with a white marble front and steps on the site of the former O'Leary house and barn. Still, much of the Near West Side below Taylor Street had all the markings of a slum. Halsted Street, the area's main thoroughfare, was usually impassable, and crowding and sanitation remained perennial problems.

In 1889 Jane Addams and Ellen Gates Starr opened a social settlement in the old C.J. Hull mansion at Halsted and Polk Streets. Known as Hull House, this settlement soon achieved an international reputation, and it remained one of the neighborhood's liveliest institutions throughout the 1950s.

(Top left) St. Patrick's parish complex, Desplaines at Adams Street, early 1870s. The oldest church building in Chicago, St. Patrick's was constructed between 1852 and 1856; the steeples were added in 1885. Over the years, frame houses in the neighborhood were replaced by commercial structures. Today Old St. Pat's stands in the shadow of Presidential Towers, a new luxury apartment complex.
(Courtesy The Chicago Catholic)

(Bottom left) C.J. Hull mansion, built in 1856 at Halsted and Polk Streets, housed the pioneering social settlement founded in 1889 by Jane Addams and Ellen Gates Starr. Now owned by the University of Illinois at Chicago, Hull House has been completely restored.
(Courtesy Jane Addams Hull House Museum, University of Illinois at Chicago)

Interior, Hull House Museum, 800 S. Halsted, c.1980. This fascinating museum documents the history of Hull House and the Near West Side.
(Courtesy Jane Addams Hull House Museum)

Jane Addams (1860-1935). During her long career as head resident of Hull House, Jane Addams sought to improve living and working conditions for Near West Side residents. Among other causes, she championed child labor laws and factory inspections as well as public playgrounds and the first juvenile court in the nation.

(Right) Ellen Gates Starr (1859-1940). In 1890, Jane Addams and her friend and co-worker Ellen Starr decided to call their settlement Hull House, "the name by which it is already known to old residents & the neighborhood."
(Both photos courtesy Jane Addams Collection, University of Illinois at Chicago Library)

In the 1890s the area around Hull House was rapidly changing. In early speeches about the settlement, Jane Addams captured the neighborhood's diversity:

> Between Halsted Street and the river live about ten thousand Italians—Neapolitans, Sicilians, and Calabrians . . . To the south on Twelfth Street are many Germans, and side streets are given over almost entirely to Polish and Russian Jews. Still farther south, these Jewish colonies merge into a huge Bohemian colony . . . To the northwest are Canadian-French, clannish in spite of their long residence in America, and to the north are Irish and first-generation Americans. On the streets directly west and farther north are well-to-do English-speaking families, many of whom own their houses and have lived in the neighborhood for years . . .

Jane Addams took the lead in supporting organized labor, and she was an early advocate of children's rights. In 1895 the *Hull-House Maps and Papers* provided case histories of young children in the area who were employed in sweatshops and as runners in local stores. Despite the efforts of trade union organizers, children often worked thirteen-hour days, especially during the Christmas season. Hull House workers supported legislation aimed at curtailing child labor and improving working conditions in factories. While school attendance laws and minimum age laws helped to alleviate the problem, families continued to eke out an existence through piecework and the sweatshop system of labor.

The influence of Hull House extended beyond Polk and Halsted Streets into the surrounding neighborhood. Jane Addams and her settlement workers launched campaigns for improved sanitation, playgrounds, milk stations, and dispensaries. Aside from its work in the neighborhood, Hull House was one of the few institutions on the Near West Side where immigrants of different ethnic and religious backgrounds socialized. Although not as sensitive as religious institutions were to cultural differences, the settlement endeavored to bring together children and adults of various nationalities for educational and recreational enrichment.

For the majority of the Near West Side's newcomers, however, community life was linked to ethnic institutions. By 1890 an estimated fifteen thousand Eastern European Jews lived in Chicago, mostly west of the river. In contrast to the earlier German-Jewish migration, recent arrivals tended to be poor, and they were predominantly Orthodox in belief. As the Russian *pogroms* intensified, more Eastern European Jews fled to America where they formed new Jewish communities. By the turn of the century Chicago's West Side ghetto extended south from Polk Street to 16th Street and west from Canal Street to Blue Island Avenue. Because so many Jewish immigrants got their start as peddlers on Maxwell Street, the market soon became synonymous with the West Side Jewish community.

In addition to supporting numerous synagogues, West Side Jews were enthusiastic patrons of Yiddish theater, whose productions ranged from adaptations of Shakespeare and Tolstoy to vaudeville. According to Jim Popkin, Wisenfreund's Pavilion Theater on 12th Street near Halsted featured live stage shows as well as "one-reel silent films and . . . short Yiddish skits . . ."

Like Irish, German, and Bohemian residents before them, Jewish families put their mark on the neighborhood. Irving Cutler has noted that more than forty Orthodox synagogues were located within walking distance of the Maxwell Street market. In her history of Congregation Rodfei Zedek, Carole Krucoff painted a vivid portrait of an emerging Jewish neighborhood:

> . . . it served as a haven amidst a strange and confusing world. It had the small synagogues where men went daily to pray. Women, who took no official role in religious services, usually came to the synagogue only on the Sabbath, and they sat apart from their men in a curtained gallery. . . . In the streets, women could be seen wearing wigs, the traditional symbol of a Jewish wife. Bearded men walked the wooden sidewalks wearing Russian boots and caps. Everybody spoke Yiddish, the language of their old home. Life, for the most part, centered around home and synagogue, with few people venturing outside the neighborhood.

Among the largest West Side Jewish institutions were Anshe Sholom at Canal and Liberty, Anshe Kneseth Israel at Judd (12th Place) and Clinton, and the Jewish Training School on Judd, near Clinton. Just as Irish Catholic and German Lutheran immigrants had battled for control of the neighborhood, now Catholic and Jewish newcomers continued the fight. Neighborhood toughs taunted Jewish peddlers and tried to remove the phylacteries and beards of Orthodox Jews. Catholic nuns had been familiar figures in the area since the 1860s, but as Catholic families moved away from the West Side, women religious felt they were in alien territory.

By the 1890s, for example, St. Aloysius Convent and High School at 13th and Jefferson Street was a Catholic institution in a predominantly Jewish neighborhood. Catholic-Jewish rivalries intensified, and on Christmas Day, 1895, the sisters' convent was the target of an attack. According to the Chicago *Times*, a crowd of hoodlums hurled stones and missiles at the building, "while the mob,

Children of the Hull House area, c.1915. Thousands of youngsters regarded the Near West Side's unpaved streets and alleys as their playground. The proud owner of a tricyle poses with his friends.

(Courtesy Chicago Historical Society)

shouting with epithets of derision, cheered each new recruit and yelled with delight as glass was broken in windows . . ."

Although the Sisters of Charity of the Blessed Virgin Mary continued to staff Holy Family grammar school, they closed St. Aloysius High School in 1896. Three years later the nuns opened St. Mary High School, the first central Catholic high school for girls in Chicago. This institution, located at Taylor and Cypress (Hoyne), drew its pupils from all sections of the city, especially from Catholic parishes which had been established west of Holy Family in the 1880s and 1890s.

When the Religious of the Sacred Heart established their academy on Taylor Street in 1860, the surrounding neighborhood was nearly all prairie. By the turn of the century, however, the Near West Side had become one of the most densely populated districts in all of Chicago. In 1907 when the nuns merged the day school on Taylor Street with their new boarding school in Lake Forest, they sold the former Sacred Heart Academy and its eight-acre site to the Chicago Hebrew Institute. Incorporated in 1903, this institution touched the lives of thousands of West Side Jewish families.

Through the generosity of Julius Rosenwald, the Chicago Hebrew Institute established its headquarters on Taylor Street between Lytle and Throop. When three leaders of the Jewish community visited the old academy early in 1908, they found "The beautiful spacious gardens were somewhat neglected and the walls around them were high and solid permitting no view to the outer world." After inspecting the property, they stretched "full-length on the long grass and dreamed of the great possibilities these grounds held for Jewish Chicago."

From the moment it opened its doors in September 1908, Chicago Hebrew Institute was a bustling community center. Although a fire in 1910 leveled the old Sacred Heart Academy, a new $135,000 gymnasium was built on the site in 1915. Even as the Hebrew Institute was becoming the West Side's best known Jewish institution, however, Jewish families were leaving the neighborhood. Like German and Irish families of an earlier generation, they moved further west in the city into the Lawndale area.

The congregation known as Anshe Sholom, for example, built a magnificent new temple in 1910 at Ashland and Polk. But after only fifteen years at this location, the congregation decided to move further west, to Lawndale. In 1927 a new Anshe Sholom Temple was dedicated at Polk Street and Independence Boulevard, three miles west of the old Jewish ghetto.

Another pioneer West Side congregation which moved to Lawndale was Congregation Anshe Kneseth Israel, founded in 1886. After the Baltimore & Ohio Railroad purchased the old synagogue at Clinton and Judd Streets, the congregation built a magnificent 3,500-seat synagogue at Douglas Boulevard and Homan Avenue in 1913.

Unlike the Jews and Italians who emigrated with their families to the Near West Side in the 1890s, the early wave of Greek immigrants tended to be single males. While Greek immigrants worked at a variety of occupations, many were employed in the Randolph Street market where they competed with Italians for control of the city's fruit and vegetable business. So many Greeks settled in the area bounded by Harrison, Halsted, Polk, and Blue Island that it became known as the Delta, after the triangular shaped Greek letter. According to Andrew T. Kopan, the Delta "became Chicago's famous 'Greektown'—the oldest, largest and most important settlement of Greeks in the United States." In addition to coffeehouses and numerous businesses along Halsted Street, the Near West Side supported one of the Greek community's oldest parishes, Holy Trinity.

The first Italian Catholic parish on the West Side, Holy Guardian Angel Church was located at 717 W. Forquer (Arthington) Street from 1899 to 1959. A new church building constructed at 860 W. Cabrini Street was razed in 1963 to make way for the University of Illinois Chicago Circle Campus.
(Courtesy Madonna Center Archives)

Beginning in 1897, members of this congregation worshiped in an old Episcopal church at 1101 S. Peoria Street. After a division in Holy Trinity Church, however, a new congregation known as St. Basil's was formed in 1926. In the following year the new Greek congregation purchased the former Anshe Sholom temple at Polk and Ashland. Although few Greeks now live in the area, St. Basil's continues to thrive, especially during the Easter season when families return from all over the city and suburbs to participate in the liturgy.

Of all the newcomers to the Near West Side in the 1890s, the Italians stayed the longest and formed a community that lingers on in the shadow of the University of Illinois. Although the Italians shared a common religion with their Irish, French, and German neighbors, they were not welcomed by the congregations at Holy Family, Notre Dame, or St. Francis of Assisi. A small group of Italians who worshiped in the basement of Holy Family Church formed the nucleus of the West Side's first Italian parish, Holy

Guardian Angel. While the Italian church, built in 1899 at 717 W. Forquer (Arthington) Street, could not rival older ethnic churches in size, it became an important institution in the lives of Italian Catholic families. Indeed, when Holy Guardian Angel church and school were razed to make way for the Dan Ryan Expressway, parishioners built another complex at 860 W. Cabrini Street in 1959.

By the 1920s Italians were the most numerous ethnic group on the Near West Side as well as the area's largest Catholic group. Once unwelcome at Holy Family and Notre Dame parishes, Italians now formed the backbone of these older ethnic churches. They also supported a range of new Catholic institutions, among them Our Lady of Pompeii parish at Lexington and Lytle; Columbus Extension Hospital, 811 S. Lytle, later renamed St. Frances Cabrini Hospital; St. Callistus parish at Bowler and Leavitt; and Madonna Center, the city's first Catholic settlement house, 718 S. Loomis Street.

Over the years many Catholic pastors were less than enthusiastic about Hull House and its influence on their parishioners. Some priests charged that Jane Addams was anticlerical because she permitted groups such as the Giordano Bruno Society to meet at the settlement on Halsted Street. Other Catholic critics charged that women religious accomplished as much as Jane Addams, but that their work was ignored by the press. Whatever their differences, local churches and Hull House battled together against the influence of bootleggers. During the Prohibition era, Taylor Street was the scene of many gun battles between police and the Genna gang. Indeed, the intersection of 12th and Halsted Streets was known as Bootlegger's Square, after the beer runners who operated in the area. The prospect of easy money appealed to youths who had grown up in one of the city's poorest neighborhoods, and local settlements and churches offered none of the excitement associated with gangsters. Even after Prohibition, gangs continued to exert tremendous influence among West Side youth.

In the 1920s blacks and Mexicans moved to the Near West Side, and to a certain extent they replaced earlier Jewish immigrants who had moved further west in the city. Although Chicago's black population was concentrated on the South Side, a number of black families settled west of Blue Island Avenue. Among the early black institutions in the area were Zion Hill Baptist Church, 1515 W. Hastings Street; Tercentenary A.M.E. Church, 1324 W. 14th Street; and St. Joseph's Catholic Mission, 1413 W. 13th Street.

Mexican immigrants recruited to work on railroad gangs formed the core of the Near West Side's Hispanic community. As the last major Catholic ethnic group to settle in the area,

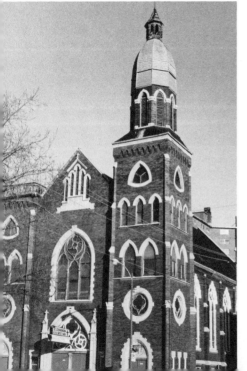

Zion Hill Missionary Baptist Church, northeast corner Ashland and Hastings, 1985. Zion Hill was organized in 1925 with Rev. H.R. Stephenson, pastor; the congregation now worships in a new building one block north. This original building is used by the St. Stephenson M.B. Church. (G. Lane)

the Mexicans also put their mark on the neighborhood. In 1927 George Cardinal Mundelein designated St. Francis of Assisi church at 12th Street and Newberry Avenue as a Spanish-speaking parish. The former German parish soon flourished, becoming Chicago's preeminent Spanish parish. Indeed, although few Mexican families live in the area today, they still come to St. Francis of Assisi in large numbers for Masses, baptisms, weddings, and funerals.

Continuing the West Side's tradition of separate ethnic institutions, the Cordi Marian Sisters from Mexico established a settlement in 1936 at 1100 S. May Street, in the former St. Joseph's Home for Working Girls. Like nearby Hull House, the Mexican center offered English classes as well as instructions in art, music, and crafts. However, the Cordi Marian settlement was one of the few places in the neighborhood where Mexican parents allowed young boys and girls to socialize. Sister Marie Ramirez, who began her work in Chicago in 1939, recalled that Mexican parents in the neighborhood refused to allow their daughters to go on dates without chaperones. In addition to interceding on behalf of young women for changes in this age-old custom, the nuns also responded to the needs of working mothers during World War II. Since the dedication of a new facility in 1957, Cordi Marian Center has been an agency of Catholic Charities in Chicago, and it now serves children of many different ethnic and religious backgrounds.

By the 1950s the Near West Side was still a neighborhood divided along ethnic, racial, and religious lines. The area's public housing projects further reinforced racial divisions in the neighborhood. The first public housing project, begun in the midst of the Depression, was known as the Jane Addams Homes. Built on the site of the former Sacred Heart Academy and the Chicago Hebrew Institute, the project included three- and four-story walk-up apartments which stretched from Cabrini Street on the north to 12th Street on the south. Although the Addams Homes (1938) remained racially integrated throughout the 1940s, the housing complex soon became all-black thereafter.

In large part because it was built on the site of the West Side's old black settlement, the Robert Brooks Homes at 14th and Loomis housed a population that was predominantly black. Like the Addams Homes, the Brooks project (1943) provided modern living quarters in one of the city's oldest neighborhoods. While the need for new housing continued, increased construction costs forced the Chicago Housing Authority to build high-rise apartments rather than walk-ups. The Grace Abbott Homes, named for the director of the Immigrants' Protective League at Hull House,

Cordi Marian Center, 1100 S. May Street, 1985. Cordi Marian was founded in 1936 to serve Mexican families on the Near West Side. The present facility, dedicated in 1957 and enlarged in 1980, has a large day-care enrollment as well as other social and religious services. (G. Lane)

dramatically changed the character of this part of the West Side. This complex, which opened in 1955, included seven high-rise buildings which dominated a ten-square-block site just south of 12th Street (Roosevelt Road). According to Devereux Bowly, the Abbott Homes were the forerunner of the massive public housing highrises built on the South Side in the 1950s and 1960s: "the overall feeling is forbidding and the human scale is completely lost."

Although many Italian families moved further west to Austin, Oak Park, and River Forest as they climbed the economic ladder, a sizable number remained in "Little Italy" purchasing homes and improving their property. Unlike other Chicago neighborhoods in the 1950s where ethnic and racial groups clashed, this part of the Near West Side was relatively peaceful. While Italians, blacks, Mexicans, and Puerto Ricans lived in close proximity to one another, there was little overt hostility—and little sense of unity. In a report on the history of the Near West Side's Planning Board, Paul B. Johnson noted that, "Suspicion and fear between groups were matched by suspicion within groups."

The announcement on February 24, 1961 that the University of Illinois's new Chicago campus would be constructed on urban renewal land at Harrison and Halsted Streets came as a shock to area residents, especially those who had worked closely with the local planning board. Although construction of the Congress Street (Eisenhower) and Dan Ryan expressways had resulted in the relocation of many families, residents were confident that their neighborhood had a promising future. According to Anthony Sorrentino, the Near West Side was one of the most important neighborhoods in Chicago:

> There were fifty thousand residents, some fifteen hundred small-business people, and three or four hundred larger businesses and industries within its' boundaries. It is close to downtown Chicago and Lake Michigan and is situated in the front yard of the medical center, which by 1949 had renovated several blocks of old, long-neglected buildings . . . The results demonstrated the possibilities of reclaiming blighted neighborhoods when concerted action by owners could be organized.

As George Rosen has recounted in his book, *The Siting of the University of Illinois at Chicago Circle*, the Harrison-Halsted location was not the first choice for the university's new campus. Mayor Richard J. Daley, for example, favored a rail terminal site east of the river between Congress Street and Roosevelt Road. Since 1946 students had attended classes in makeshift quarters on Navy

Pier. Among the sites considered for a permanent campus were the Riverside Golf Club west of Chicago, Meigs Field, and the Garfield Park neighborhood.

Florence Giovangelo Scala, a member of the Near West Side Planning Board, organized pickets to protest the city's decision to locate the university on the Near West Side. Few neighborhoods in Chicago possessed the resources for such a fight. Undeterred, Scala and local women picketed City Hall, and she pleaded the neighborhood's cause at mass meetings and in interviews with the press. Members of Holy Guardian Angel parish felt especially betrayed since their new parish complex on Cabrini Street would be demolished to make way for the university.

Although legal action in state and federal courts continued into 1963, these efforts did not result in a change of site for the university campus. According to Rosen, business groups and newspapers which had endorsed the earlier railroad site for the University of Illinois campus eventually approved the Harrison-Halsted site because it would protect and strengthen the city's business district.

To make way for the new campus, eleven buildings in the Hull House complex were demolished. University officials agreed to restore the original Hull House built in 1856 and the residents' dining room, which dated from 1905.

The stark, modern campus of the University of Illinois opened on February 22, 1965. Its location near the circle interchange of the Eisenhower, Kennedy, and Dan Ryan expressways led to its designation as the University of Illinois, Chicago Circle campus. Unlike the University of Chicago, Loyola, and Northwestern, Chicago Circle had no dormitories. Strictly a commuter college, the University of Illinois provided thousands of Chicago area students with the opportunity to attend college while they lived at home.

View of Lexington Avenue across Vernon Park, c.1930s. In the 1880s, Macalister Place (Lexington) was the Near West Side Irish Gold Coast. Alderman Johnny Powers, who controlled the old 19th Ward from 1888 until 1927, lived in the frame house (far left). The row houses built by William J. Onahan still stand today at 1254-62 W. Lexington. The street's changing ethnic composition is reflected by Our Lady of Pompeii parish (far right), founded by Italian Catholics in 1910. The park is now Victor Arrigo Park.
(Courtesy The Chicago Catholic)

By 1975 Circle campus claimed 20,000 alumni, most of whom live in the metropolitan area. Now in its twentieth year, the university has become one of the West Side's best known landmarks. But a good number of neighborhood residents still remember and mourn the loss of the Italian community which flourished in the Harrison-Halsted area. Recently, the university changed its name to the University of Illinois at Chicago, and plans are underway for a $20 million student dormitory, which will be the first on campus.

As city and university officials had hoped, the construction of the University of Illinois sparked a residential and institutional building boom on the Near West Side. During the 1970s new townhouses and apartments were constructed throughout the area ranging from the Campus Green complex at 901 S. Ashland; Circle Park Apartments, 1111 S. Ashland; Westgate Condominiums, just west of Harrison and Racine; Garden Court Townhomes at Polk and Racine; Academy Circle at Jackson and Loomis; and Uplift Village at Morgan and Maxwell. Among the new institutions built in the area were the Circle Court Shopping Center, 500 S. Racine; Whitney Young Magnet High School, 211 S. Laflin; the Chicago Police Training Academy, 1300 W. Jackson; and the Illinois Regional Library for the Blind and Handicapped, 1055 W. Roosevelt Road.

Third- and fourth-generation Italian families who were not displaced by the university soon discovered that the value of their homes had increased dramatically. In 1980, for example, the median value of owner-occupied units in the area bounded by Polk, Loomis, Roosevelt, and Ashland was $102,000. This figure is all the more significant because the area adjoins the Jane Addams public housing project.

Since the mid-1970s, widespread rehabilitation has occurred north of the Eisenhower Expressway as well as west of the University of Illinois Medical Center complex. Residents in the 1500 block of Jackson Boulevard, for example, have carefully restored the street's nineteenth-century homes. In the process, they have reclaimed their block's reputation as a fashionable residential area, now officially known as the Jackson Boulevard Historic District.

The Tri-Taylor Historic District, located in the shadow of the West Side Medical Center, is another part of the Near West Side which provides a link with the past. In contrast to the Jackson Boulevard mansions, the streets west of Ogden are lined with row houses, frame structures, and flat buildings. Established as a working-class district in the 1870s and 1880s, Tri-Taylor remains a tightly knit residential community of Italians and Mexicans. Area residents no

University Hall, administration building, University of Illinois at Chicago. 1985. Opened in 1965 on the site of the old Italian community near Halsted and Harrison, the University of Illinois campus is located just west of Chicago's Loop. (G. Lane)

longer fear that the Medical Center will claim their homes under eminent domain. Indeed, through the efforts of the State of Illinois Medical Center Commission, more than ten buildings in the area were sold in 1984 to owners who promised to restore building exteriors as part of an overall renovation program.

In the l980s the old garment district bounded by Monroe Street, Halsted Street, the Eisenhower Expressway, and Racine Avenue experienced a rebirth as the Westgate Mill district. Five- and six-story brick buildings, where Jewish and Italian immigrants once earned their livings, have been converted into commercial lofts, offices, and condominiums. Among the renovated structures are the Westgate Center, 910 W. Van Buren, 310 and 331 S. Peoria; the Rice building, 815 W. Van Buren; and the Sangamon Lofts, 913 W. Van Buren and 411 S. Sangamon. Artist Richard Haas has transformed the exterior of the Reliable Corporation, 1001 W. Van Buren, with a trompe l'oeil mural which depicts the Civic Center along Congress Street as proposed by city planner Daniel Burnham in 1909.

One of the newest developments to occur on the Near West Side has been the construction of high-rise apartments just east of the Kennedy Expressway along Madison Street. In 1980 only 500 persons lived in the area bounded by Madison Street, the Chicago River, l6th Street, and Halsted Street. Presidential Towers, the new apartment complex at Madison and Clinton, will change all that. Built on the site of the old Madison Street skid row, the four sleek high-rise towers contain more than 2,300 rental apartments. With its inter-connected buildings and shops, Presidential Towers promises to be a "complete in-town residential community."

For more than one hundred years the Near West Side has been one of Chicago's most ethnically diverse neighborhoods. Now known for its restaurants and its renovated homes, the neighborhood's days as an immigrant slum and ghetto seem far removed indeed. Anchored by the Medical Center on the west and the University of Illinois at Chicago on the east, the Near West Side is emerging as one of Chicago's new middle-class neighborhoods. Since the l970s hundreds of young urban professionals have moved into the area, drawn by its proximity to the Loop and to the world's largest medical complex. In addition to new housing, the neighborhood's homes and apartments have been carefully restored, and the Taylor Street shopping district continues to thrive. To a great extent the area now resembles the neighborhood envisioned by the Near West Side Planning Board in the l950s, with one exception—its ethnic communities have all but disappeared.

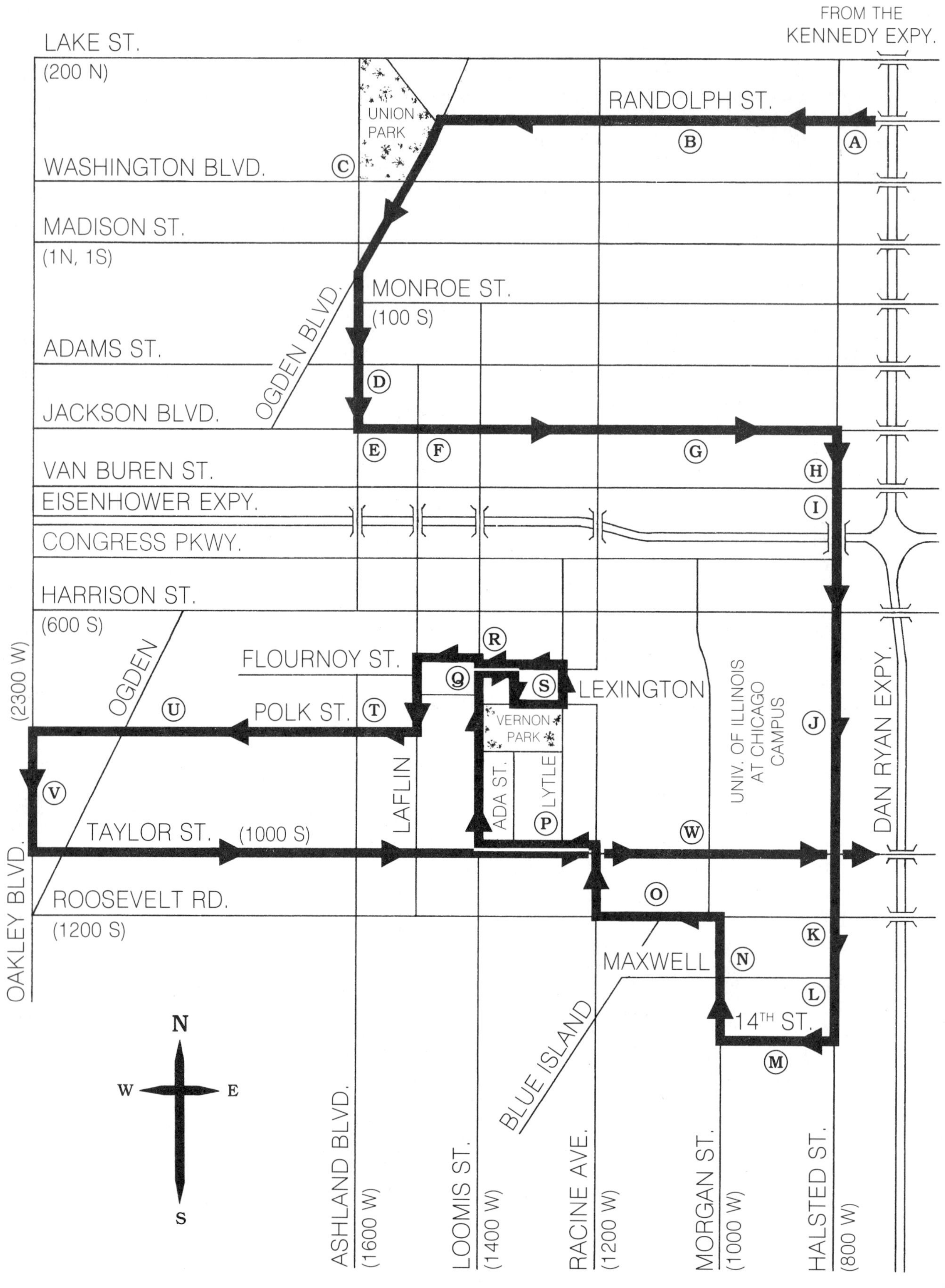

FROM THE
KENNEDY EXPY.

LAKE ST.
(200 N)

UNION PARK

RANDOLPH ST.

Ⓑ   Ⓐ

WASHINGTON BLVD.   Ⓒ

MADISON ST.
(1N, 1S)

MONROE ST.
(100 S)

OGDEN BLVD.

ADAMS ST.

JACKSON BLVD.   Ⓓ

Ⓔ   Ⓕ   Ⓖ   Ⓗ

VAN BUREN ST.

EISENHOWER EXPY.   Ⓘ

CONGRESS PKWY.

HARRISON ST.
(600 S)

OGDEN

FLOURNOY ST.   Ⓡ

Ⓠ   Ⓢ   LEXINGTON

POLK ST.   Ⓣ

Ⓤ

(2300 W)

VERNON PARK

LAFLIN

ADA ST.

LYTLE

Ⓟ

Ⓙ

UNIV. OF ILLINOIS AT CHICAGO CAMPUS

DAN RYAN EXPY.

Ⓥ

TAYLOR ST.   (1000 S)   Ⓦ

ROOSEVELT RD.
(1200 S)

OAKLEY BLVD.

Ⓞ

MAXWELL   Ⓝ   Ⓚ

BLUE ISLAND   Ⓛ

14TH ST.

Ⓜ

N
W   E
S

ASHLAND BLVD.
(1600 W)

LOOMIS ST.
(1400 W)

RACINE AVE.
(1200 W)

MORGAN ST.
(1000 W)

HALSTED ST.
(800 W)

Near West Side Tour

This tour begins in the Randolph Street Market, travels west to the Ashland Boulevard district, then east again through the Jackson Boulevard Historic District, through Greektown, south to the Maxwell Street Market, then through the Near West Side's old ethnic neighborhoods, to the West Side Medical Center and the Tri-Taylor Historic District.

Driving time: about 2 hours.

(A) Exit the Kennedy Expressway at Randolph Street (150 North) and proceed west to Ogden Avenue (1500 West). The **Randolph Street Market** developed around Haymarket Square at Randolph and Desplaines (640 West), which drew farmers from outlying areas of the city. Now bounded by the expressway on the east, the Randolph Street district continues as Chicago's oldest produce market.

(B) In the 1860s and 1870s, this part of the Near West Side, especially nearby Washington Boulevard, was a well-to-do residential district. The area's homes and institutions are long gone, replaced by wholesale produce companies and light manufacturing plants.

(C) Keep to the left and follow Ogden Avenue south to Ashland Boulevard (1600 West); then continue three blocks south on Ashland to Jackson Boulevard (300 South). To your right across **Union Park** is the **First Baptist Congregational Church**, 60 N. Ashland Boulevard. The Union Park Congregational Church began construction of this limestone edifice in 1869. It was dedicated just after the Great Chicago Fire, on November 12, 1871. Following a merger with the city's original Congregational church in 1910, the building was renamed the First Congregational Church. The Victorian Gothic structure on Ashland Boulevard was the last of Chicago's pioneer Congregational churches. Since 1970, the edifice has taken on new life as a black Baptist Congregational church.

222

Church of the Epiphany, southeast corner Ashland and Adams, 1985. When the Episcopal parish of Epiphany built this splendid structure in 1885, Ashland Avenue was lined with spacious single-family homes. Epiphany Church has been a Near West Side institution since 1868.
(G. Lane)

Jackson Boulevard mansions looking east from Ashland, 1985. In 1976, the 1500 block of Jackson Boulevard was designated an Historic District by the Commission on Chicago Historical and Architectural Landmarks.   (G. Lane)

Union Park was one of Chicago's earliest parks, and it became the center of the Near West Side's Gold Coast in the 1880s and 1890s. Beginning in the 1920s, nearby mansions were converted into headquarters of local labor unions, giving new meaning to "Union" Park. In 1922, for example, the Milk Wagon Drivers Union, Local 753, established its offices in the Charles H. Case mansion at 220 S. Ashland. Chartered in 1903, the Milk and Ice Cream Drivers Union was the first to locate on Ashland Boulevard, and they built a new structure in 1956. Today more than thirty labor unions maintain their headquarters along Ashland Boulevard between Madison and Van Buren.

(D) The **Church of the Epiphany** at 201 S. Ashland stands as a stark reminder of the days when Ashland Boulevard was a fashionable residential district. Dedicated in 1885, this beautiful church was designed by Chicago architects Burling & Whitehouse in the Richardsonian Romanesque style, so named for Boston architect H.H. Richardson whose variations on medieval Romanesque designs were popular and innovative to American architecture. When Epiphany parish was founded in 1868, it was one of Chicago's leading Episcopal congregations. Today the parish supports a variety of social service programs, making it one of the Near West Side's most important institutions.

The Haymarket Statue, now located in the atrium of the Police Training Academy, 1300 W. Jackson Boulevard, was sculpted by Johannes Gelert in 1889. It commemorates the seven police officers killed by a bomb during a meeting at Haymarket Square, May 4, 1886.
(Courtesy Chicago Police Department)

(E) Turn left at Jackson Boulevard and go east one mile to Halsted Street (800 West). Since 1976 the 1500 block of Jackson Boulevard has been known as the **Jackson Boulevard Historic District.** Mayor Richard J. Daley supported Philip Krone's plan for the restoration of this street in 1973, sparing it from demolition. A spirited group of urban pioneers restored all thirty-one Victorian row houses to their former grandeur, making this block of Jackson Boulevard a showplace of the Near West Side.

(F) New construction along Jackson Boulevard has further anchored the Jackson Boulevard Historic District. The **Whitney Young Magnet High School** (1974) at 211 S. Laflin draws students from all over the city. Shortly after the new Police Training Academy opened at 1300 W. Jackson Boulevard in 1976, the historic Haymarket statue was installed in its atrium. The statue commemorates the seven police officers who died as the result of a bomb explosion near the Haymarket Square on May 4, 1886. Since its unveiling in 1889, the statue, modeled after Chicago policeman Thomas Birmingham, has generated controversy in the city. Long the target of labor groups, in 1969 and 1970 radical students toppled the statue from its pedestal. After four years at police headquarters, 1121 S. State Street, the Haymarket monument is once again located on the Near West Side.

(G) The brick row houses in the 1000 block of W. Jackson Boulevard stand in the midst of Chicago's old garment district. Originally a residential section, this part of the Near West Side became the center of the city's garment industry by 1910. In recent years loft buildings in the area have been adapted for residential and commercial use. Millions of dollars have been invested in the Westgate Mill District, which is bounded roughly by Madison, the Kennedy Expressway, Racine Avenue, and the Eisenhower Expressway. Within the next decade developers expect this to become one of Chicago's new mixed use residential-commercial neighborhoods.

(H) At Halsted Street turn right and go over the Eisenhower Expressway and continue south all the way to 14th Street. This stretch of Halsted north of the expressway is all that is left of Chicago's Delta, the city's West Side Greek community. Urban renewal plans for the area have come and gone, but **Greektown's** restaurants remain intact, serving patrons from all over Chicago and the suburbs.

(I) The **Rice building** at 815 W. Van Buren Street is typical of the old garment district buildings which have been rehabbed for commercial and office space. When this brick structure was built in 1910, the surrounding neighborhood was one of the city's largest manufacturing districts, employing thousands of immigrant workers.

(J) The red brick building at 800 S. Halsted is Chicago's historic **Hull House,** the pioneering settlement house established by Jane Addams and Ellen Gates Starr in 1889. Over the years, Hull House expanded to include a complex of thirteen buildings. For generations of Chicagoans, this settlement was a bright spot in the

(Top right) Green Street looking north across Jackson Boulevard, 1939. Originally a residential district, this area became the center of Chicago's garment industry after 1900. Now known as the Westgate Mill District, its brick loft buildings are being converted into offices and condominiums.
(Chicago Park District, courtesy R. Wroble)

(Bottom right) The restaurants along S. Halsted Street are all that remain of the Near West Side's original Greek community, known as The Delta. (G. Lane, 1986)

midst of the West Side's teeming slums. Halsted Street's shops and homes, as well as the rest of the Hull House complex, have been replaced by the modern buildings of the **University of Illinois at Chicago.** Although Hull House is no longer located in a tenement district, its museum recreates the vanished neighborhood. Moreover, its exhibits document the role which the settlement played in improving living and working conditions on the Near West Side. As a result of a large scale reconstruction program, Hull House looks much like it did when it was built in 1856 as the country estate of Charles Hull. **Hull House Museum** is open Monday-Friday from 10 a.m. to 4 p.m. and on Sundays in the summer from 12 to 5 p.m.

(K) Roosevelt Road and Halsted Street marks the beginning of Chicago's Maxwell Street open air market. Just west of Halsted on Roosevelt is **St. Francis of Assisi Church,** built in 1866 by German Catholics and reconstructed after a fire in 1904. When 12th Street was widened in 1916 as part of Daniel Burnham's Plan of Chicago, the church was placed on a new foundation. After a short interval as an Italian parish, St. Francis of Assisi became Chicago's largest Spanish-speaking parish in the 1920s. Although the Hispanic community is no longer concentrated near Roosevelt and Halsted, Mexican families return to St. Francis of Assisi for baptisms, weddings, and funerals.

(L) The **Maxwell Street Market** has been a Chicago institution for more than 100 years, serving the Near West Side's diverse ethnic groups. As a result of urban renewal and expressway construction, however, the size of the market has been greatly diminished. Many of Chicago's Jewish merchants got their start behind pushcarts and stalls in the open air market, hawking clothes, food, and household items. In addition to producing generations of Chicago businessmen, the Maxwell Street neighborhood also claims such distinguished alumni as actor Paul Muni; Benny Goodman, "the King of Swing"; author Meyer Levin; Supreme Court Justice and U.N. Ambassador Arthur Goldberg; and trucking magnate John L. Keeshin.

Maxwell Street Market, 1985. Although the original market has been altered as a result of expressway construction and urban renewal, it continues to draw vendors, bargain hunters, and sightseers, especially on Sunday mornings. (G. Lane)

(M) Turn right at 14th Street and go four blocks west to Morgan Street (1000 West). The area along 14th Street was once known as **The Valley** because of the steep embankment of the railroad tracks to the south. In the 1920s, bootleggers Terry Druggan and Frankie Lake made the Valley one of Chicago's most notorious gang districts. However, urban renewal did much to diminish the area's unsavory reputation. In 1925 a large section of the Valley was razed to make way for the **South Water Wholesale Market,** which relocated here after it was displaced by the construction of Wacker Drive. In recent years the area's ramshackle buildings have slowly been replaced with modern townhouses.

(N) Turn right at Morgan Street and go two blocks north to Roosevelt Road (1200 South). The red brick building at 943 W. Maxwell Street is familiar to fans of "Hill Street Blues." The former **Maxwell Street Station** of the Chicago Police Department now houses the vice control division.

Holy Family Church (1860) and St. Ignatius College Prep (1870) at 1080-76 W. Roosevelt Road are the Near West Side's most famous landmarks. When Arnold J. Damen. S.J. founded the Jesuit parish of Holy Family in 1857, the surrounding area was nearly all prairie.
(Loyola University of Chicago Archives)

(O) Turn left at Roosevelt and go three blocks west to Racine Avenue (1200 West). The modern curvilinear building at 1055 W. Roosevelt Road houses the **Illinois Regional Library for the Blind and Handicapped** (1978). The exterior of the library is painted in vivid colors, which can be seen by partially sighted persons. Architect Stanley Tigerman calls his creation "witty, beautiful and colorful."

Dominating the north side of Roosevelt Road between Blue Island Avenue and May Street is **St. Ignatius College Prep** (1869) and **Holy Family Church,** the first Jesuit parish in Chicago and a Near West Side institution since 1857. When the Gothic church was dedicated in 1860, it was said to have been the third largest house of worship in America. It subsequently was enlarged in 1866. The tower of Holy Family Church was added in 1874, making this Chicago's first "skyscraper." Although the Jesuits planned to build a college as early as 1857, nearly fifteen years passed before Father Arnold Damen's dream was fulfilled. St. Ignatius, the nucleus of Loyola University, opened for classes on September 5, 1870 in a distinctive five-story building at 413 Twelfth Street (now 1076 W. Roosevelt Road). The west wing of the school was completed in 1874, and the north or "new" wing, as it is known, in

1895. Following the transfer of the college department to Loyola's Lake Shore campus in Rogers Park in 1922, St. Ignatius continued as a secondary school for boys. Since 1979 it has been coeducational, one of the few such Catholic secondary schools in Chicago.

Not only are Holy Family Church and St. Ignatius College Prep "an enduring physical feature of the Near West Side landscape," but they constitute an important legacy from the city's pioneer days before the Great Chicago Fire. In 1983 the tower of Holy Family Church was restored and an ambitious multi-million dollar renovation program is now underway to restore St. Ignatius to its 1870s splendor.

Ⓟ Turn right on Racine, go one block north to Taylor Street (1000 South), then left on Taylor and go three blocks west to Loomis (1400 West). The northwest corner of Taylor and Lytle Streets has a rich history. At this site in 1860 the Religious of the Sacred Heart established the **Sacred Heart Convent school for girls,** the premier Catholic institution in the city for the next four decades. When the nuns relocated their boarding school to Lake Forest, Illinois, they sold the Taylor Street property to the Chicago Hebrew Institute, later known as the Jewish People's Institute. Although the old Sacred Heart buildings were destroyed by fire in 1910, the CHI built a new complex which became the heart of the Near West Side's Jewish community. In the 1930s the site was cleared to make way for the **Jane Addams Housing Project,** named after the founder of Hull House.

Jane Addams Homes, northwest corner Taylor and Lytle, 1985. This was the original site of the Sacred Heart Convent School for Girls, established in 1860. In 1908, the Chicago Hebrew Institute purchased the convent academy and grounds for its community center, later known as the Jewish People's Institute. In the late 1930s, the site was redeveloped as a public housing project. (D. Pacyga)

Ⓖ Turn right onto Loomis Street and go four blocks north to Flournoy (700 South). In the 1890s Loomis Street, with its three-story greystones, was one of the Near West Side's newest and most fashionable streets. D.F. Bremner's house at 718 S. Loomis was typical of the high-class construction which occurred in the immediate area. Later known as Madonna Center, the city's first Catholic settlement, the old Bremner house continues in use today as the headquarters of the **Midtown Center.**

Ⓡ Turn right at Flournoy and go one block east to Ada Street (1326 West), then one block south on Ada to Lexington. When **Notre Dame de Chicago church** at 1336 W. Flournoy was dedicated in 1892, it was Chicago's most beautiful French church. Although the Near West Side's French community subsequently diminished, the church remained, serving new Italian residents in the area. Following a fire in 1978, there was talk of razing this magnificent Romanesque structure. But the pastor and parishioners prevailed, and in 1981 restoration work began. William L. Lavicka, head of Historic Boulevard Services, with Rev. Norman Pelletier developed a plan to "restore and renew the original art and structure of the church." The final stage in the building's restoration occurred in 1982 when a new nine-foot statue of the Blessed Mother, *Notre Dame,* was hoisted atop the cupola.

Ⓢ Turn left on Lexington and go one block east to Lytle Street (1235 West), then north on Lytle to Flournoy. Originally known as Macalister Place, Lexington Avenue in the nineteenth century was the Near West Side's Irish Gold Coast, home to such well known Chicagoans as William J. Onahan and Johnny Powers, who controlled the 19th Ward from 1888 to 1927. Although Alderman Powers' Victorian home at 1284 W. Lexington has been razed, Onahan's row houses remain at 1254-62 W. Lexington. The oldest structure on the block is an 1871 Italianate house built by John Coughlan at 1246 W. Lexington. By 1910, ethnic change on the Near West Side was clearly visible along Macalister Place. In that year Italian Catholics established **Our Lady of Pompeii** parish, and in less than fifteen years they built the present Romanesque church which stands at the northeast corner of Lexington and Lytle.

(Top left) Madonna Center, 718 S. Loomis Street, 1948. The D.F. Bremner house was a showplace on the Near West Side in the 1880s. It became Madonna Center, 1922-64, the first Catholic settlement house in Chicago. The building houses the Midtown Center today. In the background is Notre Dame de Chicago Church, built by French Catholics at 1336 W. Flournoy between 1887 and 1892. (Courtesy Madonna Center Archives)

(Bottom left) San Gennaro procession, Laflin and Lexington Streets, September 1985. Although greatly reduced in numbers, the Near West Side Italian community continues to celebrate special feast days with parades. (G. Lane)

Garden Court Townhouses at Polk and Racine, begun around 1980, represent the new housing developments on the Near West Side. (G. Lane)

Across the park at 811 S. Lytle is **Cabrini Hospital,** founded by Mother Cabrini as Columbus Extension in 1911 to serve Italian immigrants in the neighborhood. The hospital is named in honor of St. Frances Xavier Cabrini, who also established Columbus Hospital on the North Side.

(T) Go three blocks west on Flournoy to Laflin (1500 West), two blocks south on Laflin to Polk (800 South), then turn right on Polk Street and go west one mile through the West Side Medical Center to Oakley Boulevard (2300 West).

The Greek revival temple at the northeast corner of Polk and Ashland was built in 1910 by **Anshe Sholom,** one of the Near West Side's oldest Jewish congregations. The synagogue moved to Ashland Boulevard from Canal and Liberty in the heart of the old Jewish ghetto. Following the path blazed by earlier German and Irish families, members of Anshe Sholom continued to move farther west in the city. After building a new temple at Polk Street and Independence Boulevard in the Lawndale neighborhood, the Jewish congregation sold its Ashland Boulevard synagogue to **St. Basil Greek Orthodox Church** in 1927. The Greek congregation redecorated the interior with beautiful icons and paintings. Although Chicago's Greek community is now predominantly suburban, St. Basil's continues as an important center of Greek worship.

St. Basil Greek Orthodox Church, northeast corner of Polk and Ashland, 1980. Originally built as a synagogue in 1910, this beautiful building was purchased by St. Basil's in 1927 when the Jewish congregation built a new temple in the Lawndale neighborhood. (G. Lane)

Ⓤ The **West Side Medical Center** is one of the largest in the world. It occupies the area bounded roughly by the Eisenhower Expressway, Ashland Boulevard, Roosevelt Road, and Oakley Boulevard. The first institution to locate in the area was **Cook County Hospital,** established in 1873 at Harrison and Wood. Other prominent medical facilities followed, including **Rush Medical College** and **Hospital** and the **University of Illinois Hospital.** In 1941 the Illinois legislature established the Medical Center District with power of eminent domain. As a result, homes located north of Roosevelt Road between Ashland and Damen were razed to provide land for hospital expansion. The West Side Medical District now includes the massive hospital complexes of Cook County, the University of Illinois, **Rush-Presbyterian-St. Luke's, Illinois State Psychiatric Institute,** and the **Veterans Administration.**

The Polk Street elevated station of the CTA was dedicated on January 17, 1984 in memory of Dr. David Jones Peck, an 1847 graduate of Rush Medical College. Peck was the first American black to receive a doctor of medicine degree from an American medical college.

Damen Avenue at 2000 West was originally known as Robey Street. One of the West Side's most important thoroughfares, it was renamed in 1927 for Rev. Arnold J. Damen, S.J., founder of Holy Family Jesuit parish on Twelfth Street (now Roosevelt Road).

In 1984 ground was broken on a 56-acre site at Polk and Bowler Streets for **Chicago Technology Park,** an $8 million facility that will provide laboratory space to biotechnology firms. A joint project of the University of Illinois and Rush-Presbyterian-St. Luke's, with support from the City of Chicago and the State of Illinois, this lab will establish the Near West Side as a biotechnology research center.

(V) At Oakley Boulevard turn left and go one block south to Taylor Street (1000 South). The **Tri-Taylor District** with its 1870s row houses and frame cottages was added to the National Register of Historic Places in 1983. Bounded on the east by the Medical Center, this part of the Near West Side has survived intact, one of the few such districts of its kind in Chicago. For decades Tri-Taylor was a tightly knit Italian community with its own parish and school, **St. Callistus,** at Bowler and Leavitt Streets. Since the 1950s, Mexican families have been well represented in the parish and neighborhood.

(W) Turn left at Taylor Street and go east two miles to the Dan Ryan Expressway. Taylor Street remains the heart of the Near West Side's Little Italy, and it includes many of the neighborhood's best known stores and restaurants from the **Original Ferrara Bakery,** 2210 W. Taylor, to the **Florence Restaurant,** 1030 W. Taylor. One of Little Italy's newest restaurants, Florence's (1980) is run by Florence Scala. In 1961 she launched a spirited but unsuccessful campaign to halt the construction of the University of Illinois campus on land at Harrison and Halsted that previously had been designated for new housing. Scala's restaurant occupies part of the building where she was born and in which her father operated a dry cleaning-tailor shop.

The West Side Medical Center traces its origins to the 1870s when Cook County Hospital and Rush Medical College opened facilities near Wood and Harrison Streets. (G. Lane, 1986)

The brick row houses on the west side of Bowler Street are typical of working-class homes constructed after the Chicago Fire in the area now known as the Tri-Taylor Historic District. (G. Lane)

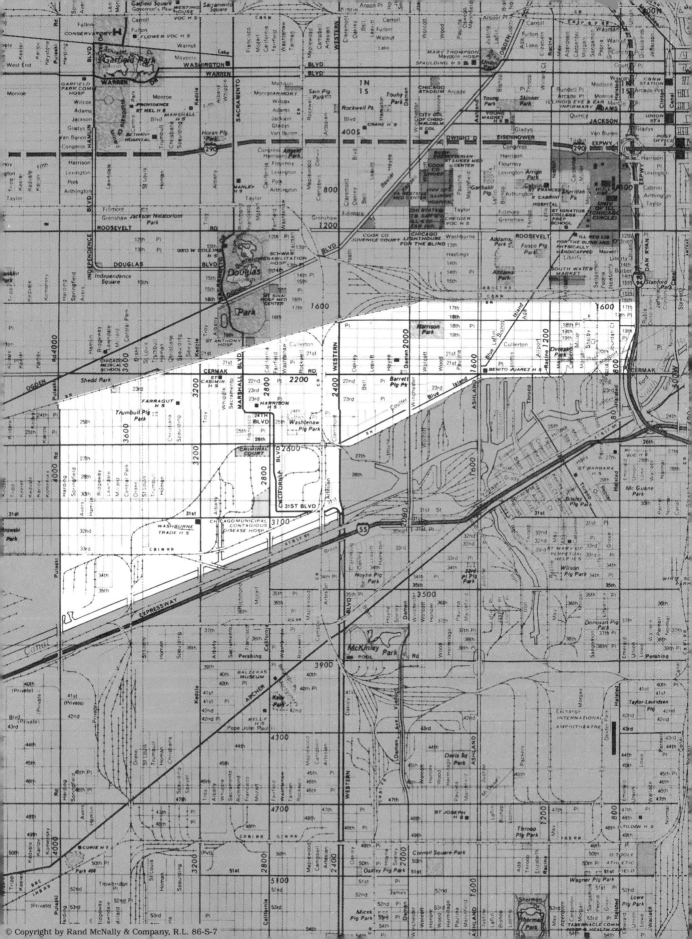

Lower West Side

7

From the 1870s through the 1950s, the Lower West Side of Chicago was a port of entry for thousands of Europeans: Irish, Bohemians, Germans, Poles, Swedes, Slovaks, Slovenes, Lithuanians, Italians, and Croatians. Today, the neighborhoods known as Pilsen, Heart of Chicago, and Little Village form the center of Chicago's flourishing Mexican community. Not only have Mexican newcomers revitalized older ethnic institutions here, but they have established their own businesses, restaurants, and social centers.

Throughout its history, the Lower West Side has been a relatively isolated area, bounded by railroad tracks on the north and west and by the South Branch of the Chicago River on the south and east. Despite the fact that the Burlington Railroad linked this part of the city to the downtown business district, the area developed as a working-class neighborhood. Large manufacturing plants such as the McCormick Reaper Works (later known as International Harvester) and the Western Electric Company's Hawthorne Works in Cicero were responsible for much of the growth of the Lower West Side, and they reinforced its character as an industrial neighborhood.

Like the Back of the Yards district on Chicago's South Side, Pilsen and its adjoining communities supported a wide range of ethnic institutions and businesses. In addition to building homes in the area, residents established churches and fraternal organizations which met their special needs, first as immigrants and later as second- and third-generation Americans. Home ownership set these neighborhoods apart from the nearby Lawndale district, where families rented apartments in multi-unit buildings. While social mobility did occur in each of the area's ethnic groups, the Lower West Side has remained a stable area. Just as Bohemians who settled in Pilsen relocated further west as they moved up the economic ladder, so Mexican families have also purchased homes, especially in Heart of Chicago and Little Village. These latter neighborhoods are in many respects "suburbs" of Pilsen, which continues to be the port of entry for Spanish-speaking families from rural Mexico and Texas.

▼

Pilsen

The Bohemian community known as Pilsen emerged after the Chicago Fire of 1871 when Bohemian immigrants began to move west of the South Branch of the river. The old Bohemian colony which had grown up around St. Wenceslaus Church at DeKoven and Desplaines Streets in the 1860s was called "Prague." The new settlement on the Lower West Side took its name from Bohemia's second largest city, Pilsen.

One of the pioneer industries in this area was the Schoenhofen Brewery, established in 1862 at 18th and Canalport by Peter Schoenhofen, a German Jewish immigrant. The largest factory to locate in the area was the McCormick Reaper Works, which moved from the North Side to Blue Island and Western Avenues in 1873.

By 1875 Pilsen was one of Chicago's major industrial centers, supporting such diverse companies as the Chicago Stove Works Foundry at 22nd and Blue Island, the McCormick Reaper Works at Blue Island and Western, and the Goss & Phillips Manufacturing Co. at 22nd and Fisk (Carpenter), which specialized in sashes, doors, and "Kelly's Patent Weather-Proof Blind."

The nearby yards of the Chicago, Burlington & Quincy Railroad provided jobs for thousands of unskilled Pilsen workers, as did the vast lumberyards along the South Branch of the river. Labor historians William Adelman and Richard Schneirov have documented the role Bohemian immigrants played in the 1870s and 1880s in the battle for improved wages and shorter working hours. Bohemian laborers joined unions and supported benevolent groups such as the Czech Slavic Benefit Society of the United States (CSPS). These lodges provided financial assistance to families whose wage earners died or sustained injuries on the job.

More than any other ethnic group in Chicago, Bohemians tended to be socialists and freethinkers, and they were closely identified with the "Battle of the Viaduct" on July 26, 1877 when Chicago police and U.S. soldiers killed nearly thirty workers and injured two hundred persons, among them women and children. According to Schneirov, Bohemian lumbershovers spontaneously joined the railroad strike of 1877, expanding it beyond the Michigan Central railroad yards near the lakefront to the area west of the Chicago River. Bohemian women filled their aprons with stones, thereby aiding their husbands and sons in the conflict with the police and militia. At one door and sash factory on 22nd Street, Bohemian women "stoned the hated bluecoats till they dispersed."

(Right) One of Pilsen's many Bohemian institutions was the lodge headquarters of the Czech Slavic Benevolent Society (CSPS), built in 1879 at 1226 W. 18th Street. At the turn of the century, Chicago's Czech population was outnumbered only by those of Prague and Vienna.

(Courtesy Chicago Historical Society)

1829

ROVNOST. SVORNOST. BRATRSTVI.

Č.S.P.S.

400

So intense were the confrontations between workers and police on Chicago's Lower West Side that Blue Island Avenue came to be known in labor circles all over the nation. Built as a plank road in 1854 linking Western Avenue to downtown Chicago, Blue Island Avenue was filled in with cinders from nearby factories, hence its name "Black Road." In 1877 and again in 1886, battles between police and strikers outside the McCormick Reaper Works gave new meaning to the sobriquet "Black Road."

In addition to the struggle for economic survival, religious differences shaped the Bohemian community in Pilsen. Freethinkers, Catholics, and Protestants all formed their own institutions, especially schools and sokols where Czech values could be transmitted to American-born children. The Bohemian community also supported a wide range of newspapers, from the liberal Czech *Svornost* to the Socialist weekly, *Spravedlnost*, and the Catholic daily, *Narod.*

By the 1880s, an estimated 45,000 Bohemians lived in the area bounded by 16th Street, Halsted, 20th Street (Cullerton), and Ashland Avenue. One of Pilsen's first Bohemian institutions was St. Procopius parish, established in 1875. So quickly did the membership of this congregation grow that within eight years they were able to build and dedicate the massive Romanesque church which stands today at the northeast corner of 18th and Allport, a link with the neighborhood's Bohemian past.

Not only did St. Procopius parish overshadow the older Irish parish of Sacred Heart at 19th and Peoria, but it became the "mother church" of Chicago's West Side Bohemian parishes. As early as 1888, Bohemian Benedictine priests from St. Procopius established a mission at 18th Place and Paulina which developed into the flourishing parish of St. Vitus. More than just a neighborhood church, St. Procopius was the largest Bohemian congregation in the United States, and it supported an abbey, the printing plant for *Narod*, a large grammar school, and a boys high school (1887), which would later evolve into Illinois Benedictine College in Lisle.

Heart of Chicago

Although a number of German immigrants lived in Pilsen, the largest German community on the Lower West Side developed west of Robey Street (Damen Avenue), in the area now known as Heart of Chicago. In 1872 German Lutherans established St. Matthew parish, and ten years later they opened a new school at the southwest corner of

St. Paul Church, 22nd Place and Hoyne, c.1900. Henry J. Schlacks designed this Gothic masterpiece which was built by German-American craftsmen between 1897 and 1899. The church has become a landmark in the Heart of Chicago neighborhood.
(Courtesy The Chicago Catholic)

21st and Hoyne. In 1887 the congregation build a brick church across the street from their "Schule." German Catholics organized St. Paul parish in 1876, and men of the congregation contributed their labor to build the massive structure which towers over the neighborhood at 22nd Place and Hoyne. Known as the church "built without a nail," St. Paul's (1899) is said to be the first all-brick Gothic church in America.

Not only did the German parish of St. Paul boast a magnificent house of worship, but it was also the birthplace of St. Paul Federal Savings and Loan (1889). One of Chicago's largest savings institutions, St. Paul Federal has expanded beyond the neighborhood into the city and suburbs. Savings and loan associations were popular among German, Polish, and Bohemian immigrants, and they made it possible for thousands of families to become property owners, a tradition which continues today among the area's Mexican residents.

Polish immigrants on the Lower West Side followed the same path set out by Bohemian families. From their original settlement around St. Adalbert Church at 1656 West 17th Street, Polish families built homes in Heart of Chicago and Little Village as they moved up the economic ladder. In addition to becoming the majority in the old Irish parish of St. Pius at 19th and Ashland, the Polish community established a network of national parishes that extended west to the suburb of Cicero. The location of their new parishes illustrates how the Polish settlement on the Lower West Side expanded, from St. Adalbert's (1874) to St. Casimir's (1890) at 22nd and Whipple; to St. Ann's (1903) at 18th Place and Leavitt; to Good Shepherd (1907), at 28th and Kolin.

In the 1880s and 1890s, Chicago's Protestant churches established a number of missions in Pilsen as a way to combat the influence of Bohemian freethinkers who denounced religion and advanced socialism as a means of promoting the rights of working men. Bethlehem Congregational Church, built in 1890 at 1853 S. Loomis, was financed by the Chicago City Missionary Society. In a report detailing the Society's work among Bohemians in Pilsen, Rev. E.A. Adams noted that:

> When we began, no word in favor of temperance was ever seen in any Bohemian paper. Now not a few adult Bohemians practice total abstinence and several papers are strong in condemnation of drunkenness, and the whole tone is entirely changed.

As in other working-class areas on the city's South and West Sides, Orthodox Jews established synagogues in close proximity to their homes and shops. B'nai Jehoshua Temple at the southwest corner of 19th and Ashland was the neighborhood's premier Bohemian synagogue. Established in 1893 as the First Hebrew Educational and Charitable Association, this congregation continued in existence until 1965 when it merged with Beth Elohim of Glenview, Illinois.

Just a few weeks before the Haymarket Riot in 1886, the Chicago *Tribune* declared that the city's Bohemians "are looked upon as some of the thriftiest members of the community, useful citizens, capable and efficient workingmen, and large contributors to the wealth and growth of Chicago." In addition to describing Pilsen's varied workforce, the newspaper noted that, "There is not a more cleanly or better built workingmen's section in Chicago." While the *Tribune* denounced the demands workers were making for unions and an eight-hour day, it could not ignore the fact that Bohemian, German, Swedish, and Polish

laborers had transformed the prairies west of the river into a community of modest homes.

In 1886, an estimated sixty percent of Chicago's Bohemians were property owners, and they supported twenty-eight building and loan associations. According to the *Tribune*, nearly all the "fine brick buildings" in Pilsen were financed by these local savings groups. Once the area west of Halsted Street was built up, Bohemians, Germans, Scandinavians, and Poles began to erect houses in the district between Ashland and Western.

By the 1890s, Blue Island Avenue from 18th to 22nd Streets was a bustling shopping district. In addition to the shops which catered to the needs of the expanding community, Blue Island Avenue included a large number of saloons and tailor shops where garments were "finished." Strikes in the garment district located just west of the Loop also spread to Pilsen, where immigrants worked for low wages as part of the infamous piecework system.

The Garment Workers' Strike of September 1910 began in Pilsen at 18th and Halsted in shop No. 5 of Hart, Schaffner & Marx, the country's largest clothing manufacturer. More than 20,000 men and women joined in the strike as it spread to other clothing firms throughout the city. Although the four-month strike did not result in immediate improvements in working conditions, it led to the creation of the Amalgamated Clothing Workers of America.
(Courtesy Chicago Historical Society)

Thalia Hall, built in 1892 at 1807 S. Allport, was an important center of Bohemian community life. Constructed at a cost of $145,000 and designed by Faber & Pagels, the building symbolized reinvestment in the neighborhood.
(J. Fiener)

(Top right) Gads Hill Center, 1919 W. Cullerton, c.1960. Founded in 1898, Gads Hill remains one of the leading institutions on the Lower West Side.
(Gads Hill Center, courtesy Brockie Dilworth)

New construction such as Thalia Hall (1892) at the southeast corner of 18th and Allport provided Pilsen residents with a theater, stores, and "flats." While brick homes and shops in the neighborhood testified to the stability of the district, congestion remained a serious problem. In 1894 the Chicago *Times* painted a graphic picture of overcrowding in the Bohemian Quarter. When a smallpox epidemic ravaged the area bounded by 18th, Loomis, 20th, and Carpenter, the *Times* reported that:

The block on Allport street where the disease is worst contains over 360 families. The houses are frequently three deep; one set of families occupying the house facing the street and others the (frame) dwellings one behind the other in the rear.

According to Robert Hunter, in 1901 more than 7,000 persons lived on nine blocks in the heart of the Bohemian Quarter. Then as now, there were many children in Pilsen. Because of the lack of parks and yards, youngsters played in the neighborhood's crowded streets and alleys and along the railroad tracks. Local churches and settlement houses provided much-needed clubrooms and activities for neighborhood children.

In 1898 Leila A. Martin, a Protestant, and Hettie Peary French, a convert to Roman Catholicism, joined forces to establish Gads Hill Social Settlement at 22nd and Robey Street (Damen Avenue). Unlike other local settlements, Gads

Hill was nondenominational and nonsectarian. In its early years the chief concerns of the settlement were temperance, social activity, and citizenship classes. Although Gads Hill has always promoted music and art, it was not named for Charles Dickens's birthplace in Rochester, England. According to a history of the center, a lieutenant in the local police station in the 1870s named this rough-and-tumble part of Chicago after Gads Hill, Missouri, the scene of "a notoriously bold bank robbery." The name stuck, but following the opening of the social center, Gads Hill became synonymous with "good fellowship, brotherly love, the true Christ spirit." Since 1916, Gads Hill Center has been located at 1919 W. Cullerton Street.

Another institution which has served the Lower West Side since 1905 is located at 1831 S. Racine Avenue. Established as the Howell Neighborhood House and supported for many years by the Fourth Presbyterian Church, this center is now an independent organization known as Casa Aztlan.

South Lawndale

As Bohemian families on the Lower West Side prospered, many moved further west to South Lawndale, below Douglas Park. In the 1870s, A.C. Millard and E.J. Decker developed a residential community just south of the Burlington Railroad station at Ogden Avenue. According to an 1875 advertisement, the community boasted eight new buildings, among them the Millard Avenue Baptist Church at 24th and Millard, and the Lawndale Hotel. Around 1880, John G. Shedd, an up-and-coming young executive with Marshall Field's, built a spacious brick home at 2316 S. Millard Avenue. Other substantial homes and new institutions followed, such as the Muscoda Club, 2340 S. Lawndale, and the Fowler Methodist Episcopal Church (1891) at 2255 S. Millard. As a result of building restrictions imposed after the Chicago Fire of 1871, brick homes predominated in the Millard & Decker subdivision.

According to the Chicago *Times*, the streets in the area were all paved with either block or asphalt, and sewers, water, gas, and shade trees were in place. Despite the fact that property in this neighborhood was "cheaper than in some of the suburban towns," South Lawndale did not develop into an exclusive residential area like Austin, Edgewater, or Kenwood. Although fifty-eight trains a day passed through the area en route to the city's business district, it remained isolated from the rest of Chicago. As late as 1891, travel to other parts of the city was difficult. The streetcar line along 21st Street extended only as far as Western Avenue, and the Blue Island cable line, the last one built in Chicago, made commuting to this part of the West Side tedious.

In 1895 South Lawndale lost its most prominent resident, John G. Shedd, to Kenwood, a South Side neighborhood that was becoming an enclave of Chicago's most powerful businessmen. Shedd's rise from stockboy to partner at Marshall Field's had been rapid. He was named partner in 1896, and became president of the department store ten years later. (The Aquarium on South Lake Shore Drive which bears his name was opened to the public in 1929.)

But Shedd's decision to build a gabled mansion at 4515 S. Drexel Boulevard did not signal the end of the Millard & Decker subdivision's glory days. On the contrary, the area took on new life as a Bohemian community which became known as Czech California. Among the Bohemian immigrants who moved to this area from Pilsen was Albert V. Cerny, a noted musician. His home at 2347 S. Lawndale became a gathering place for Bohemian intellectuals, artists, and musicians. Indeed, his daughter Zdenka was immortalized in the works of artist Alphonse Mucha. Another Bohemian immigrant who settled in Czech California at 2348 S. Millard was Anton J. Cermak, mayor of Chicago from 1931 to 1933.

The relocation of the Western Electric Company from 12th and Clinton to suburban Cicero in 1903 had important consequences for the future of this part of the Lower West Side. Just as the McCormick Reaper Works had been one of the area's main employers in the 1870s, the Western Electric Company provided jobs for thousands of area residents. Moreover, the extension of the Metropolitan branch of the Douglas Park "L" to Cicero Avenue in 1907 offered fast, inexpensive transportation to the Hawthorne plant and nearby factories. The population of South Lawndale grew rapidly as new homes and two-flats were constructed on Marshall and Sacramento Boulevards and along the side streets between Western and Crawford (Pulaski) Avenues.

As Bohemians moved into South Lawndale, they established new institutions and transplanted old ones. The Hubbard Memorial Bohemian Presbyterian Church, for example, traced its roots to the John Hus Methodist Church, established in 1891 at 24th and Sawyer. In 1915 the congregation dedicated a new church at 2520 S. Lawndale. Bohemian Catholics who moved to South Lawndale did not care to worship at the English-speaking parish of Blessed Sacrament at 22nd and Central Park. Instead, they formed two new parishes, St. Ludmilla (1891) at 24th and Albany and Blessed Agnes (1904) at 27th and Central Park. These Bohemian congregations built massive churches as well as parochial schools.

Just as they had in Pilsen, sokols and "free thought" schools took root in Czech California. Sokol Chicago, 2345 S. Kedzie, and Sokol Havlicek-Tyrs at 2619 S. Lawndale were important recreation and cultural centers in the new Bohemian neighborhood. In addition to supporting Czech language classes at Harrison and Farragut high schools, the community also maintained free thought schools such as Vojta Naprster, 2548 S. Homan, and Jan Neruda, 2659 S. Karlov.

Anton Cermak, the Lower West Side's most prominent politician, served as chairman of the Cook County Board before being elected mayor of Chicago in 1931. Cermak was responsible for the construction of a $7.5 million Criminal Court building at 26th and California, which opened—in his ward—on April 1, 1929. In 1871 this location was so remote from the center of the city that officials deemed it an appropriate spot for Chicago's bridewell, formerly at Polk and Wells Streets. Sixty years later the area was still inaccessible by public transportation. According to one publication:

> To get to the loop from this area is a tedious proposition at the best. Blue Island avenue cars on 26th street offer practically the only method.

But lack of convenient transportation to downtown Chicago did not hamper residential development. By the 1920s, the area around Marshall Boulevard had been completely built up. Indeed, when the parish of St. Roman was established in 1928 to relieve overcrowding at the older Polish parish of St. Casimir, there was no vacant land in the area. Eleven houses had to be razed to make way for the new church at 23rd and Washtenaw.

Although Pilsen ceased to be predominantly Bohemian after the turn of the century, it remained a Slavic community. By 1930, for example, immigrants from Poland and Yugoslavia accounted for more than one-fourth of the 16,000 persons who lived in the area bounded by 16th, Carpenter, 22nd, and Ashland. As Bohemians moved further west in the city and to suburbs such as Berwyn and Riverside, Croatians, Slovaks, Slovenes, and Lithuanians took their place. While these groups formed their own churches and fraternal groups, they patronized Bohemian-owned businesses such as the Leader Department Store at 1700 West 18th Street.

In Heart of Chicago and South Lawndale, the ethnic population also expanded to include Eastern Europeans of

The new Carter H. Harrison Technical High School at the intersection of Marshall and 24th Boulevards, c.1916. Marshall Boulevard formed the "last link in the chain of boulevards thirty miles in length" which connected parks on Chicago's South, West, and North Sides. In 1983, Harrison was converted into a grammar school and renamed Maria Saucedo.

(Courtesy G. Schmalgemeier)

many different backgrounds. One indication of this change appeared in the formation of Slovene and Italian parishes. In 1898 Slovenian Catholics purchased a Swedish church at 22nd Place and Lincoln (Wolcott), which they rededicated as St. Stephen Church. Likewise, in 1903 Italians from Tuscany began the parish of St. Michael in the basement of the former Swedish Emmanuel Methodist Episcopal Church on 24th Place near Oakley.

While Bohemians continued to form the largest national group in South Lawndale well into the 1940s, Polish families moved into the neighborhood in large numbers. According to the 1930 census, nearly 11,000 immigrants from Czechoslovakia and 3,700 foreign-born Poles lived in the area bounded by the Burlington railroad tracks, California, 30th, and Crawford. Statistics indicate that the area of heaviest Polish concentration was along 22nd Street, renamed Cermak Road after the mayor's assassination in 1933. The area south of 26th Street between Kedzie and Crawford, however, was still a Bohemian stronghold in 1930, with large numbers of Czech immigrants.

Despite the onset of the Depression, the Lower West Side continued to be a stable area. In her 1935 canvass of the area around 20th and Loomis, sociologist Edith Abbott reported that the district showed no deterioration since 1908. "It still had a foreign look, but the rather well-built Czech tenements had weathered the years, and industry had made slight encroachments there."

As late as 1944, city planners agreed that the Lower West Side could not be described as a slum. Although more

Homan Avenue south from Ogden Avenue, c.1909. This section of South Lawndale was rapidly built up after the Douglas Park elevated line was extended to Crawford Avenue (Pulaski Road) in 1912.
(C.R. Childs, courtesy G. Schmalgemeier)

than half of Pilsen's homes were built between 1885 and 1895, and ninety-two percent of the structures lacked central heating, Homer Hoyt concluded that area residents "have sought to preserve a semblance of neatness in their drab surroundings." The housing picture for South Lawndale was much brighter. Harold M. Mayer described the area as "a foreign island in the city of Chicago, . . . a residential island in a sea of industry." Although half the homes in the area dated from before 1902, Mayer found that ninety-seven percent of the dwelling units were located in buildings that needed only minor repairs. Among the other positive factors cited by Mayer were the neighborhood's high rate of owner occupancy and the tendency of families to live in their homes for more than fifteen years.

All three neighborhoods on the Lower West Side declined in population from the 1930s on. This decrease did much to relieve the problems of overcrowding which had characterized industrial neighborhoods throughout the city. Even more critical for the future of these areas, however, was the change in the neighborhood's industrial base. Although some businesses remained in the area, such as the Edward Hines Lumber Company, 2431 S. Wolcott, and Ryerson Steel, 2558 West 16th Street, others such as International Harvester closed their operations along the South Branch of the river in the 1950s. Ironically, at the time some manufacturing plants were moving out of the area, plans were underway for the construction of a new expressway paralleling the old Sanitary & Ship Canal. The Adlai E. Stevenson Expressway, which opened in 1964, linked the

Lower West Side to the city and to the western suburbs, making this part of Chicago one of the city's most accessible. (The recent closing of Western Electric Company's Hawthorne Works in Cicero along with other factory shutdowns has further changed the economic picture of this part of Chicago.)

As a result of urban renewal in the area around Halsted Street and Roosevelt Road, Mexican families moved into Pilsen in the 1950s and early 1960s. Since that time Pilsen has become the port of entry for thousands of Spanish-speaking families from rural Mexico and Texas. Moreover, the newcomers have followed the same path taken by the earlier Bohemian and Polish residents. As soon as Mexican families could afford to do so, they purchased homes in the Heart of Chicago and South Lawndale neighborhoods. By the late 1960s Spanish businesses along 18th and 26th Streets stood side-by-side with shops which catered to the Eastern Europeans who still lived in the area. According to one estimate, more than seventy-five percent of businesses along 26th Street are now owned by Mexican-Americans. In a relatively short time, South Lawndale took on a new identity as a Mexican neighborhood. Just as earlier Bohemian immigrants referred to their neighborhood as Czech California, Mexican families now call it "Pueblo Pequeno" (Little Village).

Little Village

Because of its stability as a residential area, Little Village has attracted black as well as Mexican families. Beginning in the early 1960s, blacks moved into the neighborhood from North Lawndale. In the 1950s the area around Douglas Park experienced rapid racial change from a Jewish community to a black neighborhood. Primarily a district of apartment buildings, North Lawndale soon became one of the most densely populated black districts in the city. As a result of the riots which occurred following the assassination of Dr. Martin Luther King, Jr., in 1968, North Lawndale lost a large portion of its local businesses.

According to the 1980 census, Mexicans accounted for two-thirds of Little Village's 75,000 residents. On the whole, families of Spanish origin were more dispersed in the community than the 6,500 blacks who lived in the area. By and large, the transition from an Eastern European neighborhood to a predominantly Hispanic one has been peaceful.

Historically, the Lower West Side was divided into ethnic communities which supported their own churches, fraternal and social institutions, and newspapers. While Bohemians, Poles, and Slovenes lived in the same area, they shared few common institutions. Although Mexicans form the largest group on the Lower West Side and predominate in the area's sixteen Catholic parishes, the tradition of separate ethnic institutions persists. The General Mihailovich Veterans Group, for example, continues to meet in the old Masonic hall at 2300 S. Millard, and the Serbian Orthodox Church of St. Nikola is still located at 2754 S. Central Park. While many former Protestant congregations are now Spanish-speaking Pentecostal churches, a small number of them have become black institutions. The original Fowler Methodist Episcopal Church at 2255 S. Millard, for example, is now the Greater Zion Hill M.B. Church.

In the past few years much controversy has surrounded the area's public schools. The Mexican community on the Lower West Side scored a major victory in 1977 when the Benito Juarez High School opened at 2150 S. Laflin. Designed by Mexican architect Pedro Ramirez Vazquez, this

Commonwealth Edison's oldest generating plant at 1111 W. Cermak Road is known as the Fisk Street station. It was built in 1903 when the Lower West Side was one of the city's most important industrial areas.
(D. Pacyga)

Benito Juarez High School, 2150 S. Laflin, 1985. This school has been the pride of the Lower West Side's Mexican-American community since its opening in 1977. In 1985, ground was broken at 1805 S. Loomis for a new public library which will include 6,000 Spanish-language books donated by the Mexican government.

(J. Ficner)

new high school symbolizes the emerging political power of the Mexican community. Mexican families have successfully fought the Chicago Board of Education's attempts to bus their children outside the neighborhood to underutilized schools. At a time when the city's public school population is declining, grammar schools on the Lower West Side remain at peak capacity, with mobile units used to handle the overflow. In the Little Village neighborhood, for example, several new schools have been constructed, among them the Gerald Delgado Kanoon Magnet School at 2233 S. Kedzie. So great is the number of young children in the area that in 1983, Harrison High School at 2850 West 24th Boulevard was converted into a grammar school, and renamed Maria Saucedo.

A recent study of Chicago's Latino communities funded by Northwestern University's Center for Urban Affairs concluded that Pilsen has the highest density of any Hispanic community in Chicago. As one of the poorest areas of the city, it includes its share of dilapidated housing. Aside from the problems of economic survival, hundreds of Pilsen residents are classified as "undocumented," persons who lack proper naturalization papers. The roundup of undocumented workers by the Immigration and Naturalization Service (INS) is a familiar and dreaded event in the neighborhood. Many Mexican workers who are sent back to their native land return once again to the Lower

West Side where they are willing to work at jobs for low wages. Despite the problems of poverty, language, poor housing, and gangs, Pilsen provides hope for thousands of Mexicans in Chicago.

The annual Fiesta del Sol is one of many celebrations in Pilsen which reminds Mexican families of their cultural heritage. Every August since 1973, the Pilsen Neighbors Community Council has sponsored the event which includes live entertainment, music, carnival rides, refreshments, and crafts. This celebration of "hope and achievement" takes place along Blue Island Avenue from 18th to 21st Streets, once the heart of the Bohemian shopping district.

In Little Village, the community's main event is the annual Mexican Independence Day Parade (September 16), which wends its way down 26th Street from Sacramento to Kildare. Sponsored by the 26th Street Businessmen's Association, the parade is a testament to the thriving Mexican-American community once known as South Lawndale.

Every year Pilsen residents continue a centuries-old ritual known as the *Via Crucis*, the Way of the Cross. On Good Friday, Mexican Catholics reenact the Last Supper of Jesus Christ at Providence of God Church at 18th and Union. Following a mock trial, the crowd follows "Christ" as he carries his cross along 18th Street to Harrison Park where he is "crucified." The body of "Christ" is then carried on a bier to St. Adalbert Church where the ceremony concludes. Unlike any other celebration, the *Via Crucis* symbolizes the suffering endured by local families as they struggle for economic survival in the city.

One of the most significant developments to occur on the Lower West Side in the past decade is a new spirit of cooperation among local Catholic churches and community groups. Once divided along ethnic lines, parishes in Pilsen, Heart of Chicago, and Little Village have pooled their resources to combat gangs and address the problems of Hispanic youth. In addition to supporting parochial schools, local parishes have waged a spirited campaign to establish the Pilsen Catholic Youth Center. This project is aimed at providing Hispanic youngsters with academic support, social activities, and religious guidance. On September 10, 1984, more than 1,200 residents braved the rain to show their support for the Youth Center, and they cheered young men and women as they marched along 18th Street.

The future of Pilsen as a Mexican community seems assured. And it is likely that as Mexican families move up the economic ladder, they too will follow the path taken by earlier Bohemian, Polish, and Mexican-Americans who moved to the "suburbs" of Heart of Chicago and Little Village and beyond.

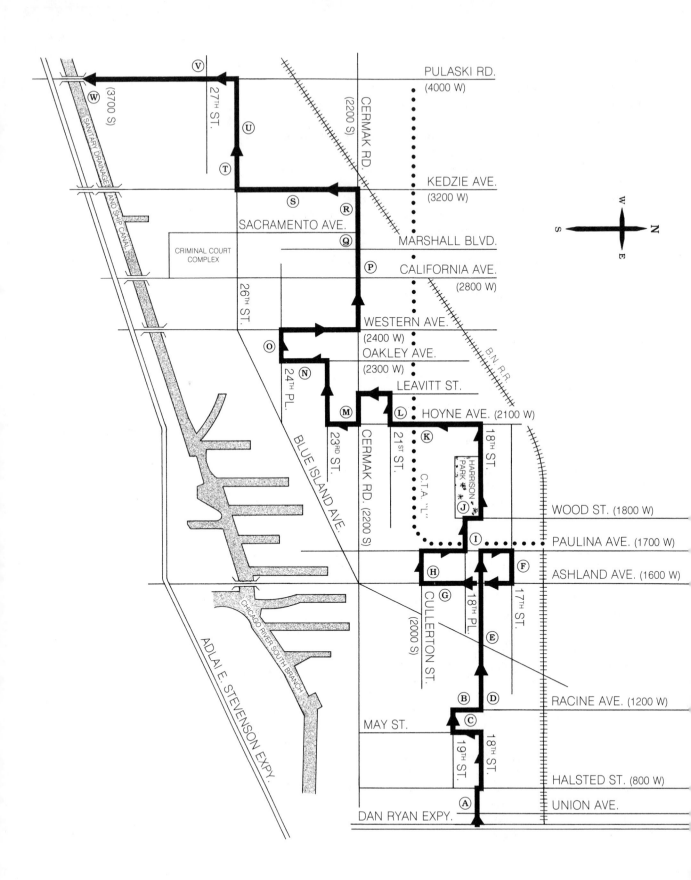

Lower West Side Tour

This tour begins at the 18th Street exit of the Dan Ryan Expressway and ends at the Pulaski Road entrance to the Adlai Stevenson Expressway. From 18th and Union in the Pilsen neighborhood, the oldest area on the Lower West Side, the tour goes west through Pilsen and Heart of Chicago to the 26th Street Little Village neighborhood.

Driving time: about 2 hours.

(A) Exit the Ryan Expressway at 18th Street and go eight blocks west on 18th to May Street (1132 West). Almost beneath the expressway at 18th and Union is **Providence of God Church (1927).** Originally a Lithuanian parish, Providence of God is now one of Pilsen's most active Spanish-speaking parishes. In 1979 Pope John Paul II stopped here on his visit to Chicago, the only Hispanic parish included on his tour. More than just a center of worship for local families, Providence of God is known throughout the Lower West Side for its efforts on behalf of undocumented workers. Few families in Pilsen are untouched by the plight of the undocumented. Despite the constant threat of deportation, men and women from Mexico make the long trip to Pilsen where they are willing to work for low wages.

At 18th and Halsted is the **Pilsen East Artists Colony,** established in the 1960s by John Podmajersky and his wife, Ann. A lifelong resident of Pilsen, Podmajersky has rehabbed buildings along Halsted Street for use as artists' studios. An estimated 300 sculptors, painters, ceramicists, photographers, writers, and actors now live in buildings which were once used as finishing shops for the West Side garment district. Each October, the local residents sponsor an art fair which draws patrons from all over the city. (18th Street jogs to the right at Halsted.)

(B) Turn left at May Street, go south to 19th Street, then turn right and go one block west on 19th to Racine Avenue (1200 West). Turn right and go north on Racine back to 18th Street. One of the few new buildings to be

constructed in Pilsen during the past twenty years is **Emmanuel Presbyterian Church** (1965) at the northwest corner of 19th and Racine. It contrasts sharply with neighboring buildings that date from the 1880s when Pilsen was a predominantly Bohemian neighborhood. Established as a Bohemian Presbyterian church, Emmanuel is now a Spanish-speaking congregation formed by the merger of three local churches in 1960.

(C) **Casa Aztlan** at 1831 S. Racine with its colorful murals symbolizes the ethnic and cultural changes which have taken place in Pilsen. Founded in 1905 as the Howell Neighborhood House, this was a Presbyterian settlement serving Bohemian and Slavic children in the area. Since 1970 the institution has been known as Casa Aztlan, reflecting its role as a Mexican-American center. After years of support by church groups, the institution is now sustained by grants from foundations such as the Illinois Arts Council and the National Endowment for the Arts. In addition to sponsoring traditional settlement activities such as English language classes, Casa Aztlan places special emphasis upon Mexican culture—dance, art, and theater. It also provides alternative activities for young people who might otherwise join local gangs.

(D) Turn left on 18th Street and go six blocks west to Paulina Street (1700 West). **St. Procopius Church** (1883) at the northeast corner of 18th and Allport (1235 West) was the first Bohemian Catholic church built in Pilsen, the "mother parish" of Bohemian Catholic communities throughout the West Side. Institutions which trace their origins to this Czech parish include Illinois Benedictine College and St. Procopius Abbey in suburban Lisle, Illinois.

(E) The 18th Street business district continues to be as important today as it was a century ago when Pilsen was strictly a "pedestrian neighborhood." Spanish signs now dominate the first floor shops, which run the gamut from Mexican bakeries, to grocery stores and butcher shops, bookstores, small clothing shops, taverns, and restaurants.

(Top left) Casa Aztlan, 1831 S. Racine, 1985. The Casa is an important center of Mexican and Mexican-American culture in the Pilsen neighborhood. Its exterior murals, painted by Ray Patlan from 1970 to 1973, have recently been refurbished. (J. Ficner)

(Bottom left) 18th Street looking east toward Allport, 1985. Once the center of Chicago's West Side Bohemian community, Pilsen is now a port of entry for Mexican families. St. Procopius Church, visible in the distance, has been a neighborhood landmark since 1883. (J. Ficner)

(F) Turn right at Paulina and go one block north to 17th Street, then right and one block east on 17th to Ashland (1600 West). The magnificent Roman basilica known as **St. Adalbert's** was built by the West Side's leading Polish Catholic congregation in 1914, forty years after the parish was founded. The church's murals and stained glass windows established St. Adalbert's as a Polish shrine. In recent years the church has taken on a new identity as predominantly Mexican. Symbolic of this change is the shrine in honor of Our Lady of San Juan de los Lagos (1975) with its traditional picture of Our Lady of Guadalupe.

(G) Turn right on Ashland and go four blocks south to Cullerton Street (2000 South). **St. Pius Church** at the southeast corner of 19th and Ashland is another of Pilsen's churches built on the grand scale. When the parish was founded in 1873, this part of the Lower West Side was not yet densely populated. By the time the imposing red brick structure on Ashland Avenue was dedicated in 1893, St. Pius was a large Irish parish. According to the Chicago *Inter-Ocean* in 1899, St. Pius was one of the poorest parishes in the city, with not "a single wealthy person in the congregation." It subsequently became a thriving Polish-American parish under the direction of the Dominican Fathers who took charge in 1922. Like Pilsen's other Catholic parishes which were divided along ethnic lines, St. Pius is now an Hispanic parish.

(H) Turn right at Cullerton and go one block west to Paulina (1700 West). The house at 1632 W. Cullerton Street was the family home of Alderman Edward F. Cullerton, one of Chicago's most notorious Irish-American politicians. Known as "Foxy Ed" because of his machinations as one of the City Council's "Grey Wolves," Cullerton was re-elected again and again by his constituents on the Lower West Side. During his thirty-odd years as alderman, he provided city jobs for local residents and did much to improve city services in one of Chicago's most congested neighborhoods. A year after his death in 1920, the City Council renamed 20th Street "Cullerton."

*Interior of St. Adalbert Church, 1656 W. 17th Street, 1980. Henry J.
Schlacks designed this magnificent Polish shrine, dedicated in
1914—forty years after St. Adalbert parish was founded.*   (A. Kezys)

Some of the brick cottages in the Heart of Chicago neighborhood were constructed before the street grade was elevated. Beneath the vaulted sidewalks, homeowners cultivate small gardens. (J. Ficner)

(I) Turn right on Paulina and go two blocks north to 18th Place, then one block west on 18th Place to Wood Street (1800 West). At the northwest corner of 18th Place and Paulina is the Bohemian church of **St. Vitus.** Between the time the parish was founded in 1888 and the present church was dedicated in 1897, this part of the Lower West Side was rapidly built up with workingmen's homes. Indeed, when the tracks of the Metropolitan branch of the Douglas Park "L" were laid in the 1890s, they passed perilously close to the neighborhood's homes—and to the old frame church of St. Vitus. The parish used the $25,000 settlement from the railroad to build a beautiful new church designed by the firm of Kallal and Molitor.

(J) **Harrison Park** at 18th Place and Wood, with its
distinctive brick fieldhouse (1924), is one of the few
open spaces on the Lower West Side. Because so many
of the neighborhood's homes are built close to the
sidewalk, there is little room for front yards where
children can play. Once the scene of Bohemian
gatherings, Harrison Park is now the site of Mexican
celebrations and athletic events.

(K) Turn right on Wood Street and go one block north to
18th Street, then left on 18th Street three blocks to
Hoyne Avenue (2100 West). Turn left and follow Hoyne
five blocks south under the "L" tracks to 21st Street. In
recent years the neighborhood known as **Heart of
Chicago** has been overshadowed by the Pilsen
community to the east. Area residents have responded
by proclaiming their neighborhood's identity through
colorful banners.

(L) Turn right at 21st Street and go one block west to Leavitt
Street (2200 West), then two blocks south on Leavitt to
Cermak Road. **St. Matthew's** parish complex at 21st and
Hoyne is a classic example of ethnic succession in the
neighborhood. The parish was founded in 1872 by
German Lutherans. The brick Gothic church on the
northwest corner of the street (1887) is also known as
Iglesia San Mateo. Lutheran services are now held in
both Spanish and English. Directly across the street, the
former German Lutheran school (1882) has been
converted into the Living Word of Faith Community
Pentecostal Church. Since the late 1960s many of the
Lower West Side's churches have taken on new life as
Evangelical houses of worship.

(M) Go one block east on Cermak to Hoyne (2100 West),
then right on Hoyne two blocks south to 23rd Street,
then turn right and go three blocks west on 23rd Street
to Oakley (2300 West). The German Catholic church of
St. Paul at 22nd Place and Hoyne has been rediscovered
in recent years by a new generation of architecture and
music lovers. Henry J. Schlacks designed this
magnificent Gothic structure with its twin towers, and it
was said to be his favorite among his Chicago churches.
St. Paul's was built in 1899 by German craftsmen from
the parish, a common practice in Europe. As finances

permitted, the interior of the church was embellished with spectacular mosaics; these were completed in 1930. St. Paul's is now well known throughout Chicago as a location for Music of the Baroque concerts.

(N) Turn left on Oakley and go south to 24th Place. Oakley Avenue with its restaurants and bakeries forms the heart of **Little Italy** on the Lower West Side. Around the turn of the century Italians from Tuscany displaced Swedish residents in this area. After World War II, immigrants from the Piedmont region of Italy moved into the neighborhood. The restaurants along Oakley and Western, which once served workers in the nearby International Harvester plant, now draw patrons from the city's North Side and suburbs. Although local residents are predominantly Italian-American, groups such as the Po-Piedmont Club testify to the persistence of ethnic identity.

(O) Turn right at 24th Place and go one block west to Western Avenue (2400 West), then right, going five blocks north on Western to 22nd Street (Cermak Road). **St. Michael Church** at 2325 W. 24th Place is one of Chicago's historic Italian Catholic parishes. Not only did Italians replace Swedes in this neighborhood, but in 1903 they constructed the superstructure of their church on the foundation of a former Swedish Methodist Episcopal church!

(P) Turn left on Cermak and go west one mile to Kedzie Avenue (3200 West). On March 15, 1933 the City Council renamed 22nd Street Cermak Road after Anton J. Cermak, Chicago's "martyred mayor," who had died nine days before. Cermak was one of South Lawndale's most famous residents, and his influence extended to the city at large. A former state representative, he was elected alderman of the old 12th Ward five times and served as Democratic ward committeeman for twenty years. Cermak's stand against Prohibition earned him the continuing support of South Lawndale's Czechs, Germans, and Poles. After serving as president of the Cook County Board and chairman of the Democratic Party, Cermak was elected mayor in 1931. His term of office was cut short by an assassin's bullet meant for President Franklin Delano Roosevelt. At the time of his death, Cermak still lived in South Lawndale, at 2348 S. Millard.

(Right) St. Matthew Church, northwest corner of 21st and Hoyne, 1980. German Lutherans founded this parish in 1872 and built the present church in 1887. Like other churches on the Lower West Side, St. Matthew's now holds services in Spanish and English. (G. Lane)

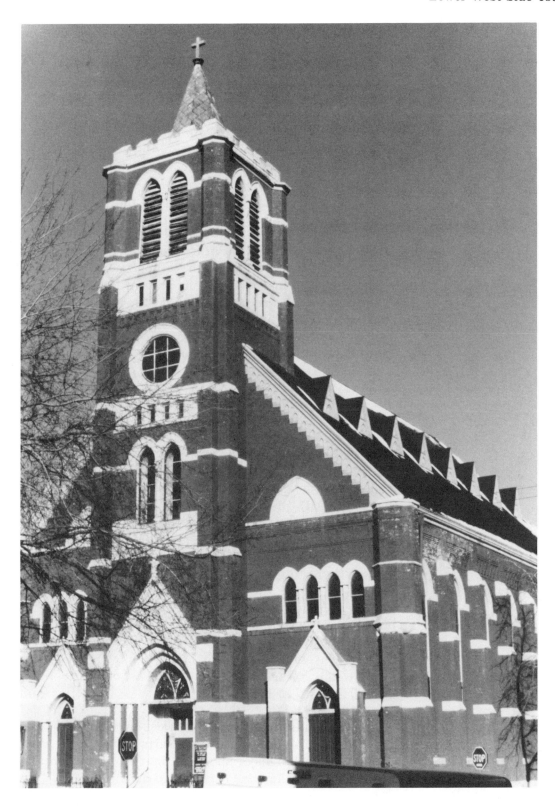

(Q) Although 26th Street has long been the area's major shopping center, Cermak Road still contains a number of institutions from the days when the neighborhood was known as South Lawndale. The **St. Paul Federal Savings and Loan** branch at 2854 W. Cermak, for example, recalls the role building and loan associations played in the development of the Lower West Side.

The **Marshall Square Theater** at 2875 W. Cermak Road now shows Spanish language fims. Named after the nearby Marshall Square Boulevard, the theater was one of South Lawndale's showplaces in the 1920s.

(R) **St. Casimir Church** at 22nd and Whipple is one of South Lawndale's most beautiful houses of worship, beloved by generations of Polish Catholics. The parish was established in 1890, and the present Baroque-style church was dedicated in 1919. Today St. Casimir's is the "old neighborhood" parish for hundreds of Polish-American families who have moved away from South Lawndale to other parts of Chicago and the western and southern suburbs.

(S) Turn left on Kedzie and go four blocks south to 26th Street. The **Kanoon Magnet School** at 2233 S. Kedzie continues an important tradition on the Lower West Side. Just as earlier public schools memorialized Bohemian and Polish figures such as Dvorak, Jirka, and Paderewski, so also new buildings reflect the neighborhood's Hispanic majority. The Kanoon School (1980) is named after Gerald Delgado Kanoon, a Mexican-born bilingual teacher and administrator in Pilsen and Little Village who died in 1978. He was well known for his interest in science and bilingual education.

The **Kedzie Avenue Municipal Public Baths** building at the southeast corner of 24th and Kedzie is a link to the days when neighborhood homes lacked modern conveniences. As late as 1944, fifteen percent of local dwellings, especially in the area east of Kedzie, had no private toilet or bath.

(T) Turn right on 26th Street and go west one mile to Pulaski Road (4000 West). For decades, 26th Street was South Lawndale's major shopping district, a function it continues today for the Little Village neighborhood.

Since the 1960s, Mexican-owned businesses have replaced older Bohemian and Polish establishments making 26th Street the city's most important Hispanic commercial center. In addition to establishing businesses, Mexican families have purchased homes in the neighborhood, following a pattern established generations ago by the pioneers of "Czech California." The **Lawndale Trust and Savings Bank** at 3333 W. 26th Street, founded in 1912, is the community's major financial institution.

Kedzie Avenue Municipal Baths, southeast corner 24th and Kedzie, 1985. As in other industrial neighborhoods throughout Chicago where homes lacked indoor plumbing, the Kedzie Avenue Municipal Baths offered modern bathing facilities.   (J. Ficner)

Little Village Shopping District, 26th and Spaulding. 1985. Formerly the commercial hub of South Lawndale, 26th Street is now a bustling Mexican-American shopping strip in the heart of Little Village. (J. Ficner)

Ⓤ Now known as **"Avenida Mexico,"** 26th Street contains a number of important institutions, among them the Little Village Community Council, the Chamber of Commerce, and the *El Heraldo* newspaper at 3610 W. 26th Street. Nearby at 2700 S. Harding are the offices of *El Manana*, Chicago's daily Spanish-language newspaper, the only one of its kind in the Midwest. The 26th Street Businessmen's Association (of which Mayor Cermak was once a director) remains a powerful group in the neighborhood.

(V) Turn left at Pulaski Road and go south to the Stevenson Expressway. The **Toman Branch of the Chicago Public Library** at the southwest corner of 27th and Pulaski was built when South Lawndale was a predominantly Czech neighborhood. It is named in honor of John R. Toman, alderman of the old 34th Ward and a close friend of Anton J. Cermak. Alexander V. Capraro designed this handsome building which opened June 5, 1927.

The 3100 block of S. Pulaski is typical of the housing that made South Lawndale a desirable neighborhood after the turn of the century. Substantial three-story brick buildings with their European-looking fronts provided countless families with the opportunity to become homeowners and landlords at the same time. Now as then, extended families are a familiar part of life in the Little Village neighborhood.

(W) Just beyond the Commonwealth Edison Crawford station, Pulaski Road crosses the **Sanitary and Ship Canal.** In 1892 construction began on a main channel known as the "Big Ditch" which would reverse the flow of the Chicago River and thus protect the city's water supply. This channel paralleled the old Illinois and Michigan Canal, constructed from Bridgeport to La Salle, Illinois in the 1840s. According to Louis P. Cain, the completion of the Sanitary and Ship Canal in 1900 had an immediate impact on the health of Chicago's citizens. Because raw sewage was no longer discharged directly into Lake Michigan, the typhoid death rate dropped dramatically, from 67 persons per 100,000 in the 1890s to 14 per 100,000 by 1910.

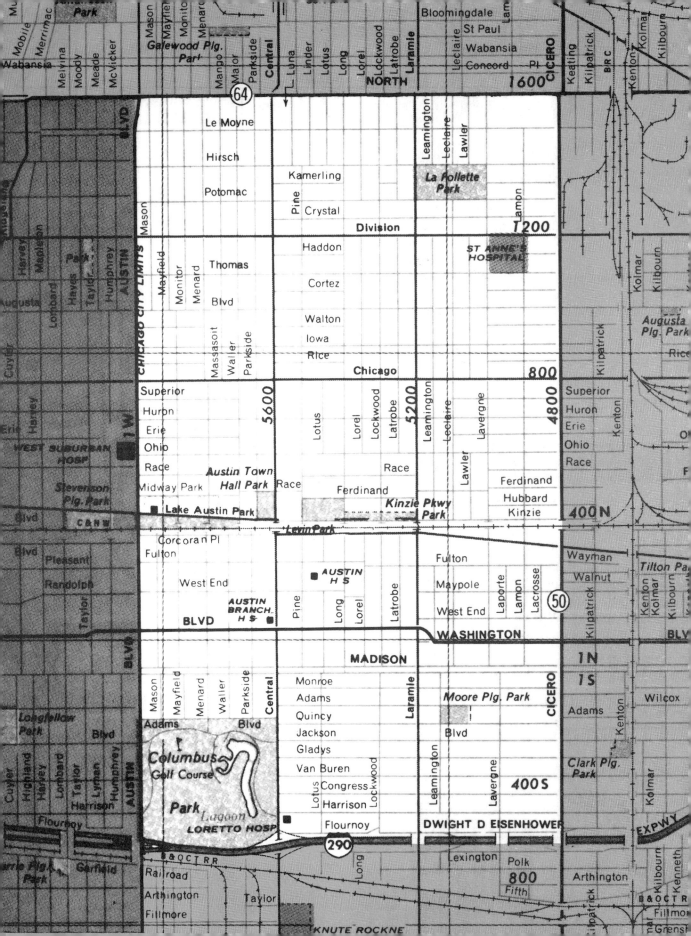

Austin

8

The Austin neighborhood on the Far West Side of Chicago
has experienced several transformations since its founding
in 1866. Originally a modest village located in the township
of Cicero, Illinois, it developed into an exclusive residential
suburb in the 1880s. Following a bitter battle over the
extension of the Lake Street Elevated Railroad, Austin was
annexed to Chicago in 1899.

As the city grew west to engulf Austin, the area took on
a new identity as a Chicago neighborhood. Not only did
Austin's housing stock change from frame houses to
multi-unit brick apartments and bungalows, but the
community's makeup also widened to include different
ethnic groups, among them Swedes, Irish, Germans, Greeks,
Jews, and Italians.

Between 1920 and 1960 Austin retained its reputation
as a middle-class white community. The area's well-built
homes and tree-lined streets gave the neighborhood a
suburban flavor, which was reinforced by its proximity to
Oak Park, Illinois. Beginning in the 1960s, Austin
experienced rapid racial change from a white to a black
community. As in scores of other neighborhoods on the
South and West Sides of the city, this transition completely
altered the composition of the community. Whereas Austin's
white residents had been predominantly middle aged, the
black newcomers were young and they supported larger
families. So great was the influx of young black children in
the 1960s that Austin's public schools became immediately
overcrowded.

By 1980 most of South and Central Austin had become
an established black community. New public schools were
constructed to meet the needs of the black children, and the
area's churches took on new life as black institutions. Like
other relatively new black communities in Chicago, Austin
includes a cross section of residents, from homeowners in
the neighborhood's bungalow belt to single-parent families
who live in rental units. To a certain degree Austin shares
the problems associated with Chicago's black ghettos: crime,
poor schools, high unemployment, and gangs. However,
unlike many other communities in Chicago, black or white,
Austin has retained its historic houses, which for decades
have symbolized the neighborhood's genteel character. In
recent years, white and black "urban pioneers" as well as
long-term owners have restored many old homes to their
former grandeur. Restoration of these homes has provided

Bird's eye view of Austin, looking southwest from the town hall, 1888. Young shade trees and new frame houses line the streets south of the Chicago and North Western Railway tracks.

(from *Picturesque Austin*, courtesy T. Barton)

the impetus for the nomination of Central Austin as an historic district, focusing new attention on one of the city's oldest neighborhoods.

Our history covers the area bounded roughly by North Avenue, Cicero Avenue, the Eisenhower Expressway, and Austin Boulevard. It encompasses the historic district in Central Austin as well the apartment house district along Jackson and Washington Boulevards to the south and the community's bungalow belt to the north.

Austin's beginnings were inauspicious. In 1835 Henry DeKoven purchased 280 acres of land from the federal government. This property, bounded by what is now Lake Street, Central Avenue, Augusta Boulevard, and Austin Boulevard, forms the heart of historic Austin. Although the Galena & Chicago Union Railroad (later the Chicago and North Western) began service from downtown Chicago along

Lake Street as early as 1848, little settlement occurred in the area. Indeed, when Henry Austin purchased DeKoven's farm and property in 1865, only five families lived in the vicinity.

Henry Austin was the Midwestern representative of the Gould Manufacturing firm, a hardware company based in his native New York State. Although he was not primarily a real estate dealer, Austin purchased a large amount of land in the area, and he used conventional methods to promote the development of his new subdivision; it included the area north of Lake Street to Chicago Avenue between Central and Waller. As a resident of nearby Oak Park, Austin was well aware of the important connection between suburban growth and commuter railroad service. According to one account, for years Henry Austin was the only resident of Oak Park "going regularly to the City to do business, and was frequently the only passenger from the station."

In the spring of 1866, Henry Austin built a depot at Central Avenue, which linked his subdivision to Chicago's business district. Next, he donated thirty acres of land to the U.S. Brass and Clock Company of New Haven, Connecticut. His efforts soon paid off. As a result of the establishment of the clock works at Lake and Waller in October 1866, nearly one hundred homes were built in the area over the next three years.

In 1868 Austin donated a four-acre block to the township of Cicero for a park and a town hall. With the construction of the town hall at Central and Lake in 1871, Austin became the seat of Cicero government. Henry Austin served briefly as township supervisor, and in that role he was responsible for the widening of Madison Street, Lake Street, and Chicago Avenue, as well as for the laying out of nine north-south streets, among them Central and Austin.

A fire in 1868 destroyed most of the clock works and prompted the relocation of many workers to Connecticut. According to the Chicago *Times*, this calamity forced the "aspiring burgh" of eight hundred residents to look to its future as a residential suburb. Although a shoe factory operated for a time in the shell of the clock works, Austin failed to attract any other large businesses. After 1873 the largest employer in the area was the North Western Railroad car shops at Lake Street and Cicero Avenue.

Another reason why Austin did not develop as a manufacturing district had to do with its prohibition of liquor. During his tenure as an Illinois legislator, Henry Austin drafted and introduced the Illinois Temperance Law, which was passed in 1872. Like other towns and villages outside Chicago's city limits in the nineteenth century, Austin remained "dry." Local boosters were firm in their

Austin Town Hall, Central and Lake, c.1909. From 1871 until 1899, this building served as the seat of government for the township of Cicero.
(C.R. Childs, courtesy G. Schmalgemeier)

Chicago and North Western Railway depot, Austin, 1888. Beginning in the 1880s, the North Western provided hourly service from Austin to downtown Chicago, making this an attractive residential district.

(from *Picturesque Austin*, courtesy T. Barton)

(Upper right) Intersection of Austin and South Boulevard (Corcoran Place), 1939. The elevated tracks are those of the North Western Railway. Until 1962, the Lake Street "L" operated at ground level from Laramie to Harlem.

(Chicago Park District, courtesy R. Wroble)

(Lower right) The Charles Hitchcock house, 5704 W. Ohio, is one of Austin's oldest structures, built in 1871.

(T. Barton, Commission on Chicago Landmarks)

belief that "the better class of people" would continue to build their homes "away from the contaminating influences of the Chicago saloons and under the purer and better air and freedom of the village of Austin . . ." Indeed, even after Prohibition ended in 1933, local residents waged a spirited battle to keep saloons out of their community.

The first building boom in Austin occurred after the Chicago Fire of 1871, when Chicagoans began to move beyond the city center in record numbers. Because Austin was not restricted by Chicago's fire code, frame construction was permitted. This factor, together with the relatively low price of land, did much to enhance Austin's future as a residential community. Whereas the first homes built in Austin were located north of the Chicago and North Western tracks, before long new houses appeared south of Lake Street also. Although many of the area's buildings in the 1870s were modest cottages, typical of a working-class community, a number of them, such as the Seth Warner mansion (1869) at 631 N. Central and the Charles Hitchcock house (c. 1871) at 5804 W. Ohio, embodied the suburban ideal. Warner's Italianate home was located on a six-acre lot, and the house was set far back from Central Avenue, the area's main thoroughfare.

Improved transportation contributed greatly to the development of Austin as a residential district during the 1880s and 1890s. In 1881 Henry Vandercook, a resident of Austin, inaugurated the West Chicago Dummy Railway which operated over West End Avenue from Madison and

Pulaski to Forest Park, Illinois. In 1889 Oak Park residents E.A. Cummings and D.J. Kennedy started the Cicero and Proviso Street Railway along Lake Street, from Cicero Avenue to Maywood, Illinois. By 1891 a streetcar line was in operation along Madison Street, and a Lake Street line was established three years later.

By 1881, the Chicago *Daily Times* estimated Austin's population at 1,600, "mostly Americans, whose moral, intellectual, and social status is of the best." During the next few years a number of substantial frame houses were built on both sides of the North Western tracks, between Pine Avenue and Austin Boulevard. One of the more elaborate of these which survives from that era is at 5804 W. Midway Park, designed by Frederick Schock for his family. Schock designed many homes in the area, giving the community an architectural continuity. His own house with its shingled surface and array of gables, turrets, and Victorian detailing epitomized Austin's identity as an exclusive suburban enclave.

Henry Austin was an early advocate of public parks, and during his years as a legislator he introduced the West Parks bill, aimed at increasing Chicago's greenery. Long after his death this legislation had important consequences for the Austin area. In the 1920s Columbus Park was developed as part of the West Parks system from land which had belonged to the Archdiocese of Chicago. Columbus Park was designed by the famous landscape architect, Jens Jensen, and was the last major park to be built on the West Side.

▼

According to A.T. Andreas, most real estate developers in Austin planted shade trees along the area's streets. Henry Austin went even further. He established parkways in the middle of such streets as Midway Park and Race Avenue in which to plant "evergreens and nut-bearing trees." In 1885 Austin also set aside property north of the railroad tracks between Austin and Waller for use as a public park.

Building and zoning regulations further enhanced Austin's desirability as a residential district. Until after the turn of the century, most of the area's housing stock consisted of single-family homes which were set well back from the street. Saloons were conspicuously absent, and until the late 1880s, the area's commercial strip was confined to the west side of Parkside Avenue between Lake and Ohio. Austin's fine homes and suburban setting had a powerful appeal to those upwardly mobile Chicagoans who wished to keep the city at arm's length. Many Austinites shared the feelings of a Chicago businessman who exclaimed that:

Columbus Park, looking west from Jackson Boulevard, 1937. The light standards at Central Avenue provided a gracious entrance to Columbus Park, the last major park on the city's West Side.
(Chicago Park District, courtesy R. Wroble)

Chicago is a great city, the place to make money. I like her during business hours. But my admiration is transformed into joy as I gaze upon her from the rear of a 5 o'clock train running at the rate of 30 miles an hour.

In the 1890s, improved transportation to Austin continued to be a major issue. Austinites generally favored the extension of the Lake Street elevated railroad beyond its Laramie Avenue terminus. They believed that a second rail link with Chicago would advance Austin's residential and commercial development, since "cheap and rapid transit is indispensable to the great mass of down-town workers." Oak Parkers vigorously opposed the extension of the "L" to Austin Boulevard, the dividing line between the two communities. Because the cost of commuting via the "L" was less expensive than the North Western, Oak Parkers feared their community would be inundated with residents of a lower social status.

Although Austinites won the battle of the Lake Street "L," their victory had a surprise ending. As the seat of Cicero government, Austin wielded a disproportionate share of political power. Critics charged that the vote on the "L" line had been rigged by board members from Austin. In retaliation, representatives from other villages in the township of Cicero promoted Austin's annexation to Chicago!

Menard Avenue, looking north across Augusta Boulevard, 1939. These two-flats were typical of the brick homes constructed in North Austin after 1910.

Less than three weeks after the opening of the Lake Street "L" station at Austin Boulevard, a township-wide referendum on April 25, 1899 decided Austin's fate. After more than thirty years as a village, Austin became Chicago's newest neighborhood.

Although annexation did not immediately alter the suburban character of the community, it had long term consequences for the neighborhood's future. Unlike Oak Park, for example, Austin was not able to restrict the construction of multi-unit apartment buildings, and this accelerated the transition of the community from a suburban to an urban neighborhood. As one of Chicago's many communities, Austin could exert far less control over its public schools than neighboring Oak Park, a fact which became increasingly clear as the community faced the challenge of racial change in the 1960s and 70s. Still, as Tim Barton has noted in his research on the Austin Historic District, the community retained its image as an affluent district through the maintenance of its historic homes long after Austin's population expanded to include blue collar workers and clerks in downtown offices and stores. Nowhere was the community's changing ethnic makeup more evident than in its churches.

Like other railroad suburbs in the metropolitan area,

First Baptist Church of Austin, 515 N. Pine Avenue, c.1910. Founded in 1871, the congregation built this edifice in 1902. The building now houses a black congregation known as the Original Providence Baptist Church. (Courtesy G. Schmalgemeier)

Austin was predominantly Protestant. In the l870s and 1880s, families of New England Yankee descent were well represented in the community, and they supported a network of churches, among them Baptist, Presbyterian, Methodist, Episcopal, Congregational, and Disciples of Christ. Many of these churches were located in "old Austin," the area's initial square-mile settlement, north of Madison Street, between Laramie and Austin. The First Methodist Episcopal Church of Austin, founded in 1867, selected a site at 502 N. Central, close to the town hall, which was considered by early residents to be the center of the community.

Irish, Scandinavian, and German newcomers did much to extend Austin's community, both geographically and institutionally. In 1889, for example, Irish Catholics built St. Catherine of Siena Church on Washington Boulevard at Parkside Avenue. This section of Austin was built up with modern "flat" buildings by the 1920s, which provided a middle-class lifestyle without the burden of home ownership. The first apartment house building in Austin was completed in 1892 at the southwest corner of Washington and Pine. Financed by T.A. Snow, the building was known simply as "The Washington."

While many of the new multi-unit apartment buildings blended in with older single-family homes, they were largely

Park Av. and Lake St., Austin, Chicago, Ill.

N. Central Av. Looking N. from O...

responsible for the neighborhood's rapid growth in population. Another contributing factor was the construction of the Garfield Park branch of the Metropolitan West Side Elevated Railroad in the 1890s. Now known as the Congress Street line, running just south of Harrison Street, the "L" included stops at Laramie, Central, and Austin. Like its counterpart on Lake Street, the Garfield Park "L" provided rapid, inexpensive transportation from Austin to downtown Chicago.

In the 1880s and 1890s a Scandinavian community grew up in the area called Moreland, located just west and south of the North Western car shops. As the Swedes and Norwegians moved up the economic ladder, many of them purchased newly built two-flats and bungalows west of Cicero Avenue, between Chicago and North Avenues. Unlike South Austin, which supported two elevated railroads, North Austin remained without rapid transit service to the Loop. However, this part of the neighborhood experienced rapid development after the streetcar line along Division Street was extended to Austin Boulevard in 1915.

According to a 1920s Sanborn fire insurance atlas, Austin was then a modern Chicago neighborhood with a wide range of housing and institutions. Extending northward from the old suburban settlement at Lake and Central was a district of bungalows and two-flats. There were many Scandinavian churches in this area. The Moreland Norwegian Danish Methodist Episcopal Church, for example, was located at 5101 W. Ohio Street, and the Swedish Evangelical Lutheran Mission occupied a church at 900 N. Waller. In keeping with its origins as a bungalow belt, North Austin included a high proportion of homeowners. This situation remained unchanged when Irish and Italian families moved into the neighborhood. Like earlier Scandinavian residents, Catholic newcomers established church-based communities within North Austin, notably Our Lady Help of Christians at Iowa and Leclaire and St. Angela parish at Potomac and Massasoit.

South Austin also reached residential maturity in the 1920s. Unlike the bungalow belt to the north, multi-unit apartment buildings predominated here, especially along Washington and Jackson Boulevards. Among the newcomers who settled in this part of Austin were Russian Jews who operated stores along Lake Street, Madison Street, and Cicero Avenue. The community's first synagogue, Congregation B'nai Israel, was formed in 1924. Three years later Jewish Austinites dedicated a massive temple at 5433 W. Jackson Boulevard.

In 1925, Greek Americans established the Assumption Greek Orthodox parish at the terminus of the Harrison

(Top left) Parkside Avenue and Lake Street, c.1909. Although Austin's commercial district had expanded since the 1880s, it still bore the markings of a suburban development thirty years later.
(Courtesy G. Schmalgemeier)

(Bottom left) Central Avenue north from Ontario (Ohio) Street, c.1910. This section of Central Austin was built up with spacious single-family homes in the 1890s.
(Courtesy G. Schmalgemeier)

William H. Byford School, Iowa Street between Parkside and Central, c.1908. The Byford, one of the city's oldest public schools, was constructed in 1892.

(C.R. Childs, courtesy G. Schmalgemeier)

streetcar line. After worshiping for many years in a frame church, West Side Greeks financed the construction of a splendid building at 601 S. Central Avenue, immediately north of the Frances E. Willard Hospital. This hospital, originally built as a hotel, was dedicated in 1928 in honor of the founder of the Women's Christian Temperance Union. Not long after the new Greek church was dedicated in 1938, the Willard Hospital changed ownership and assumed a new identity as Loretto Catholic Hospital.

Just as Austin's mainline Protestant congregations all built new churches after the turn of the century, so too Catholics participated in the church-building boom as they became the area's largest denomination. In 1909 Resurrection and St. Thomas Aquinas parishes were established to serve the rapidly increasing Irish Catholic population in the area bounded by Kinzie, Kenton, 12th (Roosevelt), and Central. Two years later the mission of St. Lucy at 5920 W. Lake Street was raised to the status of a parish. In 1917 St. Catherine of Siena Church moved to the Oak Park side of Austin Boulevard where an imposing parish complex was constructed over the next four decades. In 1925 the Sisters of Mercy reestablished St. Catherine Academy for girls in a new building at the northwest corner of Washington Boulevard and Central Avenue.

Assumption Greek Orthodox Church, 601 S. Central, 1980. Constructed just east of Columbus Park in 1938, this magnificent Byzantine structure continues as a center of Greek worship. (G. Lane)

As in other urban neighborhoods throughout Chicago, Austin supported a number of theaters and banks, all of which were built on the grand scale. The Ambassador Theater, built in 1925 at 5825 W. Division, was one of North Austin's showplaces. Later renamed in honor of Knute Rockne, of Notre Dame football fame, the theater catered to the area's large Scandinavian population as well as to the growing Irish Catholic community.

Chicago Avenue contained its share of community institutions, and it rivaled the Madison Street business district in size and influence. At the east end of Chicago Avenue was the Symphony Theater (4937 W.) and at the west end, the Iris Theater (5743 W.). Almost in the middle of the Chicago Avenue shopping strip was the Citizens Bank, at Laramie, a stunning example of Art Deco architecture.

According to the 1930 census, Austin was a multi-ethnic neighborhood. While foreign-born Swedes, Norwegians, Danes, and Germans predominated in North Austin, foreign-born Irish, Italians, Greeks, and Russian Jews were well represented in the area south of Lake Street. In addition to being divided along ethnic lines, Austin's

827.

Ohio St. West from Prairie Av.
Austin, Chicago, Ill.

population was far from being evenly distributed. Indeed, nearly 50,000 of the community's 113,258 residents were concentrated in the district bounded by Lake, Kenton, Harrison, and Austin. Because South Austin contained more apartment buildings than single-family homes, as late as 1970 its population was greater than that of North Austin.

Although the community declined in numbers during the post-World War II era, Austin remained one of the most stable neighborhoods in the city. While many Austinites commuted to Loop offices and stores via the "L," others worked nearby in the factory district between Lexington and Roosevelt and the industrial district east of Cicero Avenue. Beginning in 1960, the Congress (now Eisenhower) Expressway linked Austin to downtown Chicago as well as to the western suburbs.

By the early 1960s Austin was located in the path of the West Side's expanding black ghetto. As the neighborhood around Garfield Park changed from white to black, Austinites feared that their community would soon be resegregated. According to the 1960 census, Austin was then an all-white community with a sizable ethnic population. In less than ten years, however, South Austin had become a predominantly black neighborhood. Nowhere was racial change more evident than in the local public schools. Austin High School, for example, at 231 N. Pine, enrolled only one black student in 1963. By 1972 it was nearly an all-black institution.

As elementary schools in South Austin became overcrowded, the Chicago Board of Education inaugurated a busing program. Beginning in 1968, black children who lived south of Lake Street between Laramie and Cicero were bused to eight underutilized schools in North Austin and on the Northwest Side of the city. Despite opposition from white residents in North Austin, the program remained in effect for several more years. As racial change continued in South Austin, new facilities were built to meet the needs of the community's expanding black population.

In 1967 the Organization for a Better Austin was formed with the support of area churches. In addition to launching a campaign against panic peddling by unscrupulous real estate dealers, OBA established a housing referral service as a way to attract white families to Austin. However, as Carole Goodwin notes in her study, *The Oak Park Strategy,* OBA was unable to effect racial integration in predominantly white North Austin, and the group had to compete with "the many private real estate firms that were more than willing to place black families in the fringe areas."

The Organization for a Better Austin focused attention on the economics of racial change. They opposed the federal

(Top left) Austin High School, c.1917. This structure was replaced by a new school building at 231 N. Pine in 1930. Austin High School's enrollment peaked at 4,000 students in the early 1970s during a period of rapid racial change.
(Courtesy G. Schmalgemeier)

(Bottom left) Race Street looking west from Menard, c.1910. These frame houses are typical of the architecture built in Central Austin between 1880 and 1910.
(C.R. Childs, courtesy G. Schmalgemeier)

government's policy of granting FHA mortgages for homes and apartment buildings that did not meet building codes, and they demonstrated against realtors who engaged in panic peddling. According to sociologist Robert Bailey, OBA organizers paid home visits to absentee slum landlords: "Often a visit by twenty or thirty black tenement-dwellers is sufficient to pressure a white suburbanite to repair his inner-city buildings."

However effective, the controversial tactics adopted by OBA organizers alienated many long-time Austinites. They supported the group known as the Town Hall Assembly, named for Austin's historic meeting place. Unlike the Organization for a Better Austin, the Town Hall Assembly eschewed confrontation politics and preferred to emphasize the neighborhood's fine housing stock and the community's many churches and fraternal groups. In the end, as Goodwin argues, both groups failed in their attempt to stabilize Austin.

By 1980 South Austin was virtually an all-black community with a population of 54,000. As in other Chicago neighborhoods, racial succession had occurred from east to west. Unlike the South Side, however, racial change in Austin proceeded from south to north. The last section of South Austin to experience racial transition was located west of Central, between Madison and the Chicago and North Western tracks. From twenty-one percent black in 1970, this part of South Austin was ninety-nine percent black by 1980. Of all the census tracts in Austin, this district had the lowest percentage of owner-occupied units in 1970 and 1980, a fact directly related to the area's preponderance of apartment buildings.

Despite the complete racial transition in South Austin, North Austin was still predominantly white in 1970. Thereafter, change occurred swiftly. By 1980, the neighborhood between the Chicago and North Western tracks and Division Street was eighty-two to ninety-seven percent black. But because of the large number of bungalows and two-flats in the area, the percentage of owner-occupied units did not change dramatically as North Austin became a black community.

Present-day Austin encompasses several communities: South Austin, with its high percentage of apartments; historic Central Austin, with its elegant Queen Anne homes; and the North Austin bungalow belt.

In addition to middle-class black homeowners, Austin includes many poor families. Unemployment in the area has skyrocketed, and Austin High School's drop-out rate is one of the city's highest. Abandoned buildings remain a persistent

Frederick R. Schock House, 5804 W. Midway Park (right) and the Frederick C. Beeson House, 5810 W. Midway Park. These elegant Queen Anne style homes, designed by Schock in 1886 and 1892, are showplaces in the Austin Historic District. (G. Lane)

problem. Apart from health and safety factors, vacant apartment buildings undermine the efforts of area residents to maintain their property.

One of the most positive developments to occur in the neighborhood has been the designation in 1985 of a portion of Central Austin to the National Register of Historic Places. In addition to elaborate wooden Queen Anne homes from the 1880s and 1890s, this district contains splendid examples of modern "flat" buildings which hastened the transformation of Austin from a suburban to an urban neighborhood. The Austin Schock Neighborhood Association sponsors an annual house tour, which attracts crowds from all over Chicago. However, the interest in Austin's homes has sparked charges of gentrification from some local community groups. On the whole, long-term black homeowners in Austin welcome the efforts of urban pioneers who have carefully restored many of the area's gracious homes. As in the past, property owners hold the key to Austin's future as a stable residential neighborhood.

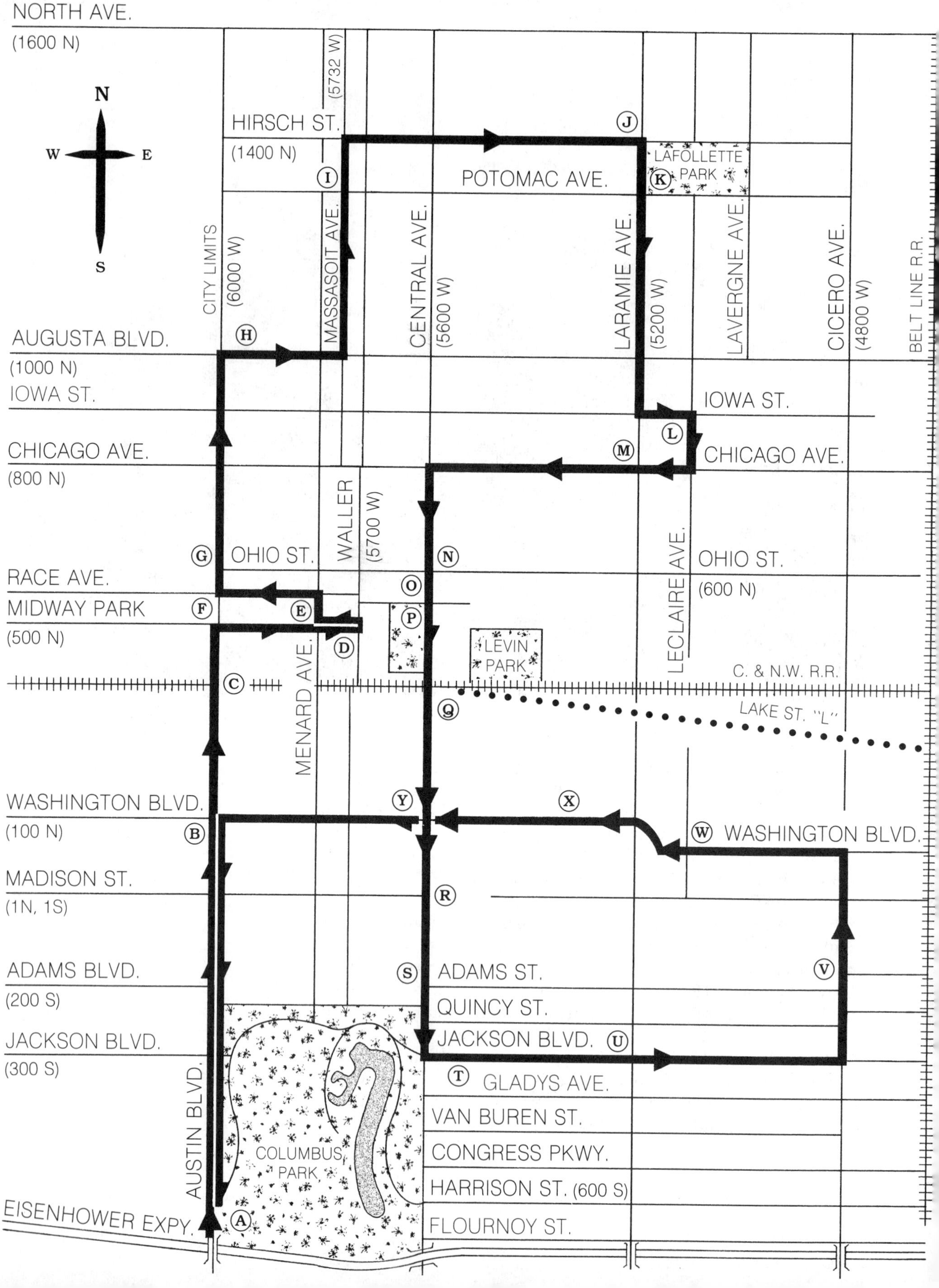

NORTH AVE.
(1600 N)
N
W
E
S
HIRSCH ST.
(1400 N)
(5732 W)
POTOMAC AVE.
LAFOLLETTE PARK
CITY LIMITS
(6000 W)
MASSASOIT AVE.
CENTRAL AVE.
(5600 W)
LARAMIE AVE.
(5200 W)
LAVERGNE AVE.
CICERO AVE.
(4800 W)
BELT LINE R.R.
AUGUSTA BLVD.
(1000 N)
IOWA ST.
IOWA ST.
CHICAGO AVE.
(800 N)
CHICAGO AVE.
WALLER
(5700 W)
OHIO ST.
OHIO ST.
(600 N)
LECLAIRE AVE.
RACE AVE.
MIDWAY PARK
(500 N)
MENARD AVE.
LEVIN PARK
C. & N.W. R.R.
LAKE ST. "L"
WASHINGTON BLVD.
(100 N)
WASHINGTON BLVD.
MADISON ST.
(1N, 1S)
ADAMS BLVD.
(200 S)
ADAMS ST.
QUINCY ST.
JACKSON BLVD.
(300 S)
JACKSON BLVD.
GLADYS AVE.
VAN BUREN ST.
CONGRESS PKWY.
HARRISON ST. (600 S)
FLOURNOY ST.
AUSTIN BLVD.
COLUMBUS PARK
EISENHOWER EXPY.
A
B
C
D
E
F
G
H
I
J
K
L
M
N
O
P
Q
R
S
T
U
V
W
X
Y

Austin Tour

This tour of the West Side neighborhood of Austin begins and ends at the Austin Boulevard ramp of the Dwight D. Eisenhower Expressway. It goes through the Old Austin Historic District, the bungalow district of North Austin, and the apartment neighborhoods of South Austin.

Driving time: about 1½ hours.

(A) Exit the Eisenhower Expressway at Austin Boulevard (6000 West) and go about eleven blocks north on Austin to Midway Park (500 North). Bordering Austin Boulevard on the east is **Columbus Park,** the West Side's last major park. Noted landscape architect Jens Jensen used indigenous plants and shrubs to create a setting that would reflect the beauty of the Midwest's prairies. Like Washington Park on the South Side, Columbus Park was not primarily an active recreational center but a passive suburban retreat for city dwellers. Indeed, at the time Columbus Park was laid out in the 1920s, Austin was just completing the transition from a suburban to an urban community.

(B) Austin Boulevard is the historic dividing line between Oak Park on the west and Austin on the east. "Working Together" banners along the boulevard proclaim a new spirit of cooperation between these two communities.

St. Catherine of Siena parish complex occupies the southwest corner of Austin and Washington Boulevards. Founded in 1889 as Austin's first Catholic parish, St. Catherine's relocated to this site in Oak Park in 1917. Like other "boulevard" churches in the city, St. Catherine's was built on the grand scale. Joseph W. McCarthy designed the present Tudor Gothic edifice, which was opened for use in 1931. As a result of racial change, nearby St. Lucy parish at 5920 W. Lake Street was consolidated with St. Catherine of Siena in 1974. St. Catherine's has a long tradition as an activist community, and for more than fifteen years it has maintained its status as an integrated parish.

Just north of St. Catherine's at 2 W. Washington Boulevard is another house of worship which draws its congregation from both Austin and Oak Park. Established as the Washington Boulevard Methodist Church, the institution is now known as **Holy Trinity Church of God in Christ.**

(C) Just north of Corcoran Place, Austin Boulevard passes under the tracks of the Chicago and North Western Railroad and the Lake Street "L." Few city neighborhoods have such excellent links to downtown Chicago. Both the commuter railroad and the rapid transit line played a central role in Austin's development, and they did much to assure its desirability as a middle-class neighborhood.

(D) Turn right on Midway Park (500 North) and go three blocks east to the end of the cul-de-sac near Waller Avenue. This is the heart of **Old Austin,** which was named to the National Register of Historic Places in 1985. **Midway Park** is the sole reminder of Henry Austin's scheme to embellish the village's streets with parkways. Ironically, Austin was a lifelong resident of Oak Park; and although his name is associated with this Chicago neighborhood, he never lived within its confines.

In addition to its historic Victorian homes, Midway Park includes two of Austin's most prominent churches. William Drummond, an associate of Frank Lloyd Wright and an Austin resident, designed the First Congregational Church of Austin at 5701 W. Midway Park in 1905. It is now known as the **Greater Holy Temple of God in Christ.** Since 1880 the land at 5700 W. Midway Park has been the site of **St. Martin's Episcopal Church.** The present building was designed by A.M. Barrows in 1901.

Part of Henry Austin's legacy is visible to the east, across Waller Avenue. Austin donated land at Central and Lake for a town hall (1871) which became the village's municipal center. In 1927 the site was cleared and a Chicago Park District recreation center was built. The impressive structure continues to be known as the **Austin Town Hall.**

(Top right) Interior of First Congregational Church of Austin, 5701 W. Midway Park, 1911. William Drummond, an Austin resident and head draftsman for Frank Lloyd Wright, designed this Prairie-style church in 1905. Over the years, several congregations have worshiped here, including Seventh Day Adventists and Eastern Rite Catholics. Since 1973, the church has been known as the Greater Holy Temple, Church of God in Christ. (Western Architect, courtesy Commission on Chicago Landmarks)

(Bottom right) Austin Town Hall, Central and Lake, 1985. Now a Chicago Park District facility, this building was designed by Michaelsen & Rognstad and was built in 1929 on the site of the original town hall. It is a replica of Independence Hall in Philadelphia. (G. Lane)

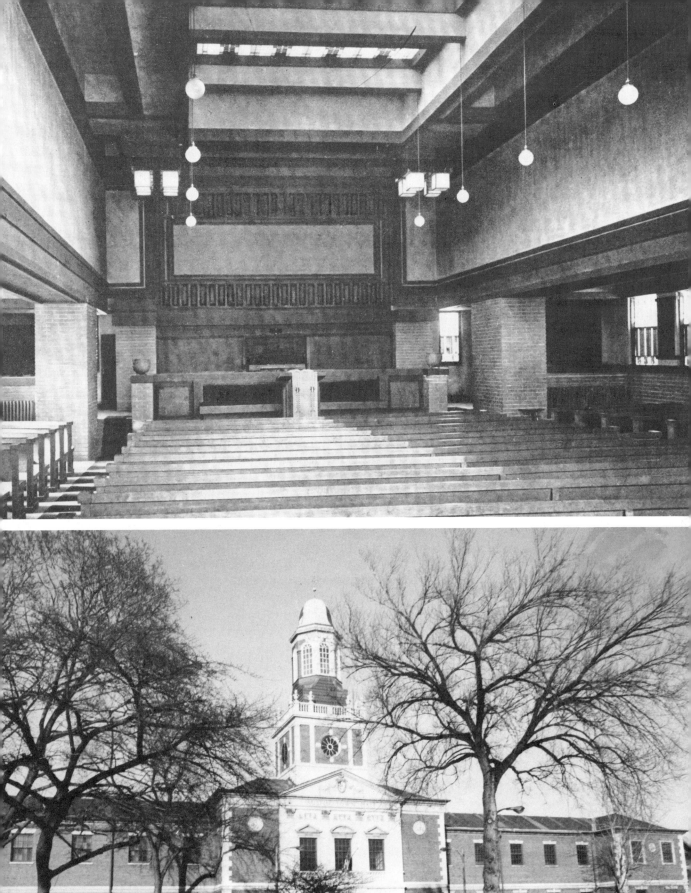

(E) Follow Midway Park as it loops back to Menard Avenue (5800 West). Turn right at Menard and go one block north to Race Avenue (543 North), then two blocks west on Race to Austin Boulevard. The Queen Anne style house at 5804 W. Midway Park was designed and built in 1886 by Austin architect Frederick Schock. Now one of the showplaces on the Austin Schock Neighborhood Association's Home Tour, the architect's family house received the 1981 City House award for excellence in interior rehabilitation and exterior maintenance. Nearby at 5804 W. Race Avenue is another Queen Anne style home designed by Schock and restored to its former grandeur.

(F) Turn right on Austin Boulevard and go nine blocks north to Augusta Boulevard (1000 North). **West Suburban Hospital** at Erie and Austin in Oak Park has been serving the Austin and Oak Park communities since 1911. A modern structure was completed in 1982.

(G) Another of the many institutions located on the Oak Park—Austin border is **Austin Boulevard Christian Church,** 634 N. Austin. Organized in 1898, the congregation built a church in 1910 at Race and Pine known as the "bungalow church." In 1923 the present church was built on the Oak Park side of Austin Boulevard; the educational wing dates from 1960. Unlike many mainline Protestant churches in America's small towns and villages which adhered to strict divisions, the Christian Church has been an ecumenical congregation with a strong belief in Christian unity. The Austin Boulevard Christian Church is known as the "border church," and part of its mission is to bridge the gap between Austin and Oak Park.

(H) Turn right on Augusta Boulevard and go five blocks east to Massasoit Avenue (5734 West). Augusta is one of Chicago's little known boulevards. Beginning near Racine Avenue on the Near Northwest Side in the old "Polonia" district, it continues west through the Ukrainian Village, past Humboldt Park, to Austin. Unlike Jackson and Washington Boulevards to the south, Augusta Boulevard was built up with bungalows and two-flats, making it one of North Austin's most desirable streets.

Lorel Avenue looking north across Augusta Boulevard, 1939. These bungalows, built between 1910 and 1930, attracted middle-class families to North Austin.
(Chicago Park District, courtesy R. Wroble)

(I) Turn left at Massasoit and go four blocks north to Hirsch Street (1400 North). **St. Angela Church** at the northwest corner of Potomac and Massasoit was one of Chicago's first "bungalow belt" parishes in 1916, established when this part of North Austin was just beginning to be built up. As the Catholic population in the district increased, so did the parish complex. At the time the present church was dedicated in 1952, St. Angela's was an ethnically diverse parish with an average Sunday Mass attendance of 7,000 people. As a result of racial change in the area, the parish membership is smaller now, but its school continues as an important neighborhood institution.

Turn right on Hirsch and go twelve blocks east to Laramie (5200 West).

Sketch of La Follette Park fieldhouse, 1333 N. Laramie Avenue. This massive building, designed by Michaelsen & Rognstad, was completed in 1929.
(Courtesy, T. Barton)

(J) **Trinity Evangelical Lutheran Church** at 1400 N. Laramie was begun in 1924 by a German Lutheran congregation which had moved to North Austin from Chicago Avenue and Ada Street on the Near Northwest Side. Founded in 1870, Trinity Lutheran escaped destruction in the Chicago Fire of 1871. The church on Ada continued in use until 1924, when it was converted into a factory. Like many of Austin's houses of worship, Trinity was built in stages, over a twenty-five year period, with the main sanctuary dedicated in 1949. Now an integrated parish, Trinity still holds an annual "homecoming celebration" each November for families who have moved to other parts of the city and suburbs.

(K) Turn right at Laramie and go six blocks south to Iowa Street (900 North). **La Follette Park** on your left was named for the Wisconsin senator who ran for president in 1924 under the banner of the Progressive Party. In the 1920s urban planners sought increased cooperation between local public schools and parks. Although La Follette Park was located close to the **Lewis School,** the cooperative venture never materialized. Nevertheless, La

Follette was one of the few open spaces in North Austin, and it came to be an important neighborhood institution. The present fieldhouse was completed in 1929 according to the plans of Michaelsen & Rognstad, who also designed the Austin Town Hall building in the same period.

(L) Turn left at Iowa Street and go two blocks east to Leclaire Avenue (5100 West), then right on Leclaire one block to Chicago Avenue (800 North). When **Our Lady Help of Christians** parish was established in 1901, this part of Austin was predominantly Swedish. Within twenty-five years, however, the Irish population of the neighborhood had increased to such an extent that larger quarters were needed for the church. The present Italian Renaissance style church at Iowa and Leclaire was designed by Gerald A. Barry and dedicated in 1927. Over the years Our Lady Help of Christians has been one of Austin's most ethnically diverse congregations serving Irish, Italian, Polish, Filipino, Spanish-speaking, and black Catholics.

(M) Turn right on Chicago Avenue and go eight blocks west to Central Avenue (5600 West). The **Citizens National Bank of Chicago,** 5200 W. Chicago Avenue, was one of Austin's largest public buildings. The architectural firm of Meyer & Cook designed this magnificent Art Deco structure, which continues to be a neighborhood landmark after more than fifty years.

(N) Turn left on Central and go twelve blocks south to Jackson Boulevard (300 South). The **Seth P. Warner house** at 631 N. Central (1869) is Austin's oldest building. As Austin grew in popularity during the 1870s, Central Avenue became the village's most fashionable street, a distinction it retained for several decades. Unlike most of Austin's early structures, the Warner house was built of brick. By the 1880s, however, it was no longer a country estate. The Warner property subsequently was subdivided, and new homes were constructed, such as the **Thomas J. Langford house** at 621 N. Central. From 1924 to 1979 the Warner house contained the Austin Academy of Fine Arts. Once again a private residence, the large brick house is one of Austin's showplaces.

(O) Another building which recalls Central Avenue's heyday as a fashionable street is the **Gammon United Methodist Church** at 502 N. Central. Established in 1867 as the Austin Methodist Episcopal Church, the present structure dates from 1910.

(P) Few Chicago neighborhoods can claim a landmark as impressive as the **Austin Town Hall** (1929) located at the corner of Lake and Central. Its architecture inspired by Independence Hall in Philadelphia, this building marks the spot of the original town hall, which was constructed in 1871 when Austin was the seat of Cicero township government. The architectural firm of Michaelsen & Rognstad designed the town hall, and the library north of it at 5615 W. Race Avenue was designed by Alfred Alschuler in 1930.

(g) Reflecting South Austin's identity as a black neighborhood is the **Kingdom Baptist Church** at 301 N. Central. This structure was built in 1926 as the Fifteenth Church of Christ Scientist. Today it is a flourishing black Baptist congregation.

The **J.J. Walser house** (1903) at 42 N. Central was designed by Frank Lloyd Wright and designated a Chicago landmark in 1984. It is a good example of Wright's mature Prairie style adapted to a rather narrow city lot.

(R) At Madison Street, look east toward the Loop. On a clear day the highrises of Chicago's business district are visible in the distance. More than just an important transportation artery, Madison Street was also a commercial link between Oak Park, Austin, and the larger city.

(S) **Pleasant Ridge Missionary Baptist Church** at 116 S. Central is a classic example of ethnic succession in the Austin neighborhood. The building, which formerly housed the Austin Jewish Community Center, has taken on new life as a black institution.

(Top left) Three of Austin's historic houses are located in the 600 block of N. Central Avenue: the Seth P. Warner house (1869), the Henry Beyer house (1902), and the Thomas Langford house (1895). (G. Lane)

(Bottom left) Frank Lloyd Wright designed the J.J. Walser house at 42 N. Central in 1903. It was designated a Chicago Landmark in 1984. (Frank Lloyd Wright: Chicago, courtesy Commission on Chicago Landmarks)

(T) Turn left at Jackson Boulevard and go six blocks east to Cicero Avenue (4800 West). The **Bethel Apostolic Church** at 5433 W. Jackson Boulevard occupies the former Congregation B'nai Israel. Austin's first Jewish congregation built this synagogue in 1927.

(U) One of the few new buildings constructed in Austin in recent years is the **Friendship Baptist Church** at 5200 W. Jackson Boulevard. In contrast to other black congregations which purchased existing churches in Austin, Friendship Baptist dedicated this impressive structure on April 3, 1983. According to Pastor Shelvin J. Hall, it is one of the few black churches in Chicago designed in an African motif. Friendship Baptist is the second oldest black congregation on the West Side, organized in 1897. Over the years the church has occupied several locations among them one at Damen and Washington and more recently, the former Anshe Kneseth Israel (Russishe Shul) synagogue at 3411 W. Doulgas Boulevard in the Lawndale neighborhood.

Just east of Friendship Baptist Church on Jackson Boulevard is the parish complex known as **Resurrection.** Irish Catholics established this parish in 1909, and in less than ten years they had built a twin-spired Romanesque structure at the northeast corner of Jackson and Leamington. At the time "Res" celebrated its golden jubilee in 1960, this Catholic community claimed 79 priests and brothers and 71 nuns among its former members. Increasing heating and maintenance costs contributed to the decision to raze the church in 1984. Resurrection is now one of the West Side's best known black Catholic parishes, continuing its long tradition of education and community service.

(V) Turn left on Cicero (4800 West) and go five blocks north to Washington Boulevard (100 North). Cicero was once a thriving commercial district at the east end of the Austin neighborhood. Today vacant lots and a few small stores are all that is left of this shopping strip.

(W) Turn left on Washington and go twelve blocks west to Central Avenue (5600 West). **St. Thomas Aquinas Church** at 5120 W. Washington Boulevard stands in the heart of the apartment house district of South Austin. The Tudor Gothic structure designed by parishioner Karl

(Top right) Friendship Baptist Church. 5200 W. Jackson, 1983. In keeping with the congregation's desire for a church that would represent their black African culture, Weese Hickey Weese developed a "hut" form which rises above the surrounding urban landscape.
(P. Turner, courtesy Weese Hickey Weese)

(Bottom right) Jackson Boulevard looking east across Lockwood, 1936. In the distance are the twin towers of Resurrection Church, which dominated Jackson Boulevard from 1918 until 1984.
(Chicago Park District, courtesy R. Wroble)

Washington Boulevard looking east across Mayfield, c.1937. This apartment house district in South Austin was enhanced by the generous use of setbacks and shade trees reminiscent of suburban developments.

(Chicago Park District, courtesy R. Wroble)

Vitzthum was begun in 1923. George Cardinal
Mundelein protested that the height of the twelve-story
tower was excessive—but to no avail. Although the Irish
pastor blessed the cornerstone himself, he did not live to
see the church completed. Still the tallest structure in
Austin, St. Thomas Aquinas Church remains one of the
community's most beautiful buildings. St. Thomas has
been a predominantly black parish for fifteen years, and
it continues as one of Austin's most important
institutions.

(X) The north side of Washington Boulevard between Lorel
and Lockwood was once part of **"Hill Town,"** named after
Oak Park-Austin developer F.A. Hill. These homes,
designed by Frederick Schock, were scale-down versions
of the Victorian structures he created along Midway Park
and Race Avenue.

(Y) The northwest corner of Washington and Central (5600
West) symbolizes the vast changes which have occurred
since Austin was a suburban village. Originally known
as the Woodbury estate, the mansion on this property
became the nucleus of St. Catherine Academy in 1895.
As the institution grew, the Sisters of Mercy made plans
for a modern Gothic structure, which was dedicated in
1925. Renamed Siena High School in 1931, the
institution was the central Catholic secondary school for
girls on the far West Side of Chicago and the western
suburbs. As Austin changed racially from a white to a
black community, enrollment declined dramatically, and
in 1973 the building became a branch of Austin High
School. It is now headquarters of the **Circle Urban
Ministries.**

Drive six blocks west on Washington to Austin
Boulevard, turn left and go six blocks south to the
Austin ramp of the Eisenhower Expressway.

Old South Side

Chicago grew up on the South Side. It was here that the first residential development of any importance took place. The village first expanded to the south from Lake Street towards the marshy land along the lakefront. No obstacles like the Chicago River separated this part of the prairie from the developing core of the village that residents later called the Loop. The South Side was the first home for some of the most prominent families and businesses of the city.

In the early days of Chicago, many trade routes led through the future South Side. Most of these came from the south and east around Lake Michigan. They converged and led to Fort Dearborn on the south bank of the river near the lake. When the soldiers and white settlers abandoned the fort in 1812 to make their way toward Detroit, the Indians attacked them along the south lakefront near what is now 18th and Calumet Avenue. United States soldiers returned along this same route to reestablish the fort four years later.

As time went by and the village grew, it seemed natural for farmers and others to move south away from the center of town. In the 1830s the Clarke family house, the oldest building in Chicago, provided a country retreat at what is today 16th and Michigan. The Clarkes were soon joined by more illustrious neighbors as Chicago's middle and upper classes fled the quickly expanding city and moved south along Michigan and Wabash Avenues. The city's well-to-do first lived in what would be the southeast quadrant of the Loop. After the Great Fire of 1871, they moved south to Prairie Avenue creating Chicago's first Gold Coast.

The South Side's history would not, however, be simply the history of the rich and famous. This part of the city was soon engulfed by economic, racial, and social developments that would eventually transform Chicago from a sleepy trading post into a world class city. The city's vice district, which became known as the Levee, extended south from the Loop along State Street. Al Capone later had his headquarters in the Lexington Hotel on 22nd and Michigan. Irish, Jewish, Italian, Chinese, black, and other Chicagoans followed the white Anglo-Saxon Protestants down the great boulevards away from the city. Industry, too, made its way to the South Side eventually establishing itself in heavy concentrations on the Southwest and Southeast Sides. Two great universities also settled on the South Side, forever changing the economic and demographic character of their surrounding communities. Worn out neighborhoods, housing projects, gentrified areas, and lakefront middle-class developments have all appeared in this part of town. Two world fairs, the Columbian Exposition of 1893 and the Century of Progress of 1933, have also made their marks here. Certainly many of Chicago's problems as well as many answers to them have been fashioned in that part of the city which lies south of the Congress Expressway.

Near South Side

The area just south of the Loop today seems to be a haphazard collection of railroad yards, warehouses, and vacant lots. It is hard to visualize, even with the establishment of the Prairie Avenue Historic District and the opening of Dearborn Park, that this area once contained Chicago's most fashionable and most notorious communities.

That section of the city south of Roosevelt Road to 26th Street and from the lake west to the Rock Island tracks (Wells Street) has often been referred to as one neighborhood. In reality, however, it a collection of separate enclaves. Actually, the residential and political history of the area forces the northern boundary as far as Van Buren Street and the "L" tracks. But even this is an artificial demarcation, because the State Street commercial zone has had a very important effect on the Near South Side's development.

In 1836 when Chicago was still a log cabin settlement nestled close to the river, Henry B. Clarke built his splendid home "out in the country" near 16th and Michigan. The Clarke House stands today as part of the Prairie Avenue Historic District, not far from its original location. It is the oldest house in the city, and in its time it was a focal point for the residential development of the neighborhood. The house was moved to the 4500 block of South Wabash in 1871, but it was replaced by the mansions of the "Prairie Avenue Set" who settled in the eastern portion of the Near South Side.

Elegant, even opulent homes lined Prairie Avenue from 16th to 22nd Street and the area attracted many wealthy Chicagoans. The corner of 18th and Prairie became the social center of Chicago. Here stood the Pullman, Kimball, and Glessner mansions. The development of the district was the culmination of a movement of the upper middle-class south along Michigan Avenue which dated back to the Civil War. The southern portion of the city was more accessible to the downtown area, and so early residential development took place here. The location of the well-to-do on Prairie

Henry B. Clarke house, Prairie Avenue Historic District, 1985. Built in 1836, the Clarke house is Chicago's oldest building. It was recently restored and is now open to the public for tours. (G. Lane)

Avenue benefited the Near South Side in several ways—not the least of which was the development of public transportation, including streetcar lines and the Illinois Central Railroad, which stopped at 16th Street.

When the Chicago Fire struck in 1871, it did not burn the Near South Side; but it radically changed the future of the district. While the merchants were building their homes along the great avenues leading away from the central business district, their businesses were destroyed by the conflagration. The stores reopened temporarily along Wabash Avenue in a residential area. But when the new stores were built along State Street, the old homes on Wabash were turned into boarding houses or wholesale stores, permanently changing the character of the district.

Residential sections located in the southern and western portions of today's central business district were also destroyed by the fire. Many of the people moved further south. Among these were the prostitutes, gamblers, and other inhabitants of the vice district. They moved down State Street between Polk and 16th Streets, creating the infamous Levee District. The relocation of the vice district south and just to the west of the fashionable residential neighborhood along the lake created a problem for Prairie

Polk Street Depot, Polk at Dearborn, c.1915. Once a busy passenger and freight station, this historic landmark at the south end of Printer's Row is now being remodeled for office use.
(Courtesy T. Samuelson)

Avenue and led, along with other pressures, to the eventual decline of the South Side's Gold Coast.

The black community was also forced to move by the fire, relocating around 22nd and State Streets. Before the turn of the century Chicago's black population was very small and not as concentrated as it would become in later years; nevertheless, eighty percent of these people lived south of the Loop. But there was no ghetto. This would not develop until after the turn of the century with the rapid increase of the black population.

By 1880 all the basic elements which would determine the future of the neighborhood were in place, with one exception: the railroad depots. Of Chicago's six major depots, the Near South Side would have four of them. The construction of the Polk Street or Dearborn Station in 1885 heralded the beginning of railroad dominance in the community. It was followed by the erection of the Grand Central Station at Harrison and Franklin in 1891, the Illinois Central Station at 12th and Michigan in 1893, and the LaSalle Street Station at Van Buren and LaSalle in 1903. When the Santa Fe Railroad purchased the area west of State Street from Polk to 16th Street and developed it as a freight yard in the 1880s, it pushed the vice district further south into the area near 22nd and State (then known as the Tenderloin). Parts of the old vice district, however, did not move and they remained in operation, especially near the train stations. Some of Chicago's most notorious houses of prostitution were located along Plymouth Court to serve the hotels and the train stations. Nothing is left today of the old Levee.

The coming of the railroads, while they symbolized economic growth, meant the end of the Near South Side as an attractive residential area. The depots pushed out the slums and the vice districts, which in turn put pressure on Prairie Avenue. The exodus of wealthy families began in earnest in the 1890s, but it had already begun when the Potter Palmers moved to North Lake Shore Drive in the early 1880s. Prairie Avenue soon became known as the "Avenue of Widows," as the children of the rich abandoned the area. Within less than one generation Prairie Avenue fell prey to the changing economics of the "boom town." Chicago was a quickly developing American industrial city.

While Prairie Avenue was thriving and then going into decline, the vice district was flourishing and setting the image of the Near South Side in the eyes of most Chicagoans. The two politicians who "presided" over the various parts of the vice district known as the Levee, Cheyenne, and the Tenderloin were "Hinky Dink" Kenna and "Bathhouse John" Coughlin. In 1905 Mayor Carter Harrison II attempted to drive vice out of the downtown area. He cracked down on the houses of prostitution near the train stations and hotels. The most infamous of these was Custom House Place. Seven years later, however, vice still flourished a short streetcar ride away on 22nd Street near State, Wabash, and Michigan. Houses of prostitution operated openly in this area under the protection of Kenna and Coughlin. In 1915 the vice district was officially closed down, but the area continued to be a red-light district for years afterward. Vice had moved south with or without official sanction, and after 1905 it was dumped on the black community—which was also centered at that time around 22nd and State.

The ethnic composition of the Near South Side was as varied as that of the city itself. While white Anglo-Saxon Protestants predominated in the communities along the lake, other ethnic groups settled in the rest of the district. At first Irish and German settlers came into the neighborhood. A large part of the area was known as Conley's Patch, named after the Irish matriarch, Mother Conley. This patch or slum ran from 12th to 16th Street and from Michigan Avenue to the lake. By the time of the Fire in 1871, the Irish patch had spread to the west, all the way across the river. In fact, the neighborhood where Mrs. O'Leary's house and barn were located was known as the Patch. The eastern part of the Patch was destroyed by the second Chicago Fire in 1874, which cleared the area for development as a wholesale and warehouse district. Of course, the Patch was also adjacent to the vice district; and this would continue to be the case even when the inhabitants of the slum changed.

The Irish and Germans, who made up the bulk of Chicago's early immigrant population, began to move south by the turn of the century, along the major streets into Douglas, Grand Boulevard, Washington Park, and Englewood. And new immigrants took their places. By 1910 an Italian settlement developed on Federal Street below 22nd. The black population also began to grow at this time. The "Black Belt," as the ghetto used to be called, first appeared on the Near South Side.

From 1890 to 1915 Chicago's black population grew from less than 15,000 to more than 50,000. This growth was overshadowed in the next four years by the so-called Great Migration which brought another 50,000 Southern blacks to the city. This burgeoning population was confined in a way that it had never been before. While the majority of black people had always lived on the South Side, there was now a growing tendency to force them to live in a prescribed area.

In 1890 the black population was still fairly well distributed across the city. In the early years blacks were less segregated from white native Americans than the Italians were. But when the number of black people in Chicago so grew so dramatically during World War I, they did not settle evenly throughout the metropolitan area but became concentrated in certain neighborhoods. An obviously segregated housing pattern had developed. Yet even as late as 1910, not more than a dozen blocks were entirely inhabited by blacks. In many areas blacks and whites lived together in relative harmony. But as the black community spread south and east into more middle-class areas, violence erupted.

By 1910 the Black Belt stretched as far south as 39th Street. And over the next four years this area absorbed more than 10,000 new immigrants, so that it became almost totally segregated. Most of the southerners settled between Federal and State Streets. This was the poorest and most rundown part of the area. As the flood of newcomers continued during World War I, housing costs and demands skyrocketed in an already inflated market.

Blacks tended to pay higher rents for the same amount of space than did other ethnic groups. In a 1912 survey, one-half of the residents of the Polish Northwest Side, the Bohemian West Side, and the Back of the Yards paid less than $8.50 a month for a four-room apartment; half of the tenants in the Black Belt at the same time paid at least $12. Besides this, the apartments and houses in the Black Belt were in worse condition than those in the Back of the Yards neighborhood and in South Chicago's Bush.

The situation which pitted black against white in competition for housing and jobs was an explosive one. On

July 27, 1919 Eugene Williams, a seventeen-year-old black youth, was swimming off the 27th Street beach. He and several friends had built a raft and drifted across the invisible boundary that separated the black and white beaches. A lone white man began throwing rocks. Williams was struck in the head and drowned. The incident quickly grew into a full-scale race riot that changed the course of history on the South Side. Before the fighting ended, 38 people were killed and 537 were injured. Much of the fighting took place on the Near South Side and in the neighborhoods to the south of it. The conflict was finally ended by a rainstorm and the state militia.

As time went on, the Black Belt spread further south, and the black middle class abandoned the Near South Side. In 1926 the Chicago *Daily News* described this neighborhood as having the city's worst slums. The article pictured the area as having endless junkyards, a "purgatory of delinquent and incorrigible used cars." Despite the blighted conditions, State Street south of 22nd was still the principal black business district.

The Near South Side experienced a decline in population from 1920 until the decade of the 1940s, when there was an increase of over 4,000. This latter was the result of another large-scale black migration to Chicago during World War II. The following decade saw another decline in population. This was among the white population, while the number of blacks remained about the same. But the rise in population during the 1940s was not matched by a corresponding growth in housing units. Only five hundred units were added despite the huge increase in population. The result was a tremendous pressure on the black community, which was forced to live within a segregated housing market. The area fell prey to poverty and crime. The lack of housing and the pressure of a growing population accelerated white flight by people who could move more easily into better housing elsewhere.

The first attempt to deal with the slum problem was the construction of the Harold Ickes Homes on 22nd and State between 1952 and 1955. An unfortunate result of the project was that it put added pressure on neighborhood schools and reinforced the segregated housing pattern on the Near South Side.

Today the Near South Side still has warehouses, vacant lots, railroad yards, and slum housing. But it is also the site of the Prairie Avenue Historic District, R.R. Donnelley's Lakeside Press, the McCormick Place Exposition Center, and the Dearborn Park, Burnham Park, and River City housing developments on the community's northern edge. Much of the hope of renewal for this area revolves around these projects and the fact that the area is well served by mass transportation.

But the problems of the past remain, including the housing projects with their great concentrations of people and their especially large populations of children. It will take more than the revival of Prairie Avenue and the development of new housing to make a neighborhood community. It is significant that many of the new housing developments have few, if any, shops, taverns, grocery stores, hardware stores, drug stores, or other "third places" where people can socialize outside the home and workplace. Perhaps planners imagine that the Loop provides such conveniences. But the typical housing in these developments consists of highrises and townhouses.

As an avowed attempt to attract middle-class families back to the city, it is amazing that no detached housing with the traditional middle- and working-class yard has yet been built. Dearborn Park was intended for families, but it is actually occupied by singles and by couples with few or no children. While it is an economic success, Dearborn Park is neither a neighborhood nor a suburb. Its long-range benefit to the city will depend on urban planning that will take into account people's needs on a more human scale.

One saving grace are the old shops and stores surrounding the district on Dearborn and east of State Street. It seems inevitable, however, that many of these will be torn down and replaced with office buildings or more townhouses. There must be a more conscious effort to humanize urban renewal. Chicago cannot survive as a city of highrises and townhouses.

Douglas

The Douglas community area lies south of 26th Street along the lakefront. Its southern boundary is an irregular line that runs along 35th Street from the lake to Vincennes Avenue and then down to Pershing Road. The western border is formed by the railroad tracks which run just to the east of the Dan Ryan Expressway.

This neighborhood was first designated as a community area in the 1920s when the University of Chicago School of Sociology divided the city into districts in order to study the patterns that were emerging on the local level. More recent studies, however, by Albert Hunter and Gerald Suttles have demonstrated that Douglas is really no longer a community, if it ever was. Suttles referred to it as a "contrived community," contrived, that is, by researchers.

John J. Glessner house, 1800 S. Prairie Avenue, 1985. This historic building, the only one remaining in Chicago designed by Henry Hobson Richardson, was built in 1886. It is now the headquarters of the Chicago Architecture Foundation.   (G. Lane)

The Vincennes Apartments, 36th and Vincennes Avenue, c.1913. Fine apartment buildings and homes once filled the streets of the Douglas neighborhood.
(C.R. Childs, courtesy G. Schmalgemeier)

R.R. Donnelley & Sons Co., 350 East 22nd Street, 1985. The Lakeside Press was designed by Howard Van Doren Shaw and built in 1912 when the printer outgrew its previous facility on Plymouth Court. The building was expanded in 1929. Donnelley now has fourteen plants throughout the United States.   (G. Lane)

Entrance to Groveland Park, Cottage Grove at 33rd Place, 1985. This private enclave of homes and townhouses was first established by Senator Stephen A. Douglas before the Civil War.   (G. Lane)

Douglas is actually a large area that encompasses several communities. A discussion of the district begs the question of just what a neighborhood is. The housing between 26th and 39th Streets is of tremendous diversity. There are high-rise projects running along the eastern and western boundaries of Douglas, and yet there is little similarity between the two. In the middle there is housing which ranges from slums to fine old greystones which are being restored. Changes over the past fifty years have produced an area that is actually several neighborhoods. These developments are all grounded in the neighborhood's history.

The first settlement in this area owes its existence to two Indian trails which crossed at 35th Street and were later known as Vincennes and Cottage Grove Avenues. Livestock herders used these trails to bring their animals to Chicago. They used to stop at Myrick's Tavern on 29th Street and Cottage Grove where there were pens to keep the animals. In 1856 John B. Sherman bought the Myrick establishment and opened a stockyard on the property. This became one of the more popular livestock markets near the city. It continued in operation until Sherman opened the Union Stock Yard in 1865 to the southwest of his Cottage Grove establishment.

In 1852 Stephen B. Douglas had purchased a seventy-acre tract of land which ran along the lakeshore from 31st to 35th Street. He hoped to attract well-to-do residents to his subdivision, which he called Oakenwald. In 1855 Senator Douglas designated three acres of his subdivision for specific purposes. One was to be the site of an educational institution, and the other two were to be elegant residential parks. These latter became Groveland and Woodland Parks.

Douglas took up residence at 34 East 35th Street in 1854 and attempted to spur residential development in the area by offering the Presbyterian Church a ten-acre site for an educational institution. They turned down the offer, but the Baptists accepted a similar offer in 1856 and opened the University of Chicago in this vicinity four years later. This brought some residential development to Groveland and Woodland Parks. But the university, which was the forerunner of the present University of Chicago, closed in 1886 because of financial difficulties.

The Civil War brought further changes to this community. In 1861 the Union Army opened Camp Douglas here to train soldiers. The camp was located just to the west of the university on a site which ran from 31st to 33rd Streets and from Giles to Cottage Grove Avenue. In 1862 it was converted to a prisoner of war camp for Confederate soldiers. After the Civil War the camp was dismantled; but during its short existence it proved to be a magnet for residential development.

In the twenty years that followed the war, the two parks attracted wealthy residents. Groveland Park in particular attracted some of Chicago's prominent citizens. By 1880 Joy Morton, founder of the Morton Salt Co., was a resident of the park. The Douglas community was now developing as its founder had hoped.

Groveland Park and Woodland Park were not the only residential developments. In fact, the diversity of housing we see in present-day Douglas was there almost from the beginning. In the 1880s large single-family homes began to appear along Dearborn, State, Wabash, Indiana, and Michigan Avenues. These housed Chicago's growing upper-middle-class population as it moved away from the center of town. Michigan Avenue's 3400 block became known as the "Avenue of Mansions." Wealthy people settled here because Douglas was well served by transportation. The Illinois Central commuter trains stopped at 35th Street, and the major avenues were also served by horsecar lines. In 1881 a cablecar ran down State Street, and eleven years later the South Side elevated trains began to stop at 31st, 33rd, and 35th Streets. The excellent transportation made it

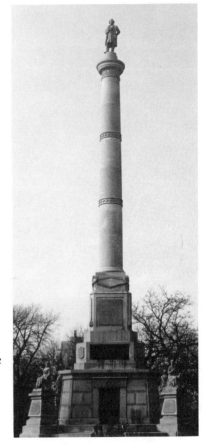

Stephen A. Douglas Monument and Tomb, 636 East 35th Street, 1985. This sculpture, completed in 1881 by Leonard W. Volk, commemorates "the Little Giant," probably the most illustrious national political figure to call Chicago his home. (G. Lane)

easy for white collar workers and management to live along the streets of Douglas and to get to work quickly and easily. While the wealthy people settled on the main streets, the middle class built comfortable homes on the sidestreets.

But this group of well-to-do people was different from those who lived in Groveland and Woodland Parks or to the northeast along Prairie Avenue. The families who settled along these streets had Irish and Jewish names. They were part of the emerging ethnic middle class of the city. Unlike those who settled to the east and northeast, they were Chicago's equivalent of nouveau riche. They built institutions, some of which still remain in the community. The Irish built and worshiped at St. James Church at 29th and Wabash. It was originally a working-class parish, but it soon took on the new character of the neighborhood. In 1863 the Sisters of Mercy relocated their Mercy Hospital and Orphan Asylum, as it was then known, to 26th and Calumet, where it would continue to serve the area with excellent medical care up to the present day. A new, twelve-story, 526-bed hospital was built to replace the older buildings in 1968. Meanwhile the Jewish community built Kehilath Anshe Ma'ariv Synagogue in 1890 at 33rd and Indiana. This distinguished building, designed by Chicago's famous architects, Adler & Sullivan, has housed the Pilgrim Baptist Church since 1922. The Irish and Jewish communities also established other institutions in Douglas which have continued to serve and grow since their beginnings in the nineteenth century. The Jews established Michael Reese Hospital in 1881 at 29th and Cottage Grove, on the site of the old Sherman Stockyards. And the Irish built De LaSalle Institute in 1892 at 35th and Wabash, a boys' school run by the Christian Brothers.

At the same time that these two communities were building their institutions, another minority group was making its way south along the boulevards from the Loop to the Douglas area.

In 1853 the first meeting of the Olivet Baptist Church took place in "downtown" Chicago. The black congregation grew quickly, and the church followed its membership out of the central business district to the South Side. In 1893 Olivet built a new church at 27th and Dearborn Streets, just a few blocks north of the Irish parish of St. James. The black community of Chicago was expanding south from the Loop.

Douglas was not only divided ethnically and racially by the turn of the century, but also by class. As the neighborhoods to the north and to the south of it, the community was divided in two by State Street. To the east

פתחו לי שערי צדק אבא בם אודה יה

OPEN FOR ME THE GATES OF RIGHTEOUSNESS,
THAT I MAY ENTER THROUGH THEM, TO PRAISE THE LORD.

Pilgrim Baptist Church, southeast corner 33rd and Indiana, 1985. This landmark building, designed by Adler & Sullivan for Chicago's oldest Jewish congregation, K.A.M., has been the home of Pilgrim Baptist since 1922.
(A. Kezys)

lived the rich, to the west the poor. While middle-class housing was erected along the boulevards, working-class homes were built on Federal Street which ran along the railroad tracks a couple of blocks west of State Street. At first Irish railroad and stockyard workers lived near the tracks along with some Germans. It was for this Irish community that the parish of St. James was first established in 1855. The whole length of Federal Street from 22nd to 54th Street soon became the longest slum in the world. The early division of the Douglas community in this way laid the groundwork for its later development.

The black community moved down the avenues west of State Street. New arrivals from the South first settled along Federal Street, and the slum soon became predominantly black. The black middle class, meanwhile, was looking for housing east of State Street; and that area became a battleground in the period during and after World War I. The war effort, in fact, set off the Great Migration of blacks from the South. The narrow Black Belt soon exploded, and the area populated by blacks expanded south and somewhat to the east. The intersection of 35th and State Streets became the center of Chicago's black community in the 1920s.

Mercy Hospital, 26th Street, Michigan, 25th, and Calumet, 1968. This
photo shows both the old buildings and the new construction of this South
Side Catholic hospital.   (Courtesy Mercy Hospital)

(Top left) Ida B. Wells Homes, 37th and Vincennes, 1985. This project was
the first federal housing built in Chicago. It remains a successful
residential area built on a human scale as opposed to the highrises of a
later period.   (J. Ficner)

(Bottom left) Armour Institute, 33rd and Federal Street, 1985. This
handsome building (1891) originally housed the Armour Institute, which
merged with the Lewis Institute in the 1930s to form the Illinois Institute
of Technology.   (G. Lane)

The huge migration of black people to Chicago changed Douglas dramatically. The ethnic middle-class people who could afford to leave did, many of them moving further south to Washington Park and eventually to South Shore. The white Anglo-Saxon Protestant middle class also moved south along the lakefront. By 1920 Douglas had a population of 58,388, seventy-four percent of whom were black. Ten years later the number of residents had dropped to 50,285, while the proportion of blacks rose to eighty-nine percent.

The segregated housing market in the city perpetuated the development of the ghetto, and by 1940 ninety-three percent of the population in Douglas was black. Douglas also became a slum. The old middle-class homes were subdivided into apartments, and the black middle-class population left, moving further south to the Grand Boulevard and the Washington Park areas.

In the early 1940s, plans for the renewal of Douglas began to take shape. The Chicago Housing Authority (CHA) opened the Ida B. Wells Housing Project at 37th and Vincennes in 1941. Nine years later the CHA opened another project on 27th and State Streets. This development, the Dearborn Homes, added 800 apartments to the community's housing stock. It replaced part of the old Federal Street slum. More developments were soon to come.

In 1937 Armour Institute and the Lewis Institute merged to form the Illinois Institute of Technology (IIT). The old Armour Institute building at 35th and Federal became the center of a new campus which changed the structure of Douglas. The school's decision to stay on the South Side meant that any renewal of the neighborhood would have firm institutional support. In 1946 IIT and Michael Reese Hospital combined efforts to organize the South Side Planning Board (SSPB). This new organization was to draw up plans for the redevelopment of the area. Meanwhile Mercy Hospital began to debate whether to stay or leave the area immediately north of Douglas. The debate ended in plans for a new hospital on the old site, another anchor for redevelopment.

The immediate effect of IIT's and Michael Reese's actions was the creation of a new campus which cleared more of the old Federal Street slum and removed the dilapidated housing along State, Wabash, and Michigan Avenues. A further development was the construction of new, moderate-income, high-rise apartment buildings east of King Drive. The SSPB's plan was attractive enough to bring in outside capital, and the New York Life Insurance Company invested in the neighborhood by financing the construction of the 2000-unit Lake Meadows apartment complex between 31st and 35th Streets. This was built between 1953 and 1968. At just

about the same time, the five Prairie Shores apartment buildings were constructed between 26th and 31st Streets, also east of King Drive.

Government-sponsored redevelopment away from the lake soon paralleled the private developments along the lakeshore. In 1955, 650 units were added to the Ida B. Wells project at 37th and Vincennes. Three years later the Prairie Avenue Court Apartments opened with 326 units for senior citizens at 3245 S. Prairie. The major event, however, was the opening of the Stateway Gardens south of 35th Street along State. This project along with the Robert Taylor Homes, its neighbor to the south, replaced all that was left of the Federal Street slum. The longest slum in the world was

Adult Education Class, Wendell Phillips High School, c.1940s. Blacks found new educational opportunities in the North. Education was one of Chicago's major attractions for Southern blacks who were often denied the right to schooling in the South.
(Courtesy Chicago Historical Society)

Slum Clearance, 35th to 39th Streets along railroad tracks. 1959. The buildings of the Stateway Gardens replaced much of the old Federal Street slum in the 1950s.
(C.W. Hines, courtesy Chicago Historical Society)

replaced by the longest housing project. The 1960s saw even more public housing come to Douglas.

The demographic effects of the new construction in Douglas were tremendous. In 1950 the population of the area had reached a high of 78,745 people, of whom ninety-seven percent were black. The destruction of slum buildings in the 1950s saw the population drop to 52,325 by 1960. The percentage of blacks also dropped to 91.8, reflecting the new integrated middle-class apartments constructed along the lake.

The population continued to decline through the 1960s, and by 1970 there were only 41,276 residents, 85.7 percent of whom were black. Ten years later the population fell to 35,700 with the racial percentages staying about the same. These demographic changes resulted from the construction of middle-class apartments and the destruction of slum dwellings which had housed large families.

31st Street looking east across South Parkway, 1937. Olivet Baptist Church (1876) dominates the intersection of 31st and South Park (King Drive). Today only the church has survived the urban renewal program of the post-World War II period.

(Chicago Park District, courtesy R. Wroble)

Douglas is a community that has been shaped by history. Decisions made in the early 1850s, 60s, 70s, and 80s have shaped the neighborhood. If the trends of the last thirty years continue, those decisions will continue to affect the area. The middle-class housing in the eastern part of the district has been replaced, after a period of decline, by middle-class units. The working-class slum on Federal Street has been replaced by today's equivalent—federal housing projects. Everywhere in Douglas the hand of the past seems to be at work. Even in "The Gap," which is located between the two high-rise developments, the past seems to be having its way. Many of the old homes are being renovated by middle-class and professional black people. The Frank Lloyd Wright townhouses on 32nd and Calumet have received the most publicity, but others are being refurbished too. Also, new townhouse construction is evident in the community as well as a condominium development across from Olivet

Baptist Church on 31st Street and King Drive. And while the 35th Street shopping strip seems shabby, the Lake Meadows Shopping Center is a success.

The past has also left Douglas with a valuable inheritance in these energy-conscious days—it is still served by an excellent transportation system. A trip to the Loop on public transportation is quick and easy by bus, elevated, or the Illinois Central Railroad, which now stops at 27th Street. Douglas is also easily accessible by car. All of these transportation factors point to the possibility of more real estate development in the neighborhood.

The institutional base of the community is also strong with IIT, Michael Reese, and Mercy Hospital giving the district a firm institutional backbone. Olivet Baptist Church has remained in the neighborhood, as have other churches like Pilgrim Baptist, Trinity Episcopal, and St. James. With this firm base residents should be optimistic about the future. Moreover, the area along the lakefront has remained at least partially integrated. Prairie Shores and Lake Meadows have withstood the test of time.

But there are difficulties. Much of the housing stock may be beyond repair. And the federal housing projects remain a problem. They are a problem that has been constant in the history of the community and one that residents will have to face for a long time to come. In reality Douglas has never been one neighborhood, it has always been several. Groveland Park remains a separate enclave, as it has been from the beginning when Senator Douglas plotted it out. The Federal Street slum has in part been born again. IIT is a community unto itself, as is Prairie Shores, Lake Meadows, and South Commons.

The problem of diversity is one that this neighborhood and the city will have to face if the future of Chicago is to be a bright one. Douglas must continue to attract investment if it is going to succeed. To do so, it must face its past in order to deal with its future.

*Prairie Shores housing, northeast corner 31st and King Drive, 1985.
These modern twenty-story apartment buildings were constructed as
moderate income rental units between 1953 and 1968.* (G. Lane)

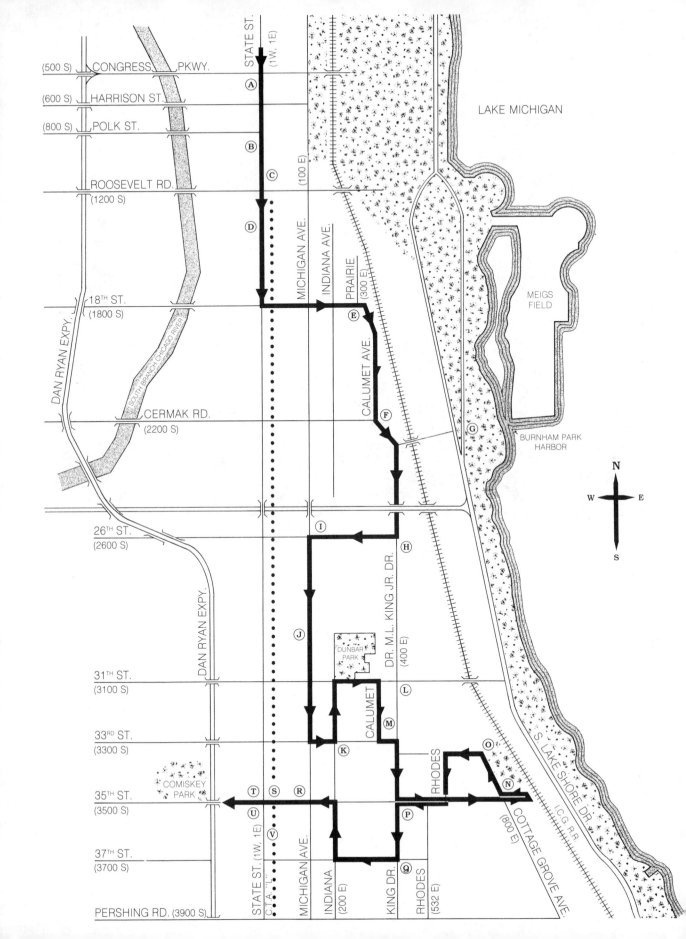

Old South Side Tour

This tour begins at Congress and State, just below the State Street Mall. It makes its way through the Prairie Avenue Historic District and the Near South Side, and then into the Douglas community area.

Driving time: about 1½ hours.

(A) As you drive south on State Street, you will be passing through the **old Levee district.** At the turn of the century this was the most notorious section of the city. Located first here and then farther south along State Street, Chicago's vice district was controlled by two of the city's most colorful politicians, "Hinky Dink" Kenna and "Bathhouse John" Coughlin, aldermen of the First Ward. Later on, Al Capone controlled most of the "action" on the Near South Side. Much of the vice district was replaced by railroad yards and warehouses that located near the downtown area. Today these are being replaced by housing, as the area south of the old retail center gradually becomes a residential area.

(B) **Dearborn Park,** located west of State Street from Polk Street to Roosevelt Road, symbolizes this new phase in the history of the area. Heralded as the city's newest neighborhood when construction began in the late 1970s, Dearborn Park has been a successful housing development.

(C) Located at 1121 S. State, directly across the street from the fashionable townhouses and condominiums, is the **James Riordan Chicago Police Headquarters.** The First District police station has been at this location since well before the turn of the century.

Kimball mansion, southeast corner 18th and Prairie, c.1980. This elegant residence, designed by Solon Beman in the French chateau style, was the home of W.W. Kimball, the piano manufacturer.

(S. Benjamin, courtesy Commission on Chicago Landmarks)

Ⓓ Proceeding south along State Street you will pass under the Roosevelt Road overpass. To the right are abandoned railroad yards, which are scheduled for residential development. At 1526 S. State stands the **Chicago Cold Storage Warehouse/Beatrice Foods Co.** This building and others nearby are all that remain of the South Side warehouse belt that serviced the Loop during the late part of the nineteenth century and the early part of the twentieth.

Ⓔ At 18th Street turn left and go four blocks east to the **Prairie Avenue Historic District.** The corner of 18th and Prairie was once the center of Chicago's most fashionable district. Located here are the **W.W. Kimball House** (1890) on the east side of Prairie, and the **John J. Glessner House** (1886) on the west side. Just off of the corner are other examples of the housing that constituted Chicago's first Gold Coast. Also situated here is the **Henry B. Clarke House,** dating from 1836, the oldest surviving building in the city. The Chicago Architecture Foundation maintains both the Glessner and Clarke houses. The foundation's bookstore is in the Glessner's old carriage house.

McCormick Place Convention Center, 23rd Street at Lake Shore Drive. 1985. Chicago's principal convention center was built in 1960 and then rebuilt after it burned down in January of 1967.
(G. Lane)

(F) Go one block east of Prairie to Calumet Avenue. This is the approximate **site of the Fort Dearborn massacre** of 1812. Then make a right turn and proceed south. This will take you past the Illinois Central Gulf Railroad yards and **R.R. Donnelley & Sons Company, The Lakeside Press**, at Cermak Road and Calumet Avenue.

(G) As you go south across Cermak Road, take the overpass to King Drive, and continue south to 26th Street. To the left of the overpass is the McCormick Place convention complex (1971 and 1986) which replaced an earlier building (1960), which burned on January 16, 1967.

(H) The **Prairie Shores housing complex** is situated on the east side of King Drive between 26th and 31st Streets. Just beyond the Prairie Shores apartments stand the buildings of **Michael Reese Hospital.** On the west side of King Drive below 26th Street are the Prairie Courts apartments, a Chicago Housing Authority project. Both the private and the public housing projects here represent the dramatic changes that took place in this area after World War II.

(I) Turn right at 26th Street and go four blocks west to Michigan Avenue. **Mercy Hospital** will be to your right, north of 26th Street; while the middle-class **South Commons housing development** is to your left, extending along Michigan Avenue all the way south to 31st Street. South Commons provides a solid housing anchor for the surrounding community.

At the southeast corner of 26th and Michigan is **Trinity Episcopal Church,** dating from 1873. Its architecture recalls the time when much of Chicago's middle class lived on the Near South Side.

(J) Turn left and go five blocks south on Michigan to 33rd Boulevard. One block to your right, at 2940 S. Wabash, you will see **Old St. James Catholic Church,** built between 1875 and 1880. Founded in 1855, St. James is the mother church of all South Side Catholic parishes and was beautifully restored after a fire in 1972.

At 2944 S. Michigan stands **"The Mansion,"** an apartment complex that occupies the former home of John W. "Bet-A-Million" Gates, who made a fortune selling barbed wire to Texas ranchers. Gates bought the house from lawyer Sidney Kent who had it built in 1882-83 according to plans by Burnham & Root. From 1929 to 1950 the house became a Catholic Youth Organization home for boys. Between 1950 and 1982 it served as the convent of St. James' parish. The house now recalls the time when Michigan Avenue was lined with magnificent homes. Just south and west of the old mansion lies the campus of the Illinois Institute of Technology. IIT provides much of the institutional base of the Douglas community area.

(K) Turn left and go one block east on 33rd to Indiana Avenue (200 East), make a left and go two blocks north to 31st Street. At the southeast corner of 33rd and Indiana stands the **Pilgrim Baptist Church,** which now houses a black congregation. Before the turn of the century this corner was the center of a growing middle-class Jewish community, often referred to as the Golden Ghetto, that had moved south along the major boulevards from the Loop. The famous Chicago architectural firm of Adler & Sullivan designed this edifice in 1890 as the synagogue for Kehilath Anshe Ma'ariv (K.A.M.). Dankmar Adler's father had been the

(Top right) The Gates mansion, 2944 S. Michigan, 1985. This is all that remains of Michigan Avenue's "Mansion Row." It once served as the convent for St. James parish, and has recently been renovated into apartments.
(G. Lane)

(Bottom right) St. James Catholic Church, 2940 S. Wabash, 1980. This historic church, built between 1875 and 1880, recalls the original Irish community in Douglas. Upwardly mobile Irish Catholics flocked to this area after the Chicago Fire, transforming it into an Irish-American middle-class neighborhood.
(A. Kezys)

Olivet Baptist Church, southeast corner 31st and King Drive, 1980. This building was built in the mid-1870s by the First Baptist Church. It was purchased in 1917 by Olivet Baptist to house its large and influential black congregation. (G. Lane)

rabbi of the congregation for over twenty years. Today K.A.M. is located in the Hyde Park—Kenwood community. The Pilgrim Baptist congregation moved to this location in 1921.

(L) At 31st Street turn right and proceed three blocks east to Calumet (325 East). Ahead of you, at the southeast corner of 31st and King Drive (400 East), stands the **Olivet Baptist Church,** an important landmark in the history of black Chicago. The building, designed by Willcox and Miller, was erected in 1875-76 to house the First Baptist Church of Chicago, which had moved south from the Loop. Olivet acquired the building in 1917 when the neighborhood underwent racial change. The First Baptist Church moved to Hyde Park, where it later became a black congregation and is located today.

(M) Turn right one block short of King Drive and proceed south on Calumet Avenue to 33rd Boulevard. This two-block section of the Douglas area is located in the "Gap," a neighborhood that is known for its old homes and the restoration process that has been taking place

there. On the east side of the 3200 block (3213-19) four Frank Lloyd Wright row houses have been restored. The **Robert W. Roloson houses** were built in 1894 and their English Tudor style shows the young architect's experiments with traditional styles before the development of his distinctive Prairie style. They were named city landmarks in 1979.

Robert W. Roloson houses, 3213-19 S. Calumet Avenue, 1985. Frank Lloyd Wright designed these striking urban townhouses in 1894. They are located in the "Gap" neighborhood and were designated Chicago landmark buildings in 1979. (G. Lane)

(N) Take 33rd Boulevard one block east to King Drive (400 East), make a right turn and go one long block south to 35th Street, make a left and go east to the end of the street. Two landmarks in the history of Chicago stand at the east end of 35th Street. The **Stephen A. Douglas** monument is on the north side of the street overlooking the neighborhood which was named for this Illinois legislator, Supreme Court justice, U.S. congressman, U.S. senator, and rival of Abraham Lincoln. Leonard Volk designed the monument for his late friend and benefactor. The Civil War and a lack of funds held up construction, but the "Little Giant's" body found its final resting place here in 1881. The monument and grounds are maintained by the State of Illinois.

(Top right) 35th Street looking east across South Parkway, 1937. On the southeast corner is the Supreme-Liberty Life Insurance building. It is the second largest black-owned insurance company in the country and still has offices at this location. Today the Lake Meadows Shopping Center is on the northeast corner.
(Chicago Park District, courtesy R. Wroble)

(Bottom right) 37th Street looking west across South Parkway, 1937. Large mansions and townhouses lined South Park Boulevard (King Drive) by 1900. The white ethnic, and later the black, middle class moved down the South Side boulevards to more desirable outlying neighborhoods. Many of these elegant old homes still stand on King Drive south of 35th Street.
(Chicago Park District, courtesy R. Wroble)

Victory Monument, 35th and King Drive, 1985. This monument was dedicated in 1928 to honor black soldiers who fought in World War I. (G. Lane)

Across the street stands another reminder of the Civil War period. **St. Joseph's Carondelet Child Center** occupies a building that once housed a Civil War Veteran's Home designed by W.W. Boyington and opened in 1866. Just to the east, the Illinois Central Gulf Railroad suburban line passes through the Douglas area, stopping at 27th Street.

(O) Return west on 35th Street and make a right turn (north) on Cottage Grove to 33rd Place. As you drive north on your right is **Groveland Park,** one of the two private residential parks established by Stephen Douglas before the Civil War.

(P) Go one block west on 33rd Place to Rhodes Avenue (532 East), make a left turn on Rhodes, and proceed one block south to 35th Street, then make a right turn (west) one block to King Drive and make another left. At the intersection of 35th and King Drive stands Leonard Crunelle's *Victory* monument. It was erected to honor the 370th Infantry, 93rd Division of the United States Army, a black unit that fought in World War I. The monument originally consisted only of the shaft, which was unveiled in 1928. In 1936 the figure of a black doughboy was added to complete this tribute to Chicago's black veterans.

On the southeast corner of the intersection stands the **Supreme Life Insurance Company,** a result of the merger of several black insurance companies. The direct predecessor of this company was the Liberty Life Insurance Company, begun in Chicago in 1919 during the Great Migration of Southern blacks to Chicago and other Northern cities.

(Q) Go one block south on King Drive to 37th Street. On the southeast corner of this intersection is the **Ida B. Wells housing project,** one of the oldest and most successful projects in Chicago. This project opened on January 18, 1941 and originally consisted of two-story row houses and three-story apartment buildings which housed 1,662 low income black families. The project covered nearly forty-seven acres. 641 new units were added to the project in 1955 as part of an urban renewal development of the area.

(R) Turn right on 37th Street and go three blocks west to Indiana Avenue (200 East). Make another right and go three blocks north to 35th Street. Turn left and proceed west. At the northwest corner of 35th and Michigan Avenue stands **De La Salle Institute.** De La Salle opened in 1892 in the original building which stood on the northeast corner of 35th and Wabash. The "old" building, which contained many fond memories for thousands of "D" graduates, was demolished in 1984. De La Salle alumni include former mayors Martin J. Kennelly, Richard J. Daley, and Michael J. Bilandic. Dan Ryan, Bernard Carey, State's Attorney Richard M. Daley, and many other notable figures in Chicago politics and the professions have also graduated from the school.

(S) Continue west on 35th to the corner of State Street. Just before the intersection you will pass under the **South Side Alley "L,"** which came to this neighborhood in the early 1890s. It was built to connect the Loop with Jackson Park and the World's Columbian Exposition. At approximately the location of the "L" station, Senator Douglas had his home "Oakenwald" at 34 East 35th Street. Proceed west on 35th Street.

(T) At the northwest corner of 35th and State the campus of the **Illinois Institute of Technology** begins. This school expanded from five buildings on seven acres in 1940 to fifty buildings on 114 acres by 1964. The internationally renowned architect Ludwig Mies van der Rohe designed the campus and headed the architecture department. IIT has proved to be an important anchor for the redevelopment of the South Side north of 35th Street.

(U) Directly south across the street from IIT's campus stand the apartment towers of **Stateway Gardens,** another Chicago Housing Authority project. This massive public housing development was built in 1958 and includes 1,684 units. Many of these were constructed to house large families. Stateway Gardens and its neighbor to the south, **Robert Taylor Homes,** which contains 4,312 units, have replaced much of the old Federal Street slum, which ran parallel to the Rock Island Railroad tracks and made up the Old South Side's western boundary.

Crown Hall, Illinois Institute of Technology, 1985. Ludwig Mies van der Rohe left his imprint on Douglas by designing IIT's landmark campus in the 1950s. Over two hundred structures are included in this tribute to modern architecture. (J. Ficner)

(V) The area on the east side of State Street, just south of 35th Street is all that is left of the **old Black Metropolis business center** which developed after the Great Migration of 1915 to 1920. The intersection of 35th and State was black Chicago's equivalent of State and Madison from the World War I years until the Great Depression. At 3633-37 S. State stood the Binga State Bank built in 1908 and the Bates Apartments built in 1894. Both of these have fallen to the wrecker's ball, but other structures like the Art Deco terra-cotta **Chicago Bee Building** still stand at 3647-55 South State Street to remind us of the heyday of the black "Downtown."

Complete the tour by following 35th Street west under the Rock Island Railroad tracks to the Dan Ryan Expressway.

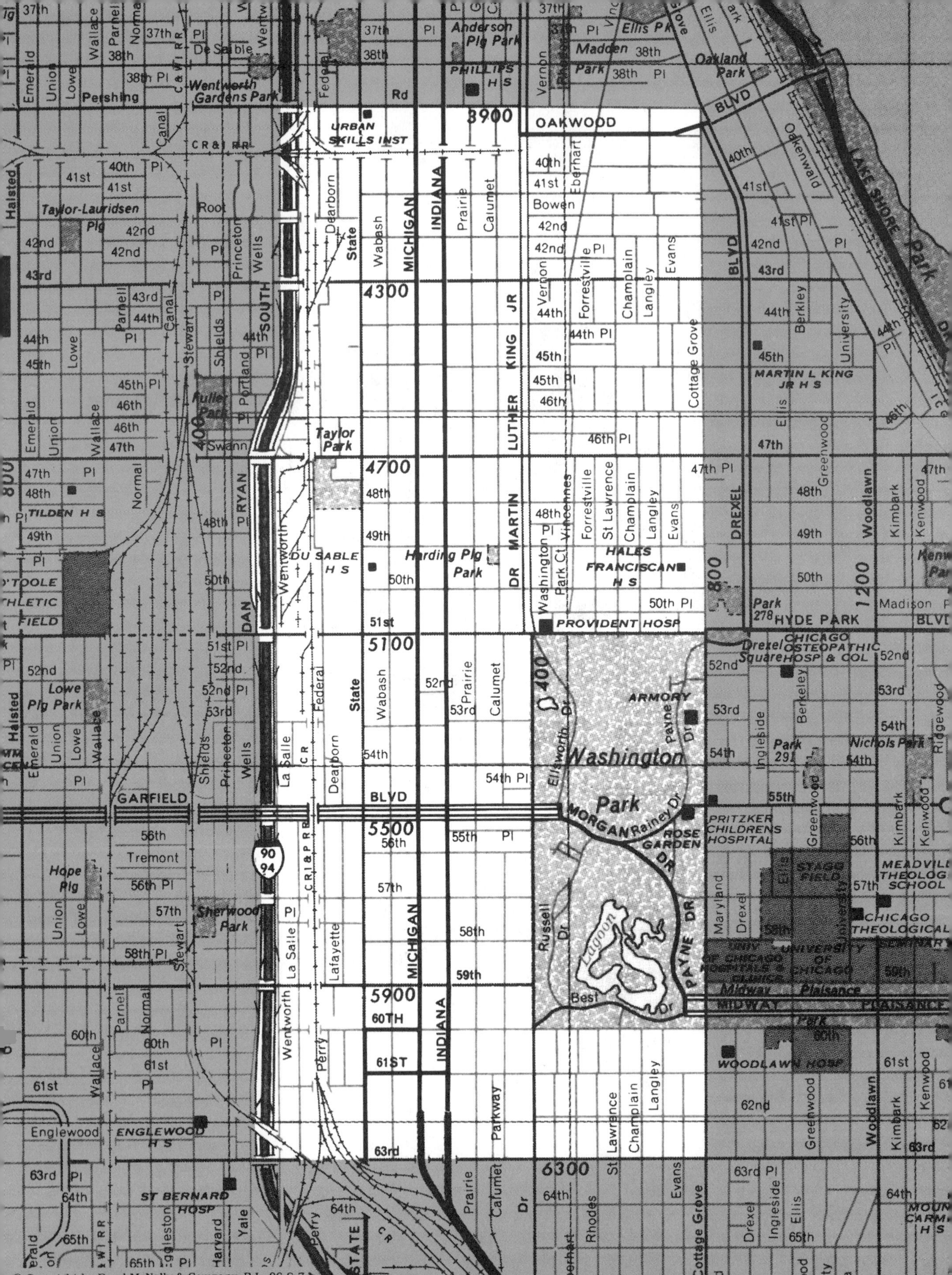

37th
Wallace
Parnell
Normal
37th Pl
De Sable
Wentworth
Anderson Plg Park
Ellis Pk
Madden
38th
Oakland Park
38th Pl
Emerald
Union
Lowe
Pershing
Wentworth Gardens Park
Federal
Rd
PHILLIPS H S
Vernon
Park
BLVD
3900
OAKWOOD
URBAN SKILLS INST
Canal
CR&I RR
40th
Eberhart
Oakenwald
Halsted
41st
Taylor-Lauridsen Plg
Root
Dearborn
MICHIGAN
INDIANA
Prairie
Calumet
Bowen
42nd
Princeton
Wells
State
Wabash
Forrestville
Champlain
Langley
Evans
LAKE SHORE
43rd
4300
SOUTH
Vernon
44th
44th Pl
Cottage Grove
Berkley
University
Stewart
Shields
Portland
Fuller Park
45th
45th Pl
46th
MARTIN L KING JR H S
46th Pl
Ellis
Greenwood
47th
Swann
400
Taylor Park
LUTHER
KING
JR
DR
MARTIN
4700
47th Pl
800
48th
TILDEN H S
RYAN
St Lawrence
Vincennes
49th
Woodlawn
Kimbark
Kenwood
DU SABLE H S
Harding Plg Park
Washington Pl
Park Ct
HALES FRANCISCAN H S
DREXEL
O'TOOLE ATHLETIC FIELD
50th
50th Pl
1200
DAN
51st
PROVIDENT HOSP
Park 278
HYDE PARK
Madison
BLVD
Drexel Square
CHICAGO OSTEOPATHIC HOSP & COL
5100
51st Pl
52nd
Lowe Plg Park
ARMORY
Ellsworth Dr
Payne Dr
53rd
Ingleside
Berkeley
Ridgewood
La Salle
CR
Washington
Park 291
Nichols Park
54th
54th Pl
GARFIELD
BLVD
MORGAN DR
Rainey Dr
PRITZKER CHILDRENS HOSPITAL
ROSE GARDEN
55th
5500
56th
55th Pl
CRI&PRR
90
94
Tremont
Hope Plg
56th Pl
MEADVILLE THEOLOGICAL SCHOOL
STAGG FIELD
57th
Sherwood Park
Lafayette
58th
58th Pl
Russell Dr
Lagoon
PAYNE DR
Maryland
Drexel
CHICAGO THEOLOGICAL SEMINARY
UNIV OF CHICAGO HOSPITALS & CLINICS
UNIVERSITY OF CHICAGO
59th
5900
Best Dr
Midway Plaisance
MIDWAY
PLAISANCE
60TH
Park
60th
Perry
61ST
61st
WOODLAWN HOSP
Parkway
Lawrence
62nd
Englewood
ENGLEWOOD H S
63rd
6300
63rd Pl
64th
ST BERNARD HOSP
Eggleston
Harvard
Yale
STATE
Rhodes
65th
MOUNT CARMEL H S

In few Chicago neighborhoods has ethnic succession been more dramatic than in the Grand Boulevard—Washington Park area on Chicago's South Side. Between 1890 and 1920 thousands of native-born Protestants, German Jews, and Irish Catholics lived in the territory bounded by 39th Street, Cottage Grove Avenue, 63rd Street, and Wentworth Avenue. By 1930 Grand Boulevard and Washington Park formed the heart of Chicago's black community, and they remained the city's premier black neighborhoods throughout the 1950s.

In the past thirty years, the exodus of middle-class black families has left its mark on Grand Boulevard and Washington Park. Whereas these two neighborhoods once included a cross section of Chicago's black community, they now contain a population that is overwhelmingly poor, with few resources. Many of black Chicago's pioneer businesses, clubs, and churches have vanished, and the growing number of vacant lots testifies to the area's demise as a residential district. Like other parts of the city, the Grand Boulevard—Washington Park district has become the "old neighborhood" for thousands of black Chicagoans.

The history of this South Side area is linked to Washington Park, which was laid out in 1873 according to the designs of the famous landscape architect, Frederick Law Olmsted. In its early years, the park was located outside the city proper and was accessible only by private carriages. With its landscaped gardens and its meadows, Washington Park embodied the suburban ideal of leisure. The opening of the Washington Park Club in 1884 at 61st and South Park Avenue further enhanced the district's reputation as an exclusive area. For an initiation fee of $150, members could enjoy "all the advantages of a country club." But the club's main attraction was its racetrack. Each June thousands of spectators gathered from all parts of the city for the running of the American Derby, an event which continued from 1884 to 1905.

Prior to the 1890s, most of the district east of State Street between 41st and 63rd Streets was prairie. A small community of Irish and German workers lived near the Rock Island Railroad car shops, but this area, with its one- and two-story frame cottages, had little impact on the development of Grand Boulevard—Washington Park. Until 1889 State Street was the boundary line between the Town of Lake and the township of Hyde Park. But long after this section became part of Chicago, State Street continued to

Young boys play on railroad tracks on Cox (40th Street) near State in the old Federal Street area. In the background the Alley "L" curves east and south toward Jackson Park. (Courtesy Rev. J.J. Keehan)

symbolize the division between the poor and the middle class. Indeed, it is no coincidence that the public housing project known as the Robert Taylor Homes (1960-62) was built on the site of the old State-Dearborn-Federal slum.

The subdivision of the district between State Street and Cottage Grove Avenue was tied to improvements in public transportation. By 1887 cable cars were running along Cottage Grove as far as 63rd Street, supplementing the horse-drawn railway lines on State and Wentworth. But it was the completion of the "Alley L" to Jackson Park for the Columbian Exposition of 1893 that spurred the development of this part of Chicago. The elevated railroad, with its stations at 43rd, 47th, 51st, 55th, 58th, and 61st Streets did more than connect Grand Boulevard and Washington Park with the city's business district. It played a crucial role in the formation of the modern urban neighborhood with its characteristic brick apartment buildings, shopping strips, and a concentrated but highly mobile population.

Grand Boulevard (King Drive) looking south from 42nd Street, c.1910. These fine homes represent the high quality housing built in the Grand Boulevard neighborhood between 1880 and 1900.

(C.R. Childs, courtesy G. Schmalgemeier)

Grand Boulevard

Because of its proximity to the center of the city, Grand Boulevard developed at a faster rate than the Washington Park district. The most desirable location for single-family homes was Grand Boulevard itself, a beautifully landscaped thoroughfare which extended from 18th Street to 51st Street, where it formed the entrance to Washington Park. (South of 51st Street the avenue was known as South Park; the street is now Dr. Martin Luther King, Jr., Drive.) Wealthy Chicagoans, many of them sons and daughters of immigrant entrepreneurs, built elegant houses along the boulevard, while middle-class families purchased spacious brownstones on side streets such as Forrestville, Champlain, and Langley. West of Grand Boulevard, two- and three-story apartments filled up the long city blocks, especially Michigan, Indiana, and Prairie Avenues.

The building boom of the 1890s transformed the prairies east and west of Grand Boulevard into a city neighborhood. While most of the pioneer settlers remained, the community expanded to include second generation German Jews and Irish Catholics who had moved up and out of congested areas

Temple Isaiah, 4501 S. Vincennes Avenue, c.1910. The last major work of architect Dankmar Adler, this temple was dedicated in 1899 by German Jews who had moved to the Grand Boulevard neighborhood from the Near West Side. In 1920, Ebenezer Baptist Church purchased the former temple.

(C.R. Childs, courtesy G. Schmalgemeier)

Brick flat buildings with bay windows and spacious porches line the west side of Grand Boulevard (King Drive), just across the street from Washington Park. In the distance are the buildings of the Chicago Orphan Asylum, 5120 S. Grand Boulevard, now the Chicago Baptist Institute.

(C.R. Childs, courtesy G. Schmalgemeier)

on the South and Near West Sides of the city. These families quickly put down roots and established synagogues, churches, and charitable institutions. The history of Temple Isaiah illustrates the speed with which a Jewish community was formed in Grand Boulevard.

Temple Isaiah was established in 1895 by men and women who had formerly belonged to Zion Temple at the corner of Washington Boulevard and Ogden Avenue on the West Side. According to the Chicago *Inter Ocean,* by the early 1890s "practically the entire society of Zion temple had settled in the neighborhood of Fortieth Street, between Drexel and Grand boulevards." The new Reform congregation worshiped in Oakland Club Hall at 39th and Cottage Grove until the temple at 4501 S. Vincennes Avenue was dedicated in 1899. Temple Isaiah was an innovative congregation, admitting single and married women to membership, and its magnificent synagogue was the last major work of architect Dankmar Adler.

The Jewish population of Grand Boulevard continued to increase after the turn of the century, and by 1915 the neighborhood included such important synagogues as Sinai Temple, 46th and Grand Boulevard; Beth Hamedrash Hagadol (Anshe Dorum), 5129 S. Indiana Avenue; and B'nai Sholom Temple Israel, 53rd and Michigan Avenue.

Among the newcomers to Grand Boulevard in the 1890s were a large number of Irish Catholics. Irish immigrants had lived west of State Street since the 1860s, and they had formed three parishes, St. Anne (1869) at 55th and Wentworth, St. Elizabeth (1881) at 41st and Wabash, and St. Cecilia (1885) at 45th and Wells. Although St. Elizabeth's included wealthy families who lived along Wabash, Michigan, and Indiana Avenues, the congregation was predominantly working class. Indeed, the majority of contributors to a new Gothic church in 1892 lived in frame cottages on Armour (Federal), Dearborn, and State Streets.

Like their Jewish neighbors in Grand Boulevard, second-generation Irish were eager to put their imprint on the neighborhood. In 1901 Corpus Christi parish was formed to serve Catholic families who lived east of Indiana Avenue. This new congregation included Irish-American families who had moved south from the old parishes of St. John and St. James as well as former residents of the stockyards district. For example, in 1900 Tom Gahan, a well-known political figure "Back of the Yards," moved to a mansion at 4619 S. Grand Boulevard, thereby becoming one of Corpus Christi's earliest benefactors.

Not to be outdone by the Italian Renaissance style synagogue of Sinai Congregation (1912) and its adjoining

social center at 46th and Grand Boulevard, the people of Corpus Christi built a massive parish complex at 49th Street. The twin towers of Corpus Christi Church (1915) proclaimed the Irish presence in Grand Boulevard, and the church's rich interior, with its stained glass windows and coffered ceiling, symbolized the prosperity of the "steam heat" Irish.

Grand Boulevard's location and the availability of vacant land made it an attractive area for institutions as well as residences. Between 1890 and 1910 important social service agencies and schools constructed new buildings in the neighborhood. Among the institutions to relocate in Grand Boulevard from the Near South Side were the Erring Women's Refuge (1890) at 5024 S. Indiana, the Chicago Orphan Asylum (1899) at 5120 S. Grand Boulevard, the Chicago Home for the Friendless (1897) at 5059 S. Vincennes, and St. Francis Xavier Academy and College (1901) at 49th and Cottage Grove.

In addition to supporting the work of the Chicago Home for Jewish Orphans and Aged Jews at 62nd and Drexel in nearby Woodlawn, Jewish families in Grand Boulevard contributed to such charitable and social institutions as Resthaven, 4401 S. Grand Boulevard; the Deborah Boys Club, 4720 S. Grand Boulevard; the Miriam Club, 4501 S. Forrestville; and the Ruth Club, 6001 S. Indiana. Catholic charitable institutions included the Chicago Industrial School for Girls (1899) at 4910 S. Prairie and St. Joseph Home for the Aged (1894) at 5148 S. Prairie.

Washington Park

Whereas Grand Boulevard was nearly all built up by the turn of the century, Washington Park experienced sporadic development. The first settlement emerged in the 1870s as railroad workers purchased two-story frame homes which had been built west of State Street and south of 51st Street. The area's principal institution was St. Anne Church at Garfield Boulevard (55th Street) and Wentworth, dedicated in 1880. This working-class district was a stable one, and St. Anne's pastor attributed the prosperity of his parish to the fact that "a larger number of its families own their own homes than is usual."

While the extension of the State Street car line to Englewood and the completion of the "L" sparked residential construction north of Garfield Boulevard, large tracts within Washington Park remained prairie. The Washington Park Club at the east end of the district had once been the

(Top left) From 1912 to 1944, Sinai Temple dominated the southwest corner of 46th and Grand Boulevard (King Drive). Alfred Alschuler designed this Italian Renaissance style temple for Chicago's first Reform synagogue, founded in 1861. The building now houses Mt. Pisgah Missionary Baptist Church, one of the largest black congregations in Grand Boulevard. (G. Lane)

(Bottom left) Corpus Christi Church, southwest corner 49th and Grand Boulevard, c.1920. Irish Catholics built this splendid edifice in 1915. When the parish was founded in 1901, the neighborhood was a new residential district of substantial brick houses and flat buildings. In 1933. Corpus Christi took on a new identity as a black Catholic parish. (Courtesy The Chicago Catholic)

Washington Park Race Track, 61st and South Park (King Drive), c.1900.
Beginning in 1884, the American Derby race at Washington Park
attracted the elite of Chicago society.
(Courtesy Chicago Historical Society)

Washington Park, c.1908. The noted landscape architect Frederick Law Olmsted laid out Washington Park in 1873. Its cultivated gardens and meadows provided much-needed greenery for nearby apartment dwellers.
(C.R. Childs. courtesy G. Schmalgemeier)

meeting place of Chicago's elite. But a betting scandal in 1894 closed the track for three seasons, and the death knell sounded in 1905 when city officials shuttered all Chicago race tracks as a way to curb gambling. The Washington Park Club disbanded and its putting greens were transplanted to South Shore where they formed the nucleus of South Shore Country Club's golf course.

Although the grounds of the old Washington Park Club and race track were subdivided for apartments, the area retained its reputation as an entertainment district. The same excellent transportation facilities which had made the Washington Park Club so attractive to Chicagoans also assured the success of similar ventures. The *Sans Souci* Amusement Park, which opened in 1899 at 60th and Cottage Grove, featured vaudeville shows, band concerts, electric gondola rides, an arcade, an electric fountain, a beer garden, and a Japanese tea garden. The admission fee was ten cents, and the management boasted that, "Every attention is paid ladies and children."

In 1914 a new entertainment complex designed by Frank Lloyd Wright was constructed on the grounds of *Sans Souci* Park. Despite its elegant facilities for music and dancing, however, the new Midway Gardens failed to catch on as a performing arts center, and in 1916 it was sold to the Edelweiss Beer Company. Its days as a drinking establishment were cut short by Prohibition in 1920, and thereafter Midway Gardens operated as a garage and car wash until it was razed in 1929.

Garfield Boulevard (55th Street) looking west from Dearborn (Lafayette Avenue). c.1910. The prohibition of streetcars made Garfield Boulevard an attractive residential street at the turn of the century.
(C.R. Childs, courtesy G. Schmalgemeier)

When the White City Amusement Park opened in 1906 at 63rd and South Park, it was located in a sparsely settled district. It soon developed into the South Side's major entertainment center featuring carnival rides, side shows, and ballroom dancing. But the crown jewel of the Washington Park amusement district was Andrew and William Karzas' Trianon Ballroom, which opened in 1922 at 62nd and Cottage Grove. Constructed at a cost of $1.2 million, the Trianon was known as the "World's Most Beautiful Ballroom," and its name bands attracted thousands of Chicago dancers through the 1940s.

Although residential construction in Washington Park lagged behind Grand Boulevard, the area between State Street and South Park Avenue was rapidly built up after the turn of the century. The most popular form of housing in the neighborhood was the three-story flat building which featured a marble foyer, steam heat, hot water, electric lights, tile bathrooms—in short, "all the latest improvements." The 5800 block of Prairie Avenue, for example, consisted exclusively of apartment buildings which ranged in size from six to thirty "flats."

In the midst of this apartment building boom, an extension of the "Alley L" was completed to Englewood in 1907. The branch line left the main tracks just south of

Jackson Park "L", crossing Garfield Boulevard, c.1939. The construction of the elevated line to Jackson Park for the World's Columbian Exposition of 1893 spurred residential development in Grand Boulevard and Washington Park.

(Chicago Park District, courtesy R. Wroble)

59th Street, and it included new stations at State Street and Wentworth Avenue. Far from diminishing the desirability of Washington Park as a residential district, the new elevated line made the area even more accessible to downtown Chicago.

In many ways Washington Park was the prototype of urban neighborhoods which grew up along Chicago's lakefront in the l920s. In addition to excellent transportation and recreation facilities, the area's apartments provided a middle-class standard of living. While Washington Park included more renters than homeowners, this situation did not adversely affect church formation. Indeed, the concentration of so many families in the district actually accelerated the process of church-building. In 1910 alone, four new churches opened their doors in the area south of Garfield Boulevard: Washington Park Baptist Church, Woolley Memorial Methodist Episcopal Church, St. Anselm Catholic Church, and SS. Constantine and Helen Greek Orthodox Church.

St. Anselm's and SS. Constantine and Helen's reflected the ease with which white ethnic groups established themselves in Washington Park. Less than six months after their parish was organized in 1909, Irish Catholics of St. Anselm's had financed a combination church-and-school building on 6lst Street, just east of Michigan. Nearby, at 6107 S. Michigan, Greek families began to worship in a two-story brick structure which also contained classrooms. When the Koraes elementary school opened in 1910, Greek was the primary language of instruction, but by 1922 the program was bilingual and accredited by the Chicago Board of Education.

Like Irish and Greek families, Jewish newcomers to Washington Park also made provisions for the education of their children. In May 1915 the South Side Hebrew Congregation dedicated its new Jewish Educational Center, which had been completed at the northeast corner of 59th and Michigan.

At the same time that Irish and Jewish families were establishing communities within Grand Boulevard and Washington Park, racial change was occurring at the west end of the district. So great was the demand for housing that black families began to purchase homes in the area bordering the Rock Island Railroad tracks along LaSalle Street. For years this district had been known for its "floating population" and saloons. In contrast to the new steam heat apartments in Grand Boulevard, the cottages between 43rd and 51st Streets were relics of another era. Not only did many of them lack sanitary facilities, but their concentration along the long narrow stretches of LaSalle, Federal, and Dearborn Streets gave this district the appearance of a "shantytown."

As black families replaced Irish and German workers, new institutions emerged at the west end of Grand Boulevard. In 1897 blacks organized St. Mary A.M.E. Church in rented quarters at 4838 S. Armour (Federal). Two years later the congregation built a small frame church on Dearborn near 49th Street. In 1900 a group of blacks purchased the old State Street Methodist Church near 47th Street and renamed it St. Mark's. This congregation included a number of property owners who banded together in 1905 to force local saloons to close at midnight. Black homeowners believed that eight saloons on 47th Street between Federal and State were too many, but they were powerless to change the long-established character of this strip.

White homeowners who lived on Dearborn Street south of Garfield Boulevard (55th Street) reacted to racial change in the area by petitioning the City Council in 1901 to rename their street Lafayette. According to the *Stockyards Sun*, Dearborn Street between 22nd and 55th Streets "has become synonymous with the colored community." The name change notwithstanding, Lafayette between 55th and 59th Streets soon became an enclave of black homeowners. The 5700 block had once formed the grounds of the John Raber estate, which dated from the 1860s. The original house,

St. Mary A.M.E. Church, 5251 S. Dearborn, was the first black congregation established in the area in 1897. Once surrounded by frame houses, St. Mary's is now overshadowed by the highrises of the Robert Taylor public housing project. (Courtesy Rev. D. Blake)

though somewhat altered, is still standing at 5760 S. Lafayette. By the l920s blacks owned twenty-two of the twenty-four houses in this block of Lafayette, and they worked to beautify their neighborhood by planting gardens, whitewashing trees, and removing fences from all front yards.

The black population of Chicago grew dramatically during World War I as thousands of Southern blacks sought jobs in the city's packing houses and steel mills. Although a black community had existed along Dearborn Street since the l890s, white families living west of the Rock Island Railroad tracks vigorously resisted the attempts of blacks to settle in their neighborhood. During the Race Riot of July 1919, white gangs burned down homes west of Wentworth that were owned or rented by blacks. After the riot black families were afraid to return to the district, and for the next thirty years Wentworth Avenue remained the dividing line between white and black neighborhoods.

At the east end of Grand Boulevard, resentment against black newcomers took the form of a mass meeting on October 20, 1919. Nearly 1,200 white residents and property owners living on Grand Boulevard and adjacent streets gathered to protest the increasing number of blacks in their neighborhood. According to the Chicago *Tribune*, the whites adopted the slogan "They Shall Not Pass," a warning that Chicago's blacks were unwelcome on Grand Boulevard. Under the auspices of the Hyde Park—Kenwood Property Owners' Association, Grand Boulevard residents launched a campaign to make it impossible for black families to acquire mortgages and insurance. A smaller group known as the

The Lakeside Club, northeast corner Grand Boulevard and 42nd Street, c.1910. One of Grand Boulevard's most important Jewish institutions, the Lakeside Club was designed by Solon Beman in 1893. Located in the midst of the expanding Black Belt, the club was destroyed by arsonists in 1924 shortly after it was sold to the Greater Bethel A.M.E. Church.
(C.R. Childs, courtesy G. Schmalgemeier)

Washington Park Court Improvement Association vowed not to sell or rent property to blacks.

Increasingly, attempts to hold the color line resulted in violence. Black homeowners as well as realtors who sold or rented property to blacks were targets of a bombing campaign which continued throughout the early 1920s. The office and home of Jesse Binga, a black banker and real estate dealer, were bombed nearly ten times between March 1919 and November 1920. Black homeowners in the 4500 block of Vincennes and the 4400 block of Grand Boulevard also were victims of unidentified bombers. Undeterred, black families continued to move into the neighborhood. And in 1920 the congregation of Ebenezer Missionary Baptist Church purchased the former Temple Isaiah at 45th and Vincennes after the Jewish congregation moved to Hyde Park.

The demand for black institutions in Grand Boulevard intensified, and before long black congregations bought two of the finest buildings in the neighborhood—with disastrous results. In 1924 the Greater Bethel A.M.E. Church at 42nd and Grand Boulevard was completely destroyed by a fire of suspicious origin. Since the 2,500-member congregation purchased the former Jewish Lakeside Club in 1922, they had been the target of the Ku Klux Klan, which was then active in nearby Hyde Park. Early in January 1925 the Bethesda Baptist Church at 53rd and Michigan sustained $50,000 damage after it was bombed. This former synagogue had been built in 1914 by the congregation of B'nai Sholom Temple Israel.

Chicago's relatively small black population of 44,000 in 1910 increased to nearly 250,000 by 1930. For years the outlines of the city's "Black Belt" had been sharply defined: 31st to 55th Streets along Federal and State. But new areas of black settlement were emerging. Indeed, the line of march for the 1923 Elks parade illustrated how the old Black Belt boundaries were being realigned. The parade began in the heart of the old black district at 35th and Prairie, proceeded south along State Street to 46th Street, then east to Grand Boulevard. Crowds of blacks gathered along the parade route to cheer the 10,000 marchers, and the Chicago *Defender* proudly noted that no parade had ever before marched on Grand Boulevard.

As the black population of Grand Boulevard increased, 47th Street between Indiana and St. Lawrence Avenues became the new black shopping district. By 1927, 47th and Grand Boulevard was the cultural and business hub of black Chicago, and the new Regal Theater dominated this intersection for the next forty-five years. Further proof that

Grand Boulevard was the *bon ton* black neighborhood
occurred in August 1929 with the opening of the Michigan
Boulevard Garden Apartments. Philanthropist Julius
Rosenwald contributed nearly $3 million toward the
construction of these model apartments, which were all
rented before the complex at 47th and Michigan was
completed. The five-story walk-up known as The Rosenwald
remained one of the most prestigious addresses in Grand
Boulevard throughout the 1940s.

*The Michigan Boulevard Garden
Apartments, 54 E. 47th Street,
1951. Philanthropist Julius
Rosenwald donated nearly $3
million toward the construction of
these five-story walk-up
apartments which opened in
1929. "The Rosenwald" was home
to thousands of middle-class
blacks constrained by segregation
to live in the South Side Black
Belt.*

(M. Mead, courtesy Chicago Historical Society)

Whereas racial change in Grand Boulevard spanned a
ten-year period between 1920 and 1930, the Washington
Park neighborhood experienced a much swifter
transformation from a white to a black community. Despite
the fact that Washington Park developed later than Grand
Boulevard, it did not remain a white stronghold. Although its
population was half the size of Grand Boulevard's,
Washington Park was composed mainly of apartment
dwellers. Not only did thousands of white families move out
of the area as soon as their leases expired, but many left
even before blacks moved into their neighborhood.

In his famous trilogy *Studs Lonigan*, James T. Farrell
recreated the world of 58th Street, and he dramatized the
response of Irish families to the expansion of the South Side
Black Belt. Farrell drew heavily upon his boyhood

350

St. Anselm Church, northeast corner 61st and Michigan, 1985. Built by Irish Catholics in 1924-25, this Gothic church was immortalized in James T. Farrell's trilogy, Studs Lonigan. (G. Lane)

(Below) Interior, St. Anselm's, late 1930s. At the time this photograph was taken, St. Anselm's was a predominantly black parish.
(Courtesy The Chicago Catholic)

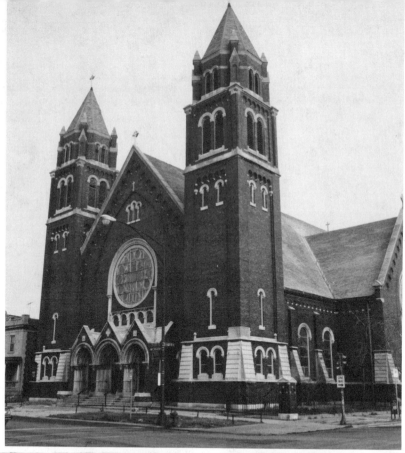

experiences in St. Anselm parish, and he accurately portrayed the confusion and fear of parishioners in the face of racial change. While a number of families in St. Anselm's moved to South Shore in the early l920s, others hoped the construction of a new Gothic church on Michigan Avenue might keep the neighborhood white. St. Anselm's new church was dedicated in 1925, but within five years nearly all the white parishioners had moved away.

Like most of the Grand Boulevard and Washington Park houses of worship, St. Anselm's soon became a thriving black church. The few white institutions that decided to stay in the area generally adhered to the color line, excluding blacks from membership. As Thomas Philpott has documented in his book, *The Slum and the Ghetto,* white Catholics and Protestants often used the recreation facilities at Sinai Temple, but black residents in Grand Boulevard were not welcome. This situation changed somewhat in 1944 when Sinai Temple relocated to Hyde Park and sold its buildings to the Catholic Archdiocese of Chicago. From 1945 to 1962 the former temple operated as Corpus Christi High School, but its student body was composed almost exclusively of young men and women from Chicago's black Catholic parishes. Now known as Mt. Pisgah Missionary Baptist Church, the temple at 46th and King Drive is one of the most important institutions in the Grand Boulevard community.

In Washington Park SS. Constantine and Helen parish remained long after the surrounding neighborhood had become a black community. But the major change that took place in this parish had to do with acculturation, not integration. As Andrew T. Kopan has observed, the new basilica-style church dedicated in 1928 included permanent pews and an organ, sure signs that the Greek Orthodox congregation was becoming "Americanized." When SS. Constantine and Helen parish finally sold its church and school to St. Edmund Episcopal parish in 1948, the Greeks followed the path taken by earlier residents of Washington Park—to South Shore.

While Chicago's black community expanded tremendously during the l920s, the Black Belt did not disappear. Rather, its boundaries were redefined. Blacks who moved into Grand Boulevard—Washington Park soon discovered that it was unsafe to travel west of Wentworth or east of Cottage Grove. Within these boundaries, however, a separate black world existed with flourishing theaters, clubs, churches, and businesses. More than any other event, the Bud Billiken Parade on August 16, 1930 symbolized the transformation of Grand Boulevard and Washington Park into black communities. Sponsored by the Chicago *Defender,* the parade began at 35th and Grand Boulevard in the heart of the old "Bronzeville" district and ended in Washington Park. In the midst of a downpour of rain, 8,000 black children participated in the line of march, and they were greeted by nearly 5,000 children who waited for the festivities to begin in the park.

Fully three-fifths of Chicago's black residents lived in Grand Boulevard and Washington Park in 1930, and both neighborhoods continued to increase in population during the next twenty years. The subdivision of apartments into kitchenettes contributed to overcrowding in the area, and these conversions seriously affected the quality of neighborhood life. While the east section of Grand Boulevard retained its prestige as a black "Gold Coast," the western edge of the neighborhood, especially along Federal Street, continued to deteriorate. The situation in Washington Park was much the same. Although the apartments nearest the park were of fairly recent origin, illegal conversions had turned much of the neighborhood into little more than a rooming-house district.

Just as Grand Boulevard and Washington Park felt the effects of black Southern migration during World War I, the area continued to attract newcomers from the Deep South during World War II. By 1950 nearly 175,000 black people lived in these twin communities, an incredible density for a district without highrises. As white neighborhoods on Chicago's South Side changed racially in the 1950s, the market for black homeowners expanded. The exodus of middle-class black families from Grand Boulevard and Washington Park had important consequences for the stability of this part of the South Side. While many families returned to the area for worship on Sunday, local businesses did not command the same loyalties as churches. The district's public schools also were affected. Du Sable High School at 4934 S. Wabash Avenue had been the pride of the black community since its opening in 1935. By the late 1950s, however, the school was losing many of its best students to newly integrated high schools located further south in the city.

Redevelopment in Grand Boulevard—Washington Park occurred in the form of two public improvement programs, the Robert Taylor Homes and the Dan Ryan Expressway. Over the years housing surveys had documented deteriorated conditions in the Federal Street corridor, and it came as no surprise to residents that city planners described their homes as "slum and blighted." In the 1950s the Chicago Housing Authority inaugurated a new policy of building high-rise public housing projects. These elevator buildings

These frame houses at 3903-5 S. Federal were typical of the dwellings that were demolished to make way for the Robert Taylor housing project, completed in 1962.
(Courtesy Commission on Chicago Landmarks)

soon replaced vast stretches of single-family dwellings, apartments, and businesses in the city's original Black Belt. In 1958, for example, eight highrises of the Stateway Gardens project were completed in the area bounded by 35th, State Street, Pershing (39th), and the Rock Island railroad tracks. Two years later construction began on the Robert Taylor Homes, now recognized as the world's largest public housing project.

In the old slum bordering the Rock Island tracks, there had been no east-west streets between 47th and 50th Streets to break up the long narrow stretches of Federal and Dearborn. The new Taylor highrises continued this land use pattern. The twenty-eight brick buildings, each sixteen stories in height, formed an island bounded by 39th Street, State Street, 54th Street, and the Rock Island tracks. Increasing the isolation of the public housing project was the new Dan Ryan Expressway which was completed to 95th Street by 1962. For more than four miles this expressway parallels Wentworth Avenue, the historic dividing line between white and black neighborhoods on the South Side.

In contrast to the housing east of State Street, where the streets follow Chicago's grid pattern, the Taylor highrises were all grouped together. While this design increased the space available for playgrounds and parking lots, its scale was such that virtually all sense of a conventional neighborhood disappeared. As Devereux Bowly notes in his book, *The Poorhouse,* the Taylor Homes opened as a segregated project with a population of 27,000 blacks, 20,000 of whom were children. The major change to occur in these highrises since 1962 has been the decrease of two-parent households in favor of single mothers and children. In one sense the Taylor Homes merely replaced slums of single-family dwellings with high-rise apartments. But the irony of it all is that the project memorialized Robert Taylor, the first black resident manager of the successful Michigan Boulevard Garden Apartments.

Despite the addition of thousands of black residents in the Taylor Homes, Grand Boulevard and Washington Park lost nearly 40,000 residents between 1960 and 1980. Like the Irish and Jews before them, black families moved further south in the city. A number of the district's pioneer churches refused to leave the area, among them St. Mary's A.M.E. at 5251 S. Dearborn and Ebenezer Baptist at 4501 S. Vincennes. Others such as St. Mark A.M.E. Zion and Antioch Missionary Baptist followed their congregations to other neighborhoods on the South Side.

Shiloh Seventh Day Adventist Tabernacle illustrates the way in which a black church grew, prospered, and relocated further south in the city—the same path taken by earlier residents. Shiloh Tabernacle began in a storefront at 43rd and State Street in 1910. The following year the congregation built a church at 4806 S. Dearborn in the heart of the South Side Black Belt. By 1929 the congregation had moved to 46th and St. Lawrence Avenue at the east end of Grand Boulevard, and here the church remained for nearly thirty years. Today Shiloh Seventh Day Adventist Church of Christ is located at 70th and Michigan Avenue in the former Immanuel Church, which had moved to this neighborhood in 1914 from 46th and Dearborn!

In recent years several Grand Boulevard—Washington Park institutions have been revitalized. The Old Peoples Home at 4724 S. Vincennes Avenue has been remodeled into apartments for low-income families, the elderly, and the handicapped. In the summer of 1982, Provident Hospital opened a 300-bed facility at 51st and Vincennes Avenue, overlooking Washington Park. Founded in 1891 as Chicago's first black hospital, Provident moved to this area in 1929, occupying the University of Chicago's original Lying-In Hospital.

The Michigan Boulevard Garden Apartments, long a landmark on the South Side, have been added to the National Register of Historic Places, and in 1982 a $15 million rehabilitation program was inaugurated with backing from the City of Chicago and the Chicago Urban League. Although some new residential construction has taken place in the district, most new buildings such as Good Shepherd Tower on Garfield Boulevard are intended for the elderly

The Robert Taylor Homes, looking north from Garfield Boulevard (55th Street), 1985. The largest public housing project in the world, the Taylor highrises were constructed on the site of the old Federal Street slum. (J. Ficner)

rather than for families. As a result of declining population, business strips along 43rd, 47th, 55th, 58th, and 61st Streets have deteriorated dramatically in the last twenty years. Whereas neighborhood business strips once supported a variety of shops and restaurants, the only new businesses to emerge in recent years have been fast-food franchises. So many buildings have been torn down that Grand Boulevard and Washington Park now contain nearly as many prairies as they did in the 1890s. Indeed, the new Life Center Church of Universal Awareness at 5500 S. Indiana Avenue presents a stark contrast to the vacant lots which dot both sides of Garfield Boulevard.

Although only Cottage Grove Avenue separates Grand Boulevard and Washington Park from Kenwood and Hyde Park, these two districts remain as separate today as they did in 1930. Despite their proximity to the University of Chicago, Grand Boulevard and Washington Park have not been considered potential areas for renovation. Unlike "the Gap" at 35th and King Drive, where black professionals are renovating brownstones, the district around Washington Park has yet to be discovered by urban pioneers.

One of the most important events to occur in the area has been the opening of the Du Sable Museum of African-American History at 740 E. 56th Place. Dr. Margaret Burroughs donated her private collection of black art to this museum which is now housed in the old Washington Park Administration Building, designed in 1910 by D.H. Burnham & Co. Not only has the museum become the main attraction in historic Washington Park, but it is a powerful symbol for black Chicagoans who remember the days when Grand Boulevard and Washington Park formed the cultural and business center of the South Side Black Belt.

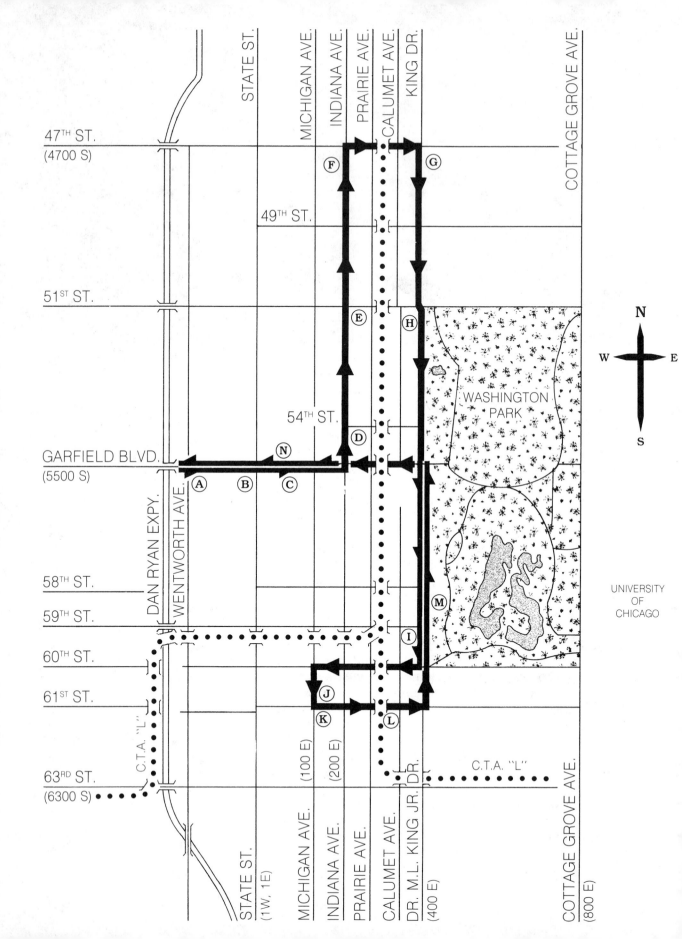

Grand Boulevard—Washington Park Tour

Exit the Dan Ryan Expressway at Garfield Boulevard (55th Street) and go east to Indiana Avenue. Because so much of the surrounding neighborhood is in the process of decline, this tour confines itself to the boulevards, going north through the Grand Boulevard area and then south on King Drive through the Washington Park district.

This tour begins at Wentworth Avenue (200 West), the historic dividing line between Chicago's white and black communities. From its northern terminus at 16th Street to 63rd Street, Wentworth cut through the heart of the city's South Side working-class neighborhoods. By the time the Dan Ryan Expressway opened in 1962, black families had moved west of Wentworth, bringing an end to the street's history of racial division.

Driving time: about 1 hour.

(A) **St. Charles Lwanga Church** at Garfield Boulevard and Wentworth is the oldest institution in the area. When it was founded in 1869 as **St. Anne's parish,** this area was only sparsely populated. In a few years, however, it was built up by railroad employees who worked in the nearby Chicago, Rock Island & Pacific car shops. Irish Catholics financed the present Gothic structure (1875-80). In keeping with its status as a "boulevard church," a limestone facade was added to the brick exterior in the 1920s. Although the neighborhood to the east became part of Chicago's black community after 1919, St. Anne remained a white parish until the 1940s. In a sharp break with tradition, St. Anne parish changed its name in 1971 to reflect its identity as a black institution. The parish commemorates St. Charles Lwanga, the first black African martyr in the Catholic Church.

(B) **Midway Liquors** building at 5500 S. State Street was one of the first brick buildings constructed in the area following the extension of the cable car line to 63rd Street in Englewood in the late 1880s. State Street was the boundary line between the towns of Lake and Hyde Park until 1889, when both areas were annexed to

Chicago. The new cable line transformed State Street from "a succession of sand hills and mud ponds" into one of the city's most important thoroughfares. The resulting building boom filled up the "long sweeps of prairie" with brick flat buildings, which in turn hastened the creation of a modern urban neighborhood.

(C) At 55 E. Garfield Boulevard is the **Good Shepherd Tower,** a privately owned seven-story highrise for senior citizens and the handicapped. The first new housing constructed in the area in more than fifteen years, the project was initiated by a black congregation and built by a black contractor, C.F. Moore. Members of the Church of the Good Shepherd (Congregational), 5700 S. Prairie, established a non-profit corporation and secured financing from the U.S. Department of Housing and Urban Development (HUD) under Section 8. The first tenants moved into the building in August 1984, and the formal dedication occurred on June 2, 1985. Longtime property owners in this section of Washington Park who remember Garfield Boulevard's heyday welcomed the construction of Good Shepherd Tower.

Another recent building on the boulevard is the **Life Center Church of Universal Awareness** (1982) at 5500 S. Indiana Avenue. Every Sunday hundreds of black Chicagoans attend services here to hear Rev. T.L. Barrett preach "the gospel of success."

Detail of Beth Hamedrash Hagadol Anshe Dorum synagogue, 5129S. Indiana. 1985. Built by a Jewish congregation about 1912, this building now houses the Unity Baptist Church. (J. Ficner)

(D) Turn left on Indiana Avenue and go eight blocks north to 47th Street. On a clear day Chicago's Loop is visible in the distance. Like Michigan and Wabash Avenues, Indiana was one of the South Side's most fashionable streets. In 1873 the Chicago *Times* noted that these three streets were "wide, handsome, perfectly straight and level," suitable for housing Chicago's "middle classes and substantial *bourgeois.*"

(E) Over the years, white Protestants, German Jews, Irish Catholics, and black families have lived in the brick flat buildings along Indiana Avenue. **The Unity Baptist Church** at 5129 S. Indiana offers a classic example of ethnic succession. It was built as a synagogue about 1912 by members of Beth Hamedrash Hagadol Anshe Dorum congregation, which moved here from the Douglas neighborhood. In 1928 Antioch Missionary Baptist Church purchased the building. Like earlier

Jewish congregations, this black church also began on the Near South Side, at 3140 S. LaSalle Street. In 1958 Antioch moved again, to 415 W. Englewood Avenue, in the Englewood neighborhood and sold the Indiana Avenue church to Unity Baptist. When Antioch pastor Rev. Wilbur N. Daniels learned that Unity Church might lose the Indiana Avenue building in foreclosure, he repurchased the church and sold it back to the congregation.

(F) Turn right at 47th Street and go two blocks east to King Drive. Forty-seventh Street between State and Cottage Grove was once the commercial and cultural hub of black Chicago. In addition to black-owned businesses and nightclubs, the 47th Street area included the five-story apartment complex at 4638 S. Michigan known as the **Michigan Boulevard Garden Apartments,** financed by philanthropist Julius Rosenwald. From its opening in 1929 through the 1950s, 4638 S. Michigan was one of Grand Boulevard's most fashionable addresses, home to scores of middle-class black families. Although the 47th Street business district has fallen on hard times, the Michigan Boulevard Garden Apartments recently received a facelift and was listed on the National Register of Historic Places in 1981.

(G) Turn right on King Drive and go south all the way to 60th Street. On July 31, 1968, South Parkway was renamed **King Drive** in honor of slain civil rights leader, Dr. Martin Luther King, Jr. For generations of Chicago blacks, 47th and South Parkway was the best known corner of their city. The **Regal Theater,** built in 1927 at 4719 South Parkway by Balaban & Katz, featured such important entertainers as Duke Ellington, Louis Armstrong, Ethel Waters, Cab Calloway, Lena Horne, and Nat King Cole. By the 1960s, however, 47th and South Parkway no longer marked the geographical center of Chicago's black community. The South Side Black Belt, which thrived precisely because of the color line against blacks, was profoundly affected by racial integration in the larger city. As black families moved to new neighborhoods on the South Side, they no longer returned to 47th Street for shopping or entertainment. While the demolition of the Regal Theater in 1973 was a sad day for black Chicagoans, it underscored the fact that black families had moved beyond the confines of the old Black Belt.

Black churches such as **Liberty Baptist,** 4849 S. King Drive, and Corpus Christi, 4900 S. King Drive, were among the most important institutions to develop in Grand Boulevard after the neighborhood became part of Chicago's Black Belt. Originally located at 27th and Dearborn, Liberty Baptist moved to 46th Street between Michigan and Wabash in 1930. In 1952 the congregation began construction of the present complex on South Parkway, which was dedicated in 1956. Known as the "Church with a Common Touch," Liberty Baptist was in the forefront of the black civil rights movement. It served as the Chicago headquarters for Dr. Martin Luther King, Jr., after whom the boulevard is named. Dr. King was scheduled to preach at Liberty Baptist on the fourth Sunday of April 1968. His assassination in Memphis on April 4, 1968 shook the nation. Before his death, Dr. King planned a Poor Peoples March to Washington, D.C. In May 1968, more than thirty busloads of civil rights activists and supporters left Liberty Baptist for Washington and the tent city known as "Resurrection City, U.S.A." Rev. A. Patterson Jackson, son of the church's first minister, has been pastor of Liberty Baptist since 1951. Under his leadership the congregation has earned the title, "Common Folks in an Uncommon Cause."

Corpus Christi Church, built by Irish Catholics in 1915, became the third black Catholic parish in Chicago in 1933. In addition to supporting a grammar school, beginning in 1945 black parishioners sent their children to Corpus Christi High School, housed in the former Sinai Temple at 4622 South Parkway. (In 1962, a modern all-boys high school known as Hales Franciscan opened at 4930 S. Cottage Grove, on the site of the old St. Francis Xavier College and Academy.) Although it is no longer one of the South Side's largest black parishes, Corpus Christi remains a vital link with Chicago's early black Catholic community. Indeed, present and former parishioners contributed generously to the restoration of Corpus Christi's ornate coffered ceiling in 1977.

(H) The **Chicago Baptist Institute,** 5120 S. King Drive, occupies buildings completed in 1899 for the Chicago Orphan Asylum, a charitable institution founded in 1849. Shepley, Rutan & Coolidge designed the brick "cottages" which were financed in part by the sale of stock from the nearby elevated railroad. Racial change in the neighborhood, coupled with new attitudes about orphanages, led to the institution's relocation in Kenwood in 1931. In addition to changing its address,

(Top left) 47th Street looking east across South Parkway (King Drive), 1937. From its opening in 1927 until it was razed in 1973, the Regal Theater was the Black Belt's most famous landmark.
(Chicago Park District, courtesy R. Wroble)

(Bottom left) Liberty Baptist Church, 4849 S. King Drive, 1985. A South Side institution since the 1920s. Liberty Baptist dedicated this new house of worship in 1956.
(G. Lane)

This spacious single-family dwelling at 5922 S. King Drive was the home of Jesse Binga, the South Side's foremost black banker and real estate dealer. Between 1919 and 1920, the Binga home was bombed nearly ten times by whites who sought to halt black migration into the Grand Boulevard and Washington Park neighborhoods. (J. Ficner. 1985)

the institution also changed its name and function. Now known as the Chicago Child Care Society, 5467 S. University, it provides day care for children in the Kenwood—Hyde Park community.

In 1937 Good Shepherd Congregational Church at 5700 S. Prairie purchased the former orphanage buildings, and the Parkway Community Center flourished at this location for the next twenty years. The Chicago Baptist Institute, founded in 1935 at 3816-18 S. Michigan, moved to 5120 South Parkway in 1957, where it continues its educational work on behalf of the city's black Baptist churches.

(I) In 1919 and 1920 **Jesse Binga's home** at 5922 South Parkway was bombed nearly ten times. One of the South Side's leading black bankers and real estate men, Binga was the first black to live in this section of Washington Park. His home as well as his bank at 36th Place and State were repeatedly bombed by whites who sought to halt the movement of blacks into Grand Boulevard and Washington Park.

(J) Turn right at 60th Street and go four blocks west to Michigan Avenue. Go one block south on Michigan to 61st Street, then turn east. **St. Anselm Church** at the northeast corner of 61st and Michigan was immortalized by James T. Farrell in his trilogy, *Studs Lonigan.* Founded in 1909 by Irish Catholics, this parish built a new church in 1925. Pastor Michael S. Gilmartin and his congregation fervently hoped that the $350,000 church would keep the neighborhood white. But four years after its dedication, St. Anselm's claimed only a handful of white parishioners. In 1932 George Cardinal Mundelein turned the church and school over to the Divine Word Fathers, and St. Anselm's subsequently became a thriving black parish. Like Corpus Christi, the other parish of Farrell's youth, St. Anselm's is now the "old neighborhood" parish for hundreds of Chicago's black Catholics.

This greystone apartment building at 5816 S. King Drive, now demolished, was the home of James T. Farrell in the early 1920s. In the second floor apartment overlooking Washington Park young Farrell "dreamed . . . and resolved to write." Studs Lonigan, as well as Farrell's Danny O'Neill novels, recreate the Washington Park neighborhood in vivid detail. (J. O'Malley)

(K) The church building at the southeast corner of 61st and Michigan also traces its beginnings to 1909, when Greek immigrants organized SS. Constantine and Helen parish. Like St. Anselm's, **SS. Constantine and Helen's** boasts a famous novelist, Harry Mark Petrakis, author of the award-winning book *Pericles on 31st Street,* among others. Harry's father, Mark E. Petrakis, came to the Greek parish as its pastor in 1923. The present church was constructed following a fire in 1926. Among the prominent Greeks who served on the building committee was Andrew Karzas, the wealthy theater owner, who with his brother built the lavish Trianon Ballroom at 62nd and Cottage Grove in 1922.

In 1948 the Greek congregation sold their Michigan Avenue church to the Episcopal congregation of St. Edmund's and moved to South Shore where they built a massive temple at 74th and Stony Island Avenue. Once again as a result of racial change, the Greeks relocated in 1972, this time to suburban Palos Hills. In addition to a new $2.3 million church complex (1976), SS. Constantine and Helen parish supports the Koraes Elementary School in Palos Hills, the second oldest Greek Orthodox day school in the country.

Although **St. Edmund's Episcopal Church** did not move to 61st and Michigan until 1948, the parish was one of Washington Park's early institutions. Founded in 1905, the congregation moved three years later to a church building at 5831 S. Indiana. As white families left the neighborhood in response to racial change, many moved to Kenwood and Hyde Park where they affiliated with St. Paul Episcopal Church at 50th and Dorchester. On July 1, 1928, St. Edmund's took on a new identity as a black parish, and twenty years later the congregation moved into the former Greek Orthodox church at 61st and Michigan.

(L) Continue four blocks east on 61st Street to King Drive. The 61st Street shopping strip is typical of the small commercial centers which grew up around stations of the Jackson Park line of the South Side Elevated Railroad. The "L" played an important role in the development of the modern urban neighborhood with its characteristic "flat" buildings and its concentrated population. Like earlier suburban developments established along commuter railroad lines, neighborhoods like Washington Park were attractive to Loop workers as well as to office workers in the

St. Edmund's Episcopal Church, southeast corner of 61st and Michigan, 1980. Built in 1928 by the Greek Orthodox congregation of SS. Constantine and Helen, this church was sold in 1948 to St. Edmund's, one of Washington Park's oldest black congregations. (G. Lane)

stockyards district to the west. In contrast to the bungalow belts where residents owned their homes, the apartment district near the "L" experienced continual turnover. This pattern of mobility, which was set by Irish and Jewish newcomers in the 1910s, was continued by the black families who moved into Grand Boulevard and Washington Park.

(M) Turn left and go north on King Drive to Garfield Boulevard (55th Street). King Drive forms the western boundary of **Washington Park,** which stretches from 51st to 60th Streets. Originally planned as a suburban retreat, the park provided much-needed open space for apartment dwellers in the adjoining Grand Boulevard and Washington Park communities. Since the 1920s Washington Park has also served as the boundary line between Chicago's Black Belt and Hyde Park and Kenwood. While the University of Chicago played a crucial role in maintaining Kenwood and Hyde Park as integrated communities, its influence did not extend across Cottage Grove Avenue into the Grand Boulevard and Washington Park neighborhoods.

The first all-black park in Chicago, Washington Park is the scene of the annual **Bud Billiken Parade,** the city's oldest neighborhood parade. As a young black reporter on the Chicago *Defender,* Willard Motley wrote a weekly column in the early 1920s under the name "Bud Billiken." So great was the appeal of this Buddha-like comic figure that *Defender* editor Robert S. Abbott named the parade Bud Billiken. Nearly twenty years after the parade had become an established institution, Motley achieved critical acclaim for his novel, *Knock on Any Door.*

(N) Turn west onto Garfield Boulevard and continue three-quarters of a mile to the Dan Ryan Expressway. This section of Garfield Boulevard once contained major businesses such as the Wanzer Milk Company and the Schulze Baking Company. In an area plagued by high unemployment and crime, the **Butternut Bread Company** remains as one of the few large businesses in the old Black Belt. It occupies the white terra-cotta building at 40 E. Garfield Boulevard, which was constructed in 1914 by the Schulze Baking Company.

(Top left) The Du Sable Museum of African-American History, 740 E. 56th Place, 1985. Founded by Dr. Margaret Burroughs, the museum documents the experience of American blacks with special emphasis on art and music. (G. Lane)

(Bottom left) The Schulze Baking Company building, 40 E. Garfield Boulevard, 1985. John Ahlschlager designed this imposing terra-cotta structure in 1914 for Chicago's largest wholesale concern. Known throughout the country as the home of Butter-Nut Bread, this building was added to the National Register of Historic Places in 1982. (G. Lane, 1985)

11

South Lakefront

In the period just before the Civil War, Chicago's upper
middle class began to look toward the south lakefront below
47th Street for a possible suburban refuge and for summer
homes. While most of the very rich were settling on Prairie
Avenue to the north, others were starting to be attracted to
Hyde Park, Kenwood, and South Shore. The turning point for
the area was the decision of the Illinois Central Railroad in
the mid-1850s to run a commuter line south from downtown
along the lakefront.

These areas soon prospered as the white Anglo-Saxon
Protestant middle class came in search of a refuge from an
increasingly crowded working-class Irish and German city.
All of the South Side below 39th Street remained a suburb of
Chicago until the annexation of 1889. The residents of the
south lakefront from 47th to 79th Street generally opposed
this "surrender" to Chicago, but their working-class
neighbors overruled them just before the World's Fair
of 1893.

The World's Columbian Exposition in Jackson Park had
a tremendous impact on these lakefront neighborhoods. It
greatly affected the residential development of Hyde Park,
Kenwood, and South Shore. It also changed the character of
Hyde Park. Storefronts, hotels, and outsiders suddenly
appeared everywhere in the once quiet suburb. Another
fundamental change also came in 1893 when the University
of Chicago opened its doors just north of the Midway
Plaisance. The fair and the university both shaped the early
history of the south lakefront.

Still more demographic and economic changes came in
the twentieth century. The ethnic middle class, originally
Jewish and Irish, followed the Anglo-Saxon Protestants to
the lakefront. By mid-century blacks joined them. The urban
renewal programs of the 1950s and 1960s were a response to
demographic and economic change, as much of the old
middle class left the area.

Today all three of these community areas, Hyde Park,
Kenwood, and South Shore, are racially integrated, at least
to some degree. The Hyde Park—Kenwood area is the
largest, most stable integrated area in Chicago and perhaps
in the country. And yet the success of Hyde Park's
integration and stability was purchased at quite a price. To a
large extent Hyde Park remains a middle-class enclave as it
was in the nineteenth century. Racial integration has proved
to be less successful in South Shore where the white middle
class tends to locate along the lakefront and in the Jackson

Park Highlands. The entire area south of 47th Street remains attractive to both black and white middle-class people, especially those interested in historic preservation.

Hyde Park — Kenwood

Hyde Park—Kenwood is generally recognized as an island surrounded by the rest of the South Side. Lying south of 47th Street along the lakefront to 60th Street, the Hyde Park—Kenwood Community in many ways has always been different from nearby areas; although the distinct flavor of the present-day neighborhood became more pronounced in the 1950s because of massive urban renewal. Before that twenty-year process began, the district's boundaries were more flexible to the north and south. With the changes of the postwar period, however, Hyde Park's future became different from that of its surrounding South Side neighbors. In many ways those changes returned the neighborhood to the pattern that its founder, Paul Cornell, had intended for it from the beginning.

Dr. John A. Kennicott, a Chicago dentist, moved to the south suburbs in 1856 and founded Kenwood. Kennicott's estate stood near the Illinois Central Railroad tracks at 43rd Street. The name Kenwood is the same as that of his mother's ancestral home in Scotland. Several other wealthy families moved to Kenwood, and in 1859 the Illinois Central agreed to make a stop at 47th Street to serve the new and growing community. By 1875 Kenwood was the gem of the South Lakefront. Stately homes and mansions were constructed along its tree-lined streets. Institutional development soon followed. St. Paul's Episcopal Church and a Congregational church came to the neighborhood. Some time later the First Baptist Church moved to 50th Street in the community. In the 1890s many of Chicago's leading families who derived their fortunes from meatpacking, steel, and stocks, built mansions in Kenwood. In the twentieth century such names as Swift, Rosenwald, and Morris were listed in the social register as Kenwood residents. With the opening of the Kenwood branch of the "L" in 1910—the terminus of which was at 42nd and Lake Park Avenue—middle income families were attracted to the neighborhood, and they took up residence in newly constructed apartment buildings. Meanwhile, the servants in the mansions of Kenwood and middle-class Catholics who lived north of 47th Street founded St. Ambrose parish in 1904. Later on well-to-do Irish families joined the wealthy Protestants in Kenwood and contributed to the growth of St. Ambrose at 47th and Ellis Avenue.

(Top right) George R.T. Ward Residence. c.1880. Fine homes lined the streets of Kenwood after the Chicago Fire of 1871. The "Jewel" of the South Side attracted some of the most prominent names on the city's social register.

(Courtesy Chicago Historical Society)

(Bottom right) Woodlawn Avenue, looking north from 48th Street, c.1910. Many illustrious Chicagoans lived along Woodlawn in the early part of the twentieth century, including Thomas E. Wilson, the meat packer, and H.M.S. Montgomery, the grain merchant.

(C.R. Childs, courtesy G. Schmalgemeier)

Woodlawn Av. N. from 48th St., Chicago, Ill.

1303.

Many of Kenwood's wealthy residents had businesses in the nearby stockyards. The neighborhood was conveniently located about three miles east of the livestock market. While this at first proved to be a benefit to Kenwood, by the 1920s the odor of the meatpacking process helped to bring about the decline of the district. Many of the very rich left the neighborhood for less polluted environs.

As Kenwood changed, the southern portion became more closely identified with Hyde Park. Faculty members of the University of Chicago and other professional people began to settle in the area. In the 1950s and 1960s the two neighborhoods were closely joined by the urban renewal process and by the fact that their populations were so similar. Moreover, the neighborhood north of 47th Street experienced a complete racial turnover and became more closely associated with the all-black Oakland neighborhood to the north. South Kenwood, which remained middle class and racially integrated, tended to identify with Hyde Park.

Hyde Park was a sparsely settled area in the 1830s and 1840s. Only a few people had ventured into the vicinity. Obadian Hooper, a farmer, claimed a homestead between 55th and 59th Streets, between Woodlawn and Dorchester Avenues, but he soon lost the land for nonpayment of taxes. Dr. William Egan was also an early settler who purchased a large tract of land in the area and attempted to build an Irish country estate. His plans never fully materialized. Earlier, Nathan Wilson constructed a log cabin at 53rd and the lake and operated a tavern for those taking the lakefront trail to Chicago. The real estate market, however, remained dormant until the 1850s.

In 1852 a young lawyer named Paul Cornell paid for a topographical survey of the lakefront area along the South Side. Stephen Douglas, then associated with the Illinois Central Railroad, advised him to invest in land between Chicago and the Calumet region. Cornell had arrived in town five years earlier and had worked for several law firms. He met Douglas while associated with the firm of Skinner and Hoyne.

A year after the survey, Cornell purchased a 300-acre tract of lakefront land between 51st and 55th Streets. He also decided to deed sixty acres of land to the Illinois Central Railroad in return for a promise that the railroad would build a station in the settlement. Cornell named his proposed suburb Hyde Park. Years later he admitted that he was unsure whether London's Hyde Park or the settlement of the same name on the Hudson River influenced him. In either case, Cornell wanted to create an upper-middle-class sanctuary and summer resort. The name Hyde Park, long associated with elegant and gracious living, would help achieve that goal.

In 1856 the Illinois Central opened the first Hyde Park station at 53rd Street, linking the suburb to the city and causing the little town to grow along the IC tracks. Encouraged by this expansion, Cornell built a hotel, the Hyde Park House, on 53rd Street a short walk from the train station. He hoped the hotel, which opened in 1857, would be a summer resort for upper-class Chicagoans and provide potential real estate developers with a place to stay while they considered the purchase of land.

Cornell's next move was to establish a firm economic base for Hyde Park. Having seen the first push by the middle class out of the center of the city, he took advantage of this demographic movement. Cornell was aware of his competition, such as Stephen Douglas's enterprise just north of Hyde Park, which had attracted the first University of Chicago and provided the Douglas area with an apparently stable anchor.

Paul Cornell was related by marriage to John Evans, after whom Evanston had been named, and to Orrington Lunt, another Evanston father and founder of Northwestern University. He was also familiar with Evanston's success, and this influenced his idea of what Hyde Park should be. As Jean Block has pointed out in in her book, *Hyde Park Houses*, Cornell wanted an institution like Northwestern University to be the economic and cultural base of his settlement. He set aside land along the lakefront south of 53rd Street as a site for a Presbyterian theological seminary. His plans, however, were not successful, and Hyde Park remained without an institutional base until the 1890s.

Despite this setback, the settlement continued to grow. Many of those who invested in Hyde Park early on were related to Cornell and kept up their support. The Illinois Central railroad connection with Chicago was of utmost importance, and lots that were for sale were generous in size. Thus those who were attracted to Hyde Park were precisely of the class and character that Cornell wanted.

During the 1850s Hyde Park was situated within the Township of Lake, which stretched south from 39th Street and included several working-class towns. However, in 1861 the small middle-class settlements along the IC tracks petitioned and received separate township status from the Illinois General Assembly. This new district, known as the Township of Hyde Park, stretched from 39th to 130th Street and from State Street to the lake. When it was first created, the township had only 350 residents who hailed the move as an advance in participatory democracy. Hyde Parkers would no longer have their destiny controlled by the working-class

Fraternity house. 923 E. 60th Street. c.1913. This building faced the Midway and the University of Chicago. University buildings now occupy the site.
(Courtesy G. Schmalgemeier)

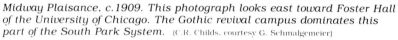

Midway Plaisance, c.1909. This photograph looks east toward Foster Hall of the University of Chicago. The Gothic revival campus dominates this part of the South Park System. (C.R. Childs, courtesy G. Schmalgemeier)

Harvard School for Boys, 47th and Drexel, c.1907. Several private schools opened in the Kenwood community to serve its upper-class residents. Among them were the Harvard and Faulkner Schools for Boys and the Starrett School for Girls. (C.R. Childs, courtesy G. Schmalgemeier)

politicians of the Town of Lake. Four years later, in 1865, the Union Stock Yard opened on 43rd Street west of Halsted and further changed the future of the two towns. Hyde Park continued as a middle-class enclave, while the Town of Lake thrived as an industrial center.

This division fit in perfectly with Cornell's plans. The founder of Hyde Park wanted no industry in his settlement. His was to be a strictly residential suburb with just enough commerce to provide for its residents' daily needs. There were to be institutions, but no smelly packinghouses or smoky steel mills. These would be located far to the south in the Calumet Region, not in the heart of Hyde Park.

Institutional growth began in 1858 when residents organized a Presbyterian congregation. Their first house of worship was a small chapel at what is now 53rd Street and Lake Park Avenue. In 1860 they built a larger church on the same site. This was followed eight years later by a new and larger edifice constructed at 53rd Street and Blackstone Avenue, and the town remodelled the old church into a combination town hall and jail. The Episcopalians shared the same church with the Presbyterians. Schools were also constructed. A small grammar school opened on 46th Street, and the first Hyde Park High School was established at 50th and Lake Park Avenue in 1870.

Hyde Park began to take on the characteristics of a small New England town, reflecting the background of most of its early residents. The suburb even had a small commons located on 53rd Street and the lakefront. Moreover, as with many other small towns, the train depot became the center of activity. Before the town hall was constructed, the IC station served as a meeting place for community organizations. By the late 1860s the entire township, stretching to 130th Street, numbered about 3,000 people, and Paul Cornell and other real estate developers began to look for ways to speed up development on the South Side.

At the end of the Civil War, Cornell headed a group which called for the creation of a park system south of Chicago. After suffering several defeats, pro-park forces succeeded in getting a bill through the Illinois General Assembly. Cornell was considered the "father of the South Park System," so it is not surprising that his settlement was surrounded by the largest and most beautiful of the parks. Jackson Park and the Midway Plaisance formed the southern boundary of Hyde Park, while Washington Park bordered it on the west; thus the community took on the appearance of an island surrounded by greenery. The parks became strong selling points for Hyde Park developers, and years later they provided natural boundaries between Hyde Park and the economic and demographic changes going on around it.

*Old Field Museum building, 57th
at Lake Shore Drive, 1924.
Originally built as the Palace of
Fine Arts for the Columbian
Exposition of 1893, this building
later housed the Field Museum
until 1919, and from 1933 the
Museum of Science and Industry.*
(Kaufmann & Fabry, courtesy The Chicago
Catholic)

Meanwhile, transportation improved for Hyde Park residents. In 1869, the same year the South Park System was created, the Chicago and Calumet Railroad began to run a "steam dummy" train along 55th Street and up Cottage Grove Avenue. This rail line connected with the horsecar line at 39th Street and provided residents of western Hyde Park with easy access to Chicago. In 1870 the town had 1,000 inhabitants, while the township as a whole had grown to 3,600. Cornell's original settlement continued to be populated by businessmen and professionals, though others were moving in to provide services for the middle class. In 1872 the township was granted a "village" government by the General Assembly in order to expand services for the growing population.

During the next decade Hyde Park experienced tremendous growth. The town was suddenly caught up in the quick expansion of Chicago, overwhelming Cornell's dream of an elite suburb. Row houses and working-class cottages appeared on side streets adjacent to mansions. City services became inadequate. The new mass transit system encouraged the development of commercial shopping strips, which sprang up near the IC stops and along 53rd and 55th Streets. The 1880s saw Hyde Park change from a quiet village to an urban neighborhood.

Faced with this changed environment, township residents proposed annexation to the City of Chicago. In 1887 a referendum was defeated, but two years later it

Promontory Point, 1937. This photograph taken for the Chicago Park District by a W.P.A. photographer shows the construction of Promontory Point at 55th Street and Lake Michigan. The newly constructed Lake Shore Drive can also be seen.
(Courtesy R. Wroble)

passed, and the entire township disappeared from the map, becoming part of the city. In both instances, however, those who lived in the original core settlement voted against annexation. They were overruled after a bitter struggle, and Hyde Park became a part of Chicago in 1889.

Two events soon occurred which pushed Hyde Park into the modern era. In 1890 Chicago won the fight to host the World's Columbian Exposition in the parks which surrounded Hyde Park. This victory resulted in a surge of new construction. Hotels, stores, and apartment buildings sprang up everywhere, but especially near the site of the fair. In the midst of this development, Hyde Park almost lost its identity. It was on the verge of becoming just another South Side neighborhood swallowed up by the city's tremendous growth following the Civil War. It seemed that the golden age of the settlement was gone forever.

At this point, however, Cornell's dream of an institutional anchor for Hyde Park was revived, and this changed the destiny of the community. The Baptist Church, with support from John D. Rockefeller, decided to create a new University of Chicago on land donated by Marshall Field. The school was to be located just north of the Midway Plaisance. And so the most important event in the history of Hyde Park came to pass. Cornell's settlement finally had a firm institutional, economic, and cultural base. From that time on, the destiny of the neighborhood was intertwined with that of the university.

The history of the University of Chicago is well known to those who live in the area. Its impact on Hyde Park's housing market was immediate. The university encouraged faculty, students, and staff to live close to the campus, and by 1900 this new population dominated the area south of 55th Street. Students competed with residents and with ethnic groups who were pushing south along the avenues seeking housing in the area. Hyde Park took on the atmosphere of a major university town. The new residents changed Hyde Park from a conservative bastion to one that was still economically conservative, but socially liberal and politically independent. This change was significant because it would shape Hyde Park's response to urban problems fifty years later.

The aftermath of World War I brought sweeping changes to Chicago's South Side. Not the least of these was the dramatic growth of the city's black population. The Black Belt expanded south and east from the original settlement around 22nd and State Streets. That part of the city sometimes called "greater" Hyde Park lay in the path of this population movement. This area included Oakland, Kenwood, parts of Washington Park, as well as Hyde Park itself. Because the housing was of a better quality in these neighborhoods, they attracted middle-class black people. This resulted in racial violence and the use of restrictive covenants by whites in an attempt to fend off racial change.

Hyde Park homeowners, businessmen, and others banded together to form the Hyde Park—Kenwood Property Owners Association. This group used political, economic,

*Hull Gate, University of Chicago,
c.1913. Hull Gate faces 57th
Street and marks the original
entrance to the biological
laboratories; it also leads to the
main quadrangle. Charles J. Hull
is the same person that Chicago's
famous Hull House is named after.*
(C.R. Childs, courtesy G. Schmalgemeier)

and other kinds of pressure to prevent the racial
transformation of the South Side. The fact that bombings
took place in the Grand Boulevard and Kenwood areas
during the height of the Association's power is indicative of
the atmosphere at the time. And while there is no proof that
the Association was involved in such activities, there is
strong evidence that they did not frown on such practices.
More than twenty bombings preceded the tragic race riot in
1919.

The use of restrictive covenants was more successful
than acts of violence in stemming the tide of racial change.
Hyde Park homeowners pledged not to rent their homes to
non-Caucasians. The Supreme Court declared this practice
unconstitutional in 1948 in a case argued by Earl Dickerson,
a black attorney and insurance executive, who later lived in
Hyde Park. Until that court decision, however, covenants
remained a partially effective way of segregating the area.

Like World War I, World War II also brought upheaval in
its wake. A wartime boom resulted in a new migration of
Southern blacks to Chicago. The South Side Black Belt
expanded again as memories of the 1919 race riot faded.
The neighborhood to the north of Hyde Park witnessed
significant racial change, and by the end of the 1940s the
combination of two decades of depression, war, and neglect
had caused vast new slums to develop. Hyde Park and
Kenwood seemed to be in store for the same fate. Many of
the old wealthy families, who for years had made Kenwood
their home, moved. The odor from the nearby stockyards
and the pollution from the lakefront steel mills in South

Chicago lessened the area's desirability. Lower-middle-class and white-collar workers replaced the old aristocracy. By 1950 German and Russian Jews made up the largest ethnic group in the neighborhood. Japanese Americans, displaced by World War II, also constituted a large part of the area's population. Blacks accounted for about six percent of the local population, many living in housing units that had deteriorated badly. An irreversible trend seemed to be underway.

But Hyde Park—Kenwood was different. While blockbusting, illegal conversions, and the spread of slums hit the area, the neighborhood did not dissolve. In 1949 the 57th Street Meeting of Friends (Quakers) began the first organized program to combat the neighborhood's problems. This was the Hyde Park—Kenwood Community Conference, an organization which proposed two objectives for the neighborhood: to stop decay and to promote racial integration. Another organization, the South East Chicago Commission, was organized in 1952 and was backed by more conservative elements in the neighborhood, especially the University of Chicago. These two organizations often distrusted each other and had different aims. Yet they avoided open clashes because their memberships overlapped, and ultimately they both wanted to make Hyde Park—Kenwood work. Yet by the middle 1950s, the fate of the neighborhood was still in doubt. The police district to which the neighborhood belonged had the highest crime rate in the city.

In 1954 the new Federal Housing Act set the stage for the first large-scale neighborhood urban renewal program in the nation, and it decisively determined the future of the Hyde Park—Kenwood community. Leaders in the community were familiar with the legislation because some of the legal research for the Housing Act had been done at the University of Chicago Law School. As former resident Muriel Beadle has pointed out, "much of the experience gained by both the Conference and the Commission was reflected in the new law."

Unlike the communities which underwent irrevocable racial change to the north and south of it, two important factors kept Hyde Park—Kenwood integrated; it had a firm economic and institutional base in the University of Chicago and the neighborhood was already well organized. Hyde Parkers have a long tradition of being joiners. Local residents came to meetings, voiced their opinions, and supported causes. It was a factor that was often missing in other middle-class areas where residents saw decline and simply left.

Once the 1954 Federal Housing Act was passed, these local organizations gave Hyde Park—Kenwood a definite

Looking south on Lake Park at 50th Street, 1950. Urban renewal brought about the demolition and complete reconstruction of this area. Lake Park Avenue was moved to the east and Kenwood Academy now stands on this site. (Courtesy Chicago Historical Society)

advantage for receiving federal aid. The law required public meetings, and this was a requirement the neighborhood could easily meet. Hyde Park also had the administrative ability to carry out programs, and it met federal financial requirements as well. It was as if the 1954 law was written specifically for the area between 47th Street and the Midway, Cottage Grove Avenue and the lake.

Add to this a major economic and symbolic force like the University of Chicago, and the district had a good chance to protect itself. The economic power of the university should not be underestimated. This institution was able to expand and influence the real estate market as none other had before it. Buying up buildings and turning them into student housing was one tactic; political influence was another. The university used the South East Chicago Commission to develop a broad plan of attack using the wrecking ball as well as the recycling of buildings for a major urban renewal project. Fifty-fifth Street would never again be the same.

It began in May 1955. Nearly forty-three acres of buildings were slated for demolition in an area from 54th Street to 57th, and from Kimbark to Lake Park Avenues. Then another 909 acres of buildings were added to the list to be pulled down. Hyde Park underwent radical surgery. The Chicago Land Clearance Authority spent $9,800,000 to acquire the buildings to be torn down. The city, the university, and the community cooperated in the effort. Mayor Richard J. Daley called the demolition of the first building "one of the most important events in the city's history." The program to rebuild Hyde Park was under way.

But was there a vision that would remold the neighborhood? Many were bitter. Merchants and other small businessmen were uprooted. The old art colony on 57th Street was pulled down during the fifteen-year operation. The artists could hardly afford the "new colony" in Harper Court, so they moved, taking with them much of the soul of the neighborhood. And some who moved once were forced to move again and again. Ted and Bea Ciral's House of Tiki was moved from Hyde Park Boulevard near Harper Avenue so that Kenwood Academy could be built. Their other businesses had already been forced off Lake Park Avenue by the wrecker's ball. The old Compass Bar, the birthplace of the Second City Players, was replaced by a fire station at 55th Street and University Avenue. One after another of Hyde Park's business and entertainment landmarks disappeared.

Elaine May and Mike Nichols once described Hyde Park as "black and white united against the poor." Was this, then, the ultimate plan for the new Hyde Park? The Hyde Park—Kenwood Conference opted for keeping the area a socially as well as racially integrated community. Many had been attracted to the neighborhood precisely because of its cosmopolitan character. The art colony, the university, the wealthy, and the poor seemed to mingle. Memories may have turned the previous times into romantic visions, but some of them were based in reality. The Hyde Park of 1919 died sometime during the Great Depression, and another more pluralistic Hyde Park had replaced it. The neighborhood was socially more liberal, but that too was changing. A third Hyde Park has been created since 1954, economically more secure, but less so culturally. The South East Chicago Commission's vision of the new Hyde Park was for it to be an elite enclave, thus bringing the district full circle. It was this vision which won out in 1954 and which prompted Elaine May's and Mike Nichol's remarks.

Hyde Park—Kenwood tried for a time to have it both ways. Indeed it looked for a while like it might have worked. By the mid-1960s the district regained its confidence. There was still some entertainment left. The Hyde Park Shopping Center designed by architect Harry Weese was stable. The Fifth Ward's liberal politicians were once again offending the regular Democratic organization, and murals were appearing under the IC tracks. Hyde Parkers were active in the anti-war movement and smug in their integrated, liberal enclave. Meanwhile, the city began falling apart.

In 1968 the Judy Robert's Trio played at the Baroque Lounge on 53rd Street. The Last Stage Players fled the wrecker's ball next door to the House of Tiki and had settled in the Harper Theatre. A controversial play was being shown at the Shoreland Hotel. That same year the Democratic Convention and the assassination of Martin Luther King, Jr. and Robert Kennedy jolted the nation. The riots that shook the Black Belt shook Hyde Park as well. The enclave mentality was reinforced.

The spirit of a neighborhood is a delicate thing. In the 1850s Paul Cornell envisioned his Hyde Park, the first Hyde Park, as an elite suburb on the edges of a great city. He worked hard to reach that goal, and by 1900 the area became a Chicago neighborhood and was one of the finest in the city. The first Hyde Park was a bastion of Republican politics and was socially and economically conservative. This original Hyde Park, however, died in the 1930s and a new liberal Democratic community took its place. The changes of the war years meant that its days were numbered too. 1954 signaled the birth of a third Hyde Park that struggled through an intense identity crisis which has not yet been resolved. Paul Cornell's ideas still haunt the neighborhood, as do the visions of the 1930s and the 1940s. They all mingle together on 53rd and 55th Streets.

South Shore

South Shore has always been a special place for South Siders. Located south of 67th Street from Stony Island Avenue to the lake and running as far south as 79th Street, it has been the destination for countless middle-class families since the 1890s.

One of the first settlers in the district was Ferdinand Rohn, who operated a farm near 71st and the lake in the 1850s. Rohn traveled into Chicago to sell his produce, and the round-trip took him anywhere from twelve to sixteen hours. The area must have seemed fairly forbidding at the time. South Shore was mostly swamp land with some high ground over which rough trails had been cut. Sparsely settled, the community had to wait until 1881 for the Illinois Central Railroad to open its South Kenwood Station at 71st Street and Jeffery Boulevard connecting it with Chicago.

By the early 1890s a small settlement was established near the IC station in an area which became known as Bryn Mawr—the train station soon adopted the name which it still has today. Just west of Bryn Mawr, a neighborhood called Parkside developed. This district ran from 67th to 71st Street. South of Parkside to 75th Street another small settlement took the name of Essex. It was an outgrowth of a small residential area organized by Paul Cornell, the father of Hyde Park.

In 1889 the entire district became part of the city of Chicago when the Township of Hyde Park voted in favor of annexation. The area was greatly affected by two events: the annexation and the Columbian Exposition, which followed soon afterwards in 1893. Paul Cornell was one of the first to try to capitalize on the World's Fair that was held in Jackson Park. The park, which separated Hyde Park from South Shore, promised to be a boon to all the surrounding areas. Cornell opened a huge wooden hotel, The Calumet, at 75th Street and the IC tracks. The railroad connected the fairgrounds with downtown and, of course, with South Shore.

A housing explosion followed the fair, and developers quickly subdivided the farm land. The Windsor Park Golf Club, located between 75th and 79th Streets east of Yates Boulevard was sold to Charles Ringer shortly after the fair. He hoped to attract the Armour Institute to the site, but failed, and eventually he sold the land to apartment house developers.

With the construction of more and more housing, South Shore took on the characteristics of a middle-class neighborhood. In 1905 the Jackson Park Highlands west of

South Shore Country Club, c.1910. This postcard view of the once private club shows the main gate at 71st Street. The restored club is operated today for the public by the Chicago Park District.
(Courtesy G. Schmalgemeier)

Jeffrey and south of 67th Street were subdivided and developed. This was followed the next year with the opening of the South Shore Country Club. Both of these developments were related to events which were happening to the northwest of the neighborhood in the Washington Park community. In fact, these same events set a trend that would continue to shape the history of South Shore for the rest of the century.

By the 1880s Washington Park had become an exclusive residential neighborhood. With the coming of the fair and the elevated trains to the South Side, this quickly changed. Washington Park was soon full of real estate developers who constructed large apartment houses within easy walking distance of the "L." The entertainment district that emerged along the "L" tracks further changed the neighborhood. And finally, the good transportation brought an entirely new ethnic group to Washington Park, the Irish. These people arrived in large numbers in the neighborhood, and they built Catholic churches on the main streets, thus changing the character of the district. In 1905 the city closed the Washington Park Race Track, and along with it went the Washington Park Club, an exclusive social institution. Already the white Protestant middle class was making its way into South Shore.

When the Washington Park Club was closed, its former members organized the South Shore Country Club, which soon became one of the most exclusive meeting places in Chicago. The neighborhood also took on an upper-middle-class character..

Bathing Beach, Chicago Beach Hotel, c.1912. This was one of many private beaches that occupied the south lakefront before World War I. The Chicago Beach Hotel at Hyde Park Boulevard and the IC Railroad tracks was one of the fancier "off-Loop" hotels.
(Courtesy G. Schmalgemeier)

But the new settlers in the area had blazed a new social and demographic trail from Washington Park to South Shore. The ethnic groups which had followed them to Washington Park would now follow them to South Shore. By 1910 the Irish middle class was firmly entrenched in Washington Park with German Jews following them in large numbers. These in turn were followed by Russian Jews. The novels of Chicago author James T. Farrell, best known for his Studs Lonigan trilogy, portray the communities along the elevated tracks during this period. In fact, the community of Washington Park served as a corridor through which various ethnic groups would quickly pass. These "L" neighborhoods funneled people further south as they climbed the economic ladder. South Shore was the destination of many people who had formerly lived in Washington Park.

This movement of ethnic groups rolling like waves southward in the city can be traced through census materials and through the various institutions which they established to serve their needs.

In 1920 the population of South Shore was 31,832 and predominately Protestant. The leading nationality groups were Swedish and English. But there was already a considerable number of Irish and English Catholics in the community. It was around this time that racial change began to occur in Washington Park. The Irish who lived in the communities along the "L" tracks moved out in large numbers, and those who were upwardly mobile moved to South Shore. By 1920 fifteen percent of Washington Park's population was made up of black people.

The following decade saw the transformation of South Shore from a Protestant enclave to an ethnically mixed Chicago neighborhood. Once again the Washington Park influence was felt. In the early 1920s the dividing line between black and white Chicagoans in Washington Park had been Garfield Boulevard; but as the decade progressed, blacks pushed across that boundary line. Jews quickly left the Washington Park area and moved to South Shore, following the Irish who had followed the Protestants. Many of the Jews settled in the new apartment buildings under construction in the neighborhood.

By 1930 the population of Washington Park was 44,016, of which ninety-two percent was black. The racial transformation of Washington Park was complete. The ethnic transformation of South Shore quickly followed.

The 1920s saw the population of South Shore more than double, from 31,832 to 78,755. This was the result both of natural growth and of white flight from the areas which were becoming part of the city's Black Belt. Much of the natural growth resulted from the opening of the Outer Drive and the development of the lakefront. Developers constructed large apartment hotels along the lakefront from Hyde Park Boulevard south.

The most numerous American-born ethnic groups in the area became the Germans and the Irish. Behind these were the English and Welsh, the Swedes and the Russians. Both the Irish and the German populations were about twice the size of any of the other groups. Most of the Germans and the Russians were Jews; and among the foreign-born, the Swedes were the most numerous, with the Irish and Germans coming next. In 1930, 171 black people lived in the South Shore community. They were probably employed in the apartment hotels.

Statistics show that the Washington Park connection continued to operate. A group of Jews who had lived in Washington Park founded the South Side Hebrew Congregation, the first synagogue in the lakefront community.

The Irish and the Jews quickly established their distinctive institutions in South Shore. The parishes of St. Philip Neri at 72nd and Merrill, St. Bride at 78th and Coles, and Our Lady of Peace at 79th and Jeffrey became the centers of Irish religious and communal life. Jewish institutions also prospered. The two ethnic groups appeared to have created a barrier between themselves and the Black Belt. South Shore became a Mecca for the rising ethnic middle class.

A 1939 description of the neighborhood characterized

St. Phillip Neri Church, 2126 E. 72nd Street, 1985. This huge church was built in the 1920s to serve the Irish Catholic community in South Shore. Today it is home to a racially integrated Catholic congregation. (G. Lane)

South Shore as "predominately middle-class—upper middle-class, to be sure, but not social register." The groups who had fled Washington Park as the Irish moved in had by now also left South Shore, and by 1940 there were 249 black people living in the neighborhood.

Old South Shore residents have many memories of the South Shore Country Club. Blacks and Jews were excluded, as well as those who could not afford the membership. But for the upwardly mobile Irish-American middle class it became a magic place, with parties, dances, receptions, and celebrations in the club, on the golf course, and along the private beach. The club introduced the Irish to the world of cotillions and champagne.

Organizational life was also important for the Irish. The Holy Name Society, the Knights of Columbus, and the Catholic Order of Foresters among others, provided the Catholic parishioners with rich neighborhood experiences. Seventy-first Street was well known for its St. Patrick's Day celebrations.

Not all the Irish and Jewish residents of South Shore fit the upwardly mobile middle-class pattern. Many were middle-class families who had made their way to Chicago's famous bungalow belt. South Shore had many modest single-family homes as well as the apartments which seemed to dominate the housing stock.

By the 1940s the neighborhood contained fifteen Protestant churches, four Catholic churches, and four Jewish synagogues. The institutional and residential maturity of the community was complete.

World War II brought many changes to the South Side. It definitively ended the Depression and brought a new prosperity to the city. It also brought a new migration of black people from the South. Because of the restricted housing patterns in Chicago, the Black Belt began to swell under the pressure of a quickly expanding population. Woodlawn, the neighborhood immediately northwest of South Shore, saw its black population almost triple during the war. The Irish and Jewish people of South Shore now saw the Black Belt, from which they had fled, appear on their very doorsteps. For upwardly mobile black people, South Shore began to look like an attractive place to live.

The white community in South Shore seemed determined to hold on, and the 1950 census actually showed a decrease in the black population there, probably because black people who worked in the area could now find housing in neighboring Woodlawn. But the phenomenon of neighborhood change in Chicago was already ocurring south of Jackson Park.

The following decade saw a dramatic increase in the black population of South Shore. By 1960 black people comprised ten percent of the population, but they were restricted for the most part to the area west of Stony Island Avenue. A rapid increase in the black population followed another instance of white flight. By 1970, 55,483 blacks lived in South Shore out of a total population of 80,529. The 1970s saw a further increase in this trend.

White people in South Shore tried to deal with the problems of racial change in the 1960s, but they could not stop the transition. The Washington Park connection continued to operate as it had before. Upwardly mobile black people looking for better housing naturally looked to South Shore, just as white Protestants, Irish Catholics, and German and Russian Jews had before them. They simply followed the trail that had been blazed two generations earlier.

Today South Shore faces many of the problems of other inner-city neighborhoods. Seventy-first Street declined as a fashionable shopping district. Much of the housing stock has deteriorated. The community is nominally integrated, with most of the white people living in the Jackson Park Highlands or along the lakefront.

The South Shore Country Club is no longer the preserve of local privilege. It is now owned by the Chicago Park District, and its golf course, beach, and party facilities are available to the general public. The Irish and the Jews have, for the most part, moved on to other parts of the city or to the suburbs. The South Side Hebrew Congregation is now located on the Near North Side. Many of the Irish live on the Southwest Side of Chicago. As in 1930, the change has been complete.

Just when South Shore was beginning to show many signs of urban decay, it began to stabilize and make a comeback in the 1970s. New housing has been built along the lakefront, and plans are under way for the revitalization of 71st Street. The Academy of St. James College Preparatory School, housed in a former Jewish high school at 7550 S. Phillips Avenue, was opened in 1970 and offers no-nonsense secondary education. A South Shore Historical Society has also been founded. Other organizations dedicated to making the community a bright spot on the South Side abound, including the South Shore Commission, the Neighborhood Institute, the Revitalization Center, and the South Shore Open House Organization. These organizations, plus the fact that the area is well served by mass transportation and is easily accessible by auto, make South Shore an attractive place for Chicagoans.

But there are still problems. Drugs and crime have hurt the community. Seventy-first and Jeffrey continues to be a problem corner. Even the Highlands have been touched by violence. Unlike neighboring Hyde Park with its University of Chicago, South Shore has no large institution that has enough political influence to bring about major improvements. The work of the South Shore Bank at 71st and Jeffery in helping the community make a comeback has been sizable, but problems remain. The city's economic problems have also plagued the area, and racism has prevented investment here as it has in other parts of the South Side.

Perhaps one lesson to be learned from South Shore is that no community in a metropolitan area can stand alone. Those early residents who fled Washington Park in order to leave the problems of the city behind eventually found themselves surrounded by them. They or their children moved again. Chicagoans have long thought that as long as problems remain on the other side of the tracks, there is little that can or should be done. The truth, however, is that problems, like people, cross tracks.

Elijah Muhammad Mosque #2, 7351 S. Stony Island, 1980. Black Muslims purchased this structure from a Greek Orthodox congregation in 1972. Built between 1948 and 1952 for the parish of SS. Constantine and Helen, it was the largest Greek Orthodox church in North America until its sale.   (G. Lane)

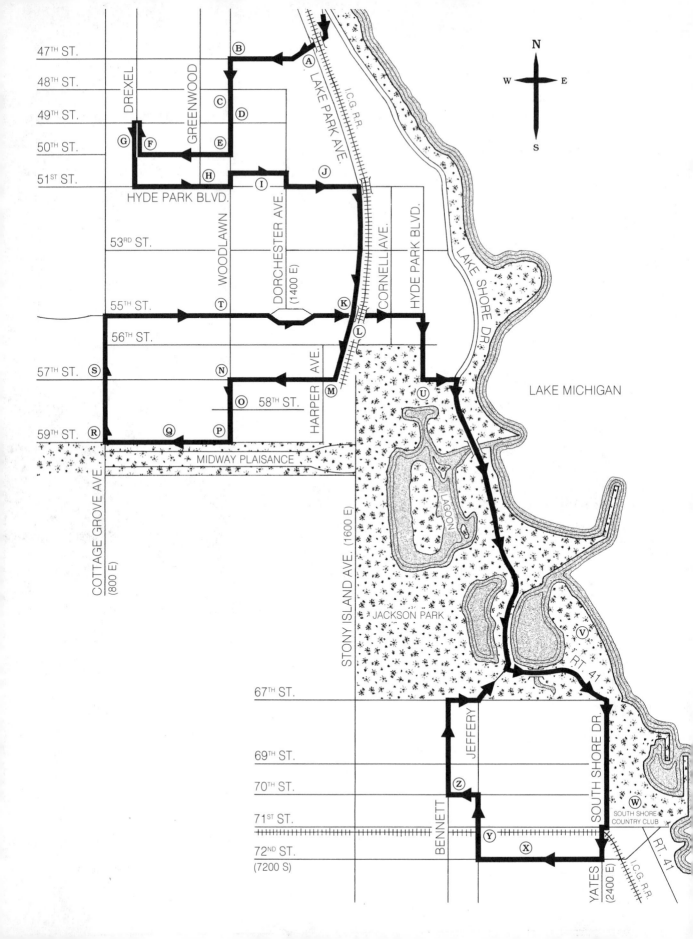

South Lakefront Tour

This tour begins at 47th Street and South Lake Shore Drive. It goes through the Kenwood, Hyde Park, and South Shore neighborhoods, and ends at the 67th and Jeffery entrance to Jackson Park.

Driving time: about 2 hours.

(A) Proceed three blocks west on 47th Street to Woodlawn (1200 East). A twenty-six story high-rise apartment building containing 200 units towers above the intersection of 47th and Lake Park Avenue. This is **Lake Village East,** part of the Lake Village complex that stretches along 47th Street to Ellis Avenue. Designed in 1971 by Harry Weese and his associates Ezra Gordon and Jack Levin, this is an example of the later stages of urban renewal for the Hyde Park—Kenwood area. Just to the south stand two high-rise co-op apartment buildings developed by the Amalgamated Clothing Workers Union and designed by George Fred Keck and William Keck.

(B) Turn left on Woodlawn and go three blocks south to 50th Street. On the northeast corner of 47th and Woodlawn, Chicago Muslims are constructing the **Muhammad Mosque.** Dana Ave., Ltd. is the architectural firm.

(C) A fine Italianate style house stands at 4812 S. Woodlawn. C.S. Bouton of the Union Foundry Works built this home in 1873. It is a good example of the type of housing that was constructed in the Kenwood area after the Civil War as the community came into its own as a fine suburban development connected to the city by excellent commuter train service.

(D) The Black Muslim presence in Kenwood is apparent at the corner of 49th and Woodlawn. On both the northeast and northwest corners are buildings that serve that religious community. The **home of the late Elijah Muhammad,** with its beautiful stained glass windows, stands on the northeast corner. The opposite corner contains several townhouses for the Muslim sisterhood. The Black Muslims had a very positive impact on Kenwood in the 1960s and 1970s through construction of new housing for its members and through social programs.

(E) As you continue south on Woodlawn, you will see many examples of fine residential architecture on both sides of the street. The second house from the corner of 50th Street on the west side of the street is the former home of boxing great Mohammad Ali, who moved to Kenwood in the 1960s to be near his spiritual mentor, Elijah Muhammed.

(F) Make a right turn on 50th Street and go three blocks west to Drexel Boulevard. The huge Greek revival building on the northeast corner of 50th and Drexel is now the home of **Operation Push.** Kehilath Anshe Ma'ariv (K.A.M.), the oldest Jewish congregation in Chicago, built this building in 1923 when they moved from their old synogogue on 33rd and Indiana. Architects Newhouse and Bernham designed this house of worship. Operation Push bought the building in 1971 when K.A.M. merged with Temple Isaiah and moved to Hyde Park Boulevard and Greenwood Avenue.

(G) Turn right on Drexel and go one block north to 49th Street. Make a left, or U turn, and go south on Drexel two blocks to Hyde Park Boulevard and make another left (east). After you make the U turn south on Drexel from 49th Street, the historic McGill Parc Apartments at 4938 S. Drexel will be on your right. Henry Ives Cobb, the original architect of the campus of the University of Chicago, designed this structure as a single-family residence. He used the same type of Bedford stone here that he used on the first university buildings. The private residence was completed in 1891. After additions, the home eventually contained 40,000 square feet. It was built for Dr. John McGill, a prominent

(Top left) Elijah Muhammad House and Chapel, northeast corner 46th and Woodlawn, 1985. This Kenwood home was the center of Chicago's Nation of Islam during the last years of the Right Honorable Elijah Muhammad. (D. Pacyga)

(Bottom left) Operation PUSH Headquarters, northeast corner 50th and Drexel, 1980. The magnificent home of Operation PUSH in Kenwood was built by and formerly housed the Kehilath Anshe Ma'ariv Hebrew congregation. (G. Lane)

physician whose family founded McGill University in Montreal. The French Gothic structure opened as an apartment complex in 1983 after being used for several purposes including a YMCA and a center for wayward juveniles. Architect Carl Klimek developed the plan for the apartment project.

At the southwest corner of Hyde Park (51st Street) and Drexel Boulevards stands an elegant fountain in a small park known as **Drexel Square.** It is the oldest fountain in Chicago. Henry Manger designed this tribute to Austrian-born Francis Martin Drexel, founder of the world famous financial house of Drexel and Company. Drexel's sons presented the fountain to the South Park Commission in 1883.

(H) Go east (left) on Hyde Park Boulevard. On the northeast corner of Hyde Park and Greenwood stands an imposing Byzantine structure, a synagogue designed by Alfred Alschuler and built in 1923-24 for the **Isaiah Israel** congregation. In 1971 K.A.M. merged with Isaiah Israel and moved its services to this magnificent place of worship. The building's smoke stack is designed to look like a minaret. Both the synagogue and its neighbor to the south, the **Chicago College of Osteopathic Medicine and Medical Center,** have provided important anchors for this part of the South Lakefront.

(I) Continue one block east on Hyde Park Boulevard to Woodlawn (1200 East) and turn left (north). Just north of the intersection on the east side of the street is a private driveway, turn right into **Madison Park.** This private park and development, which lies between Hyde Park Boulevard and 50th Street, between Woodlawn and Dorchester, is isolated from the rest of the neighborhood. The small strip of green grass with trees along it is lined on both sides with closely adjoining homes and apartment buildings. Among these are the award-winning **Y.C. Wong atrium townhouses.** The old **Madison Park Hotel** on the northwest corner of Dorchester and Hyde Park Boulevard is being renovated as an apartment complex.

K.A.M.—Isaiah Israel Temple,
northeast corner Greenwood and
Hyde Park Boulevard, 1980. This
prominent Jewish congregation
has played a vital role in the
stabilization of the Hyde
Park-Kenwood community.   (G. Lane)

(J) Turn right at Dorchester and return to Hyde Park
Boulevard. Make a left and go three blocks east to Lake
Park Avenue (400 East). **Kenwood Academy** stands at
the northeast corner of Blackstone and Hyde Park
Boulevard. This magnet public high school draws
students from all over the South Side. Merchants
threatened by the decision to build the school at this
location opposed its construction in 1969.

Across the street from Kenwood Academy, on Harper
and Lake Park, is the **Village Shopping Center,** which
leads to Harper Court on 53rd and Harper Avenue.
These developments were intended to provide space for
Hyde Park merchants and artisans displaced by the
massive urban renewal projects of the 1950s and 1960s.
Many of the artists who were forced to move because of
the demolition of the old artists' colony on 57th and
Stony Island expected to relocate in **Harper Court.**
Unfortunately, the Harper Court rents proved too high
for many of the artists, and they left Hyde Park for Old
Town and other North Side locations. Among the
buildings demolished to make way for the Village Center
was Theodore Starrett's Hyde Park Hotel, which stood on
51st Street between Harper and Lake Park from 1888
until 1963.

(K) Turn right on Lake Park and go four blocks south to 55th Street. The **New Hyde Park Shopping Center,** designed by Harry Weese, is located on the northwest corner of 55th and Lake Park Avenue. This small version of a suburban-type mall is part of the urban renewal plan that changed 55th Street in the 1950s and 1960s. The city demolished most of the commercial structures on 55th Street and all of the commercial structures on Lake Park Avenue north of 55th Street to make way for the new shopping center. The University of Chicago has owned this property since 1984.

(L) Continue south on Lake Park Avenue to 57th Street and turn right. Architect John Vinci restored the cable car station at 5529 S. Lake Park for the **Hyde Park Historical Society.** This neighborhood organization is among the best of its kind in the city. Many of its members are professional historians, writers, and others who are interested in the community's past.

At 56th Street the Illinois Central Gulf Railroad underpass is the site of **"Women's Struggle,"** a mural painted by Astrid Fuller in 1975. This work of art traces the history of the women's movement. Ms. Fuller has another mural about women's history on the northeast corner of the 57th Street underpass; it is entitled **"Pioneer Social Workers."** Fuller's 1973 **"Spirit of Hyde Park"** decorates the south side of the same underpass. "Justice Speaks: Delbert Tibbs/New Trial or Freedom" by William Walker is presented on the northwest corner of the underpass. The 57th Street Art Colony was located just east of the underpass on Stony Island Avenue. Artists had settled in a group of concession stand storefronts which were originally built for the Columbian Exposition in 1893. The storefronts were demolished as part of the urban renewal program in the early 1960s. The only vestige of the art colony that remains today is the famous 57th Street Art Fair held every summer.

(M) Turn right on 57th Street and go one block west to Harper Avenue. Park if you can. This section of Harper, from 57th to 59th Street, was originally known as Rosalie Villas. According to historian Jean F. Block, this

ROSALIE INN & CAFE.
COR. 57TH ST. & HARPER AV.
CHICAGO, ILL.

development was Hyde Park's first planned community. In 1883 Rosalie Buckingham purchased these two blocks and called upon Solon S. Beman, the designer of Pullman's model town, to create a series of elegant homes here. There is evidence that many of these houses were originally conceived of as summer homes. The railroad ran at ground level at the time they were built, so that originally the homes looked out over the lagoon and prairie which stood between them and Lake Michigan. This is a good place to stop and take a leisurely walk up the street to get a look at the houses. While Beman supervised the project, he did not design all of the houses. W.W. Boyington, the architect who designed the Water Tower on Michigan Avenue, drew up the plans for 5752, which Charles Bonner, a brick manufacturer, built in 1889. The house at 5736, **"Villa Armour,"** was originally built for M.C. Armour, an iron merchant, and is unaltered. A large building, formerly on the southeast corner, once housed the Cafe Red Roses. The singer Mary Garden made her debut in this building at the age of seventeen. A small park, **Sylvia Court,** serves Harper Avenue just south of 57th Street.

Rosalie Inn and Cafe, southeast corner 57th and Harper, c.1910. This building marked the entrance to Rosalie Court. The apartment building behind the inn was the first in the area when it was built in 1889. It still stands, but Powell's Bookstore now occupies the corner lot.
(Courtesy G. Schmalgemeier)

Rosalie Court residence, 1985.
This house has been restored to
resemble its original appearance
as one of the homes on Rosalie
Court. (D. Pacyga)

(N) Continue five blocks west on 57th Street to Woodlawn
(1200 East). The **First Unitarian Church of Chicago**
dominates this intersection with its 200-foot English
Gothic steeple. Denison B. Hull designed this house of
worship, which was the last stone-on-stone church built
in Chicago. It was completed in 1931 at a cost of one
million dollars.

(O) Turn left on Woodlawn and go one block south to 58th
Street. Frank Lloyd Wright's magnificent **Robie House,**
built in 1909, stands on the northeast corner of the
intersection. The building is used today by the
University of Chicago for offices. William Zeckendorf
donated the house to the university, and it has been
renovated by funds coming from public subscriptions.
This house is probably the best example of Wright's
Prairie style.

(P) Continue one block south on Woodlawn to the **Midway Plaisance.** On the northwest corner of 59th and Woodlawn stands the neo-Gothic **Rockefeller Chapel,** designed by Bertram G. Goodhue and built in 1926-28. Originally called University Chapel, it was named after John D. Rockefeller after his death in 1937. Rockefeller founded the University of Chicago and donated the chapel to the university.

(Q) Turn right at the Midway Plaisance and go two long blocks west to Cottage Grove Avenue. **The Midway** was designed as part of the South Park System by Frederick Law Olmsted. It served as the carnival midway for the 1893 Columbian Exposition. Today it acts as the "main street" of the University of Chicago, whose buildings line it on both sides. The original campus designed by Henry Ives Cobb faces the Midway between University and Ellis Avenues on the north side of 59th Street. The main quadrangle lies behind the massive **Harper Library.** The quadrangle can be entered by foot from 59th Street or by auto from 58th and University. **Cobb Hall** (named after Silas B. Cobb, no relation to the architect) on the east side of Ellis Avenue was the first building to open. It set the pattern for most of Cobb's work at the University of Chicago. The architect chose blue-gray Bedford cut stone for the buildings of the university.

Hutchinson Court, University of Chicago, 1985. Mitchell Tower stands tall above Hutchinson Court. This group of buildings was opened on December 22, 1903. This court was the original site of the Court Theatre.
(D. Pacyga)

(R) Turn right at Cottage Grove and proceed north to 55th Street. As you make the turn, you will see a large concrete sculpture on your left at the edge of Washington Park facing east towards the Midway Plaisance. This is Lorado Taft's famous *Fountain of Time.* It was dedicated in 1923 after fourteen years in the making. This sculpture was reportedly cast in the largest plaster piece-mold in the world. The *Fountain of Time* is the only part of Taft's plan for the Midway which was actually carried out. Taft envisioned the whole Midway as a sculpture garden dedicated to the great ideas of mankind.

Ciral's House of Tiki, 1612 E. 53rd Street, 1985. The House of Tiki is one of the few cocktail lounge/restaurants to survive the trauma of the urban renewal years in Hyde Park. (D. Pacyga)

(Left) Rockefeller Chapel, northwest corner 59th and Woodlawn, 1980. This huge chapel, completed in 1928, was built with the last million dollar bequest of John D. Rockefeller to the university he founded.
(A. Kezys)

Ⓢ The **DuSable Museum of African-American Culture** stands on the northwest corner of Cottage Grove and 57th Street. It is one of Chicago's foremost black institutions. An impressive sculpture garden decorates the museum's northern entrance in Washington Park.

Ⓣ Turn right at 55th Street and follow it thirteen blocks east to Hyde Park Boulevard, which is a north-south street in East Hyde Park. Fifty-fifth Street probably represents the starkest example of the impact of urban renewal on Hyde Park. Once a busy commercial street, this thoroughfare has been completely changed. It was once known for good jazz at various bars and clubs. Today **Jimmy's Woodlawn Tap** is the only reminder of 55th Street's former commercial character. The street is now dominated by **I.M. Pei's University Apartments,** which stand in the middle of the street between Dorchester and Blackstone. Gone are the bars, delicatessens, coffee houses, and much of the diversity that marked Hyde Park as a truly urban neighborhood before the wrecker's ball fell in 1955. And yet, despite the laments of critics, the plan which transformed 55th Street probably also stabilized Hyde Park. Without the urban renewal effort, many critics of this suburban, park-like strip might be making their laments out in Park Forest instead of on the streets of Hyde Park. In one way the new 55th Street has realized the vision of Frederick Law Olmsted, who felt in 1871 that there was no reason for any part of Hyde Park to develop as a commercial district. Urban planners have made Olmsted's vision come true, at least along 55th Street.

The church of **St. Thomas the Apostle** survived the urban renewal period. Located on the northwest corner of 55th and Kimbark, this church is on the National Register of Historic Places and is recognized as the first modern-style Catholic church in America. Barry Byrne, a disciple of Frank Lloyd Wright, designed this house of worship, which was built in 1922-24. Irish Americans founded the parish in 1869. Today it serves a multi-ethnic and multi-racial congregation.

(U) Turn right on Hyde Park Boulevard and drive one block south. You are now in East Hyde Park, the home of Mayor Harold Washington, who lives several blocks north at 53rd Street in the **Hampton House apartments.** Proceed south on Hyde Park Boulevard.

On the northwest corner of Hyde Park Boulevard and 56th Street (just before the traffic light) stands the newly renovated **Windermere House.** This South Side landmark can trace its history back to the 1893 Columbian Exposition. Edna Ferber (who actually lived in the hotel with her mother), Philip Roth, and Richard Stern have made the place famous in their novels. This grand old hotel-turned-apartment building underwent rehabilitation in the early 1980s.

Across from the Windermere stands one of Chicago's most popular attractions, the **Museum of Science and Industry.** The museum is housed in the rebuilt Palace of Fine Arts of the Columbian Exposition. This structure also housed the Field Museum for a time, until that institution moved to its present location south of Roosevelt Road on the lakefront in 1920. The Museum of Science and Industry opened in this building after the Century of Progress Exposition in 1933-34.

La Rabida, Jackson Park, 1911. This postcard shows the replicas of the La Rabida Monastery and Columbus's Santa Maria flagship. The building later became the home of the famous children's hospital. (Courtesy G. Schmalgemeier)

(V) Turn left at the traffic light just before the Museum of Science and Industry and follow the parkway to Lake Shore Drive. Turn right and follow Route 41 south through Jackson Park. Be sure to stay to your left so as not to exit to Jeffery Avenue. Stay on Route 41 (South Shore Drive), passing the **Jackson Park Marina** on the left.

Just beyond the marina is **La Rabida Children's Hospital and Research Center.** This important charitable institution owes its existence to the World's Columbian Exposition. The original hospital building was erected by Spain to serve as the Columbus Memorial during the fair. It was a reproduction of the Franciscan monastery of La Rabida near the city of Palos. The monks of Palos befriended Columbus and helped him convince the Spanish monarchy to finance his journey to the new world. The Spanish consul in Chicago offered the building as a children's sanitarium after the fair. The original reproduction was demolished in 1935 and was eventually replaced with the three buildings we see today. La Rabida cares for chronically ill children of all economic levels who pay according to their family's ability.

Jackson Park Life Saving Station, c.1910. Jackson Park, designed by Frederick Law Olmsted, included a marina and a coast guard station by the time of World War I.
(Courtesy G. Schmalgemeier)

(W) Continue south on South Shore Drive to 71st Street. As you leave **Jackson Park** going south on South Shore Drive, you will notice a golf course on your left. This was once the exclusive **South Shore Country Club.** The clubhouse is located just off the intersection of 71st and South Shore Drive. The architectural firm of Marshall & Fox designed it early in the century after the closing of the Washington Park Club and Race Track. The South Shore Country Club became a bastion of Chicago's South Side WASP elite. The Irish soon joined the club as they came to dominate South Shore along with their Jewish neighbors. Jews, however, along with blacks, were not allowed to join the club. Membership peaked in 1957 at 2,200, but already affluent white South Siders were leaving the neighborhood. The property was sold to the Chicago Park District in 1974 for just under ten million dollars. The Park District planned to demolish the elegant old building, but South Shore residents organized to save it. Neighbors created the Coalition to Save the South Shore Country Club. Out of this experience residents also established the **South Shore Historical Society.** The Country Club has become an important symbol of a positive future for South Shore. Because of local efforts, an important part of Chicago's history has been saved. The Park District has spent over six million dollars in renovating the elegant old structure. Several successful celebrations have already taken place on the grounds including a jazz festival.

(X) Do not make a lefthand turn at 71st Street, but keep to the right and go south across the I.C.G. railroad tracks one block to 72nd and Yates. Turn right at 72nd Street and go five blocks west to 2126 East 72nd Street. Joseph McCarthy's massive Tudor Gothic church of **St. Philip Neri** (1928) overlooks a neighborhood of well-built homes which were once occupied by its Irish-American parishioners, but are now predominantly black-owned. This church seats 1,700 people and is one of the largest in Chicago. St. Philip Neri parish was founded in 1912 to serve forty Catholic families in the area.

(Y) Continue two blocks west on 72nd street to Jeffery Avenue (2000 East). Turn right and go three blocks north to 70th Street. At 71st and Jeffery you will pass through a neighborhood shopping strip which was once one of the most exclusive outlying shopping strips in Chicago. After years of decline it is now experiencing a revival, thanks to local investment. Still, there are considerable problems here which are tied to the general economic picture of South Shore.

(Z) Turn left at 70th Street and go two blocks west to Bennett (1900 East). Make a right and go three blocks north to 67th Street. You are now driving through the **Jackson Park Highlands,** an integrated residential community that boasts some of the finest homes in Chicago. Rev. Jesse Jackson, jazz pianist Ramsey Lewis, and other notables live in this neighborhood. Playwright David Mamet also lived here for some time. Many University of Chicago professors and other professionals live here.

At 67th Street turn right and go two blocks east to Jeffery. Turn left and you will be back on South Shore Drive heading north into the city.

Southeast Side

12

The Southeast Side of Chicago owes its existence to the railroads and industries that came to the area in the last half of the nineteenth century. Steel played a major role in the growth of this highly industrialized district. The huge mills which line the lakefront below 79th Street and cover the banks of the Calumet River not only dominated the skyline of the neighborhoods crowded up against them, but also the lives of the local residents. Nowhere on the Southeast Side can one escape the presence of steel. Even today in the so-called post-industrial era, steelmaking fills the conversations of the people who live here as they face a future that may well include the end of the local steel industry. It is certainly safe to say that steel will never again dominate the area as it once did.

The four community areas covered in this chapter all have or had an economy based on heavy industry. South Chicago, the East Side, South Deering, and Pullman were all built around large manufacturing concerns. In South Chicago, U.S. Steel's South Works dominated the neighborhood. South Deering centered on Wisconsin Steel. Republic Steel was the East Side's major employer. The Pullman Company, of course, created the Pullman neighborhood. All of this has changed in the last ten years as the steel industry and other heavy manufacturing have declined in the United States. Today the hope for these neighborhoods revolves around other economic developments, though they still try to hold on to as much of the steel industry as they can. Local leaders have come up with various plans, like having Chicago construct a third major airport in the district. Much of this is hopeful speculation. Whatever happens, the steelworkers will have to make major adjustments to a changing local economy. These neighborhoods originally benefited from the Industrial Revolution. Today they must readjust as that revolution gives way to new developments.

South Chicago

The South Chicago community is the nucleus for the Southeast Side of Chicago. Because of its location at the mouth of the Calumet River, it developed early on as a small settlement of fishermen and of squatters who farmed the nearby area. The Pottawatomie Indians had a burial ground here, which they occasionally returned to visit long after they had left the area. Before the 1850s South Chicago, originally called Ainsworth, enjoyed a small town, rural atmosphere despite its proximity to the quickly expanding city to the north.

Irish Catholics and Western Europeans made up the population of the original settlement. The residents were few, and the town remained only loosely organized for some time. Catholics established St. Patrick's parish in 1857 and built a frame church two years later at 93rd and Houston. Other institutions followed. The town developed quickly over the next thirty years because of its all-important Chicago connection.

When the first railroad came to Chicago in 1848, it ushered in a new era in the history of the city and of the entire Midwest. At this time South Chicago and all of the Southeast Side was a remote suburb of Chicago. After 1861 the area developed as part of the Township of Hyde Park, which remained independent until 1889 when the city annexed the entire area. Despite its political independence, the small town and future urban neighborhood grew within the economic influences of Chicago. Decisions made along the banks of the Chicago River had a great impact on the settlement along the banks of the Calumet.

As more and more Eastern railroads reached Chicago, many cut across the prairie in or near South Chicago. This provided the impetus for industrial development. Car shops for the railroads and grain elevators offered much of the early employment in the area. These industries attracted various immigrant groups to the district, including Swedes, Scots, Welsh, and Germans who joined the small Irish and American communities. These people provided a skilled work force which in turn attracted more and more industry to South Chicago.

Meanwhile, industry was filling up the banks of the Chicago River. That waterway soon became crowded with ships and barges moving goods and supplies for the quickly expanding plants. Industrialists began to look for other locations as the downtown district overflowed with people and factories. Chicago was quickly expanding beyond its original boundaries. The Chicago Fire of 1871 accelerated the movement of people and industry away from the center city. South Chicago as well as other outlying areas benefited from this movement.

In 1875 the Brown Steel and Iron Company opened a mill on the Calumet River. This marked the beginning of the age of steel in South Chicago and its environs. Five years later the North Chicago Rolling Mill Company chose the

83rd Street looking east across South Shore Drive, 1938. The smokestacks of the South Works fill the skyline of the Bush. This photo shows St. Michael's Catholic Church (left), the Kuzniar Funeral Parlor, an ice cream store, and the tip of Russell Square Park.
(Chicago Park District, courtesy R. Wroble)

mouth of the Calumet River as the location for its new plant, the South Works. Over the next twenty years steel mills appeared throughout the area and even spilled over the Indiana-Illinois border. In 1900 the newly-formed United States Steel Corporation, which by this time also owned the South Works, built Gary, Indiana as a company town. South Chicago became the center of the Midwestern steel industry.

The arrival of this heavy industry determined the future of South Chicago and of the entire Southeast Side. The area near the river developed first. Much of the housing was wooden, as it generally was throughout the Chicago area. Wood buildings were especially popular in working-class districts.

Wooden construction also prevailed in the neighborhood near the South Works. Residents called this area the Bush, and it grew quickly as the work force at the South Works increased. Block after block of frame two-flats were built near the mill gates. These were interspersed with cottages and occasionally with larger tenements, some of them brick. The Bush was a typical Victorian industrial slum. The unpaved streets all led to the mill. Indoor plumbing was not common until after the turn of the century; and even then, many houses relied on outhouses and the illegal privy. Conditions in the Bush continued to be harsh well into the twentieth century.

A large cloud of black smoke hung over the entire district. At night the blast furnaces lit the sky with a

diabolic glow. Huge smokestacks, buildings, and cranes towered over the neighborhood. Women who hung their wash outside often found it covered with soot from the mills. South Chicagoans could not escape the effects of the huge plants.

Native-born Americans made up most of the original settlers in this area. Western Europeans of the old immigration joined them. Many of these Welsh, Scotch, Swedish, and English immigrants had the skills that the early steel industry needed. As the industry expanded, however, more and more workers were needed, and many of these new jobs were in the unskilled category. By the mid-1880s the source of immigration began to change. Eastern Europeans, mainly Polish people, flooded into the area. As early as 1882 Polish steelworkers organized Immaculate Conception parish at 88th and Commercial in South Chicago. This church joined German SS. Peter and Paul parish and Irish St. Patrick's to serve the Roman Catholic community. German and Swedish Protestants also had congregations in the district.

Immigration continued to grow, and the Eastern European community expanded. Lithuanians settled near the Poles. Serbs, Croatians, and Slovenes arrived from the Balkans. Italians and Hungarians came in large numbers. It was not long before the neighborhood took on a completely different cultural and ethnic quality as older ethnic groups made their way across the Calumet River to the East Side. By the end of the 1920s, four Polish Roman Catholic churches and one Polish National Catholic parish served South Chicago. In the 1930s Polish Americans made up about ninety percent of the Bush neighborhood's population.

World War I was a turning point in the ethnic development of the South Chicago area. The fighting in Europe cut off immigration at the same time that steel production was increasing. Steel companies began to look for new sources of unskilled labor. Hispanics, Mexicans in particular, and blacks began to be hired in large numbers.

Continental Grain Company, Elevator B, 11700 S. Torrence Avenue, 1985. Railroad lines and international shipping converge at the huge grain elevators on the Calumet River. (G. Lane)

(Top left) Looking north across the Wisconsin Slip at the idled Wisconsin Steel Works, 1985. (G. Lane)

(Bottom left) Bush neighborhood cottage, 1985. This wooden house in the 8500 block of S. Mackinaw Avenue is typical of early construction in the Bush area of South Chicago. Notice the South Works in the background. (D. Pacyga)

Our Lady of Guadalupe Church, 91st and Burley, 1928. George Cardinal Mundelein dedicated this church on September 30, 1928. The building was built at a cost of $150,000.

(Courtesy The Chicago Catholic)

Both groups had arrived earlier in South Chicago and taken their places in local industries. As early as 1900 black people lived in the oldest section of South Chicago, near the mouth of the Calumet River. Mexicans had been working on the railroads and living in the southeastern part of South Chicago before World War I. But it was during the war that both groups began to work in the mills in large numbers. The Mexican community developed along the lines of a traditional South Chicago ethnic group in the 1920s. Blacks proved to be more transient. Many of them worked as stevedores in South Chicago, which was a major Great Lakes port. Black South Chicagoans, however, always lived within the shadow of the larger black community to the west of the district.

About 1923 the Catholic Church began to address the needs of its Mexican members in South Chicago. Father William Kane, a Jesuit, served the community by organizing Spanish-speaking residents into the congregation of Our Lady of Guadalupe at 3200 East 91st Street. In 1924 the Claretian Fathers came to serve South Chicago's Mexicans, and they have had charge of the parish ever since. Our Lady of Guadalupe gave the Mexican community in the steel mill district a strong institutional base which allowed them to create a large and stable community.

As in other industrial districts, South Chicago's ethnic groups tended to settle first in the core of the neighborhood, generally close to the mills or to the river. As time went by they moved away from the old wooden slums to better outlying areas. In the 1920s a large number of brick bungalows were built in the western section of South Chicago. New housing also appeared on the East Side, attracting the better established ethnic groups. Many Poles moved into the western parts of South Chicago, where they founded St. Bronislava parish at 87th and Colfax in 1928. The Western European groups moved across the river in large numbers. Eventually, Poles and other East European ethnic groups also crossed the Calumet River to the East Side and beyond to Hegewisch. The outward movement of these groups caused their old neighborhoods to undergo ethnic succession. In 1930, despite this outward movement, South Chicago reached its population peak with 56,583 people, a forty percent increase over 1920.

The population of South Chicago dropped by a little more than 1,000 people in the 1930s. This was due to the Great Depression, which hit this community very hard. The 1940s and the Second World War saw only a slight increase in the area's population. While the population continued to drop in the 1950s and 1960s, it increased slightly in the 1970s as younger minority group families replaced older white ethnics. The 1980 population stood at 46,422, a decrease of about 10,000 since 1930.

The big demographic change, however, has been in the ethnic and racial makeup of South Chicago. In 1960 white people made up 94.8 percent of the population. Twenty years later they accounted for only 27.5 percent. The decrease in white European ethnics as compared to white Latino groups proved to be even greater. Black people made up 47.8 percent of South Chicago's population in 1980, while Hispanics counted for nearly forty percent. Most of the Roman Catholic parishes in South Chicago now offer Masses in Spanish as well as in various East European languages and English. The huge Polish church of St. Michael at 83rd and South Shore Drive serves both ethnic communities. A painting of the Polish Black Madonna as well as the image of Our Lady of Guadalupe decorate the church's interior. Most of the black people who now live in South Chicago have little to do with the traditional black millgate neighborhood. The South Side Black Belt expanded towards South Chicago from the northwest and from neighboring South Shore north of 79th Street.

After the relatively prosperous period following World War II, and after the Vietnam conflict ended in 1975, the 1970s proved to be bad years for the steel industry. Cutbacks and layoffs resulted. In the spring of 1980, Wisconsin Steel closed in South Deering. This plant was a direct descendent of the Brown Steel Company, the area's first steel mill. Some 3,500 workers were immediately laid off. Companies that depended on Wisconsin Steel also cut back. This closing provided the most dramatic symbol of the decline of the local steel industry. Other mill cutbacks and closings followed. The South Works has become a ghost town. As late as the early 1970s, some 12,000 steelworkers and management personnel worked in the huge mill alongside the lake in South Chicago. The work force fell to about 900 in 1985. Despite several attempts by the State of Illinois, the City of Chicago, the United Steelworkers of America, and even the Roman Catholic Archdiocese of Chicago, these men and women know their jobs will be eliminated. South Chicago, like Back of the Yards, now faces the post-industrial period with a good deal of uncertainty.

The decline of the steel industry presents basic problems for South Chicago and for Chicago as a whole. South Chicago has traditionally been a receiving station for working-class immigrants to Chicago, whether these were Irish, Swedish, Polish, Mexican, black, or any other group which has called the place home. The magnet which drew these people in the past and helped them reach some sort of security in the city is weakening. If working-class neighborhoods like South Chicago are to continue to exist, some substitute will have to be found. Unemployment is high in this district. Local political, economic, and social leaders have tried to solve the problem with little success. The area is now part of an enterprise zone, but that program is not yet fully developed. Fifty thousand black, brown, and white residents of South Chicago now face a fairly uncertain economic future. And yet South Chicago holds on. Its ethnic churches, stores, and restaurants still symbolize a vital area with a rich history on the Southeast Side of Chicago.

East Side

The East Side is virtually an island. The Calumet River cuts it off from South Chicago and South Deering. Lake Michigan borders it on the east. To the south, Wolf Lake provides part of its boundary, as does Hegewisch and Indiana. Its name derives from the fact that it is on the east bank of the Calumet River. It once served as the east side of South Chicago. Before it developed a separate identity about the time of World War I, outsiders and residents alike identified it with the older community to the north. Actually, early residents identified more with the names of Taylorville, Goosetown, and Colehour than they did with the name East Side until they realized their common commercial interests in the 1920s.

As in South Chicago, early settlers lived off the land and the great number of game animals and fish that inhabited

Avenue L looking south from l03rd Street, c.1910. This postcard view shows St. Petri United Church of Christ and the surrounding neighborhood. Notice the streetcar tracks down the middle of the street. (Courtesy G. Schmalgemeier)

the area. Whereas South Chicago began to develop before the arrival of the steel industry in the mid-1870s, it was this event which sparked the development of the East Side. Both the Colehour and Taylor subdivisions followed upon the announcement that the Silicon Steel Company had chosen the Calumet River area for its new plant. At just about the same time the Pennsylvania Railroad opened its Colehour Station at 100th and Ewing Avenue. The Silicon Steel plant never materialized, but the opening of the Brown Steel Company mill in 1875 saved the subdivisions. The new plant caused a population explosion on the East Side. At the begining of the 1870s, only about six families lived on the East Side. By the end of the decade, the population reached about 1,000.

The community greatly benefited from its location on the Southeast Side. The East Side was right on the route for railroads approaching Chicago from the East. Three passenger railroads soon connected the neighborhood with downtown Chicago. Freight lines also criss-crossed the district. By the end of the nineteenth century, the East Side could rightly claim the title "Gateway to Chicago."

As new industry continued to locate along the Calumet River, more and more people made their homes on the East Side. Various plants opened in the 1880s. Among these were a sash company, a brewery, and many steel-related manufacturers. Workers followed them south of South Chicago.

In 1874 the first religious congregation, the Colehour German Lutheran Church, opened. Today the parish still serves the community as Bethlehem Lutheran Church at 103rd and Avenue H. The following year the Evangelical Association arrived in the area. The East Side United Methodist Church at 110th and Ewing carries on the Evangelical tradition on the East Side. In 1882 the German Baptist Church of Colehour, South Chicago opened. Parishioners renamed it the East Side Baptist Church in 1930. By 1888 there were enough German Catholics on the East Side for them to organize the parish of St. Francis de Sales at 102nd and Avenue J. The parish opened not as an ethnic parish, but as a territorial parish. Nevertheless, German pastors have always served it, and a number of the congregation's members were of Luxembourger descent.

Swedes quickly joined the Germans in the neighborhood. In 1880 the Swedish Lutheran Evangelical Bethany Church opened. Two years later the Swedish Mission of the Covenant Church began to serve the area. Swedes provided an important segment of the neighborhood. Though other Chicago area Swedish settlements were much larger than that on the East Side, the community here was fairly large. The Swedes tended to settle along Avenues M, N, and O, north of the railroad tracks. In the 1920s Swedes and Germans predominated on the East Side. They both quickly underwent an Americanizing process. The arrival of Eastern and Southern Europeans hastened this process. The Germans and Swedes regarded themselves as Americans when they were confronted by the Slavs and Italians.

The late 1880s saw Slovenes arrive on the Southeast Side from that part of the Austro-Hungarian Empire which would later become Yugoslavia. The Catholic Slovenes generally lived near South Chicago's Germans and attended Mass at SS. Peter and Paul on East 91st Street at Exchange. A Slovene priest, Rev. John Plevnik, visited this community periodically from his parish on Chicago's Lower West Side. Before long, however, it was obvious that South Chicago's Slovenes needed a parish of their own. In 1893 Slovenes organized the Knights of St. Florian, a fraternal group, which led the movement for a parish. Ten years later the people broke ground for a new church, St. George's, on 96th and Ewing Avenue on the East Side. This church originally served both the Slovenian and Croatian Catholic communities.

Croatians arrived in large numbers at about the same time that the Slovenes and Serbians did. All of these groups originated in that part of Europe which later became Yugoslavia. On November 3, 1912 the Southeast Side Croatians decided to leave St. George's and form their own

parish. Sacred Heart parish at 96th and Escanaba was the third Croatian Catholic parish to be organized in Chicago. Although technically located in South Deering, it serves Croatian families on both sides of the Calumet River. The Croatian community developed many local institutions. Post-World War II migration to the United States gave this community new ethnic life. The Sacred Heart Croatian Tamburitza and Kolo Group is a very popular exponent of traditional folk dances and songs on the Southeast Side, especially in South Deering and the East Side.

Meanwhile as the Croatians left St. George, they were replaced by Italians who began to cross the river from South Chicago and South Deering around 1914. Italians settled in the parish and played an important role in the development of the East Side. They and the Slavs tended to settle in the older parts of the community close to the river. Many Italians originally lived on Commercial Avenue south of 95th Street in South Deering and South Chicago. They attended St. Patrick's Catholic Church.

The East Side in many ways served as a suburb for the older community of South Chicago. As the newer ethnic groups came to the East Side, they met hostility from the older groups. This was especially true among the youth. There were frequent gang fights among German, Swedish, and Italian youths. Anti-Catholicism also marked this community in the early twentieth century. As South Chicago came to be inhabited more and more by Eastern Europeans, the East Side developed a local identity of its own based to a large extent on ethnicity. The movement of Eastern and

(Left) 112th Street looking west across Avenue H, 1937. This section of the Southeast Side was not developed as the Fair Elms community until after the Depression. At the end of World War II more than twenty percent of the land within the boundaries of Chicago had not yet been built upon.
(Chicago Park District, courtesy R. Wroble)

(Above) St. Simeon Mirotocivi Serbian Orthodox Church, 114th and Avenue H, 1980. This church, modeled after a fifteenth-century Serbian monastery, was built in 1969 by Serbian Americans, most of whom work in the steel mills.
(G. Lane)

Southern Europeans across the river after 1900 was not appreciated. The East Side has always had a reputation for being more conservative than South Chicago, especially with regard to ethnic and racial relations.

After World War I the ethnic divisions began to subside. This was partly because many German and Swedish families became assimilated. The East Side did not benefit much from the housing boom that saw so many bungalows built in the 1920s. In 1930 only 16,839 people lived in the East Side neighborhood. The decade of the Depression saw the population there decline by 326.

The East Side witnessed much turmoil in the 1930s. In 1937 the Congress of Industrial Organization's Steelworkers Organizing Committee (SWOC-CIO) attempted to organize Republic Steel. On Memorial Day 1937 picnicing union members and their supporters decided to march on the Republic Steel plant which they had struck. The Chicago Police met them at the mill gates. The confrontation resulted in the Memorial Day massacre in which ten people, either steelworkers or their sympathizers, died. This battle remains a sensitive issue in the community nearly fifty years later. The battle broke the strike, but the CIO eventually organized the plant in the 1940s.

World War II proved to be a watershed in the history of the East Side. Increased steel production during the war brought an end to the effects of the Depression. It also brought pressure on the limited housing stock of the far South Side. In 1940 residential construction resumed on the East Side in the area south of 108th street. This district contained the Fair Elms development. Included in the new residential area was Annunciata parish formed at 111th and Avenue G in July 1941. Many Polish Americans came to Fair Elms in the 1940s and 1950s. By the end of the 1940s the population of the East Side had risen to 21,619. Much of this resulted from new home construction in the southern portion.

The postwar period saw the continuation of several trends which had begun somewhat earlier in the history of the East Side. The most important of these was that the East Side continued to be a "suburb" of the South Chicago area. Polish Americans and others continued to cross the river in large numbers in the 1950s. By the end of the decade, the East Side population rose by just under 1,600 people. The East Side reached its population peak in 1970 with 24,649 people. Ten years later 21,331 people lived here. Hispanics made up 2,600 of these, living for the most part in the older sections of the East Side. Over ninety-four percent of the population was white.

Today the East Side, like its neighbors, faces the post-industrial period with misgivings. It remains a white ethnic part of Chicago, and politically it is an important component of the white ethnic block in the city council. The East Side is the home of Edward R. Vrdolyak, a Croatian American, who is chairman of the Cook County Democratic Party and leader of the majority block in the city council.

Racial confrontations have rocked the East Side several times in the postwar period. Riots occured at Calumet Park in the 1950s, and East Siders took part in the Trumbull Park riots across the Calumet River in South Deering. In the early 1980s several racial confrontations took place, one of which revolved around the purchase of an East Side home by a black family from South Shore. Once a suburb of South Chicago, the East Side today faces both the problems of the inner-city and the decline of its industrial base.

South Deering

South Deering is located to the south of 95th Street and west of the Calumet River. It is an old industrial district with several well defined neighborhoods whose names recall the history of the area. Among these are Irondale, Slag Valley, Veterans Park, and the Manors. Various ethnic and racial groups live in these sections of South Deering. Much of the history of these residential areas, with the exception of the Manors, is associated with the Southeast Side's industrial past.

The oldest of these neighborhoods is Irondale. In the 1870s the federal government spent more than a quarter of a million dollars improving the Calumet River and its harbor. The Calumet Canal and Dock Company also developed the river with a view to what it believed to be a bright industrial future for the area. As a result of these improvements, industry was attracted to the Calumet River. The coming of the steel industry in 1875 created Irondale, a community of steelworkers. On July 5, 1875 the Joseph H. Brown Iron and Steel Works opened on the west bank of the river. That November the first iron ore boat to enter the waterway delivered its cargo at Brown's mill and began a whole new era in the life of South Deering, and of the entire Southeast Side. Irondale's original location was on the west bank just north of 106th Street. The community moved further west to Torrence Avenue and beyond as the mill expanded.

In 1880 Irondale had 926 residents. Most of these were Irish, Welsh, and English. German and Swedish workers followed. These same groups composed a large part of the

Idled buildings of Wisconsin Steel, looking northwest across the Wisconsin Slip, 1985. International Harvester's giant steel mill was the principal employer in South Deering.
(G. Lane)

early migration to South Chicago. This is not surprising because immigrants from the British Isles and Western Europe had experience in the iron industry, and employers welcomed skilled employees in the early steel mills in America. Except for the Irish, who filled many of the unskilled and construction jobs in South Deering, these people were Protestants. In 1875 the Evangelical Association held the first religious service in South Deering in Watson's Dining Hall. Five years later the Methodist Episcopal Congregation opened the first church in the district. The Irish organized St. Kevin's Catholic church in 1884.

The Irondale Irish belonged to St. Patrick's parish before St. Kevin's was formed. Many of the Irish lived on the edge of South Deering and identified more readily with South Chicago and with St. Patrick's, which had opened in 1857. Only after the Irish moved to South Deering in large numbers did a separate parish seem neccessary. The priests from St. Thomas the Apostle parish in Hyde Park established a mission which served Irondale Catholics until 1881. That year St. Patrick's took over the spiritual care of the district. Until then Irondale Catholics celebrated Mass at Gagne's Hall on 106th and Torrence and later in the local public school until they could erect their own church at 105th and Torrence in 1887.

Except for the steel mill, Irondale resembled a frontier settlement on the edge of the prairie. Unpaved streets and wooden cottages predominated. Everything revolved around the success of Brown's mill. That company in fact had a very troubled early history. It changed hands in 1882 with little success. The nail mill, which once produced 12,000 kegs of nails per day, closed in 1884. By 1891 a local newspaper described the area as almost deserted. In 1895 much of the mill closed down. The turn of the century, however, brought an economic upswing to the entire Southeast Side. The South Chicago Furnace Company purchased the plant in 1899. The Deering Harvester Company took control of the furnace company in 1900 and then merged with the McCormick Harvester Company to form International Harvester by 1902. The new corporate giant announced plans to build a huge new plant in Irondale that was to begin operation in 1903. The leaders of the neighborhood then renamed the district South Deering, and the economic future of the area looked bright. South Deering became a boom town. In 1905 International Harvester renamed the mill Wisconsin Steel. Residents became so optimistic about the neighborhood's future that they organized the South Deering Marathon in 1915 with the hope that the race would be as popular as the famous Boston event. The 1915 race was the only marathon in the history of the community. Residents organized the South Deering Improvement Association in 1917, just before the American entry into World War I. Its main concern was the improvement of streets and the construction of Trumbull Park at 103rd and Yates.

Other industries also built plants in the South Deering neighborhood, among them the Gold Medal Flour Mill, By-Products Coke Corporation, Illinois Slag and Ballast Company, and the Federal Furnace Company. Ships crowded the Calumet River. In 1906 the amount of shipping on the Calumet equaled that on the Chicago River. Ten years later the Calumet carried five times the traffic of the Chicago River.

Wisconsin Steel became the largest employer in South Deering. In many ways the district resembled a company town. The mill supplied funds and even electricity to local churches. It dominated the neighborhood. The entire steel mill district saw an upsurge in production during the 1920s. The success of International Harvester and therefore of Wisconsin Steel meant a happy and prosperous South Deering.

The older residents in this area were joined in the early twentieth century by Eastern and Southern Europeans. Large Croatian, Serbian, Polish, and Italian communities appeared in the neighborhood. Many of these had ties to similar communities in South Chicago. For example, South Deering Poles often belonged to the parish of the Immaculate

Conception in the neighboring district. By 1920 South Deering was a residentially mature community dominated by Catholic and Orthodox Christian ethnic groups. One non-European group, the Mexicans, also lived in the older sections of South Deering in the 1920s. They arrived in large numbers after World War I. Like the Poles, they often belonged to a parish outside their immediate neighborhood. Our Lady of Guadalupe Church in South Chicago served all Southeast Side Hispanics. Nevertheless, St. Kevin's also tried to serve the mixed Catholic ethnic groups in South Deering. This parish certainly embraced a polyglot community by 1920.

The 1920s saw more construction and more expansion at Wisconsin Steel. Just before the end of the decade, the steel company announced plans for a new building program. These plans ended with the economic crash of 1929. The Depression hit Wisconsin Steel and South Deering very hard. The plans to expand the mill came to nothing.

As war clouds gathered over Europe and Asia in the mid-1930s, the steel industry revived. As early as 1935 the Depression began to release its grip on South Deering. Wisconsin Steel took another look at its expansion plans. In March 1936 it closed its Bessemer mill. Hereafter the steel maker would only produce high grade steel. The slight economic recovery also brought changes in the neighborhood. Residents reorganized the South Deering Improvement Association to work for local improvements and political influence.

Also for the first time a large number of homes began to be built just outside the traditional borders of Irondale. The developer was not an individual or even the mill, but the federal government. The Public Works Administration built the Trumbull Park Homes. This housing project covered some twenty acres bounded by Yates, Bensley, and Oglesby Avenues between 105th and 109th Streets. The Trumbull Park Homes contained 462 units and housed about 1,735 people. They cost $3,558,000. Only white people lived in the project when it opened in the late 1930s. The homes provided housing for workers attracted to the area by increased steel production. While South Deering residents originally applauded the project, it soon became a object of derrision. Locals felt that the Homes brought unwanted outsiders into the community. As a result of the construction of the federal project, South Deering's population increased in the 1930s from 7,898 inhabitants to 9,662. The population was all white in 1940.

The next decade brought even more change to South Deering as the population jumped to 17,476 by 1950. While over 2,000 employees of Wisconsin Steel marched off to war, women entered the mill as laborers for the first time. "Rosie the Riveters" made the steel that earned the coveted "E" award from the government for increasing wartime production.

Chicagoans faced with a housing shortage looked to the open prairie north of Irondale for residential expansion. Development of **Jeffery Manor** began in 1941. **Merrionette Manor** construction started six years later. The Manors proved to be different from the older neighborhoods of South Deering. The residents, for the most part, did not work in the mills. They were not part of the traditional working-class communities of the mill district. The new brick homes held fewer foreign-born residents. Jews made up a large part of the population. These upwardly mobile families had ties to South Shore rather than to South Chicago. Meanwhile the Hispanic population of Irondale and the older steel communities was also growing. In 1950 Mexicans made up 23.5 percent of the foreign-born population of the area. Despite the increase in population for South Deering as a whole, Irondale lost people.

Race and ethnicity soon came to the forefront as major problems in South Deering. On the morning of August 5, 1953 the Donald Howard family moved into the Trumbull Park Homes. A racial confrontation resulted which lasted throughout the decade. The Trumbull Park riots focused the nation's attention on South Deering. This confrontation followed an unsuccessful attempt by another black family to purchase a home in Merrionette Manor. The incident in the Manors set the stage for the Trumbull Park disturbances.

The majority of those arrested during South Deering's racial battles of the 1950s lived within twelve blocks of the housing project. Torrence Avenue became a battleground as crowds of whites attacked black people in automobiles. According to historian Arnold Hirsch, the South Deering community carried out a veritable war of attrition against the projects. Irondalers saw the coming of black people into the Trumbull Park Homes as a direct attack on their community.

The Irondale riots were not the only ones on the Southeast Side. Conflicts also broke out in Calumet Park and at Rainbow Beach. On occasion one disturbance led to another. A riot broke out on July 28, 1957 at Calumet Park on the East Side and spread back to Trumbull Park. During the 1950s, hot weather occasioned battles over control of local parks and beaches. The postwar era proved to be one of racial change. South Deering residents tried to fight a holding action against these changes, and in part they succeeded. Although the South Deering population rose to

18,794 in 1960, black people made up less than 0.7 percent of the residents. During the 1960s no more than thirty-one black families lived in the projects. During most of the time the number hovered around twenty-five.

The 1960s saw a modest expansion of production at Wisconsin Steel. The company built a merchant mill in 1961, and the basic oxygen furnaces began production in 1964. The Vietnam years produced a boom period for the steel industry. As the 1960s came to an end, the economic situation of South Deering looked very strong. The next decade, however, brought change to the industry which supported the neighborhood.

As the recession of the 1970s took its toll on the American steel industry, the Wisconsin Steel plant appeared to be a white elephant for the struggling International Harvester Company. The parent company sold the South Deering plant to the Envirodyne Corporation in 1977. It did not, however, sell the profitable ore fields that fed the 300-acre plant. As foreign steel flooded the American market, the new owners had a difficult time keeping the mill operating. On March 28, 1980 Wisconsin Steel closed its gates. Envirodyne collapsed after International Harvester and the Chase Manhattan Bank foreclosed on its $65,000,000 mortgage on March 26. The mill became the property of the Economic Development Administration, a federal agency, which had guaranteed the loans to the bankrupt Envirodyne Corporation. The abandoned plant soon became a political football used by local and national politicians to try to win votes. As the new decade began, the economic base of South Deering was gone.

Demographic change also occurred. In 1960, 125 black people lived in South Deering, mostly in the Trumbull Park Homes. The census reported 813 foreign-born Mexicans. Ten years later the neighborhood's population grew to a record high of 19,405, including 3,065 blacks and 3,220 Hispanics. The 1970s brought more change as white ethnics continued to leave. The black population crossed 103rd Street into Irondale proper. By 1980, 10,631 blacks and 4,763 Hispanics lived in South Deering out of a total population of 19,400. Irondale, Veterans Park, and Slag Valley remain the stronghold of the white ethnic and Hispanic population. The Manors saw the first racial change other than the few black families in the Trumbull Park Homes.

Despite several attempts to stabilize the population, the problem of a quickly disappearing economic base has not helped. Many white South Deering residents have made their way to the East Side or to Hegewisch, if not to the suburbs. Still those who have remained behind have worked with the

newer ethnic and racial groups to try to make a better future
for the area. The South Deering Improvement Association
recently reestablished the once famous Fourth of July
parties. A new group called Irondalers Against the Chemical
Threat (IACT) has been fighting the dumping of waste
material in the community. There still is a good deal of
institutional life in the neighborhood. St. Kevin's parish
recently celebrated its centenary with a pledge to keep
serving the people of South Deering. Blacks, Hispanics, and
whites are active participants in these local organizations.
As in other parts of the Southeast Side, residents of South
Deering look to the future with caution while the mill that
gave rise to the community has been dismantled.

Pullman

George Mortimer Pullman was still in his twenties when he
made his first fortune by devising an ingenious method for
raising Chicago out of the mud. In the mid-1850s the city
council ordered the grade of Chicago's streets to be raised in
order to allow for better drainage. The young entrepreneur
saw the challenge and met it; he invented a way of using
jacks to lift whole downtown buildings to the new grade
level. Not long afterwards, in 1863, Pullman began to
develop his ideas about traveling in comfort. Out of this
came the Pullman Palace Car Company, organized in 1867
and capitalized at $1,000,000. This firm would play a
significant role in the future of the American railroad
industry, American labor relations, and the development of
the Southeast Side of Chicago.

The railroad strikes and riots of 1877 troubled George
Pullman. In this period after the Civil War, many people
openly discussed the possibility of another war in America,
not between the states, but between the classes. Conflict
between the rich and the poor seemed to be an everyday
occurrence. Chicago, a city which had grown and prospered
with the industrial expansion of America, witnessed much of
the class conflict which Pullman feared. The Pullman Palace
Car Company was one of the most successful corporations at
the time. It employed many skilled wood workers and other
craftsmen to make its famous railroad cars. The threat of
radicalism seemed very real to Pullman. He also had a
certain fear of the city and the vices generally associated
with it. Like other industrialists, Pullman saw the urban
slums and wondered out loud about their inhabitants. He
believed that if the workers' environment could be
controlled, class conflict could be eliminated through a

process of moral uplift. The Palace Car prince often referred to his employees as "my children."

This paternalistic attitude led Pullman to plan and construct a model town on the Illinois prairie about ten miles south of downtown Chicago. Influenced by Saltaire, a planned community in Northern England, Pullman hired architect Solon Spencer Beman and landscape designer Nathan F. Barrett. This was perhaps the first time in the United States that an architect and a landscaper were brought together to create an entirely new town.

Ground was broken on April 24, 1880 for the 600-acre industrial town, two miles long and one-half mile wide, between the Illinois Central railroad tracks and Lake Calumet. Benzette Williams, formerly superintendent of sewage for the city of Chicago, took on the task of draining the marshy area west of Lake Calumet and installing water, sewer, and gas mains. Once started, the work progressed rapidly. The first resident of the town, Lee Benson, moved into Pullman on January 1, 1881. Benson had worked as a foreman in Pullman's Detroit shop. Several hundred more workers came to the town over the next few months. The car repair shops began operation on March 2, 1881, when Pullman's daughter Florence pushed a button to start the huge Corliss engine which powered the plant and the town on the prairie. By late spring Pullman had a population of over six hundred people. One year later the works were almost complete. Five million dollars had been spent on the construction of the Pullman plant and the town itself. More homes were built over the next ten years as Pullman expanded.

The town of Pullman, Illinois was an experiment in social control. George Pullman believed that the problems associated with slum housing and even those of morality could be controlled in an ideal community. Pullman did not allow taverns in his town. All the buildings were made of brick. Even religious life was to be controlled. One church was built, the Greenstone Church at 112th and St. Lawrence, and it was leased to the different religious groups, while it remained the property of the Pullman Land Association. Moreover, to insure complete control, workers could not own their own homes or any other real estate in the town. The company indirectly regulated the sale of vegetables and other food products. The town had its own library of about 8,000 volumes, selected for "moral uplift." Pullman was a company town, and its creator believed that it should turn a profit of six percent.

At its height, more than 11,000 people lived in Pullman under the protecting hand of "practical philanthropy." The Pullman car works were built for efficiency. So was the

Town of Pullman

(Top left) Workers' row houses, 11200 block S. Champlain Avenue, Pullman, 1985. Many houses have recently been restored and renovated in the historic town of Pullman. (G. Lane)

Workers' housing, northwest corner 113th and Langley, 1985. These recently renovated houses reflect the best aspects of George Pullman's company town. (G. Lane)

Greenstone Church, 112th and St. Lawrence, 1980. This church, designed by Solon S. Beman, was intended to serve all the congregations of the Pullman community. Since 1907 it has housed the Pullman United Methodist Church. (G. Lane)

town. Beman and Barrett received high praise for their designs. The housing was utilitarian. Observors called the architecture of the public buildings "secular gothic." Beman used the Queen Anne style for the detached housing and the Hotel Florence, which was named for Pullman's daughter. He wanted to make handsome as well as practical structures. Class distinctions could easily be seen in the construction of the houses. Management personnel lived in impressive buildings, while the unskilled lived in tenements on the edge of town.

Pullman quickly drew the attention of the nation and the world. During the 1893 World's Columbian Exposition in Chicago, visitors flocked to see the model town on the prairie.

But it was not long before criticism arose. Workers soon reacted against the complete control that the company exerted over their lives. More and more of them moved to nearby Roseland and Kensington. In 1889 when the

question of annexation to Chicago came up, Pullman
residents voted overwhelmingly to join the city to the north
despite George Pullman's objections. Not everything was rosy
in the Palace Car town. The experiment that was devised to
eliminate class warfare soon became the scene of some of
the most intense class conflicts in American history.

In 1893 the American economy fell into a severe
depression. Chicago managed to avoid the full impact of the
crisis for a while because of the Columbian Exposition. But
by the spring of 1894, the city suffered with the nation. By
this time George Pullman could boast that his company was
capitalized at $34,000,000. The Pullman Palace Cars ran on
three-quarters of all American railroads, and the company
manufactured many different railroad cars besides the
much-heralded sleepers. Meanwhile, in order to maintain
the eight percent profit he demanded from his company in
the face of diminishing orders, Pullman ordered a cutback in
the labor force and a cut in pay for those who stayed on. He
instructed the Pullman Land Association, however, to
maintain rent levels in order to insure the six percent profit
he demanded from the town. The cut in wages without a cut
in rents put the workers in an economic vice grip. Like a
stern father, Pullman preached frugality to his workers from
his mansion on Prairie Avenue.

Cutback in the company and payment of salary)

At the beginning of the depression, 5,816 people worked
at Pullman. The roll call fell to about 2,000 men and women
when the company announced a call back at wages that
were reduced anywhere from thirty to seventy percent. In
April of 1894 about 4,200 employees entered the gates each
day. Pullman announced that he had taken action to protect
his employees, and he said that work at reduced wages was
better than no work at all. The Pullman Land Association
also announced that it would hold rents and prices at the
same level. The Pullman Palace Car Company continued to
pay an eight percent dividend to its stockholders and had
undivided profits of nearly $25,000,000. Labor and
management were clearly on a collision course.

In the spring of 1894, many Pullman employees joined
the new American Railway Union headed by Eugene V.
Debs. They were eligible to join because they built the
railroad cars. As the crisis worsened, the union aproached
management for negotiations. On May 9, 1894 a meeting did
take place; but the following day the company laid off three
of the workers' negotiators. So a strike was called for the
next day, and about ninety percent of the Pullman workers
walked out. The following month they sent a delegate to the
American Railway Union convention in Chicago to ask for
aid. The A.R.U. voted, against Debs's advice, to boycott
railroads using Pullman cars until George Pullman agreed to

strike

arbitration. He refused, and the strike suddenly became a national issue as railroads all over the country ground to a halt.

Meanwhile, George Pullman received help from the General Managers Association in Chicago. This organization of twenty-four railroads agreed to support Pullman in his struggle. The member railroads immediately fired all A.R.U. members. The Managers Association had a lot of influence in Washington D.C. and won President Grover Cleveland to its cause. The Democrat ordered federal troops to Chicago and virtually seized the railroads under the pretext of guaranteeing the U.S. Mail. Illinois Governor John Peter Altgeld and Chicago Mayor John Patrick Hopkins opposed the move by the president, but to no avail. Chicago became an armed camp, and blood flowed freely in several working-class neighborhoods which supported the strike. The conflict which Pullman had tried to avoid by creating his own town now engulfed it. The Palace Car king pulled no punches in his battle with labor. Eugene V. Debs was painted as a revolutionary and arrested for disobeying an injunction. Clarence Darrow defended the future founder of the Socialist Party of America.

The strike ended in failure. Pullman emerged victorious, but the hopes for his ideal town lay buried in the ashes of the conflict. The town of Pullman never fulfilled its promise. The 1,750 residential units and paternalistic control did not satisfy the workers. The desire for profit on the one hand and the desire for decent wages on the other could not be balanced in the company town.

In 1897 George Pullman died a bitter man. His remains were interred in Chicago's Graceland Cemetery under a massive monument. Robert Todd Lincoln became the new president of the Pullman Palace Car Company, and there was a change in the relationship between the company and the town. By the end of the century control of the town passed to the city and its residents. The dream of a model industrial town ended completely in 1908 when the Illinois Supreme Court decreed there was no longer any relationship between the town, now neighborhood, and the company.

The neighborhood went into decline after the transfer of title from the Pullman Company. The company remained a major employer hiring, like many other Southeast Side companies, more and more unskilled laborers. Many Poles, Italians, and Czechs lived in the community, which had a population in 1920 that was forty-two percent foreign born. The population of Pullman continued to decline in the 1920s and 1930s, so that by 1940 it stood at its lowest point with only 6,523 residents, down roughly 5,000 from the time of the strike. In 1930 the Italians replaced the Poles as the

Troops camped outside of the Hotel Florence, Pullman, 1894. Federal troops occupied Pullman during the tragic railroad strike which shook the city and the nation in 1894.
(Courtesy Chicago Historical Society)

MARKET HOUSE FROM ARCADE, PULLMAN, ILL.   45-B-17

largest ethnic group in Pullman. Mexicans moved into the town on Langley Avenue and would eventually become an important group in the community.

The 1940s brought an increase in the population of Pullman to 8,899. The twentieth century peak was reached in 1970 when 10,893 people lived there. At that time white people were moving out while black families were moving in. In 1970 whites made up more than fifty percent of the population. Ten years later they made up less than twenty percent. White and Hispanic families tend to live in the old town proper, south of 111th Street.

In 1970 Pullman was placed on the National Register of Historic Places. Two years later the City of Chicago granted landmark status to the South Pullman District (south of 111th Street). The last railroad car rolled out of the Pullman Standard plant in 1981, symbolizing the end of an era. Today many rehabbers have purchased homes in Pullman and are restoring them. An ambitious development plan for the old Pullman Wheelworks resulted in new housing for the area. The Historic Pullman Foundation has played an important role in giving the community a sense of its past. It saved the Hotel Florence in 1975 and is in the process of restoring it to its former grandeur.

(Top left) Doctor's house, Market House, and Greenstone Church, looking east from the Arcade, Pullman, c.1909.
(Courtesy G. Schmalgemeier)

(Bottom left) Market Hall, 112th and Champlain, Pullman, c.1909. This building, originally owned and operated by the Pullman Company, served the town as its only market.
(Courtesy G. Schmalgemeier)

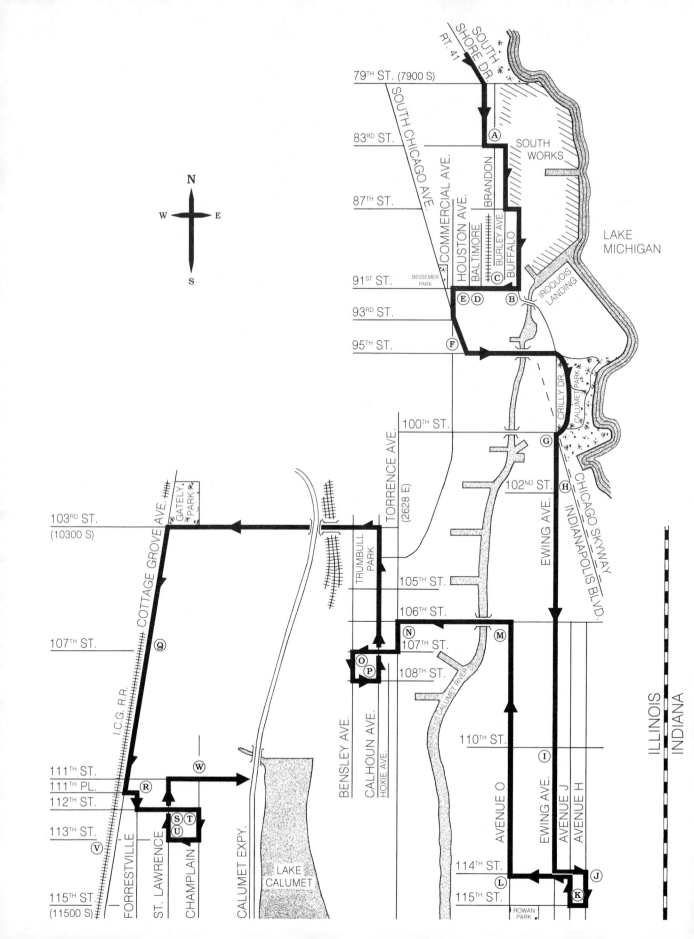

Southeast Side Tour

This tour begins at 79th Street and South Shore Drive in South Chicago's Bush neighborhood. It moves through South Chicago and over the 95th Street bridge into the East Side. After touring this neighborhood, it proceeds into South Deering, and finally into Pullman where you will see what remains of America's most famous planned industrial community.

Driving time: about 2 hours.

(A) Go four blocks south on South Shore Drive to 83rd Street. The huge 250-foot steeple of **St. Michael's Catholic Church** towers over South Shore Drive as you make your way past wooden and brick apartment buildings and single-family homes to 83rd Street. William J. Brinkman designed this Gothic church for the Polish community of South Chicago's Bush neighborhood in 1907. The church seats 1,500 people and took two years to build. Rev. Paul Rhode, the first Polish American Roman Catholic bishop in the United States, served the community as pastor at the time the church was built. Polish immigrants founded the congregation in 1892 as an outgrowth of Immaculate Conception BVM parish on Commercial Avenue. Large numbers of Mexican families have moved into the Bush in the last twenty years. Today Polish, English, and Spanish Masses are offered at St. Michael's. Shrines to Our Lady of Czestochowa and to Our Lady of Guadalupe are included in the church.

St. Michael's parish also served as the home of the Russell Square Community Committee, which was organized as part of the Chicago Area Project to combat juvenile delinquency in the 1930s. Rev. John Lange, then pastor of St. Michael's, played a crucial role in gaining community support for the youth program. Today St. Michael's continues to provide the working-class community of South Chicago with a strong institutional base.

438

St. Michael Church, northeast corner 83rd and South Shore Drive. 1980. This stately Gothic church was completed in 1909 by Polish Catholics who lived in this Bush neighborhood of South Chicago. It has a sizeable Mexican-American population today. (G. Lane)

(B) Continue south about twelve blocks on Rt. 41. Signs are posted along the streets it follows. Turn right at 91st Street and go west. While you are making your way south to 91st Street, you will be passing along the side of the massive, but now nearly abandoned, **South Works.** This plant is owned by U.S. Steel, but its future seems doubtful at best. Once among the most modern steel mills in the nation, it is outdated today and awaiting the wrecker's ball. In the 1970s as many as 13,000 men and women were employed at South Works. By 1983 this number had dropped to less than 1,000. U.S. Steel, despite attempts by the union, the State of Illinois, and the Roman Catholic Archdiocese of Chicago to save the mill and its jobs, has decided to close the plant, which is more than a century old. This announcement has been a major economic and psychological blow to the South Chicago area.

The South Works gave birth to the Bush neighborhood, which makes up that part of South Chicago north of the railroad tracks at 87th Street. Irish and German families originally settled this area, but Poles soon outnumbered them and came to dominate the Bush until the late 1960s when Mexican families moved in in large numbers. The Bush is not the oldest part of South Chicago. The area around 91st Street is actually older, as South Chicago grew up around the mouth of the Calumet River.

The **Pilgrim Baptist Church,** which stands on the southeast corner of 91st and Burley, was founded in 1917 and is the oldest black congregation in South Chicago. The first black neighborhood in South Chicago was located here, south of the Bush and close to the mill. This area is called Millgate, and blacks have lived here since the early 1900s. In the late 1960s another black community grew up in South Chicago to the west of Millgate. This is a rather new development and has more to do with the expansion of Chicago's South Side Black Belt than with the original settlement of black stevedores and unskilled workers in South Chicago. Pilgrim Baptist received national media attention in the late 1970s when part of the movie *The Blues Brothers* was filmed at the church.

Ⓒ Continue one block west on 91st Street to Brandon Avenue (3200 East). The church of **Our Lady of Guadalupe** stands on the northeast corner. This parish traces its history back to the arrival around 1923 in South Chicago of Rev. William Kane, S.J. to serve the spiritual needs of Mexican immigrants in the South Chicago area. In November 1924 the Claretian Fathers arrived to administer the parish. On April 1, 1928 the Most Rev. Pascual Diaz, exiled Bishop of Tabasco, Mexico, laid the cornerstone of the present church. This church is well known for its **National Shrine of St. Jude** established in 1929. Three years later, four hundred members of the Chicago Police Department formed a branch of the St. Jude League here. The church then became the policemen's shrine in Chicago. Today Our Lady of Guadalupe still serves South Chicago's large and expanding Mexican-American community. Solemn novenas in honor of St. Jude which are attended by Catholics from all over the metropolitan area continue to be held at the shrine.

(D) Continue two blocks west on 91st Street to Houston (3026 East). The large and recently remodeled **South Chicago YMCA** stands on the southeast corner. The YMCA can trace its history on the East Side back before the turn of the century. At one point it was a predominantly German institution. It disappeared for awhile, but a new YMCA was organized by local residents in the 1920s. The "Y" gained much support from local businessmen and from the steel companies. In the early 1980s, while many local YMCAs faced a grim economic picture and even the prospect of closing, the South Chicago YMCA went through a renaissance as local leaders organized support for this valuable community asset. Today its modern facilities help continue the tradition of the "Y" in South Chicago.

(E) Go one more block and turn left on Commercial Avenue (3000 East), then go two blocks south to South Chicago Avenue. This retail center acted like a small town's downtown for many years. It was indeed the center of the Southeast Side. Theaters, stores, and offices lined Commercial Avenue, 92nd Street, and South Chicago Avenue. The 9100 block of South Commercial Avenue still contains many of the structures that made this such an important neighborhood center. On the whole, however, this strip has suffered from the ravages of time and from competition with outlying shopping malls. The once proud **Commercial Theatre** (1919), which stood on the northwest corner of 92nd and Commercial Avenue, was converted into a shopping arcade in 1978. 92nd Street now includes many empty lots where various furniture, music, and food stores once did business.

(F) Turn left at South Chicago Avenue and go southeast to 95th Street. **Steelworkers' Hall** stands at 9350 S. South Chicago Avenue. The hall is the home of Local 65 of the United Steelworkers of America, AFL-CIO. This local organized the workers at U.S. Steel's South Works in the 1930s. It, along with other USWA locals, received their first contract from U.S. Steel in 1937. Local 65 is the local that led the Sadlowski rebellion against traditional union leaders in the 1970s. Today, because of the closing of the South Works, it looks like Local 65 will go out of business.

(G) Turn left at 95th Street and cross the Calumet River.
You are now entering the East Side. Continue east past
Ewing Avenue and into Calumet Park. As you cross the
river on 95th Street, you can see the industry which
transformed this waterway from a fisherman's haven to
a bustling lake port. The 95th Street Bridge is often up
to allow lake vessels to pass through to reach local
industries. The recent decline of Chicago's steel industry
has brought several proposals for the Calumet River.
Some consideration has been given to turning part of
the waterway into parkland and creating a boat marina.

*95th Street Bridge over the
Calumet River, 1985. The S.S.
Roger M. Keyes passes under the
95th Street Bridge. Bridges
connect the East Side
neighborhood with the rest of
Chicago.* (D. Pacyga)

As you enter **Calumet Park** at 95th Street, **Iroquois
Landing** is just to your left. This was once the site of the
Iroquois Steel Company, founded by Roger Brown in
1890. The mill was later owned and expanded by the
Youngstown Sheet and Tube Company, which eventually
closed it. Much hope for the industrial future of the
Southeast Side is tied up in Iroquois Landing, but so far
little of its promise has been fulfilled. The new, larger
lake vessels find it difficult to use the facilities here and
many cannot navigate the Calumet River.

The 176-acre **Calumet Park** is built on landfill made
up primarily of slag dumped from the local mills. South
Park Commissioners opened the park in 1904. It was

originally called Park No. 11. The Douglas and Esther
Taylor estate made up the center of the park. This estate
included nineteen acres of land above water and
thirty-one acres under water. Officials dedicated the
huge fieldhouse in 1924. In its basement is one of the
largest model railroads in the world. A museum
celebrating the history of the surrounding community is
planned for the first floor of the complex. In the 1950s
and 1960s Calumet Park was the scene of several race
riots when black people attempted to use the facilities
and the beach. Today, however, white, black, and
Mexican families share the beach and park. The south
beach lies in the shadow of a huge power plant just
across the state line in Indiana.

As you follow Crilly Drive south you will leave the
park going west toward Ewing Avenue. The street winds
to 100th Drive. Pass under the viaduct and approach
Ewing. Ahead of you, just under the Chicago Skyway,
stands the **East Side Memorial,** which celebrates this
community's past. The monument is on the site of the
former Chicago Host House for the Century of Progress
Exposition. Before that, a commuter station of the
Pennsylvania Railroad was located at approximately this
same site. A small street runs past the monument. It is
named after James Fitzgibbons, a local historian who
died in the spring of 1983. He was the driving force
behind the construction of this memorial. The street and
the memorial are a fitting monument to his memory and
to the memory of the people of the East Side.

(H) Turn left on Ewing and go two blocks south to 102nd
Street. At 102nd and Ewing stands the parish and high
school complex of **St. Francis de Sales.** This parish
began as a mission of SS. Peter and Paul Church in
South Chicago in 1888. While established as a territorial
church, in reality St. Francis de Sales was a national
parish serving German-speaking families on the East
Side. Luxembourgers have made up a large part of the
parish's population throughout its history. In 1908 the
parish began a commercial high school course. In 1930
the program was expanded to a three-year course. A
modern high school building was dedicated on April 20,
1958. Today the parish still serves many German ethnic
families as well as large numbers of parishioners from
other ethnic backgrounds.

*Calumet Park fieldhouse, 9801 S.
Avenue G, 1985. This park was
partly built on landfill created by
the dumping of slag from nearby
mills.* (G. Lane)

*St. Francis de Sales Church,
102nd and Ewing, 1985. This very
old parish served mostly
German-speaking Catholics on the
East Side. Today it conducts a
grade school, a high school, and
many other services.* (G. Lane)

(I) Continue eight blocks south on Ewing to 110th Street. The **East Side United Methodist Church** stands on the southwest corner of the intersection. There are many Protestant churches in certain parts of the East Side. Many immigrants who came from Northern and Western Europe moved to the East Side in the last quarter of the nineteenth century. In the years after World War II, a good number of these Protestant families moved south into the newly developed Fair Elms section of the East Side. The East Side United Methodist Church followed its parishioners to 110th Street in 1955.

(J) Continue four blocks south on Ewing to 114th Street and turn left, going two blocks east to east to Avenue H. An authentic reproduction of the fifteenth-century Serbian monastery of Kalenich stands on the southeast corner of 114th and Avenue H. **St. Simeon Mirotocivi Serbian Orthodox Church** stands out among the post-World War II houses which surround it. This parish developed out of a theological disagreement in the Serbian Orthodox community which led 300 families to leave St. Michael Archangel Serbian Orthodox Church on Commercial Avenue. They built this church in 1968-69. Unlike most American churches, there are no pews. The tradition of standing and kneeling during the Orthodox service is maintained. The iconography in the interior of the church is beautiful.

(K) Turn right on Avenue H and go one block south to 115th Street, then turn right (west) once again. The house with the tennis court on the northeast corner of 115th and Avenue J belongs to Alderman Edward R. Vrdolyak. Vrdolyak is chairman of the Cook County Regular Democratic Organization. He also represents the 10th Ward, which includes a large part of Southeast Chicago, and he is the leader of the majority block in the City Council.

(L) Turn right on Avenue J and drive one block north to 114th Street. Turn left on 114th and go five blocks west to Avenue O. Smokestacks once again fill the horizon. The **East Side plant of the Republic Steel Company** stands to the southwest of the intersection on the Calumet River. In 1901 the Chicago Tack Company opened a plant on the East Side. The company eventually developed into a part of the Republic Steel

Republic Steel, South Chicago Works, 11600 S. Burley, 1985. This view looks east across the Calumet River at Republic Steel, one of the principal employers in the South Chicago area. (G. Lane)

Company. This mill, however, is best known as the site of the Memorial Day Massacre in 1937. Just south of the intersection, at 11731 Avenue O, is **Memorial Hall of Local 1033** of the United Steelworkers of America. A plaque on the cornerstone recalls the day when ten steelworkers were killed and many others were injured in a clash with the Chicago police outside Republic Steel's gates. The police fired on the workers while they picketed the plant. The newly formed CIO Steel Workers Organizing Committee led the strike for union recognition. The battle at Republic Steel was the most famous of several clashes throughout the Midwest during the Little Steel Strike in the summer of 1937. After the shooting, the CIO lost the strike. But workers eventually organized the plant during World War II.

(M) Turn right on Avenue O and drive eight blocks north to 106th Street. Turn left on 106th and cross the 106th Street Bridge over the Calumet River. The river is the center of industrialization at this point. Once you cross the bridge, you are in South Deering. Just to your left stands the massive plant of the **Valley Mould and Iron Corporation** which began production here in the 1890s under the name of the Thomas D. West Company. While much industry has left the Calumet Region in the last ten years, there is a large industrial base still in operation on the Southeast Side. Nevertheless, the unemployment rate for Steel Mill District neighborhoods is very high.

(N) Continue west on 106th Street to Torrence Avenue (2628 East). Keep to the left. As you approach Torrence Avenue, the remains of a steel mill appear on your left. This is **Wisconsin Steel.** The huge mill, which once produced steel for International Harvester, closed in 1980. About 3,500 workers lost their jobs, even their pensions were in doubt. The impact on the Irondale section of South Deering was tremendous. Many stores and taverns closed on Torrence Avenue, which had been a busy strip since the 1880s. Several attempts have been made to get developers interested in the abandoned site, but to no avail. South Deering owes its origin to this mill's predecessor, the Joseph H. Brown Steel and Iron Company, which opened here in 1875.

(O) Turn left on Torrence Avenue and go south one block to 107th Street. Make a right turn and go three blocks west to Bensely (2500 East). The low-rise housing project which stands just ahead of you is the **Trumbull Park Homes.** This project was built in 1937 and 1938. The homes cover some twenty acres and cost $3,558,000 to build. They contain 462 units and house about 1,735 people. On August 5, 1953 the Donald Howard family moved into the Trumbull Park Homes. This precipitated a race riot that lasted on and off for most of the summer. Racial fighting then broke out periodically over the next ten years. Today Hispanics, blacks, and whites live in the Irondale community.

(P) Turn left on Bensely and go one block south to 108th Street. Make another left on 108th and go one block east to Calhoun (2525 East). Turn left again on Calhoun and proceed five blocks north to 103rd Street. The large public school on the northwest corner of 108th and Calhoun is the **Bright School.** The first public school in Irondale opened in 1876 in a rented building on Torrence Avenue. Later that year a two-room school house opened at 107th and Hoxie. In 1884 the Cummings School started classes on the current site of the Bright School, which replaced it in 1922. The operation of a public school in the area marked the beginning of permanent institutions in the early community. Schools and churches gave early Irondale a sense of stability.

(Q) Turn left at 103rd Street and go west almost two miles to Cottage Grove Avenue. After making the turn on 103rd, you will pass **Trumbull Park** on your left. The South Park District acquired the land for this park in 1908 and 1909. In the latter year the first improvements were made for ball playing. The park was originally laid out according to a plan presented by the sons of Frederick Law Olmstead, who had designed Washington and Jackson Parks. Park commissioners named the park after Lyman Trumbull in 1917. Before that it was called Park No. 16.

Go west on 103rd Street to Cottage Grove Avenue, then turn left and proceed south. The row houses on 107th and Cottage Grove mark the beginning of the Pullman community. Solon S. Beman laid out these houses on a slight angle to break up the usual monotony of row houses. This is the **North Pullman** community, and it has not drawn as much attention as that part of Pullman below 111th Street.

(R) Continue south on Cottage Grove to 111th Place and turn left. To your left will be the **Hotel Florence,** named after George Pullman's daughter. The hotel is being restored to its former beauty. In front of the hotel is a group of historical markers. At one time the Hotel Florence contained the only bar in Pullman's "perfect" town. George Pullman maintained a suite at the hotel for those nights when he could not return to his home on 18th and Prairie. The suite is now open for viewing.

(S) Turn right at Forrestville and go one block south to 112th Street. Turn left on 112th and go one block east to St. Lawrence. The **Greenstone Church** stands on the southeast corner of 112th and St. Lawrence. This was the only church Pullman allowed in his company town. It cost $57,000 to build in 1882. The Pullman Methodist Church purchased the building in 1907 when the Pullman Company was forced to sell their interests in the company town now turned neighborhood.

(T) Continue east on 112th Street to Champlain and the **Pullman Market Center.** Fire destroyed the original center market building. The present structure was erected in 1892. This marketplace sold vegetables raised

The Pullman Stables, southeast corner 112th and Cottage Grove, 1985. This building once housed all the community's horses as well as the volunteer fire department.
(G. Lane)

on the Pullman farm. The market was owned and operated by the Pullman Company, and the rent for the market stalls was set by the company. It was the only produce market in Pullman itself.

(U) Turn right on Champlain and go one block south to 113th Street. Turn right again and go one block west to St. Lawrence. Just before St. Lawrence, at 614 East 113th Street, is the **Historic Pullman Center.** This building originally served as a boarding house, but after the town was sold, it became a Masonic temple. The center puts on slide presentations and is a valuable resource for learning more about Pullman.

(V) The steeple of **Holy Rosary Church** can be seen to the west from the corner of 113th and St. Lawrence. The church stands on the corner of 113th and King Drive, just outside of Pullman proper. The parish was established in 1882 to serve Irish Catholics who lived in Pullman. Although George Pullman did not allow churches other than the Greenstone Church to be built in his town, he donated the land for Holy Rosary Church and stipulated that Solon Beman design the building so that it would not conflict with the architectural style of the model town. The church was dedicated in 1890 by Archbishop Feehan. It was rebuilt after a fire in 1937.

(W) Turn right on St. Lawrence and go two blocks north to 111th Street. The old main gate of the Pullman plant stood on 111th Street, just to the east of here, at the head of Champlain Avenue. A wire fence and gate stand at the location now.

Continue east on 111th Street to I-94 where the tour ends.

(Left) Historic Pullman Center, 614 E. 113th Street, 1985. (G. Lane)

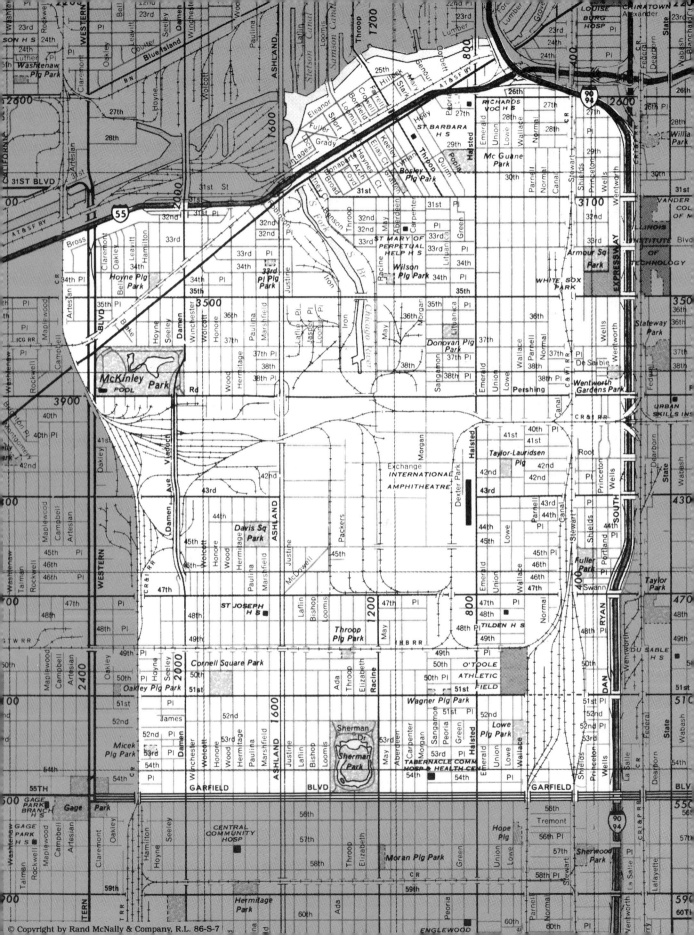

Stock Yard District

13

On Christmas Day 1865 the Union Stock Yard opened its gates and pens for the first time. The joyous occasion was celebrated in a regal way at Hough House, the livestock market's new hotel on Halsted Street. Business leaders thus inaugurated a new era in the history of Chicago and the American Midwest. Around the four hundred acres of cattle, hog, sheep, and horse pens would soon develop a series of neighborhoods that would be involved in the history of Chicago's working-class population. The history of the Stock Yard District has been told in prose and poetry, song and theater. The neighborhoods which surround the Union Stock Yards remain as important markers in Chicago's past and present.

Bridgeport, Back of the Yards, McKinley Park, and Canaryville all served as important way stations for immigrants from all over Europe, Latin America, and most recently from the American South, as they made their way to Chicago and hopefully to the middle class. First the Irish and Germans lived in the frame cottages, brick bungalows, and two-flats of the district. Then came the great Slavic invasion between 1880 and 1920. Poles, Slovaks, Czechs, Ukrainians, Lithuanians, Jews, and others left their East European homelands and came to this square mile of pens and packinghouses to find work and to live under the smokestacks and church steeples of the Stock Yard District. Mexican Americans followed, as did Southern whites and blacks who now predominate in certain parts of the area.

Out of the Stock Yard District have come some of the most famous and infamous names in Chicago's short but turbulent history. "Dingbat" Obierta invented the "one-way ride" here as a member of Al Capone's gang. Ragen's Colts, perhaps Chicago's largest ethnic gang, patrolled the streets of this district during the 1919 race riot. Richard J. Daley, Dan Ryan, Joseph Powers, John Kluczynski, and John "Mr. Bingo" Fary made political history in these neighborhoods. So did Joe Burke and his son Edward Burke, the alderman. During the 1930s and 1940s Joe Meegan and Saul Alinsky organized neighborhood people in order to change conditions in what Upton Sinclair once called "The Jungle" in his famous novel of the same name. Church leaders, too, have made their mark on Chicago and on the nation from the Stock Yard District. Father Maurice J. Dorney served Irish and other Catholics from his landmark church, St. Gabriel's, in Canaryville. Rev. Louis Grudzinski made history as a leader of Chicago's Polish community from St. John of God parish, and the Rev. Harry Ward helped start the Social Gospel movement from the Union Avenue Methodist Church, which was founded by the Swift family. These and other churchmen shaped much of the urban American religious experience from their pulpits near "the yards."

In the mid-1950s the major packinghouses began to close their Chicago operations, and the economic base of the Stock Yard District began to dwindle. Those who managed the Chicago stockyards claimed that the yards had been there before the packers and would still be there after they left, but the reality of the situation was clearly otherwise. After a decade of struggling to stay open and a brief stay from the federal court, the Union Stock Yards closed forever on August 1, 1971. It was truly the end of an era for Chicago, and the closing of the yards heightened the economic problems of the area. Back of the Yards was no longer in back of anything. Today the district faces the realities of a post-industrial world. The loss of the meatpacking industry was Chicago's first economic crisis after World War II. Residents have tried to maintain their faith in prosperity, but the economic base of this once-great industrial community is rapidly changing. New immigrants are still attracted to the area, however, by cheap rents and ethnic institutions like Spanish-speaking Holy Cross/Immaculate Heart of Mary Church at 46th and Hermitage and St. Joseph's Church at 48th and Hermitage Streets. The Yards are gone, but the neighborhoods are a reminder of the past and a hope for a better future.

Our history will begin with Bridgeport and then McKinley Park, Back of the Yards, and Canaryville. Much is gone from the old neighborhoods and industrial center, but enough remains to bring back the memories of the district that made Chicago famous and more than a little aromatic in the days of the Big Packers.

Bridgeport

On the South Side just west of Sox Park and south of the South Branch of the Chicago River lies one of the city's most famous neighborhoods. Over the past thirty years it has been known as the home of Mayor Richard J. Daley and the heart of the Democratic organization. The district is back in the news once again as a younger Daley makes his bid for a bright political future. Bridgeport has been the home of four Chicago mayors since 1933.

Long before the Daleys, however, Bridgeport was a bastion of the Democratic party and the South Side Irish. The community which adjoins the old Union Stock Yards has a rough-and-tumble history. Out of the rows of frame cottages, bungalows, and two-flats came machine politicians, gangsters, union leaders, and just plain hardworking Chicagoans. Bridgeport has perhaps the most colorful history of all Chicago neighborhoods.

In 1836 Chicago embarked on one of its earliest public works, a canal to connect the city with the Mississippi River system. The new Illinois and Michigan Canal would open up the hinterlands to the southwest and help to enhance Chicago's economic position in the Midwest. Someone had to dig the canal; and the Irish responded. They lived in shanties along the river. The panic of 1837 delayed the construction of the canal, and the population of the area, then called Hardscrabble or Lee's Place, remained small. But by 1850 there were enough Irish Catholics in the area to establish the parish of St. Bridget on Archer Avenue.

The district was christened Bridgeport in the 1840s when a low bridge was built across the river at Ashland Avenue. Barges making their way to Chicago were forced to unload there. The cargoes were then loaded on barges on the other side of the bridge—thus the name.

The canal was finally completed in 1848, and Bridgeport became a boom town as industries moved into the area. Chief among these were slaughterhouses which were being pushed out of the downtown area. A large steel mill opened on the southeast corner of Archer and Ashland Avenues in the 1860s, and breweries and brickyards also became important local employers. In 1865 the Union Stock Yard opened to the south of the community. Eventually most of the packinghouses moved again to the area just west of the livestock market, but they were still close enough to Bridgeport to remain an important source of employment and income for its residents. The railroads which served the various factories and packinghouses also employed many Bridgeporters. Finally, in 1905 the creation of the Central Manufacturing District, the country's first planned industrial development, on Bridgeport's western border signaled the completion of the community's industrial base.

The Irish inhabitants of Bridgeport were followed by the Germans who held many of the skilled positions in the meatpacking industry. The First Lutheran Church of the Trinity was built at 25th Place and Canal Street in 1863. This German congregation moved to 31st and Lowe in 1913. The parish grew rapidly and another, Holy Cross Lutheran Church, was founded to the west, at 31st Place and Racine Avenue.

First Trinity Lutheran Church, southwest corner 31st and Lowe, 1980. This German Lutheran congregation was founded in 1863 and moved to this site in 1913.
(G. Lane)

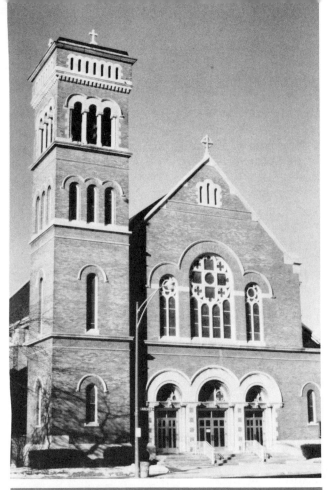

The churches of Bridgeport are the best way to trace the waves of immigrants who came into the neighborhood. Irish Catholics founded St. Bridget's (1850), Nativity of Our Lord (1868), All Saints (1875), and St. David's (1905); the Germans established St. Anthony (1873) and Immaculate Conception (1883). And these parishes were soon followed by others. The Czechs founded the parish of St. John Nepomucene in 1871. Poles, who began to settle in the community in large numbers in the early 1880s, established St. Mary of Perpetual Help in 1886 and St. Barbara's in 1910. Lithuanians built their first church in Chicago, St. George's, in 1892 on Lituanica Avenue.

The parishes played a central role in the immigrant communities. They served not only religious, but social and economic purposes as well. Every one of the congregations maintained a parochial school, which helped immigrant children adjust to life in America and maintained the cultural and religious traditions of the various groups. Fraternal and religious societies were also organized, and they added to the social life of Bridgeport.

But while the churches were important social and religious institutions, they were not the only places where Bridgeporters met and discussed matters. The neighborhood saloon was and is an important local institution on the South Side. Many of Chicago's labor unions and political organizations originated in the back rooms of taverns. Chicagoans discussed important social and political problems "out back."

Bridgeport drinking establishments were made legendary by Finley Peter Dunne in his Mr. Dooley newspaper columns. These gave vivid descriptions of life along Archer Avenue at the turn of the century. Here the Irish working-class philosophers waxed eloquent on the issues of their time. It was not merely coincidental that Dunne's mythical Irish bar on Bridgeport's main street was just down the road from St. Bridget's.

The tavern was the natural habitat of the political organization. Schaller's Pump on 37th and Halsted is probably Chicago's most famous political bar. It is located directly across the street from the 11th Ward Regular Democratic headquarters. Some say it is the real headquarters for Bridgeport Democrats.

In ethnic working-class neighborhoods like Bridgeport, the saloon was a social center and a source of information for newcomers. The bartender was confessor and banker, newsman and politician. He knew all the "important people" and how to get around in "the city of the big shoulders." The back room not only provided a place for political and labor

(Top left) St. Bridget's Church, 2928 S. Archer, 1980. This Roman Catholic parish, originally Irish, today serves a multi-ethnic community comprised mostly of Irish, Polish, and Mexican Catholics.

(Top right) Nativity of Our Lord Church, southeast corner 37th and Union, 1985. This parish was founded in 1868 to serve Irish Catholics who lived near the Union Stock Yards.

(Bottom left) All Saints-St. Anthony, 2849 S. Wallace, 1980. This church, St. Anthony, was built by German Catholics, and later the Irish parish of All Saints was merged with it.

(Bottom right) St. Mary of Perpetual Help, 1039 West 32nd Street, 1980. This is the oldest of several churches built by Polish Catholics in Bridgeport.

(All photos G. Lane)

meetings, but also for celebrations. Wedding, christening, and confirmation parties, as well as funeral dinners were held there. The tavern played an important role in the life of the community.

Other businesses did too, because they also provided communal meeting places. Chief among these were grocery stores, newspaper stands, restaurants, and drugstores. Chicago was once rich in what some experts call "third places," a location outside both the home and the work place where people can meet and socialize. The main streets of Bridgeport were, and to an extent still are, filled with such places. But they are diminishing in this neighborhood as they are in other parts of the city as well. As these third places disappear, so does the lively street life and the feelings of communality and safety in the neighborhood. The more people on the street, the more secure they become.

Even the architecture of Bridgeport supported an active street life. The small cottages with their porches and front steps were and are natural places for families to spend their summer evenings. The two-flats and tenements encouraged the same thing during hot July and August nights. The fact that Bridgeport is like a small town, and most people on the block know one another means than an information and security network has been developed by the "front porch police." This is what made some of Chicago's toughest neighborhoods safe for those who lived in them. The destruction of this lifestyle by architects who build huge buildings or townhouses which face away from the street has made once-safe streets unbearably dangerous. This has not happened in Bridgeport.

Bridgeport has had a longstanding public reputation. During the Civil War the neighborhood, which had become a part of Chicago only in 1863, was a center for Democratic politics. Some local residents supported the Confederacy and actually celebrated Union Army defeats. By the turn of the century the area became widely known through the Dunne newspaper columns and by a host of native sons who climbed the political and business ladders of the city. In 1933, after the assassination of Mayor Anton Cermak, Ed Kelly and Pat Nash took over and recast the Democratic party organization. For the next forty-five years a son of Bridgeport occupied the mayor's office. And Bridgeport's reputation as the political capital of Chicago stood firmly in place until the great snow of 1979 when Jane Byrne defeated Michael Bilandic in the Democratic mayoral primary election. Much of the reputation, of course, was made during the long reign of Richard J. Daley.

Daley, who was elected mayor for the first time in 1955, came from a section of Bridgeport known as Hamburg. It was here that he built his political base. Early in Daley's career he became the leader of the Hamburger SAC, a local "social athletic club" and quasi political organization. From that foundation he rose in the 11th Ward and eventually in city and national politics. While the events of Daley's political life are generally well known, one of the most important facts to be remembered was his loyalty to Bridgeport and Hamburg. Daley lived his entire life on the 3500 block of Lowe Avenue. He did not make the political mistake of those Bridgeport mayors before him who moved out of the old neighborhood. He stayed in Hamburg, raised his family there, and eventually died there.

Bridgeport benefited from Daley's residence. City services were excellent during the Daley-Bilandic years. Local government also became a large employer during that period, even if not as large as is popularly thought. Bridgeport's privileged political position not only made municipal jobs available, but it also gave local politicians a definite influence with private employers. All in all, Bridgeport prided itself as the political heart of the city.

The neighborhood also had another, less praiseworthy reputation. Bridgeport's connection with Chicago's underworld goes back to the early days of the city. Street gangs were notorious in the neighborhood. Names like the Shields, Dukies, Hamburgers, and Ragen's Colts are well remembered among old-timers. Some of these gangs took part in the 1919 race riot. For the most part, however, the gangs were more concerned with fighting among themselves and with local mischief. Eventually some of them, like the Hamburgers, became involved in politics. Some of the neighborhood kids, however, did grow up to be involved in more serious crime. Bridgeport's "Smiling Jack" O'Brien was one of the last criminals to be hanged in the Cook County jail, and Martin "Sonny Boy" Quirk was tried several times for murder before being killed by rival racketeers.

Another indictment of the neighborhood is that of parochialism and racism. Perhaps the most widely known criticism of Bridgeport came from Mike Royko in his book *Boss* and in his newspaper column. Racial conflict has been common in the area and in the surrounding neighborhoods.

The immigration of large numbers of Europeans to America and to Bridgeport has shaped the history of that community. The Irish, Germans, Poles, Lithuanians, Italians, Czechs, Croatians, and others rarely got along. Neighborhood territory was divided along ethnic lines. For years Morgan

Street in the northwestern part of the neighborhood was the dividing line between Poles and Lithuanians. Hamburg, despite its Germanic name, was mostly Irish. Dashiel, the area north of 31st Street and east of Halsted, has long been German and Italian. That is not to say that each area did not have representatives of other groups living within it, but only that these groups were in the majority and dominated the street life there. The story of Bridgeport and Chicago has been one of ethnic segregation and rivalry. This has sometimes led to pitched battles, as in the case of the almost legendary fight between the Bridgeport Irish and Germans in 1856.

The racial factor has further complicated the matter. To the east of Bridgeport and Armour Square, just beyond the Rock Island railroad tracks, is the Douglas community. At the turn of the century this was a middle-class white community with large numbers of Irish and Jews. The Douglas neighborhood began to undergo racial change during World War I, and control of the district was hotly contested by the Irish and blacks. Racial violence broke out there and elsewhere in the city in 1919. Since the 1920s Douglas has been a predominantly black area bordering on Italian, Croatian, and Chinese North Armour Square. Since the 1940s the southern part of Armour Square has also been black. Bridgeport stands like an island surrounded by railroads, industry, and the ghetto. It is not hard to understand the reason for Bridgeport's defensive attitude.

Bridgeport today faces many of the same problems that other urban communities do. The housing is old, but generally well maintained. City services have diminished somewhat. White flight remains a problem, as do relations between older ethnic populations and newer Hispanic residents. Still, Bridgeport has reason to be optimistic about the future. The streets of the neighborhood are safe. The local shopping district seems prosperous enough, and much of the old ethnic flavor of the area has been preserved. Irish bars, Lithuanian and Mexican restaurants, Italian bakeries, and the usual delights of ethnicity in a big city are readily found on the commercial and side streets of Bridgeport. The neighborhood is close to the Loop and connected to the city by excellent transportation. It has great potential for growth. The White Sox remain for now in their "palace" on 35th Street, and the art of people watching can be practiced on any hot summer night when the Sox are in town and fans fill the streets of Bridgeport while making their way to Comiskey Park.

▼

McKinley Park

Across the South Fork of the South Branch of the Chicago River from Bridgeport lies the neighborhood of McKinley Park. The river at this part of the South Side had a notorious reputation as an open sewer for the old stockyards and its adjoining industries. Local residents still refer to the remaining section of the once larger water system as Bubbly Creek. True to form, the river still bubbles on occasion, and the "fermenting" can still be seen from the short bridge that crosses it at 35th Street. Today Bubbly Creek is no longer a refuse drain for the world's largest packinghouses, but it does provide a border between McKinley Park and Bridgeport, and it is a reminder of the city's earlier history.

McKinley Park is a quiet working-class neighborhood just northwest of the old stockyards. Some people used to call it the "American" section of the Stock Yard District because English was the principal street language in this part of the heavily immigrant-populated industrial area. Nevertheless, large numbers of foreign-born people also found their way to this community in the years before the First World War. The history of McKinley Park, like that of its surrounding neighborhoods, reflects the waves of migration that shaped Chicago and the nation.

The McKinley Park area was originally settled by Irish families who came to work on the construction of the Illinois and Michigan Canal. These were mostly squatters who worked the marshy land to harvest cabbages and potatoes. These pioneers were driven out in the 1840s when farm families began to purchase the land and settle the area. One of the more important of these was the Beers family who located here after leaving their native New England. They were, in fact, part of that important migration of Yankees to Chicago which had so much influence on the cultural and economic life of the early city. The Beers scouted the area near what is today Pershing Road and Ashland Avenue and decided to settle there in 1847. This once-wooded area reminded them of New Hampshire.

The future of the neighborhood, however, was not to be in farming, though farm products would play an important part in the industrial development of what would come to be called McKinley Park. The area quickly developed from a small farming community to an industrial center, as Chicago reached out from its origins at the mouth of the river to transform its immediate hinterland. As early as the 1830s, an attempt was made to develop the area for residential and industrial purposes when the Town of Canalport was laid out. The western part of this town lay in the future neighborhood of McKinley Park. The town proved unsuccessful, however, since Bridgeport was in a much better location for development. Developers also planned the Town of Brighton in 1840, though it was not incorporated until 1851. The town included the Brighton Race Track, opened in 1855 by Long John Wentworth on the present site of McKinley Park, as well as the Brighton Stock Yard which lay to the north of Archer Avenue. The stockyard hosted a state fair organized by the United States Agricultural Society in 1861. Inclement weather caused the fair to fail, and the Brighton yards never recovered from the venture. They closed in 1865 when the Union Stock Yard opened to the southeast. Two years earlier, in 1863, Chicago annexed most of the McKinley Park area north of 39th Street.

A steel mill opened at the southeast corner of Archer and Ashland Avenues in 1863. The plant had an immediate economic and physical effect on the area. Workers began to settle on land bounded by Archer Avenue, 35th Street, and Ashland Avenue. This section of the neighborhood came to be known as Mount Pleasant. Like most of the surrounding area, Mount Pleasant suffered from poor drainage, and at certain times of the year it found itself under a good deal of water. Residents began to call the place Ducktown because of the frequent flooding problem.

Among the early developers of the area was Samuel E. Gross. In 1891 Gross offered his Archer Avenue Cottages, located on Hoyne Avenue north of 34th Street, for $50 to $100 dollars down, with $8-dollar monthly payments. The developer built some two hundred of these four-room houses for workers who wished to live in the area. Gross also developed housing to the south of Mount Pleasant on land formerly owned by the Beers family. This High View subdivision was located on Wood, Honore, and Lincoln (Wolcott) Streets, between 38th and 39th Streets (Pershing Road). These buildings sold for $750 dollars in the late 1880s.

More industries soon arrived in the district, and the remaining farm land was soon subdivided for housing. The success of the Union Stock Yards brought packinghouses to the east of Ashland Avenue and south of Pershing Road. These added to the economic base of the community. By the turn of the century, when the original Union Steel Company plant closed and moved to South Chicago to become part of Illinois Steel's South Works, the McKinley Park community already depended on the meatpacking industry for most of the income of its residents. Other local employers included makers of iron and steel products and over twenty brickyards which produced the famous Chicago common bricks needed for the rapidly growing city.

McKinley Park, 1985. This park opened as part of the South Park System in 1901. The land now occupied by the park was formerly the site of the Beers family farm, Long John Wentworth's Brighton Race Track, and the ill-fated Brighton Stock Yards which closed in 1865. (D. Pacyga)

Industrial development attracted many different ethnic groups to this area. In the 1870s Northern and Western Europeans along with native-born Americans settled along the streets of the neighborhood. Irish, German, Swedish, English, and Welsh settlers arrived in large numbers. By 1900 Poles and other East Europeans came to the district. These various groups are reflected in the different churches of the neighborhood. German Catholics founded the parish of St. Maurice on 36th and Hoyne Avenue in 1890. German Protestants established St. Phillipus United Church of Christ on 36th Street near Damen in 1902. The Poles organized SS. Peter and Paul Catholic parish at 38th and Paulina in 1895. The Rev. Paul P. Rhode was the first pastor of the new Polish parish. Rhode later became the first Polish American to be named a bishop of the American Catholic Church. The large number of Irish Catholics in the neighborhood originally attended St. Bridget's in Bridgeport or St. Agnes' in Brighton Park. In 1901 the Irish Catholics in the area organized the parish of Our Lady of Good Counsel in the 3500 block of South Hermitage Avenue to serve the English speaking, that is Irish, residents in the community. The various ethnic groups thus left their marks in brick and mortar on the neighborhood.

The twentieth century brought significant changes to the area. In 1901 the city established a park on the land north of 39th Street and east of Western Avenue that was formerly occupied by Wentworth's race track and was later a cabbage patch. The construction of this park changed the history of the surrounding neighborhood. It suddenly became a much more desirable place to live, despite its proximity to the Chicago stockyards and other industrial developments. Sixty-nine acres in all were set aside for the park. When President William McKinley was assassinated, the South Park commissioners decided to name the new green spot in the Stock Yard District after him. In 1905 a monument was raised at the northwest corner of the park in honor of the slain president. Charles J. Mulligan recast the statue from the bronze of a controversial statue of Christopher Columbus, which public pressure had put on the scrap heap. Up until this time the area adjoining the park to the east had consisted mostly of frame working-class houses. Single- and two-family brick homes now began to appear. The area reached residential maturity before 1914. In 1920, 22,016 people lived in the McKinley Park neighborhood.

Something else happened in the early years of the century which added to the economic stability of this neighborhood. In 1902 a group of investors headed by Frederick H. Prince began to buy up land north of the Union Stock Yard. The Prince interests had earlier purchased the Union Stock Yard & Transit Company and its belt line railroad, the Chicago Junction Railway. Prince soon became one of the most important investors in the city. In 1905 he announced plans for a new Central Manufacturing District (CMD), and the construction of the planned industrial community to the east of McKinley Park began. The new real estate development proved to be a pioneering effort. The original East District, along 35th Street and east of Ashland Avenue, was an immediate success. In 1912 the William Wrigley Company moved its chewing gum factory to 35th and Ashland Avenue in the CMD. The company remains at the same site to this day. By 1915 other thriving industries had filled the original 265-acre development. A former cabbage patch and lumber yard had been turned into a major industrial complex by the time World War I broke out in the summer of 1914.

The success of the CMD meant further industrial development in the McKinley Park area. In 1916 the CMD began to construct a series of large manufacturing buildings along the south side of 39th Street between Ashland and Western Avenues. The new buildings stood on land bordering the Chicago Junction Railway's classification yards. This was crucial because all CMD tenants agreed to use the railroad for their products. One of the major tenants of the development along Pershing Road, as 39th Street was called after the war, was the United States Army, which took up residence in October 1921. They remained at this site until 1961.

McKinley Park thus found itself surrounded by both heavy and light industry in the 1920s. It had come a long way in eighty years from an agricultural community to a major urban neighborhood.

The population of the community remained stable during the 1920s. The following decade saw a loss of about 2,000 people; but a pattern of population loss seems to have been set at between one and two thousand residents every decade, so that by 1980 the population of McKinley Park stood at 13,248. Over ninety percent of these people were white. The leading ethnic groups continued to be Americans of Polish, Irish, and German descent. While no black people lived in McKinley Park or apparently ever have, a growing number of Hispanics have moved into the community, and they now make up over sixteen percent of the population. Hispanic families seem to be younger and are increasing in number as time goes by.

The big change in this community since the 1920s has been in its industrial base. Like the rest of the Stock Yard District, McKinley Park suffered from the loss of jobs in the meatpacking industry and then from the general decline of the CMD. While the community was once surrounded by industry, the old plants to the east have been gradually abandoned or are no longer major employers, and the stockyard area remains only partially rebuilt after the collapse of the meat industry in the 1950s and 1960s. According to the 1980 census, the median family income in this area was just under $20,000, and twenty-three percent of McKinley Park families had an income over $30,000. Over fifty percent of local residents claimed white collar status.

McKinley Park is a neighborhood with a long history. The housing stock is good. Public transportation is excellent. It is, in fact, the geographical center of Chicago. The city determined this fact and erected a plaque commemorating it at 37th and Honore in 1977. The area continues to have reasonable rents, and the value of its homes remains stable. Up until 1985 there has been no real gentrification of this neighborhood. And yet some professionals have been drawn to the area because of its easy access to the Loop and to the

highway system via Damen Avenue and the Stevenson
Expressway. The future of McKinley Park, like neighboring
Bridgeport, seems to lie in the hope of industrial
development on one hand and in its proximity to the Loop
and other major professional employment centers on the other.

Back of the Yards *"Packingtown"*

Just south and west of the old Union Stock Yards lies a
neighborhood that has been the inspiration for songs,
poems, a classic muckraking novel, television
documentaries, and one of the most successful neighborhood
organizations in the United States. The Back of the Yards,
once counted among the nation's worst slums, became a
model for local groups trying to deal with urban problems.
Whether slum or model community, this neighborhood
always was and still is a port of entry for Chicago's
newcomers. The story of the Back of the Yards neighborhood
is the story of immigrant America, be it immigrant Irish,
Polish, Mexican, or native-born American from some other
part of the country.

Originally a part of the Town of Lake, the stockyard area
was sparsely settled before the Civil War. In fact, the entire
district was far removed from the populated parts of the city.
All this would change in 1865 as engineers and construction
crews began to build the new stockyard. This construction
resulted from a campaign begun during the war years by the
Chicago Pork Packers Association and supported by the
Chicago *Tribune* for the creation of a Union Stock Yard
where all of Chicago's livestock business could be carried on.
Nine railroads quickly got behind the movement and
provided much of the financial support.

The Union Stock Yard and Transit Company was formed,
and it purchased 320 acres of land from John Wentworth.
The new livestock market would be located between 39th
Street and 47th Street, and between Halsted Street and
Center Avenue (Racine Avenue). The site was swampy, and
Octave Chanute, who would later become a famous aviation
pioneer, designed an ingenious method for draining the area.
Soon the yards themselves, railroad tracks, offices, and a
market hotel appeared. The Union Stock Yard opened on
Christmas Day, 1865 with pen space for 21,000 cattle,
75,000 hogs, 22,000 sheep, and 200 horses.

Suddenly the western part of the Town of Lake took on
the appearance of a city. Workers' houses began to rise on
the prairie to the west of the yards. The first homes were
built near the corner of 43rd and Loomis, but these were
later relocated when packinghouses moved into the area and

needed the land for expansion. Most of these early settlers moved to the vicinity of 47th Street and Ashland Avenue, just to the southwest of the original settlement.

As the yards grew, so did the neighborhood. Although Chicago was the principal meatpacking center in the United States as early as 1861, it was not until twenty years later that the city would usher in the modern age of the industry. The G.H. Hammond Company was the first to successfully ship beef in a refrigerated railroad car in 1868, but it was Chicago's Swift & Company that used the cars to revolutionize the marketing of meat. Gustavus F. Swift began experimenting with them in the 1870s. Both Swift and Armour manufactured the new carriers, and they soon dominated the refrigerated car industry.

Fearing a loss of revenue, the railroads at first refused to carry the "reefers," but eventually the Grand Trunk agreed, and the other lines followed. The railroad transportation

Packingtown, Chicago, 1909. This photograph shows Chicago's packinghouses just four years after the publication of Upton Sinclair's novel, The Jungle. *The total value of the livestock killed in Chicago in 1910 was about $225,000,000, making Chicago the center of the nation's meatpacking industry.*
(M. Riott, courtesy Chicago Historical Society)

network became the means of distribution for the meatpacking industry, and the Chicago packers used it to the utmost. Chicago beef was soon being sold all over the United States. Chicago, in fact, became the livestock market of the world. Meat prices were set by the packers in their offices, all of which were located within one square mile in the area simply referred to as "the yards."

Meanwhile, the neighborhood to the south and west of the stockyards filled up with new houses for the thousands of workers who were needed to operate the livestock market and the packinghouses. Ethnicity was readily apparent in the growing population of the district.

The first to move into Back of the Yards in large numbers were the Irish. The Germans joined them almost immediately. Both left their institutional marks on the community. The Irish organized St. Rose of Lima parish at 1546 West 48th Street in 1881 with the help of Father Dorney from neighboring Canaryville. The Germans in turn established both the Catholic parish of St. Augustine in the 5000 block of South Laflin and the Lutheran church of St. Martini at 1624 West 51st to serve their settlement. Parochial schools and other ethnic institutions were also established. The neighborhood streets definitely took on a German and Irish character.

But even as these two groups came to dominate the neighborhood and the meatpacking industry, another type of immigrant appeared on the scene. When the Zulawski family came to the Back of the Yards in 1877, there were no other Poles in the area. Seven years later Polish immigrants were building homes on Justine Street and along Loomis near 48th Street. Like the earlier immigrants, they gathered together in certain sections of the neighborhood. The Eastern Europeans came in large numbers as the decade of the 1880s went on. Their numbers grew tremendously after the packinghouse strike of 1886.

At first the religious needs of the small Polish community were met by priests from St. Adalbert's, more than three miles to the north, and from the Polish church in Bridgeport. Eventually the Poles needed a church of their own, and in 1887 they established St. Joseph's at 48th and Hermitage, the first Polish parish in Back of the Yards.

This was the first of three such parishes in the neighborhood as the Polish population of the community expanded. While the first Poles came from German and Russian Poland, others from Galicia soon outnumbered them. Sacred Heart parish in the 4600 block of South Wolcott became the institutional center for the Polish mountaineers who settled in large numbers in the area north of 47th Street and east of Damen Avenue.

The Poles were not the only Eastern Europeans to come to Back of the Yards in the 1880s and 1890s. They were joined by large numbers of Lithuanians, Slovaks, Czechs, Ukrainians, Russians, Jews, and others who made their way into the neighborhood. By the end of the century, Back of the Yards had become a Polish and Slavic enclave on the South Side. Each one of these groups left some reminder of their stay in the community. This was usually a church, but other institutions also evolved.

The neighborhood which these immigrants came to was congested and made up of wooden houses, mostly two-flats, which lined dirt streets. Many of the homes had no connection with the city's water system, and few had gas lights, much less electricity. The wooden sidewalks were in disrepair, and most of the streets were unlighted.

Perhaps the first thing that struck the newly arrived immigrants as they got off the streetcar in their new neighborhood was the odor. An all-pervasive odor filled the community: a result of the packing process. Longtime residents joked about it and claimed they could tell the time of day by slight changes in the smell. The odor and the heavy smoke from the factories hung over the whole community.

Still, the stockyard smell was not the only offense to people's nostrils in the neighborhood. While the yards made up the eastern boundary of the neighborhood, Bubbly Creek, the infamous open sewer for Packingtown, stood to the north, and the largest garbage dumps in the city cut it off from the open prairie to the west.

[handwritten margin note: description of the neighborhood dirt, smell, pollution]

Tuberculous and death (handwritten margin note)

The scars of the industrial revolution were everywhere in Back of the Yards. Flies, mice, rats, and other vermin were a constant problem. A fine soot from the smokestacks covered everything. Children died at an alarming rate, and tuberculosis was a major killer of the adult population. Back of the Yards was a classic Victorian slum. The usual characteristics of urban poverty were everywhere; a high crime rate, juvenile delinquency, disease, and alcoholism plagued the residents.

Much of this was related to the fact that packinghouse wages were low, and, much worse, the work year was irregular. The workers had no labor organizations. Nineteenth-century strikes ended in terrible defeats for the workers. As the twentieth century arrived, so did a new labor organization. The Amalgamated Meat Cutters and Butcher Workmen led unsuccessful strikes in 1904 and 1921. Although the strikes failed for the most part, they did lead to some improvements in the packinghouses. The work week and work year became more regular. And the threat of unionization brought improved conditions in the plants.

While labor unions were trying to organize the packinghouses, another type of organizing also took place. In 1894 Mary E. McDowell came to Back of the Yards to head the new University of Chicago Settlement House. A friend of Jane Addams, she planned to settle in the neighborhood and help organize it for its own betterment. McDowell supported the union in 1904 and attempted to bring change. She worked to close the garbage dumps and to fill in Bubbly Creek. These goals were eventually achieved, and much of the success was due to McDowell's early efforts to bring pressure on City Hall and the meat packers.

Sociologists had little hope (handwritten margin note)

Sociologists and reformers who visited the neighborhood pointed out that it was disorganized. They saw little hope for the residents, who seemed condemned to live out their lives in the slum. But the neighborhood was actually highly organized. What Upton Sinclair and other commentators missed was the tremendous amount of institutional life based on ethnicity. Twelve Catholic churches stood in the neighborhood and ethnic institutions flooded the area. This organizational richness was never mentioned in Sinclair's book, *The Jungle,* or in more objective reports on living conditions. Yet this was a firm base on which a more powerful type of organization would later be built.

After World War I immigration from Europe diminished to a trickle. A new type of immigrant began to appear on the streets of Back of the Yards. Mexican workers and blacks joined the older ethnic groups in the packinghouses. There was some friction in the parishes between the East

(Top left) Making link sausages, c.1912. Mechanization helped make Chicago the meatpacking center of the world. One of the machines pictured could stuff seven miles of sausage in one hour.

(Top right) Trimming and skinning hams, c.1912. These hams are being prepared by skilled butchers for market.

(Bottom left) Splitting backbones, c.1912. This photograph, taken at Swift and Company, shows workers splitting carcasses before placing them in the huge coolers.

(Bottom right) Washing beef carcasses, c.1912. This was the last process of dressing beef in the Chicago packinghouses.

(All photos courtesy T. Samuelson)

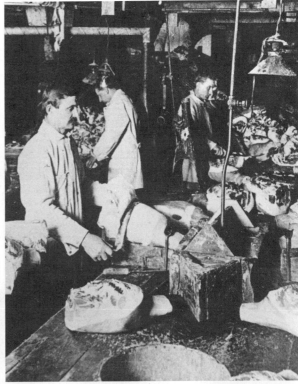

46th and Gross Avenue playlot. The development of playgrounds was an important outgrowth of the settlement house movement. This photograph, taken from the roof of the University of Chicago Settlement House before World War I. shows an early attempt to provide such a recreation space. Notice the wooden working-class housing in the background.
(Courtesy Chicago Historical Society)

Europeans and the Mexicans, but the newcomers quickly set up a mission to serve the Spanish-speaking community. This eventually became the Immaculate Heart of Mary Vicariate on 45th and Ashland. The present building, which resembles a Spanish mission, was built with the help of the entire community and is referred to as "La Capilla" by local residents. Once again Back of the Yards served as a receiving station for a new immigrant group.

The 1920s brought some degree of prosperity to the neighborhood after the Harding Depression and the unsuccessful strike of 1921. The institutional life of the community became even richer than before, but the end of the decade brought the disaster of the Great Depression. With the economic collapse, Back of the Yards, like the rest of the country, went through hard times. Conditions which had been improving, now got worse. No unions in the packinghouses meant no protection against lay-offs or against wage and hour reductions. Out of the chaos of the early Depression came a call to organize not only the labor force in the yards, but the people in the neighborhood as well.

In the late 1930s a new labor group, the Packinghouse Workers Organizing Committee of the new CIO, appeared in Chicago. Led by Herb March and others, it quickly made inroads in the stockyards. At the same time a young University of Chicago student named Saul Alinsky and a local resident, Joseph Meegan, with the aid of Roman Catholic bishop Bernard J. Sheil, set up the Back of the Yards Neighborhood Council (BYNC). The new organization got support from the CIO through Sheil and quickly moved to change conditions in the area. One of the immediate concerns of Alinsky, Meegan, and Sheil was juvenile delinquency. The Council moved to lower crime rates by organizing activities for local youth. Sheil, of course, also founded the Catholic Youth Organization (CYO), and he helped to organize amateur sports in Back of the Yards with the Council.

Housing was another concern of the Council. The old wooden tenements were in terrible condition, so the organization led a campaign to clean up the area. The BYNC became a powerful political pressure group and was able to exert force on City Hall in a way Mary McDowell had never dreamed of. In the first twenty years of its existence, BYNC helped local residents to transform the Back of the Yards from "the Jungle" into a model community. The Back of the Yards Council was the first and one of the most successful organizations to be founded on what would come to be known as the "Alinsky Plan." The connection with local ethnic organizations, especially the churches, and with the packinghouse union gave it a broad base for political influence.

As success seemed within reach of the Back of the Yards Council, changes came to transform the neighborhood again. World War II unleashed economic forces that altered the South Side forever. Returning veterans sought jobs away from the packinghouses. In 1939 about eighty percent of the families in the neighborhood depended on the meatpacking industry for their income; twenty years later only about thirty-five percent drew all or part of their income from the slaughterhouses. The residents of Back of the Yards went outside the neighborhood to work. They kept living in the community for reasons of family and because of the ethnic institutions which made it "home," but they traveled outside to work. Meanwhile, the work force in the plants was being drawn more and more from the black community. By 1959 about eighty percent of the packinghouse workers were black. The result was that the neighborhood was less dependent on the packinghouses than it had ever been before.

At the same time, changes in the means of transportation were transforming the meatpacking industry. The truck and the new interstate highway system made the old railroad-based stockyard obsolete. Slowly but surely, the packers decentralized their plants. This process began in the early part of the century, but it picked up speed as time went on. In the 1950s Wilson and Company led the way for the modernization of the industry with their new Kansas City plant. By the mid-1950s Wilson's closed their Chicago operation, and the other major packers soon followed. The Union Stock Yard & Transit Company held on until 1971, when the stockyards closed forever.

The Central Manufacturing District has been trying to redevelop the stockyards area with some success as a light industrial park, but the 60,000 jobs associated with meat packing during World War I are gone and will not be replaced by the small plants now being built in the area.

The loss of the packinghouses did not at first hurt the Back of the Yards to the extent that most people feared, because the largest part of the population no longer worked in the industry. The black community to the east of the neighborhood was hurt the most by the closings. The loss of income had a tremendous impact on the immediate stability of the black South Side and only later on the white communities of the city.

Demographic change also affected the Back of the Yards. The Mexican community grew by leaps and bounds. Today the neighborhood has a distinctly Hispanic flavor to it. The older groups are still around, but Back of the Yards has become a predominantly Mexican area. Also, black people have moved in in large numbers on the edge of the neighborhood.

The Back of the Yards Council has been criticized for not responding to the new groups. The Hispanics and the blacks have established rival organizations. Like other areas in Chicago, Back of the Yards is facing the realities of a shrinking economic base. Racial and ethnic conflict are also major problems. But these are problems that the neighborhood has faced before.

Canaryville

Canaryville is located directly east of the Union Stock Yards. The U.S. Census Bureau includes the neighborhood in the New City community area along with Back of the Yards. Many outsiders get Canaryville confused with Bridgeport, its neighbor to the north; but Canaryville is a distinct and separate place from its more famous neighbors. The neighborhood is cut off from other parts of the city by railroad tracks on the east, the old stockyards area on the west (Halsted Street), and an industrial belt on the north, which once included many of Chicago's small independent meatpackers. Because of these boundaries Canaryville has developed as a discrete part of Chicago. Longtime residents call it "The Village."

Although a family named Gaffney settled here as early as 1853, Canaryville principally owes its existence to the Union Stock Yards. The building of the yards brought the first workers to the area. The grand hotel, constructed at Exchange Avenue and Halsted to serve the new livestock market, was the social center of the early community. Originally called the Hough House and later the Transit House, this hotel was one of the finest in the Chicago area. Behind the hotel the new stockyard sprawled across the prairie after it opened on Christmas Day in 1865. Canaryville was definitely "in front" of the yards.

One part of Canaryville originally had a very middle-class character. The new industry booming at its doorstep required all kinds of white collar workers as well as blue collar operatives. Moreover, the first generation of packinghouse owners wanted to stay close to their investments in the stockyards. In the mid-1870s the Swifts, Libbys, and Hutchinsons lived on Emerald Avenue, creating a sort of Stock Yard District Gold Coast. In 1877 the Swift family founded the Union Avenue Methodist Church at 47th Place and Union. Neighbors still call it "Swift's Church." Furthermore, Canaryville played an important role in the early history of the Town of Lake, a suburb of Chicago that included the stockyards and remained independent until its annexation in 1889. The town's economic and political life revolved around the yards and the new packinghouse owners. In 1873 Sam Goodall began publication of the *Drover's Journal* which served the industry. The *Stock Yard Sun* was also published in Canaryville and carried news of the Town of Lake. These early days were the golden years of Canaryville.

The middle-class character of Canaryville soon changed. As the packinghouses prospered and the city engulfed its former suburb, the owners and white collar workers moved to the lakefront communities to the east. Meanwhile, more and more Irish workers and their families moved into the neighborhood. Many of these came from Bridgeport to the north. They followed the packinghouses that before the 1870s had been located along the South Branch of the Chicago River in Bridgeport. When the meat plants moved, so did their workers. Irish Catholics organized the parish of St. Gabriel in 1880 under the leadership of Rev. Maurice J. Dorney. The new pastor soon became well known in the yards and was the principal figure in Canaryville's religious and social life until his death in 1914. Dorney knew many of the packinghouse owners on a first name basis. He personally intervened in several labor strikes, and he could always get a deserving neighborhood boy a job in Packingtown. St. Gabriel church was built in 1887-88 and was designed by the prestigious Chicago architectural firm of Burnham and Root. St. Gabriel's is the only Catholic church designed by these legendary founders of the Chicago School of Architecture. John Wellborn Root designed the church. Daniel Burnham was the son-in-law of John Sherman, president of the Union Stock Yard & Transit Company. Dorney's stockyard connections are memorialized in this landmark church at 45th and Lowe Avenues. When Father Dorney died the flags in the stockyards were lowered to half-mast.

Father Dorney managed to keep the saloons off of the side streets in most of Canaryville. Halsted Street, however, soon developed as the major business center of the community, and by 1900 it sported a "Whiskey Row" that rivaled the infamous one on Ashland Avenue in Back of the Yards. Chief among the saloons was Big Jim O'Leary's at 4183-85 S. Halsted, directly across the street from the main gate of the Union Stock Yards. Big Jim was the son of Chicago's famous Mrs. O'Leary, in whose barn the Chicago Fire began in 1871. The family moved to Canaryville soon after the accident, and Jim grew up to be the gambling king of the Stock Yard District. After Jim O'Leary became a success he, like many other "villagers," left the neighborhood for the Irish "lace curtain" neighborhood of Englewood to the south.

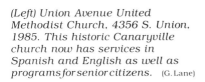

(Left) Union Avenue United Methodist Church, 4356 S. Union, 1985. This historic Canaryville church now has services in Spanish and English as well as programs for senior citizens. (G. Lane)

(Below) Canaryville houses, 500 block of West 45th Street, 1985. Typical houses built mostly for the people who worked in the Union Stock Yards nearby. (G. Lane)

St. Gabriel's Church, southeast corner 45th and Lowe, 1985. This beautiful structure, designed by John W. Root in 1887, serves the predominantly Irish-American parish of St. Gabriel. The congregation was founded by the legendary Rev. Maurice Dorney, the "King of the Yards," in 1880. It is an institutional anchor for the Canaryville community. (A. Kezys)

Just as the middle-class residents had done before, many of the Irish left the old neighborhood as they climbed the economic laddder in Chicago. These Irish Americans often followed the path of the white Anglo-Saxon Protestants who moved toward the lake or into neighboring Englewood. Visitation parish, just to the south on Garfield Boulevard (55th Street), was a favorite destination for those who continued to work in the stockyards. This middle-class community was still close to the stockyards and close to friends and family in Canaryvillle.

Some Mexican Americans moved into the neighborhood in the 1920s, but Canaryville remained primarily Irish in ethnicity. Today many Appalachian whites as well as Hispanics live in Canaryville with the Irish. Canaryville is bordered to the east and south by black communities. Fewer than 8,000 people lived in the neighborhood in 1980.

While many changes have taken place in Canaryville over the last few years, the most significant was the decline of the stockyards and then of the International Amphitheatre at 42nd and Halsted. When the major meatpackers left Chicago, the stockyards continued to employ many local people. Others made their living either working for the Amphitheatre or for firms that prospered from the convention and trade show business. When McCormick Place opened on the lakefront in 1960, the writing was on the wall for the Amphitheatre and for the economic base of Canaryville. The small meatpackers, who provided a good deal of the area's economic vitality, also began to leave the area. 47th Street, never a well developed shopping strip, fell into decline, and Halsted Street suffered from the loss of the stockyard and Amphitheatre business. The history of Canaryville was built on industry. Most of that industry is now gone, and Canaryville waits to see what will happen in the former stockyard area that once gave it life.

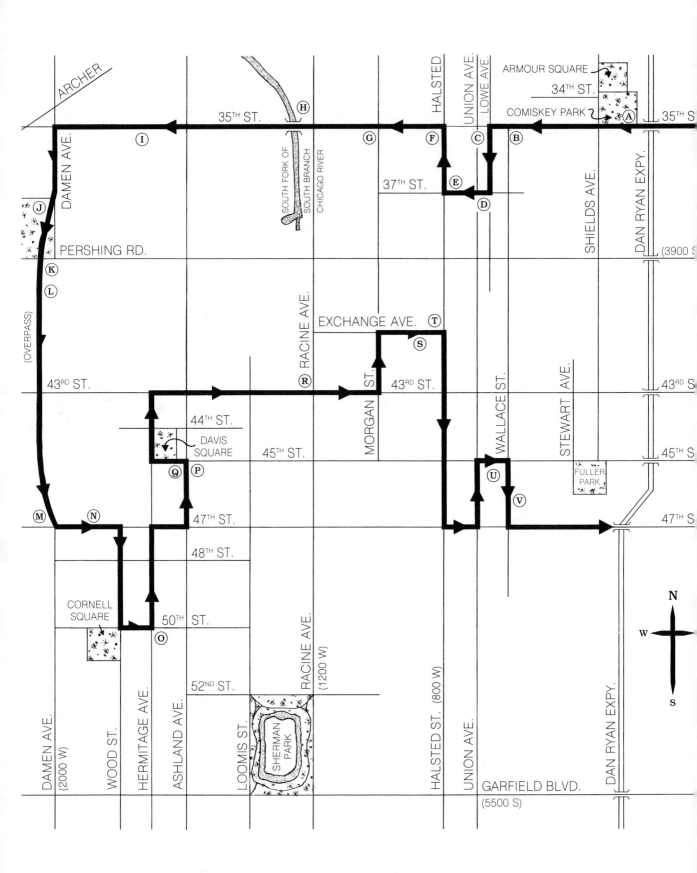

Stock Yard District Tour

This tour begins at 35th Street and the Dan Ryan Expressway. It proceeds through Bridgeport and McKinley Park, then south through Back of the Yards, and finally through the Canaryville neighborhood.

Exit the Dan Ryan at 35th Street and drive seven blocks west to Lowe Avenue.

Driving time: about 2 hours.

(A) Just west of the Dan Ryan on the north side of 35th Street stands **Comiskey Park,** home of the 1917 World Champion White Sox. In 1908 the "Old Roman," Charles Comiskey, bought fifteen acres of land from the estate of "Long John" Wentworth for his new baseball palace. As early as the 1860s the land had been used as an athletic field. The White Sox played their first game there on April 15, 1910. The park was officially dedicated on July 2 of that year. After the White Sox moved to Comiskey Park, their old ballpark at 39th (Pershing Road) and Wentworth became the home of the Chicago Giants of the Negro League.

(B) Going west on 35th Street, you will pass the **George B. McClellan Public School** (1881) on the southeast corner of 35th and Wallace. The McClellan school building is typical of working-class public school architecture in the nineteenth century. The little red schoolhouse of rural areas gave way to the massive public schools of urban America as cities like Chicago boomed in the years after the Civil War.

(C) Turn left at Lowe Avenue (632 West) and go two blocks south to 37th Street. On the right side of the street you will see a modest bungalow at 3526 S. Lowe. This was the home of the late great **Mayor Richard J. Daley** from 1936 until his death. Mayor Daley spent his entire life

Comiskey Park, 35th and Shields, c.1951. The home of the Chicago White Sox baseball team. In 1985 White Sox management announced that they were looking at several sites in the Chicago area to build a new stadium. Notice that this photograph predates the construction of the Dan Ryan Expressway in the late 1950s and early 1960s.
(Courtesy The Chicago Catholic)

(Right) Home of the Daley Family, 3526 S. Lowe, 1985. This modest brick bungalow is the family home of the late Mayor Richard J. Daley. The mayor lived his entire life on Lowe Avenue in the Hamburg section of Bridgeport. (D. Pacyga)

Schaller's Pump, 37th and Halsted, 1985. This neighborhood institution is probably the most politically oriented neighborhood bar-restaurant in the city.
(J. Ficner)

as a resident of this part of Bridgeport, having been born down the street at 3602 S. Lowe. Mrs. Daley still lives here. This dwelling is typical of the block and this part of Bridgeport known as Hamburg. Most of the houses on this well-kept street between 35th and 37th were built before World War I, and they give a sense of the typical working-class home at the turn of the century.

(D) Turn right at 37th Street and go three blocks west to Halsted Street (800 West). **Nativity of Our Lord Church** (1885) stands on the southeast corner of 37th and Union. Irish Catholics organized this parish in 1868. At one time 2,800 families belonged to Nativity. The congregation was comprised in large part of packinghouse and stockyard workers. The parish provided the major institutional base for the Hamburg area. Mayor Daley, a lifelong member of the parish, was buried from this church in December of 1976.

(E) Turn right at Halsted and drive two blocks north to 35th Street. At the intersection of 37th and Halsted stand two major political and social institutions. **Schaller's Pump,** perhaps the most famous political bar in Chicago, guards the end of 37th Street. Directly across the street on the northeast corner is the headquarters of the **11th Ward Regular Democratic Organization.** The connection between the tavern and politics is long established in the ethnic working-class neighborhoods of Chicago. Democratic regulars often stop at Schaller's to hear a little political gossip or to get a bite to eat.

(F) Turn left and drive west on 35th Street. The intersection of 35th and Halsted Streets marks a neighborhood shopping district. This strip is a fairly small one because it grew up well within the shadow of 63rd and Halsted, which by the 1920s was the most important neighborhood shopping district in the city. Still this strip is a busy one that serves Bridgeport and the surrounding neighborhoods. Several ethnic businesses here draw customers from many parts of the city.

(G) Continue west on 35th Street. At the corner of 35th and Morgan (1000 West) a series of industrial buildings begins. This is the **Central Manufacturing District** (CMD) established in 1905. Three years earlier the New Jersey Company, the parent organization, began to acquire land north of the Union Stock Yards for a planned real estate development that would cater to industry and use their Chicago Junction Railway; it was, in effect, the first industrial park in the nation. By 1915 the CMD's original East District, along and south of 35th Street, was filled with important industries.

(H) As you continue west on 35th Street, you will cross a small bridge over a narrow river. This is the South Fork of the South Branch of the Chicago River. It is all that remains of notorious **Bubbly Creek,** the open sewer for the stockyards and the plants of the CMD. On a warm day you can still see the river bubble because of decomposing debris on the bottom. Most of the South Fork of the Chicago River was filled in around the time of World War I. The South Fork marks Bridgeport's western boundary. You will now be entering the McKinley Park community area.

(I) Continue west along 35th Street about nine blocks to Damen Avenue (2000 West). Another small neighborhood shopping strip developed along this part of 35th Street. It never grew to be very big, because it developed more as a local convenience market than a large regional marketplace. It also grew under the shadow of larger neighborhood shopping centers at 47th and Ashland, along Archer Avenue, and the Bridgeport strip at 35th and Halsted. Nevertheless, the area is interesting because it exemplifies a mixed residential/commercial strip popular in American cities during the era of the streetcar. Private transit companies introduced public transportation to the area in the late 1880s and early 1890s. One of the results of this was the development of taverns and coffee shops at strategic corners where the streetcars stopped.

(J) Turn left at Damen Avenue and go south to 47th Street using the **Damen Avenue Overpass.** The overpass opened in 1962 connecting 37th and 47th Streets and the Stevenson Expressway with the communities to the south. **McKinley Park,** from which the neighborhood gets its name, is situated at the southwest corner of 37th and Damen, just before you get on the overpass. The park is one of the most attractive on the Southwest Side and is heavily used during the spring, summer, and fall. It includes a lagoon stocked with fish and ample playing fields, as well as a large fieldhouse near Western Avenue at the opposite end of the park.

(K) As you drive up the overpass on both the right and left you will notice large manufacturing buildings. These are part of the CMD's **Pershing Road Development.** After the initial success of the East District, the CMD developed along Pershing Road from Ashland to Western Avenue during the World War I era. The developers tried to blend the new buildings in with the surrounding environment by designing them to complement the houses and the park. Even the CMD watertower, just to the east of the overpass, was designed to look like a clocktower on a college campus. The U.S. Army occupied many of the buildings to the east of Damen Avenue until the 1960s. Today the Chicago Board of Education is a major tenant of the Pershing Road Development.

Old Chicago Junction Railroad Yards, looking east, 1985. These railroad yards were once among the busiest in the nation. In the distance are the abandoned packinghouses once operated by Swift and Company. Today they stand as a stark reminder of the problems Chicago faces in the post-industrial era. (J. Ficner)

(L) Just south of the CMD are the freight yards of the **Chicago Junction Railway.** These yards were once among the busiest in the nation. They served not only the CMD, but also the Union Stock Yards and the adjacent packinghouses. Today the freight yards are still used, but the abandoned packinghouses to the east tell the story of diminishing rail transportation and industrial decline in this part of Chicago.

As you continue south on the Damen Avenue Overpass, the church spires of the **Back of the Yards** neighborhood will appear just south of 43rd Street and the rail yards. The neighborhood contains twelve Roman Catholic parishes, as well as several Protestant churches. The nearest set of twin spires you see to the left are those of **Holy Cross/Immaculate Heart of Mary Church.** This parish was originally Lithuanian, today it is primarily Mexican.

(M) At the south end of the overpass, on your right, is a large field that is used today as an athletic field and as the grounds for the Chicago County Fair run by the

Back of the Yards Neighborhood Council to raise funds for its activities. At the turn of the century, this field and the surrounding area contained the largest garbage dumps in the city of Chicago. Upton Sinclair memorialized them in 1905 in his classic novel of the stockyards, *The Jungle.*

Turn left at the end of the overpass and go five blocks east on 47th Street to Wood Street (1800 West), then make a right turn (south). Notice the various shops and stores on 47th Street. This east-west street intersects Ashland Avenue just east of here to create a major shopping center for the Stock Yard District. Many of the shops have an ethnic character. As time goes on, more and more of the old Slavic businesses are changing hands, reflecting the growing number of Hispanics in the area. The **Kubina-Tybor Funeral Home** at 1938 West 47th has traditionally served the Slovak community of St. Michael's parish on 48th and Damen Avenue. Farther down the street, at 1745 West 47th, the **Bafia Funeral Home** serves primarily the local Polish parishes of Sacred Heart and St. Joseph.

Housing on 4800 block of S. Paulina Street, 1985. This row of two-flats shows the change which took place in Back of the Yards housing stock after 1880. The growth of the packing industry called for more workers' housing; two-flats soon replaced many of the original wooden cottages. These buildings have housed wave after wave of immigrants as they came to this neighborhood to find employment. (J. Ficner)

47th Street looking toward Paulina, 1985. This thriving commercial strip reflects the ethnic change that has swept over the Back of the Yards community in the last twenty years. Mexican-American businesses now predominate on the street along with a few surviving Polish stores. The corner of 47th and Ashland is the economic heart of the neighborhood. (J. Ficner)

(O) Go three blocks south on Wood Street to 50th and make a left, go one block east on 50th Street to Hermitage, then three blocks north on Hermitage to 47th Street. On the southeast corner of 50th and Hermitage you will see the beautiful **SS. Cyril and Methodius Church,** built by Bohemian Catholics in 1912. On the corner of 48th and Hermitage stands the magnificent Polish church of **St. Joseph.** This parish was the first of three Catholic parishes to be founded in Back of the Yards to serve the Polish community of stockyard workers. Although the recognized date of the founding of the parish is 1887, property was purchased in 1885, and the original church was dedicated on December 19, 1886. The parish remained a mission of St. Mary of Perpetual Help parish in Bridgeport until 1889 when it received independent status. The imposing church was dedicated on September 27, 1914. This parish maintains a coeducational grammar school and high school. Its present congregation includes foreign-born as well as second-, and third-generation Poles.

(P) Turn right on 47th Street and go three blocks east to Ashland (1600 West). Turn left on Ashland and go two blocks north to 45th Street. You will be passing through the Ashland Avenue shopping area. The major store is a **Goldblatt's** department store at the corner of 47th Street. On your right, just before you reach 45th Street, is a building that looks like a Spanish mission in the old Southwest. It is the **Immaculate Heart of Mary Vicariate** at 4515 S. Ashland. This Catholic parish serving the Mexican community has recently merged with the former Lithuanian parish, Holy Cross, at 46th and Hermitage. The building on Ashland is actually a series of storefronts with a common facade. The Mexican community built this church through generous contributions of money and volunteer labor in the late 1950s. It is still in use, and both churches of the parish are served by the Claretian Fathers, a missionary order.

(Q) Turn left at 45th Street and go three blocks west to Hermitage (1734 West). **Davis Square Park** will be on your right. Make a right turn on Hermitage and go two blocks north to 43rd Street. Davis Square Park opened in 1904. Its fieldhouse contains a boys' and a girls' gym, a library, meeting rooms, and showers. The park served as a rallying place for the Stock Yard Labor Council at the time of the First World War. On December 8, 1921 it was the scene of a riot between workers and the Chicago police during the packinghouse strike of that year.

(R) Turn right on 43rd Street and go east as far as you can, to Morgan Street in the heart of the old stockyards. As you drive along this stretch of the old stockyard area, you will see abandoned packinghouses to your left. These are all that remain of **Swift & Company's** Chicago operations. Supporters of the United Packinghouse Workers CIO referred to the corner of 43rd and Packers Avenue as **Union Square.** Detractors called it Red Square, referring to the radicalism of the union in the

488

Old Stone Gate, Exchange at Peoria, 1985. This gate was the original entrance to the Union Stock Yards. It was very likely built in 1879, and was probably designed by John W. Root. A two-story watchman's building stood to the south of the gate until the yards closed in 1971. Exchange Avenue originally ran through the center arch, but it was routed around the structure when the gate was made a landmark. (J. Ficner)

1930s and 1940s. It was here that mass meetings were often held. When you cross Racine Avenue (1200 West), you will actually be in the area that made up the Union Stock Yards until August 1, 1971, when the yards closed forever. To your left is AMPAC, the last packinghouse left on former yard's property. The building once served as Armour and Company's garage and employee gymnasium. Far to the south at 46th Street is all that remains of the Hammond Packing Company. Part of this huge building is still used for cold storage, but most of it lies vacant, another reminder of the technological changes that brought about the decline of Chicago as a meatpacking center.

(S) Turn left at Morgan Street and go one block north to Exchange Avenue (4124 South), make a right on Exchange and go east to Halsted Street. At Exchange and Peoria stands the **old stone gate.** This triple-arched entranceway is a historical landmark attributed to Burnham and Root, which replaced an older wooden gate in 1875. The original watchman's building, which stood next to the gate to the south, was demolished in 1971 when the yards closed. Originally eastbound traffic passed through the main arch of the gate as it left the yards.

(T) Turn right at Halsted and go seven blocks south to 47th Street. The old **Livestock National Bank** building stands at the northwest corner of Exchange and Halsted facing an empty lot to the south where the famous Stock

Yard Inn once stood. Just beyond the lot stands the **International Amphitheatre,** once one of the largest and most widely used convention and exhibit places in the nation. It has held several national political conventions, perhaps the most famous being the 1968 Democratic Convention. The Amphitheatre also served as the home of the International Livestock Show and Rodeo until the early 1970s.

(U) Turn left at 47th Street, go two blocks and make another left at Union Avenue (700 West); go three blocks north on Union and then right on 45th Street. You are now in the Canaryville neighborhood. Like Back of the Yards, wooden frame buildings make up the majority of the housing stock in this area. After more than a century Irish Americans are still the dominant group in Canaryville. At the corner of 45th and Lowe stands **St. Gabriel's Catholic Church.** The legendary Father Maurice J. Dorney, known as "The King of the Yards," founded the parish in 1880. It was the first Catholic parish in the Town of Lake. The current church building was designed by John W. Root and consecrated in 1888. The 160-foot tower stands high above the neighborhood and remains a monument to Father Dorney and to the Irish immigrants who settled in Canaryville after the opening of the stockyards.

(V) Go one block east on 45th to Wallace (600 West); make a right turn and go four blocks south on Wallace to 47th Street. **McInerney's Funeral Chapel** at 4635 S. Wallace is a neighborhood and city institution. Founded in 1873, the parlor has been memorialized in a poem entitled "Bring Out the Lace Curtains" by T.J. O'Donnell. McInerney's hands out copies of this poem printed on the inside of matchbooks. The funeral parlor was a very important local institution in Canaryville and throughout the city. Undertakers served specific ethnic groups in immigrant neighborhoods, and they often expanded by opening new parlors in areas of second and third settlement. McInerney's, for example, has another funeral parlor at 79th and Komensky on the Southwest Side where many families from Canaryville now live.

Make a left at 47th Street and exit the Stock Yard District via the Dan Ryan Expressway just to the east.

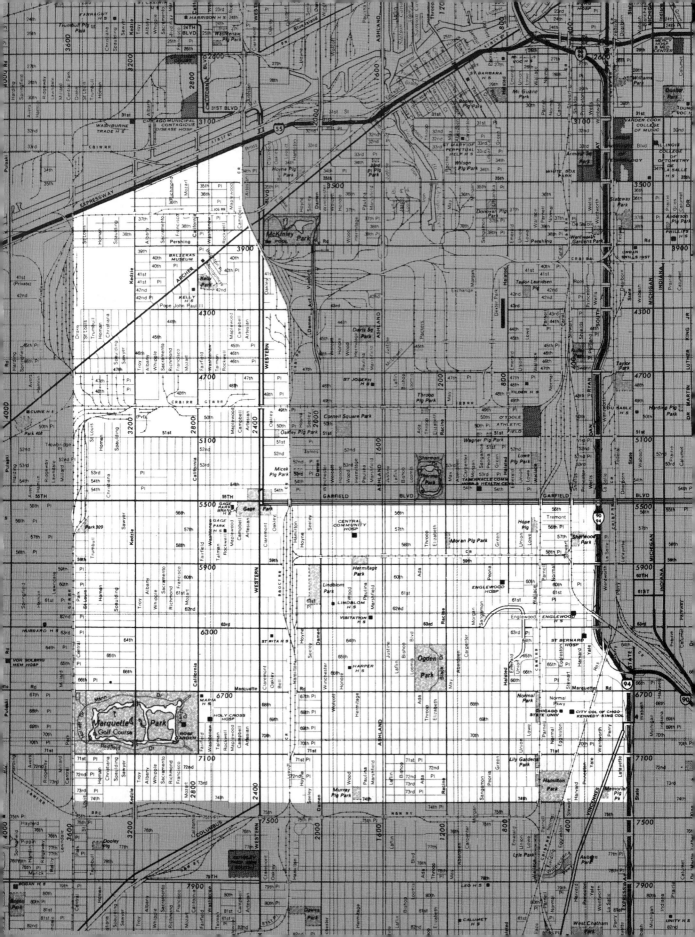

As the stockyards expanded and the neighborhoods around
them filled up with workers and their families, the area to
the south and west of the packinghouses also felt the impact
of the Industrial Revolution. To a large extent these
communities grew up as suburbs of the Stock Yard District.
They filled up with families who had left the immediate
yards area in search of better housing as they gained a
stronger foothold in Chicago. It is not surprising that
native-born whites, Irish and German Americans first
settled these areas. These are the people, of course, who had
made up the majority of residents in the early days in the
neighborhoods which adjoined the Union Stock Yards. After
a while they made their way down Halsted or 47th Street or
Archer Avenue to areas further removed from the dirt and
the noise of the yards. Soon the Poles and other Slavic
groups followed the Irish and Germans out to Englewood,
Gage Park, Marquette Park, and Brighton Park. The
institutions established in these neighborhoods, lying to the
south and southwest of the stockyards, vividly show the
ethnic migration away from the old economic heart of the
Southwest Side.

Marquette Park, Gage Park, and Brighton Park are
obviously neighborhoods of second settlement for many of
Chicago's white ethnic groups. The housing is newer, as are
the institutions that serve the various communities.
Englewood, on the other hand, has served as the destination
for two different migrations across the cityscape. The first
was composed of middle-class Anglo-Saxon Protestants,
followed in turn by Irish, Germans, and Swedes who moved
out of the Stock Yards District. The second major migration
occurred after World War II as large numbers of black people
moved into Englewood from neighborhoods to the east. All of
these groups followed the same basic migratory patterns
along the main streets and Garfield Boulevard. The history
of ethnic and racial change in Englewood has often been a
difficult one. The neighborhood also went through much
economic change, and different visions of its future have
complicated the tasks that residents have had to face to
make their neighborhood livable. It could be argued that this
resulted from the different urban migrations which crossed
each other's paths in Englewood.

The history of the Southwest Side is very much the
history of the movement of working-class and middle-class
people not only across the city, but up the economic ladder.

The Southwest Side benefited in the years after World War II by the development of industries other than the packinghouses. The Central Manufacturing District and other such developments widened the employment base of this part of the city. And yet today the area suffers from a loss of blue collar jobs, as Chicago continues to make the painful readjustment toward the service sector economy.

Englewood

The history of the area south of Garfield Boulevard and west of the Dan Ryan Expressway goes back to the 1840s when the first white settlers arrived. Englewood, like much of the South Side, was originally swamp and forestland. The community developed because of the railroads that crisscrossed it. In February 1852 the first steam engine cut across the district; it was owned by the Michigan, Southern, and Northern Indiana Railroad which laid tracks that year. Several months later the Rock Island Railroad was built, and 63rd and LaSalle Streets became known as Chicago Junction. The Wabash Railroad also arrived that year, and in 1854 the Fort Wayne Railroad joined it. Most of the early settlers in Englewood were German and Irish railroad workers, some of whom maintained truck farms, especially around what is today 63rd and Halsted. Residents, for the most part, lived along Junction Avenue, in an area called Junction Grove, now 63rd Street from Indiana to Halsted.

In 1860 local residents and developers looked at the Douglas community near the lake and saw that the establishment of the first University of Chicago there had created the type of community which they desired. So they began to seek a similar institutional base. The area at this time was still a suburb of Chicago and part of the Town of Lake, which was organized in 1865.

In 1868 community members got what they wanted when the Cook County Normal School opened on ten acres of land donated by L.W. Beck, a prominent land developer. This event changed the history of Junction Grove. The new school attracted a group of professionals and businessmen. In 1869 Beck subdivided the land to the southeast of the new Normal School, and over the next few years he further developed the land which surrounded the school.

The name Junction Grove, however, kept alive memories of the old railroad community. In 1868 Henry B. Lewis, a wool commission merchant on South Water Street and a member of both the Cook County and the Town of Lake Boards of Education, suggested the name of this part of the

Englewood High School, Chicago, Ill.   1016.

Town of Lake be changed to Englewood, since the area was heavily wooded. The name itself is supposedly derived from Englewood, New Jersey, and before that from Englewood Forest outside of Carlisle, England, which was the legendary home of Adam Bell, Clym of the Clough, and William of Cloudsley, outlaws before the time of Robin Hood. Influential professionals like Lewis felt that, like nearby Hyde Park, the name Englewood gave the image of middle-class prominence rather than lower-class railroad workers.

Within a few years the area became an important suburb of Chicago. Local institutional development occurred quickly. The first Presbyterian Mission was organized as early as 1860, and after the construction of the Normal School, congregations multiplied. In 1869 Catholics established the parish of St. Anne's, primarily for the remaining railroad community at 55th and Wentworth. Soon afterwards there was an "explosion" of Protestant parishes. Within six years Baptist, Methodist, Universalist, Episcopalian, Swedish Lutheran, German Evangelical, Unitarian, and Congregational churches opened in Englewood. More schools were built, and in 1873 Englewood High School opened its doors. Civic organizations sprang up. Many of the new settlers were veterans of the Civil War, and in February 1880 a Union Veterans Club was organized with twenty-five members.

Englewood High School, c.1910. The original Englewood High School building was constructed in 1887 before the neighborhood became part of Chicago. The Neo-Gothic structure gives a hint to the upper-class pretensions of the district's early residents.
(C.R. Childs, courtesy G. Schmalgemeier)

Byrne Building, southwest corner Halsted and Garfield Boulevard, c.1909. This huge building stood on this corner until the late 1960s providing housing and business rentals to the community. The spire in the background is that of Visitation Catholic Church.
(Courtesy G. Schmalgemeier)

What had begun as a small settlement of railroad workers and truck farmers changed within ten years to a prosperous middle-class community. The squatters and truck farmers gradually moved away and the oak woods were chopped down. While a pocket of working-class settlers remained to work at industrial developments to the north, the fundamental nature of the community had changed.

Meanwhile, the stockyards opened just to the north in 1865. Farmers brought their livestock on hoof to the yards, often down Halsted Street. This traffic encouraged taverns to open on 63rd Street to serve the drovers as they made their way north. A small shopping district for residents also developed. The railroad lines which gave birth to the neighborhood provided easy transportation to and from Chicago and to other parts of the South Side. This transportation connection, which centered on 63rd Street, meant that the area's commercial enterprises were ideally located for further expansion in the Chicago market.

Perhaps more than any other, the northeast corner of 63rd and Halsted exemplifies the history and development of the Englewood shopping district. In 1887 the horsecar line had just reached 63rd Street. That year the northeast corner of 63rd and Halsted Streets was sold for the then unheard of price of $50 a front foot or $13,750 for the entire lot. In 1889 the Boldenweck Dry Goods store opened on the property in a magnificently constructed brownstone building. This was the same year that Englewood, along with the rest of the Town of Lake, became a part of Chicago. It was also the year that Richard W. Sears decided that country banking was not for him, and he returned to Minneapolis to found Sears, Roebuck & Company's mail order business. 1889 was also the year that Louis Becker, a general store owner in Goshen, Indiana, left for Chicago to find his fortune. He became associated with Morris Rosenwald, brother of Julius Rosenwald, who would lead Sears, Roebuck & Co. through its greatest period of expansion. Becker and Rosenwald eventually gave up their mail order business, and in 1901 Becker bought the retail store on 63rd and Halsted Streets from Simeon Lederer. In 1901 John Ryan joined the business, and for thirty-two years the Becker-Ryan Store flourished in the building which had been constructed in 1889.

The Becker-Ryan building contained other offices and businesses. Mahoney Brothers' Saloon occupied the corner; a Chinese restaurant rented the ground floor. Justice of the Peace Peter Caldwell held court on the third floor until about 1895. Becker-Ryan purchased the land which fronted 124 feet on 63rd and 167 feet on Halsted Street from Edward A. Uihlein of the Schlitz Brewing Company in 1919 for about $585,000. This was more than forty-two times what speculators had paid for it thirty-two years earlier. The period was marked by economic growth, and 63rd and Halsted Streets took off as a regional shopping district. The Englewood "L" opened in 1907, and surface transit lines converged on the neighborhood. In 1920 over 86,000 people lived in Englewood. Yet the corner of 63rd and Halsted was still to see more changes in the future.

In 1934, at the height of the Great Depression, the Becker-Ryan building closed, not as a sign of economic disaster but as a symbol of growth. For Sears, Roebuck & Co. had announced that a new $1,500,000 retail store would be built on the site. The giant mail order firm headed by Julius Rosenwald had purchased the capital stock of the Becker-Ryan Company in 1929 from a syndicate which had acquired it four years earlier. Sears purchased and leased other properties for its block-long building, including the property of the Chicago City Bank and Trust Company, for which Sears paid $8,000 per front foot on Halsted Street in 1931. This was 160 times what speculators had paid for nearby property in 1887.

Such growth in the midst of economic stagnation resulted from the continued development of the Englewood shopping district. By the end of the 1920s, 63rd and Halsted was the second busiest intersection in the city. It was the regional shopping center for the entire South and Southwest Sides. In many ways it was the forerunner of today's

63rd and Halsted Streets, looking southwest, 1948. This corner was the heart of the Englewood shopping strip. Local boosters claimed this intersection was the second busiest in the city. Several transit lines converged at or near this corner making the intersection easily accessible to urban shoppers.

(R. Stevens, courtesy Chicago Historical Society)

suburban shopping malls. The major difference was that its prosperity was based on the streetcar, elevated, and interurban transit lines that moved people across the city. 63rd and Halsted was an easy place to get to.

Success meant change. The elevated lines gave impetus to the construction of apartment buildings in Englewood's eastern section. The district west of Halsted Street developed as a working-class neighborhood. Most of the residents there were Irish and German packinghouse workers who were moving up the ladder at the stockyards and moving out of the Back of the Yards and Canaryville. Many of these newcomers in the 1880s, 1890s, and early 1900s were Roman Catholics. Englewood's Protestant majority opposed this "change" in the neighborhood, but could do little about it. Many of the older families, in turn, moved on to Beverly. By 1920 Catholics dominated Englewood, supporting magnificent parochial complexes such as St. Martin's, St. Bernard's, and Visitation, which were among the city's most prosperous parishes.

Although the building of the Sears store marked large-scale growth, the Depression hit the little Englewood businessman hard. Practically all of Englewood's banks collapsed early in the economic crisis. Real estate declined in

63rd Street looking east towards Halsted, 1985. This photograph shows the mall which replaced the busy traffic arteries which dominated this part of Englewood until the 1970s. (J. Ficner)

value and appearance. Much of 63rd Street east of Halsted was an entertainment area. The Depression hurt these enterprises despite the lifting of prohibition.

At this time the Irish, German, and Swedes dominated the community. Also living in the area were considerable numbers of English, Welsh, and families of Dutch descent. Some Poles and Croatians lived in Englewood, but most of them lived west of Racine Avenue. The great majority of residents were members of highly mobile ethnic groups. They could move out quickly if the need or opportunity presented itself. There were also two small black communities in Englewood, one located on the western border, the other on the eastern border of the neighborhood.

As in so many other neighborhoods, the outbreak of World War II meant considerable change for Englewood. First, due to a lack of manpower and materials, the area's real estate continued to deteriorate. Since the district had been residentially mature for forty years, many homes were considerably older than that. Second, the wartime emergency brought another migration of blacks from the South. Most settled in the already crowded neighborhoods to the east, but the expanding Black Belt population began to move into Englewood.

Just as Protestant settlers had resisted the coming of Catholics to Englewood after the 1880's, now Catholic residents tried unsuccessfully to halt black immigration. In 1940 blacks made up 2.2 percent of Englewood's population. Ten years later, 10.5 percent of the residents were black. By 1960 the community was 68.9 percent black. Today Englewood is nearly 100 percent black. Like the founding Protestant residents who moved on, the Irish and Germans moved southwest, many to Beverly, Mount Greenwood, and to the suburbs beyond.

The neighborhood's racial change did not take place without hostility. Riots, fighting, even bombings occurred, but change happened nevertheless. The key which unlocked the barrier to change was the fact that many residents were economically mobile. They could and did move out. Unsurprisingly, the last sections to undergo racial change were the white working-class areas where families lived who could least afford to move. Caught in the transition swirling about them, lower middle-class and poor families of both races were hurt in the panic of block busting. The results were classic, one by one blocks turned from white to black.

Along with racial change came a continuing decline in the housing stock. Local leaders pushed for government aid, and the big stores like Sears, Wieboldt's, and others attempted to keep the shopping district alive. By 1960, however, the strip along 63rd and Halsted Streets was a slum. The Englewood Businessmen's Association and local leaders led a fight to designate the strip a conservation area. It was so designated, and for the first time a shopping strip was helped by the Department of Urban Renewal. Plans were drawn up for a concourse mall. The businessmen's association claimed that 750,000 shoppers could be attracted. Homes were torn down for parking lots and traffic was banned from the street. The mall was dedicated on October 15, 1969. Despite all the plans and new development, further decline ensued.

At the time the mall opened, Englewood still attracted outside shoppers. The final decline of the shopping district began when shoppers were attracted to outlying regional centers. The first to have an impact was the Evergreen Shopping Center on 95th Street and Western Avenue, which served the area that many former Englewood residents had moved to. Another competitor, the Ford City Shopping Center to the southwest, opened in the 1960s. The mall's attempt to compete with these larger shopping centers proved unsuccessful. Sears, Wieboldt's, and other stores in the area closed. Today small shops are being refurbished on the northeast corner of 63rd and Halsted for use by local residents.

Englewood exemplifies an urban neighborhood that benefited from technological advances in transportation. Ultimately it was bypassed by more sophisticated transportation technology and it declined. The upwardly mobile middle-class people who lived in Englewood in 1940 could afford cars after the wartime shortage; and cars allowed them to move to newer housing. As racial change took place, it forced the middle-class population to run to the suburbs. Mass transit created the Englewood shopping district. The auto subsequently allowed shoppers to travel easily to the suburban malls. When given the choice between an increasingly black, integrated Englewood or white neighborhoods with amenities like shopping malls, the white middle-class moved on. Englewood is a microcosm of a racial problem that has plagued Chicago for years, making it one of the most segregated cities in the nation.

Gage Park - Marquette Park

To the southwest of Back of the Yards and west of Englewood lies a community of mixed ethnicity that originally served as a suburb of the the Stock Yard District. The area south of 51st Street to the Belt Line Railroad tracks south of 71st street and west of Western Avenue to Central Park Avenue consists of several neighborhoods. Generally speaking, however, these residential areas share much of a common history and are considered to be closely related by the rest of the city. The census bureau refers to the area south of 59th Street as Chicago Lawn, but residents more often use the name Marquette Park. The area north of 59th Street is known as Gage Park. Moreover, local organizations often treat both areas as part of the same community.

This section of the Southwest Side has had a tumultuous recent history. Race relations have been uneasy, and the district is known for the conflicts that have, on occasion, erupted over black-white issues. Nevertheless the Gage Park—Marquette Park area remains a relatively stable residential community which boasts a good degree of institutional development. The area has given birth to several organizations that are working for residential stability and economic growth.

This part of Chicago developed relatively late. Most of the district was originally marshland, and residents often referred to the northern part of it as "Little Venice." Early settlers included a group of German farmers. George W. Gage owned much of the property in the eastern section of the future Gage Park community area. This land began to rise in value when a rumor circulated that the South Park District planned to establish a park at Garfield Boulevard (55th Street) and Western Avenue. In 1873 land for the park was purchased, and it became the southwest corner of a series of parks and boulevards which circled the city. The Gages continued to own much of the land south of the new park. In 1877 the heirs to the Gage estate defaulted on a loan, and multimillionaire real estate speculator Hetty Green took title to the land. She kept the area undeveloped until 1911 when her son sold the land to the Bartlett Realty Company which began a subdivision known as Marquette Manor. This development and one farther to the southwest, known as Chicago Lawn, provided the two economic centers from which the neighborhood later developed.

Developers James Webb and John Eberhart organized a model community near 63rd and Central Park Avenue in 1876. The Chicago and Southern Railroad connected what was then a suburban community with the city. Purchasers of homes in the new Chicago Lawn development were given three-year passes on the railroad. About forty structures stood on the prairie by 1885. Chicago Lawn, like much of the Southwest Side, remained a part of the Town of Lake until it was annexed to the City of Chicago in 1889.

There were reasons for the late development of the Near Southwest Side, which were related to the growth of industry and mass transportation. The fact that the Green interests did not allow the land in Gage Park to be subdivided until 1911 slowed up the development of the area. The general economy of the Southwest Side was closely related to that of the Union Stock Yards. It was in that immediate vicinity that most of the residential development took place. Later, as skilled and managerial personnel began to look for better housing, the Gage Park—Marquette Park area seemed ready for development.

At the turn of the century, streetcar lines reached out to the Near Southwest Side, but large scale development had not yet taken place. The population of the Town of Lake remained concentrated in the Stock Yard District. In 1905 when the Augustinian priests, a Catholic teaching order, announced that they would build a large church and a college at 63rd and Oakley, there were few potential parishioners in the neighborhood. Only seven Catholic families, or about fifty people, resided in the neighborhood south of 59th Street between Kedzie and Damen Avenues. While the Augustinians dedicated St. Rita College (St. Rita High School) at 6310 S. Claremont on April 22, 1906, the parish of St. Rita of Cascia did not build its church on 63rd Street until 1916. The Augustinians celebrated Mass for Southwest Side Catholics in the school chapel for ten years.

Apartment house, 67th and Marquette Park, c.1920. This building is typical of many constructed in Chicago around the time of World War I. The courtyard design enabled middle-class Chicagoans to enjoy maximum sunlight and fresh air while enabling developers to build a large structure on a limited amount of land.

(P.L. Huckins, courtesy G. Schmalgemeier)

The parish opened its grammar school in 1916 staffed by the Dominican Sisters of Adrian, Michigan. By this time a larger Catholic population had settled in the neighborhood.

While St. Rita's was the mother parish of many Catholic parishes on the Southwest Side, St. Gall's at 55th and Kedzie in Gage Park actually opened earlier as a mission of St. Agnes' parish in Brighton Park. In 1890 Catholics in Elsdon, a small railroad workers' settlement, met for Mass in a cottage at 5151 S. St. Louis Avenue. Although a permanent pastor was assigned in 1899, St. Gall's grew slowly.

By World War I several small, distinct settlements were located in the Gage Park—Marquette Park area. The two major concentrations in the western section (west of Kedzie) were associated with the railroad line that passed through that district. Chicago Lawn was a planned community of larger homes. The Elsdon settlement consisted of small frame working-class cottages. While many Catholics settled in Elsdon, Protestants predominated in the Chicago Lawn area. Protestant congregations can be found throughout the Gage Park—Marquette Park area. Included among these are the Elsdon United Methodist Church, 5258 S. Christiana; the Chicago Lawn United Methodist Church, 3500 West 63rd Place; and the Chicago Lawn Presbyterian Church, 6210 S. St. Louis. The Elsdon church, founded in 1892 by a twenty-member congregation of railroad workers in the back of a saloon, had a mixed ethnic identity. Bohemians, however, seem to have been in the majority among the founders.

Bungalows, 5900 block S. Troy Street. 1985. These homes are typical of many constructed in Chicago during the 1920s. These single-family homes range from five to eight rooms. The "Bungalow Belt" attracted many upwardly mobile ethnic families both before and after the Depression.
(D. Pacyga)

After 1906 the priests at St. Rita's began to serve a rapidly expanding Catholic community. In 1909 the Augustinians opened two missions in the area and built a new church for the parish of St. Gall. The parishes of St. Clare of Montefalco at 55th and Washtenaw and St. Nicholas of Tolentine at 62nd and Lawndale both trace their histories to this period when Irish, German, Bohemian, and other Catholics began to move southwest out of the Stock Yard District. That area, meanwhile, changed from a basically German and Irish community to one that was increasingly Slavic in character. All three of these churches represent the ethnic diversity of the area. Their parishioners are of mixed ethnic backgrounds. For the most part, this has been the history of the Near Southwest Side. The area was a neighborhood of second settlement where many different ethnic groups lived after making their first settlement in the Stock Yard District. To a large extent this ethnic mix is a legacy of the early twentieth century.

World War I created a housing boom in the area. In 1905, 575 residential structures stood in the Gage Park area. Fifteen years later nearly 14,000 people lived in the neighborhood. By 1920 the Germans and the Irish began to move on. Poles and Bohemians predominated in the area north of 59th Street as they claimed the better jobs in the stockyards. This population explosion continued to involve the entire Gage Park—Marquette Park area. In 1920 the district south of 59th street also had a population of about 14,000. This jumped to 47,462 ten years later! North of 59th Street the residents numbered 31,535 in 1930. By the beginning of the Great Depression both Gage Park and Marquette Park (Chicago Lawn) had reached residential maturity and were successful urban neighborhoods.

The housing which corresponded with this population increase consisted, for the most part, of brick homes, mostly brick bungalows. Gage Park—Marquette Park is one segment of the huge bungalow belt that grew up in the outlying neighborhoods of Chicago in the prosperous 1920s.

The 1920s saw the continued movement of ethnic groups out of Back of the Yards and other parts of the Stock Yard District into the neighborhoods of the Southwest Side. In 1926 Slovak Catholics organized St. Simon's parish at 52nd and California Avenue. Lithuanians, meanwhile, moved into the Marquette Park area in large enough numbers to create the Nativity of the Blessed Virgin Mary parish at 69th and Washtenaw in the far southeastern part of the district in 1927. Today this congregation of 2,500 families is considered to be the largest Lithuanian parish outside of Lithuania. It is the heart of the large ethnic community that lives in the Marquette Park neighborhood east of California Avenue. Other groups also moved into the area. On 53rd Street just west of Western Avenue stands a fine example of Byzantine architecture. St. Peter and Paul Carpatho-Russian Orthodox Church serves a part of Gage Park's Slavic community. A predominantly Polish American congregation of Catholics organized St. Turibius Parish in 1927 on 57th and Karlov in the western part of the community. All of these churches represent the outward movement of ethnic groups from the Stock Yard District. In 1930 about twenty-five percent of the population of Marquette Park was foreign born. The concentration of foreign-born people was even higher in Gage Park, north of 59th street.

Other institutions, like Talman Home Federal Savings and Loan, founded by Ben F. Bohac, a Czech American, in 1922 at 51st and Talman, also reflect this ethnic movement.

The combined population of the Gage Park and Marquette Park areas in 1930 was 78,997. While the decade of the Great Depression saw a decline in Gage Park's population from 31,535 to 30,343, the Marquette Park or

Chicago Lawn community area rose from 47,462 to 49,291. Gage Park's population continued on a downward trend from 1930 on. The Marquette Park area, however, continued to grow until 1960, when it reached its population peak of 51,347. It declined to 46,568 residents by 1980.

This demographic history has much to do with the economic and social history of the two communities. Gage Park and Marquette Park had originally developed as "suburbs" of the Stock Yard District. Various ethnic groups entered the area during the first thirty years of the twentieth century. The Southwest Side is a classic example of a second settlement area, neighborhoods to which established ethnic groups migrated after a period of residence in Chicago. To a certain extent they originally benefited from the upward mobility of ethnics from the older industrial neighborhoods like Bridgeport and Back of the Yards. By the 1950s and 1960s, however, Marquette Park began to grow from the effects of white ethnic flight from neighborhoods to the east, especially Englewood and West Englewood. This in-migration from racially changing communities offset the natural movement of the ethnic middle class within Marquette Park and Gage Park themselves.

In the mid-1960s civil rights coalitions made Gage Park and Marquette Park the object of open housing marches. Dr. Martin Luther King, Jr. marched into these neighborhoods, which greeted him with mob violence. Racial conflict also erupted over the integration of Gage Park High School. For a period of time, the American Nazi Party occupied headquarters in the Marquette Park area on 71st Street. This hate organization, along with the Ku Klux Klan, attempted to make political progress by playing on the racial fears of the neighborhoods on the Southwest Side. They had little success. Few local ethnics, many of whom had suffered or saw their relatives suffer under Nazi oppression during World War II, supported these groups. In the late 1970s racial conflict broke out again over another series of open housing marches. Although racial conflict in the area occasionaly makes the evening news, times have definitely changed.

Southwest Side ethnics have seen the cycle of integration and resegregation occur repeatedly in the neighborhoods east of Western Avenue. While racism played a role in their reaction to the open housing marches, so did economic fear. Perhaps a more important fear was that their sense of community would be lost through racial integration. Unlike Hyde Park—Kenwood, the Southwest Side did not have a major institution like the University of Chicago to protect it. Nor did it have powerful financial institutions to come to its aid, as did the Loop and the Near North Side. With some justification, working-class whites on the Southwest Side felt that they stood alone and were being sacrificed by powerful groups in other parts of the city. This feeling of abandonment was just as powerful a force as racism on the Southwest Side.

Today several neighborhood organizations are working to stabilize and renew the Gage Park—Marquette Park area. The Southwest Community Congress, the Southwest Parish and Neighborhood Federation, and the Greater Southwest Development Corporation (DEVCORP) have all attempted to put an end to the racial violence of the past two decades. These groups have often been divided among themselves by ideology and politics, but over the last few years they have put together a coalition that is designed to create a vital stable community.

In 1983 the Southwest Parish Federation convinced the State of Illinois to arrange for the American City Corporation to conduct a feasibility study for the redevelopment of 63rd Street from Bell to Central Park Avenue. The 63rd Street Growth Commission, which acts as an umbrella organization, is today attempting to implement this plan which calls for the revitalization of the shopping strip as an ethnic shopping center. Critics, including some community members, have called this plan racist. However, blacks patronize shops in the area and it is likely that they will continue to do so in the future. Sixty-third Street remains one of the few vital commercial districts bordering the Englewood area.

Meanwhile the Gage Park—Marquette Park area continues to act as an area of second settlement for Chicago's ethnic groups. Just as Eastern and Southern Europeans followed the Western European ethnics out of the older industrial neighborhoods after 1900, now newer groups are following them. A quick trip down 63rd Street reveals a large number of Arab restaurants, groceries, and businesses. Hispanics, too, have left Back of the Yards to move into this traditional community of second settlement. They are simply doing what the English, Irish, Germans, Poles, and Lithuanians did before them. To a large extent this in-movement of Arab and Hispanic families has offset the continuing out-migration of European ethnic families to the far Southwest Side and the suburbs. The result on 63rd Street is a fascinating mix of Lithuanian and Polish restaurants along with Arab and Mexican businesses, not to mention an occasional German bakery and delicatessen, or an Irish bar. It makes the Gage Park—Marquette Park area one of the most ethnically cosmopolitan in Chicago.

Brighton Park

Despite Brighton Park's location to the southwest of the Loop, its history predates its neighbors which are closer to the center of Chicago. The area originally consisted mostly of marsh and swampland, but as early as the mid-1830s developers were looking to the district for possible investment. The name Brighton first appeared in 1840 with the dedication of an unincorporated subdivision below 35th Street and west of the future Western Avenue. Real estate speculators hoped that the area would prosper as an industrial center. The land company that built the Blue Island Avenue Plank Road (Western Avenue) through the area incorporated the town of Brighton or Brighton Park in 1851. The name Brighton gives a hint to the future the developers envisioned for their community. Despite some people's claims that Brighton Park took its name from the Brighton Park Race Track built by John Wentworth on the present site of McKinley Park in the 1850s, the opposite seems to be true. An advertisement for the Town of Brighton which appeared in the early 1850s associated Chicago's Brighton with the Brighton markets in Boston, Cincinnati, and other cities. Brighton was also the name of the livestock market in London, England. In Chicago the name was closely connected with the livestock trade. Indeed the Blue Island Plank Road provided easy access to the city's packinghouses for outlying farmers. The advertisement cited above also mentions the Brighton Stockyards to be built on the corner of Archer and Western Avenue as a major attraction. All of this happened before Wentworth's race track opened.

Brighton Park, however, did not develop into the central livestock market for the Midwest, as early investors had hoped. Other stockyards soon competed with the Brighton market. Railroad lines coming into Chicago made other locations more profitable. The Sherman yards on 29th Street and Cottage Grove Avenue proved to be formidable competition for the Brighton market. In 1861 the owners of the Brighton yards tried to revive their business by hosting a state fair organized by the United States Agricultural Society. The fair failed, however, and the Brighton yards never fully recovered. At the close of the Civil War, a group of investors formed the Union Stock Yard and Transit Company and opened a huge new stockyard that would incorporate all of the older and smaller Chicago yards. When this new market opened just to the southeast of the Brighton yards on Christmas Day 1865, Brighton Park's future as a livestock market ended. The town fell under the influence of its

Brighton Park Police Station, southwest corner California and Pershing Road, c.1914. This station is still in operation today.
(C.R. Childs, courtesy G. Schmalgemeier)

neighbors to the east. Both the economic and demographic history of Brighton Park would subsequently be closely tied with the emerging Stock Yard District.

But other industries located in Brighton after the Civil War. Chief among these was the Laflin and Rand Company which manufactured explosives. On August 29, 1886 an explosion at the Laflin and Rand powder mill rocked the town. The next day a mass meeting of residents called for the removal of all powder mills from Brighton. The mills eventually moved to Blue Island, Illinois, several miles south of Brighton Park. Brickyards and other manufacturing plants remained in the area, however, providing a small, but growing industrial base.

The big change for the future prospects of Brighton Park occured in 1887 when the Santa Fe Railroad built its Corwith Yards at 35th Street and Central Park Avenue. These yards are still among the busiest in the nation. This important rail connection with the West meant that Brighton Park could look forward to continuing industrial growth as the twentieth century approached. This transportation link foreshadowed events in the early years of the twentieth century which would see Brighton Park develop into a major industrial neighborhood.

In 1889 Brighton Park joined the City of Chicago through resolution (north of 39th Street) and by an annexation election (south of 39th Street). This change sparked further land speculation in the neighborhood, and Brighton Park's population continued to grow.

The original settlers in this area included Germans and Irish. These two immigrant groups made up the majority of the population by the 1870s. In 1878 Roman Catholics organized the parish of St. Agnes. The church served Irish families who had moved southwest along Archer Road from Bridgeport. An abandoned powder mill served as the first church. The congregation grew, and a parochial school opened in 1884 under the direction of the Sisters of Mercy. Another teaching order, the Sisters of Providence, came to St. Agnes in 1889.

That same year French Catholics requested and received permission to establish a national parish in Brighton Park. The French formerly worshiped at the church of St. Jean Baptiste at 33rd Place and Wood Street. On November 3, 1889 the French celebrated Mass in Farrell Larney's Hall on 38th Street as the congregation of St. Joseph. The French Provincial Gothic church which stands today at the corner of 38th Place and California Avenue was dedicated in 1892. In 1900 the parish established the Shrine of St. Anne de Brighton Park and celebrated a special novena to the saint. Shortly thereafter the parish changed its name to St. Joseph and St. Anne.

German Lutherans attended services at St. Andrew's Church in neighboring McKinley Park until they organized Peace Lutheran Church in 1902. Their present church dates from 1911 and is located on the southwest corner of 43rd and California Avenue. Many of the German immigrants worked in the packinghouses which were located adjacent to the Union Stock Yards to the east. These skilled butchers moved west along 43rd and 47th Streets to Brighton Park. The neighborhood was already beginning to act like a suburb of the Stock Yard District. The more mobile ethnic groups tended to move further away from the stockyards in search of better housing and a cleaner environment. Eastern Europeans replaced the Irish and the Germans in the Back of the Yards neighborhood by the 1890s. The movement of these older groups into Brighton Park was a natural result of their upward mobilty and of neighborhood succession. Eastern Europeans soon followed and challenged the dominance of the Irish and Germans in Brighton Park.

After 1900 Poles and Lithuanians began to move into the neighborhood. By 1908 enough Polish families lived in Brighton Park to request the establishment of a Polish Roman Catholic parish. In November of that year Rev. Joseph H. Kruszka organized the parish of Five Holy Martyrs at 43rd and Richmond Streets, the third Catholic congregation to be founded in the neighborhood. Six years later sixty Lithuanian families asked permission to form a

Brighton Park Housing, 1985. This row of two-flats was built in the 1920s as part of the housing boom of that decade. Stockyard workers in search of better homes made their way west along 47th and 43rd Streets to the Brighton Park neighborhood. (J. Ficner)

parish of their own. These people first celebrated Mass in the basement of the French church. But their parish soon prospered, and they built a church of their own, Immaculate Conception, at 44th Street and California Avenue. A Lithuanian parochial school opened in 1916. The Sisters of St. Casimir staffed it in 1922. Like the Germans and Irish before them, Poles and Lithuanians moved west from Back of the Yards in large numbers. Another Polish Catholic church, St. Pancratius, opened in 1924 to serve Polish families living north of Archer Avenue. A Polish National Catholic Parish, St. John's, also opened in the neighborhood at 4555 S. Kedzie.

The various ethnic groups continued to be attracted to Brighton Park by the industry developing around the Santa Fe yards and by the better housing available in the neighborhood. Moreover, excellent public transportation linked the neighborhood to the center of the city and to the Stock Yard District. Both of these factors, industry and transportation, made Brighton Park attractive for working-class and lower-middle-class families. And so Brighton Park became a boom town in the first three decades of the twentieth century.

Industry expanded throughout the Chicago area at this time; but Brighton Park was in an especially good position to benefit from it. The Chicago stockyards continued to be a major employer of its residents. As the meatpacking industry expanded, so did the population of Brighton Park. The opening of the Central Manufacturing District in 1905 also provided jobs for the people of Brighton Park. In 1915 the Crane Manufacturing Company moved to 41st and Kedzie from its old location at 15th and Canal. Meanwhile, the Kenwood Manufacturing District opened on the southern boundary of the neighborhood.

The 1920s saw a continuing expansion of the housing stock in Brighton park. More and more families came to the area. Back of the Yards had already achieved residential maturity, and its wooden housing was crowded and in poor condition. Brighton Park provided an attractive alternative for upwardly mobile working-class families. The neighborhood also offered alternate employment for workers. Developers constructed much of Brighton Park's housing stock during this period to attract working-class families. Row after row of brick two-flats appeared on the side streets of the district. The first of these appeared before World War I, but the real building boom took place afterwards in the relatively prosperous 1920s. In 1930 Brighton Park reached its peak population with 46,552 residents. Poles formed the largest ethnic group, accounting for thirty-seven percent of all the residents.

The population of Brighton Park went into a gradual decline after 1930. By 1980, census figures showed that 30,770 people lived in this community. Foreign-born persons made up 20.6 percent of the residents. The largest percentage of these continued to be Poles and Lithuanians, though Hispanics make up a growing percentage of neighborhood people. The post-World War II immigration of Poles and Lithuanians replenished the populations of these two ethnic communities in Brighton Park. The Poles at St. Pancratius Church dedicated a new house of worship in 1959, and their co-ethnics at Five Holy Martyrs remodeled their church in 1964. Lithuanians built the new parish church of Immaculate Conception that same year. This new construction demonstrates the continuing vitality of ethnic working-class neighborhoods in Chicago.

Five Holy Martyrs parish hosted Pope John Paul II's Mass for the Polish community of Chicago on October 5, 1979. Over seventeen thousand people attended the outdoor Mass which the Pope celebrated in the parking lot of the Polish parish. In honor of His Holiness' visit, the city renamed 43rd Street from Western Avenue to Kedzie Avenue Pope John Paul II Drive.

The ethnic diversity of Brighton Park is still one of its great attractions. The major shopping strip along Archer

Five Holy Martyrs Church, southeast corner Richmond and Pope John Paul II Drive, 1985. This parish is the center of Brighton Park's Polish Catholic community. Polish Masses are offered every Sunday morning at 7:15 and 11:00. This photo shows the crowd at the 11:00 o'clock liturgy. (J. Ficner)

Avenue boasts Polish, Lithuanian, and other ethnic shops. The Balzekas Museum of Lithuanian Culture is located at 4012 S. Archer Avenue in the community, and the Polish Highlanders Alliance of North America built its Chicago headquarters on the same street in the western part of the neighborhood in the early 1980s. The Highlanders' building resembles a mountain chateau in the Polish Tatra Mountains. The Polka Music Hall of Fame and Museum is located on Kedzie Avenue.

Brighton Park, however, faces the same uncertain future that all old industrial neighborhoods in Chicago do. The Crane Company is gone. The piggyback yards of the Santa Fe Railroad replaced the massive plant in the early 1980s. Still the neighborhood is well situated and well served by public transportation. Like neighboring McKinley Park, the housing stock is solid and reasonably priced. The ethnic population is stable, and the neighborhood enjoys a good deal of residential loyalty. Since the closing of the yards in 1971, Brighton Park no longer looks to the Stock Yard District for its future. Today the neighborhood looks to the Loop as its major source of employment, and the Archer Avenue bus line continues to be a vital link between Brighton Park and the downtown business district.

Archer Avenue and Chinatown

The Chicago street system, for the most part, is a based on a grid. There are several streets in the city, however, which do not conform to this pattern. On the Southwest Side, Archer Avenue is a major diagonal thoroughfare which cuts a southwestern path across the South Side beginning at State Street near 19th Street. Archer Road was originally a path along the South Branch of the Chicago River and along the Illinois and Michigan Canal leading to Joliet. It was used to supply the workers digging the canal in the twelve-year period between 1836 and 1848. Colonel William Archer, the engineer of the canal project, gave his name to the street. Archer Avenue became a major entryway into the city from the southwest. Drovers herded livestock along the road to the slaughterhouses that were located in Bridgeport in the 1860s, and farmers used it to bring their produce to market. Stores, taverns, and hotels sprang up along the road to serve the procession of people who were coming to Chicago.

Indeed, the Archer Avenue corridor has long served Chicagoans as a gateway to the southwest. The South Branch of the Chicago River, which parallels Archer Avenue, provided the original path of discovery for Europeans. Father Jacques Marquette and Louis Jolliet traveled the river and used the portage to the southwest in 1673. This waterway provided a natural connection between the Mississippi River and the Great Lakes. Accordingly, it became a popular passageway for the French fur traders and explorers in the seventeenth and eighteenth centuries.

In the nineteenth century the canal was built, and the railroads soon paralleled the canal, providing yet another important means of transportation along the Archer Avenue corridor. In the twentieth century still another form of transportation joined the river, the street, and the railroad. Namely, the Stevenson Expressway, which was built by the federal government in the 1960s. The Archer Avenue corridor still serves Chicago as its major outlet to the southwest.

Many of the ethnic groups of the South and Southwest Sides used Archer Avenue as an escape route from the inner-city. In Bridgeport, the Irish who worked on the Illinois and Michigan Canal organized the parish of St. Bridget at 2940 S. Archer in 1850. As they moved further west to Brighton Park, they organized St. Agnes Church. The Poles followed the Irish down Archer Avenue, as did the Lithuanians, and then the Mexicans. Archer Avenue not only brought goods and produce into the city, but it also allowed people to search for better housing beyond the city's core.

The Chinese are one of the ethnic groups who live along Archer Avenue. They have not, however, used Archer Avenue as a route to the Southwest Side. Instead, they have stayed in the vicinity of Archer and Cermak and along Wentworth Avenue.

The neighborhood known today as Chinatown was not the first Chinese settlement in Chicago. The Chinese originally lived in the South Loop area. The federal government forced a large number of Chinese merchants and residents to leave the Loop in 1912 to make way for the construction of federal buildings in their old neighborhood. About fifty merchants made a contract through the H.O. Stone Company to lease stores in the Cermak and Wentworth area. They assumed ten-year leases totalling approximately $50,000 in annual rents. This Archer-Wentworth area originally included a large number of Italian, Irish, and German residents. The Italians still play an important role in the demographics of the area.

The Chinese who settled on Chicago's South Side tended to be connected with the On Leong Tong. The Hip Sing Tong dominated the downtown Chinatown. These two societies were involved in tong wars of one kind or another for some

Chinese Boy Scouts Parade, Wentworth Avenue, 1941. The Chinese presence in Chicago is most evident in Chinatown, near Archer and Wentworth. Here a group of Boy Scouts from St. Therese Chinese Catholic Mission parade down Wentworth Avenue.
(Courtesy The Chicago Catholic)

3,000 years. A Chicago resident, Chin Kung Fong, acted as an important mediator between the two rival factions. Today the On Leong Merchants Association is still headquartered in the ornate building on Wentworth Avenue just south of Cermak, which is often referred to as the Chinatown city hall.

Chinese Americans seem determined to stay in their famous enclave along Wentworth Avenue. A symbol of this determination is the Chinatown Gate which spans Wentworth Avenue at Cermak. Designed by Peter Fung, it is an important sign of Chinatown's prosperity. There has been considerable investment in Chinatown in recent years. Plans now include the possible expansion of the neighborhood into the old Santa Fe railroad yards north of Archer Avenue. Local government officials support this move into the old yards. Both Mayor Harold Washington and Alderman Fred Roti have asked the federal government not to consider the area as a site for a new post office complex.

Whatever the outcome of the redevelopment program, Chinatown remains a vital community. The Chinese have spilled over traditional boundaries into Italian and Croatian

禮 義 廉 耻

Armour Square and Bridgeport. Those neighborhoods may see more Chinese moving into them in the future if the Santa Fe yards project is not a success. A good deal of money continues to be invested here not only by Chinese Americans, but also by Hong Kong investors.

The Chinatown Gate, on Wentworth Avenue just south of Cermak Road, 1985. This dramatic symbol of Chinese-American pride and identity was erected in 1975.
(G. Lane)

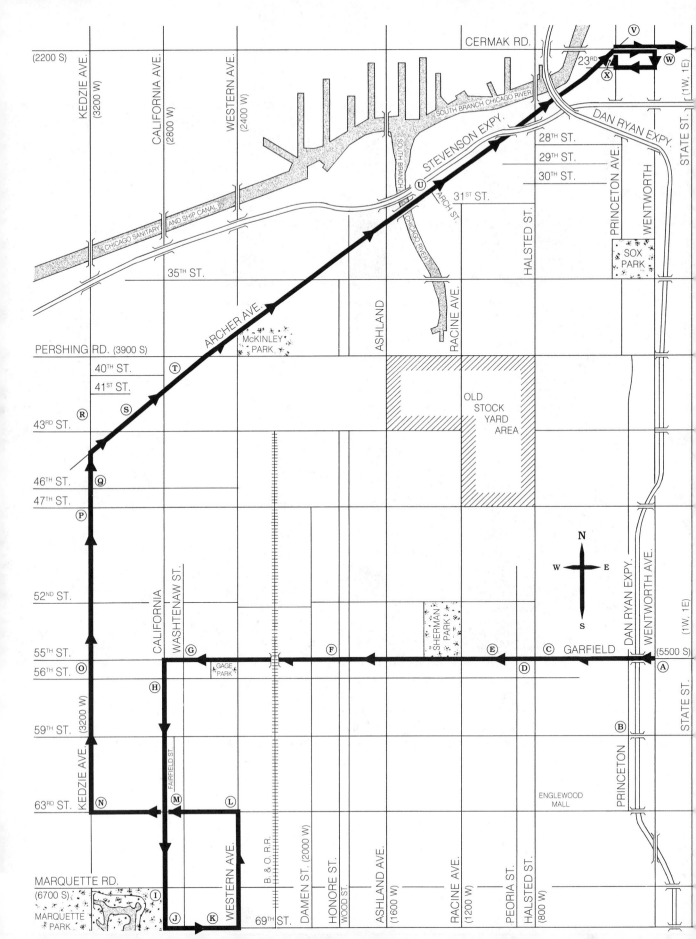

Near Southwest Side Tour

This tour begins in Englewood and makes its way through Marquette Park, Gage Park, and Brighton Park, ending with a trip up Archer Avenue into Chinatown.

Exit the Dan Ryan Expressway at Garfield Boulevard (5500 South) and go west on the boulevard. Turn right if you had been going south on the expressway. Turn left if you were driving north.

Driving time: about 2 hours.

(A) The church of **St. Charles Lwanga** overlooks the Dan Ryan from the southeast corner of Wentworth and Garfield. This black Catholic parish represents the consolidation of three South Side parishes in 1971, St. George, St. Cecilia, and St. Anne. Charles Lwanga was a Ugandan Christian who died a martyr for his faith in 1886. The church itself was built in 1880 for a predominantly Irish parish. St. Anne's was the first Catholic parish in Englewood when it was established about 1865 as a mission of St. James in the Douglas community. Soon afterward, the parish of St. Thomas the Apostle in Hyde Park took over the mission. The former Kehilath Anshe Ma'ariv synogogue, which stood at Adams and Wells Streets, was purchased and moved to 55th and Wentworth to serve as a Catholic church when the Jewish congregation moved into larger quarters. In 1870 St. Anne's received its first permanent pastor, Rev. Thomas F. Leydon. The parish's immediate neighborhood remained working-class in character throughout its entire history. Notice the wooden homes on Garfield Boulevard as you drive west. We will compare these homes to others just a few blocks farther west on the boulevard.

This is the first of several Catholic churches on Garfield Boulevard. They will help us trace the movement of ethnic groups across the Southwest Side, in particular the movement of Irish Americans.

St. Charles Lwanga Church, southeast corner Wentworth and Garfield Boulevard, 1985. Originally St. Anne's, this church was built in 1880 for the oldest Catholic parish in Englewood.
(G. Lane)

518

St. Martin Church, 59th and Princeton, 1980. This splendid example of German Gothic architecture was completed in 1895 by a German Catholic community in Englewood. (G. Lane)

(Below) O'Leary mansion, Sweeney home, and former Chicago Bicycle Club, 700 block W. Garfield Boulevard, 1985. These houses reflect the quality homes which lined Garfield Boulevard. (G. Lane)

(B) Four blocks south of Garfield Boulevard and one block west of the Dan Ryan stands the magnificent **St. Martin Catholic Church** at 5848 S. Princeton. It is one of the finest examples of German Gothic architecture in the United States. The steeple, which you can see from Garfield and the Dan Ryan, rises 228 feet into the air. Originally named after St. Martin of Tours, the parish today also honors St. Martin de Porres, the black Dominican brother of Lima, Peru. German Catholics organized the parish in 1886 in what was then the suburb of Englewood. By the time the church was dedicated in 1895, Englewood was a Chicago neighborhood. Today St.Martin's is a very active black Catholic parish.

(C) Continue west on Garfield Boulevard. A group of three homes stands on the north side of the 700 block, just before Halsted. The first, at 718, is the former clubhouse of the **Chicago Bicycle Club.** Members of the club bicycled the Columbian Exposition's Midway in 1892. The building immediately to the west was the **home of Margaret Sweeney,** a popular radio entertainer. The last home, at 726, is the **O'Leary mansion** built by "Big Jim" O'Leary, the son of Mrs. O'Leary of Chicago Fire fame. Big Jim became "Chicago's real and only gambler king" at the turn of the century. His headquarters were located in his saloon across the street from the Union Stock Yards on 41st and Halsted. The actual gaming operations took place next door to the saloon in a building now occupied by the Stock Yards Hardware & Supply Company. The O'Learys moved to Canaryville after the Fire in 1871. Once Jim O'Leary had "made it" as an entrepreneur, he moved his family to Garfield Boulevard in Visitation parish. This geographic move also showed a rise in social status for the O'Leary family. Over the years a move to Garfield Boulevard, and to Englewood beyond it, was a sign of increased status for Stock Yard District families. This was especially true for Irish-American families from Canaryville, Bridgeport, and Back of the Yards.

(D) Continue one block west on Garfield Boulevard to Peoria (900 West). On the southeast corner of the intersection stands **Visitation Church.** The diocese established this parish in 1886 to serve the growing number of Irish Catholics south of 47th Street, east of Racine, and west of Wallace. These people were moving away from the older Stock Yard District to the newer developments in Englewood. The present Gothic church was dedicated in 1899. Visitation's boundaries have changed over time, as has the ethnicity and race of its parishioners. For many years Visitation was one of the largest parishes in Chicago. Although race riots broke out in this area in the late 1940s, the parish remained all white. In 1959, 2,155 students attended Visitation grammar school, and 1,100 girls attended the parish high school. Four years later racial strife broke out again after black families moved onto the 5600 and 5700 blocks of South Morgan Street. White families began to move out of the area. By 1966 the student population of the girls's high school had dropped to 761. Many of the families who left Visitation moved west to the Gage Park and Marquette Park communities. Others moved to Beverly and the southwest suburbs. Today the parish high school is closed, but the grammar school is still very active. The parish serves the Puerto Rican and black communities of the area, centering on Garfield Boulevard and Halsted Street.

Visitation Church, southeast corner Garfield and Peoria, 1985. The Celtic cross on the spire reflects the Irish origins of this parish, for many years one of the largest and most prominent Catholic parishes in the city. (G. Lane)

(E) Continue west on Garfield Boulevard. The boulevard contains many fine homes. Some of these date back to the 1890s; others are of more recent construction. All of them remind us of the time when Garfield Boulevard was the Gold Coast of the Stock Yard District. The materials used and the size of these homes differ signifiantly from those farther east on Garfield Boulevard near the Dan Ryan. The parish of St. Anne's (St. Charles Lwanga) always served a working-class population. Visitation, on the other hand, served Catholics of a higher economic status. The boulevard was the goal of many upwardly mobile families on the South and Southwest Sides.

St. Basil's Church, 1840 W. Garfield Boulevard, 1985. The present church opened in 1904. The first building to house the congregation was a blacksmith's shop at 53rd and Ashland. Today St. Basil's serves a mostly black and Hispanic congregation.

(A. Kezys)

(F) Continue west on Garfield Boulevard. You will pass **Sherman Park** on your right, named after the founder of the Chicago Stockyards, John Sherman. The park was built by the South Park commission in the early 1900s. It includes a lagoon stocked with fish and a branch of the **Chicago Public Library.** Just north of the park stands the large Polish Catholic church of **St. John of God.** This church contains the "weeping" Madonna, which became a center of attraction in the Catholic community in 1984 when "tears" inexplicably appeared on the face of the statue.

Irish Americans continued to move west from the parish of the Visitation along Garfield Boulevard. By the turn of the century enough Irish and German families had moved south from Back of the Yards to call for the establishment of another Catholic parish. In 1904 **St. Basil's** was established at Garfield Boulevard and Honore Street (1826 West). Construction of the present Byzantine-style church took place in 1925-26. The dome is modeled after that of Hagia Sophia in Constantinople. Poles, Italians, Croatians, Slovaks, Lithuanians, and other white ethnics moved into the parish in large numbers by the time of the Great Depression. In the late 1960s blacks began to arrive, and Garfield Boulevard underwent rapid racial change. At the present time St. Basil's is a mostly black and Latino community. The parish's newly-opened **Boulevard Arts Center** and a medical dispensary serve the neighborhood, which today includes many poor families.

(G) Continue fourteen blocks west to California Avenue (2800 West). As you go under the railroad overpass between Damen Avenue and Western Boulevard, you are entering the Gage Park community area. **Gage Park,** which gives the neighborhood its name, is located at Garfield and Western. It marks the southwest corner of the original plan for the South Park System. The South Park Commission purchased the land for the park in 1873.

Garfield Boulevard ends at Western Avenue. West of this point it is known as 55th Street, and it becomes a pleasant major thoroughfare lined with Chicago-style bungalows and brick two-flats. **Gage Park High School** and **Richards Vocational High School** are located just west of Western Avenue.

The church of **St. Clare of Montefalco** stands on the northeast corner of 55th and Washtenaw. It opened as a mission of St. Rita College in 1909. World War II presented a turning point for the parish and the community. The postwar period was one of tremendous growth for the neighborhood. Construction of the present church began in 1953. St. Clare's is an ethnically diverse parish. Many of the residents can trace their families back to older ethnic settlements in Back of the Yards and Bridgeport.

(H) Turn left on California and go twelve blocks south to Marquette Road (6700 South). You are driving through the heart of the Southwest Side's Bungalow Belt. Much of the land in the outlying neighborhoods of Chicago had not been developed before World War I. The "boom" times of the 1920s saw land speculators and developers reach out to these places on the prairie. In the 1920s some 20,000 bungalows were built in Chicago. The small single-family dwellings along California Avenue

Gage Park housing, 5500 block of S. Talman Avenue, 1985. These substantial brick two-flats, along with the single-family bungalows, are typical of the housing in Gage Park and Chicago Lawn. (G. Lane)

are typical of this construction. The Gage Park—Marquette Park area has an abundance of these structures. Some of the homes are quite impressive, ranging from huge bungalows to rather delicate Prairie-style stucco homes, such as those located south of 63rd Street and west of Kedzie Avenue. The side streets reveal some real surprises. Old Victorian homes, Prairie homes, and Cape Cod houses are mixed in with the standard bungalows in this residential district.

(I) Continue south on California Avenue to 69th Street. At the southwest corner of Marquette Road (6700 South) and California Avenue stands a monument which Chicago's Lithuanian community erected in 1934 in honor of two Lithuanian aviators, **Stephen Darius** and **Stanley Girenas,** who attempted to set a record by flying from New York to Kaunas, Lithuania in 1933. Unfortunately they crashed in Germany about four hundred miles short of their goal. The French-American artist, Raoul Josset, sculpted the reliefs.

Marquette Park Lithuanian Festival, Lithuanian Plaza Court, 1985. This annual summer event is the largest of its kind in Chicago. Lithuanian merchants, artists, and craftspeople display their goods along West 69th Street in the Marquette Park area.
(D. Pacyga)

Across from the park on the southeast corner stands **Maria High School.** The Sisters of St. Casimir founded the school as the St. Casimir Academy in 1911. It is a leading educational institution in the Lithuanian community and marks the beginning of the Lithuanian Plaza which covers several square blocks to the east of California Avenue. Included in the plaza are **Holy Cross Hospital,** dedicated in 1928, and the motherhouse of the Sisters of St. Casimir. The Lithuanian community is one of the best organized ethnic communities in Chicago.

(J) Turn left at **Lithuanian Plaza Court** and go eight blocks east to Western Avenue (2400 West). To your left stands the original building of Holy Cross Hospital (1925), which is still in use. Next to it, at the corner of Washtenaw, stands a beautiful example of Lithuanian architecture, the church of the **Nativity of the Blessed Virgin Mary.** This parish is named after the famous shrine to the Blessed Virgin at Siluva, Lithuania. Lithuanians in the Marquette Park area founded the

St. Rita of Cascia Church, northeast corner 63rd and Fairfield, 1985. This stately Romanesque church was dedicated in 1950. The parish, however, begun by Augustinian priests in 1905, has a very large grade school, established St. Rita High School, and founded four other parishes in the area.
(G. Lane)

parish in 1927. The present church, designed by John Mulokas, was dedicated in 1957. Mulokas incorporated Lithuanian folk architecture with a Baroque design. The result is as impressive an example of Lithuanian architecture as can be found in the United States.

(K) Continue east on **Lithuanian Plaza Court.** The small neighborhood commercial strip which runs from Washtenaw to Western Avenue includes Lithuanian-American restaurants, delis, taverns, and other businesses. The Lithuanian Homeowners Association of Marquette Park sponsors a Lithuania Festival on this street every summer. It is the largest gathering of its kind in Chicago, though Brighton Park Lithuanians also hold a festival during the summer on Western Boulevard and 44th Street.

(L) Turn left on Western and go six blocks north to 63rd
Street and make another left (west). Until recently
automobile dealerships predominated along this part of
Western Avenue. In the last few years some of them
have closed down, though many still remain. Except for
the car dealerships, this strip never developed as a
strong commercial zone. The best area was at the corner
of 63rd Street, where a movie house and a Sears store
provided an important anchor for the commercial strip.
A good amount of economic investment has taken place
recently in the 63rd and Western area, including the
construction of a new food store and drugstore, and the
expansion of the Sears outlet. **St. Rita High School** is
located just east of Western Avenue on 63rd Street.

Sixty-third Street itself has traditionally been the
major commercial district of this part of the South Side.
Many of the stores on 63rd Street were owned and
operated by European ethnic entrepreneurs. In recent
years Arab and Hispanic merchants have joined their
Italian, Lithuanian, Irish, German, and Jewish
neighbors in opening businesses. Some of the best Arab
food stores and restaurants are located here. Despite the
growth of Arab-American businesses, 63rd Street has
come upon hard times. Many of the storefronts are
vacant. A recent study of the strip by the American City
Corporation found it overbuilt for modern use. In reality,
63rd Street grew up under the influence of the streetcar.
The change in transportation habits to the automobile
has proved to be a problem for this strip. Over the years
there have been several attempts to revive 63rd Street,
but none have yet proved successful. A recent plan calls
for the establishment of an ethnic village type of
shopping district to prevent economic decline in the
surrounding neighborhoods. Only time will tell if such a
plan can be successful.

(M) Continue seven blocks west on 63rd Street to Fairfield
(2733 West). Between Washtenaw and Fairfield stands
the magnificent church of **St. Rita of Cascia.** This
parish is the mother parish of many Catholic
congregations on the Southwest Side. It was established
by the Augustinian Fathers in 1905 at the invitation of
Archbishop James A. Quigley. Cardinal Stritch dedicated
the present Romanesque church in 1950. It dominates

the surrounding neighborhood and 63rd Street with its high towers and stately entrance. The parish is a very active one. Although Irish and Germans were the majority in the early years, parishioners have always included families of many ethnic backgrounds.

(N) Continue nine blocks west to 63rd and Kedzie (3200 West) and turn right (north). This intersection has many commercial structures built around the time of World War I. During the summer of 1985 many of the storefronts were empty, while others had attracted discount retail businesses. In the same proposal that calls for an "ethnic village" farther east on 63rd Street, this intersection is earmarked for a discount retail zone. The plan also calls for a small park on the site of the shuttered Marquette Theatre.

(O) Drive eight blocks north on Kedzie to 55th Street. The modern structure that stands on the southwest corner of 55th and Kedzie is the church of **St. Gall.** Founded in 1890 as a mission of St. Agnes in Brighton Park, this parish gained secure footing when the Augustinians from St. Rita's took it over in 1909. Diocesan control returned in 1916. Polish Americans are the most numerous in this ethnically mixed congregation, though Bohemians made up a large number of the original parishioners.

The modernistic church, designed by Radoslav Kovacevic, was built between 1955 and 1958. It has a seating capacity of 1,400. The edifice anticipated many of the liturgical reforms called for by the Second Vatican Council. A tall stainless steel cross stands in front of the church facing the intersection.

Directly across the street from St. Gall's is another important neighborhood and citywide institution. The offices of **Talman Home Federal Savings and Loan** recall the Bohemian community that settled here early in the history of the Elsdon—Gage Park area. Founded by Ben F. Bohac in 1922, Talman has long been a trusted name in the financial community. Mayor Martin H. Kennelly dedicated the corner building in 1949.

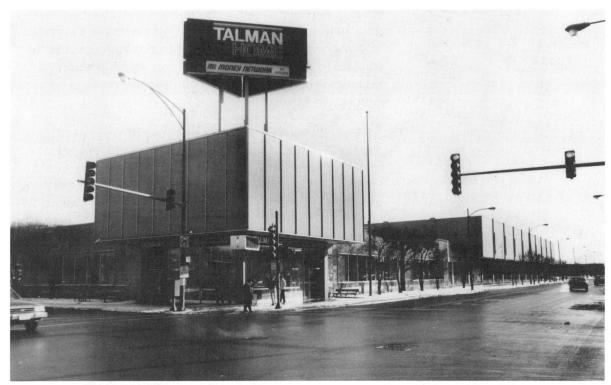

(P) Continue north on Kedzie to 47th street. You are now entering **Brighton Park.** The southeast and southwest corners of 47th and Kedzie have seen much change over the last few years. The early 1980s brought the demolition of light manufacturing plants on the west side of Kedzie and an old hotel on the east side of the street. These were replaced by small shopping centers. They symbolize some of the neighborhood investment that has occurred in the last few years. This shopping center, with its ample parking, may prove to be a strong competitor for the traditional shopping strip along Archer Avenue to the north. The Taxman Corporation developed this project with support from the city of Chicago and an Urban Development Action Grant (UDAG).

(Q) Continue north to 46th Street. The **Polish National Catholic Church of St. John's** stands on the northeast corner. The cornerstone of this church was laid in 1953. The Polish National Catholic Church was founded in America at the end of the last century as a result of

Talman Home Federal Savings and Loan Association, southeast corner 55th and Kedzie, 1985. Begun as a neighborhood savings institution in 1922, Talman Home has grown throughout the city and northern Illinois. (G. Lane)

clashes between Polish Americans and the Irish-dominated Roman Catholic hierarchy. It was the first major schism to take place in the Roman Catholic Church in North America. Brighton Park's population includes one of the highest concentrations of Polish Americans in the city.

(R) Go three blocks north on Kedzie and turn right on Archer Avenue. Just to the north and west of this intersection are the **Corwith Yards** of the Santa Fe Railroad, established in 1878. Taking advantage of the excellent freight-handling capabilities of the Corwith Yards, the Crane Company opened its huge manufacturing plant on this site in 1915 and became Brighton Park's major employer. By the late 1970s, however, the Crane Company was in the process of closing down its plant. Finally in the 1980s the company left the area completely. The huge office building that fronts on Kedzie Avenue at 41st Street once contained Crane's offices. Today the Santa Fe Railroad occupies the building, while most of the manufacturer's other structures have been torn down and the space used for Santa Fe's piggyback terminal. The Corwith Yards remain an important railroad link for the city and for the Midwest.

(S) Continue northeast on Archer Avenue. The original Archer Road was built to service the construction of the Illinois and Michigan Canal (1836-1848). It developed into a major thoroughfare connecting the southwest hinterland with the Chicago market. The street actually parallels the route of discovery used by Father Jacques Marquette and Louis Jolliet in 1673. Today it serves the Brighton Park community as a major shopping district. Along with the famous **Archer Avenue Big Store,** ethnic shops line the street, providing services to the surrounding community.

(T) Continue up Archer Avenue. The **Balzekas Museum of Lithuanian Culture** is located at 4012 S. Archer. This Lithuanian-American cultural institution contains artifacts and archives pertaining to the history of Lithuanians in Europe and America. It was founded by Stanley Balzekas, who also operates an auto dealership on Archer Avenue.

Santa Fe Tower, Corwith Yards, 41st and Kedzie, 1985. This building once housed the offices of the Crane Company. Today Santa Fe occupies the building on the east side of their vast Corwith Yards. (J. Ficner)

At the southeast corner of Archer and Western you will see McKinley Park, and you will be entering the McKinley Park neighborhood.

(U) Continue up Archer Avenue and take the overpass at Ashland. The top of the overpass will afford you a view of the **Stevenson Expressway,** the **Chicago River,** the railroads, and Archer Avenue as it makes its way back into the city via Bridgeport and Chinatown. Bridgeport derives its name from a low-hanging bridge that crossed the South Branch of the Chicago River at Ashland Avenue. Barges and boats could not pass under it, so they were forced to unload at this point. Hence the name Bridgeport.

As you continue up the avenue, you will come to a church at the intersection of Archer and Arch Street. This is **St. Bridget's Catholic Church.** Its history is the history of Bridgeport and much of the Southwest Side that touches Archer Avenue. The parish began in 1847 as a mission of St. Patrick's at Adams and Desplaines. Irish canal workers made up most of the original congregation. The present church was dedicated in 1906. It resembles a cathedral built by Irish monks in Novara, Italy in 1170. This neighborhood played an important part in the literary lore of Chicago. It was along "Archie" Avenue in the parish of St. Bridget that Finley Peter Dunne placed his fabled Irish-American philosopher, Mr. Dooley. Today Polish, German, and Mexican families attend St. Bridget's, as well as some remaining Irish families. Eleanor Guilfoyle married the future mayor Richard J. Daley at St. Bridget's in 1936.

The On Leong Merchants Assn. building, northwest corner Wentworth and 22nd Place, 1985. This ornate building is sometimes called the Chinatown "City Hall."
(G. Lane)

(V) Continue up Archer Avenue to Cermak Road. Just past Cermak, you will notice abandoned railroad yards on your left. These are the former downtown yards of the Santa Fe Railroad. Since the curtailment of rail service there in the late 1970s, the yards have been the subject of much speculation. The U.S. Postal Service hoped to build a new central facility on the land. Chinese-American developers want to build housing here for the expansion of Chinatown. Others have called for the building of a giant domed sports complex along the river near 16th Street. All of these plans are still up in the air. A look at the property easily reveals its value. It is just south of the Dearborn Park complex and the new River City development. This area is one of the largest parcels of land open for development in Chicago's central area. The success of South Loop redevelopment has made this prime property for developers.

(W) Turn right on Cermak Road and go one block east to Wentworth Avenue (200 West). Make another right (south). You will pass under the famous **Chinatown Gate,** designed by Peter Fung and erected in 1975 at a cost of $70,000. **Chinatown** remains the largest Chinese community in Chicago, despite the fact that Chinese Americans are now spread throughout the city. Wentworth Avenue is the main street of the neighborhood, which still numbers many Italian Americans in its population. Both Chinese and Italian residents hold annual celebrations in the neighborhood.

Procession in front of Santa Maria Incoronata Church, 200 block of W. Alexander Street, 1946. This Italian-American parish in the midst of Chinatown was given over to the Chinese Catholic parish of St. Therese in 1963.
(Courtesy The Chicago Catholic)

(X) Turn right at 23rd Street and go one block west to Princeton (300 West). Follow Princeton north (right) to Cermak and Archer Avenue. The **Archer Courts** housing project stands at Princeton and Cermak. The Chicago Housing Authority built this complex, designed by Everett F. Quinn and Alfred Mell, in 1952. Archer Courts contains 147 units on a little more than four acres. This housing project contrasts with the nearby Chinese-style apartment buildings that have been constructed over the last few years as Chinatown has tried to expand its housing stock.

The tour ends at Cermak and Princeton. Take Archer Avenue northeast to State Street and go north to the Loop. Or take Cermak east where just beyond Wentworth you can turn right and get onto the Dan Ryan or Stevenson Expressways.

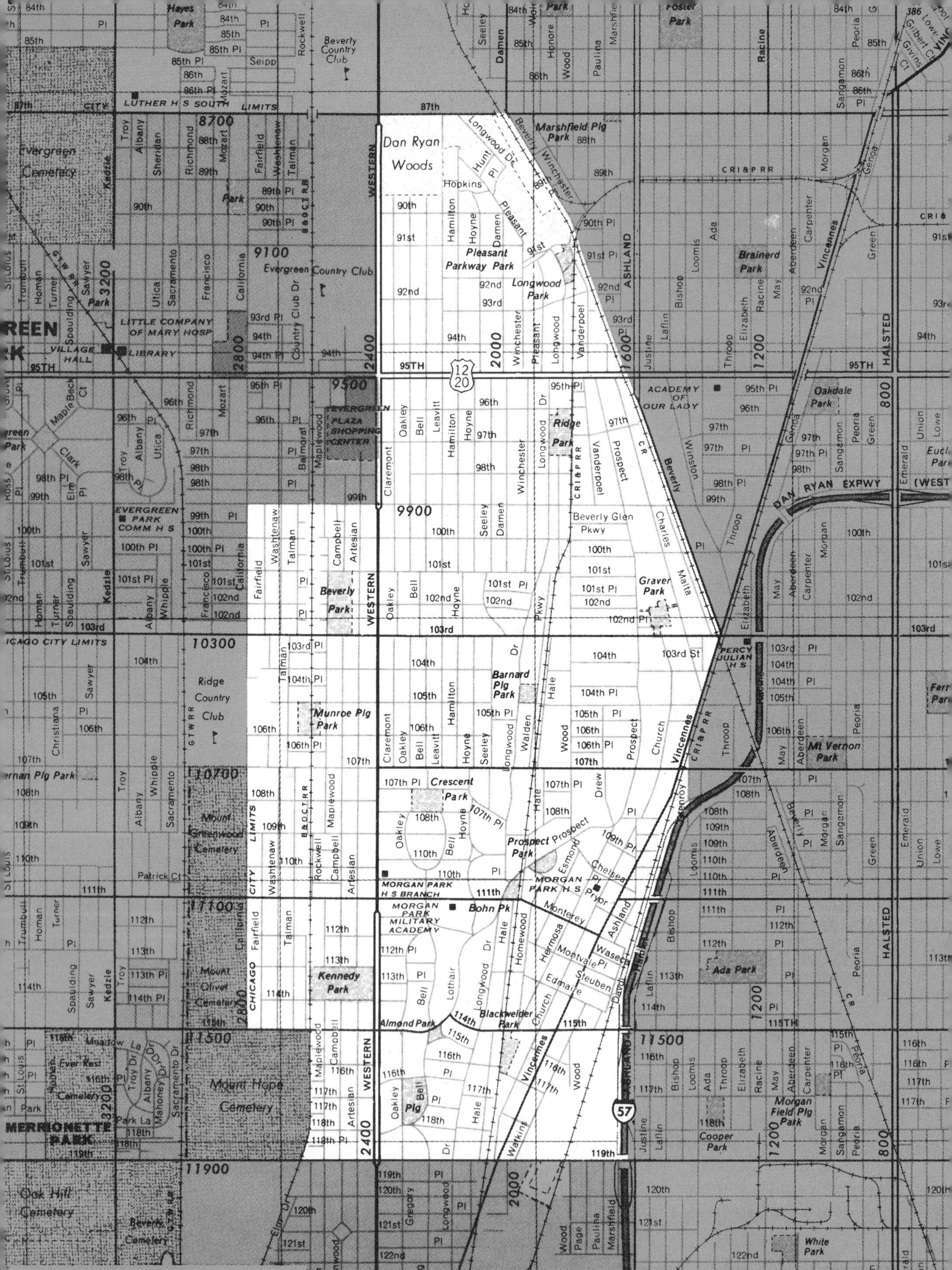
Hayes Park
Beverly Country Club
Foster Park
LUTHER H S SOUTH
CITY LIMITS
87th
8700
Evergreen Cemetery
Dan Ryan Woods
Marshfield Plg Park
CRI&PRR
9100
Evergreen Country Club
Pleasant Parkway Park
Longwood Park
Brainerd Park
ASHLAND
Vincennes
LITTLE COMPANY OF MARY HOSP
VILLAGE HALL
LIBRARY
95TH
2800
2400
2000
1600
1200
HALSTED
12
20
9500
EVERGREEN PLAZA SHOPPING CENTER
ACADEMY OF OUR LADY
Oakdale Park
800
Ridge Park
Beverly
DAN RYAN EXPWY
9900
EVERGREEN PARK COMM H S
Beverly Glen Pkwy
Beverly Park
Graver Park
WESTERN
103rd
CHICAGO CITY LIMITS
10300
PERCY JULIAN H S
Ridge Country Club
Barnard Plg Park
Munroe Plg Park
Mt Vernon Park
10700
Crescent Park
Mount Greenwood Cemetery
Prospect Park
MORGAN PARK H S BRANCH
MORGAN PARK H S
111th
11100
MORGAN PARK MILITARY ACADEMY
Bohn Pk
Kennedy Park
Ada Park
Mount Olivet Cemetery
Almond Park
Blackwelder Park
11500
Ever Rest Cemetery
Mount Hope Cemetery
Plg
57
Morgan Field Plg Park
MERRIONETTE PARK
Cooper Park
119th
11900
Oak Hill Cemetery
Beverly Cemetery
White Park

Beverly Hills—Morgan Park

The Beverly Hills—Morgan Park neighborhoods on Chicago's Southwest Side contain some of the city's finest residences, built by upper-middle-class families between 1870 and 1930. In 1975 the National Register of Historic Places noted that of all Chicago's residential districts, Beverly—Morgan Park was unique because it had "successfully retained its building stock and the congruent sense of an almost organic evolution." Once suburban outposts linked to downtown Chicago by the Rock Island Railroad, Beverly and Morgan Park were gradually transformed into city neighborhoods. But unlike other urban neighborhoods, ethnic and racial changes occurred only gradually, with the result that these twin neighborhoods have lost little of their middle-class, small town flavor.

Although Beverly Hills and Morgan Park developed at different rates, both areas originated as New England Protestant communities. For decades, the village life centered around its churches, and both communities shared reputations as temperance towns. Even after Beverly and Morgan Park were annexed to Chicago, they clung tenaciously to their old village ways.

In 1844 Thomas Morgan, an Englishman, purchased all the land along the Blue Island Ridge from 91st to 119th Streets. This prehistoric glacial ridge, which rises nearly one hundred feet above the current level of Lake Michigan, provides a spectacular setting for neighborhood homes. But during Morgan's lifetime this hilly area remained undeveloped.

The transformation of the Ridge area from a small farming settlement to a suburban community began in 1869 when the Blue Island Land and Building Company acquired Thomas Morgan's property and platted it for residential use. Thomas F. Nichols, a British designer, laid out the curving streets and open green spaces in the area's first subdivision, known as Morgan Park. Unlike Chicago, where streets formed a grid pattern, Morgan Park boasted broad winding thoroughfares and roundabouts. An early village map shows in detail how the area west of the Ridge was platted with large, deep lots suitable for spacious Victorian homes. East of the Ridge and south of 111th Street, lots were small and narrow. This section developed primarily as a working-class community. To attract potential homeowners to the district

Victorian mansions, 10910-34 S. Prospect, 1892. In the 1880s, Prospect Avenue was Morgan Park's most fashionable street, containing the homes of prominent village residents.
(Courtesy Ridge Historical Society)

between 107th and 119th Streets, the Blue Island Co. sponsored land auctions and advertised in Chicago newspapers and building journals.

Like other suburbs in the nineteenth century, Morgan Park's future growth depended on the railroad. Although the Panhandle Railroad inaugurated service to downtown Chicago as early as 1865, its accommodation train primarily served the village of Washington Heights with stops at 103rd and Vincennes, 95th and Charles, and 91st and Beverly. Of greater benefit to the new subdivision of Morgan Park was the "dummy" line established by the Rock Island Railroad in 1870. This branch line provided commuter service from Blue Island to downtown Chicago with stops at Morgan (111th), Tracy (103rd), 99th and Prospect, and "Dummy Junction" at 97th and Vincennes.

In 1877 the Blue Island Land and Building Co. convinced the Baptist Union Theological Seminary to move to Morgan Park from the Douglas area of Chicago. Under the leadership of Thomas W. Goodspeed and William Rainey Harper, the Baptist seminary put Morgan Park "on the map," and it played a crucial role in attracting families to the area. According to an early guidebook, the seminary, together with Morgan Park Military Academy (1873) and the Chicago Female College (1875), "form the chief attraction of the place."

Following Morgan Park's incorporation as a village in 1882, the area experienced its first real estate boom. Gracious Victorian homes were constructed near the Baptist seminary on Morgan Avenue (111th Street), and a business district developed around the Rock Island depot. Before long Episcopal, Congregational, Methodist, and Presbyterian churches were built, rivaling in size and influence the Morgan Park Baptist Church at 110th and Bell Avenue.

Despite these signs of growth, Morgan Park lost its bid as the location for the new University of Chicago, an institution supported by the American Baptist Education Society and endowed by John T. Rockefeller. Although Morgan Park boosters claimed their community was "more accessible than the majority of homes in the city," prominent Baptist educators successfully argued that the village was too remote for a university. Thus in 1891 construction began in the 5800 block of Ellis Avenue on a Gothic campus for the University of Chicago, and thereafter the names of Harper and Goodspeed were linked to Hyde Park rather than to Morgan Park.

In 1892 *The Budget*, a local newspaper, advocated streetcar connections with nearby villages as the way to build up Morgan Park. Although service along Vincennes Avenue began in 1896, Morgan Park and Beverly remained isolated from the expanding city. Community leaders believed that streetcar lines threatened the exclusivity of the area, and consequently no public transportation was available along Western Avenue, 103rd, or 95th Streets until the 1930s.

By 1900 Morgan Park was well on its way to becoming an elite residential community. Among those who built homes in the village were executives of the Rock Island line, the Chicago stockyards, and the Chicago Bridge and Iron Company, which opened in 1889 on nearby Vincennes Avenue. But it was improved rail transportation that made the larger Ridge area attractive to businessmen who worked in Chicago's financial and commercial center. Indeed, increased suburban service and the opening of new stations at 99th, 95th, and 91st Streets were responsible for the growth of the area now known as Beverly Hills.

Prior to 1900 small residential communities had developed around the Rock Island suburban stations at Belmont (107th), Tracy (103rd), and Walden (99th) within the village of Washington Heights. The area's main institution was Bethany Union Church, built in 1874 at 103rd and Prospect by an alliance of Baptists, Methodists, and Presbyterians. Although these settlements along the Rock Island's "dummy" line became part of Chicago in 1890 with

(Top left) Morgan Park Congregational Church, northwest corner 112th and Hoyne, 1890s. When this church was dedicated in 1890, Hoyne Avenue was just being built up with homes. After they built a modern brick church across the street, the Congregationalists sold their frame building in 1917 to the Morgan Park Masonic Lodge.
(Courtesy Ridge Historical Society)

(Bottom left) Blake Hall was built in 1888 as the chapel and administration building of the Baptist Union Theological Seminary, which moved to Hyde Park in 1892. Until it was destroyed by fire in 1962, Blake Hall was a landmark on the campus of Morgan Park Academy. The Beverly Art Center, 2153 W. 111th Street, now occupies the site. (Courtesy Ridge Historical Society)

the annexation of Washington Heights, they remained suburban in character and outlook. Far from assuming an urban identity, the residents merely switched their affiliation from Washington Heights to Beverly Hills.

When the Rock Island Railroad realigned its suburban tracks in 1889, thereby expanding local service north of 99th street, it named the 91st Street station Beverly Hills. Although a few homes were built along the Ridge in the 1880s and 1890s, nearly three decades passed before the area reached residential maturity. Like Morgan Park, the Beverly district was built up from east to west, mostly with single-family homes. The building boom which occurred in these two neighborhoods between 1910 and 1930 reinforced earlier patterns of settlement. No saloons, factories, or businesses were permitted along the Ridge, and developers took care to remove "only trees that actually interfere with building." Thus the district retained its suburban character as its housing stock expanded to include brick mansions, "Chicago" bungalows, and a small number of apartment buildings. What distinguished Morgan Park—Beverly from other Chicago neighborhoods in the 1920s was its high quality housing and its small town atmosphere: "no noisy

Armida (Hoyne) Avenue between 111th and 112th Streets, c.1910. Sidewalks, shade trees, and carefully tended lawns enhanced Morgan Park's high quality housing. Despite a vigorous campaign against annexation, Morgan Park became a Chicago neighborhood in 1914.
(C.R. Childs, courtesy G. Schmalgemeier)

street cars, no heavy traffic, no smoke or smells of industries, no hustle and bustle of business, no glittering movie palaces or dance halls."

Before Morgan Park was annexed to Chicago in 1914, a black community developed in the area around 111th and Ashland Avenue. Although early maps showed Loomis Street as the village's eastern boundary, Vincennes Avenue became the dividing line between black and white residents. In 1921 the Chicago Commission on Race Relations reported that whites and blacks in Morgan Park "maintain a friendly attitude," but it also noted that "there seems to be a common understanding that Negroes must not live west of Vincennes Road . . ." Although the swampy land between Ashland and Halsted subsequently developed into a middle-class black residential area and was included as part of Morgan Park on city maps, the black community remained separate from "Old Morgan Park."

Since the 1880s most of the newcomers to Beverly and Morgan Park had been Protestant families. Many of them moved to this area from Englewood and Normal Park, located north and east of Beverly along the Rock Island line. These neighborhoods were originally suburban communities of large frame homes, but they were built up with apartments beginning in the 1890s. As the ethnic composition of Englewood and Normal Park changed, old-line families moved to Beverly and Morgan Park where they swelled the membership of the district's many Protestant churches.

The Morgan Park Methodist Church at 11030 S. Longwood is typical of the imposing churches constructed along Longwood Drive between 1892 and 1940. Henry H. Waterman designed the first section of this church in 1913; the 1927 addition was designed by Dwight Perkins. (G. Lane)

By the 1920s Longwood Drive had emerged as the area's most prestigious street, eclipsing Prospect Avenue as the main north-south thoroughfare. Not only did Longwood contain some of the neighborhood's most beautiful homes, but it was also the setting for several prominent churches. Between 1892 and 1916 the Presbyterians, Methodists, Christian Scientists, and Episcopalians built stately churches along Longwood Drive from 110th to 95th Street. The announcement that Roman Catholics planned to build a church at 100th and Longwood Drive shattered the peace of the Ridge district and began a new chapter in the community's development.

Catholics had been among the early settlers in nearby Washington Heights, but they did not become a visible presence in Beverly—Morgan Park until the 1920s. Although the Irish newcomers entered communities that were organized along religious lines, their attempts to form St. Barnabas parish met with stiff resistance. In 1924 area residents succeeded in having the parish property at the southwest corner of 100th and Longwood condemned for a

park. Undaunted, the Catholic pastor purchased another site further south on Longwood Drive (through a third party) and let contracts for a church-and-school building. The Catholic population of the Ridge area increased slowly, but by 1936 enough Catholic families had purchased homes in Beverly to warrant the formation of another parish, Christ the King, at 93rd and Hamilton Avenue.

The third building boom which shaped Beverly—Morgan Park occurred in the years following World War II as tracts of land along both sides of Western Avenue were built up with homes. In 1952 a 45-store shopping plaza complete with parking opened in the 9500 block of S. Western Avenue, just beyond the city limits in suburban Evergreen Park. Evergreen Plaza was the first major suburban shopping center in the Chicago area, and as its developer Arthur Rubloff predicted, it dramatically changed the shopping habits of city dwellers and suburbanites alike. In Beverly—Morgan Park, however, the tradition of neighborhood shopping persisted. While 95th Street remained the largest commercial district in the area, small shopping strips which had developed around the Rock Island stations continued to thrive. But improvements in public transportation and the widespread use of the automobile meant that Beverly—Morgan Park residents were not as dependent as earlier generations upon the Rock Island Railroad. Although ridership remained high, many people began to drive downtown by car, especially after the west leg of the Dan Ryan Expressway (I-57) was completed in 1967.

On March 17, 1979, these youngsters revived the South Side St. Patrick's Day Parade which had been a tradition along 79th Street from 1953 to 1960. The Irish parade down Western Avenue is now one of Beverly-Morgan Park's largest events, involving families and organizations throughout the Ridge area.

(S. Lewellyn, courtesy G. Hendry)

Throughout the 1950s and 1960s, Beverly Hills and Morgan Park continued to be divided along religious lines. Although Protestants and Catholics took pride in their homes, they rarely cooperated in civic ventures. This situation might have continued were it not for the threat of racial resegregation. Area residents had long believed that Beverly and Morgan Park would escape block-by-block resegregation. Not only had a black community existed east of Vincennes Avenue for more than fifty years, but Morgan Park High School was one of the few Chicago public schools to maintain racial diversity. Unlike other city neighborhoods where apartments predominated, Beverly and Morgan Park were essentially areas of single-family homes with a stable residential population. Moreover, both neighborhoods east of Western Avenue were "dry," a prohibition demanded by early Baptist settlers and upheld by Catholic newcomers. But change was coming swiftly, aided in part by the federal government's Section 235 housing program which subsidized the construction of small homes along Vincennes Avenue and south of Morgan Park High School. Between 1969 and 1974 nearly four hundred such homes were built in Morgan Park, the highest number for any community area in the city. While this program provided black families with the opportunity to own their own homes, the Section 235 houses were a modern version of the nineteenth-century workingman's cottage.

As Morgan Park and Beverly had developed at different rates, so integration in the two communities occurred at a different pace also. While Vincennes Avenue ceased to be the dividing line between black and white residents of Morgan Park in the 1960s, Beverly remained virtually an all-white community. However, as bungalow-belt neighborhoods east of Ashland and north of 91st Street changed from white to black with lightning speed, Beverly residents began to realize that their neighborhood and Morgan Park might be resegregated also. Community leaders responded by reorganizing the Beverly Area Planning Association (BAPA), a federation of local civic groups founded in 1947. BAPA succeeded in halting panic peddling by unscrupulous real estate dealers with the result that in 1975 the Ridge area had stabilized and home values began to rise.

Just as the Blue Island Land and Building Co. advertised the fledgling subdivision of Morgan Park in the 1870s, BAPA publicized the neighborhood's fine housing in the 1970s. In addition to sponsoring home tours, which attract thousands of Chicagoans to Beverly and Morgan Park every year, BAPA promoted the inclusion of the area on the National Register of Historic Places. Interest in the neighborhood's past has also been sparked by the Ridge Historical Society, which operates a museum at 10616 South Longwood Drive. Since its organization in 1971, the Society has identified landmark homes throughout the area and established an oral history program and archives. While home renovation continues to occupy the energies of many families in the Ridge area, residents have not neglected such issues as increased police protection, quality education in local public schools, expanded commuter service to downtown Chicago, and the upgrading of the commercial district along 95th Street.

In recent years a number of families have moved to Beverly Hills and Morgan Park from the suburbs as well as from out of state. But the majority of new homeowners, white and black, are longtime South Siders. Once a minority in the district, Catholics now form the largest religious denomination. Indeed, the St. Patrick's Day Parade down Western Avenue, organized in 1979, has become a symbol of the Catholic presence in the Ridge area. Although parish and congregational identities continue to be important to Southwest Side Catholics and Protestants, religious hostility has given way to cooperation between denominations. Moreover, racial tensions have eased, and Beverly—Morgan Park has emerged as one of the few Chicago neighborhoods to maintain racial diversity.

With a population of more than 40,000, Beverly and Morgan Park are now very much a part of the larger city. In terms of their present ethnic and racial composition, they have ceased to resemble nineteenth-century New England communities. Yet they have retained much of their former village character. Because of the building and zoning restrictions imposed by early Yankee settlers, the Ridge district experienced a relatively controlled development. Not only have the majority of homes built between 1870 and 1930 survived intact, but Beverly and Morgan Park have remained middle-class residential communities, even as they changed from suburban outposts to city neighborhoods.

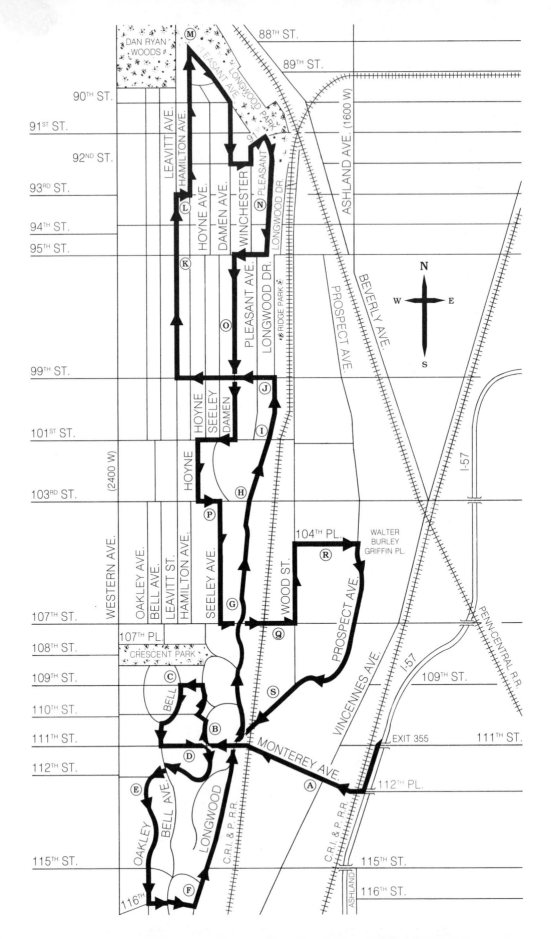

Beverly Hills — Morgan Park Tour

This tour visits the residential neighborhoods of Morgan Park and Beverly.

Exit the Dan Ryan Expressway (I-57) at 111th Street, then continue on the frontage road to the stoplight at Monterey Avenue. From the south suburbs, exit Monterey Avenue. Turn west, cross the railroad tracks, and follow Monterey seven blocks west to Longwood Drive (1826 West).

Driving time: about 2 hours.

(A) From the 1880s to the 1970s Monterey Avenue was the business center of **Old Morgan Park.** After urban renewal, all that remains of the former commercial district is the high school, post office, police station, train station, and a few stores west of Hale Avenue.

(B) Proceed up the hill, turn north at the top onto Hoyne Avenue (2100 West), past the **Walker Library,** constructed in 1890. After Morgan Park was annexed to Chicago in 1914, the village library became a branch of the Chicago Public Library system.

(C) Go three blocks north on Hoyne, turn left at 109th Street and go one block west to Bell Avenue (2234 West), then go left on Bell, curving south around the **Morgan Park Baptist Church** on your right to 111th Street. When Morgan Park Baptist's first church was dedicated in 1874, it was located "on the high ground, a number of blocks away from any other buildings..." With the arrival of the Baptist Union Theological Seminary in 1877, Morgan Park Baptist Church became one of the most powerful institutions in the community. The present church was built in stages from 1896 to 1954.

George C. Walker, president of the Blue Island Land and Building Company, donated this library at 11071 S. Hoyne to the village of Morgan Park in 1890. Charles Frost designed the limestone building, which was later enlarged after it became a branch of the Chicago Public Library.
(G. Lane)

(D) Turn left on 111th Street and go one block east to Hoyne Avenue (2100 West). The townhouses on the north side of 111th Street mark the site of the Baptist Union Theological Seminary which flourished from 1877 until 1892 when it became the Divinity School of the University of Chicago in Hyde Park.

Beverly-Morgan Park is one of the few neighborhoods in Chicago to have its own art center. The **Beverly Art Center,** 2153 West 111th, was constructed in 1969 on the campus of Morgan Park Academy and financed by community contributions. The center contains a large collection of paintings by John H. Vanderpoel (1857-1911), a local resident who was head of the instruction department at the Art Institute of Chicago. The **Vanderpoel Gallery** is open to the public on Tuesdays, Thursdays, and Saturdays from 1 to 4 p.m., except during August.

(E) Turn right on Hoyne and go one block south to 112th, following 112th as it curves past **Morgan Park Academy.** Formerly a military academy, this private coeducational grammar school and high school draws students from all over the South Side and suburbs.

Turn left onto Oakley Avenue and continue south all
the way to 116th Place. The white frame house at 11216
S. Oakley was the residence of Thomas W. Goodspeed
when he served as pastor of Morgan Park Baptist
Church and secretary of the Baptist Union Theological
Seminary. On your right at 113th and Oakley are the
grounds of the **Washington and Jane Smith Retirement
Home.** On your left at 114th and Oakley is the new
Bellhaven Nursing Home. It occupies the site of the
Fridhem Swedish Baptist Old People's Home, founded in
Morgan Park in 1902.

(F) Turn left at 116th Place, jog right at Bell, then go east
down the hill to Longwood Drive. Turn left onto
Longwood Drive and go past the **Cenacle,** a Catholic
retreat house established in 1946 in the former Charles
Walgreen home. Continue north on Longwood, across
111th Street, past the **Morgan Park Presbyterian Church**
(1940) and the **Morgan Park Methodist Church** (1912).

(G) Go north on Longwood Drive all the way to 99th Street.
This is a typical section of Longwood Drive—mansions
built atop the hill with more modest homes located on
the east side of the street. The former Driscoll home at
10616 S. Longwood is now the headquarters of the
Ridge Historical Society. Its museum is open to the
public on Thursdays and Sundays from 2 to 5 p.m.

(H) The **Irish castle** at the northwest corner of 103rd and
Longwood was built in 1886 as a residence for Robert
Givins. It symbolized the aristocratic kind of community
which real estate developers like Givins hoped to create
along the Ridge. It now houses the **Beverly Unitarian
Church** and the **Beverly Community Nursery School.**

(I) When **St. Barnabas** parish was founded in 1924, local
residents protested the construction of a Catholic church
on Longwood Drive. This Catholic parish with its
modern church (1969) is now the largest congregation
along the Ridge. The small park at 101st and Longwood

The Irish castle, northwest corner 103rd and Longwood, 1930. Built in 1886 by Robert Givins, a real estate developer along the Ridge, the castle is Beverly-Morgan Park's most famous landmark. Originally a private residence, the castle has been the home of Beverly Unitarian Church since 1942.

(C.R. Childs, courtesy, G. Schmalgemeier)

has recently been renamed **Timothy J. Hurley Park.** It commemorates the founding pastor of St. Barnabas as well as his first choice of property for the church.

(J) Turn left at 99th Street, go up the hill, and continue six blocks west to Leavitt Street (2200 West). **Trinity United Methodist Church** at 99th and Winchester reflects the east-to-west development of the Beverly neighborhood. When this church was completed in 1924, its congregation literally moved up the hill, from 99th and Prospect Avenue.

(K) Turn right on Leavitt and go six blocks north to 93rd Street. This stretch of Leavitt, with its stop signs and stoplight at 95th Street, provides easy access into the heart of Beverly Hills where the 1920s building boom "plowed right ahead through the worst of the depression."

Turn right at 93rd Street, go one block east to Hamilton Avenue, past the **Kellogg Grammar School** and **Christ the King** parish complex, memorialized in Andrew M. Greeley's novel, *Lord of the Dance.* Turn left on Hamilton and go six blocks north to the intersection of Pleasant Avenue at 8819 South. The **Beverly Hills Tennis Club** at 9121 S. Hamilton was founded in 1919 when this part of the neighborhood was just being built up with homes. The tennis courts date from 1926, and the clubhouse was built in 1928.

North Beverly contains many fine examples of homes designed by Murray Hetherington, a local architect who began his practice in the early 1920s. Hetherington adapted the English manor style of architecture for many of the homes, especially his own at 8918 S. Hamilton (1925). Examples of his work may be seen along Hamilton Avenue at 9014, 8947, and 8929. He also designed the following homes along Pleasant Avenue: 8828, 8841, 8848, 8929, and 8944.

This brick home at 8929 S. Pleasant, designed by Murray Hetherington for the Mickleberry family, is typical of the high-class construction throughout the Beverly neighborhood.
(Courtesy Ridge Historical Society)

552

Robey Street (Damen Avenue), looking north from 91st Street, 1926. Generous setbacks contributed to the suburban atmosphere of this section of North Beverly.
(C.R. Childs, courtesy G. Schmalgemeier)

Pleasant Avenue, looking north from 93rd Street, 1926. Many of the frame homes along Pleasant Avenue were constructed in the early l900s by William Ashton and his son.
(C.R. Childs, courtesy G. Schmalgemeier)

Southwest corner 93rd and Pleasant, 1926. Architect John Todd Hetherington designed this Prairie-style home with its dramatic roof line in 1908. It is now the parish house for the Episcopal Church of the Holy Nativity.
(C.R. Childs, courtesy. G. Schmalgemeier)

(M) Make a sharp right turn onto Pleasant Avenue. Even
longtime Ridge residents get lost in North Beverly, where
the **Dan Ryan Woods** provide a dramatic setting for
neighborhood homes. Follow Pleasant Avenue three
blocks southeast to 90th Street, then go two blocks
south along Damen to 92nd Street. At 92nd Street turn
left and go one block east to Winchester Avenue. Turn
left on Winchester and go north, then right on 91st
Street one block as it curves around to Pleasant Avenue.

(N) Turn right onto Pleasant Avenue and go two blocks
south to 95th Street. The **Episcopal Church of the Holy
Nativity** (1954) stands at the southwest corner of 93rd
and Pleasant. Founded in 1899, the Episcopal parish
moved to this part of North Beverly from 95th and
Longwood Drive. Pleasant Avenue between 92nd and
95th contains an interesting mix of Victorian and
Prairie-style homes. The **W.M.R. French mansion** (9203)
was built in 1894 for the first director of the Art
Institute of Chicago. Artist John H. Vanderpoel, a friend
and colleague of French, lived in the house at 9319 S.
Pleasant from 1897 to 1910. Frank Lloyd Wright
designed the **Jessie M. Adams house** at 9326 S.
Pleasant in 1900.

(O) Turn right on 95th Street and go two blocks west to
Damen Avenue (2000 West). Turn left on Damen and go
six blocks south to 101st Street. This stretch of Damen
Avenue contains a wide variety of housing, from
Chicago-style bungalows in the 9700 block to Georgians
in the 100th block. Over the years Beverly's mixture of
mansions and modest homes has made it one of
Chicago's most stable communities. Solidly middle class,
the area is one of the few city neighborhoods to achieve
peaceful racial integration.

Turn right on 101st Street and go three blocks west
to Hoyne, then two blocks south on Hoyne to 103rd
Street. Turn left and go two blocks east on 103rd to
Seeley Avenue (2032 West).

(P) Turn right on Seeley and go four blocks south to 107th Street. Seeley Avenue at approximately 10350 south was once the second tee of the Ridge County Club golf course. In 1908 neighborhood golfers were divided over the liquor question. The "wets" withdrew and joined members of the Auburn Park Club to form the Beverly Country Club at 87th and Western. In 1916 Ridge Country Club moved to 104th and California Avenue, and its old golf course was subdivided for spacious single-family homes.

(Q) Turn left on 107th and go east down the hill and across the railroad tracks to Wood Street (1800 West). The small shopping area known as **Belmont Square** is a vestige of the community which developed in the 1890s around the Belmont station of the Rock Island Railroad. Belmont Food Mart and the nearby Java Express draw patrons from all over Beverly—Morgan Park and are classic examples of neighborhood meeting places, as important today as when the area was first built up with homes.

(R) At Wood Street turn left and go five blocks north to Walter Burley Griffin Place (104th Place). Turn right and go one block east to Prospect Avenue. One of the longest residential blocks on the South Side of Chicago, Griffin Place is named after **Walter Burley Griffin,** a local architect who once served as Frank Lloyd Wright's chief draftsman. The street contains several Prairie-style homes designed by Griffin. They include: 1741, 1736, 1731, 1727, 1724, 1712, and 1666 W. Griffin Place.

(S) Turn right and go about ten blocks south on Prospect Avenue as it curves around to 111th Street. The 10900 block of Prospect Avenue was Morgan Park's most fashionable street in the 1880s and 1890s. Its mansions recall the days when the village was a sparsely settled suburban outpost. Morgan Park's historic houses include the **Ingersoll/Blackwelder home** (10910); the **German house** (10924) which contained the office and home of the village's first doctor; the **Ferguson home** (10934); and the **Lackore home** (10956).

At 111th Street, turn left and return to the I-57 Expressway via Monterey Avenue.

(Top left) Beverly Country Club, 87th and Western Avenue, c.1909. Prominent Beverly residents built this clubhouse as a refuge from their "dry" neighborhood. In addition to a golf course, the club was the scene of excellent "meals . . . dances and card parties."
(Courtesy G. Schmalgemeier)

(Bottom left) This distinctive house at 1736 W. 104th Place was one of several on the block designed by Walter Burley Griffin between 1909 and 1914. Griffin, a former colleague of Frank Lloyd Wright, incorporated Prairie School elements in his designs. The Chicago City Council renamed 104th Place in honor of Griffin in 1981. (G. Lane)

Acknowledgments

In researching and writing CHICAGO: CITY OF NEIGHBORHOODS we drew upon the resources of many individuals and institutions. At every step of the way George A. Lane, S.J. offered encouragement and assistance. In addition to editing the manuscript and driving all the tours, he offered valuable suggestions based on his extensive knowledge of Chicago. We would also like to thank Rev. Daniel L. Flaherty, S.J., Director of Loyola University Press, for his support of this project.

Tim Barton and Tim Samuelson of the Commission on Chicago Historical and Architectural Landmarks reviewed the manuscript. Tim Barton was especially helpful in suggesting neighborhood source material and photographs.

The staffs of the Chicago Historical Society, Chicago Public Library Archives, Chicago Board of Education Administrative Resource Center, Municipal Reference Library, and Newberry Library provided generous assistance. We are grateful to the many Chicagoans who took time to answer our questions and supply us with information about the institutions which played a crucial role in the development of Chicago's neighborhoods.

Joseph Ficner, Andrzej Chruscinski, Algimantas Kezys, and George Lane provided us with contemporary photographs and Joseph A. Mulac with the assistance of Jane Mostert drew the maps for the neighborhood tours.

Special thanks are due the following persons who assisted us in gathering historical photographs: Richard Wroble; Robert L. Johnston, editor, and Frederick J. Olk, librarian, *The Chicago Catholic*; Rev. Leland Issleib, pastor, Edgewater Presbyterian Church; LeRoy Blommaert, Edgewater Community Council; Bro. Michael J. Grace, S.J., archivist, Loyola University; Robert J. White, Ridge Historical Society; Brockie Dilworth, Gads Hill Center; Sr. M. Josetta Phoenix, BVM, archivist, Mundelein College; Becky Haglund, special collections, Sulzer Regional Library; Sr. Vivian Ivantic, OSB, St. Scholastica Priory Archives; Edith Johnson, Swedish American Museum Association of Chicago; Jayne Fitzsimmons, Henrotin Hospital; George Lamparter; Rev. David Blake, pastor, St. Mary AME Church; Sr. Gwendolyn Durkin, RSM, and Judith Traynor, Mercy Hospital; George Hendry; and Mary Ann Johnson, Hull House Museum. We also wish to thank Grant Schmalgemeier who shared with us his collection of historic postcards.

Among the many people who helped make this book possible, we thank Catherine Blaho, Shelley Brown, Diane Williams, the James M. Conniff family, John Corrigan, Anne Coyne, Elizabeth Howard, Deborah and Michael Kennedy, Louise Killie, Jerome and Joseph McGovern, William J. McLaughlin, Catharine M. O'Malley, John Posluszny, Jr., and Margaret M. Skerrett.

Thanks to the Macmillan Publishing Company for permission to reprint material from *Twenty Years at Hull House* by Jane Addams.

Thanks are also due Eugene Forrester III, publisher of The Chicago *Journal.* Some of the material on South Side neighborhoods appeared in the *Journal* in a different form.

We are particularly indebted to our spouses, Kathleen Alaimo and John C. O'Malley, for their love, understanding, and help charting neighborhood tours.

Bibliography

General Books

Andreas, A.T. *History of Chicago*. 3 vols. Chicago: 1884-86.

——*History of Cook County, Illinois*. Chicago: 1884.

Bach, Ira J. *Chicago on Foot*. Chicago: Rand McNally, 1977.

The Chicago Fact Book Consortium. *Local Community Fact Book, Chicago Metropolitan Area*. Chicago: 1984.

City of Chicago, Department of Development and Planning. *Historic City: The Settlement of Chicago*. Chicago, 1976.

Duis, Perry. *Chicago: Creating New Traditions*. Chicago: Chicago Historical Society, 1976.

—— *The Saloon: Public Drinking in Chicago and Boston, 1880-1920*. Urbana: University of Illinois Press, 1983.

Gutstein, Morris A. *A Priceless Heritage: The Epic Growth of Nineteenth Century Chicago Jewry*. New York: Block Publishing Co., 1953.

Heimovics, Rachel Baron. *Chicago Jewish Sourcebook*. Chicago: 1981.

Hirsch, Arnold R. *Making the Second Ghetto: Race and Housing in Chicago, 1940 to 1960*. Cambridge: Cambridge University Press, 1983.

Hofmeister, Rudolph A. *The Germans in Chicago*. Urbana: University of Illinois Press, 1976.

Holli, Melvin G., and Jones, Peter d'A., eds. *Ethnic Chicago*. Grand Rapids: William Eerdmans, 1984.

Holt, Glen E., and Pacyga, Dominic A. *Chicago: A Historical Guide to the Neighborhoods, The Loop and South Side*. Chicago: Chicago Historical Society, 1979.

Inglehart, Babette, ed. *Walking With Women Through History*. Chicago: Salsedo Press, 1981.

Koenig, Rev. Msgr. Harry C., ed. *A History of the Parishes of the Archdiocese of Chicago*. 2 vols. Chicago: Archdiocese of Chicago, 1980.

Lane, George A., *Chicago Churches and Synagogues: An Architectural Pilgrimage*. Chicago: Loyola University Press, 1981.

Mayer, Harold M., and Wade, Richard C. *Chicago: Growth of a Metropolis*. Chicago: University of Chicago Press, 1969.

Nelli, Humbert S. *The Italians in Chicago, 1880-1930: A Study in Ethnic Mobility.* New York: Oxford University Press, 1970.

Pierce, Bessie Louise. *A History of Chicago.* 3 vols. New York: Knopf, 1937-57.

Poles of Chicago, 1837-1937: A History of One Century of Polish Contribution to the City of Chicago, Illinois. Chicago: The Polish Pageant, 1937.

Riedy, James L. *Chicago Sculpture.* Urbana: University of Illinois Press, 1981.

Spear, Allan. *Black Chicago: The Making of a Negro Ghetto, 1880-1920.* Chicago: University of Chicago Press, 1967.

The Loop

Cutler, Irving. *Chicago: Metropolis of the Mid-Continent.* 3rd ed. Dubuque: Kendall-Hunt, 1982.

Lewis, Lloyd, and Smith, Henry Justin. *Chicago: The History of Its Reputation.* New York, 1929.

Siegel, Arthur. *Chicago's Famous Buildings.* Chicago: University of Chicago Press, 1965.

Near North Side

Beijbom, Ulf. *Swedes in Chicago: A Demographic and Social Study of the 1846-1880 Immigration.* Stockholm: University of Uppsala Press, 1971.

Hilliard, Celia. "Rent Reasonable to Right Parties": Gold Coast Apartment Buildings 1906-1929." *Chicago History* 8:2 (1979): 66-77.

Palmer, Vivien M. *Social Backgrounds of Chicago's Local Communities.* Typescript, Chicago, 1930.

Tessendorf, K.C. "Captain Streeter's District of Lake Michigan." *Chicago History* 5:3 (1976): 152-60.

Zorbaugh, Harvey Warren. *The Gold Coast and the Slum: A Sociological Study of Chicago's Near North Side.* Chicago: University of Chicago Press, 1929.

Mid-North Side

Clark, Stephen Bedell. *The Lake View Saga.* Chicago: Lake View Trust and Savings Bank, 1974.

Lindberg, Richard. "The Chicago Whales and the Federal League of American Baseball, 1914-1915." *Chicago History* 10:1 (1981): 2-12.

Warren, Elizabeth. *Chicago's Uptown: Public Policy, Neighborhood Decay, and Citizen Action in an Urban Community.* Chicago: Center for Urban Policy, Loyola University, 1979.

Far North Side

Davis, James Leslie. *The Elevated System and the Growth of Northern Chicago.* Evanston: Northwestern University, 1965.

Marciniak, Edward. *Reversing Urban Decline: The Winthrop—Kenmore Corridor in the Edgewater and Uptown Communities of Chicago.* Washington, D. C.: National Center for Urban Ethnic Affairs, 1981.

Ratcliffe, Jane E. *A Community in Transition: The Edgewater Community.* Chicago: Center for Research in Urban Government, Loyola University, 1978.

Milwaukee Avenue Corridor

Greene, Victor. *For God and Country: The Rise of Polish and Lithuanian Ethnic Consciousness in America, 1860-1910.* Madison: State Historical Society of Wisconsin, 1975.

Kantowicz, Edward R. *Polish-American Politics in Chicago, 1888-1940.* Chicago: University of Chicago Press, 1975.

Parot, Joseph. *Polish Catholics in Chicago.* DeKalb: Northern Illinois University Press, 1981.

Sommers, Nicholas. *The Historic Homes of Old Wicker Park.* Chicago: The Old Wicker Park Commission, 1978.

Near West Side

Addams, Jane. *Twenty Years at Hull House.* Reprint. New York: New American Library, 1960.

Berkow, Ira. *Maxwell Street: Survival in an Ethnic Bazaar.* Garden City: Doubleday, 1977.

Krucoff, Carole. *Rodfei Zedek: The First Hundred Years.* Chicago, Congregation Rodfei Zedek, 1976.

Rosen, George. *Decision Making Chicago-style: The Genesis of a University of Illinois Campus.* Urbana, University of Illinois Press, 1980.

Sorrentino, Anthony. *Organizing Against Crime: Redeveloping the Neighborhood.* New York: Human Sciences Press, 1977.

Suttles, Gerald D. *The Social Order of the Slum: Ethnicity and Territory in the Inner City.* Chicago: University of Chicago Press, 1968.

Lower West Side

Adelman, William J. *Pilsen and the West Side: A Tour Guide.* Chicago: Illinois Labor History Society, 1983.

Cain, Louis P. *Sanitation Strategy for a Lakefront Metropolis: The Case of Chicago.* DeKalb: Northern Illinois University Press, 1978.

Casuso, Jorge and Camacho, Eduardo. *Hispanics in Chicago.* Chicago: The Chicago *Reporter* and The Community Renewal Society, 1985.

"Hispanics and the Church: Today, tomorrow . . . together." Supplement to *The Chicago Catholic,* Dec. 16, 1983.

Reichman, John J. *Czechoslovaks of Chicago: Contributions to a History of a National Group.* Chicago: Czechoslovak Historical Society of Illinois, 1937.

Schneirov, Richard. "Chicago's Great Upheaval of 1877." *Chicago History* 9:1 (1980): 2-17.

Austin

Goodwin, Carole. *The Oak Park Strategy: Community Control of Racial Change.* Chicago: University of Chicago Press, 1979.

Bailey, Robert, Jr. *Radicals in Urban Politics: The Alinsky Approach.* Chicago: University of Chicago Press, 1972.

Old South Side

Bowly, Devereux, Jr. *The Poorhouse: Subsidized Housing in Chicago, 1895-1976.* Carbondale: Southern Illinois University Press, 1978.

Hunter, Albert. *Symbolic Communities: The Persistence and Change of Chicago's Local Communities.* Chicago: University of Chicago Press, 1974.

Suttles, Gerald D. *The Social Construction of Communities.* Chicago: University of Chicago Press, 1972.

Wendt, Lloyd, and Kogan, Herman. *Bosses in Lusty Chicago.* Bloomington: Indiana University Press, 1971.

Wright, Richard. *Native Son.* New York: Harper & Bros., 1940.

Grand Boulevard—Washington Park

Fanning, Charles, and Skerrett, Ellen. "James T. Farrell and Washington Park: The Novel as Social History." *Chicago History* 8:2 (1979): 80-91.

Farrell, James T. *Studs Lonigan.* New York: Random House, 1938.

Philpott, Thomas Lee. *The Slum and the Ghetto: Neighborhood Deterioration and Middle-Class Reform, Chicago, 1880-1930.* New York: Oxford University Press, 1978.

South Lake Front

Annis, Barbara, ed. *Our Hyde Park.* Chicago: Hyde Park Herald, 1976.

Berry, Brian J. L., et al. *The Impact of Urban Renewal on Small Business.* Chicago, University of Chicago Press, 1968.

Block, Jean F. *Hyde Park Houses.* Chicago: University of Chicago Press, 1978.

Rossi, Peter H., and Dentler, Robert A. *The Politics of Urban Renewal.* Glencoe: The Free Press, 1961.

Southeast Side

Adelman, William. *Touring Pullman.* Chicago: Illinois Labor History Society, 1972.

Brosch, David, Bulanda, Robert, and Kijewski, Marcia. *The Historical Development of Three Chicago Millgates: South Chicago, East Side, South Deering.* Chicago: Illinois Labor History Society, 1972.

Buder, Stanley. *Pullman: An Experiment in Industrial Order and Community Planning 1880-1930.* New York: Oxford University Press, 1967.

Kornblum, William. *Blue Collar Community.* Chicago: University of Chicago Press, 1974.

Stock Yard District

Leech, Harper, and Carroll, John Charles. *Armour and his Times.* New York: D. Appleton-Century Co., 1938.

Philpott, Thomas Lee. *The Slum and the Ghetto.* New York: Oxford University Press, 1978.

Swift, Louis F. *Yankee of the Yards.* Chicago: A. W. Shaw Co., 1927.

Sinclair, Upton. *The Jungle.* Reprint. New York: New American Library, 1960.

Southwest Side

Hamzik, Joseph. "Gleanings of Archer Road." Typescript, Chicago Historical Society, 1961.

Poles of Chicago, 1837-1937. Chicago, The Polish Pageant, 1937.

Sullivan, Gerald E., ed. *The Story of Englewood, 1835-1923.* Chicago, 1924.

Beverly Hills—Morgan Park

Greeley, Andrew M. *That Most Distressful Nation: The Taming of the American Irish.* Chicago: Quadrangle Books, 1973.

"Village in the City: Beverly Hills/Morgan Park." Supplement to the Chicago *Tribune,* section , *May 23, 1984.*

Index